D0810237

The Penguin Dictionary of Science

The Penguin Dictionary of Science

E. B. UVAROV

AND

D. R. CHAPMAN

Revised for the Third and Fourth Editions by
ALAN ISAACS

SCHOCKEN BOOKS · NEW YORK

Foreword to the 1971 Edition

SINCE this dictionary was last revised in 1963–4, science has been advancing on a wide front – with a corresponding increase in its vocabulary. Many new words have therefore been added and many existing entries have been expanded and brought up to date. Although a smattering of computer terminology has been included in this edition, the general principle of selecting predominantly scientific, as opposed to technological, words has been maintained. Fuller and wider treatment of words used in computers, electronics, biology, and astronomy will be found in the Penguin dictionaries covering these subjects.

The introduction of SI units has also entailed a revision of all quantitative information, which is now expressed in these units throughout the dictionary. Comprehensive tables have been added at the end of the dictionary giving conversions from SI units to commonly used c.g.s. and f.p.s. units.

While making these revisions, it was thought desirable to expand and modernize the chemical entries. Some six hundred new compounds have been added, and where necessary names have been altered to those recommended by the British Standards Institution for chemicals used in industry.

Several new tables have been added, both in the body of the text, and at the end of the dictionary, and the number of illustrations has been approximately doubled. The network of cross-references has been maintained throughout this edition, and cross-references in the text are indicated by the use of italics. Italics have not been used for the elements, however, as the dictionary lists all the elements (including transuranic elements). Trade names are indicated by an asterisk.

Finally, once again I would like to thank all the indulgent scientists, teachers, and editors of reference books who have supplied information: unfortunately they are too numerous to allow me to make individual acknowledgements.

A. I.

Abbreviations used in the Text

At. No.   Atomic number
A.W.   Atomic weight
(astr.)   Astronomy; as used in astronomy
(bio.)   Biochemistry; as used in biochemistry (or biology)
b.p.   Boiling point
°C   Degrees on the Celsius (Centigrade) scale
cc   Cubic centimetre
(chem.)   Chemistry; as used in chemistry
cm   Centimetre
conc.   Concentrated
°F   Degrees on the Fahrenheit scale
f.p.   Freezing point
g   Gram
Hz   Hertz
J   Joule
K   Thermodynamic temperature in Kelvin
kg   Kilogram
km   Kilometre
lb   Pound
m   Metre
(math.)   Mathematics; as used in mathematics
mm   Millimetre
m.p.   Melting point
N   Newton
(phot.)   Used in photography
(phys.)   Physics; as used in physics
s   Second
S.G.   Specific gravity
sq   Square
temp.   Temperature

The Penguin Dictionary of Science

A

AB-. A prefix attached to the names of practical electric *units* (e.g. *ampere*, *volt*) to indicate the corresponding unit in the *electromagnetic system* (e.g. abampere, abvolt). See *absolute units*.

ABBE CONDENSER. An optical *condenser* used in *microscopes*, consisting of two or three *lenses* having a wide *aperture*. Named after Ernst Abbe (1840–1905).

ABERRATION (astr.). A variation in the apparent position of a *star* or other heavenly body, due to the motion of the observer with the *Earth*.

ABERRATION, CHROMATIC. The formation, by a *lens*, of an image with coloured fringes, due to the *refractive index* of *glass* being different for *light* of different *colours*. The light is thus dispersed (see *dispersion of light*) into a coloured band. The effect is corrected by the use of *achromatic lenses*.

ABERRATION, SPHERICAL. The distortion of the image produced by a *lens* or *mirror* due to different rays from any one point of the object making different angles with the line joining that point to the *optical centre* of the lens or mirror (see *mirrors, spherical*) and coming to a *focus* in slightly different positions.

ABIOGENESIS. The hypothetical process by which living *organisms* are created from non-living matter: spontaneous generation.

ABRASIVE. A substance used for rubbing or grinding down surfaces; e.g. *emery*.

ABSCISSA of a point *P*. In *analytical geometry*, the portion of the *x* axis lying between the *origin* and a point where the line through *P* parallel to the *y* axis cuts the *x* axis. See Fig. 5, page 65.

ABSOLUTE. Not relative; independent. E.g. *absolute zero* of temperature, as distinct from zero on an arbitrary scale such as the *Centigrade scale*.

ABSOLUTE ALCOHOL. *Ethanol* containing not less than 99% pure ethanol by weight.

ABSOLUTE EXPANSION of a liquid. The true *expansion*, not relative to the containing vessel. The coefficient of absolute expansion is equal to the sum of the coefficient of relative or apparent expansion of the liquid and the coefficient of volume expansion of the containing vessel.

ABSOLUTE HUMIDITY. The amount of *water vapour* present in the *atmosphere*, defined in terms of the number of grams of water in a cubic metre of air. See also *relative humidity*.

ABSOLUTE THERMODYNAMIC TEMPERATURE. See *thermodynamic temperature*.

ABSOLUTE UNITS. 1. A system of electrical *units* based on the *c.g.s. system*; e.g. the *abvolt* which is 10^{-9} practical *volts*. 2. Any system of units using the least possible number of *fundamental units*. See *SI units, coherent units*.

ABSOLUTE ZERO. The lowest temperature theoretically possible; the zero of *thermodynamic temperature*. $0K = -273 \cdot 15°C = -459 \cdot 67°F$.

ABSORPTION EDGE. The *X-ray wavelength* at which a discontinuity appears in the intensity of an X-ray *absorption spectrum*.

ABSORPTION OF GASES. The *solution* of *gases* in *liquids*. Sometimes also applied to the absorption of gases by *solids*.

ABSORPTION OF RADIATION. *Radiant energy* is partly reflected, partly transmitted, and partly absorbed by the surface upon which it falls, the absorption being accompanied by a rise in *temperature* of the absorbing body. Dull black surfaces absorb the greatest proportion of the incident energy, and brightly polished (reflecting) surfaces the least. Surfaces which are the best absorbers are also the best radiators. See *absorptivity*.

ABSORPTION SPECTRUM. A *spectrum* consisting of dark lines or bands which is obtained when the *light* from a source, itself giving a continuous spectrum, is passed through a *gas* into a *spectroscope*. The dark lines or bands will occur in the same position as the coloured lines in that substance's *emission spectrum* and will be characteristic of the substance. When the absorbing medium is in the *solid* or *liquid state* the spectrum of the transmitted light shows broad dark regions which are not resolvable into sharp lines. Characteristic *X-ray* and *ultraviolet* absorption spectra are also formed.

ABSORPTIVITY of a surface. The fraction of the *radiant energy* incident on the surface which is absorbed. The absorptivity is a pure numeric, but is often referred to as 'absorptive power'. From *Kirchhoff's laws* it follows that the absorptivity is equal to the *emissivity*.

ABUNDANCE. The ratio of the number of *atoms* of a particular *isotope* in a mixture of isotopes of an *element*, to the total number of atoms present. Sometimes expressed as a percentage, e.g. the abundance of $^{235}_{92}U$ in natural uranium is $0 \cdot 71\%$.

ACCELERATION. *a*. The rate of change of *velocity*; measured as a change of velocity per unit time.

ACCELERATION DUE TO GRAVITY. The *acceleration* of a body falling freely in a *vacuum*; varies slightly in different localities as a result of variations in the distance from the centre of mass of the Earth. Standard accepted value = $9 \cdot 80665$ metres per second per second ($32 \cdot 174$ ft per second per second). Symbol *g*.

ACCELERATOR (chem.). A substance which increases the rate of a *chemical reaction* (i.e. a *catalyst*), particularly in the manufacture of *vulcanized rubber*.

ACCELERATOR (phys.). A machine for increasing the *kinetic energy* of charged particles (e.g. *protons, electrons, nuclei*) by accelerating them in *electric fields*. In *electrostatic generators* (see also *Van der Graaff generator* and *tandem generator*) the acceleration is achieved directly by using a very high *potential difference*. In multiple accelerators a lower potential difference is used repeatedly to give the particle successive increments of energy. Multiple accelerators are classified as *linear accelerators* or cyclic accelerators. See *cyclotron*, *synchroton*, *synchro-cyclotron*, *betatron*, and *bevatron*.

ACCELEROMETER. An instrument for measuring *acceleration*, especially the acceleration of an aircraft or *rocket*.

ACCEPTOR. An imperfection in a *semiconductor* which causes *hole* conduction.

ACCESS TIME. The time taken by a *computer store* to provide information to the *C.P.U.* The access time for high-speed stores is of the order of 1 *micro*second: for *backing storage* it may be from 1 *milli*second to some minutes.

ACCUMULATOR. Storage battery, secondary cell. A device for 'storing' *electricity*. An *electric current* is passed between two plates in a *liquid*; this causes chemical changes (due to *electrolysis*) in the plates and the liquid. When the changes are complete, the accumulator is charged. When the charged plates are joined externally by a *conductor* of electricity, the chemical changes are reversed, a current flows through the conductor till the reversal is complete, and the accumulator is discharged. In the common lead accumulator, the liquid is *sulphuric acid* of *specific gravity* 1·20 to 1·28, the positive plate when charged is *lead dioxide*, PbO_2, and the negative plate is spongy lead. During discharge both plates tend to become lead sulphate, $PbSO_4$, and the specific gravity of the acid solution falls. Discharge should not be continued beyond the point at which the S.G. reaches 1·15, otherwise an insoluble sulphate of lead, not decomposed on re-charging, may be formed. When this occurs, the cell is said to be sulphated. Nickel-iron (Ni-fe*) accumulators in which the negative plate is iron and the positive plate is *nickel oxide* are also widely used. In these cells the liquid is a 20% solution of *potassium hydroxide*.

The increasing interest in all-electric cars has stimulated development of accumulators in recent years. One of the most promising devices is the zinc-air accumulator which derives its *energy* from the conversion of zinc to *zinc oxide*. The plates are made of zinc and oxygen is obtained from the air through a porous nickel *electrode*, the electrolyte is potassium hydroxide. The lead accumulator will provide some 10 *watt* hours of energy per lb (approx. 8×10^4 *joules* per kg), whereas the zinc accumulator can provide 5 times this energy density. Even higher energy densities are obtainable from Na/S (100 Whr/lb) and Li/Cl (150 Whr/lb) accumulators but these require operating *temperatures* of 300–600° C. See also *fuel cells*.

ACETAL. An *organic compound* of the general formula $RCH(OR')_2$, where R is hydrogen or an organic *radical*, and R′ is an organic radical. Term is generally applied to $CH_3CH(OC_2H_5)_2$, a liquid, b.p. 104°C, used as a *solvent*, in perfumes, and in medicine as a *hypnotic*.

ACETALDEHYDE. CH_3CHO. A colourless *liquid* with a pungent fruity smell, b.p. 21°C. Formed by the *oxidation* of *ethanol*; further oxidation gives *acetic acid*. Used as an intermediate in the manufacture of many *organic compounds*.

ACETALDOL. Aldol, 3-hydroxybutyraldehyde. $CH_3CH(OH)CH_2.CHO$. A thick oily *liquid* formed by the *condensation* of *acetaldehyde*, b.p. 83°C. Used in the vulcanization of *rubber* and in perfumes.

ACETAMIDE. CH_3CONH_2. A colourless crystalline substance, m.p. 81°C., odourless when pure. Used industrially as a *solvent*, etc.

ACETANILIDE. Antifebrin. $C_6H_5NHCOCH_3$. A white crystalline solid, m.p. 112°C. Used as an *antipyretic*.

ACETATE. A *salt* or an *ester* of *acetic acid*.

ACETATE PLASTICS. *Plastics* made from *cellulose acetate* (see also *rayon*).

ACETIC ACID. CH_3COOH. The *acid* contained in *vinegar* (3 to 6%). A colourless corrosive *liquid* with a pungent smell; m.p. 16.6°C., b.p. 118.1°C. Solidifies at low temperatures to *glacial acetic acid*. Commercially obtained from *pyroligneous acid*, from vinegar made when *alcohol* is oxidized by the action of *bacteria*, and by the *oxidation* of *acetaldehyde*. Used in the manufacture of *cellulose acetate* and in other industries.

ACETIC ANHYDRIDE. $(CH_3CO)_2O$. A colourless pungent *liquid*, the *anhydride* of *acetic acid*, b.p. 140°C., used in the manufacture of *plastics*.

ACETIC ETHER. See *ethyl acetate*.

ACETOIN. Acetylmethylcarbinol. $CH_3CH(OH)COCH_3$. A yellow *liquid*, b.p. 148°C., used in the manufacture of flavours.

ACETONE. Dimethyl ketone. CH_3COCH_3. A colourless inflammable *liquid* with a pleasant smell, b.p. 56.5°C., used as a *solvent* especially in the production of *rayon*.

ACETONITRILE. Methyl cyanide. CH_3CN. A colourless poisonous *liquid*, b.p. 82°C., with an odour like *ether*. Used in organic synthesis and as a *solvent*.

ACETOPHENONE. Acetylbenzene, phenyl methyl ketone. $C_6H_5COCH_3$. A colourless sweet-smelling *liquid*, b.p. 202.3°C., used in the manufacture of perfume.

ACETYL GROUP. The *univalent* organic *radical*, CH_3CO—.

ACETYLENE. Ethyne. C_2H_2. A colourless poisonous inflammable *gas*. Made by the action of water on *calcium carbide*, CaC_2, or by the action of an electric *arc* on other *hydrocarbons*. Used as a starting material for many *organic compounds*, and for *welding* on account of the high flame *temperature* (about 3300°C.) it produces when burnt in oxygen. (See *oxy-acetylene burner*.)

ACETYLENE SERIES. A series of *unsaturated hydrocarbons* containing a *triple bond*, based on *acetylene*, and having the general formula C_nH_{2n-2}.

ACETYLSALICYLIC ACID. See *aspirin*.

ACHROMATIC LENS. A *lens* free from chromatic *aberration*, giving an image free from coloured fringes. Consists of a pair of lenses, one of *crown glass*, the other of *flint glass*, the latter correcting the *dispersion* caused by the former.

ACID. A substance which liberates *hydrogen ions* in *solution*; substance which contains hydrogen which may be replaced by a *metal* to form a *salt*; substance having a tendency to lose *protons*. Many acids are corrosive, have a sour taste, and turn *litmus* red. See also *Lewis acids and bases*.

ACID AMIDES. See *amides*.

ACID DYES. A group of *dyes*, nearly all *salts* of *organic acids*; used chiefly for dyeing wool and natural silk from an acid dyebath.

ACID RADICAL. A *molecule* of an *acid* without the *acidic hydrogen*. E.g., the *bivalent sulphate radical* $-SO_4$, from *sulphuric acid*, H_2SO_4, is present in all sulphates.

ACID SALT. An *acid* in which only a part of the *acid hydrogen* has been replaced by a *metal*. E.g. *sodium hydrogen carbonate*, $NaHCO_3$.

ACID VALUE of a fat or oil. A measure of the free *fatty acid* present; the number of *milligrams* of *potassium hydroxide* required to neutralize the free fatty acids in one gram of the substance.

ACIDIC. Having the properties of an *acid*; the opposite of *alkaline*.

ACIDIC HYDROGEN. That portion of the hydrogen in an *acid* which is replaceable by *metals* to form *salts*.

ACIDIMETER. An instrument for measuring the strength of an *acid*.

ACIDIMETRY. Determination of the amount of *acid* present in a *solution* by *titration*. See *volumetric analysis*.

ACIDOLYSIS. *Hydrolysis* by means of an *acid*.

ACLINIC LINE. See *magnetic equator*.

ACOUSTICS. The study of *sound*.

ACOUSTOELECTRONICS. The study and use of devices in which *electronic* signals are converted by *transducers* into surface acoustic waves and passed through tiny solid strips. As acoustic signals are propagated some 10^5 times more slowly than *electromagnetic waves*, this technique enables *delay lines* to be constructed which can be up to 50 times lighter than pure electronic devices.

ACRE. British unit of area. 4840 square yards. 4046·86 square metres.

ACRIFLAVINE, 3:6-diaminomethylacridine chloride hydrochloride. $C_{14}H_{14}N_3Cl.HCl$. A yellow substance used an an *antiseptic*.

ACROLEIN. See *acrylaldehyde*.

ACRYLALDEHYDE. Acrolein, acraldehyde. $CH_2:CH.CHO$. A colourless inflammable *liquid* with an irritating smell, b.p. 52·5°C., used in the synthesis of pharmaceutical products.

ACRYLIC ACID, $CH_2:CH.COOH$. A corrosive *liquid*, m.p. 13°C., b.p. 141°C. Derivatives form the basis of the important *acrylic resins*.

ACRYLIC RESINS. Class of *plastics* obtained by the *polymerization* of derivatives of *acrylic acid*. They are transparent, colourless, and *thermoplastic*; widely used, especially if a clear, transparent material is required.

ACRYLONITRILE. Vinyl cyanide. $CH_2:CH.CN$. A colourless *liquid*, b.p. 78°C. Used in the manufacture of *plastics*, synthetic *rubbers*, and artificial textile fibres.

ACTH. Adreno-cortico-tropic hormone. A *polypeptide hormone* secreted by the pituitary gland which controls the adrenal glands.

ACTINIC RAYS. The portion of the *Sun's* radiation rich in *ultraviolet radiation*, having a strong effect on a photographic plate.

ACTINIDES. Actinons. The name of the group of *elements* with *atomic numbers* from 89 (actinium) to 103; analogous to the *lanthanides*. See Table 8, page 440.

ACTINIUM. Ac. Element. A.W. 227. At. No. 89. A *radioactive* substance, *half-life* 21·6 *years*, m.p. 1050°C., b.p. 3200°C.

ACTINON. Actinium emanation. A gaseous *radioisotope* of radon, $^{219}_{86}$ Rn, produced by the *disintegration* of actinium.

ACTION. The product of *work* and time. *Planck's constant* of action is measured in *SI units* of *joule seconds*.

ACTIVATED ALUMINA. *Aluminium oxide* which has been dehydrated in such a way that a porous structure of high surface area is obtained. Activated alumina has the power of adsorbing *water vapour* and certain gaseous *molecules*. Used for drying air and other gases.

ACTIVATED CARBON. Active charcoal. Carbon, especially *charcoal*, which has been treated to remove *hydrocarbons* and to increase its powers of *adsorption*. Used in many industrial processes for recovering valuable materials out of gaseous mixtures, as a deodorant, and in *gas masks*.

ACTIVATION (phys.). The process of inducing *radioactivity*.

ACTIVE MASS (chem.). In the Law of *Mass Action* is taken to mean the *molecular concentration* of the substance under consideration.

ACTIVITY. *A.* The number of *disintegrations* of a *radioactive* material per second. See also *specific activity* and *curie*.

ACTOMYOSIN. A complex of two *proteins*, actin and myosin, which is the major constituent of muscle. The contraction of muscles is due to the shortening of actomyosin fibrils.

ACUTE ANGLE. Angle of less than 90°.

ACYCLIC. Not cyclic; having an *open-chain* structure.

ACYL GROUP. The *univalent radical* RCO—, where R is an organic group.

ADDITION COMPOUND. A chemical *compound* formed by the addition of an *atom* or group of atoms to a *molecule*. E.g. *phosgene*, $COCl_2$, is an addition compound of *carbon monoxide*, CO, and chlorine, Cl_2.

ADDITION REACTION. A *chemical reaction* in which one or more of the *double bonds* in an *unsaturated compound* is converted to a single bond by the addition of another *atom* or group.

ADENINE. 6-aminopurine. $C_5H_3N_4NH_2$. A white crystalline *purine* base, m.p. 360–65°C., occurring in *nucleic acids*, which plays a part in the formulation of the *genetic code*. Also occurs in *adenosine triphosphate*.

ADENOSINE TRIPHOSPHATE. ATP. $C_{10}H_{12}N_5O_3H_4P_3O_9$. A *nucleotide* of importance in the transfer of *energy* within living *cells*. One of the phosphate groups can be readily transferred to other substances, in the presence of the appropriate *enzymes*, and with it goes a considerable amount of stored energy. It is as a result of the transfer of these phosphate groups that energy is made available in cells for chemical synthesis, muscle contraction, etc. ATP which has lost one phosphate group becomes the diphosphate (ADP). Adenosine is a *nucleoside* consisting of *adenine* and D-ribofuranose.

ADHESION. Sticking to a surface. The effect is produced by *forces* between *molecules*.

ADHESIVES. Substances used for sticking surfaces together; e.g. *glues, cements,* etc.

ADIABATIC. Taking place without *heat* entering or leaving the system.

ADIPIC ACID. $COOH(CH_2)_4COOH$. A white crystalline solid, m.p. 152° C., used in the synthesis of *nylon*.

ADMITTANCE. The reciprocal of *impedance*.

ADRENALINE. Epinephrine. 3, 4-dihydroxy-α-(methylaminoethyl) benzyl alcohol, $C_9H_{13}NO_3$. A *hormone* produced by the adrenal glands and synthetically. Used in medicine as a heart stimulant and to constrict blood vessels.

ADSORBATE. The substance which is adsorbed on a surface. See *adsorption*.

ADSORPTION. The concentration of a substance on a surface; e.g. *molecules* of a *gas* or of a dissolved or suspended substance on the surface of a *solid*.

ADVANCED GAS-COOLED REACTOR. A.G.R. See *gas-cooled reactor*.

ADVECTION. The process in which either *matter* or *energy* is transferred from one place to another by a horizontal stream of *gas*.

AELOTROPIC. See *anisotropic*.

AERIAL (U.S.A., antenna). That part of a *radio* system from which *energy* is transmitted into, or received from, *space* (or the *atmosphere*).

AEROBIC. In the presence of free oxygen.

AERODYNAMICS. The study of the motion and control of solid bodies (e.g. aircraft, *rockets*, missiles, etc.) in *air*. The study of air or other *gases* in motion.

AEROLITES. *Meteorites*, especially those consisting of stony material rather than iron.

AERO METAL. A casting *alloy* consisting chiefly of aluminium, zinc, and copper.

AEROSOL. A dispersion of *solid* or *liquid* particles in a *gas*; e.g. *smoke*.

AEROSPACE. The *Earth's atmosphere* and the *space* beyond.

AETIOLOGY (U.S.A., etiology). The science or philosophy of causation. Used in medicine to mean the science of the causes of disease.

AFFINITY (chem.). Chemical attraction; the *force* binding *atoms* together.

AFTERBURNING. 1. The *combustion* which results from the addition of *fuel* to the exhaust of a *jet engine* in order to increase *thrust* and reduce fuel consumption. 2. The irregular burning of residual *propellant* in a *rocket* motor when the main combustion has finished.

AFTER-DAMP. A poisonous mixture of *gases*, containing *carbon monoxide*, formed by the explosion of *fire-damp* (*methane*, CH_4) in coal-mines.

AFTER-GLOW. A glow sometimes observed high in the western sky after sunset. Caused by fine dust particles in the *upper atmosphere* scattering the *light* from the *Sun*.

AFTER-HEAT. *Heat* generated in a *nuclear reactor* after it has been shut down, by the *radioactive* substances formed in the *fuel elements*.

AGAR-AGAR. A *gelatin*-like material obtained from certain seaweeds. Chemically related to the *carbohydrates*. A *solution* in hot water sets to a firm jelly, which is used as a base for *culture media* for growing *bacteria*.

AGATE. A very hard natural form of *silica*, used for knife-edges of *balances*, for mortars for grinding hard materials, and in ornaments.

AGONIC LINE. A line of zero *magnetic declination*.

AIR. See *atmosphere*.

AIR THERMOMETER. See *gas thermometer*.

ALABASTER. Natural opaque form of *hydrated calcium sulphate*, $CaSO_4.2H_2O$.

ALANINE. A colourless crystalline *soluble amino acid*. See Table 5, page 435.

ALBUMENS, ALBUMINS. A group of *soluble proteins* occurring in many animal *tissues* and *fluids*; e.g. egg-white (egg albumen), milk (lact-albumen), and *blood* (serum albumen).

ALBUMINOIDS. See *scleroproteins*.

ALCHEMY. The predecessor of scientific *chemistry*. An art by which its devotees sought, with the aid of a mixture of mysticism, *astrology*, practical chemistry, and quackery, to transmute *base metals* into gold, prolong human life, etc. Flourished from about A.D. 500 till the Middle Ages, when it gradually fell into disrepute.

ALCOHOLOMETRY. The determination of the proportion of *ethanol* in spirits and other *solutions*; usually performed by measuring the *specific gravity* of the liquid at a standard *temperature* by a specially graduated *hydrometer*.

ALCOHOLS. A class of *organic compounds* derived from the *hydrocarbons*, one or more hydrogen *atoms* in *molecules* of the latter being replaced by *hydroxyl groups*, – OH. E.g. *ethanol* (ordinary 'alcohol') is C_2H_5OH, theoretically derived from *ethane*, C_2H_6. Alcohols which contain more than one hydroxyl group are called *polyhydric alcohols*. See also *diols* and *triols*.

ALDEHYDE. See *acetaldehyde*.

ALDEHYDES. A class of *organic compounds* of the type $R—C{\displaystyle {O \atop H}}$ where R is an *alkyl* or *aryl radical*.

ALDOL. See *acetaldol*.

ALGEBRA. The branch of mathematics dealing with the properties of, and relationships between, quantities by means of general symbols.

ALGEBRAIC SUM. The total of a number of quantities of the same kind, with due regard to sign. Thus the algebraic sum of 3, -5, and -2 is -4.

ALGIN. A loose term for *alginic acid* or its sodium *salt*.

ALGINIC ACID. $(C_6H_8O_6)_n$. A complex *organic compound* related to the *carbohydrates*, found in certain seaweeds. Used for preparing *emulsions* and as a thickening agent in the food industry; its *salts*, the alginates, can be made into textile fibres which are *soluble in alkalis* and are used for special purposes.

ALGOL. Algorithmic language. A type of *computer* language, based on *Boolean algebra*, for expressing information in an algebraic notation.

ALGORITHM. Algorism (math.). A systematic mathematical procedure which enables a problem to be solved in a finite number of steps. Problems for which no algorithms exist require *heuristic* solutions.

ALICYCLIC COMPOUND. A type of *organic compound* which is essentially *aliphatic*, but which also contains a ring of carbon *atoms*.

ALIDADE. An instrument for measuring vertical heights and distances.

ALIPHATIC COMPOUNDS. *Organic compounds* containing open chains of carbon *atoms*, in contradistinction to the closed rings of carbon atoms of the *aromatic compounds*. Comprise the *paraffins*, the *olefins* and the *acetylenes* as well as all their *derivatives* and *substitution products*.

ALIQUOT PART. A divisor of a number or quantity which will give an *integer*. Thus 3 is an aliquot part of 6, but 5 is not.

ALIZARIN. 1:2 dihydroxyanthraquinone. $C_{14}H_6O_2(OH)_2$. An orange-red crystalline *solid*, m.p. 289° C. Colouring matter formerly extracted from the root of the madder plant, now made synthetically. Used in dyeing with the aid of *mordants*.

ALKALI. A *soluble hydroxide* of a *metal*, particularly of one of the *alkali metals*; term is often applied to any substance which has an alkaline reaction (i.e. turns *litmus* blue and neutralizes *acids*) in solution. See also *base*.

ALKALI METALS. The *univalent metals* lithium, sodium, potassium, rubidium, and caesium, belonging to Group 1 of the *periodic table*.

ALKALIMETRY. The determination of the amount of *alkali* present in a *solution*, by *titration*. See *volumetric analysis*.

ALKALINE. Having the properties of an *alkali*; the opposite of *acidic*.

ALKALINE EARTH METALS. The *bivalent* group of *metals* comprising beryllium, magnesium, calcium, strontium, barium, and radium, belonging to Group 2 of the *periodic table*.

ALKALOIDS. A group of *basic* organic substances of plant origin, containing at least one nitrogen *atom* in a ring structure in the *molecule*. Many have important physiological actions and are used in medicine. E.g. *codeine, cocaine, nicotine, quinine, morphine*.

ALKANE. A member of the *paraffin series* of *saturated hydrocarbons*.

ALKENE. A member of the *olefine* series of *unsaturated hydrocarbons*.

ALKINE. Alkyne. A member of the *acetylene series* of *unsaturated hydrocarbons*.

ALKYD RESINS. See *glyptal resins*.

ALKYL GROUPS. *Univalent hydrocarbon radicals*, particularly those derived from hydrocarbons of the *paraffin series*, and having the general formula C_nH_{2n+1}. E.g. *methyl*, CH_3—; *ethyl*, C_2H_5—.

ALKYLATION. 1. The replacement of a hydrogen *atom* in a *compound* by an *alkyl group*. 2. The addition of a *paraffin hydrocarbon* to an *olefine*.

ALLO -. Prefix meaning 'other', used in *chemistry* to denote a variation from the standard or normal form.

ALLOMERISM. A similarity in the crystalline structure of substances of different chemical composition.

ALLOMORPHISM. A variability in the crystalline structure of certain substances. Allomorphs are different crystalline forms of the same *compound*.

ALLOTROPES. Allotropic forms. See *allotropy*.

ALLOTROPY. The existence of a chemical *element* in two or more forms differing in physical properties but giving rise to identical chemical *compounds*. E.g. sulphur exists in a number of different allotropic forms.

ALLOY. A composition of two or more *metals*; an alloy may be a *compound* of the metals, a *solid solution* of them, a heterogeneous *mixture*, or any combination of these.

ALLUVIAL. Deposited by rivers.

ALLYL ALCOHOL. $CH_2:CH.CH_2OH$. A colourless pungent *liquid*, b.p. $96 \cdot 5°C.$, used in the manufacture of synthetic *resins* and pharmaceuticals.

ALLYL GROUP. The *univalent radical*, $CH_2:CH.CH_2$—, derived from *propylene*.

ALLYL RESINS. Synthetic *resins* formed by the *polymerization* of chemical *compounds* containing the *allyl group*.

ALPHA-IRON. Allotropic (see *allotropy*) form of pure iron which exists up to 900°C.

ALPHA PARTICLE. Helium *nucleus*; i.e. a close combination of two *neutrons* and two *protons* (see *atom, structure of*), and therefore positively charged. Alpha particles are emitted from the *nuclei* of certain *radioactive elements*. See *radioactivity*.

ALPHA RAYS. Streams of fast-moving *alpha particles*. Alpha rays produce intense *ionization* in *gases* through which they pass, are easily absorbed by *matter*, and produce *fluorescence* on a fluorescent screen.

ALTAZIMUTH. An instrument for the measurement of the *altitude* and *azimuth* of heavenly bodies.

ALTERNATING CURRENT. a.c. A flow of *electricity* which, after reaching a maximum in one direction, decreases, finally reversing and reaching a maximum in the opposite direction, the *cycle* being repeated continuously. The number of such cycles per second is the *frequency*.

ALTERNATOR. A machine for producing electrical *alternating currents*.

ALTITUDE. 1. Height. 2. The altitude of a heavenly body is its *angular distance* from the horizon on the vertical circle passing through the body, the *zenith*, and the *nadir*. See Fig. 2, page 36.

ALUM. Potash alum. $K_2SO_4.Al_2(SO_4)_3.24H_2O$. Crystalline potassium aluminium sulphate. The *compound* occurs naturally and is used as a *mordant* in dyeing, for fireproofing, and other technical purposes.

ALUMINA. See *aluminium oxide*, Al_2O_3. Occurs naturally as *corundum* and *emery*, and in a *hydrated* form as *bauxite*. (See also *activated alumina*.)

ALUMINIUM. Al. Element. A.W. 26·9815. At. No. 13. A light white *metal*, S.G. 2·7, m.p. 659·70° C., ductile and malleable, good *conductor* of electricity. Occurs widely in nature in *clays*, etc.; extracted mainly from *bauxite* by *electrolysis* of a molten mixture of purified bauxite and *cryolite*. The metal and its *alloys* are used for aircraft, cooking utensils, electrical apparatus, and for many other purposes where its light weight is an advantage.

ALUMINIUM ACETATE. $Al(CH_3COO)_3$. A white *soluble amorphous* powder, used as an *astringent* and *antiseptic*. *Basic* aluminium acetate, $AlOH(CH_3COO)_2.xH_2O$, a white crystalline powder, is used as a waterproofing and fireproofing compound in the textile industry.

ALUMINIUM BRASS. *Brass* containing small amounts of aluminium.

ALUMINIUM BRONZE. An *alloy* of copper containing 4%–13% aluminium.

ALUMINIUM HYDROXIDE. $Al(OH)_3$. A white *insoluble amphoteric* powder used in the manufacture of *glass* and *ceramics*, and as an *antacid* in medicine.

ALUMINIUM OXIDE. Alumina. Al_2O_3. A white crystalline substance, m.p. 2015° C., used in *cement*, as a *refractory*, and in the manufacture of aluminium. See also *activated alumina*.

ALUMINIUM SULPHATE. $Al(SO_4)_3$. A white crystalline *soluble* substance, used in purifying *water*, in the manufacture of *paper*, and in *fire extinguishers*.

ALUMS. Double *salts* of the general formula
$$M_2SO_4.R_2(SO_4)_3.24H_2O,$$
where M is a *univalent metal* such as sodium, potassium, or ammonium, and R is a *tervalent* metal such as aluminium or chromium.

ALUM-STONE. See *alunite*.

ALUNITE. Alum-stone. A natural *compound* of potassium and *aluminium sulphate* and *aluminium hydroxide*, $K_2SO_4.Al_2(SO_4)_3.4Al(OH)_3$. Used as a source of *alum*.

AMALGAM. An *alloy* of mercury.

AMALGAMATION PROCESS for gold. Gold-bearing rock or sand, after crushing, is treated with mercury, which forms an *amalgam* on the surface of the gold. The amalgamated particles are allowed to stick to amalgamated copper plates, the rest of the ore being washed away; they are then removed, the mercury is distilled off in iron *retorts*, and the remaining gold purified by *cupellation*.

AMATOL. An explosive mixture of 80% *ammonium nitrate* and 20% *T.N.T.*

AMBER. Succinite. A fossil *resin*, derived from an extinct species of pine. Obtained from mines in East Prussia, and found on seashores. A yellow to brown solid, which contains *succinic acid*, used for ornamental purposes.

AMBERGRIS. Grey or black waxy material which occurs (probably as the result of disease) in the intestines of the sperm whale. Used in perfumery.

AMERICIUM. Am. *Transuranic element*. At. No. 95. *Radioactive*. A member of the *actinide* series. Most stable *isotope*, $^{243}_{95}$ Am, has *half-life* of $7 \cdot 4 \times 10^3$ years. S.G. $13 \cdot 7$, m.p. $995°$ C.

AMETHYST. A violet variety of *quartz*; impure crystalline *silica*, SiO_2.

AMIDES. A group of *organic compounds* formed by replacing hydrogen atoms of ammonia, NH_3, by *organic acid radicals*. E.g. *acetamide*, CH_3CONH_2.

AMIDOL*. 2:4-diaminophenol dihydrochloride,
$$C_6H_3(OH)(NH_2)_2.2HCl;$$
used in *photography* as a developer.

AMINASES. *Enzymes* which *catalyze* the *hydrolysis* of *amines*.

AMINES. Compounds formed by replacing hydrogen *atoms* of *ammonia*, NH_3, by organic *radicals*. Classified into primary amines of the type NH_2R; secondary, NHR_2; and tertiary, NR_3. See also *quaternary ammonium compounds*.

AMINO ACID. A *carboxylic acid* which contains the *amino group* —NH_2. These acids are the units which link together into *polypeptide* chains to form *proteins*; they are therefore of fundamental importance to life. Some twenty different amino acids occur in nature, all of which have the general formula: R—CH—NH_2—COOH. See Table 5, page 435. 'Essential' amino acids are those which an *organism* is unable to synthesize and therefore has to obtain from its environment. There are eight 'essential' amino acids for man.

AMINO GROUP. The *univalent* group —NH_2.

AMINOPLASTIC RESINS. Synthetic *resins* derived from the reaction of *urea*, *melamine*, or allied amino compounds with *aldehydes*. They form the basis of *thermosetting* moulding materials.

AMMETER. An instrument for the measurement of *electric current*. In moving iron ammeters, a strip of soft iron is caused to move in the *magnetic field* set up by the current flowing through a coil; for the measurement of *direct current*, the more accurate moving coil instruments contain a permanent *magnet* between the poles of which is pivoted a coil carrying the current to be measured. In each type of instrument a pointer attached to the moving portion moves over a scale graduated in *amperes*.

AMMONAL. A *mixture* of *ammonium nitrate*, NH_4NO_3, and aluminium. Used an an *explosive*.

AMMONIA. NH_3. A pungent-smelling very *soluble gas*, giving an *alkaline solution* containing *ammonium hydroxide*, NH_4OH. Obtained synthetically from atmospheric nitrogen (see *Haber process*) and as a by-product of *coal-gas* manufacture. Used as a *refrigerant*, and for the manufacture of *explosives* and *fertilizers*.

AMMONIUM ACETATE. CH_3COONH_4. A white *deliquescent* solid, m.p. 114°C., used as a meat preservative and in the manufacture of *dyes*.

AMMONIUM CHLORIDE. Sal ammoniac. NH_4Cl. A white *soluble* crystalline *salt*, used in *dry cells* and *Leclanché cells*.

AMMONIUM HYDROXIDE. NH_4OH. A *compound* presumed to exist in *aqueous solutions* of *ammonia*; the name is often applied to the *solution*.

AMMONIUM NITRATE. NH_4NO_3. A white *soluble* crystalline *salt*, m.p. 169·6°C., which decomposes on heating to form *nitrous oxide*, N_2O, and water. Used in *explosives*, e.g. *ammonal*, *amatol*.

AMMONIUM RADICAL. NH_4—. A *univalent radical* which has not been obtained free, but in *compounds* behaves similarly to an *alkali metal*, giving rise to ammonium *salts*.

AMMONIUM SODIUM HYDROGEN ORTHOPHOSPHATE. Microcosmic salt. $NH_4NaHPO_4.4H_2O$. A white crystalline *soluble salt*, used as a *flux*.

AMMONIUM SULPHATE. $(NH_4)_2SO_4$. A white *soluble* crystalline *salt*, obtained as a by-product of *coal-gas* manufacture, used as a *fertilizer*.

AMMONIUM THIOCYANATE. NH_4SCN. A colourless *soluble* crystalline substance, m.p. 149·6°C., used as a herbicide and in the textile industry.

AMORPHOUS. Non-crystalline; having no definite form or shape.

AMOUNT OF SUBSTANCE. *n*. A basic physical quantity that is proportional to the number of specified particles of a substance. The specified particle may be an *atom, molecule, ion, radical electron, photon*, etc., or any specified group of such particles. The constant of proportionality, *Avogadro's constant*, is the same for all substances. The basic *SI unit* of amount of substance is the *mole*.

AMPERE. A unit of *electric current* approximately equivalent to the flow of 6×10^{18} *electrons* per second. The absolute ampere, which is one-tenth of an abampere (see *ab-*), is equal to 1·000165 International amperes. The International ampere was originally defined as the unvarying current which when passed through a *solution* of *silver nitrate*, deposits silver at the rate of 0·00111800 grams per second. Redefined in 1948 as the intensity of a constant current which, if maintained in two parallel, rectilinear *conductors* of infinite length, of negligible circular section and placed at a distance of one *metre* from one another in vacuo, will produce between the conductors a *force* equal to 2×10^{-7} *newton* per *metre* of length. The ampere so defined is the basic *SI Unit* of current. Symbol A.

AMPERE-HOUR. The practical unit of quantity of *electricity*; the amount of electricity flowing per hour through a *conductor* when the current in it is one *ampere*. 3600 *coulombs*.

AMPERE-TURNS. A measure of *magnetomotive force*. The product of the number of turns in a coil and the current in *amperes* which flows through it.

AMPERE'S LAW. The strength of the *magnetic field* induced by a *current* flowing through a *conductor* is, at any point, directly proportional to the *product* of the current and the length of the conductor and inversely proportional to the *square* of the distance between the point and the conductor. The direction of the field is perpendicular to the *plane* joining the point and the conductor. Named after A. M. Ampère (1775–1836).

AMPHETAMINE. $C_6H_5CH_2CHNH_2CH_3$. A *drug*, used in the form of the *sulphate*, which stimulates the central nervous system in cases of depression. Also known under the trade name, Benzedrine*.

AMPHIBOLES. A group of complex *silicate minerals* which includes *hornblende* and *asbestos*.

AMPHICHROIC. Amphichromatic. Giving one colour on reaction with an *acid* and another colour on reaction with a *base*.

AMPHOTERIC. Chemically reacting as *acidic* to strong *bases* and as *basic* towards strong *acids*. E.g. the amphoteric *oxide, zinc oxide*, gives rise to zinc *salts* of strong *acids* and zincates of the *alkali metals*.

AMPLIFIER. An *electronic* device which increases the strength of a signal fed into it, by obtaining *power* from a source other than the input signal.

AMPLITUDE (phys.). If any quantity is varying in an oscillatory manner about an equilibrium value, the maximum departure from that equilibrium value is called the amplitude; e.g. in the case of a *pendulum* the amplitude is half the length of the swing. For a *wave motion*, e.g. *electromagnetic waves* or *sound* waves, the amplitude of the wave determines the amount of *energy* carried by the wave.

AMPLITUDE MODULATION. The principal method of transmitting information by *radio* waves. The *amplitude* of a *carrier wave* is modulated (see *modulation*) in accordance with the *frequency* of the signal to be transmitted.

AMU. See *atomic mass units*.

AMYL GROUP. *Pentyl group*. The *univalent radical* C_5H_{11}—.

AMYL ACETATE. See *pentyl acetate*.

AMYL ALCOHOL. $C_5H_{11}OH$. A colourless *liquid* with a characteristic smell. Exists in several isomeric forms (*see isomerism*). Commercial amyl alcohol consists mainly of *iso*-amyl alcohol,
$$(CH_3)_2:CH.CH_2.CH_2OH,$$
b.p. 131·4° C., and is obtained from *fusel oil*. Used as a *solvent*.

AMYLASES. A group of *enzymes* capable of splitting *starch* and *glycogen* into *sugars*. Found in many plants and animals (e.g. the pancreatic juices of mammals).

AMYLOPECTIN. A form of *starch* which consists of *molecules* containing between 10 and 25 chains, each chain comprising about 20 *glucose* units. In amylopectin molecules, unlike *amylose* molecules, these chains are joined by cross-linkages so that a highly branched structure is formed.

AMYLOSE. A *starch* component structurally related to *cellulose*. Consists of *molecules* containing between 10 and 25 chains, each chain comprising about 20 *glucose* units. In amylose molecules, unlike *amylopectin* molecules, these chains are joined end to end, giving an unbranched chain of between 200 and 500 glucose units.

AMYLUM. See *starch*.

ANABOLISM. Part of *metabolism*, comprising the building-up of complex substances from simpler material, with absorption and storage of *energy*.

ANAEROBIC. In the absence of free oxygen.

ANAESTHETIC. A substance used in medicine to produce insensibility or loss of feeling.

ANALGESIC. A substance used in medicine to relieve pain.

ANALOG COMPUTER. A *computer* in which numerical magnitudes are represented by physical quantities such as *electric current, voltage,* or *resistance*. See also *digital computer*.

ANALYSIS (chem.). Decomposition of substances into their *elements* or constituent parts; term usually applied to chemical or physical methods of determining the composition of substances. See *colorimetric, gravimetric, qualitative, quantitative, spectrographic,* and *volumetric analysis*.

ANALYTICAL GEOMETRY. Coordinate geometry. Form of *geometry* based upon the use of *coordinates* to define positions in *space*. See *Cartesian coordinates* and *polar coordinates*.

ANASTIGMATIC LENS. A *lens* designed to correct *astigmatism*.

ANATASE. Crystalline form of natural *titanium dioxide*, TiO_2.

ANDROGEN. A *steroid*, or other substance, which promotes male characteristics in vertebrates; e.g. *testosterone*.

ANECHOIC. Having a low degree of reverberation.

ANEMO−. Prefix denoting the wind.

ANEMOMETER. Instrument for measuring the speed of wind or any other moving gas.

ANEROID. Without liquid. The aneroid *barometer* is an instrument for measuring atmospheric *pressure*; it consists of an exhausted metal box with a thin corrugated metal lid. Variations in atmospheric pressure cause changes in the displacement of the lid; this displacement is magnified and made to actuate a pointer moving over a scale by means of a system of delicate levers.

ANETHOLE. $CH_3CH:CHC_6H_4OCH_3$. A white crystalline powder, m.p. $22 \cdot 5°C$., used in perfumes, flavouring, and in medicine.

ANEURIN. See *thiamin*.

ANGLE. The space between two intersecting lines or *planes*. Measured in degrees, $360°$ being the angle traced by the complete revolution of a line OA about a point O until it returns to its original position, or in *radians* (see *circular measure*).

ÅNGSTRÖM UNIT. Å.U., 10^{-10} *metre*. A unit of length, formerly used for measurement of *wavelengths* of *light* and intra-molecular distances.

ANGULAR ACCELERATION. Rate of change of *angular velocity*.

ANGULAR DISPLACEMENT. The *angle* through which a point, line, or body has been rotated in a specified direction, about a specified *axis*.

ANGULAR DISTANCE. The distance between two bodies, measured in terms of the *angle* subtended by them at the point of observation; used in *astronomy*.

ANGULAR FREQUENCY. The *frequency* of a periodic process expressed in *radians* per *second*; equal to 2π times the number of *cycles* per second.

ANGULAR MOMENTUM. The product of *moment of inertia* and *angular velocity*. For the angular momentum of *elementary particles* see *spin*.

ANGULAR VELOCITY. Rate of motion through an *angle* about an *axis*. Measured in *degrees*, *radians*, or revolutions per unit time.

ANHYDRIDE. The anhydride of a substance is that which, when chemically combined with *water*, gives the substance. A *basic* anhydride is the *oxide* of a *metal* which forms a *base* with *water* (e.g. $Na_2O + H_2O = 2NaOH$): an *acidic* anhydride is the oxide of a non-metal which forms an *acid* with water (e.g. $SO_3 + H_2O = H_2SO_4$).

ANHYDRITE. Naturally occurring form of *calcium sulphate*, $CaSO_4$.

ANHYDROUS. Without *water*; often applied to *salts* without *water of crystallization*.

ANILIDE. An *organic compound*, derived from *aniline* or *acetanilide*, which contains the *univalent radical* C_6H_5NH—.

ANILINE. Phenylamine, aminobenzene. $C_6H_5NH_2$. A colourless oily *liquid* with a peculiar smell, b.p. 184·4°C. Made by the reduction of *nitrobenzene*, $C_6H_5NO_2$, which is obtained from *benzene*, C_6H_6, extracted from *coal-tar*. Used in the manufacture of many important products, including *dyes*, *drugs*, and *plastics*.

ANILINE DYES. *Dyes* prepared or chemically derived from *aniline*.

ANILINIUM CHLORIDE. Aniline hydrochloride. $C_6H_5NH_2.HCl$. A white crystalline *soluble* solid, m.p. 198°C., used in the manufacture of *dyes*.

ANIMAL CHARCOAL. Bone black, bone char. Material containing 10% carbon and 90% inorganic matter, chiefly *calcium phosphate*, $Ca_3(PO_4)_2$, obtained by charring bones and other animal substances. Used as a decolorizing agent.

ANIMAL STARCH. See *glycogen*.

ANION. Negatively charged *ion*; ion which during *electrolysis* is attracted towards the *anode*.

ANISALDEHYDE. Aubepine. A colourless oily *liquid*, the *para-* form of $CH_3OC_6H_4.CHO$. B.p. 247°C., used in cosmetics and perfumes.

ANISOLE. Methyl phenyl ether. $CH_3OC_6H_5$. A colourless *liquid* with an aromatic odour, b.p. 155·4°C., used in perfumes and as a *vermicide*.

ANISOMETRIC. Not *isometric*. Applied to *crystals* which have *axes* of different lengths.

ANISOTROPIC. Aelotropic. Possessing different physical properties in different directions; e.g. certain *crystals* have a different *refractive index* in different directions.

ANISYL ALCOHOL. Anisalcohol. $CH_3OC_6H_4CH_2OH$. A colourless *liquid*, b.p. 258·8°C., used in perfumes.

ANNEALING. Very slow regulated cooling, especially of *metals*, to relieve *strains* set up during heating or other treatment.

ANNIHILATION RADIATION. The *electromagnetic radiation* which results from the collision, and subsequent annihilation, of a particle and its corresponding *anti-particle*. In the collision between an *electron* and a *positron* the annihilation radiation usually consists of two *photons* of γ-radiation emitted in opposite directions. The *energy* of the annihilation radiation is derived from the *mass* of the annihilated particles according to the *mass-energy equation*.

ANNUAL VARIATION of *magnetic declination*. A very small regular variation which the magnetic declination undergoes in the course of a year.

ANNULAR. Ringed. An annular space is the space between an inner and outer ring.

ANNULAR ECLIPSE. An *eclipse* of the *Sun* in which a ring of its surface is visible surrounding the darkened *Moon*.

ANODE. Positive *electrode*. See *electrolysis* and *thermionic valve*.

ANODIZING. Producing an *oxide* coating on a metallic surface by making it the *anode* in an electrolytic bath (see *electrolysis*).

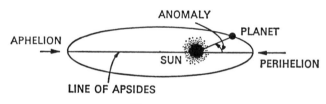

FIGURE I.

ANOMALY (astr.). A term used to describe the position of a *planet* in its *orbit*. The 'true anomaly' is the *angle* between the *perihelion*, the *Sun*, and the planet, in the direction of the planet's motion. See Fig. I. The 'mean anomaly' is the angle between the perihelion, the Sun and a fictitious planet having the same *period* as the real planet, but assumed to be moving with a constant *velocity*.

ANTENNA. See *aerial*.

ANTHRACENE. $C_6H_4(CH)_2C_6H_4$. A white crystalline *hydrocarbon* with a blue *fluorescence*; often yellowish due to impurities. M.p. $217^\circ C$. Obtained from *coal-tar*; used in the manufacture of *dyes*.

ANTHRACITE. A hard form of *coal*, containing more carbon and far less *hydrocarbons* than other forms. Probably the oldest form of coal.

ANTHRAQUINONE. $C_6H_4(CO_2)_2C_6H_4$. A yellow *insoluble* powder, derived from *anthracene* and used as a *dye*.

ANTI-. Prefix denoting opposite, against. E.g. *antichlor*.

ANTIBIOTICS. Chemical substances produced by *micro-organisms* such as moulds and *bacteria*, which are capable of destroying bacteria or preventing their growth. Numerous antibiotics have been discovered, the

25

ANTIBODY

first of which was *penicillin*. See *aureomycin, streptomycin, chloromycetin, erythromycin, terramycin*, and *nystatin*.

ANTIBODY. A *protein* produced by animal plasma *cells* (of the reticulo-endothelial system) as a result of the presence of an *antigen*. Specific antigens stimulate the formation of specific antibodies. The function of the antibodies is to combine chemically with antigens and thereby to render them harmless to the *organism* which they are invading. As parasitic *organisms* and *viruses* produce, or are associated with, specific antigens, the consequent antibody formation provides a defence mechanism against these invading parasites. Once produced, antibodies persist in the bloodstream and therefore confer enduring immunity against the infecting organisms of antigens. Immunity to disease by inoculation is brought about by injecting antigens into the blood-stream with the object of stimulating the formation of antibodies. See also *vaccine*.

ANTICHLOR. A substance used to remove chlorine from materials after *bleaching*. E.g. *sodium thiosulphate*, $Na_2S_2O_3$.

ANTIDOTE. A remedy for a particular poison, which generally acts chemically upon the poison, thus neutralizing it, making it *insoluble*, or otherwise rendering it harmless.

ANTIFEBRIN. See *acetanilide*.

ANTI-FREEZE. A substance added to water in radiators of motor-car engines in order to lower the *freezing point* of the water. *Ethanediol* (ethylene glycol), $CH_2OH.CH_2OH$, is frequently used.

ANTIGEN. A *protein* or *carbohydrate* which is foreign to an *organism* and which is capable of stimulating the formation of *antibodies*.

ANTIHISTAMINES. A group of *drugs* which counteract the effect of *histamine* in the body and are therefore used in the treatment of allergic diseases.

ANTILOGARITHM. Antilog. The number represented by a *logarithm*.

ANTI-MATTER. Hypothetical *matter* composed of *anti-particles*. Anti-hydrogen, for example, would consist of an anti-*proton* and an orbital *positron*. While theoretically possible, the existence of anti-matter in the *Universe* has never been detected. Contact between anti-matter and matter would result in the annihilation of both with the production of *annihilation radiation*.

ANTIMONY. Sb. (Stibium.) Element. A.W. 121·75. At. No. 51. A brittle crystalline silvery-white *metal*, S.G. 6·69, m.p. 630°C., expands on solidifying. Occurs as the *element, oxide*, and *sulphide* (*stibnite*, Sb_2S_3). Extracted from its ores by roasting the ore and reducing with carbon. Used in *type metal* and other *alloys*.

ANTIMONY HYDRIDE. See *stibine*.

ANTIMONY PENTASULPHIDE. Sb_2S_5. A yellow *insoluble* powder, used as a *pigment* and in the *vulcanization* of *rubber*.

ANTIMONY POTASSIUM TARTRATE. Tartar emetic. Potassium antimonyl tartrate. $2K(SbO)C_4H_4O_6.H_2O$. A white *soluble* poisonous powder, used as an emetic and as a *mordant*.

26

ANTIMONY SULPHATE. $Sb_2(SO_4)_3$. A white crystalline *insoluble* solid, used in *explosives*.

ANTIMONY TRISULPHIDE. Stibnite. Sb_2S_3. A black or red *insoluble* crystalline solid, m.p. 550°C., used as a *pigment* and also in fireworks and *matches*.

ANTINODES. Points of maximum displacement in a series of *standing waves*. Two similar and equal *wave motions* travelling with equal *velocities* in opposite directions along a straight line give rise to antinodes and *nodes* alternately along the line. The antinodes are separated from their adjacent nodes by a distance corresponding to a quarter of the *wavelength* of the wave motions.

ANTI-PARTICLE. Every *elementary particle* has a corresponding real or hypothetical anti-particle, of equal *mass* but opposite *electric charge*, with which annihilation can take place. The anti-particle of the *electron* is the *positron*. Anti-*neutrons*, anti-*neutrinos*, and anti-*protons*, amongst others, have been detected. The anti-neutron has the same mass and *spin* as a neutron, but opposite *magnetic moment*.

ANTIPYRETIC. Febrifuge. A substance used medically to lower the body *temperature*.

ANTISEPTIC. Preventing the growth of *bacteria*.

APATITE. Natural *phosphate* and *fluoride* of calcium, $CaF_2.3Ca_3(PO_4)_2$. Used in the manufacture of *fertilizers*.

APERTURE. Opening; in optical instruments, the size of the opening admitting *light* to the instrument. In spherical *mirrors* or *lenses*, the diameter of the reflecting or refracting surface.

APERTURE SYNTHESIS. The use of two small *aerials* in a *radio telescope* to synthesize a large *aperture*. This principle can be used both with *parabolic reflectors* and *radio interferometers*, but is usually best employed in conjunction with an *unfilled aperture*.

APHELION. The time, or point, in a *planet's orbit* when it is furthest from the *Sun*. The opposite of *perihelion*. See Fig. 1, page 25.

APLANATIC. If any reflecting or refracting surface produces a point image at *B* of a point object at *A* irrespective of the angle at which the rays fall on the surface from *A*, then that surface is said to be aplanatic with respect to *A* and *B*.

APOCYNTHION. The time, or point, of greatest distance of a *satellite* in lunar *orbit* from the *Moon's* surface. The opposite of *pericynthion*.

APOGEE. The *Moon* or any other Earth *satellite* is said to be in apogee when it is at its greatest distance from the Earth. The opposite of *perigee*.

APOMORPHINE. $C_{17}H_{17}NO_2$. A crystalline *alkaloid*, derived from *morphine*, used in the form of its hydrochloride as an emetic.

APOTHECARIES' FLUID MEASURE.

1 minim	= 0·0591 cc (about 1 drop)	
60 minims	= 1 fluid drachm	= 3·55 cc
8 fl dr	= 1 fluid ounce	= 28·41 cc
20 fl oz	= 1 pint	= 568 cc

These measures are now largely replaced by *metric units*.

APOTHECARIES' WEIGHTS. See *Troy weight*.

APOTHEM. A *perpendicular* from the centre of a regular *polygon* to one of its sides.

APPARENT DEPTH of a *liquid* viewed from above is less than the true depth, owing to the *refraction* of *light*. The ratio of the true depth to the apparent depth is equal to the *refractive index* of the liquid.

APPARENT EXPANSION. Relative expansion of a *liquid*. See *expansion of liquids*.

APPLETON LAYER. See *ionosphere*.

APSIS (plural APSIDES). One of the extremities of the major *axis* of the *orbit* of a *planet* or *comet*. See *perihelion* and *aphelion*. The 'line of apsides' joins one apsis to the other. See Fig. 1, page 25.

AQ. (chem.). Symbol denoting *water*; e.g. H_2SO_4.aq. is *aqueous sulphuric acid*.

AQUA FORTIS. Concentrated *nitric acid*, HNO_3.

AQUA REGIA. Mixture of concentrated *nitric* and *hydrochloric acids* (1 to 4 by volume). Highly corrosive *liquid* which dissolves gold and attacks many substances unaffected by other reagents. Turns orange-yellow owing to the formation of nitrosyl chloride, $NOCl$, and free chlorine.

AQUAMARINE. Bluish form of *beryl*.

AQUEOUS. Watery. Usually applied to *solutions*, indicating that *water* is the *solvent*.

ARABINOSE. Pectinose. $C_5H_{10}O_5$. A white *soluble* crystalline solid, m.p. 164·5° C., obtained from *gums* or synthetically from *glucose*, used as a *culture medium* in *bacteriology*.

ARACHIDIC ACID. Arachic acid. $CH_3(CH_2)_{18}COOH$. A white crystalline *insoluble* solid, m.p. 76·3° C., obtained from peanut oil and used in lubricants, plastics and *waxes*.

ARC, ELECTRIC. A highly luminous discharge, accompanied by a *temperature* of over 3000° C.; produced when an *electric current* flows through a gap between two *electrodes*, the current being carried by the *vapour* of the electrode; e.g. the common carbon arc is formed between two carbon rods, and constitutes a very bright source of *light*. In the same way metallic arcs are formed between two similar metallic surfaces.

ARC LAMP. A technical application of the electric *arc* to produce a very bright *light*. The *carbon arc* lamp consists of an electric arc between two carbon *electrodes*, with suitable automatic mechanism for striking the arc and drawing the carbons closer together as they are vaporized away. The mercury arc lamp is important for laboratory use.

ARC OF CIRCLE. See *circle*.

ARC SIN, TAN, COS. See *inverse trigonometrical functions*.

ARCHIMEDES' PRINCIPLE. The apparent loss in *weight* of a body totally or partially immersed in a *liquid* is equal to the weight of the liquid displaced. See *buoyancy*. Named after the Greek mathematician (287–212 B.C.).

ARE. *Metric unit* of *area*, 1 square dekametre, 100 square *metres*, 119·60 square yards.

AREA. Measure of surface; measured in 'square' units of length, e.g. square *metres*.

AREA, BRITISH UNITS.

$$
\begin{aligned}
1 \text{ square inch} &= 6\cdot4516 \text{ square cm} \\
144 \text{ sq ins} &= 1 \text{ sq foot} = 929 \text{ sq cm} \\
9 \text{ sq ft} &= 1 \text{ sq yard} \\
30\tfrac{1}{4} \text{ sq yds} &= 1 \text{ sq pole} \\
40 \text{ sq pls} &= 1 \text{ rood} \\
484 \text{ sq yds} &= 1 \text{ sq chain} \\
4 \text{ roods} = 4840 \text{ sq yds} &= 1 \text{ acre} \\
640 \text{ acres} &= 1 \text{ sq mile}
\end{aligned}
$$

See also Table 1, page 426.

AREA, METRIC UNITS.

$$
\begin{aligned}
1 \text{ sq centimetre} &= 0\cdot155 \text{ sq inch} \\
10\ 000 \text{ sq cm} &= 1 \text{ centare} = 1 \text{ sq metre} \\
100 \text{ sq m} &= 1 \text{ are} \\
100 \text{ ares} &= 1 \text{ hectare} = 2\cdot47105 \text{ acres} \\
100 \text{ hectares} &= 1 \text{ sq kilometre}
\end{aligned}
$$

See also Table 1, page 426.

ARGENTIFEROUS. Silver-bearing.

ARGENTITE. Silver glance. Natural silver sulphide, Ag_2S. An important *ore* of silver.

ARGININE. An essential *amino acid*. See Table 5, page 435.

ARGOL. Tartar. A reddish-brown crystalline deposit consisting mainly of *potassium hydrogen tartrate*, which separates in wine-vats.

ARGON. Ar. Element. A.W. 39·948. At. No. 18. An *inert gas*, which occurs in the air (0·9%). Used for filling electric lamps and in fluorescent tubes at a pressure of about 3 mm of mercury (400 N_m^{-2}).

ARGUMENT (math.). An independent *variable* that forms part of a *function*.

ARITHMETICAL PROGRESSION. *Series* of quantities in which each term differs from the preceding by a constant common difference. For an A.P. in which the first term is a, the common difference d, the number of terms n, the last term L, and the sum of n terms S,

$$S = \frac{n}{2}\left\{2a + (n-1)\,d\right\}$$

$$S = \frac{n}{2}(a+L)$$

$$L = a + (n-1)d.$$

ARMATURE. The coil or coils, usually rotating, of a *dynamo* or *electric motor*. Also more widely used as any part of an electric apparatus or machine in which a *voltage* is induced by a *magnetic field*, e.g. in gramophone pick-ups, electromagnetic loudspeakers, *relays*, etc.

AROMATIC COMPOUNDS (chem.). *Organic compounds* derived from *benzene*.

29

ARSENATE. A *salt* or *ester* of *arsenic acid.*

ARSENIC. As. Element. A.W. 74·9216. At. No. 33. Exists in three *allotropic* forms; ordinary grey crystalline arsenic, S.G. 5·727, black metallic arsenic, S.G. 4·5, and yellow arsenic, S.G. 2·0. Occurs combined with sulphur as *realgar*, As_2S_2, *orpiment*, As_2S_3; with oxygen as *white arsenic*, As_2O_3; with some *metals* and as the *element*. *Compounds* are very poisonous, and are used in medicine and for destroying pests.

ARSENIC ACID. $H_3AsO_4.\frac{1}{2}H_2O$. A white *soluble* crystalline powder, m.p. 35·5° C., used in the manufacture of *arsenates.*

ARSENIC DISULPHIDE. *Realgar.* As_2S_2. A red *insoluble* poisonous powder, m.p. 307° C., used in the manufacture of fireworks.

ARSENIC TRIOXIDE. White arsenic, arsenous oxide, arsenous anhydride, arsenous acid. As_2O_3. A white *amorphous* powder used in the manufacture of *pigments* and as an *insecticide.*

ARSENIC TRISULPHIDE. *Orpiment.* As_2S_3. A yellow *soluble* solid, m.p. 300° C., used as a *pigment.*

ARSENICAL PYRITES. See *mispickel.*

ARSINE. Hydrogen arsenide. AsH_3. An intensely poisonous colourless *gas.*

ARTIFICIAL RADIOACTIVITY. See *induced radioactivity.*

ARYL GROUPS. Organic *radicals* or groups of *atoms* derived from *aromatic compounds*; e.g. *phenyl*, C_6H_5—.

ASBESTOS. A variety of fibrous *silicate* minerals, mainly calcium magnesium silicate. Used as a heat-insulating material and for fire-proof fabrics.

ASCORBIC ACID. *Vitamin* C. $C_6H_8O_6$. A white crystalline *solid*, m.p. 192° C., occurs in fruits and vegetables. Deficiency causes scurvy.

ASEPTIC. Free from *bacteria.*

ASH. Incombustible residue left after the complete *combustion* of any substance. Consists of the non-*volatile*, *inorganic* constituents of the substance.

ASPARAGINE. A white crystalline *soluble amino acid* obtained from some leguminous plants. See Table 5, page 435.

ASPARTIC ACID. Asparaginic acid, aminosuccinic acid. A white crystalline *amino acid* found in sugar beet. See Table 5, page 435.

ASPHALT. A black semi-solid sticky substance composed of *bitumen* with mineral matter. Consists mainly of complex *hydrocarbons.* Occurs naturally in asphalt lakes or in deposits mixed with *sandstone* and *limestone*; made artificially by adding mineral matter to bitumen. Used in road-making and building.

ASPIRATOR. Apparatus for drawing a current of air or other *gas* through a *liquid.*

ASPIRIN. Acetylsalicylic acid. $CH_3COOC_6H_4COOH$. A white solid, m.p. 133° C., used in medicine as an *antipyretic* and *analgesic.*

ASSAYING. Analysing for one constituent of a *mixture*, particularly the estimation of *metals* in *ores.*

ASSOCIATION (chem.). Under certain conditions, e.g. in *solution*, the *molecules* of some substances associate into groups of several molecules, thus causing the substance to have an abnormally high *molecular weight*.

ASTATIC COILS. An arrangement used in sensitive electrical instruments; coils so arranged that the *resultant* external *magnetic field* which they produce when an *electric current* passes through them, and the *electromotive force* induced in them by an external magnetic field, are zero.

ASTATIC GALVANOMETER. A type of moving *magnet galvanometer*, in which two equal small magnets are arranged parallel but in opposition at the centres of two oppositely wound coils, the system being suspended by a fine torsion fibre. Since the resulting *magnetic moment* is zero, the Earth's *magnetic field* exerts no controlling *torque* on the moving system. Instead, the restoring torque is supplied by the suspending fibre and is made very small by using a fine *quartz* fibre; the sensitivity of the galvanometer is thus very large.

ASTATIC PAIR of magnets. Arrangement of *magnets* used in *astatic galvanometers*.

ASTATINE. At. Element. At. No. 85. The last member of the *halogen* group and the only one without a stable *isotope*. The most stable isotope, $^{210}_{85}$ At, has a *half-life* of only 8·3 hours.

ASTEROIDS. Planetoids, minor *planets*. A belt of some 1500 small bodies, none exceeding 300 miles in diameter, rotating round the *Sun* in orbits between those of *Mars* and *Jupiter*.

ASTIGMATISM. A defect of *lenses* (including the eye) caused by the curvature being different in two mutually perpendicular *planes*; thus *rays* in one plane may be in focus while those in the other are out of focus, producing distortion. Astigmatism of the eye is corrected by the use of cylindrical lenses.

ASTRINGENT. A substance which by contracting body *tissues*, veins etc, reduces the discharge of mucus or *blood*.

ASTRO-COMPASS. An instrument for determining direction relative to the *stars*. Unaffected by the errors to which *magnetic* or *gyro compasses* are subject; used to determine the errors of such instruments.

ASTROLABE. An instrument used by early astronomers to measure the *altitude* of heavenly bodies. The simplest form consists of a graduated circular ring with a movable sighting arm. Now replaced by the *sextant*.

ASTROLOGY. The ancient art, or pseudo-science, of predicting the course of human destinies by indications derived from the positions and movements of the heavenly bodies.

ASTRONAUTICS. The scientific study of travel outside the *Earth's atmosphere*.

ASTRONOMICAL UNIT. The mean distance from the centre of the *Earth* to the centre of the *Sun*. 149·6 × 10⁹ *metres*, approximately 92·9 × 10⁶ miles.

ASTRONOMY. Scientific study of the heavenly bodies, their motion, relative positions, and nature. See also *astrophysics* and *cosmology*.

ASTROPHYSICS. The branch of *astronomy* concerned with the physical properties of celestial bodies, and the interaction between *matter* and *energy* within them (and in the *space* between them).

ASYMMETRIC. Not possessing *symmetry*.

ASYMMETRIC CARBON ATOM. A carbon *atom* in a *molecule* of an *organic compound* with four different atoms or groups attached to its four *valencies*. Such a grouping permits of two different arrangements in space, leading to the existence of optical isomers. See *stereoisomerism*.

ASYMPTOTE. A line approaching a curve, but never reaching it within a finite distance.

-ATE. Suffix used in the naming of chemical *compounds*; in the case of *salts*, denoting a salt of the corresponding -*ic* acid; e.g. *sulphate* from *sulphuric acid*.

ATHERMANCY. The property of being opaque to *radiant heat*; i.e. of absorbing heat radiations.

ATHERODYDE. Athodyd. See *ram jet*.

ATMOLYSIS. The separation of a *mixture* of *gases* through the walls of a porous vessel by taking advantage of the different rates of *diffusion* of the constituents.

ATMOMETER. Evaporometer. An instrument for measuring the rate of *evaporation* of *water*.

ATMOSPHERE. The gaseous envelope surrounding the *Earth* (or other heavenly body). The composition of the Earth's atmosphere varies very slightly in different localities and according to altitude. Volume composition of dry air at sea-level (average values): nitrogen, $78 \cdot 08\%$; oxygen, $20 \cdot 95\%$; argon, $0 \cdot 93\%$; *carbon dioxide*, $0 \cdot 03\%$; neon, $0 \cdot 0018\%$; helium, $0 \cdot 0005\%$; krypton, $0 \cdot 0001\%$; xenon, $0 \cdot 00001\%$. Air generally contains, in addition to the above, *water vapour*, *hydrocarbons*, *hydrogen peroxide*, sulphur *compounds*, and dust particles in small and very variable amounts. See also *upper atmosphere*.

ATMOSPHERE. A unit of *pressure*. The pressure which will support a column of mercury 760 mm high (29·92 inches) at $0°$ C., sea-level and latitude $45°$. 1 normal atmosphere = 101,325 *newtons* per square *metre* = 14·72 lb/sq in (approx.). Atmospheric pressure fluctuates about this value from day to day.

ATMOSPHERICS. Electrical discharges which take place in the atmosphere, causing crackling sounds in *radio* receivers.

ATOM. The smallest portion of an *element* which can take part in a *chemical reaction*. See *atom, structure of*; *atomic theory*.

ATOM SMASHER. A popular name for an *accelerator*.

ATOM, STRUCTURE OF. The *atom* consists of a positively charged central core, the *nucleus*, surrounded by one or more negatively charged planetary *electrons*. The openness of atomic structure is indicated by the following approximate dimensions:

Effective radius of atom $\quad 10^{-10}$ m

Effective radius of nucleus $\quad 10^{-14}$ m

Effective radius of electron $\quad 10^{-15}$ m

Almost all the *mass* of the atom resides in the nucleus, which is composed of two different types of stable particle of almost equal mass, the *proton* which is positively charged, and the *neutron* which is electrically neutral. The mass of the electron is 1/1836th of that of the proton, and although its charge is opposite in sign, it is numerically equal to that of the proton. The number of planetary electrons in the electrically neutral atom is therefore equal to the number of protons in the nucleus. The chemical behaviour of an atom is determined by its number of planetary electrons (characterized by the *atomic number*), chemical combination between atoms taking place by the transfer or sharing of outer electrons between combining atoms. See *valency, electronic theory of*.

According to the *Bohr theory*, the planetary electrons of an atom were to be thought of as moving in well defined *orbits* about the nucleus, corresponding to specific *energy levels* – the emission or absorption of a *photon* of *electromagnetic radiation* occurring when an electron made a *quantum* jump from one permitted orbit, or energy level, to another. In the more modern *wave mechanics* the electrons are regarded as having a dual wave particle existence which is expressed mathematically by a *wave function*. The precise position of the electron in the Bohr model of the atom is therefore replaced in the wave mechanical model by a *probability* that a particular planetary electron, visualized as a particle, may be found at a particular point in the path of a wave. Thus, in this model the atom is visualized as a central nucleus surrounded by a distribution of probabilities that individual electrons will exist at certain points at certain instants of time.

Atoms of an *element* which have the same number of protons, p, in their nuclei, but a different number of neutrons, n, are called *isotopes* of that element. When a particular isotope is being considered the following notation is used: to the chemical *symbol* of the element, the *mass number* (n+p) of the isotope is added as a superscript. The atomic number of the element may also be added as a subscript; e.g. $^1_1$H, $^{12}_6$C, $^{197}_{79}$Au, are the most abundant isotopes of hydrogen, carbon, and gold.

ATOMIC BOMB. See *nuclear weapons*.

ATOMIC CLOCK. A very accurate form of clock in which the basis of the time scale is derived from the vibrations of *atoms* or *molecules*. E.g. caesium clock, ammonia clock.

ATOMIC CONSTANTS. See Table 2, page 430.

ATOMIC ENERGY. See *nuclear energy*.

ATOMIC HEAT. The numerical product of the *atomic weight* and the *specific heat capacity* of an *element*. *Dulong and Petit's law* states that the atomic heat of all *solid* elements is approx. 6·4 *calories* per *mole* per degree. The law is obeyed by many elements at ordinary *temperatures*, but at lower temperatures the atomic heat of all elements falls below this value, tending to zero as *absolute zero* of temperature is approached. Actual values of atomic heat for some elements are: Ca 6·3, Cu 5·9, Fe 6·6, Pb 6·4, Ni 6·2, K 7·0, Ag 6·1, Sa 6·3, Zn 6·1. All at *N.T.P.*

ATOMIC MASS. The *mass* of an *isotope* of an *element* measured in *atomic mass units*.

ATOMIC MASS UNIT. AMU. Unit used for expressing the masses of individual *isotopes* of *elements*: approximately equal to $1·66 \times 10^{-27}$ kg. Formerly defined so that the most abundant isotope of oxygen, $^{16}_{8}O$, had a mass of 16 atomic mass units. In 1961 the 'unified atomic mass unit' was defined as 1/12 of the mass of an *atom* of $^{12}_{6}C$, and was adopted by the International Union of Pure and Applied Physics and the International Union of Pure and Applied Chemistry. *Atomic weights* given in this dictionary are based upon this scale. See Table 3, pages 432–4.

ATOMIC NUCLEUS. See *nucleus, atomic*.

ATOMIC NUMBER. Proton number. Z. The number of *electrons* rotating round the *nucleus* of the neutral *atom* of an *element*, or the number of *protons* in the nucleus. (See *atom, structure of* and Table 3, pages 432–4.)

ATOMIC ORBITAL. The volume containing all the points within a free *atom* at which the *wave function* of an *electron* has an appreciable magnitude.

ATOMIC PILE. The original name for a *nuclear reactor*.

ATOMIC THEORY. Hypothesis as to the structure of *matter*, foreshadowed by Democritus, put forward as a formal explanation of chemical facts and laws by Dalton in the beginning of the nineteenth century. Assumes that matter is made up of small indivisible particles called *atoms*; the atoms of any one *element* are identical in all respects, but differ from those of other elements at least in *weight*. Chemical *compounds* are formed by the union of atoms of different elements in simple numerical proportions. Modern views on the structure of the atom (see *atom, structure of*) diverge considerably from Dalton's hypothesis, but it is still of value in affording a simple explanation of the laws of *chemical combination*.

ATOMIC VOLUME. The *atomic weight* of an *element* divided by its *density*.

ATOMIC WEIGHT. Relative atomic mass. The ratio of the average *mass* per *atom* of a specified isotopic composition of an *element* to 1/12 of the mass of an atom of $^{12}_{6}C$. The natural isotopic composition is assumed unless otherwise stated. The atomic weights of the elements are given in Table 3, pages 432–4.

ATP. See *adenosine triphosphate*.

ATROPINE. $C_{17}H_{23}NO_3$. A colourless crystalline *insoluble alkaloid*, m.p. 115°C.; extremely poisonous, has a powerful effect upon the nervous system, used in medicine to dilate the pupil of the eye. Occurs in the deadly nightshade and henbane.

ATTENUATION (phys.). The loss of *power* suffered by *radiation* as it passes through *matter*.

ATTO-. Prefix denoting one million million millionth; 10^{-18}. Symbol a, e.g. am $= 10^{-18}$ *metres*.

AUDIBILITY, LIMITS OF. The limits of *frequency* of *sound* waves which are audible as sound to the human ear. The lowest is about 30 *hertz*, corresponding to a very deep vibrating rumble, and the highest in the region of 20,000 *hertz*, corresponding to a shrill hiss.

AUDIO-FREQUENCY. A *frequency* between 30 and about 20 000 *hertz*, which in the case of *sound* waves would be audible.

AUDIOMETER. An instrument for measuring the level of human hearing.

AUER METAL. A *pyrophoric alloy* of 65% *misch metal* (a mixture of cerium and other metals) and 35% iron. Used as 'flint' in lighters.

AUGER EFFECT. The emission of an *electron* by an *atom*, without the emission of *X*- or *γ-radiation*, as a result of a change from an excited state (see *excitation*) to a lower energy state. Named after Pierre Auger (born 1899).

AUREOMYCIN*. Chlortetracycline. $C_{22}H_{23}N_2O_8Cl$. A broad-spectrum *antibiotic* used against many *organisms* which are resistant to *penicillin*; also used to stimulate growth of animals.

AURIC. Containing *trivalent* gold.

AURIC CHLORIDE. Gold chloride. $AuCl_3$. A red *soluble* crystalline solid, used in *photography* and in gilding glass.

AURIFEROUS. Gold-bearing.

AURORA BOREALIS, Northern lights. A display of coloured light streamers and glows, mainly red and green, visible in the regions of the North and South Poles. Probably caused by streams of electrified particles from the *Sun*; most prominent when large *sunspots* are observed. See *solar wind*.

AUROUS. Containing *univalent* gold.

AUSTENITE. *Solid solution* of carbon or of iron carbide in the *gamma* form of iron; normally stable only at high *temperatures*, but may be preserved at normal temperatures by certain alloying *elements* or by rapid cooling.

AUTOCLAVE. A thick-walled vessel with a tightly fitting lid, in which substances may be heated under pressure to above their *boiling points*. Used in the manufacture of chemicals, for sterilizing medical instruments, etc., and in cooking.

AUTOLYSIS. The self-destruction of biological *cells* after death, as a result of the action of their own *enzymes*.

AUTOMATION. The application of mechanical, or more commonly *electronic*, techniques to minimize the use of manpower in any process.

AUTORADIOGRAPH. Image obtained by placing a thin biological or other specimen, containing a *radioactive isotope*, in contact with a photographic plate, exposing for a suitable period and *developing*. The image shows the distribution of the radioactive *element* in the specimen.

AUTOSOME. Any *chromosome* other than a sex chromosome.

AUXINS. Phytamins, plant hormones. Substances promoting or directing the growth of plants.

AVALANCHE (phys.). A *shower* of particles caused by the collision of a high *energy* particle (e.g. a *cosmic ray*) with any other form of *matter*.

AVOGADRO'S CONSTANT. Avogadro's number. The number of atoms or molecules in a mole of a substance: $6{\cdot}02252 \times 10^{23}$ mol -1. Symbol L or NA.

AVOGADRO'S LAW. Avogadro's hypothesis. Equal *volumes* of all *gases* contain equal numbers of *molecules* under the same conditions of *temperature* and *pressure*. Named after Count Amadeo Avogadro (1776–1856).

AVOIRDUPOIS WEIGHTS. System of *weights* used in the English-speaking countries. See *weight, British units of*.

AXIS. An imaginary line about which a given body or system is considered to rotate.

AXIS OF MIRROR. See *mirrors, spherical*.

AXIS OF SYMMETRY. A line about which a given figure is symmetrical; e.g. the diameter of a *circle*.

AXON. A long nerve fibre which carries impulses away from the body of a *neurone*.

AZEOTROPIC MIXTURE. Constant boiling mixture. A mixture of two or more *liquids* which distils at a given constant *temperature* and has a constant composition, at a given *pressure*.

AZIDE. A *compound* containing the *univalent* azido group, $-N_3$, e.g. *sodium azide*, NaN_3. A derivative of *hydrazoic acid*.

AZIMUTH (astr.). The *angular distance* from the north or south point of the horizon to the foot of the vertical circle through a heavenly body. The azimuth of a horizontal direction is its deviation from the north or south. See Fig. 2.

CELESTIAL SPHERE

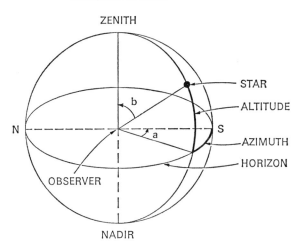

a = azimuth angle
b = zenith angle

FIGURE 2.

AZINE. A *heterocyclic organic compound* containing a six-membered ring in which at least one member of the ring is a nitrogen *atom*.

AZOBENZENE. $C_6H_5N:NC_6H_5$. A red *insoluble* crystalline powder, m.p. 68° C., used in the manufacture of *dyes* and as an *insecticide*.

AZO-DYES. Class of organic *dyes*, mainly red or yellow, derived from *azobenzene*.

AZO GROUP. The *bivalent* group —N:N—.

AZOTE. Former name for *nitrogen*.

AZURITE. Natural *basic* copper carbonate, blue in colour. $2CuCO_3.Cu(OH)_2$.

B

BABBITT METAL. A class of *alloys* with a high proportion of tin, and small amounts of copper and antimony. Part of the tin may be replaced by lead. Used for bearings. Named after I. Babbitt (1799–1862).

BABO'S LAW. The addition of a non-volatile *solid* to a *liquid* in which it is *soluble* lowers the *vapour pressure* of the *solvent* in proportion to the amount of substance dissolved.

BACILLUS. In general, a rod-shaped *bacterium*. In particular, a genus of spore-producing bacteria.

BACK E.M.F. OF CELL. When the poles of a *cell* become polarized (see *polarization, electrolytic*) a back *E.M.F.* is set up opposing the natural E.M.F. of the cell.

BACK E.M.F. OF ELECTRIC MOTOR. *E.M.F.* set up in the coil of an *electric motor*, opposing the current flowing through the coil, when the *armature* rotates.

BACKGROUND (phys.). The counting rate of a *counter tube* caused by sources other than the one being measured. Due primarily to natural *radioactivity* in the soil, and *cosmic rays*.

BACKING STORAGE. *Computer stores* which have a capacity to store enormous quantities of information, but with an *access time* much greater than the main store. The commonest types are *magnetic tape* decks, fixed magnetic disc stores, and exchangeable magnetic disc stores.

BACTERICIDE. A substance which kills *bacteria*.

BACTERIOLOGY. The study of *bacteria*.

BACTERIOPHAGE. Phage. A *virus* which requires a *bacterium* in which to replicate.

BACTERIUM. A cellular *micro-organism* incapable of *photosynthesis*. Usually single celled and usually reproduced by *mitosis* although there are exceptions. Bacteria are the causes of many diseases, most of which can now be treated by the use of *antibiotics*. However, bacteria also perform an indispensable function in nature by bringing about the decay of plant and animal debris in the *soil*. Bacteria are broadly classified by their shape into three main groups: the spherical or *coccus* form, the spiral-shaped organism called a *spirillum*, and the rod-shaped or *bacillus* type.

BAKELITE*. Trade name for various synthetic *resins* of which *phenol-formaldehyde resins* are amongst the most widely known.

BAKING POWDER. A *mixture* which produces *carbon dioxide* gas, CO_2, on wetting or heating, thus causing the formation of bubbles in dough and making it 'rise'. Usually contains *sodium hydrogen carbonate*, $NaHCO_3$, and *tartaric acid* or *cream of tartar*.

BAKING SODA. *Sodium hydrogen carbonate*, $NaHCO_3$.

BALANCE. An apparatus for weighing. In principle consists of a lever with two equal arms, with a pan suspended from the end of each arm.

Masses placed in the pans are subject to pulls of *gravity*; when these *forces* are equal, as indicated by the beam being horizontal, the masses themselves must be equal. Sensitive balances have beam and pans poised on knife-edges of *agate* resting on agate surfaces. An accurate balance will weigh to the nearest 0·0001 g. More sensitive balances have been designed for special work, for example, *microbalances* have been made which are capable of detecting differences in weight of only $0·25 \times 10^{-6}$ *milligrams* in a load of 250 milligrams.

BALANCED REACTION. See *chemical equilibrium*.

BALATA. A natural *rubber*-like material very similar to *gutta-percha*.

BALLISTIC GALVANOMETER. An instrument for measuring the total quantity of *electricity* passing through a circuit due to a momentary current. Any *galvanometer* may be used ballistically provided that its period of oscillation is long compared with the time during which the current flows.

BALLISTIC MISSILE. A ground-to-ground missile with a parabolic flight path. A missile which is propelled and guided only during the initial phase of its flight.

BALLISTIC PENDULUM. A device for measuring the *velocity* of a *projectile*, such as a bullet. Consists of a large *mass* freely suspended from a horizontal beam and a means of measuring the displacement of the mass when it is struck by the projectile. The displacement of the mass is a function of the projectile's velocity.

BALLISTICS. The study of the flight path of *projectiles*.

BALMER SERIES. The visible *spectrum* of hydrogen. Consists of a series of sharp distinct lines, the *wavelengths*, λ, of which may be represented by the formula $\frac{1}{\lambda} = R\left(\frac{1}{2^2} - \frac{1}{n^2}\right)$; $n = 3$, 4, 5, etc., R is a constant known as *Rydberg's Constant* which has the value $1·09677 \times 10^7 \text{m}^{-1}$. Named after J. J. Balmer (1825–98).

BAND SPECTRUM. An *emission* or *absorption spectrum* consisting of a number of fluted bands each having one sharp edge. Each band is composed of a large number of closely spaced lines. Band spectra arise from *molecules*.

BANDWIDTH. The range of *frequencies* within which the performance of a *circuit*, *receiver*, or *amplifier* does not differ from its maximum value by a specified amount. The bandwidth of a *radio* emission is the width of the *frequency band* which carries a specified proportion (usually 99%) of the total *power* radiated.

BAR. Unit of *pressure* in the *C.G.S. system*; a pressure of 10^6 *dynes* per sq cm. Equivalent to a pressure of 0·986923 *atmospheres* (approx. 75 cm of mercury). 1 bar $= 10^5$ *newtons* per sq *metre*.

BARBITONE. Barbital, 5,5-diethyl barbituric acid. $CO(HNCO)_2(C_2H_5)_2$. A crystalline substance derived from *barbituric acid*, m.p. 191°C., used in the form of its sodium *salt* as a *hypnotic*.

BARBITURATES. Class of *organic compounds* derived from *barbituric acid*.

39

Many of these compounds have a powerful and sometimes dangerous soporific effect. Used in medicine.

BARBITURIC ACID. Malonyl urea. $CO(NH.CO)_2CH_2$. A white crystalline powder, m.p. 248° C., used in the synthesis of *barbiturates*.

BARFF PROCESS. Prevention of rusting of iron by the action of *steam* upon the surface of the red-hot metal, resulting in a surface coating of black oxide of iron, Fe_3O_4.

BARIUM. Ba. Element. A.W. 137·34. At. No. 56. A silvery-white soft *metal*, tarnishes readily in air. S.G. 3·5, m.p. 710° C. Occurs as *barytes*, $BaSO_4$, and as *barium carbonate*, $BaCO_3$. *Compounds* resemble those of calcium but are poisonous. Compounds are used in the manufacture of *paints*, *glass*, and fireworks.

BARIUM CARBONATE. $BaCO_3$. A white poisonous *insoluble* powder, used in *paints* and *dyes*.

BARIUM HYDROXIDE. Caustic baryta. $Ba(OH)_2.8H_2O$. A colourless crystalline solid, m.p. 78° C., used in refining sugar beet and *vegetable oils*.

BARIUM OXIDE. Baryta. BaO. A white crystalline powder, m.p. 1923° C., used as a dehydrating agent and in the manufacture of *glass*.

BARIUM PEROXIDE. BaO_2. A white *insoluble* powder, m.p. 450° C., used as a bleaching agent.

BARIUM SULPHATE. Blanc fixe. $BaSO_4$. A white crystalline *insoluble* powder, m.p. 1580° C., used as a *pigment* and, because it is *opaque* to *X-rays*, as the basis of 'barium meal' in X-ray diagnosis.

BARIUM TITANATE. $BaTiO_3$. A crystalline substance with good *ferroelectric* and *piezo-electric* properties, used in *transducers*.

BARKHAUSEN EFFECT. The effect observed when a *ferromagnetic substance* is magnetized by a slowly increasing *magnetic field*; the magnetization does not take place continuously, but in a series of small steps. The effect is due to orientation of *magnetic domains* present in the substance. Named after H. Barkhausen (born 1881).

BARN. Unit of area for measuring the *cross-section* of *nuclei*. 1 Barn equals 10^{-24} sq cm.

BAROGRAPH. An instrument used in *meteorology* for recording on paper the variations in atmospheric pressure over a period of time.

BAROMETER. (See also *aneroid* barometer.) An instrument for measuring atmospheric pressure. Consists of a long tube closed at the upper end filled with mercury and inverted in a vessel containing mercury; the vertical height of the mercury column which the atmospheric pressure is able at any time to support being taken as the atmospheric pressure at that time.

BARRIER-LAYER RECTIFIER. A *rectifier* which consists of a *semiconductor* between rectifying and non-rectifying metal *electrodes*.

BARYCENTRE. *Centre of mass*: particularly the centre of mass of the *Earth/Moon* system.

BAYRE. Unit of pressure in the *C.G.S. system*, equal to one *dyne* per sq cm.

BARYON. A collective name for *nucleons* and *hyperons*. The number of baryons minus the number of corresponding anti-baryons taking part in a process is called the baryon number – a quantity which appears to be conserved in all processes. All baryons have *spin* $\frac{1}{2}$. See Table 6, page 436.

BARYTA. See *barium oxide*.

BARYTES. Heavy spar. Natural *barium sulphate*, $BaSO_4$.

BASALT. A rock of volcanic origin, chemically resembling *felspar*.

BASE (chem.). A substance which reacts with an *acid* to form a *salt* and *water* only; substance which has a tendency to accept *protons*; substance which yields *hydroxyl ions* if dissolved in water. See also *organic base* and *Lewis acids and bases*.

BASE (math.). 1. The horizontal line upon which a geometric figure stands. 2. The number which is a starting point for a numerical or logarithmic system. E.g. the *binary notation* is a numerical system to the base 2; common *logarithms* are to the base 10.

BASE (phys.). The part of a *transistor* which separates the *emitter* from the *collector*.

BASE EXCHANGE. Cation exchange. See *ion exchange*.

BASE METALS. In contradistinction to the *noble metals*, metals which corrode, tarnish, or oxidize on exposure to air, moisture, or heat.

BASIC (chem.). Having the properties of a *base*; opposite to *acidic*; reacting chemically with *acids* to form *salts*.

BASIC DYES. A group of *dyes* which are *salts* of *organic bases*, and are used for dyeing wool and natural silk, especially if bright shades are needed. Also used for staining *nucleic acids* in *biochemistry*.

BASIC SALT. A *salt* which has been formed by the partial neutralization of a *base*; consists of the normal salt combined with a definite molecular proportion of the base. E.g. *white lead*, basic *lead carbonate*, $2PbCO_3.Pb(OH)_2$.

BASIC SLAG. An impure *mixture* of tetracalcium phosphate, $Ca_4P_2O_9$, *calcium silicate*, $CaSiO_3$, *lime*, CaO, and *ferric oxide*, Fe_2O_3. By-product of *steel* manufacture; its high phosphorus content makes it a valuable *fertilizer*.

BATH SALTS. The main constituent is generally sodium sesquicarbonate, $Na_2CO_3.NaHCO_3.2H_2O$, or some other *soluble* sodium *salt* to soften the *water*. See *hard water*.

BATHYMETRY. Measurement of depth, especially of the sea.

BATTERY. A number of *primary* or *secondary cells* arranged in series or parallel. In series, they give a multiple of the *E.M.F.* of the cell; in parallel, they give the same E.M.F. as the cell, but have a greater capacity, i.e. a given current can be supplied for a longer period. The common 'dry batteries' usually consist of *Leclanché cells*.

BAUMÉ SCALE. A scale of *specific gravity* of *liquids*. Named after A. Baumé (1728–1804).

$$\text{Degrees Baumé} = \frac{144 \cdot 3 (\text{S.G.} - 1)}{\text{S.G.}}; \quad \text{S.G.} = \frac{144 \cdot 3}{144 \cdot 3 - \text{Degrees Baumé}}$$

BAUXITE. Natural *hydrated aluminium oxide*, $Al_2O_3.xH_2O$. The most important *ore* of aluminium.

BAUXITE CEMENT. Ciment fondu. A rapid-hardening *cement* consisting mainly of calcium aluminate; made from *bauxite* and *lime* in an electric furnace.

BEAM (phys.). *Radiation* travelling in a particular direction.

BEAM HOLE. A hole made in the shield, and usually through the *reflector*, of a *nuclear reactor* to permit the escape of a beam of radiation, particularly *neutrons*, for experimental purposes.

BEAM RIDING. A method of *rocket* guidance in which the missile steers itself along the axis of a *beam* of *radiation*, usually a conically scanned *radar* beam.

BEAM TRANSMISSION. *Radio* transmission in which the *electromagnetic waves* are sent in a particular direction in a *beam* instead of being radiated in all directions.

BEARING (math.). The direction of a point B from a fixed point A; stated either in terms of the angle the line AB makes with the line running due North and South through A (e.g. 20° East of North), or in terms of the angle the line AB makes with the line running due North through A, considered in a clockwise direction.

BEAT FREQUENCY. The difference *frequency* resulting from the inter-action between *radio frequency* signals of different *wavelengths*.

BEATS (phys.). A periodic increase and decrease in loudness which is heard when two notes of nearly the same *frequency* are sounded simultaneously. Caused by *interference* of *sound* waves, the number of beats produced per second is equal to the difference in frequencies of the two notes.

BEAUFORT SCALE. A numerical scale for the estimation of wind force, based on its effect on common objects. The table below gives the scale:

Beaufort number	Description of wind	Wind speed metres per sec.
0	Calm	< 0·3
1	Light air	0·3–1·5
2	Light breeze	1·6–3·3
3	Gentle breeze	3·4–5·4
4	Moderate breeze	5·5–7·9
5	Fresh breeze	8·0–10·7
6	Strong breeze	10·8–13·8
7	Near gale	13·9–17·1
8	Gale	17·2–20·7
9	Strong gale	20·8–24·4
10	Storm	24·5–28·4
11	Violent storm	28·5–32·6
12	Hurricane	> 32·7

Named after Admiral Sir F. Beaufort (1774–1857).

BECKMANN THERMOMETER. A sensitive *thermometer* for measuring small differences or changes in *temperature*. The quantity of mercury in the bulb can be varied by causing it to overflow into a reservoir at the top, thus enabling the thermometer to be used over various ranges of temperature. The scale covers 6–7 degrees and is graduated to 0·01 degree.

BEESWAX. A whitish *wax* consisting of a *mixture* of *compounds*, secreted by bees for the purpose of building their honeycombs. Used in polishes and cosmetics.

BEET SUGAR. Sucrose. $C_{12}H_{22}O_{11}$. Obtained from the sugar beet; chemically identical with *cane sugar*.

BEHENIC ACID. See *docosanoic acid*.

BEL. Ten *decibels*.

BELL, ELECTRIC. A simple device making use of the magnetic effect of an *electric current*. Closing the switch (see Fig. 3) causes a current, provided by a *Leclanché cell*, to flow through a small *electromagnet*. This then attracts a piece of soft iron attached to a hammer, causing the latter to strike the gong of the bell. The movement of the iron breaks the circuit; the current ceases to flow through the electromagnet, and the iron and attached hammer spring back into their original position, thus closing the circuit again; this process continues as long as the switch is closed.

FIGURE 3.

BELL METAL. An *alloy* of copper (60%–85%) and tin.

BENDING MOMENT. The bending moment about any point in a loaded beam is the *algebraic sum* of the *moments* of all the vertical *forces* to one side of that point.

BENTONITE. A clay-like material similar to *fuller's earth.*

BENZALDEHYDE. C_6H_5CHO. A colourless oily *liquid*, b.p. 178·1°C., with a smell of almonds. Used as a *solvent*, in the manufacture of *dyes*, and in perfumes.

BENZAL GROUP. The *bivalent radical* C_6H_5CH—.

BENZEDRINE*. See *amphetamine.*

BENZENE. Benzol. C_6H_6. A colourless *liquid aromatic hydrocarbon* found in *coal-tar*, b.p. 80·1°C. Used as a *solvent*, in motor fuel, and in the manufacture of numerous *organic compounds.*

BENZENE RING. Kekulé formula. The representation of *benzene* as a six-membered hexagonal carbon ring with alternate single and *double bonds*:

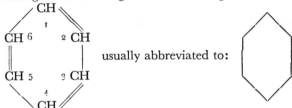

usually abbreviated to:

Derivatives are formed by substitution of hydrogen atoms, positions being indicated by numbering the ring as shown. See *ortho-, meta-, para-.*

BENZENESULPHONIC ACID. $C_6H_5SO_3H$. A crystalline *soluble* solid, m.p. 52·5°C., used in organic synthesis and as a *catalyst.*

BENZIDINE. $NH_2C_6H_4C_6H_4NH_2$. An *aromatic* base, m.p. 128°C., of importance in the dyestuff industry.

BENZINE. A *mixture* of *hydrocarbons* of the *paraffin* series, boiling 50°–65°C. Used for dry cleaning and as a *solvent.*

BENZOIC ACID. C_6H_5COOH. A white crystalline powder, the simplest of the *carboxylic acids* of the *aromatic* series, m.p. 122°C. Used as a food preservative, because it inhibits the growth of *yeasts* and moulds. Also used for this purpose in the form of its sodium *salt* which is highly water *soluble.*

BENZOIN. 1. $C_6H_5CHOH.CO.C_6H_5$. An *optically active* crystalline substance, m.p. 133-7°C., used in organic synthesis. 2. Gum Benjamin. A natural brown *aromatic resin* obtained from certain trees (Styrax Benzoin), used in incense and in the manufacture of cosmetics and perfumes.

BENZOL. Benzole. See *benzene.*

BENZONITRILE. Phenyl cyanide. C_6H_5CN. A colourless poisonous *liquid*, b.p. 190·7°C., used in organic synthesis.

BENZOPHENONE. Diphenyl ketone. $C_6H_5COC_6H_5$. A crystalline *insoluble* solid, m.p. 48·1°C., used in organic synthesis.

BENZOPYRENE. $C_{20}H_{12}$. A yellow crystalline *polycyclic hydrocarbon*, m.p. 179°C., found in small quantities in *coal-tar*. It is a *carcinogen* and is one of the most harmful constituents of tobacco smoke.

BENZOYL GROUP. The *univalent radical* C_6H_5CO—.

BENZOYL PEROXIDE. $(C_6H_5CO)_2O_2$. An *insoluble* crystalline explosive solid, m.p. 106–8°C., used in bleaching flour, fats, oils, etc., and as a *catalyst*.

BENZYL GROUP. The *univalent radical* $C_6H_5.CH_2$—.

BENZYL ALCOHOL. $C_6H_5CH_2OH$. A colourless *aromatic liquid*, b.p. 205·3°C., used as a *solvent* and in the manufacture of perfumes and flavours.

BENZYL CELLULOSE. A *benzyl ether* of *cellulose*, possessing good electrical insulating properties, which forms the basis of a *plastic* material.

BENZYLIDINE CHLORIDE. Benzal chloride. $C_6H_5CHCl_2$. A colourless oily *liquid*, b.p. 205·2°C., used in the manufacture of *dyes*.

BERBERINE. $C_{20}H_{19}NO_5$. A *soluble* crystalline *alkaloid*, m.p. 145°C., used in the form of its *sulphate* or *hydrochloride* in medicine.

BERGIUS PROCESS. A process for the manufacture of *oil* from *coal*. Coal, made into a paste with heavy oil, is heated with hydrogen under a pressure of 250 *atmospheres* to a *temperature* of 450°–470°C., in the presence of a *catalyst*. The carbon of the coal reacts with the hydrogen to give a mixture of various *hydrocarbons*. Named after F. Bergius (1884–1949).

BERKELIUM. Bk. *Transuranic element*. At. No. 97. A member of the *actinide* series. Most stable *isotope*, $^{247}_{97}Bk$, has a *half-life* of about 1400 years.

BERNOULLI'S THEOREM. At any point in a tube through which a *liquid* is flowing, the sum of pressure energy, *potential energy*, and *kinetic energy* is constant. Named after Jacob Bernoulli (1654–1705).

BERTHOLLIDE COMPOUNDS. Chemical *compounds* the composition of which does not conform to a simple ratio of *atoms* in the *molecule*.

BERYL. Natural beryllium silicate, $3BeO.Al_2O_3.6SiO_2$.

BERYLLIUM. Glucinum. Be. Element. A.W. 9·0122, At. No. 4. Hard white *metal*, S.G. 1·85, m.p. 1280°C. Occurs as *beryl*, from which it is obtained by *electrolysis*. Used for light, corrosion-resisting *alloys*.

BESSEMER PROCESS. A process for making *steel* from *cast iron*. Molten iron from the *blast furnace* is run into the Bessemer converter, a large egg-shaped vessel with holes below. Through these, air is blown into the molten metal, and the carbon is oxidized. The requisite amount of *spiegel* is then added to introduce the correct amount of carbon for the type of steel required. In some modern converters, instead of air a mixture of oxygen and steam is blown into the molten metal to avoid the absorption of nitrogen by the steel. This is known as the VLN (very low nitrogen) process. Named after H. Bessemer (1813–98).

BETA-IRON. An allotropic (see *allotropy*) form of pure iron, stable be-

45

tween 768°C. and 910°C., similar to *alpha-iron* except that it is non-*magnetic*.

BETA PARTICLE. An *electron* or *positron* emitted by a *radioactive nucleus*. The emission of an electron involves the change of a *neutron* into a *proton* within the nucleus, while the emission of a positron involves the change of a proton into a neutron. Beta particles do not exist within the nucleus, but are created at the instant of emission. See *neutrino*.

BETA RAYS. A stream of *beta particles*; possess greater penetrating power than *alpha rays* and are emitted with velocities in some cases exceeding 98% of the *velocity* of light.

BETA TRANSFORMATION. Beta process, beta decay. The transformation of a *nucleus* caused by the emission of a *beta particle*. A beta transformation involves a unit change of *atomic number* but no change of *mass number*.

BETATRON. A cyclic *accelerator* for accelerating a continuous beam of *electrons* to high speeds by means of the *electric field* produced by a changing magnetic flux. The electrons move in stable circular orbits in an evacuated *torus*-shaped chamber. By allowing the fast electrons to strike a metal target a continuous source of *gamma rays* with energies up to 100 MeV can be produced.

BEVATRON. A cyclic *accelerator* for accelerating *protons* and other particles to very high *energies* (up to 6 *gigaelectron volts*).

BI-. Prefix denoting two; formerly used in chemical nomenclature to indicate an *acid salt* of a *dibasic acid*. See *bicarbonate*.

BICARBONATE. *Acid salt* of *carbonic acid*, H_2CO_3; carbonic acid in which half the *acidic hydrogen* has been replaced by a *metal*. E.g. sodium bicarbonate, $NaHCO_3$. However the use of 'bi-' as a prefix in such *compounds* has now been abandoned and the correct name for this substance is *sodium hydrogen carbonate*.

BI-CONCAVE. A term used to describe a *lens* which is *concave* on both sides. See Fig. 24, page 219.

BI-CONVEX. A term used to describe a *lens* which is *convex* on both sides. See Fig. 24, page 219.

BILE. A secretion of the liver of vertebrates which is important in the digestion of *fats*.

BILLION. Million million, 10^{12} (British); thousand million, 10^9 (American).

BIMETALLIC STRIP. A strip composed of two different *metals* welded together in such a way that a rise of *temperature* will cause it to buckle as a result of unequal expansion. Used in *thermostats*.

BIMORPH CELL. Two plates of *piezo-electric* material joined together so that they bend in proportion to an applied *voltage*.

BINARY CELL. An element in a *computer* which can store information by virtue of its ability to remain stable in one of two possible states.

BINARY COMPOUND. A chemical *compound* of two *elements* only. Denoted by the suffix -ide; e.g. *calcium carbide*, CaC_2.

46

BINARY NOTATION. Binary number system. A system of numbers which has only two different *digits*, usually 0 and 1. There are several ways of representing numbers in the binary notation, one common method is given below. Because it has only two digits this notation is used in *computers*.

Decimal system	Binary system
1	0001
2	0010
3	0011
4	0100
5	0101
6	0110
7	0111
8	1000
9	1001
10	1010

BINARY STARS. Two *stars* gravitationally attracted to each other, so that they revolve around their common *centre of gravity*, thus forming a *double star*.

BINDING ENERGY (phys.). The *energy* which must be supplied to a *nucleus* in order to cause it to decompose into its constituent *neutrons* and *protons*. The binding energy of a neutron or a proton is the energy required to remove a neutron or a proton from a nucleus.

BINOCULAR. Any optical instrument designed for the simultaneous use of both eyes; e.g. binocular field-glasses.

BINOMIAL. A mathematical expression consisting of the sum or difference of two terms; e.g. $a^2 - 3b$.

BINOMIAL NOMENCLATURE (bio.). The method of naming plants and animals introduced by Linnaeus in the mid eighteenth century. Every plant or animal has two Latin names; a generic name designating its genus, and a specific name indicating the species; e.g. Felis tigris, the tiger.

BINOMIAL THEOREM. The expansion of

$$(x+y)^n = x^n + nx^{n-1}y + \frac{n(n-1)}{\underline{|2}} x^{n-2}y^2 + \ldots + y^n,$$

n being a positive *integer*. In general, for n not a positive integer, the following expression is valid if the numerical value of x is less than unity:

$$(1+x)^n = 1 + nx + \frac{n(n-1)}{\underline{|2}} x^2 + \ldots \text{ to } \infty.$$

BIOCHEMISTRY. The *chemistry* of living matter.

BIOGENESIS. The biological doctrine that only life begets life, as opposed to the unsubstantiated theory that animate matter may still be spontaneously generated from inanimate matter. See *abiogenesis*.

BIOLOGY. The science of life, the main branches of which are *botany* and *zoology*. Other branches include *cytology, histology, morphology, physiology, embryology, ecology, genetics,* and *microbiology*. Related subjects are *biochemistry, biophysics,* and *biometry*.

BIOMETRY. The application of mathematical and statistical methods to the study of *biology*.

BIOPHYSICS. The application of *physics* to the study of *biology*.

BIOSPHERE. See *ecosphere*.

BIOTYPE. A group of individual *organisms* having the same genetic characteristics.

BIOTIN. $C_{10}H_{16}O_3N_2S$. A crystalline substance, m.p. 230°C.; a *vitamin* of the B complex, also known as vitamin H, widely distributed in nearly all living *cells* in very small quantities. Appears to be of importance in the *metabolism* of *carbohydrates, fats,* and *proteins*.

BIPHENYL. Diphenyl. $C_6H_5C_6H_5$. An *insoluble* colourless powder, m.p. 70°C., used in organic synthesis and in the manufacture of *dyes*.

BI-PRISM. An optical device for obtaining *interference* fringes; consists of two acute-angled *prisms* placed base to base.

BIRKELAND AND EYDE PROCESS. A process for the fixation of atmospheric nitrogen (see *fixation of nitrogen*), becoming obsolete. Nitrogen and oxygen from the atmosphere are made to combine to form *nitric oxide*, NO, by the action of an electric *arc*.

BISECTION. Division into two equal parts.

BISECTOR. A straight line that divides another line or angle into two equal parts.

BISMUTH. Bi. Element. A.W. 208·98. At. No. 83. A white crystalline *metal* with a reddish tinge, S.G. 9·7, m.p. 271°C. Brittle, rather poor *conductor* of *heat* and *electricity* which expands on solidifying. Occurs as the metal, or as the *oxide*, Bi_2O_3. Extracted by roasting the *ore* and heating with *coal*. Used in *alloys* of low *melting point* (see *Rose's metal, Wood's metal*); *compounds* used in medicine.

BISMUTH OXIDE CHLORIDE. Bismuth oxychloride. BiOCl. A white crystalline *insoluble* powder, used in the manufacture of *pigments* and artificial pearls.

BISMUTH NITRATE. $Bi(NO_3)_3.5H_2O$. A colourless *deliquescent* crystalline substance which, with a large excess of water, forms *basic* bismuth nitrate (bismuth sub-nitrate), $BiONO_3.H_2O$, a crystalline substance, m.p. 105°C., used in medicine.

BIT. A unit of information in *information theory*. The amount of information required to specify one of two alternatives, e.g. to distinguish between 1 and 0 in the *binary notation* as used in *computers*. Also used as a unit of capacity in a *store*. See also *byte, character,* and *word*.

BITTERN (chem.). The *mother-liquor* remaining after the crystallization of common *salt*, NaCl, from *sea-water*. Source of *compounds* of magnesium, bromine, and iodine.

BITUMEN. A term covering numerous *mixtures* of *hydrocarbons*, more particularly solid or tarry mixtures, *soluble* in *carbon disulphide*.

BITUMINOUS. Containing, or yielding upon *distillation, bitumen* or *tar*.

BIURET. Carbamyl urea. $NH_2CONH.CONH_2.H_2O$. An *insoluble* crystalline substance formed from *urea*. See *biuret reaction*.

BIURET REACTION. A *chemical reaction* in which an *alkaline solution* of *biuret* gives a purple colour on the addition of *cupric sulphate*. Used as a biochemical test for *protein* and *urea*.

BIVALENT. Divalent. Having a *valency* of two.

BLACK ASH. Impure *sodium carbonate* obtained in the *Leblanc process*.

BLACK BODY RADIATION. Full or complete *radiation*; radiation of all *frequencies*, such as would be emitted by an ideal 'black body' which absorbs all radiations falling upon it. As the *emissivity* of a black body is one, the radiation which it emits is a function of *temperature* only. See *Stefan's Law*.

BLACKDAMP. *Carbon dioxide* (in coal mines).

BLACKLEAD. Plumbago, graphite. Natural crystalline form of carbon. A soft grey-black *solid*; used for making vessels to resist high *temperatures*, in pencils, and as a lubricant.

BLANC FIXE. Artificial *barium sulphate*, $BaSO_2$. Used as an *extender* in the *paint* industry.

BLANKET (phys.). A layer of *fertile* material surrounding the core of a *nuclear reactor* to act as a *reflector*, or for the purpose of breeding new fuel. See *breeder reactor*.

BLAST FURNACE. A furnace for the smelting of iron from iron oxide *ores*. Constructed of *refractory* bricks covered with *steel* plates. Charged from above with a mixture of the ore, *limestone* ($CaCO_3$), and *coke*. The coke is ignited at the bottom of the furnace by a blast of hot air; the *carbon monoxide* so produced reduces the iron oxide to iron, while the heat of the action decomposes the limestone into *carbon dioxide* and *lime*, CaO. The lime combines with the sand and other impurities in the ore to form a molten *slag*. The molten iron and the slag are tapped off at the bottom of the furnace. The resulting *pig-iron* or *cast iron* contains up to $4 \cdot 5\%$ carbon.

BLASTING GELATIN. Jelly-like mixture of *gun-cotton* with *nitroglycerin*. A very powerful *explosive*.

BLASTULA. A hollow ball of *cells* which forms in the very early embryonic development of animals.

BLEACHING. Removing the colour from coloured materials by chemically changing the dyestuffs into colourless substances. *Bleaching powder* and other *oxidizing agents*, or *sulphur dioxide* and other *reducing agents* are often used.

BLEACHING POWDER. Chloride of lime. A whitish powder, consisting mainly of calcium oxychloride, $CaOCl_2$, with water; prepared by the action of chlorine on *calcium hydroxide*, $Ca(OH)_2$. The action of *dilute acids* liberates chlorine which acts as an *oxidizing agent* and so bleaches the material.

49

BLENDE. Natural *zinc sulphide*, ZnS.

BLINK MICROSCOPE. Blink comparator. An instrument for examining photographs of the sky taken in rapid succession to each other. Minor *planets* and *stars* with large *proper motions*, or rapid changes of *luminosity*, are thereby made conspicuous.

BLOOD. A *liquid* which circulates throughout the body of the higher animals, transporting oxygen and *cell* foods to all the component cells of the body, and removing their excretions. Blood consists of a liquid, *blood plasma*, in which *blood cells* are suspended. The average human male has about 11 pints (6·2 litres) of blood in his body.

BLOOD CELLS. Blood corpuscles, haemocytes. There are three types of blood cell: red corpuscles (*erythrocytes*), white corpuscles (*leucocytes*), and *blood platelets* (thrombocytes). The function of the red corpuscles is to transport oxygen throughout the body, by way of the *haemoglobin* which they contain. The function of the white cells is to combat infection.

BLOOD PLASMA. *Blood* from which all *blood cells* have been removed. Plasma is 90% water, in which the principal *solutes* are *proteins*, *salts*, *sugar*, and *urea*.

BLOOD PLATELETS. Thrombocytes. Small membrane-bounded coin-shaped particles which circulate in the *blood*. If a blood vessel should break, the platelets clump together to form a plug to stop the bleeding. Platelets contain substantial quantities of ATP, and it is now known that the diphosphate causes the agglutination. Human blood contains about 250 000 platelets per cubic millimetre.

BLOWN OIL. A thickened *oil* made by blowing air through a natural vegetable or animal oil.

BLOWPIPE. A device for producing a jet of *flame* by forcing an inflammable *gas* mixed with air or oxygen through a nozzle at high pressure.

BLUE VITRIOL. Bluestone. Crystalline *cupric sulphate*, $CuSO_4.5H_2O$. Used for copper plating and in *solution* for spraying plants.

BLUE-PRINT. Cyanotype. A device much used for reproducing electrical circuit diagrams, engineering designs, etc. Sensitive paper, coated with an organic *ferric salt* and *potassium ferricyanide*, $K_3Fe(CN)_6$, is used; the original drawing is placed over this and the whole exposed to *light*. The sensitive paper is then developed by washing with water; this gives an image of white lines on a blue background. The blue colour is caused by the reduction of the ferric salt to a *ferrous* salt by the action of light, and the interaction of the ferrous salt with the potassium ferricyanide to give *Prussian Blue*.

BLUESTONE. See *blue vitriol*.

BOARD OF TRADE UNIT. B.O.T. unit. Legal British unit of *electrical energy*, the *kilowatt-hour*. The energy obtained when a *power* of 1 *kilowatt* is maintained for 1 hour.

BOART. See *bort*.

BODY-CENTRED. A *crystal* is said to be body-centred when there is a *lattice* point at the centre of the body of the crystal as well as at the corners. It is said to be 'face-centred' when there is a lattice point at the centre of each face. See Fig. 4.

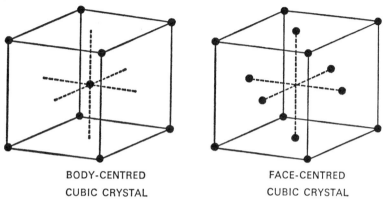

BODY-CENTRED
CUBIC CRYSTAL

FACE-CENTRED
CUBIC CRYSTAL

FIGURE 4.

BOG IRON ORE. Impure form of *hydrated ferric oxide*, $Fe_2O_3.xH_2O$, found in bogs and marshes.

BOHR THEORY of hydrogen atom spectrum. Theory of the *atom* put forward by Niels Bohr (1885–1962) to explain the *line spectrum* observed for hydrogen (see *Balmer series*). Based on three postulates: 1. The *electrons* rotate in certain *orbits* round the *nucleus* of the atom without radiating *energy* in the form of *electromagnetic waves*. 2. These orbits are such that the *angular momentum* of the electron about the nucleus is an *integral* multiple of $h/2\pi$, where $h = Planck's\ constant$. 3. Emission or absorption of radiation occurs when an electron jumps from one of these so-called *stationary states* of energy E_1 to another of energy E_2, the *frequency*, v, of the emitted (or absorbed) *light* being given by $E_1 - E_2 = hv$. If E_1 is greater than E_2, light is emitted; conversely, light is absorbed. See *quantum mechanics*. This theory has now been superseded by the application of *wave mechanics*, which has shown that for the hydrogen atom spectrum, Bohr's theory is a very good approximation. Wave mechanics has the advantage of requiring no *ad hoc* assumptions and can deal more effectively with the problem of atoms with two or more electrons. (See also *atom, structure of.*)

BOILED OIL. *Linseed oil* boiled with, or containing, a drying agent such as *lead monoxide*, PbO. Used in *paints*.

BOILING. Ebullition. The state of a *liquid* at its *boiling point* when the maximum *vapour pressure* of the liquid is equal to the external pressure to which the liquid is subject, and the liquid is freely converted into *vapour*.

BOILING POINT. B.p. The *temperature* at which the maximum *vapour pressure* of a *liquid* is equal to the external pressure; the temperature at which the liquid boils freely under that pressure. Boiling points are normally quoted for standard atmospheric pressure, i.e. 760 mm of mercury.

BOILING WATER REACTOR. BWR. A *nuclear reactor* in which *water* is used as *coolant* and *moderator*. *Steam* is thus produced in the reactor under pressure, and can be used to drive a *turbine*.

BOLIDE. A large bright *meteor*; some of these objects explode on entering the *Earth's atmosphere*.

BOLOMETER. An extremely sensitive instrument for measuring *heat radiations*. Consists essentially of two very thin, blackened platinum gratings, forming two arms of a *Wheatstone bridge* circuit. Radiant heat falling upon one of the gratings raises its electrical *resistance*, thus causing a deflection of the needle of a *galvanometer* in the circuit.

BOLTZMANN'S CONSTANT. $k = \dfrac{R}{L} = 1 \cdot 38054 \times 10^{-23}$ *joule* per *kelvin*

where $R =$ the *gas constant* and $L = Avogradro's constant$.
Named after L. Boltzmann (1844–1906).

BOMB CALORIMETER. A strong metal vessel used for measuring *heats of reaction*, especially *heats of combustion*; e.g. for determining the *calorific value* of a *fuel*. To do this, a known *weight* of the substance under test is burnt in the vessel, and by measuring the quantity of heat produced, the calorific value is calculated.

BOND. Valency bond, linkage. A representation of a *valency* link by which one *atom* is attached to another in a chemical *compound*.

BOND ENERGY. The *energy* characterizing a chemical *bond* between two *atoms*. Measured by the energy required to separate the two atoms.

BOND LENGTH. The distance between the *nuclei* of two *atoms* joined by a chemical *bond*.

BONE ASH. *Ash* obtained by heating bones in air. Consists mainly of *calcium phosphate*, $Ca_3(PO_4)_2$.

BONE BLACK. See *animal charcoal*.

BONE CHAR. See *animal charcoal*.

BONE OIL. Dippel's oil. Product obtained by the *destructive distillation* of bones. Dark oily evil-smelling liquid used as a source of *pyridine*.

BOOLEAN ALGEBRA. A branch of symbolic logic used in *computers*. Logical operations are performed by operators such as 'and', 'or', 'not-and' in a way analogous to mathematical signs. Named after George Boole (1815–64).

BOOSTER. See *rocket*.

BORACIC ACID. See *boric acid*.

BORATE. A *salt* or *ester* of *boric acid*.

BORAX. See *sodium tetraborate*.

BORAX BEAD TEST. A chemical test for the presence of certain *metals*. A bead of *borax* fused in a wire loop will react chemically with the *salts* of a number of metals, often producing colours which help to identify the metal; e.g. manganese *compounds* give a violet bead, cobalt a deep blue.

BORDEAUX MIXTURE. A mixture of *cupric sulphate*, $CuSO_4$, *calcium oxide*, CaO, and *water*. Used for spraying plants as a *fungicide* for plant diseases.

BORIC ACID. Orthoboric acid, boracic acid. H_3BO_3. A white crystalline *soluble solid*. Occurs naturally in volcanic regions; also manufactured from *borax*. Used as a mild *antiseptic* and in various industries.

BORIC OXIDE. Boric anhydride. B_2O_3. An *oxide* which exists either as a transparent crystalline substance, m.p. 460°C., or a transparent *amorphous glass*. Used in the manufacture of special glasses.

BORIDE. A *binary compound* with boron.

BORNEOL. Bornyl alcohol. $C_{10}H_{17}OH$. A white *optically active translucent* solid, m.p. 210·5°C., used in the manufacture of synthetic *camphor* and in perfumes.

BORNYL ACETATE. $C_{10}H_{17}COOCH_3$. A colourless *liquid*, b.p. 223°C., with a *camphor*-like odour. Used in the manufacture of perfumes and as a *plasticizer*.

BORON. B. Element. A.W. 10·811. At. No. 5. A brown *amorphous* powder, S.G. 2·37, or yellow *crystals*, S.G. 2·34; m.p. 2300°C. Occurs as *borax* and *boric acid*. Used for hardening *steel* and for producing *enamels* and *glasses*. As boron absorbs slow *neutrons*, it is used in steel *alloys* for making *control rods* in *nuclear reactors*.

BORON CARBIDE. B_4C. A very hard black crystalline substance, m.p. 2450°C., used as an *abrasive* and as a *moderator* in *nuclear reactors*.

BORON CHAMBER. An *ionization chamber* lined with boron or boron *compounds* or filled with boron trifluoride *gas*. Used in *boron counter tubes*.

BORON COUNTER TUBES. A *counter tube* containing a *boron chamber* used for counting *neutrons*. The counting pulse results from particles emitted when *neutrons* react with the $^{10}_{5}B$ *isotope*.

BORT. Boart. Impure or discoloured *diamond*, useless as a gem, but as hard as pure diamond, and used for drills, cutting tools, etc.

BOSCH PROCESS. An industrial process for the manufacture of hydrogen. *Water gas*, a *mixture* of *carbon monoxide* and hydrogen, is mixed with *steam* and passed over a heated *catalyst*. The steam reacts chemically with the carbon monoxide to give *carbon dioxide*, CO_2, and hydrogen. The CO_2 is then removed by dissolving it in water under pressure. Named after C. Bosch (1874–1940).

BOSE-EINSTEIN STATISTICS. The branch of *statistical mechanics* used with systems of identical particles which have the property that the *wave function* remains unchanged if any two particles are interchanged. See *bosons*. Named after S. N. Bose (1858–1937) and Albert Einstein (1879–1955).

BOSONS. Particles which conform to *Bose-Einstein statistics*, such as *photons* and *mesons*, whose numbers are not conserved in particle interactions. Bosons have *integral spin* (0, 1, 2). See Table 6, page 437.

BOTANY. The scientific study of plants.

BOUNDARY LAYER. The layer of *fluid* closest to a body over which the fluid is flowing; owing to the *force* of *adhesion* between the body and the fluid the boundary layer has a reduced rate of flow.

BOURDON GAUGE. A *pressure* gauge for steam boilers, etc. Depends on the tendency of a partly flattened curved tube to straighten out when under internal pressure.

BOYLE'S LAW. At a constant *temperature*, the *volume* of a given quantity of any *gas* is inversely proportional to the *pressure* upon the gas; i.e. $V \propto \dfrac{1}{P}$, or $PV = $ constant. True for a *perfect gas*. Named after Robert Boyle (1627–91). See also *gas laws*.

BRAGG'S LAW. When a *beam* of *X-rays*, of *wavelength* λ, strikes a *crystal* surface, the maximum intensity of the reflected ray occurs when $\sin \theta = \dfrac{n\lambda}{2d}$. Where d is the distance separating the layers of the *atoms* or *ions* in the crystal, θ is the *complement* of the angle of *incidence*, and n is an *integer*. Named after W. H. Bragg (1862–1942) and W. L. Bragg (born 1890).

BRAKE HORSEPOWER. The *horsepower* of an engine measured by the degree of resistance offered by a brake; represents the useful horsepower that the engine can develop.

BRANCHING (phys.). The occurrence of more than one *radioactive disintegration* scheme for a particular *nuclide*.

BRASS. A large class of *alloys*, consisting principally of copper and zinc.

BREEDER REACTOR. A *nuclear reactor* which produces the same kind of *fissile* material as it burns. E.g. a reactor using plutonium as a fuel can produce more plutonium than it uses by conversion of uranium-238.

BREMSSTRAHLUNG (German, meaning 'brake radiation'). *X-rays* emitted when an *electron* strikes a positively charged *nucleus*; results from the direct conversion of *kinetic energy* into *electromagnetic radiation*.

BREWING. The making of beer. *Malt* is ground and mixed with water. In the resulting 'mash', chemical changes take place, the chief of which is the conversion of *starch* into *maltose*, forming a sweetish liquid known as wort. This is boiled with the addition of hops. After cooling and removal of *solids, yeast* is added and *fermentation* occurs.

BREWSTER'S LAW. The tangent of the angle of *polarization* is numerically equal to the *refractive index* of the reflecting medium when the polarization is a maximum. Named after David Brewster (1781–1868).

BRIGHTNESS. The brightness at any point of an extended source, in a given direction, is the quotient of the *luminous intensity* of a small element of the source containing the point, and the area of the element projected on to a plane perpendicular to the given direction. Measured in *candelas* per unit area.

BRIMSTONE. Sulphur fused into blocks or rolls.

BRINELL TEST. A test for the hardness of *metals*. A ball of chrome *steel*, or other hard material, of standard size, is pressed by a heavy load into the surface of the metal, and the diameter of the depression is measured. The Brinell Number is the ratio of the load in *kilogrammes* to the *area* of the depression in square millimetres. Named after J. A. Brinell (1849–1925).

BRITANNIA METAL. An *alloy* of variable composition, containing 80%–90% tin, with some antimony and copper, and sometimes also zinc and lead.

BRITISH THERMAL UNIT. The quantity of *heat* required to raise the *temperature* of 1 lb of *water* through 1° Fahrenheit; equal to 251·997 *calories* or 1055·06 *joules*.

BROMATE. A *salt* of *bromic acid*.

BROMIC ACID. $HBrO_3$. A *compound* which is only stable in *dilute solution*. Formed by the action of *sulphuric acid* on barium bromate, and used as an *oxidizing agent*.

BROMIDE. *Salt* of *hydrobromic acid*, HBr; *binary compound* with bromine. 'Bromide' of pharmacy is *potassium bromide*, KBr.

BROMIDE PAPER. Photographic paper containing *silver bromide*, AgBr.

BROMINE. Br. Element. A.W. 79·909. At. No. 35. A dark red fuming *liquid* with a choking, irritating smell, b.p. 58·8° C. Occurs as magnesium bromide, $MgBr_2$, in *bittern* from *sea-water*, in the *Stassfurt deposits*, in marine plants and animals, and in some inland lakes. Used as a *disinfectant* and in the manufacture of some *organic compounds*. Compounds are used in *photography* and medicine.

BROMOFORM. $CHBr_3$. A colourless *liquid*, m.p. 8·3° C., b.p. 149·5° C., used in organic synthesis.

BRONZE. A class of *alloys* of copper and tin; term is also sometimes applied to alloys containing no tin, e.g. *aluminium bronze*, an alloy of copper and aluminium.

BROWNIAN MOVEMENT. Erratic random movements performed by microscopic particles in a *disperse phase*; e.g. particles in suspension in a *liquid*, or *smoke* particles in air. Caused by the continuous irregular bombardment of the particles by the *molecules* of the surrounding medium. Named after Robert Brown (1773–1858).

BRUNSWICK GREEN. See *copper oxide chloride*.

BRUSH DISCHARGE. The discharge of *electricity* from sharp points on a *conductor*. The surface density (i.e. quantity of electricity per unit area) is greatest at sharp points; the high charge at such points causes a displacement of the charge on the air particles near the points, and hence an attraction to the points. On reaching the points, the particles acquire some of the charge on the points and are repelled. This causes a stream of charged air particles to leave the vicinity of the points.

BUBBLE CHAMBER. An instrument for making the tracks of ionizing particles visible as a row of bubbles in a *liquid*. The liquid is heated to slightly above its *boiling point* and maintained under *pressure* to prevent boiling. Immediately before the passage of the particles the pressure is reduced, the ionized particles then act as centres for the formation of small *vapour* bubbles which can be photographed to give a record of the tracks of the particles.

BUCHNER FUNNEL. A funnel, usually of *porcelain*, with a flat circular base perforated with small holes. Used for filtering by suction. Named after E. Buchner (1860–1917).

BUFFER SOLUTION. A *solution* the *hydrogen ion concentration* of which, and hence the acidity or alkalinity, is practically unchanged by dilution, and which resists a change of *pH* on the addition of *acid* or *alkali*.

BULK MODULUS. *Elastic modulus* applied to a body having uniform *stress* distributed over the whole of its surface. Its value is given by the expression $\dfrac{pV}{v}$ where $p=$ intensity of stress, $V=$ original *volume* of the body, and $v=$ change in volume.

BUNSEN BURNER. A burner for *coal-gas*, used in laboratories. Consists of a metal tube with an adjustable air-valve for burning a mixture of gas and air. Named after R. W. Bunsen (1811–99).

BUNSEN CELL. A *primary cell* in which the *anode* consists of zinc and is immersed in dilute *sulphuric acid*, and the *cathode* consists of carbon immersed in concentrated *nitric acid*.

BUOYANCY. The upward thrust exerted upon a body immersed in a *fluid*; equal to the *weight* of the fluid displaced. (See *Archimedes' Principle*). Thus a body weighs less when weighed in water, the apparent loss in weight being equal to the weight of the water displaced. For accurate weighing of bodies in air, a small allowance has to be made to correct for the buoyancy of the body.

BURETTE. A graduated glass tube with a tap, for measuring the volume of *liquid* run out from it. Used in *volumetric analysis*.

BURNING. See *combustion*.

BURNT ALUM. A white porous mass of *anhydrous* potassium aluminium sulphate, $K_2SO_4.Al_2(SO_4)_3$, obtained by heating *alum*.

BUTADIENE. $CH_2:CH.CH:CH_2$. A *gas* used in the manufacture of synthetic *rubbers*. See *styrene-butadiene rubber*, *nitrile rubber*, and *stereoregular rubbers*.

BUTANE. C_4H_{10}. A *hydrocarbon* of the *paraffin series*. Gas at ordinary *temperatures*. B.p. $-0.5°$ C. Used in the manufacture of *synthetic rubber* and as a *fuel* (e.g. in cylinders under pressure under the trade name Butagas*).

BUTANEDIONE. Diacetyl, biacetyl. $CH_3COCOCH_3$. A yellow *liquid*, b.p. 89° C., which occurs in butter. Used as a flavour.

BUTANOL. Butyl alcohol. C_4H_9OH. A *liquid* which exists in three *isomeric* forms. Butan-1-ol, $CH_3CH_2CH_2CH_2OH$, has a b.p. $117.5°$ C. and is used as a *solvent*.

BUTANONE. Ethyl methyl ketone. $C_2H_5COCH_3$. An inflammable *liquid*, b.p. $79.6°$ C., used as a *solvent* and in the manufacture of *plastics*.

BUTTER OF ANTIMONY. Antimony trichloride. $SbCl_3$. A white crystalline substance, m.p. $73°C$.

BUTYL GROUP. The *univalent alkyl radical* C_4H_9—.

BUTYL RUBBER. A synthetic *rubber*; copolymer (see *polymerization*) of iso-butylene and sufficient *isoprene* (2%–3%) to enable vulcanization to be effected. Owing to its low *permeability* to *gases*, butyl rubber is used in the manufacture of tyre inner tubes.

BUTYRALDEHYDE. Butanal. $CH_3(CH_2)_2CHO$. A colourless inflammable *liquid*, b.p. $75·7°C$., used in the *plastics* and *rubber* industries.

BUTYRIC ACID. Butanoic acid. C_3H_7COOH. A *liquid* with a rancid odour, b.p. $163·5°C$., which occurs in rancid butter. Used in the form of its *esters* as a flavouring.

BUTYRYL GROUP. The *univalent radical* $CH_3(CH_2)_2CO$—.

BUZZER. A device similar in principle to the electric *bell*, but without a hammer or gong. The rapid vibration of the arm produces a definite buzzing note when the current flows.

BYPASS CAPACITOR. Bypass condenser. A *capacitor* which provides a path of low *impedance* over a certain range of *frequencies*.

BY-PRODUCT. A substance obtained incidentally during the manufacture of some other substance. Often as important as the manufactured substance itself. E.g. the by-products of *coal-gas* manufacture include *ammonia*, *coal-tar*, and *coke*.

BYTE. A single unit of information handled by a *computer*; usually 8 *bits*.

C

CABLE, COAXIAL. A cable consisting of central conducting wire together with a concentric cylindrical *conductor*, the space between the two being filled with a *dielectric* substance, e.g. *polythene*, air, etc. The outer conductor is normally connected to earth. Its main use is to transmit *high-frequency* power from one place to another with minimum *energy* loss; e.g. from a *transmitter* to its *aerial*.

CACODYL GROUP. The *univalent radical* $(CH_3)_2As—$, derived from *arsine*.

CACODYLIC ACID. Dimethyl arsinic acid. $(CH_3)_2AsOOH$. A colourless *deliquescent* crystalline solid, m.p. 200°C., used in the manufacture of *dyes* and as a weed killer.

CADMIUM. Cd. Element. A.W. 112·40. At. No. 48. A soft silvery-white *metal*, S.G. 8·642, m.p. 320·9°C. Occurs together with zinc. Used in the manufacture of *fusible alloys* and for *electroplating*. As cadmium is a good absorber of *neutrons* it is used in the manufacture of *control rods* for *nuclear reactors*.

CADMIUM CELL. Standard *primary cell*. See *Weston cell*.

CADMIUM SULPHIDE. CdS. A yellow *insoluble* powder, used as a *pigment* known as 'cadmium yellow'. In the impure natural form it is known as 'greenockite'.

CAESIUM. Cesium. Cs. Element. A.W. 132·905. At. No. 55. A silvery-white *metal* resembling sodium in its physical and chemical properties. S.G. 1·87, m.p. 28·5°C. Highly reactive. *Compounds* are very rare. Used in *photo-electric cells* and as a *catalyst*.

CAFFEINE. Theine. $C_8H_{10}O_2N_4$. A white crystalline *purine*, m.p. 237°C. Occurs in tea-leaves, coffee-beans, and other plant material. Has a powerful action on the heart; used in medicine.

CALAMINE. A zinc mineral, originally either *zinc carbonate*, $ZnCO_3$, or *zinc silicate*, $2ZnO. SiO_2.H_2O$. In English usage calamine now refers to the carbonate but in American usage it refers to the silicate. Also used for a skin preparation consisting of *zinc oxide* with $\frac{1}{2}\%$ *ferric oxide*.

CALCIFEROL. Vitamin D_2. $C_{28}H_{43}OH$. A crystalline *unsaturated alcohol*, m.p. 115°C., formed by the action of *ultraviolet radiation* on *ergosterol*. See *vitamins*. It controls the deposition of calcium compounds in the body; deficiency causes rickets.

CALCINATION. Strong heating; conversion of *metals* into their *oxides* by heating in air.

CALCITE. Calcspar. Natural crystalline *calcium carbonate*, $CaCO_3$.

CALCIUM. Ca. Element. A.W. 40·08. At. No. 20. A soft white *metal* which tarnishes rapidly in air; S.G. 1·55, m.p. 845°C. *Compounds* are very abundant, widely distributed, and essential to life. Occurs as *calcium carbonate*, $CaCO_3$ (*limestone*, *marble*, and *chalk*); *calcium sulphate*, $CaSO_4$ (*gypsum*, *anhydrite*); essential constituent of bones and teeth. Compounds are of great industrial importance; e.g. *lime*.

CALCIUM CARBIDE. Carbide. CaC_2. A greyish solid, colourless when pure; prepared by heating *calcium oxide* with carbon in an electric furnace. Reacts with *water* to give *acetylene*.

CALCIUM CARBONATE. $CaCO_3$. A white *insoluble* solid; occurs naturally as *chalk, limestone, marble*, and *calcite*. Used in the manufacture of *lime* and *cement*.

CALCIUM CHLORIDE. $CaCl_2$. A white *deliquescent* substance, m.p. $772°C.$, obtained by reacting *calcium carbonate* with *hydrochloric acid*. Used as a drying agent and preservative.

CALCIUM CYANAMIDE. Cyanamide, Nitrolime. $CaCN_2$. A black crystalline powder made by heating *calcium carbide*, CaC_2, in nitrogen at $1000°C.$ Used as a *fertilizer* and converted by *water* in the soil into *ammonia*.

CALCIUM CYCLAMATE. $(C_6H_{11}NHSO_3)_2Ca.2H_2O$. A white crystalline *soluble* powder, formerly used as a sweetening agent in soft drinks, but its excessive consumption has been shown to be undesirable and it has therefore been banned.

CALCIUM HYDROXIDE. *Slaked lime.* $Ca(OH)_2$. A white crystalline powder, obtained by the action of *water* on *calcium oxide*, used in *mortars*, plaster, and *cement*.

CALCIUM OXIDE. *Quicklime.* CaO. A white solid, m.p. $2580°C.$, made by heating *calcium carbonate (limestone)* in lime-kilns. Combines with *water* to form *calcium hydroxide* (slaked lime). Used in *cements* and *mortars* and in the manufacture of calcium *compounds*.

CALCIUM NITRATE. A white *deliquescent* solid, m.p. $561°C.$, used in the manufacture of *fertilizers*, fireworks, *matches*, and *explosives*.

CALCIUM OXYCHLORIDE. Calcium hypochlorite. See *bleaching powder*.

CALCIUM PHOSPHATE. There are several *phosphates* of calcium which occur in rocks and animal bones. Tricalcium diorthophosphate, $Ca_3(PO_4)_2$, is a white *amorphous* powder, m.p. $1670°C.$ (see *bone ash*). It is converted to the more *soluble* calcium hydrogen orthophosphate, $Ca(H_2PO_4)_2.H_2O$, a *deliquescent* crystalline substance which is the main constituent of *superphosphate*. See also *octacalcium phosphate*.

CALCIUM SILICATE. $CaSiO_3$. A colourless crystalline substance, m.p. $1540°C.$, used in the manufacture of *glass* and *cement*.

CALCIUM SULPHATE. *Anhydrite.* $CaSO_4$. Also occurs as *gypsum*, $CaSO_4.2H_2O$. If gypsum is heated to $120°C.$ it becomes $CaSO_4.\frac{1}{2}H_2O$ and is known as *plaster of Paris*.

CALCIUM SULPHIDE. CaS. A colourless crystalline substance, having an odour of bad eggs, used in the manufacture of luminous *paints* and in cosmetics.

CALCULUS. Branch of mathematics, divided into two main parts, *differential* and *integral calculus*. Deals with *variable* quantities and their rates of change. Affords a powerful method of solving numerous mathematical problems.

CALIBRATION. The *graduation* of an instrument to enable measurements in definite *units* to be made with it; thus the arbitrary scale of a *galvanometer* may be calibrated in *amperes*, thereby converting the instrument into an *ammeter* for measuring *electric current*.

CALICHE. Impure natural *sodium nitrate* $NaNO_3$, found in Chile.

CALIFORNIUM. Cf. *Transuranic element*. At. No. 98. The most stable *isotope*, $^{251}_{98}Cf$, has a *half-life* of 800 years.

CALLIPERS. Calipers. An instrument for measuring the distance between two points, especially on a curved surface; e.g. for measuring the internal and external diameters of tubes.

CALOMEL. See *mercurous chloride*.

CALORESCENCE. Absorption of *light* radiations by a surface, their conversion into *heat*, and the consequent emission of heat *radiation*.

CALORIE. Unit of quantity of *heat*. The amount of heat required to raise the *temperature* of 1 g of *water* through 1°C. The 15° calorie is defined as the amount of heat required to raise the temperature of 1 g of water from 14·5°C. to 15·5°C. This calorie is equal to 4·1855 *joules*. The International Table Calorie is defined as 4·1868 joules. The joule is the *SI unit* of *heat*.

CALORIE, LARGE. Kilogramme-calorie. 1000 *calories*. Written Calorie or kcalorie. Used for quoting energy values of foods.

CALORIFIC VALUE of a fuel. The quantity of *heat* produced by a given *mass* of the *fuel* on complete *combustion*. Expressed in *joules* per *kilogramme (SI units)*, *calories* per gram (*c.g.s.* units) or *British Thermal Units* per pound (*f.p.s* units). Determined by the *bomb calorimeter*.

CALORIMETER. Instrument for determining quantities of *heat* evolved, absorbed, or transferred. In its simplest form consists of an open cylindrical vessel of copper or other substance of known *heat capacity*.

CALX. 1. The powdery *oxide* of a *metal* formed when an *ore* or a *mineral* is roasted. 2. Quicklime (see *calcium oxide*).

CAMERA, PHOTOGRAPHIC. A device for obtaining photographs or exposing cinematic film, either coloured or black and white. A camera consists essentially of a *light*-proof box with a *lens* at one end and a light-sensitive film or plate at the other. An 'exposure' is made by opening a 'shutter' over the lens for a predetermined period during which an image of the object to be photographed is thrown upon the light-sensitive film. Focusing is carried out by varying the distance of the lens from the film by a suitable device. The amount of light which enters the camera, in order to obtain a correctly exposed photograph, is determined by the amount of light available (either sunlight or artificial light), the 'speed' of the film, the *aperture* of the lens (see *f-number*), and the shutter speed. In the simplest cameras the shutter speed and aperture are fixed, so that satisfactory photographs can only be obtained in bright sunlight. In more expensive cameras the aperture can be controlled by a variable *iris* and several separate shutter speeds are provided. In some modern cameras the iris is controlled by the current from a built-in *photo-electric cell* (*exposure meter*) which measures the light available. Thus for given film and shutter speeds the camera automatically takes a correctly exposed photograph. In cinematic cameras the opening of the shutter is mechanically synchronized with the passage of the film through the camera so that, at normal speeds, between 16 and 24 frames are exposed every second. See also *photography*.

CAMERA, TELEVISION. That part of a *television* system which converts optical images into electrical signals. Consists of an optical *lens* system similar to that used in a photographic *camera*, the image from which is projected into a 'camera tube'. The camera tube comprises a *photosensitive mosaic* which is scanned by an *electron* beam housed in an evacuated glass tube. The output signals of the camera tube are usually pre-amplified within the body of the camera.

CAMPHOR. $C_{10}H_{16}O$. A white crystalline *solid* with a characteristic smell, m.p. $178°C$. Occurs in the camphor tree. Used in the manufacture of *celluloid* and in other industries.

CANADA BALSAM. A yellowish *liquid* derived from fir trees with a *refractive index* similar to that of *glass*. Used for mounting microscopic slides and as an *adhesive* for optical instruments.

CANAL RAYS. Positively charged *ions* produced during the *discharge* of electricity in gases, driven to the *cathode* by the applied *potential difference* and allowed to pass through canals bored in the cathode.

CANDELA. New candle. The *SI unit* of *luminous intensity*. Defined as the luminous intensity, in the horizontal direction, of a surface of $1/600\ 000$ square *metre* of a *black body* at the *temperature* of freezing platinum under a *pressure* of $101\ 325\ Nm^{-2}$. The candela now replaces the *international candle*. Symbol C.

CANDLEPOWER of a light source, in a given direction, is the *luminous intensity* of the source in that direction expressed in terms of the *candela*. Formerly expressed in terms of the *international candle*.

CANDLE WAX. Usually either *paraffin wax* or *stearine*.

CANE SUGAR. Sucrose, saccharose. $C_{12}H_{22}O_{11}$. A *disaccharide* obtained from the sugar-cane. Chemically identical with *beet sugar*.

CANTON'S PHOSPHORUS. Impure *calcium sulphide*, CaS, having the property of *phosphorescence* after exposure to *light*. Used in luminous *paints*.

CAOUTCHOUC. Raw *rubber*.

CAPACITANCE. Electrical capacity. *C*. The property of a system of electrical *conductors* and *insulators* which enables it to store *electric charge* when a *potential difference* exists between the conductors. Measured by the charge which must be communicated to such a system to raise its potential by one unit. The *SI unit* of capacitance is the *farad*.

CAPACITOR. Electrical condenser. A system of electrical *conductors* and *insulators*, the principal characteristic of which is its *capacitance*. The simplest form consists of two parallel *metal* plates separated by a layer

61

of air or some other insulating material, such as *mica* (see *dielectric*). The capacitance, *C*, of such a parallel plate capacitor is given by:

$$C = \frac{A\epsilon}{d}$$

where ϵ is the *permittivity*, in *farad* per *metre*, *A* the area of plate, and *d* the distance between them.

CAPILLARY ACTION. Capillarity. A general term for phenomena observed in *liquids* due to unbalanced inter-molecular attraction at the liquid boundary; e.g. the rise or depression of liquids in narrow tubes, the formation of films, drops, bubbles, etc.

CAPILLARY TUBE. A tube of small internal diameter.

CAPROIC ACID. See *hexanoic acid*.

CAPTURE. A process by which an atomic or nuclear system acquires an additional particle, e.g. the capture of *electrons* by *ions* or of *neutrons* by *nuclei*. 'Radiative capture' is a nuclear capture process which results in the emission of *gamma rays* only.

CARAMEL (chem.). A brown substance of complex composition, formed by the action of *heat* on *sugar*.

CARAT. 1. A measure of weight of *diamonds* and other gems; formerly 3·17 grains (0·2053 g), now standardized as the international carat, 0·200 g. 2. A measure of *fineness* of gold, expressed as parts of gold in 24 parts of the *alloy*. Thus, 24 carat gold is pure gold, 18 carat gold contains 18 parts in 24 or has a fineness of 750.

CARBAMIDE. See *urea*.

CARBIDE. *Binary compound* of carbon; loose term for *calcium carbide*.

CARBOCYCLIC COMPOUNDS. *Organic compounds* containing a closed ring of carbon *atoms* within the *molecule*. E.g. *benzene*, C_6H_6, has a molecule of six carbon atoms joined in a ring, with a hydrogen atom attached to each. See *benzene ring*.

CARBOHYDRATES. A large group of *organic compounds* composed of carbon, hydrogen, and oxygen only, with the general formula $C_x(H_2O)_y$. Comprises *monosaccharides*, *disaccharides* (both *sugars*), and *polysaccharides (starch* and *cellulose)*. Carbohydrates play an essential part in the *metabolism* of all living *organisms*, starch being the principal form in which *energy* is stored and cellulose being the principal structural material of plants.

CARBOLIC ACID. See *phenol*.

CARBON. C. Element. A.W. 12·011, At. No. 6, m.p. 3550°C. Occurs in several allotropic forms (see *allotropy*) including *diamond* (S.G. 3·51) and *graphite* (S.G. 2·25); and as *amorphous* carbon (S.G. 1·8–2·1) in the forms of *lamp-black*, *gas carbon*, etc. *Compounds* occur as the metallic *carbonates*, *carbon dioxide* in the air, and an enormous number of *organic compounds*. Owing to its *valency* of four, carbon *atoms* are able to unite with each other to form the very large *molecules* upon which life is based. See *carbon cycle (bio.)*. Animals obtain their energy by the *oxidation* of carbon compounds eaten as food.

CARBON BLACK. Finely divided form of pure carbon, obtained by the incomplete *combustion* of *natural gas*. Used in the manufacture of *inks*, *rubber* products, and some *plastics*.

CARBON CYCLE (bio.). The circulation of carbon (as *carbon dioxide*) between living *organisms* and the *atmosphere*. Carbon dioxide is built into complex carbon *compounds* by plants during *photosynthesis*; animals obtain their carbon *atoms* by feeding on plants or other animals; during *respiration*, and by decay after death, some of this carbon is returned to the atmosphere in the form of carbon dioxide.

CARBON CYCLE (phys.). A cycle of six consecutive *nuclear reactions* resulting in the formation of a *helium* nucleus from four *protons*. The carbon nuclei with which the cycle starts are reformed at the end and therefore act as a *catalyst*. The *energy* liberated by the carbon cycle is thought to be the main source of energy in a large class of *stars*.

CARBON DIOXIDE. Carbonic acid gas. CO_2. A colourless *gas* with faint tingling smell and taste. Occurs in the *atmosphere*; formed by the *oxidation* of carbon and carbon *compounds*. Utilized by plants. See *photosynthesis* and *carbon cycle (bio.)*. Forms a solid at $-78.5°C$. at atmospheric pressure, and is used as a *refrigerant* in this form as *dry ice*, for the preservation of frozen foods, etc. As carbon dioxide gas is heavier than air and does not support *combustion*, it is used in *fire extinguishers*.

CARBON DISULPHIDE. Carbon bisulphide. CS_2. A colourless inflammable *liquid*, b.p. $46°C$., with a high *refractive index*. Made by heating carbon with sulphur in a *retort*. Used as a *solvent* in the vulcanization of *rubber*, in the manufacture of viscose *rayon*, and for killing pests.

CARBON FIBRE. A material consisting of black silky threads of pure carbon which can be made stronger and stiffer than any other material of the same *weight*. Typical fibres are about 7 μm in diameter and have a *tensile strength* of up to 220 000 kg per square cm. They are made by heat-treating organic textile fibres in such a way that the side chains are stripped off, leaving only the carbon backbone. This backbone is subjected to further mechanical and heat treatment so that the crystallites are pulled into orientation along the axis of the fibre. They are used to reinforce a matrix of *resin*, *ceramic*, or *metal* with up to 600 000 fibres per square centimetre of *cross-section* and in this form make a valuable constructional material where strength is required at high *temperatures*, such as in components for jet engines and *rockets*.

CARBON MONOXIDE. CO. A colourless, almost odourless *gas*. Very poisonous when breathed, as it combines with the *haemoglobin* of the *blood* to form bright red carboxyhaemoglobin. This is chemically stable, and thus the haemoglobin is no longer available to carry oxygen. Burns with a bright blue *flame* to form *carbon dioxide*. Formed during the incomplete *combustion* of *coke*, *charcoal*, and other carbonaceous *fuels*. Occurs in *coal-gas* and in the exhaust fumes of motor engines.

CARBON TETRACHLORIDE. CCl_4. A heavy colourless *liquid* with a sweetish smell, b.p. 76·8°C. Used as a non-inflammable *solvent* and in *fire extinguishers* (*pyrene*).

CARBONADO. Black, discoloured, or impure variety of *diamond,* useless as a gem but very hard and used for drills, etc.

CARBONATE. A *salt* of *carbonic acid,* H_2CO_3.

CARBONIC ACID. H_2CO_3. A very weak *acid* probably formed in small amounts when *carbon dioxide* dissolves in *water.* Term often applied to carbon dioxide itself. Never obtained pure; breaks up almost completely into carbon dioxide and water when obtained in a chemical reaction. Gives rise to two series of *salts,* the *carbonates* and *bicarbonates* (now called 'hydrogen carbonates'.).

CARBONIZATION. See *destructive distillation.*

CARBONYL CHLORIDE. See *phosgene.*

CARBONYL GROUP. The *divalent* group $= CO$.

CARBONYLS. *Compounds* of *metals* with *carbon monoxide*; e.g. nickel carbonyl, $Ni(CO)_4$.

CARBORUNDUM *Silicon carbide.* SiC. A dark crystalline *solid,* nearly as hard as *diamond,* used as an *abrasive* and as a *refractory* material. Made by heating *silica,* SiO_2, with carbon in an electric furnace.

CARBOXYL GROUP. The *univalent* group, $- COOH$, characteristic of the organic *carboxylic acids.*

CARBOXYLIC ACID. An *acidic organic compound* which contains one or more *carboxyl groups.*

CARBURETTOR. A device in the *internal-combustion* petrol engine for mixing air with *petrol vapour* prior to explosion.

CARCINOGEN. A substance capable of producing cancer (carcinoma).

CARNALLITE. Natural potassium magnesium chloride, $KCl.MgCl_2.$ $6H_2O$, found in the *Stassfurt deposits.* Important source of potassium *salts.*

CARNOSINE. $C_9H_{14}N_4O_3$. An *optically active* crystalline *dipeptide,* m.p. 260°C., found in muscle *tissue.*

CARNOTITE. Uranium potassium *vanadate* of variable composition. *Ore* of uranium.

CARNOT'S CYCLE. An ideal reversible cycle of operations for the working substance of a heat engine. The four steps in the cycle are: (a) *isothermal* expansion, the substance taking in *heat* and doing *work*; (b) *adiabatic* expansion, without heat change, external work done; (c) isothermal compression, heat given out, work done on the substance by external forces; (d) adiabatic compression, no heat change, work done on the substance. Named after N. L. S. Carnot (1796–1832).

CARNOT'S PRINCIPLE. The *efficiency* of any reversible heat engine depends only on the *temperature* range through which it works and not upon the properties of any material substance. If all the heat is taken up at *absolute temperature* T_1 and all given out at absolute temperature T_2 (as in *Carnot's cycle*), the efficiency is $\dfrac{T_1 - T_2}{T_1}$.

CARO'S ACID, H_2SO_5. See *persulphuric acids*.

CAROTENE. $C_{40}H_{56}$. A yellow *unsaturated hydrocarbon* present in carrots and butter. Converted into vitamin A (see *vitamins*) in the animal *organism*. Carotene acts as a photosynthetic pigment (see *photosynthesis*) in plant *cells* which lack *chlorophyll*.

CARRIER (chem.). 1. A substance assisting a *chemical reaction* by combining with part or all of the *molecule* of one of the reacting substances to form a *compound* which is then easily decomposed again by the other reacting substance; the carrier is thus left unchanged. See *catalyst*. 2. An inactive substance used to transport a *radioisotope* in *radioactive tracing*. A radioisotope is said to be 'carrier-free' if it can be used without a carrier.

CARRIER (phys.). The mobile *electrons* or *holes* which carry charges *in a semiconductor*.

CARRIER WAVE. A continuous *electromagnetic radiation*, of constant *amplitude* and *frequency*, emitted by a *radio* transmitter. By *modulation* of the carrier wave, oscillating *electric currents* caused by *sounds* at the transmitting end are conveyed by it to the receiver.

CARRON OIL. A mixture of *vegetable oil* (olive or cotton-seed) with *lime-water*. Used as an application for burns.

CARTESIAN COORDINATES. A system for locating a point, P, in a *plane* by specifying its distance from two *axes* at right angles to each other which intersect at a point O, called the *origin*. The distance from the horizontal or *x*-axis is called the *ordinate* of P; the distance from the *y*-axis is called the *abscissa*. See Fig. 5. The system may also be used to locate a point in space by using a third, *z*-axis. Named after R. Descartes (1596–1650).

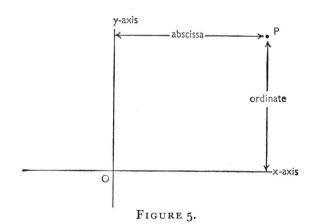

FIGURE 5.

CARVACROL. $(CH_3)_2CH.C_6H_3CH_3OH$. A colourless oily *liquid*, b.p. 237·7° C., with a mint-like odour. Used as a *disinfectant*, and in perfume.

CARVONE. Carvol. $C_{10}H_{14}O$. An *optically active liquid ketone* related to the *terpenes*, b.p. 231°C., found in *essential oils* and used in flavours and perfumes.

CASCADE LIQUEFIER. Apparatus used for liquefying air, oxygen, etc. A *gas* cannot be liquefied until it is brought to a *temperature* below its *critical temperature*. In the cascade liquefier the critical temperature of the gas is reached step by step, using a series of gases having successively lower *boiling points*. The first of these, which can be liquefied by compression at ordinary temperatures, is allowed to evaporate under reduced *pressure*; this produces a temperature below the critical temperature of the second gas, which can then be liquefied. This is similarly allowed to evaporate, and the step is repeated until finally the desired liquefaction is reached.

CASCADE PROCESS. A process used in the separation of *isotopes*. Consists of a series of stages connected so that the separation produced by one stage is multiplied in subsequent stages. In a 'simple cascade' the enriched fraction is fed to the succeeding stage and the depleted fraction to the preceding stage.

CASCADE SHOWER. See *shower*.

CASEIN. The main *protein* of milk. A pale yellow *solid* obtained from milk by the addition of *acid* ('acid casein'), by controlled souring ('self-soured casein'), or by curdling with *rennet* ('rennet casein'). Used in paper-coating, *paints*, *adhesives*, *plastics*, and for making artificial textile fibres.

CASEINOGEN. British term for *casein* before precipitation. The American terms are casein before precipitation, and paracasein after.

CASSEGRANIAN TELESCOPE. A form of astronomical reflecting *telescope* in which a hole in the centre of the primary mirror allows the light to pass through it to the *eye-piece* or the photographic plate. See Fig. 6.

CASSEGRANIAN TELESCOPE

FIGURE 6.

CASSIOPEIUM. See *lutetium*.

CASSITERITE. SnO_2. Natural *stannic oxide*. Principal *ore* of tin.

CAST IRON. Pig-iron. Impure, brittle form of iron, such as produced in the *blast furnace*. Contains from 2%–4.5% carbon in the form of *cementite* and usually also some manganese, phosphorus, silicon, and sulphur. Generally not used direct, but converted into *steel* or *wrought iron*.

CASTOR OIL. A *vegetable oil* extracted from the seed of the castor plant, consisting of *glyceryl esters* of *fatty acids*; the predominant acid (about 85%) being *ricinoleic acid*, $C_{17}H_{32}(OH).COOH$. Used in the *paint* and varnish industry as well as medically as a laxative.

CATABOLISM. Katabolism. The part of *metabolism* dealing with the chemical *decomposition* of complex substances into simple ones, with a release of *energy*.

CATALASE. An *enzyme* which decomposes *hydrogen peroxide*.

CATALYSIS. The alteration of the rate at which a *chemical reaction* proceeds, by the introduction of a substance (*catalyst*) which remains unchanged at the end of the reaction. Small quantities of the catalyst are usually sufficient to bring the action about or to produce a vast increase in its speed.

CATALYST. A substance which alters the rate at which a *chemical reaction* occurs, but is itself unchanged at the end of the reaction. Catalysts are widely used in the chemical industry; *metals* in a finely divided state, and *oxides* of metals, are frequently used. The *enzymes* are organic catalysts produced by living *cells*.

CATALYTIC CRACKING. The use of a *catalyst* to bring about the *cracking* of high boiling mineral *oils*.

CATAPHORESIS. See *electrophoresis*.

CATECHOL. Pyrocatechol, *ortho*-dihydroxybenzene. $C_6H_4(OH)_2$. A white crystalline *aromatic* substance, m.p. $105°C.$, used in *photography* and in dyeing.

CATENARY. A curve formed by a chain or string hanging from two fixed points. Equation, $y = \cosh \dfrac{x}{k}$, where k is the distance between the *vertex* of the curve and the *origin*.

CATENOID. The surface generated by rotating a *catenary* about its vertical axis.

CATHETOMETER. A *telescope* mounted on a graduated vertical pillar along which it can move. The instrument is used for measuring lengths and displacements at a distance of a few feet.

CATHODE. Negative *electrode*. Negatively charged *conductor* in *electrolysis* and in *vacuum tubes*. See *discharge in gases*.

CATHODE RAY OSCILLOSCOPE. CRO. An instrument based upon a *cathode ray tube*, which provides a visible image of one or more rapidly varying electrical quantities. Also used as an indicator in a *radar* system.

CATHODE RAY TUBE. CRT. A vacuum tube which allows the direct observation of the behaviour of *cathode rays*. Consists essentially of an *electron gun* producing a beam of *electrons* which, after passing between horizontal and vertical deflection plates, falls upon a luminescent screen: the position of the beam can be observed by the *luminescence* produced upon the screen. *Electric potentials* applied to the deflection plates are used to control the position of the beam, and its movement across the screen, in any desired manner. Used as the picture tube in *television* receivers and in *cathode ray oscilloscopes*.

CATHODE RAYS. A stream of *electrons* emitted from the negatively charged *electrode* or *cathode* when an electric discharge takes place in a vacuum tube, i.e. a tube containing a gas at very low pressure. See *discharge in gases*.

CATION. Positively charged *ion*; an ion which, during *electrolysis*, is attracted towards the negatively charged *cathode*.

CAUSALITY. The relating of causes to the effects which they produce. Many contemporary physicists believe that no coherent causal description can be given of events which occur on the sub-atomic scale.

CAUSTIC. Corrosive towards organic matter (but not applied to *acids*). E.g. *caustic soda*.

CAUSTIC (phys.). Parallel rays of *light* falling on a *concave* spherical mirror do not form a point image at the *focus* (see *mirrors, spherical*). Instead, there is a region of maximum concentration of the rays forming a curve or surface of revolution, called a caustic, the *apex* or cusp of which is at the focus of the mirror. A similar caustic occurs in the image formed by a *convex lens* receiving parallel light. Such a curve may be seen on the surface of a liquid in a cup, formed by the reflection of light upon the curved wall of the cup.

CAUSTIC ALKALI. *Sodium* or *potassium hydroxide*.

CAUSTIC POTASH. *Potassium hydroxide*, KOH.

CAUSTIC SODA. *Sodium hydroxide*, NaOH.

CELESTIAL EQUATOR (astr.). The circle in which the *plane* of the Earth's *equator* meets the *celestial sphere*.

CELESTIAL SPHERE (astr.). The imaginary *sphere* to the inner surface of which the heavenly bodies appear to be attached; the observer is situated at the centre of the sphere. See Fig. 2, page 36.

CELL (bio.). The unit of life. All living *organisms* are composed of discrete, membrane-bounded units, which usually comprise two distinct forms of *protoplasm*; the *nucleus* and the *cytoplasm*. The former contains the *nucleic acids* responsible for organizing the synthesis of the cell's *enzymes* and for controlling the characteristics of its progeny, while the latter contains the enzyme systems which control the cell's *metabolism* and manufacture its constituents. Many *micro-organisms* (e.g. *bacteria*, protozoa, etc.) consist of only one cell, whereas a man consists of some million million cells.

CELL (phys.). Device for producing an *electric current* by chemical action. See *accumulator, primary cell*.

CELLULOID. A *thermoplastic* material made from *cellulose nitrate* and *camphor*.

CELLULOSE. $(C_6H_{10}O_5)n$. A complex *polysaccharide carbohydrate* consisting of parallel unbranched chains of *glucose* units condensed together into strong fibrous structures. Found in nature as the *cell* walls of plants. Obtained from wood pulp, cotton, and other green plants; used in the manufacture of *paper, rayon, plastics,* and *explosives.*

CELLULOSE ACETATE. An *ester* obtained by the action of *acetic anhydride* on *cellulose.* A white *solid,* used in the manufacture of *rayon* and *plastics.*

CELLULOSE NITRATE. Nitrocellulose. *Nitric acid ester* of *cellulose.* A range of *compounds* formed by treatment of cellulose with a mixture of nitric and *sulphuric acids*; properties depend on the extent to which the *hydroxyl groups* of the cellulose are esterified (see *esterification*). Used in the manufacture of *plastics,* lacquers, and *explosives.*

CELSIUS TEMPERATURE. Centigrade temperature. *Temperature* measured on a scale originally devised by Anders Celsius (1701–44) in which the *melting point* of ice was 0° and the *boiling point* of water was 100°. This definition has been superseded by the *International Practical Temperature Scale* of 1968, which is expressed in both *kelvins* and degrees Celsius. The unit for both means of expressing temperature is the kelvin, and temperature differences may be expressed in kelvins even when using Celsius temperatures. The relation between the Kelvin temperature (T) and the Celsius temperature (t) is given by: $T = t + 273 \cdot 15$.

CELTIUM. See *hafnium.*

CEMENT. A powder which, after mixing with *water,* sets to a hard mass. Portland cement is made by heating a mixture of *limestone* and *clay* and grinding the product. Consists of *calcium silicates* and aluminates; complex chemical changes occur during setting.

CEMENTATION. An early process for *steel* manufacture. Bars of *wrought iron* were heated for several days in *charcoal* at red heat.

CEMENTITE. Iron carbide. Fe_3C. A hard, brittle *compound* which is responsible for the brittleness of *cast iron* and is present in *steel.*

CENTI-. Prefix denoting one hundredth of, in *metric units.* Symbol c, e.g. cm = 0·01 metres.

CENTIGRADE TEMPERATURE. See *Celsius temperature.*

CENTRAL PROCESSING UNIT. Central processor. See *C.P.U.*

CENTRE OF CURVATURE of a spherical mirror. The centre of the sphere of which the *mirror* forms a part.

CENTRE OF GRAVITY of a body is the fixed point through which the *resultant force* of *gravity* always passes, irrespective of the position of the body. This is identical to the *centre of mass* in a uniform *gravitational field.*

CENTRE OF MASS. The point at which the *mass* of a body may be considered to be concentrated. The point from which the sum of the *moments of inertia* of all the component particles of a body is zero.

CENTRIFUGAL FORCE. The outward *force* acting on a body rotating in a *circle* round a central point. The centripetal force is the radial force imposed by the constraining system, necessary to keep the body moving in its circular path. The centrifugal and centripetal forces are equal and opposite. The centrifugal force acting on a body of *mass m kilogrammes* moving in a circle radius *r metres*, with a *velocity v* metres per sec. is $\dfrac{mv^2}{r}$ *newtons*.

CENTRIFUGE. Apparatus for separating particles from a *suspension*. Balanced tubes containing the suspension are attached to the opposite ends of arms rotating rapidly about a central point; by *centrifugal force* the suspended particles are forced outwards, and collect at the bottoms of the tubes. See also *ultracentrifuge*.

CENTRIPETAL FORCE. See *centrifugal force*.

CERAMIC. Pertaining to products or industries involving the use of *clay* or other *silicates*.

CERARGYRITE. See *horn silver*.

CERENKOV (CHERENKOV) RADIATION. *Light* emitted when charged particles pass through a transparent medium at a *velocity* greater than the *velocity of light* in that medium. Named after P. A. Cerenkov (born 1904).

CERESIN. Hard, brittle *paraffin wax* with a *melting point* in the range of 70°–100°C. Used as a substitute for *beeswax* in *paints* and polishes.

CERIC. Containing *tetravalent* cerium.

CERIUM. Ce. Element. A.W. 140·12. At. No. 58. A steel-grey soft *metal*, S.G. 6·7, m.p. 795°C. Occurs in several rare minerals, e.g. *monazite* sand. Used in *pyrophoric alloys* for lighter 'flints'; *compounds* are used in the manufacture of *gas mantles* and in *glass* polishing.

CERIUM DIOXIDE. Ceria. CeO_2. A white crystalline powder, m.p. 2600°C., used in *glass* polishing.

CERMET. Ceramet. Abbreviation of CER(A)mic and METal. A very hard mixture of a *ceramic* substance and *sintered* metal, used where resistance to high *temperature, corrosion*, and abrasion is required.

CEROUS. Containing *trivalent* cerium.

CETANE. $C_{16}H_{34}$. See *hexadecane*.

CETANE NUMBER. A measure of the ignition characteristics of a diesel fuel by comparison with a range of mixtures, in which *cetane* is given a value of 100 and α-methylnaphthaline is 0.

CETYL ALCOHOL. See *hexadecanol*.

C.G.S. SYSTEM. Centimetre-gram-second system. A system of physical *units* derived from the centimetre, *gram* mass and the *second*. E.g. *velocities* in c.g.s. units may be measured in centimetres per second. Now superseded for scientific purposes by the *SI units*.

CHABASITE. A natural *zeolite*, calcium aluminium silicate. See *ion exchange*.

CHAIN REACTION. In general, any self-sustaining molecular or *nuclear reaction*, the products of which contribute to the propagation of the reaction. In particular a fission chain reaction is a process in which one nuclear transformation is capable of initiating a chain of similar transformations. For example, when *nuclear fission* occurs in a uranium-235 *nucleus*, between 2 and 3 *neutrons* are emitted, each of which is capable of causing the fission of further uranium-235 nuclei. The chain reaction so created is the basis of the atomic bomb (see *nuclear weapons*) and the *nuclear reactor*. If the average number of *transformations* directly caused by one transformation is less than one, the reaction is said to be convergent or *subcritical*; if it is equal to one, the reaction is self-sustained or critical; if it exceeds one, the reaction is divergent or *supercritical*.

CHALCEDONY. A variety of natural impure *silica*, SiO_2, which has a fibrous structure and a waxy lustre. Used for ornaments.

CHALK. Natural *calcium carbonate*, $CaCO_3$, formed from the shells of minute marine *organisms*. Blackboard chalk sticks are *calcium sulphate*, $CaSO_4$.

CHALONES. Physiologically active substances produced within *tissues* which appear to control the *mitosis* of the *cells* of the specific tissues which produce them.

CHALYBEATE. Chalybite. Natural ferrous carbonate, $FeCO_3$.

CHANGE OF STATE (phys.). The conversion of a substance from one of the *physical states* of *matter* (*solid, liquid,* or *gas*) into another. E.g. the melting of *ice*.

CHANNEL. In *telecommunications*, a path for the transmission of electrical signals, often specified by its *frequency band*. In *information theory*, a path or route along which information may flow or be stored.

CHANNEL CAPACITY. The number of signals per second which can be transmitted through a *channel*. Also, in *information theory*, the hypothetical limiting rate at which information could be communicated by a given channel, with the frequency of errors tending to zero.

CHARACTER. A unit of information as handled by *computers*, usually six bits.

CHARACTERISTIC (math.). The *integral* or whole-number part of a *logarithm*.

CHARCOAL. A general name for numerous varieties of *carbon*, usually impure; generally made by heating vegetable or animal substances with exclusion of air. Many forms are very porous and adsorb various materials readily. See *activated carbon*.

CHARGE, ELECTRIC. See *electric charge*.

CHARLES' LAW. At constant *pressure* all *gases* expand by 1/273 of their *volume* at 0°C., for each 1°C. rise in *temperature*; the volume of a fixed mass of gas at constant pressure is proportional to the *absolute temperature*. Named after J. A. C. Charles (1746–1823). See also *gas laws*.

CHEDDITE. Class of *explosives* containing *sodium* or *potassium chlorate* with *dinitrotoluene* and other organic substances.

CHELATING AGENTS. See *chelation*.

CHELATION. The formation of a closed ring of *atoms* by the attachment of *compounds* or *radicals* to a central *polyvalent metal ion* (occasionally non-metallic); usually due to the sharing of a *lone pair of electrons*, from oxygen or nitrogen atoms in the compounds or radicals, with the

71

central ion, e.g. two *molecules* of ethylene diamine ($NH_2CH_2CH_2NH_2$) form a 'chelate ring' with a cupric ion thus:

$$
\begin{array}{ccc}
CH_2-NH_2 & & NH_2-CH_2 \\
| & \searrow \; ++ \; \nearrow & | \\
& Cu & \\
| & \nearrow \quad \nwarrow & | \\
CH_2-NH_2 & & NH_2-CH_2
\end{array}
$$

Chelating agents are used for 'locking up' unwanted metal ions; for instance they are added to shampoos with the object of softening the water by locking up *ferric*, calcium, and magnesium ions. Many tests for identifying metal ions depend on the formation of coloured *insoluble* chelates. *Chlorophyll* and *haemoglobin* are naturally occurring chelate compounds in which the central ions are magnesium and iron respectively.

CHEMICAL AFFINITY. See *affinity* and *free energy*.

CHEMICAL CHANGE. A change in a substance involving an alteration in its chemical composition, due to an increase, decrease, or rearrangement of *atoms* within its *molecules*. See *equation, chemical; molecule*.

CHEMICAL COMBINATION, LAWS OF:

Law of constant composition. A definite chemical *compound* always contains the same *elements* chemically combined in the same proportions by *weight*.

Law of multiple proportions. When two *elements* unite in more than one proportion, for a fixed *weight* of one element there is always a simple relationship with the weight of the other element present.

Law of combining weights (also termed the law of reciprocal proportions, law of equivalents). *Elements* combine in the ratio of their combining weights or *chemical equivalents*; or in some simple multiple or sub-multiple of that ratio.

CHEMICAL ENERGY. That part of the *energy* stored within an *atom* or *molecule* which can be released by a *chemical reaction*.

CHEMICAL ENGINEERING. The design, operation, and manufacture of plant or machinery used in industrial chemical processes.

CHEMICAL EQUILIBRIUM. Many *chemical reactions* do not go to completion; in such cases a state of equilibrium or balance is reached when the original substances are reacting at the same rate as the new substances are reacting with each other to form the original substances. Thus, if two substances A and B react to form C and D, the state at equilibrium is denoted by the balanced equation $A+B \leftrightharpoons C+D$. If one of the substances is removed, the system readjusts the equilibrium; thus, if C is constantly removed as soon as formed, more A and B react until the action is completed. An equilibrium reaction which could thus be made to complete itself in either direction is termed a *reversible reaction*. E.g. if *steam* is passed over red-hot iron, iron oxide and hydrogen are formed, the latter being constantly removed by more steam which passes through; the reaction thus goes to completion according to the equation $4H_2O + 3Fe = Fe_3O_4 + 4H_2$. If, however, hydrogen is passed over red-hot iron oxide, the reverse action takes place, $Fe_3O_4 + 4H_2 = 4H_2O + 3Fe$. If the reaction is allowed to proceed in an enclosed space, a state of equilibrium is reached, all four substances being present. See also *equilibrium constant*.

CHEMICAL EQUIVALENTS. Combining weights. The combining proportions of substances by *weight*, relative to hydrogen as a standard. The equivalent of an *element* is the number of grams of that element which will combine with or replace 1 g of hydrogen or 8 g of oxygen. The gram-equivalent, or equivalent weight, is the equivalent expressed in grams. The equivalent weight of an *acid* is the weight of the acid containing unit weight of replaceable *acidic hydrogen*. The equivalent weight of a *base* is the weight of the base required to neutralize the equivalent weight of an acid. The combining proportions of substances by weight are in the ratio of their equivalents, or in some simple multiple or sub-multiple of that ratio. For an element, the *atomic weight* is equal to the product of its equivalent and its *valency*. The gram-equivalent as a unit quantity of substance in chemical calculations has been replaced in *SI units* by the *mole*. E.g. 1 equivalent of H_2SO_4 equals 1 mole of $\frac{1}{2}H_2SO_4$.

CHEMICAL REACTION. The interaction of two or more substances, resulting in *chemical changes* in them.

CHEMILUMINESCENCE. Cold *flame*. The evolution of *light* accompanied by some *heat* during a *chemical reaction*.

CHEMISORPTION. The process of *adsorption* in which a chemical link is formed between the adsorbing and adsorbed material.

CHEMISTRY. The study of the composition of substances, and of their effects upon one another.

CHEMOTHERAPY. The treatment of disease by chemical substances which are toxic to the causative *micro-organisms*, or which directly attack *neoplastic* growths.

CHEMURGY. The study of chemical industrial processes based on organic substances of agricultural origin.

CHERT. A natural form of *silica*, SiO_2, resembling flint.

CHILE SALTPETRE. Impure *sodium nitrate*, $NaNO_3$. Occurs in huge deposits in Chile.

CHINA CLAY. Kaolin. Pure natural form of *hydrated* aluminium silicate, $Al_2Si_2O_5(OH)_4$. On heating, it loses *water* and changes its chemical composition. Used for making *porcelain*.

CHINESE WHITE. *Zinc oxide*, ZnO.

CHITIN. A complex organic substance, related to the *carbohydrates* but containing nitrogen. It forms an essential part of the shells of crustaceans and insects. Also found in some fungi.

CHLORAL. CCl_3CHO. A pungent colourless oily *liquid*, b.p. $97 \cdot 7°$ C.

CHLORAL HYDRATE. $CCl_3CH(OH)_2$. A white crystalline *solid*, m.p.

57° C. Prepared from *chloral* by the action of *water*. Used in medicine as a *hypnotic*.

CHLORAMINE. NH_2Cl. An *unstable* colourless *liquid* with a pungent odour. The term is also applied to any *compound* obtained by replacing a hydrogen *atom* of an NH, or NH_2 group, with a chlorine atom.

CHLORANIL. $C_6Cl_4O_2$. A yellow *insoluble* crystalline substance, m.p. 290° C., used as a *fungicide* and in the manufacture of *dyes*.

CHLORATE. A *salt* of *chloric acid*.

CHLORIC ACID. $HClO_3$. A hypothetical *acid* known only in *solution* or in the form of its *salts*, the *chlorates*.

CHLORARGYRITE. See *horn silver*.

CHLORIDE. *Binary compound* with chlorine; *salt of hydrochloric acid*, HCl.

CHLORIDE OF LIME. *Calcium oxychloride*, $CaOCl_2$. See *bleaching powder*.

CHLORINE. Cl. Element. A.W. 35·453. At. No. 17. A greenish-yellow poisonous *gas* with a choking irritating smell. The first poison gas to be used in warfare (by Germany, Ypres, 1915). *Compounds* occur as common salt (*sodium chloride*), NaCl, in *sea-water* and as *rock salt*; and as *chlorides* of other *metals*. Manufactured almost entirely by the *electrolysis* of brine. Used in the manufacture of *bleaching powder, disinfectants, hydrochloric acid*. Also used as a *germicide* in drinking-water.

CHLORITE. 1. A *salt* of *chlorous acid*. 2. A group of *mineral silicates* of aluminium, iron, and magnesium.

CHLOR(O)ACETIC ACIDS. The following three substituted *acetic acids*: monochloroacetic acid, $CH_2ClCOOH$, which is a crystalline solid, m.p. 63° C.: dichloroacetic acid, $CHCl_2COOH$, a colourless *liquid*, m.p. 10° C., b.p. 192–3° C.: trichloroacetic acid, CCl_3COOH, a *deliquescent* crystalline solid, m.p. 56·3° C. All forms are used in the manufacture of *dyes* and as wart removers.

CHLOROACETONE. CH_3COCH_2Cl. A colourless poisonous *liquid*, b.p. 119° C., used in the manufacture of *insecticides* and in organic synthesis.

CHLOROBENZENE. Phenyl chloride. C_6H_5Cl. A colourless inflammable *liquid*, b.p. 132° C., used as a *solvent* and in the synthesis of *drugs*.

CHLOROFORM. $CHCl_3$. A *volatile* colourless heavy *liquid* with a powerful sweet smell, b.p. 61° C. Made from *acetone, acetaldehyde*, or *ethanol* by the action of *bleaching powder*, or by the action of chlorine on *methane*, CH_4. Used as an *anaesthetic* and industrial *solvent*.

CHLOROMETHANE. Methyl chloride. CH_3Cl. A colourless poisonous *gas*, used as a *refrigerant* and as a methylating agent.

CHLOROMYCETIN*. Chloramphenicol. $C_{11}H_{12}Cl_2N_2O_5$. A colourless crystalline *antibiotic*, active against certain *bacteria* and certain *viruses*.

CHLOROPHENOL. ClC_6H_4OH. A substituted *phenol* which exists in three *isomeric* forms. The *ortho-* form has m.p. 8·7° C. and b.p. 175° C., the *meta-* form has m.p. 32·8° C., and the *para-* form has m.p. 43° C. All forms are used in the manufacture of *dyes*.

CHLOROPHYLL. A green *pigment* found in plants, which absorbs *energy* from sunlight, enabling them to build up *carbohydrates* from atmospheric *carbon dioxide* and *water* by *photosynthesis*. Consists of a mixture of two pigments, chlorophyll-a ($C_{55}H_{72}O_5N_4Mg$) and chlorophyll-b ($C_{55}H_{70}O_6N_4Mg$).

CHLOROPICRIN. CCl_3NO_2. An oily *liquid*, b.p. $112°C$. Highly poisonous and chemically active. Used as a *disinfectant* and *fungicide*.

CHLOROPLATINIC ACID. Platinum chloride solution. $H_2PtCl_6.6H_2O$. A brown *hygroscopic soluble* substance, m.p. $60°C$., used in platinizing *glass* and *ceramics*.

CHLOROPRENE. $CH_2CH:CCl.CH_2$. A colourless *liquid*, b.p. $59·4°C$., used in the manufacture of *neoprene* synthetic *rubber*.

CHLOROQUINOL. Chlorohydroquinone. $C_6H_3Cl(OH)_2$. A white crystalline *soluble* solid, which can exist in six *isomeric* forms. Used as a photographic *developer* and in organic synthesis.

CHLOROUS ACID. $HClO_2$. A hypothetical *acid* known only in *solution*, or in the form of its *salts*.

CHOKE. Choking coil. A coil of low *resistance* and high *inductance* used in electrical circuits to pass *direct currents* whilst suppressing *alternating currents*.

CHOKE-DAMP. See *after-damp*.

CHOLESTEROL. $C_{27}H_{45}OH$. A white waxy *sterol* present in the *tissues* of the human body, in which it performs a number of vital functions. Its excessive production in man is suspected of being a contributory cause of coronary thrombosis.

CHOLINE. $OH.C_2H_4N(CH_3)_3OH$. An *organic base* which is a constituent of some *fats* and of egg yolk. Member of *vitamin* B complex.

CHONDRITE. A type of stony meteorite (see *meteor*) which contains the small round masses of *olivine* or *pyroxene* known as chondrules.

CHORD (math.). A straight line joining two points on a curve. See *circle*.

CHROMATE. A *salt* of *chromic acid*.

CHROMATIC ABERRATION. See *aberration, chromatic*.

CHROMATIDS. The two identical strands into which a *chromosome* splits during *cell* reproduction.

CHROMATOGRAPHY. Column chromatography. A method of chemical analysis developed from the fact that if a *liquid mixture* is allowed to trickle through a column of adsorbing material (e.g. *chalk*) the components of the mixture may be adsorbed in separate layers in the column. See also *gas chromatography* and *paper chromatography*.

CHROMATRON. Chromoscope. A type of *cathode ray tube* which has four screens; used as a colour picture-tube in *television*.

CHROME ALUM. See *chromic potassium sulphate*.

CHROME IRON ORE. Chrome ironstone, chromite, ferrous chromite. $FeO.Cr_2O_3$. A source of chromium *metal* and its *compounds*.

CHROME RED. *Basic* lead chromate, $PbO.PbCrO_4$. Used as a *pigment* in *paints*.

CHROME YELLOW. Lead chromate, $PbCrO_4$. Used as a *pigment*.

CHROMIC. Containing *trivalent* chromium.

CHROMIC ACID. H_2CrO_4. A hypothetical *acid* known only in *solution* or in the form of its *salts*.

CHROMIC POTASSIUM SULPHATE. Chrome alum. $K_2SO_4.Cr_2(SO_4)_3.$ $24H_2O$. A dark purple crystalline *soluble salt*, used in *dyes*, calico printing and *tanning*.

CHROMITE. 1. See *chrome iron ore*. 2. A *salt* of *bivalent* chromium.

CHROMIUM. Cr. Element. A.W. 51·996. At. No. 24. A hard white *metal* resembling *iron*; S.G. 6·92, m.p. 1890°C. Occurs as *chrome iron ore*. Extracted by reducing the *oxide* with aluminium (see *Goldschmidt process*). Used in the manufacture of *stainless steel* and for *chromium plating*.

CHROMIUM PLATING. The deposition of a thin resistant film of chromium *metal* by *electrolysis* from a bath containing a *solution* of *chromic acid*.

CHROMIUM STEEL. *Steel* containing varying amounts of chromium; strong and tough, used for tools, etc.

CHROMIUM TRIOXIDE. Chromic anhydride. CrO_3. A red *deliquescent* crystalline substance, m.p. 196°C., that is a strong *oxidizing agent*.

CHROMOPHORE. Any chemical group, such as the *azo group*, that causes a *compound* to have a distinctive colour.

CHROMOSOMES. Thread-like bodies that occur in the *nuclei* of living *cells*, the *molecules* of which carry the *genetic code*. Consist of *nucleoproteins*, the *nucleic acid* being *DNA*. The unit of genetic information is the *gene* (see also *cistron* and *operon*) and each chromosome may be regarded as comprising a number of genes. Chromosomes occur in pairs in *somatic* cells, each species being characterized by the different number of chromosomes that its cells contain (Man has 46 chromosomes per cell).

CHROMOSPHERE. Layer of the *Sun's* atmosphere surrounding the *photosphere*, which is visible during a total *eclipse*. The chromosphere is several thousand miles thick and has an estimated temperature of 20 000 K.

CHROMOUS. Containing *divalent* chromium.

CHROMYL. Containing *hexavalent* chromium, e.g. chromyl chloride, CrO_2Cl_2.

CHRONOGRAPH. An accurate time-recording instrument.

CHRONOMETER. An accurate clock; term now applied mainly to instruments used in navigation.

CHRONON. A hypothetical particle of time defined as the ratio of the diameter of an *electron* to the *velocity of light*: i.e. the time taken for light to traverse an electron. Approximately 10^{-24} *second*.

CHRONOTRON*. A device which measures the time between two events, by measuring the positions on a transmission line of pulses initiated by the events.

CIMENT FONDU. See *bauxite cement*.

CINCHONIDINE. $C_{19}H_{22}N_2O$. A white crystalline *alkaloid*, m.p. 207·2°C., used as a substitute for *quinine*. One of its *isomers*, cinchonine, m.p. 265°C., is also used for this purpose.

CINEOLE. $C_{10}H_{18}O$. A colourless oily *liquid terpene*, b.p. $176.4°$C., with an odour of *camphor*. Found in certain *essential oils* and used in perfumes and medicine.

CINNABAR. Natural *mercuric sulphide*, HgS. A bright red crystalline *solid*, S.G. 8.1. *Ore* of mercury.

CINNAMIC ACID. $C_6H_5CH:CHCOOH$. A white crystalline *insoluble* substance the *cis-form* of which has a m.p. $42°$C., and the *trans-form* has a m.p. $135°$C. Used in perfumes.

CINNAMYL GROUP. The *univalent* group $C_6H_5CH:CH.CH_2$—, derived from *cinnamic acid*.

CIRCLE (math.). A plane figure contained by a line, called the circumference, which is everywhere equidistant from a fixed point within it, called the centre. The distance from the centre to the circumference is the radius; a straight line joining any two points on the circumference is a *chord*; a chord passing through the centre, equal in length to twice the radius, is a diameter; any portion of the circumference is an arc; a portion cut off by a chord is a segment; a portion cut off by two radii is a sector. The ratio of the circumference to the diameter, denoted by π ('pi')$=3.14159\ldots$ (approx. $3\frac{1}{7}$). Length of circumference$=2\pi r$; area$=\pi r^2$, where $r=$radius.

CIRCUIT, ELECTRICAL. The complete path traversed by an *electric current*.

CIRCULAR MEASURE of angles. Measurement of *angles* in *radians*; the size of an angle stated as the ratio of the length of arc cut off by the angle at the centre of a *circle* to the radius of the circle. Thus

$$180°=\pi \text{ radians}; \text{ 1 radian}=\frac{180}{\pi}\text{ degrees}=57° 17.7'.$$

CIRCULAR MIL. A unit of area. The area of a *circle* whose diameter is 0.001 inches, i.e. 0.785×10^{-6} sq in. Used in measuring the cross-section of fine wire.

CIRCULARLY POLARIZED LIGHT. *Light* which can be resolved into two vibrations lying in *planes* at right angles, of equal *amplitude* and *frequency* and differing in *phase* by $90°$. The electric *vector* of the wave describes, at any point in the path of the wave, a *circle* about the direction of propagation of the light as axis. See also *polarization of light*.

CIRCUMFERENCE. See *circle*.

CIS-FORM. See *cis-trans isomerism*.

CIS-TRANS ISOMERISM. A form of *isomerism* associated with *compounds* containing a *double bond*. Like groups in such compounds may be either on the same side of the plane of the double bond (*cis*-form) or on opposite sides (*trans*-form). E.g. H—C—COOH, *maleic acid*, and

$$\parallel$$

H—C—COOH

H—C—COOH, *fumaric acid*, are respectively *cis*- and

$$\parallel$$

HOOC—C—H

trans-forms. See also *stereoisomerism*.

77

CISTRON. The functional unit of genetic information, taking into account the distribution of abnormal (mutant) *genes* among pairs of *chromosomes*, and the way in which an abnormal gene in one chromosome may be compensated for by a normal gene either in the same chromosome (cis-configuration) or its pair (trans-configuration).

CITRATE. A *salt* or *ester* of *citric acid*.

CITRIC ACID. $C_6H_8O_7$. A white crystalline *soluble* organic *tribasic acid*, m.p. 153°C. It has a sour taste, and occurs as the free acid in lemons (6%) and other sour fruits. Used in the preparation of effervescent salts.

CITRIC ACID CYCLE. Krebs cycle. A complex cycle of *enzyme*-controlled biochemical reactions, which occur within living *cells*, as a result of which *pyruvic acid* is broken down into *carbon dioxide* and *energy*. The citric acid cycle is a most important clearing-house of metabolic intermediates, since it deals with the final stages of the *oxidation* of *carbohydrates* and *fats* and is also involved in the synthesis of some *amino acids*.

CITRONELLAL. $C_9H_{17}CHO$. A colourless *liquid aldehyde* existing in several *isomeric* forms, b.p. 205–8°C., with a lemon-like odour. Used as a flavouring and in the manufacture of perfume.

CITRONELLOL. $C_9H_{17}CH_2OH$. A colourless *liquid alcohol* existing in several *isomeric* forms, b.p. 110°C., used in the manufacture of perfumes.

CLADDING (phys.). The covering of a *fuel element* in a *nuclear reactor* by a thin layer of another *metal*, to prevent corrosion by the *coolant* and the escape of *fission products*.

CLARK CELL. A standard *primary cell*, used as a standard of *E.M.F.*, which produces 1·4328 *volts* at 15°C. Consists of a zinc *amalgam anode* and a mercury *cathode*, both immersed in a *saturated solution* of *zinc sulphate*.

CLASSICAL PHYSICS. *Physics* prior to the *quantum theory* (or in some senses prior to the theory of *relativity*).

CLATHRATE COMPOUNDS. Chemical *compounds* formed not by the action of *valency bonds*, but by 'molecular imprisonment', the combined *molecules* being held together mechanically by virtue of their configuration in space.

CLAY. A class of complex *silicates*, e.g. kaolinite or *china clay*.

CLEAVAGE. The manner of breaking of a crystalline substance, so that more or less smooth surfaces are formed.

CLINICAL THERMOMETER. See *thermometer, clinical*.

CLOTTING. The formation of *solid* deposits or clots in *liquids*, often due to the *coagulation* of *soluble proteins* dissolved in the liquid. E.g. the clotting of *blood*.

CLOUD CHAMBER (phys.). An apparatus for making the tracks of ionizing particles visible as a row of droplets which condense from a supersaturated *vapour*. Depends on the fact that *water vapour* condenses more readily on charged *ions* than on uncharged *molecules*.

CLUSTER (astr.). An aggregation of *stars* which move together. A *globular cluster* is an aggregation of stars in a roughly spherical arrangement.

COAGULATION OF PROTEINS. When *solutions* of water-soluble *proteins* (*albumens*) are heated, the protein becomes 'denatured' at a definite *temperature*; it then becomes *insoluble* and either remains in *suspension* or is precipitated as a clot or curd. Other types of proteins, e.g. *globulins*, may be denatured and coagulated by *heat*, or by the addition of *acids* or *alkalis*. A denatured protein cannot be easily reconverted into the original *compound* (see *denature*).

COAL. A material, occurring in large underground deposits, consisting of carbon and various carbon *compounds*. Formed by the *decomposition* of vegetable matter during periods of many millions of years. The main types of coal are: *peat*, *lignite*, ordinary or *bituminous* coal, and *anthracite*.

COAL-GAS. Fuel *gas* manufactured by the *destructive distillation* of *coal* in closed iron *retorts*; often supplemented with *water-gas* or *natural gas*. Composition by *volume* (average values): hydrogen 50%, *methane* 30%, *carbon monoxide*, 8%, other *hydrocarbons* 4%, nitrogen, *carbon dioxide*, and oxygen 8%.

COAL-GAS BY-PRODUCTS. Amongst the valuable substances obtained during the manufacture of *coal-gas* are *coke*, *coal-tar*, *ammonia*, *sulphuric acid*, and *pitch*.

COAL-TAR. A thick black oily *liquid* obtained as a by-product of *coal-gas* manufacture. *Distillation* and purification yields, amongst other valuable products: *benzene*, C_6H_6; *toluene*, $C_6H_5CH_3$; *xylene*, $C_6H_4(CH_3)_2$; *phenol*, C_6H_5OH; *naphthalene*, $C_{10}H_8$; *cresol*, $CH_3C_6H_4OH$, and *anthracene*, $C_{14}H_{10}$. *Pitch* is left as a residue.

COAL-TAR DYES. *Organic compounds*, used as dyestuffs, prepared or derived from substances such as *benzene* occurring in *coal-tar*.

COAXIAL. Having a common axis. See *cable, coaxial*.

COBALT. Co. Element. A.W. 58·9332. At. No. 27. A hard silvery-white magnetic *metal* resembling iron. S.G. 8·9, m.p. 1480° C. Occurs combined with sulphur and with arsenic. Extracted by converting the *ore* into the *oxide* and reducing with aluminium, or with carbon in an electric furnace. Used in many *alloys*; compounds used to produce a blue colour in *glass* and *ceramics*.

COBALT STEEL. *Steel* containing cobalt, and often other *metals* such as tungsten, chromium, and vanadium. The addition of cobalt results in greater hardness and brittleness, improves the cutting power of *high-speed-steel* tools, and alters the magnetic properties.

COBALTIC. Containing *trivalent* cobalt, e.g. cobaltic chloride, $CoCl_3$.

COBALTOUS. Containing *divalent* cobalt, e.g. cobaltous chloride, $CoCl_2$.

COCAINE. $C_{17}H_{21}O_4N$. A white crystalline *alkaloid* which occurs in the coca plant, m.p. 98° C. It is used as a local *anaesthetic* and is a dangerous habit-forming drug.

COCCUS. A globular or spherical-shaped *bacterium*.

COCHINEAL. A natural red dyestuff obtained from the dried body of the Coccus cacti insect.

COCKROFT-WALTON GENERATOR OR ACCELERATOR. A high voltage *direct current accelerator* used for accelerating nuclear particles (particularly *protons*). The DC voltage is obtained by multiplying a low AC voltage by an arrangement of *rectifiers* and *capacitors*.

CODEINE. $C_{18}H_{21}O_3N$. A white crystalline *alkaloid*, m.p. 158° C., which occurs in *opium*. Used in medicine (often in the form of its *phosphate*) as an *analgesic*, *hypnotic*, and in the treatment of coughs.

COEFFICIENT (math.). A number or other known *factor* written in front of an algebraic expression. E.g. in the expression $3x^4$, 3 is the coefficient of x^4.

COEFFICIENT (phys.). A *factor* or multiplier which measures some specified property of a given substance, and is constant for that substance under given conditions. E.g. coefficient of expansion. (See *expansion, coefficient of*, also *restitution, coefficient of*.)

COELOSTAT. A device used in conjunction with an astronomical *telescope* to follow the path of a celestial body and reflect its *light* into the telescope. Consists essentially of two mirrors, one movable and one fixed.

COENZYME. A substance which plays an essential part in some reactions catalysed by *enzymes*, often acts as a temporary *carrier* of an intermediate product of the reaction.

COERCIVE FORCE of a substance. The strength of the *magnetic field* to which a *ferromagnetic substance* undergoing an *hysteresis cycle* must be subjected in order to *demagnetize* the substance completely. If the substance is magnetized to saturation during the cycle, the coercive force is called the *coercivity*. See Fig. 21, page 192.

COERCIVITY. See *coercive force*.

COFFEY STILL. Apparatus for the *fractional distillation* of *solutions* of *ethanol* as obtained by *fermentation* on an industrial scale; the product is known as *rectified spirit*.

COHERENT. A beam of *light*, or other *electromagnetic radiation*, is said to be coherent if its waves are in *phase*. See *laser*.

COHERENT UNITS. A system of *units* in which the *quotient* or *product* of any two units in the system yields the unit of the resultant quantity. E.g. when unit length is divided by unit time, the unit of *velocity* results. The basic units of a coherent system are arbitrarily defined physical quantities. All other units are obtained from these basic units by defining relations and are called 'derived units'. The coherent units now in scientific use are the *SI units*.

COHESION. Holding together; the *force* holding a *solid* or *liquid* together owing to attraction between the *molecules*. It decreases with rise in *temperature*.

COINAGE METALS. The *metals* copper, silver, gold.

COINCIDENCE CIRCUIT. Coincidence gate. An *electronic* circuit which produces an output only when two or more input signals arrive simultaneously, or within a specified time interval.

COKE. A greyish porous brittle *solid* containing about 80% carbon. Obtained as a residue in the manufacture of *coal-gas* ('gas coke'); also made specially in coke ovens, in which the *coal* is treated at lower *temperatures* than in gas manufacture.

COLCHICINE. $C_{22}H_{25}NO_6$. A yellow crystalline *alkaloid*, m.p. $156°C.$, obtained from the autumn crocus, which interferes with the process of *mitosis* in such a way that it causes an increase in the number of *chromosomes* in a *cell*. Used as an artificial method of obtaining new agricultural and horticultural varieties.

COLCOTHAR. Rouge, red iron oxide, *ferric oxide*, Fe_2O_3. Used as a *pigment* and for polishing.

COLLAGEN. A *protein* that is the major fibrous constituent of skin, tendon, ligament, and bone: it is, therefore, probably the most abundant protein in the animal kingdom. Collagen owes its unique properties not only to its chemical composition, but also to the physical arrangement of its individual *molecules*. The basic molecular *polypeptide* chain forms a left-handed *helix*, and three such helices are wrapped around each other to form a right-handed super-helix. On boiling with *water* collagen gives rise to *gelatin*.

COLLARGOL. A powder containing *protein* material and finely divided silver; with *water* it forms a *colloidal solution* of silver.

COLLECTOR. The *electrode* in a *transistor* through which a primary flow of *carriers* leaves the inter-electrode region.

COLLIGATIVE PROPERTIES. Those properties of a substance (e.g. a *solution*) which depend only on the *concentration* of particles (*molecules* or *ions*) present and not upon their nature; e.g. *osmotic pressure*.

COLLIMATOR. 1. A tube containing a *convex achromatic lens* at one end and an adjustable slit at the other, the slit being at the focus of the lens. *Light* rays entering the slit thus leave the collimator as a parallel *beam*. 2. An arrangement of absorbers for limiting a beam of *radiation* to the required dimensions and angular spread in *radiology*. 3. A small fixed *telescope* attached to a larger one for the purpose of accurately setting the line of sight of the larger instrument.

COLLISION DENSITY. The number of collisions per unit volume per unit time which a given *neutron* flux makes when passing through *matter*.

COLLODION. A *solution* of *cellulose nitrate* in a mixture of *alcohol* and *ether*.

COLLOID. A substance present in *solution* in the *colloidal state*. The original division, made by Graham, of all substances into *crystalloids* and colloids according to the ability of their solutions to pass through a *semipermeable membrane* is not generally accepted now, since most substances can be brought into the colloidal state by suitable means.

COLLOIDAL METALS. *Colloidal solutions* or *suspensions* of *metals*, the metal being distributed in the *solvent* in the form of very small electrically charged particles. May be prepared by striking an electric *arc* between poles made of the metal, under water; or by the chemical *reduction* of a *solution* of a *salt* of the metal. Used in medicine.

COLLOIDAL SOLUTION. Sol. A *solution* in which the *solute* is present in the *colloidal state*. Common examples include solutions of *starch*, *albumen*, *colloidal metals*, etc. The *solvent* is termed the *dispersion medium* and the dissolved substance the *disperse phase*. Several types of colloidal solution are possible, depending upon whether the dispersion medium and the disperse phase are respectively *liquid* and *solid* (suspensoid sols), liquid and liquid (emulsoid sols), *gas* and solid, etc. If the disperse phase, when removed from solution by *evaporation* or coagulation, returns to the colloidal state on merely mixing with the dispersion medium, it is termed a reversible or *lyophilic colloid*, and the solution a reversible sol. If the disperse phase does not return to the colloidal state on simple mixing, it is termed an irreversible or *lyophobic colloid*.

COLLOIDAL STATE. A system of particles in a *dispersion medium*, with properties distinct from those of a true *solution* because of the larger size of the particles. The presence of these particles, which are approximately 10^{-4} to 10^{-6} mm across, can often be detected by means of the *ultramicroscope*. As a result of the grouping of the *molecules*, a *solute* in the colloidal state cannot pass through a suitable *semipermeable membrane* and gives rise to negligible *osmotic pressure*, *depression of freezing point*, and *elevation of boiling point* effects. The molecular groups or particles of the solute carry a resultant *electric charge*, generally of the same sign for all the particles.

COLOPHONY. See *rosin*.

COLORIMETER. Apparatus used in *colorimetric analysis* for comparing intensities of *colour*. See also *tintometer*.

COLORIMETRIC ANALYSIS. A form of *quantitative analysis* in which the quantity of a substance is estimated by comparing the intensity of *colour* produced by it with specific *reagents*, with the intensity of colour produced by a standard amount of the substance.

COLOUR. The sensation of colour is the result of the interpretation by the human central nervous system of the effect produced upon the eye by *electromagnetic radiation* of a particular *wavelength*.

COLOUR TEMPERATURE. The *temperature* of a full radiator (see *black-body radiation*) which would emit visible *radiation* of the same spectral distribution as the radiation from the *light* source under consideration.

COLOUR VISION. *White light*, such as daylight, consists of a mixture of *electromagnetic radiations* of various *wavelengths* (see *spectrum colours*). A surface which reflects all of these will appear white; some surfaces, however, have the property of absorbing some of the radiations they receive, and reflecting the rest. Thus, a surface which absorbs all light radiations excepting those corresponding to green, will appear green by reflecting only those radiations. In the cases of colour seen by transmitted light, as in coloured *glass*, the glass absorbs all the radiations except those which are visible, and which pass through. See *surface colour; pigment colour.*

COLOURTRON. A type of *cathode ray tube*, used as a colour picture-tube in *television*, which has three *electron guns*, one for each *primary colour.*

COLUMBIUM. Cb. See *niobium.*

COLZA OIL. Rapeseed oil. Yellow oil obtained from the seeds of various Brassica plants. Used as an edible oil, illuminant, lubricant, and in the *quenching of steel.* 'Mineral colza' oil is a mixture of *paraffin hydrocarbons* with a boiling range of 250°–350° C.

COMA. I. The nebulous patch of *light* which surrounds the *nucleus* of a *comet.* 2. An error of a *lens* or spherical *mirror* which causes a blurred *comet*-like image.

COMBINATION, LAWS OF CHEMICAL. See *chemical combinations, laws of.*

COMBINATION (math.). A selection of a specified number of different objects from some larger specified number. The number of combinations of r different objects selected from n objects (i.e. the number of combinations of n objects taken r at a time) is denoted by the expression $^{n}C_{r}$, and is equal to $\dfrac{n!}{r!\,(n-r)!}$. (See *factorial.*)

COMBUSTION. Burning. A *chemical reaction*, or complex of chemical reactions, in which a substance combines with oxygen producing *heat, light*, and *flame.* The combustion reactions which supply most of the *energy* required by human civilization involve the oxidation of *fossil fuels* in which carbon is converted into *carbon dioxide* and hydrogen is converted into *water (steam).*

COMET. A heavenly body, moving under the attraction of the *Sun.* Consists of a hazy gaseous cloud (see *coma*) containing a brighter nucleus and a fainter tail.

COMMAND GUIDANCE. A method of missile or *rocket* guidance in which computed information is transmitted to the missile and causes it to follow a directed flight path.

COMMUNICATION SATELLITE. See *satellite, artificial.*

COMMUTATOR. A device for altering or reversing the direction of an *electric current*; used in the *dynamo* to convert the *alternating current* into a direct one if required. Consists of a cylindrical assembly of insulated *conductors* each of which is connected to sections of the winding. Spring-mounted carbon brushes make contact with the conductors and thus carry the current to external circuits.

COMPASS, MAGNETIC. In its simplest form a compass consists of a magnetized needle pivoted at its centre so that it is free to move in a horizontal plane. The effect of the Earth's *magnetic field* is to cause the needle to set along the *magnetic meridian.* The needle is usually placed at the centre of a circular scale marked with the points of the compass. As such a compass is also affected by magnetic fields other than that of the Earth, for navigation the *gyro-compass* is used.

COMPLEMENTARITY. A term introduced into *quantum theory* by Niels Bohr (1885–1962), implying that evidence relating to atomic systems which has been obtained under different experimental conditions cannot necessarily be comprehended by one single model. Thus, for example, the wave model of the *electron* is complementary to the particle model.

COMPLEMENTARY ANGLES. *Angles* together totalling 90° or one right angle.

COMPLEMENTARY COLOURS. Pairs of *colours* which, when combined, give the effect of white. See *colour vision*.

COMPLETE RADIATION. See *black body radiation*.

COMPLEX NUMBER. A complex number consists of two parts, 'real' and 'imaginary', and can be expressed in the form $x+iy$, where both x and y are real quantities and i is the square root of -1, i.e. $i^2 = -1$. The real part of the complex number is 'x' and the imaginary part 'iy'. Such numbers obey the ordinary laws of *algebra* except that in *equations* containing them the real and imaginary parts are equated separately.

COMPONENT (chem.). A term in the *phase rule*. The number of components in a system is the least number of substances from which every *phase* of the system may be constituted. E.g. each of the phases *ice, water, water vapour* in equilibrium is composed of one component, H_2O.

COMPONENT FORCES AND VELOCITIES. Two or more *forces* or *velocities* which produce the same effect upon a body as a single force or velocity, known as the *resultant*.

COMPOUND (chem.). A substance consisting of two or more *elements* chemically united in definite proportions by *weight*.

COMPOUND, INTERSTITIAL. A *compound* of a *metal* and certain *metalloids* in which the metalloid *atoms* occupy the interstices between the atoms of the metal *lattice*.

COMPRESSIBILITY. The coefficient of compressibility (*isothermal*) of a substance is given by $\kappa = -\dfrac{1}{V} \cdot \dfrac{\delta V}{\delta p}$, where δV is the change in the volume V of the substance resulting from a change of *pressure* δp, the *temperature* remaining constant. The *reciprocal* of *bulk modulus*. Measured in square *metres* per *newton*.

COMPTON EFFECT. The reduction in the *energy* of a *photon*, as a result of its interaction with a free *electron*. Part of the photon's energy is transferred to the electron (Compton or recoil electron) and part is re-directed as a photon of reduced energy (Compton scatter). Named after Arthur H. Compton (1892–1962).

COMPUTER. An *electronic* device which can accept data, apply a series of logical processes to it, and supply the results of these processes as information. Computers are used to perform complex series of mathematical calculations at very great speed; this makes them of great use for a variety of purposes, such as routine office calculations, control of industrial processes, and the control of spacecraft flight paths. Their ability to perform these operations depends not only on their mathematical capabilities, but also on their ability to store information and retrieve specified *bits* of information in the appropriate circumstances. The two main types of computer are: the *analog computer* in which numbers are represented by magnitudes of such physical quantities as *voltages*, mechanical movements, etc., and the *digital computer* in which numbers are expressed directly as *digits*, usually in the *binary notation*. This latter type is more versatile. See also, *C.P.U.*, *store, software, backing storage, peripherals*, etc.

CONCAVE. Curving inwards; thus, a concave (or bi-concave) *lens* is thinner at the centre than at the edges. See Fig. 24, page 219.

CONCAVO-CONVEX. A term used to describe a *lens* which curves inwards on one side and outwards on the other. See Fig. 24, page 219.

CONCENTRATED (chem.). As applied to *reagents*, containing the minimum of *water* or other *solvent*; the opposite of *dilute*.

CONCENTRATION. *c*. The quantity of a substance present in a given space, or defined quantity of another substance. Concentration of *aqueous solutions* is usually expressed in *moles* per cubic *metre*. See also *molarity*.

CONCENTRATION CELL. A *primary cell* whose *E.M.F.* is due to a difference in *concentration* between different parts of the *electrolyte*.

CONCENTRIC. Having the same centre. E.g. two concentric tubes would appear, in cross-section, as two concentric *circles*.

CONCHOIDAL FRACTURE. A type of break or fracture characteristic of an *amorphous solid*; an irregular break with a curved face exhibiting concentric rings.

CONCRETE. A building material composed of stone, *sand, cement*, and *water*. Reinforced concrete has *steel* rods or meshes imbedded in it to increase its *tensile strength*.

CONDENSATION (chem.). A chemical change in which two or more *molecules* react with the elimination of *water* or of some other simple substance. E.g. *acetic anhydride*, $(CH_3CO)_2O$, may be regarded as a condensation product of *acetic acid*, CH_3COOH, a molecule of the anhydride being formed when two molecules of the acid combine with the elimination of one molecule of water. See also *polymerization*.

CONDENSATION OF VAPOUR. The change of *vapour* into *liquid* which takes place when the *pressure* of the vapour becomes equal to the maximum *vapour pressure* of the liquid at that *temperature*.

CONDENSATION PUMP. Diffusion Pump. Apparatus used to obtain high vacua, i.e. *pressures* of the order of 10^{-6} mm mercury. Mercury or oil *vapour* issuing as a jet through the orifice O exhausts the system attached to the tube A. *Gas molecules* in A diffuse through the layer of mercury vapour around the orifice and are carried down with the vapour stream by molecular bombardment. The mercury vapour is cooled at the jet causing it to condense, so preventing it from diffusing back into the system which is being exhausted. See Fig. 7, page 86.

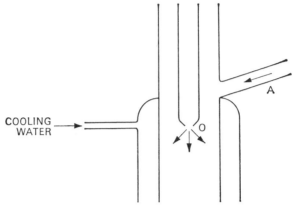

FIGURE 7.

CONDENSER (chem.). Liebig condenser. Apparatus for converting *vapour* into *liquid* during *distillation*. In its simplest form consists of a tube along which the vapour passes and is cooled, usually by cold water flowing through an outer jacket surrounding the tube.

CONDENSER, ELECTRICAL. See *capacitor*.

CONDENSER MICROPHONE. A *microphone* consisting essentially of an electrical *condenser*, one plate of which is fixed and the other plate forms the diaphragm upon which the *sound* waves fall. The vibrations of the diaphragm vary the *capacitance* of the condenser, which in turn alters the *potential* across a high *resistance*. This varying potential is then amplified in the normal way.

CONDENSER, OPTICAL. Device used in optical instruments to converge rays of *light*; e.g. in the *microscope* a condenser *lens* is used to converge upon the object to be viewed.

CONDUCTANCE. G. The conductance of a *direct current* circuit is the *reciprocal* of its *resistance*. The conductance of an *alternating current* circuit is its resistance divided by the square of its *impedance*. Measured in both cases by 'reciprocal ohms' or *mhos*. See also *siemens*.

CONDUCTION BAND. The range of energies (see *energy bands*) in a *semiconductor* corresponding to states in which the *electrons* can be made to flow by an applied *electric field*.

CONDUCTION, THERMAL. The transmission of *heat* from places of higher to places of lower *temperature* in a substance, by the interaction of *atoms* or *molecules* possessing greater *kinetic energy* with those possessing less. In *gases* the heat energy is transmitted by collision of the gaseous molecules, those possessing the greater kinetic energy imparting, on collision, some of their energy to molecules having less. Conduction in *liquids* is mainly due to the same process. In solid electrical *conductors*, the chief contribution to thermal conduction arises from a similar process taking place between the free *electrons* present. The interaction of the molecules responsible for thermal conduction in solid electrical *insulators* arises from the elastic binding *forces* between the molecules, which are effectively fixed in space.

CONDUCTIVITY, ELECTRICAL. κ. The *reciprocal* of the *resistivity* or specific resistance of a *conductor*. Measured in 'reciprocal ohms' or *mhos* per *metre*.

CONDUCTIVITY, THERMAL. Heat conductivity. λ. The rate of transfer of *heat* along a body by *conduction*. Measured in *calories* flowing per second across a centimetre cube of the substance, having a *temperature* difference of $1°C$. on opposite faces, in the *c.g.s. system*, or *watts* per *metre* cube per *kelvin* in *SI units*.

CONDUCTOR, ELECTRICAL. A body capable of carrying an *electrical current*; a body which, if given an *electric charge*, will distribute that charge over itself.

CONDUCTOR, THERMAL. A body which will permit *heat* to flow through it by *conduction*.

CONDY'S FLUID. A *solution* of sodium or calcium (or sometimes aluminium) permanganate, $NaMnO_4$ or $Ca(MnO_4)_2$. Used as a *disinfectant*.

CONE (math.). A solid figure traced by a straight line passing through a fixed point, the *vertex*, and moving along a fixed *circle*. For a cone of vertical height h, slant height s, and radius of base r, the *volume* is given by $V = \frac{1}{3}\pi r^2 h$, and the area of the curved surface $A = \pi r s$.

CONFINEMENT. See *containment*.

CONGRUENT FIGURES. Geometrical figures equal in all respects.

CONFORMATION THEORY. The principle that the three-dimensional structure of a *molecule* enables its stability and reactivity to be predicted. The theory pays special attention to the conformation of substituted hydrogen *atoms* in *organic* compounds; the axial (vertical) or equatorial (horizontal) disposition of *substituents* has been shown to be of great importance in predicting physical and chemical properties.

CONIC SECTIONS. Curves obtained by the intersection of a *plane* with a

CONIC SECTIONS

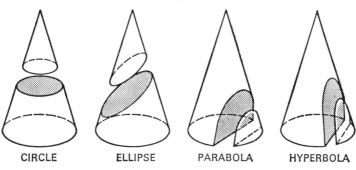

CIRCLE   ELLIPSE   PARABOLA   HYPERBOLA

FIGURE 8.

cone; include the *circle, ellipse, parabola,* and *hyperbola.* See Fig. 8.

CONIINE. $C_8H_{17}N$. A poisonous *liquid alkaloid,* b.p. 166–8°C., which is the active constituent of hemlock.

CONJUGATE POINTS of a lens. Points on either side of the *lens,* such that an object placed at either will produce an image at the other.

CONJUGATED DOUBLE BOND. In an *unsaturated organic compound* two *double bonds* separated by a single bond are said to be conjugated, e.g. *butadiene,* $CH_2:CH.CH:CH_2$.

CONJUNCTION (astr.). A *planet* (or other heavenly body) is said to be in superior conjunction when it is in a straight line with the *Sun* and the *Earth*; a planet with its orbit inside that of the Earth is in inferior conjunction when it is between the Sun and the Earth and in line with them.

CONSERVATION OF CHARGE. The principle that the total *electric charge* associated with a system remains constant: that electric charge can be neither created nor destroyed.

CONSERVATION OF MASS AND ENERGY. A principle, resulting from Einstein's special theory of *relativity,* that combines the separate laws of the conservation of *energy* and of *mass.* The law of the conservation of energy states that in any system energy cannot be created or destroyed, and the law of the conservation of mass (or *matter*) states that in any system matter cannot be created or destroyed. These laws are now seen to be approximations which can only be applied to systems not involving *nuclear reactions* or *velocities* approaching the velocity of *light.* The general principle of the conservation of mass and energy, which is of universal applicability, and which is based upon the *mass-energy equation,* states that in any system the sum of the mass and energy remains constant.

CONSERVATION OF MOMENTUM. The principle that the total *momentum* of two colliding bodies before impact is equal to their total momentum after impact. When *velocities* comparable to the speed of *light* are being considered, the variation of *mass* with *velocity* (see *relativity, theory of*) must be taken into account, and the expression for the momentum becomes:

$$\text{Momentum} = mv = \frac{m_0}{\sqrt{1 = \dfrac{v^2}{c^2}}} \times v, \text{ where }$$

$m_0 = $ *rest mass,*
$v = $ velocity of the body and
$c = $ velocity of light

CONSTANT (math., phys.). Any quantity which does not vary; e.g. π ('pi'), the ratio of the circumference to the diameter of any *circle.*

CONSTANT BOILING MIXTURE. See *azeotropic mixture.*

CONSTANT COMPOSITION, LAW OF. See *chemical combination, laws of.*

CONSTANTAN. An *alloy* of copper containing 10%–55% nickel; as its electrical *resistance* does not vary with *temperature* it is used in electrical equipment.

CONTACT ANGLE, for solid-liquid interface. The *angle* included between the tangent plane to the surface of a *liquid* and the tangent plane to the surface of a *solid* at any point along their line of contact.

CONTACT POTENTIAL DIFFERENCE. If two dissimilar *metals, a* and *b,* are in contact (see Fig. 9), then in general a *potential difference* exists between point *A,* just outside *conductor a,* and a point *B,* just outside conductor *b.* This is the contact potential difference of the two conductors.

FIGURE 9.

CONTACT PROCESS. Industrial process for the manufacture of *sulphuric acid,* H_2SO_4. *Sulphur dioxide,* SO_2, is made to combine with oxygen by passing over a heated *catalyst,* usually platinum or platinized asbestos. The *sulphur trioxide,* SO_3, which is formed is combined with *water* to give sulphuric acid.

CONTAINMENT. Confinement. In a controlled *thermonuclear reaction,* the process of preventing the *plasma* from coming into contact with the walls of the containing vessel is referred to as containment or confinement. The approximate period for which the *ions* remain trapped by the containing field is referred to as the 'containment time' or the 'confinement time'.

CONTINUOUS SPECTRUM. See *spectrum.*

CONTINUOUS WAVE. CW. *Radio* or *radar* transmissions which are generated continuously and not in short *pulses.*

CONTINUUM. A continuous series of component parts passing into one another; e.g. the three *space* dimensions and the time dimension are considered to form a four-dimensional continuum.

CONTROL GRID. An *electrode* placed between the *cathode* and the *anode* of a *thermionic valve* for controlling the flow of *electrons* through the valve.

CONTROL ROD. Part of the control system of a *nuclear reactor* which directly affects the rate of reaction therein. Usually a rod or tube, which can be moved up or down its *axis,* made of steel or aluminium containing boron, cadmium, or some other strong absorber of *neutrons.*

CONTROLLED THERMONUCLEAR REACTION. CTR. See *thermonuclear reaction.*

CONVECTION. Transference of *heat* through a *liquid* or *gas* by the actual movement of the *fluid.* Portions in contact with the source of heat become hotter, expand, become less dense and rise; their place is taken by colder portions, thus setting up convection currents.

CONVERGENCE. Coming to a point.

CONVERGING LENS. A *lens* capable of bringing to a point a *beam* of *light* passing through it; a *convex* lens. See Fig. 25, page 220.

CONVERSE. The transposition of a statement consisting of a fact or datum and a consequent conclusion. Thus the converse of the proposition 'equal chords of a *circle* are equidistant from the centre' is 'chords which are equidistant from the centre of a circle are equal'. The converse of a statement is not necessarily true.

CONVERSION. The process in a *nuclear reactor* as a result of which *fertile* material is transformed into *fissile* material, e.g. the conversion of thorium-232 into uranium-233. The 'conversion factor' is the number of fissile *atoms* produced from the fertile material per fissile atom destroyed in the fuel.

CONVERSION ELECTRON. An *orbital electron* ejected from an *atom* as a result of the *energy* it acquires from a transition of the *nucleus* from one energy state to another in the absence of *gamma-ray* emission.

CONVERTER. 1. An electrical machine for converting *alternating current* to *direct current* or vice versa. 2. The *retort* used in the *Bessemer process*.

CONVERTER REACTOR. A *nuclear reactor* which produces *fissile* material from *fertile* material by *conversion*.

CONVEX. Curving outwards; e.g. a convex *lens*, one thicker at the centre than at the edges. See Fig. 24, page 219.

COOLANT. A *fluid* used for cooling, usually extracting *heat* from one source and transferring it to another. In a *nuclear reactor* the coolant transfers the heat from the *nuclear reaction* to the steam-raising plant.

COORDINATE BOND. Dative Bond. See *valency, electronic theory of*.

COORDINATE GEOMETRY. See *analytical geometry*.

COORDINATES. Magnitudes which are used to define the position of a point or line within a fixed frame of reference. See *Cartesian coordinates* and *polar coordinates*.

COORDINATION NUMBER. The number of *anions* which surround a *cation* in a *crystal lattice*.

COPAL. A natural *resin* obtained from certain trees. Used in varnishes.

COPLANAR (math.). In the same *plane*.

COPOLYMERIZATION. See *polymerization*.

COPPER. Cu. Element. A.W. 63·54. At. No. 29. A red malleable and ductile *metal*, m.p. 1084° C., S.G. 8·95; after silver, the best *conductor* of electricity. It is unaffected by *water* or *steam*. Occurs as the free metal, and as cuprite or ruby *ore*, Cu_2O; copper glance, Cu_2S; copper pyrites, $CuFeS_2$. Extracted from *sulphide* ores by alternate roasting and fusing with sand, thus removing iron and *volatile* impurities, and leaving a mixture of *cuprous oxide* and sulphide. This is then heated in a *reverberatory furnace*, giving impure copper, which is then refined by various methods. Used for steam boilers, electrical wire and apparatus, in *electrotyping*, and in numerous *alloys*, e.g. *bronze, brass, speculum metal, gun metal, bell metal, Dutch metal, manganin, constantan, nickel silver, German silver*, etc.

COPPER OXIDE CHLORIDE. Brunswick green. $CuCl_2.3Cu(OH)_2$. A green *insoluble* crystalline substance used as a *pigment*.

COPPER SULPHATE. See *cupric sulphate*.

COPPERAS. See *ferrous sulphate*.

CORAL. Deposits of impure *calcium carbonate*, $CaCO_3$, formed of the hard skeletons of various marine *organisms*.

CORDITE. An *explosive* prepared from *cellulose nitrate* and *nitroglycerine*.

CORONA. A white irregular halo surrounding the *Sun*, which is visible during a total *eclipse*.

CORONA DISCHARGE. A luminous discharge which appears round the surface of a *conductor* due to *ionization* of the air (or other *gas* surrounding it), caused by the *voltage* gradient exceeding a critical value, but not being sufficient to cause sparking.

CORPUSCLE. See *blood cell*.

CORPUSCULAR THEORY. The theory that *light* consists of minute corpuscles in rapid motion. The original corpuscular theory was abandoned in the middle of the nineteenth century in favour of the *wave theory of light*, first put forward by Huygens in 1678. Later research has shown that light phenomena must be interpreted in terms of *photons* and waves, as the two descriptions are merely two different ways of viewing one and the same reality. See *complementarity*.

CORROSION. Surface chemical action, especially on *metals*, by the action of moisture, air, or chemicals.

CORROSIVE SUBLIMATE. See *mercuric chloride*.

CORTISONE. 17-hydroxy-11-dehydrocorticosterone. $C_{21}H_{28}O_5$. A crystalline *steroid hormone*, m.p. 215° C., secreted by the cortex of the adrenal gland. Produces healing responses and reduces local inflammation, used in the treatment of rheumatic conditions.

CORUBIN. Crystalline *aluminium oxide*, Al_2O_3. Obtained as a *by-product* of the *thermit* process.

CORUNDUM. Natural *aluminium oxide*, Al_2O_3. A crystalline substance nearly as hard as *diamond*, used as an *abrasive*.

COSECANT. See *trigonometrical ratios*.

COSINE. See *trigonometrical ratios*.

COSMIC DUST. Small particles of *matter*, probably ranging in size from one hundredth to one ten-thousandth of a *millimetre*, distributed throughout *space*.

COSMIC RAY SHOWER. Cascade shower. See *shower*.

COSMIC RAYS. Very energetic *radiation* falling upon the Earth from outer *space*, and consisting chiefly, if not entirely, of charged particles. The majority of these are most probably *protons*, although *electrons* and *alpha particles* are also present. There is also evidence that a small component (about 2%) of the primary radiation consists of heavy atomic *nuclei*. The primary particles, when incident upon our atmosphere, cause several secondary processes. Proton-*neutron* collisions in the top tenth of the atmosphere give rise to *mesons*, several different types of which are now known. High-energy electrons are created in the atmosphere by meson *decay*, by interaction of high energy protons with nuclei, by *knock-on* collisions of mesons with electrons, etc. These high-energy electrons give rise to *cosmic ray showers* resulting in the creation of *photons, positrons,* and further electrons. Energies as high as 10^{17} *electron-volts* have been observed with cosmic ray particles. The origin of cosmic rays is not known with certainty although some appear to emanate from the *Sun.* See also *east-west asymmetry.*

COSMOGONY. The science of the nature of the heavenly bodies, with particular reference to the formation of *planets, stars,* and *galaxies.*

COSMOLOGY. The science of the nature, origin, and history of the *Universe.* A more general and widely used term than *cosmogony* when referring to the Universe as a whole. See *steady state theory, superdense theory.*

COSMOTRON. A *proton accelerator* containing a very large ring-shaped *electromagnet.*

COTANGENT. See *trigonometrical ratios.*

COUDÉ SYSTEM. A form of astronomical reflecting *telescope* in which *light* from the primary *mirror* is reflected back along the axis of the telescope by means of a system of mirrors as shown in Fig. 10. This system may also be adapted for use with a refracting telescope.

COUDÉ TELESCOPE

FIGURE 10.

COULOMB, THE. The derived *SI unit* of *electric charge,* defined as the quantity of electricity transferred by 1 *ampere* in one second. 10^{-1} *electromagnetic units;* 3×10^{9} *electrostatic units.* Symbol C. Named after Charles Augustin Coulomb (1736–1806).

COULOMB SCATTERING. The *scattering* of sub-atomic particles caused by the *electrostatic* (coulomb) *field* surrounding an atomic *nucleus.*

COULOMB'S LAW. The *force* of attraction or repulsion between two charged bodies (whose charges behave as though they were concentrated at a point) is proportional to the magnitude of the charges and inversely proportional to the square of the distance between them.

COULOMETER. Coulombmeter. See *voltameter.*

COUMARIN. $C_9H_6O_2$. A white crystalline substance, m.p. $71°C.$, with an odour of vanilla. Used as a flavour and in perfume.

COUMARONE. Benzofuran. $C_6H_4OCH:CH$. A *liquid* derived from *coaltar*, b.p. $173°C.$, which polymerizes into a synthetic *resin*; used in the *paint* and varnish industry.

COUNTER TUBE. A device for counting individual ionizing events. See *Geiger counter, scintillation counter,* and *crystal counter.*

COUPLE (phys.). Two equal and opposite parallel, but not colinear, *forces* acting upon a body. The *moment* of a couple is the product of either force and the perpendicular distance between the line of action of the forces.

COVALENT BOND. See *valency, electronic theory of.*

COVALENT CRYSTAL. A *crystal* in which the *atoms* are held in the *lattice* by covalent bonds (see *valency, electronic theory of*). Typical examples are *diamond*, silicon, and most organic crystals. See also *semiconductors.*

C.P.U. Central processing unit. The central *electronic* unit in a *computer* which processes input information, and information from the *store*, and produces the output information. The C.P.U. and the store form the central part of the computer. The devices connected to them, known as *peripherals*, include the *backing storage* and the input and output equipment.

CRACKING (chem.). Pyrolysis. The *decomposition* of a chemical substance by *heat*; especially the conversion of *mineral oils* of high *boiling point* into more *volatile* oils suitable for petrol engines, by 'cracking' the larger *molecules* of the heavy oils into smaller ones. In catalytic cracking the decomposition takes place in the presence of a *catalyst.*

CREAM OF TARTAR. See *potassium hydrogen tartrate.* $C_4O_6H_5K.$

CREATININE. $C_4H_7N_3O$. A white crystalline substance, derived from the *amino acid* creatine, $C_3H_8N_3COOH$, found in urine, blood, etc.

CREEP. A permanent change in the physical dimensions of a *metal* caused by the application of a continuous *stress.*

CREOSOTE. A *distillation* product obtained from *tar*; term often restricted to the product from the tar obtained by the *destructive distillation* of wood. An oily, transparent *liquid* containing *phenol* and *cresol*, used for preserving timber.

CRESOL. Hydroxy toluene. $CH_3C_6H_4OH$. A *liquid aromatic organic compound* obtained from *coal-tar*. Consists of three *isomers* which boil in the range $191°–203°C.$ Used in the *plastics, explosives,* and *dye* industries, and as a *disinfectant.* See *lysol.*

CRITH. The *weight* of 1 litre of hydrogen at $0°C$, and a pressure of 760 mm; approximately $0·09$ g.

CRITICAL ANGLE of a medium (phys.). The least angle of *incidence* at which *total internal reflection* occurs. When a ray of *light* passing from a denser to a less dense medium, e.g. *glass* to air, meets the surface, a portion of the light does not emerge, but is internally reflected. As the angle of incidence increases, the intensity of the internally reflected beam also increases until an angle is reached when the whole beam is thrown back, total internal reflection taking place.

CRITICAL DAMPING. A measuring instrument is said to be critically damped when it takes up its *equilibrium* deflection in the shortest possible time, the oscillations of the indicator (needle) about the equilibrium position being quickly damped out. *Galvanometers* are normally used critically damped.

CRITICAL MASS. The minimum amount of *fissile* material required in a *nuclear reactor* or a *nuclear weapon* to sustain a *chain reaction*.

CRITICAL POTENTIAL. The minimum *energy* required to raise the *energy level* of an *orbital electron* (see *excitation*) or to remove it from the *atom*. See *ionization potential* and *radiation potential*.

CRITICAL PRESSURE. The *pressure* of the *saturated vapour* of a substance at the *critical temperature*.

CRITICAL REACTION. See *chain reaction*.

CRITICAL STATE. Critical point. The state of a substance when its *liquid* and gaseous *phases* have the same *density*, at the same *temperature* and *pressure*.

CRITICAL TEMPERATURE of a *gas*. The *temperature* above which the gas cannot be liquefied by *pressure* alone.

CRITICAL VELOCITY. The *velocity* at which the flow of a *liquid* ceases to be *streamline* and becomes *turbulent*.

CRITICAL VOLUME. The *volume* occupied by unit mass (1g, 1kg, or 1 *mole*) of a substance at its *critical temperature* and *critical pressure*.

CROSS-LINKAGE (chem.). The joining of polymer *molecules* (see *polymerization*) to each other by *valency bonds*. A polymer may be imagined, in the simplest case, to consist of very long chain-like *molecules*; cross-linkage would have the effect of joining adjacent chains by lateral links.

CROSS-SECTION. A term used in *nuclear physics* to represent the effective area, which has to be attributed to a particular *atom* or *nucleus*, to account geometrically for its interaction with an incident *beam* of *radiation*. The 'total' (or 'collision') cross-section, which accounts for all interactions, is subdivided into the 'elastic cross-section' and the 'inelastic cross-section'. The elastic cross-section accounts for all elastic *scattering* in which the incident radiation suffers no loss of *energy* to the atom or nuclei. The inelastic cross-section accounts for all other interactions and may be further subdivided to account for specific interactions, e.g. 'capture cross-section', 'fission cross-section', 'ionization cross-section', etc.

CROTONIC ACID. Butenoic acid. $CH_3CH:CHCOOH$. A colourless crystalline *soluble* substance which exists in two *isomeric* forms. The *trans-form* has a m.p. 71·6°C. and is used in organic synthesis. The *cis-form* (isocrotonic acid) has a m.p. of 14·5°C.

CROWN GLASS. A variety of *glass* containing potassium or barium in place of sodium; it is less fusible than ordinary *soda glass*, and is used in optical instruments.

CRUCIBLE. A vessel of heat-resisting material used for containing high-temperature *chemical reactions*.

CRYOGEN. See *freezing mixtures*.

CRYOGENICS. The study of materials and phenomena at *temperatures* close to *absolute zero*.

CRYOHYDRATES. Crystalline substances, containing the *solute* with a definite molecular proportion of *water*, which crystallize out from *solutions* cooled below the *freezing point* of pure water.

CRYOLITE. Natural sodium aluminium fluoride, Na_3AlF_6. Used in the manufacture of *aluminium*.

CRYOMETER. A *thermometer* especially designed for measuring low *temperatures*.

CRYOPHORUS. Apparatus used to demonstrate the cooling effect of *evaporation*.

CRYOSCOPIC METHOD for the determination of *molecular weights*; freezing-point method. The determination of the molecular weight of a dissolved substance by noting the *depression of freezing point* produced by a known *concentration*.

CRYOSTAT. A vessel in which a specified low *temperature* may be maintained.

CRYOTRON. A switch based on *superconductivity*. The simplest form consists of a coil of wire of one superconducting material wound round a length of wire of another superconductor, all immersed in a bath of liquid helium. A control current passed through the coil produces a *magnetic field* strong enough to destroy the superconductivity of the central wire but not of the coil. Thus the current in the coil controls the *resistance* of the wire, switching it from zero to a finite value.

CRYSTAL. A substance which has solidified in a definite geometrical form. Most *solid* substances, when pure, are obtainable in a definite crystalline form. Solids which do not form crystals are said to be *amorphous*. Crystals are classified according to the structure of their *lattices*, or according to the type of *bond* which holds them together, i.e. *electrovalent* (or *ionic crystals*), *covalent crystals*, or *metallic crystals*.

CRYSTAL COUNTER. A *counter tube* which depends upon a *crystal* in which the electrical *conductivity* is momentarily increased by an ionizing event.

CRYSTAL DETECTOR. See *detector*. A fine wire ('cat's whisker') in contact with a crystal of *galena* (PbS) or other suitable *semiconductor*. This arrangement is a good conductor of *electricity* in one direction, and suppresses most of the flow of electricity in the other direction.

CRYSTAL OSCILLATOR. A source of electrical oscillations of very constant *frequency* determined by the physical characteristics of a *quartz crystal*. See *quartz clock*.

95

CRYSTAL RECTIFIER. A *semiconductor* used as a *rectifier*, usually in a manner similar to a *diode* valve; also called a semiconductor diode.

CRYSTALLOGRAPHY. The study of the geometrical form of *crystals*. See *X-ray crystallography*.

CRYSTALLOIDS. Substances which, in *solution*, are able to pass through a *semipermeable membrane*; substances which do not usually form *colloidal solutions*.

CS. Ortho-chlorobenzal malononitrile. $C_6H_4ClCH:C(CN)_2$. A white powder, m.p. 52°C., used as a tear gas and 'harassing agent' in crowd control. Causes tears, salivation, choking, and painful breathing.

CUBE. 1. A regular hexahedron; a regular solid figure with six square faces. 2. The third power of a number. E.g. 8 is the cube of 2, 2^3.

CUBE ROOT. $\sqrt[3]{}$. The cube root of a number is the quantity which when raised to the third power gives that number. Thus 2 is the cube root of 8.

CUBIC CENTIMETRE. cc. Metric unit of volume. 1000 cc = 1 *litre*. Term used synonymously with *millilitre*, ml., one thousandth of a litre, although the litre is no longer used for accurate measurements.

CULTURE MEDIUM. A preparation used for growing and cultivating *micro-organisms* for experimental purposes.

CUPEL. A dish used in the extraction of the *noble metals* by *cupellation*.

CUPELLATION. A separation of silver, gold, and other *noble metals* from impurities which are oxidized by hot air. The impure metal is placed in a *cupel*, a flat dish made of porous *refractory* material, and a blast of hot air is directed upon it in a special furnace. The impurities are oxidized by the air and are partly swept away by the blast and partly absorbed by the cupel.

CUPRAMMONIUM GROUP. A complex of copper and *ammonia*, especially the *bivalent cation* $Cu(NH_3)_4$—. Cuprammonium *solution* is a blue *aqueous* solution containing this cation; it is used as a *solvent*, and in the manufacture of *rayon*.

CUPRIC. Containing *bivalent* copper. Most of the commoner copper compounds are cupric *salts*.

CUPRIC OXIDE. Tenorite. CuO. A black crystalline *insoluble* substance, m.p. 1326°C., used in *glass* manufacture.

CUPRIC SULPHATE. Copper sulphate, blue vitriol. $CuSO_4.5H_2O$. A blue crystalline *soluble salt*. Used as a *mordant*, an *insecticide*, and a *fungicide*.

CUPRO-NICKEL. An *alloy* of copper and nickel used in coinage.

CUPROUS. Containing *univalent* copper.

CUPROUS OXIDE. Cuprite, red copper oxide. Cu_2O. A red *insoluble* powder, m.p. 1235°C., formed when *Fehling's solution* is reduced. Used in *glass* manufacture and in *paints*.

CURARE. A very poisonous material, containing certain *alkaloids*. Obtained from various South American trees.

CURIE. A measure of the *activity* of a *radioactive* substance (see *radio-*

activity). Originally defined as the quantity of *radon* in radioactive equilibrium with 1 g of radium. Now extended to cover all radioactive *isotopes* and defined as that quantity of a radioactive isotope which decays at the rate of $3 \cdot 7 \times 10^{10}$ *disintegrations* per second. Named after Madame Marie Curie (1867–1935).

CURIE POINT. Curie temperature. The temperature for a given *ferromagnetic* substance above which it becomes merely *paramagnetic*. Named after Pierre Curie (1859–1906).

CURIE'S LAW. The *magnetic susceptibility* of a *paramagnetic* substance is inversely proportional to the *absolute temperature*. Named after Pierre Curie.

CURIUM. Cm. *Transuranic element*, At. No. 96. A radioactive *actinide* whose most stable *isotope*, $^{247}_{96}Cm$, has a *half-life* of $1 \cdot 6 \times 10^{7}$ years.

CURRENT, electric. See *electric current*.

CURRENT BALANCE. Instrument for the determination of an *electric current* in absolute *electromagnetic units*. Consists of two similar coils attached to the extremities of a balance arm. Above and below each of these coils is a fixed coil. The six coils are connected in series in such a way that when the current is allowed to pass through them, the beam experiences maximum *torque*. The beam is restored to its horizontal *equilibrium* position by means of a known torque supplied by a rider sliding along the arm. From the known torque and the geometry of the system the current can be calculated.

CURRENT DENSITY, in *electrolysis*. The current per unit area of *electrode*.

CURSOR. A transparent slider with a fine hair-line, used in *slide-rules*.

CYANAMIDE. NH_2CN. A colourless crystalline *unstable* substance, m.p. $44°C$. Name often applied to *calcium cyanamide*.

CYANATE. A *salt* or *ester* of *cyanic acid*.

CYANIC ACID. HOCN. A poisonous *gas* which decomposes in *solution* or upon freezing to a *liquid*.

CYANIDE. A *salt* of *hydrocyanic acid*, HCN. All cyanides are intensely poisonous.

CYANIDE PROCESS for gold. Extraction of gold from its *ores* by dissolving the gold in a *solution* of potassium cyanide, KCN, reducing the resulting potassium aurocyanide, $KAu(CN)_2$, with zinc, filtering off, melting down, and cupelling (see *cupellation*) the metal.

CYANITE. Al_2SiO_5. A blue mineral consisting of aluminium silicate, used as a *refractory*.

CYANOCOBALAMINE. Vitamin $B_{12}.C_{63}H_{90}N_{14}PCo$. A red crystalline *soluble* substance, obtained from liver, eggs, fish, etc., used in the treatment of pernicious anaemia, and to promote the growth of livestock.

CYANOGEN. C_2N_2. A colourless, very poisonous *gas* with a smell of bitter almonds. In its chemical properties it resembles the *halogens*, forming *cyanides* analogous to the *chlorides*, etc.

CYANO GROUP. The *univalent radical* —CN.

97

CYANOGUANIDINE. See *dicyandiamide*.

CYANURIC ACID. Tricyanic acid. $C_3H_3O_3N_3.2H_2O$. A white crystalline *soluble* substance, used in organic synthesis.

CYBERNETICS. The theory of communication and control mechanisms in living beings and machines.

CYCLAMATE. See *sodium cyclamate, calcium cyclamate*.

CYCLE (phys.). Any series of changes or operations performed by or on a system, which brings it back to its original state. E.g. the *frequency* of an *alternating current* is measured in cycles per second. (See also *hertz*.)

CYCLIC FIGURE (math.). A figure through all the vertices or corners of which a *circle* may be drawn; a figure inscribed in a circle.

CYCLIC HYDROCARBONS. *Organic compounds* of carbon and hydrogen only, some or all of the carbon *atoms* in the *molecule* being linked in a closed ring structure; e.g. *benzene*.

CYCLIC QUADRILATERAL. A four-sided plane *rectilinear* figure through the vertices of which a *circle* may be drawn. The pairs of opposite angles are *supplementary* (i.e. total 180°).

CYCLOHEXANE. C_6H_{12}. A colourless inflammable *liquid*, b.p. 81°C., consisting of a six-membered ring of *methylene groups*. Used as a *solvent* and in the manufacture of *plastics*.

CYCLOHEXANOL. $C_6H_{11}OH$. A crystalline *soluble* substance, m.p. 25·1°C., b.p. 161·1°C., used as a *solvent*.

CYCLOID. A figure traced out in space by a point on the circumference of a *circle* which rolls without slipping along a fixed straight line.

CYCLONITE. Hexogen, R.D.X.*. $(CH_2N.NO_2)_3$. A very powerful *explosive* made from *hexamine*.

CYCLOPENTANE. C_5H_{10}. A colourless *liquid*, b.p. 49·2°C., obtained from *petroleum* and used as a *solvent*.

CYCLOPROPANE. C_3H_6. A colourless inflammable *gas*, used as an *anaesthetic*.

CYCLOTRON. An *accelerator* for imparting to charged particles of atomic magnitudes *energies* of several million *electron-volts*. The *ions* or charged particles are caused to traverse a spiral path between two hollow semi-circular *electrodes*, called dees, by means of a suitable *magnetic field* applied perpendicularly to the plane of the dees. At each half-revolution the particles receive an energy increase of some tens of thousands of electron-volts from an oscillating *voltage* applied between the dees.

CYLINDER. A solid figure traced out by a rectangle rotating round one side as *axis*. For a cylinder having vertical height h and radius of base r, the volume is $\pi r^2 h$ and the total surface area $2\pi r(h+r)$.

CYSTEINE. A crystalline *amino acid*, present in most *proteins*. See Table 5, page 435.

CYSTINE. An *insoluble* crystalline *amino acid*, m.p. 247–9°C., which forms *cysteine* on *reduction*. See Table 5, page 435.

CYTOCHEMISTRY. The *chemistry* of living *cells*.

CYTOCHROME. A respiratory *pigment* widely distributed in *aerobic organisms*. Consists of *proteins* with an iron *prosthetic group* similar to that of *haemoglobin*. The *oxidation* of cytochrome by molecular oxygen, and its subsequent *reduction* in the cell, is the principal route by which atmospheric oxygen enters into cellular *metabolism*.

CYTOLOGY. The study of the structure and function of living *cells*.

CYTOLYSIS. The dissolution of *cells*, particularly by the destruction of their surface membranes.

CYTOPLASM. The *protoplasm* of a living *cell* outside its *nucleus*.

CYTOSINE. Aminopyrimidone. $C_4H_5N_3O$. A white crystalline substance, m.p. 320–25°C. One of the *pyrimidine* bases which occur in the *nucleotides* of the *nucleic acids* and which play a part in the formulation of the *genetic code*.

D

DAILY VARIATION of the Earth's magnetic field (see *magnetism, terrestrial*). The small variation of the *horizontal intensity, magnetic declination*, and *dip* recurring over a period of a day.

DALTON'S ATOMIC THEORY. See *atomic theory*.

DALTON'S LAW of Partial Pressures. The total *pressure* of a mixture of two or more *gases* or *vapours* is equal to the sum of the pressures that each component would exert if it were present alone, and occupied the same *volume* as the whole mixture. Named after John Dalton (1766–1844).

DAMPING. A decrease in the *amplitude* of an oscillation or *wave motion* with time.

DANIELL CELL. A *primary cell* having a negative pole of amalgamated zinc, standing in a porous pot containing dilute *sulphuric acid*. This pot stands in *cupric sulphate solution*, which also contains the positive pole, a copper plate. On completion of the external circuit, a current flows and the following reactions take place: at the negative pole, zinc is dissolved, *zinc sulphate* being formed; at the positive pole, copper is deposited. The *E.M.F.* is 1·1 *volts*. Named after J. F. Daniell (1790–1845).

DARAF. The practical unit of *elastance*; *reciprocal* of the *farad*.

DARK GROUND ILLUMINATION. A device used in microscopy, whereby transparent or unstained objects are made to appear as bright particles on a black background.

DARWIN'S THEORY of evolution. The theory that different species arise by genetic *mutation*, the beneficial characteristics thus caused helping *organisms* to survive by *natural selection*. Named after Charles Darwin (1809–82).

DASH-POT. A mechanical damping device which depends upon the fact that when a body moves through a *fluid* medium, viscous *forces* are set up which damp the motion of the body. It usually consists of a piston, attached to the part whose movements are to be damped, fitting loosely into a cylinder containing either air or oil.

DASYMETER. An instrument for determining the *density* of a *gas*.

DATING. The determination of the age of *mineral, fossil*, or wooden objects by measuring their *radioactivity*. See also *radiocarbon dating* and *radioactive age*.

DATIVE BOND. Coordinate bond. A *covalent type* of *bond* in which both *electrons* forming the bond are donated by one *atom*. See *valency, electronic theory of*.

DAVY LAMP. See *safety lamp*.

D.D.T. DichloroDiphenylTrichloroethane. $(C_6H_4Cl)_2.CH.CCl_3$. A white powder, m.p. 107°C., with a fruity smell. Used as a contact *insecticide*.

DEAMINASE. An *enzyme* which catalyses the removal of an *amino group* from a *compound*.

DEAMINATION. The removal of *amino groups* from a *compound*.

DEAN AND STARK METHOD. A method of estimating the quantity of *water* in an *oil* or other *liquid* substance. The liquid under examination is distilled into a special *reflux condenser* so constructed that the water is prevented from running back into the distillation flask. The *volume* of water so collected is measured and thus the water content of a known *weight* of initial liquid can be calculated.

DE BROGLIE WAVELENGTH. A moving particle, whatever its nature, has wave properties associated with it. For a particle of *mass m* moving with *velocity v*, the *wavelength* of the associated de Broglie wave is given by $\lambda = \dfrac{mv}{h}$, where h is *Planck's constant*. Named after Louis Victor de Broglie (born 1892).

DEBYE AND HUCKEL'S THEORY of electrolysis. An explanation of the phenomena of *electrolysis* put forward to overcome certain difficulties which arise in the interpretation of the phenomena on the classical theory of *electrolytic dissociation*. It is assumed that strong *electrolytes* are completely dissociated, and that the increase in equivalent *conductivity* which is observed with dilution is due not to an increase in the fraction ionized, but to an increase in the mobility of the *ions*, due to the decrease of *electrostatic forces*.

DEBYE UNIT. A unit of molecular *dipole* moment equal to 1×10^{-18} *electrostatic units* or 3.33564×10^{-30} *coulomb metre*. Named after Peter J. W. Debye (born 1884).

DECA -. Prefix denoting ten times in the *metric system*. Symbol da, e.g. dam = 10 *metres*.

DECANE. $C_{10}H_{22}$. A *liquid paraffin hydrocarbon*, b.p. 174·1°C., which occurs in several *isomeric* forms.

DECANTATION. The separation of a *solid* from a *liquid* by allowing the former to settle and pouring off the latter.

DECAY. The *transformation* of a radioactive substance into its decay (or daughter) products. (See *radioactivity*.) Also used in relation to the transformation of particles into more stable particles.

DECAY CONSTANT. See *disintegration constant*.

DECAY, PERIOD OF. See *half-life*.

DECI-. Prefix denoting one tenth in the *metric system*. Symbol d, e.g. dm = 0·1 *metre*.

DECIBEL. One tenth of a *bel*. A unit which compares levels of *power*. Two power levels, P_1 and P_2, are said to differ by n decibels when:

$$n = 10 \log_{10} \frac{P_2}{P_1}$$

This unit is often used to express *sound* intensities. In this case, P_2 is the intensity of the sound under consideration and P_1 is the intensity of some reference level, often the intensity of the lowest audible note of the same *frequency*.

DECINORMAL SOLUTION. A *solution* containing one tenth of a *gram-equivalent* per *litre*. See *normality*.

DECLINATION (astr.). The *angular distance* of a heavenly body from the *celestial equator*.

DECLINATION, MAGNETIC. See *magnetic declination*.

DECOMPOSITION (chem.). Breaking up of a chemical *compound*. E.g. *mercuric oxide*, HgO, decomposes on heating into mercury and oxygen. Also used in relation to the breaking up of organic materials as a result of the action of *bacteria, fungi*, or chemicals.

DECREPITATION. Bursting or cracking of *crystals* of certain substances on heating, mainly due to expansion of water within the crystals.

DEFECT. A discontinuity in the pattern of *atoms, ions*, or *electrons* in a *crystal*. A 'point defect' consists of a *vacancy* or an *interstitial*. A 'line defect' is caused by a *dislocation*. In a *semiconductor*, 'defect conduction' is a result of *hole* conduction in the *valency band*.

DEFERENT. See *epicycle*.

DEFICIENCY DISEASES. Diseases produced by lack of a particular *vitamin* or other essential food factor in the diet; e.g. scurvy, caused by the deficiency of vitamin C.

DEFINITION. The sharpness of an *image* formed by a *lens, mirror*, or other optical system: the accuracy of *sound* or vision reproduction in a *radio* or *television* set.

DEFORMATION. An alteration in the size or shape of a body.

DEFORMATION POTENTIAL. The *electric potential* which acts on a *free electron* in a *conductor* or *semiconductor* as a result of *deformation* of the *crystal lattice*.

DEGAUSSING. The *demagnetization* of a magnetized substance, achieved by surrounding the substance with a coil carrying an *alternating current* of ever-decreasing magnitude.

DEGENERATE GAS. A state of *matter* in which *electrons* and atomic *nuclei* are packed too closely together for the evolution of *nuclear energy*; occurs in *stars* of the *white dwarf* class.

DEGREE. 1. A subdivision of an interval in a scale of measurement; e.g. the *Celsius* degree. 2. The sum of the *exponents* of the *variables* in a mathematical expression: the exponent of the *derivative* of highest *order* in a *differential equation*. 3. See *angle*.

DEGREES OF FREEDOM (chem.). 1. A term used in the *phase rule*; the least number of independent variables defining the state of a system (e.g. the *temperature* and *pressure* in the case of a *gas*) which must be given definite values before this state is completely determined. 2. The number of independent ways in which a *molecule* may possess translational, vibrational, or rotational *energies*.

DEGREE OF LATITUDE AND LONGITUDE. See *latitude, longitude*.

DEHYDRATION. The elimination or removal of *water*; usually the removal of chemically combined water. E.g. concentrated *sulphuric acid*, H_2SO_4, acts as a dehydrating agent on substances which contain hydrogen and oxygen in the proportions in which they occur in water.

DEHYDROGENASE. An *enzyme* which catalyses *oxidation* reactions by the removal of hydrogen from the *substrate*.

DEKATRON. A gas-filled emission tube with a central *anode* usually surrounded by ten *cathodes* and associated transfer *electrodes*. Incoming pulses cause a *glow discharge* to be transferred from one cathode to the next so that the tube may be used for counting or switching.

DELAY LINE. A component or circuit designed to introduce a calculated delay in the transmission of a signal.

DELAYED NEUTRONS. *Neutrons* resulting from *nuclear fission* which are emitted with a measurable time delay. Only a small proportion of neutrons are delayed, but the average delay period must be taken into account in the control of *nuclear reactors*. See *prompt neutrons*.

DELIQUESCENT. Having the property of picking up moisture from the air to such an extent as to dissolve in it; becoming *liquid* on exposure to air.

DELTA CONNECTION. A method of connecting the three windings of a three-*phase* electrical system. The windings are connected in series, the three-phase supply being taken from, or put into, the three junctions.

DELTA-IRON. An allotropic (see *allotropy*) form of pure iron which exists between 1400° C. and the *melting point*.

DELTA METAL. An *alloy* of copper (55%) and zinc (43%) with small amounts of iron and other *metals*.

DELTA RAY. An *electron* ejected from an *atom* by a fast moving ionizing particle.

DEMAGNETIZATION. The process of depriving a body of its magnetic properties. The 'demagnetization energy' is the *energy* which would be released when a body is completely demagnetized.

DEMODULATION. The process, in a *radio, television,* or *radar* receiver, of separating information from a *modulated carrier wave*. The equipment used is called a demodulator or a *detector*.

DENATURE. 1. To denature *ethanol* is to add some poisonous substance to it to make it unfit for human consumption, e.g. *methylated spirits*. 2. To denature a *fissile* material is to add another *isotope* to it to render it unsuitable for use in a *nuclear weapon*. 3. To denature a *soluble*, or globular, *protein* is to produce a structural change in it, either chemically or by heating, so that it loses most of its solubility. Usually involves an unfolding of the *polypeptide* chain.

DENDRITE. 1. (chem.) A many-branched *crystal*. 2. (bio.) Branching processes of a *neurone* which carry impulses into the *cell* body, and which form *synapses* with the *axons* of other neurones.

DENDROLOGY. The branch of *botany* concerned with trees and shrubs.

DENITRIFYING BACTERIA. *Bacteria* in the *soil* which, in the absence of oxygen, break down *nitrates* and *nitrites* with the evolution of free nitrogen.

DENOMINATOR (math.). The number below the line in a *vulgar fraction* e.g. 4 in $\frac{3}{4}$.

DENSITOMETER. Instrument for the measurement of the *density* of an image produced by *light*, *X-rays*, *gamma rays*, etc., on a photographic plate.

DENSITY. The *mass* of unit *volume* of a substance. In *SI units* density is expressed in *kilogrammes* per cubic *metre*, in *c.g.s. units* in *grams* per cubic centimetre, and in *f.p.s.* units in *pounds* per cubic foot. $1 \text{ kg}/m^3 = 10^{-3} \text{ g}/cc = 0\cdot062428 \text{ lb}/ft^3$. The density of *water* is one gram per cc and therefore in these units density is numerically equal to *specific gravity*.

DENSITY, OPTICAL. If one medium has a greater *refractive index* than another for *light* of a given *wavelength*, then it has the greater optical density for that wavelength.

DENSITY, PHOTOGRAPHIC. The degree of *opacity* of a part of a *negative* or transparency.

DEOXYRIBONUCLEIC (DESOXYRIBOSENUCLEIC) ACID. DNA. Long thread-like *molecules* found in *chromosomes* and *viruses*, consisting of two interwound helical chains of *polynucleotides*. The *sugar* of all the *nucleotides* is 2-deoxy-D-*ribose*, but each nucleotide is characterized by one of the four following nitrogenous bases: *adenine*, *cytosine*, *guanine*, and *thymine*. DNA molecules are responsible for storing the *genetic code* by the order of the arrangement of their nitrogenous bases, three bases coding for one *amino acid*. The structure of a DNA molecule has been likened to a twisted rope-ladder, the sides of which consist of sugar-phosphate chains, the rungs of linked nitrogenous bases.

DEPILATORY. A substance used for removing hair.

DEPLETED MATERIAL. In general, a material which contains less of a particular *isotope* than it normally possesses. In particular, applied to *nuclear fuel*, a material which contains less *fissile* isotopes than natural uranium, e.g. the residue from an *isotope separation* plant or a *nuclear reactor*.

DEPLETION LAYER. The region of a *semiconductor* in which the density of mobile *carriers* is too low to neutralize the fixed charge density of *donors* and *acceptors*.

DEPOLARIZATION. The prevention of electrical *polarization* in a *cell*. In the *Leclanché cell* polarization is reduced by surrounding the positive carbon pole with *manganese dioxide*, MnO_2. This oxidizes the hydrogen liberated at the pole, the chief cause of polarization.

DEPRESSION, ANGLE OF. If B is a point below the level of another point A, the angle of depression of B from A is the *angle* which AB makes with the horizontal *plane AX* through A. See Fig. 11, page 105.

DEPRESSION OF FREEZING POINT. Lowering of the *freezing point* of a *liquid* when a *solid* is dissolved in it. With certain exceptions, the depression is proportional to the number of *molecules* or *ions* present, and the depression produced by the same *molecular concentration* of any substance is a constant for a given *solvent*. This gives rise to the *cryoscopic method* for the determination of *molecular weights*.

DEPTH OF FIELD. Depth of focus. The range over which a *camera*, or other optical instrument, will produce a distinct *image* of an object.

DERIVATIVE (chem.). A substance derived or prepared from some other substance, usually retaining the general structure of the parent substance, e.g. *nitrobenzene*, $C_6H_5NO_2$, is a derivative of *benzene*, one of the hydrogen *atoms* in every *molecule* of the latter being replaced by a *nitro group*, NO_2.

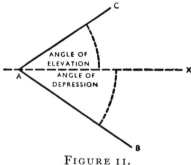

FIGURE II.

DERIVATIVE (math.). Derived function. The result of *differentiation* of a mathematical function. See Table 9, page 441.

DERIVED FUNCTION. See *derivative*.

DERIVED UNITS. *Units* of physical measurement, other than the *fundamental units* of length, mass, time, etc., but derived from these. The unit for *velocity*, for example, is derived from the units for length and time, velocity being expressed as length per unit time, e.g. *metres* per *second*.

DESALINATION. The process of removing *salt* from *sea-water* to make it suitable for agricultural purposes or for drinking. Various methods are possible, but to make the process commercially viable on a large scale, the waste heat from a *nuclear power* station is used to provide the *energy* for *distillation*.

DESICCATION. Drying; removal of moisture.

DESICCATOR. Apparatus used in laboratories for drying substances and for preventing *hygroscopic* substances from picking up moisture. Consists of a glass vessel, with a close-fitting ground lid, which contains some hygroscopic substance, e.g. *phosphorus pentoxide*, P_2O_5.

DESTRUCTIVE DISTILLATION. Carbonization. Heating a complex substance to produce chemical changes in it, and distilling off the *volatile* substances so formed. E.g. the destructive distillation of *coal* produces *coal-gas* and many other valuable products.

DETECTOR. That part of a *radio* receiver in which the information is separated from the *modulated carrier wave*. Now more usually called a demodulator. See *demodulation*, also *crystal detector*.

DETERGENT. A cleaning agent; usually restricted to substances used in *solution* for cleaning a solid surface by action other than simple dissolution; e.g. by using a *surface-active agent*. Modern synthetic detergents, unlike traditional *soaps* which are *salts* of *fatty acids,* are *alkyl aryl sulphonates* produced from *petroleum* and *sulphuric acid.* Unlike soaps they are effective in soft, hard, or salty water and they form no scum.

DETERMINANTS. An algebraic method of solving *simultaneous equations* in which an expression is written out in a square array. Thus, the determinant of $a_1b_2 - a_2b_1$ is written:

$$a_1 \ b_1$$
$$a_2 \ b_2$$

DETINNING. The recovery of metallic tin from scrap tin-plate by the action of chlorine, which combines with the tin to form *volatile stannic chloride,* $SnCl_4$.

DETONATING GAS. A *mixture* of hydrogen and oxygen in a *volume* ratio of 2:1; i.e. in the volume ratio required to form *water.* Extremely explosive when ignited.

DETONATION. Extremely rapid *combustion* which takes place within a high velocity *shock wave.* Also used loosely, but incorrectly, to describe the combustion reactions which occur during *knocking* or 'pinking' in an *internal-combustion engine.*

DEUTERIUM. D. $_1^2H$. The *isotope* of hydrogen with *mass number* 2, and *atomic mass* 2·0147. The *abundance* of deuterium in natural hydrogen is 0·0156%. It occurs in *water* as the oxide, D_2O (see *heavy water*), from which it is obtained by fractional *electrolysis.*

DEUTERIUM OXIDE. D_2O. See *heavy water.*

DEUTERON. The *nucleus* of the *deuterium atom.*

DEVARDA'S ALLOY. An *alloy* of 50% copper, 45% aluminium, 5% zinc.

DEVELOPING, PHOTOGRAPHIC. The action of certain chemicals, usually organic *reducing agents,* on an exposed photographic plate or film in order to bring out the latent image. The developer reduces those areas of the silver *salts* which had been exposed to *light* to metallic silver. This remains as a black deposit. See *photography.*

DEVIATION (statistics). The difference between one of a *set* of values and the *mean* of the set. The 'mean deviation' is the mean of all the individual deviations of the set.

DEVIATION, ANGLE OF. The difference between the angle of *incidence* and the angle of *refraction* when a ray of *light* passes from one medium to another. See Fig. 13, page 115.

DEVITRIFICATION of glass. The crystallization of *glass,* which is normally an *amorphous* mixture in a *metastable* state; when crystallization takes place, the glass loses its characteristic state of clear transparency.

DEW. Liquid *water* produced by *condensation* of *water vapour* in the air when the *temperature* falls sufficiently for the vapour to reach saturation.

DEW POINT. The *temperature* at which the *water vapour* present in the air saturates the air and begins to condense, i.e. *dew* begins to form.

DEWAR FLASK. A glass vessel used for keeping *liquids* at *temperatures* differing from that of the surrounding air. This is done by reducing to a minimum the transfer of *heat* between the liquid and the air. Consists of a double-walled flask with the space between the two walls exhausted to a very high *vacuum*, to minimize transfer of heat by *convection* and *conduction*. The inner surfaces of the walls are silvered to reduce transfer of heat by *radiation*; areas of contact between the two walls are kept at a minimum to keep down conduction of heat. See Fig. 12. Named after James Dewar (1842–1913).

MODERN THERMOS FLASK

FIGURE 12.

DEXTRIN. British gum, starch gum. A *mixture* of gummy *polysaccharide carbohydrates* obtained by the partial *hydrolysis* of *starch*.

DEXTROROTATORY. Rotating or deviating the plane of vibration of polarized light to the right (observer looking against the oncoming light). See *polarization of light*.

DEXTROSE. See *glucose*.

DIACETYL. See *butanedione*.

DIAGONAL. A line joining the intersections of two pairs of sides of a *rectilinear* figure.

DIALYSIS. The separation of *colloids* in *solution* from other dissolved substances (*crystalloids*) by selective *diffusion* through a *semipermeable membrane*. Such a membrane is slightly permeable to the *molecules* of the crystalloids, but not to the larger molecules or groups of molecules in the colloidal state.

DIALYZED IRON. A *colloidal solution* of ferric hydroxide, $Fe(OH)_3$. Deep red liquid, used in medicine.

DIALYZER. An arrangement for effecting *dialysis*. The *solution* to be dialyzed is placed in a vessel in which it is separated from *water* by a *semipermeable membrane*; this is not permeable to the substance in the *colloidal state*, which will eventually remain as a pure solution on its side of the membrane.

DIAMAGNETISM. The property of a substance which has a small negative *magnetic susceptibility*. This type of magnetism is due to a change in the orbital motion of the *electrons* in the *atoms* of the substance consequent on the application of an external *magnetic field*. The phenomenon occurs in all substances, although the resulting diamagnetism is often masked by the much greater effects due to *paramagnetism* or *ferromagnetism*.

DIAMETER. See *circle*.

DIAMINOHEXANE. Hexamethylenediamine. $H_2N(CH_2)_6NH_2$. A *soluble* organic substance, m.p. $41\cdot2°C$, b.p. $204°C$, used in the manufacture of *nylon*.

DIAMOND. Natural crystalline allotropic form (see *allotropy*) of carbon. It is colourless when pure, but is sometimes coloured by traces of impurities; it has a very high *refractive index* and *dispersive power*. Diamond is one of the hardest substances known and is transparent to *X-rays* (imitations are not). Used for cutting tools and drills, and as a gem.

DIASTASE. An *enzyme* contained in *malt* which converts *starch* into *maltose* during *brewing*. See also *amylase*.

DIATHERMANCY. The property of being able to transmit *heat radiation*; it is similar to transparency with respect to *light*.

DIATHERMY. A method of medical treatment by heating the body-tissues by the passage of a *high-frequency* electric discharge.

DIATOMACEOUS EARTH. See *kieselguhr*.

DIATOMIC (chem.). Consisting of two *atoms* in a *molecule*; e.g. hydrogen *gas*, H_2.

DIAZO COMPOUNDS. *Organic compounds* of the general formula $RN:NR'$. Many are important in the manufacture of *dyes*. In some cases diazo compounds are of the form $R:N:N$, e.g. *diazomethane*.

DIAZOMETHANE. $CH_2:N:N$. A yellow odourless explosive *gas*, used as a methylating agent.

DIAZONIUM COMPOUNDS. *Organic compounds* of the general formula $Ar : N-$, where Ar is an *aryl group*. The diazonium *salts*, of the form ArN_2X (in which X is an *anion*), are used in the manufacture of *azo-dyes*.

DIBASIC ACID. An *acid* containing two *atoms* of *acidic hydrogen* in a *molecule*; an acid giving rise to two series of *salts*, normal and acid salts; e.g. *sulphuric acid*, H_2SO_4, which gives rise to normal *sulphates* and hydrogen sulphates or bisulphates.

DIBROMOETHANE. Ethylene dibromide. $C_2H_4Br_2$. A *volatile liquid* existing in two *isomeric* forms. The common isomer 1, 2-dibromoethane, m.p. 10°C., b.p. 131°C., is used in conjunction with anti-knock compounds in *petrol* and as a *solvent*.

DIBUTYL OXALATE. $(C_4H_9OOC)_2$. A colourless *liquid*, b.p. 243·4°C., used as a *solvent* and in organic synthesis.

DICHLORODIFLUOROMETHANE. CCl_2F_2. A colourless *gas*, b.p. −29°C., used as a *refrigerant* and as a *propellant* for *aerosols*.

DICHLOROETHANE. Ethylene dichloride, Dutch liquid. $C_2H_4Cl_2$. An oily toxic *liquid* existing in two *isomeric* forms. The common isomer 1, 2-dichloroethane, m.p. −35°C., b.p. 84°C., is used as a *solvent* and in the manufacture of *polyvinyl chloride*.

DICHLOROMETHANE. Methylene chloride. CH_2Cl_2. A colourless *volatile liquid*, b.p. 40·1°C., used as a *solvent*, a *refrigerant*, and an *anaesthetic*.

DICHROMATE. A *salt* of the hypothetical dichromic acid, $H_2Cr_2O_7$, e.g. *potassium dichromate*, $K_2Cr_2O_7$.

DICHROMATE CELL. Bichromate cell. A *primary cell* having a positive pole of carbon and a negative pole of zinc in a *liquid* consisting of a *solution* of *sulphuric acid*, H_2SO_4, and *potassium dichromate*, $K_2Cr_2O_7$, the latter acting as a depolarizing agent (see *depolarization*) by its oxidizing action. The *EMF* is 2·03 *volts*.

DICHROMATISM. A form of colour blindness in which only two *colours* of the *spectrum* can be distinguished.

DICYANDIAMIDE. Cyanoguanidine. $H_2NC(NH)NHCN$. A white crystalline substance, m.p. 208°C., used in the manufacture of *plastics* and in medicine.

DIELECTRIC. Non-conductor of electricity, insulator. A substance in which an *electric field* gives rise to no net flow of *electric charge* but only to a displacement of charge.

DIELECTRIC CONSTANT. Relative *Permittivity*. Specific Inductive Capacity. The ratio of the *capacitance* of a *capacitor* with the given substance as *dielectric*, to the capacitance of the same capacitor with air (or a *vacuum*) as the dielectric. The values of the dielectric constants for a few common dielectrics are given below. Symbol ϵ_r.

Material	Dielectric constant	Dielectric strength Volts per millimetre
Air	1	—
Paraffin Wax	2·0–2·5	$6·2 \times 10^4$
Rubber	2·8–3·0	$1·2 \times 10^5$
Shellac	3·0–3·7	$3 − 9 \times 10^4$
Bakelite	4·5–7·5	$2 − 9 \times 10^4$
Porcelain	6·0–8·0	$10^4 − 10^5$
Mica	6·0–8·0	$2 − 6 \times 10^4$

DIELECTRIC HEATING. A form of heating in which electrically insulating material is heated by being subjected to an alternating *electric field*. Results from *energy* being lost by the field to *electrons* within the *atoms* and *molecules* of the material. In industrial dielectric heating the material to be heated is placed between the plates of a *capacitor* connected to a *high frequency* power source.

DIELECTRIC STRENGTH. The maximum *voltage* that can be applied to a *dielectric* material without causing it to break down; usually expressed in *volts* per mm. See table on page 109 for the dielectric strengths of some common dielectric materials.

DIELECTROPHORESIS. The motion of electrically polarized (see *electric polarization*) particles in a non-uniform *electric field*.

DIENE. An *unsaturated hydrocarbon* containing two *double bonds*, e.g. butadiene.

DIESEL ENGINE. A type of *internal-combustion engine* which burns heavy oil. Air which is mixed with the oil is compressed and thereby heated to the *ignition temperature* of the oil (about 540°C.). Named after Rudolf Diesel (1858–1913).

DIETHYL ETHER. See *ethers*.

DIFFERENTIAL CALCULUS. A branch of mathematics which deals with continuously varying quantities. It is based upon the *differential coefficient* of one quantity with respect to another of which it is a *function*. Used for solving problems involving the rates at which processes occur and for obtaining maximum and minimum values for continuously varying quantities.

DIFFERENTIAL COEFFICIENT. Derived function, derivative. See *differentiation* and Table 9, page 441.

DIFFERENTIAL EQUATION. An equation which involves *differential coefficients*. An ordinary differential equation is one in which only one independent variable is involved. The *order* of a differential equation is the same as that of the *derivative* of the highest order appearing in it; the *degree* is given by the largest *exponent*.

DIFFERENTIATION (bio.). 1. The development of *cells* so that they are capable of performing specialized functions in the organs and *tissues* of the *organisms* to which they belong. 2. In microscopic specimens, the removal of the excess stain from certain parts to show up the structure of the whole.

DIFFERENTIATION (math.). The operation, used in the *calculus*, of obtaining the *differential coefficient*; if $y = x^n$, the differential coefficient, $\frac{dy}{dx} = nx^{n-1}$. See Table 9, page 441.

DIFFRACTION. When a beam of *light* passes through an *aperture* or past the edge of an opaque obstacle and is allowed to fall upon a screen patterns of light and dark bands (with *monochromatic light*) or coloured bands (with *white light*) are observed near the edges of the beam, and extend into the geometrical shadow. This phenomenon, which is a particular case of *interference*, is due to the wave nature of light, and is known as diffraction. The phenomenon is common to all *wave motions*. See also *electron diffraction*.

DIFFRACTION GRATING. A device used to disperse a beam of *light*, *X-rays*, or other *electromagnetic radiation* into its constituent *wavelengths*, i.e. for producing its *spectrum*. It may consist of any device which acts upon an incident *wave front* in a manner similar to that of a regular array of parallel slits where the slit width is of the same order as the wavelength of the incident radiation. Such gratings may be prepared by ruling equidistant parallel lines on to a *glass* (transmission grating) or *metal* surface (reflecting grating). The grating may be plane or *concave*, the latter having self-focusing properties.

DIFFUSION OF GASES. *Molecules* of all *gases* move freely and tend to distribute themselves equally within the limits of the vessel enclosing the gas; thus all gases diffuse within the limits of any enclosing walls, and are all perfectly miscible with one another. The rates of diffusion of gases through porous bodies are inversely proportional to the square roots of their *densities*. (See *Graham's law*.)

DIFFUSION OF LIGHT. The *scattering* or alteration of direction of *light* rays, such as is produced by transmission through frosted glass, fog, etc., or by irregular reflections at matt surfaces such as blotting paper.

DIFFUSION OF PARTICLES. In *nuclear physics*, the passage of *elementary particles* through *matter* in such a way that the *probability* of *scattering* is large compared to that of *capture*.

DIFFUSION OF SOLUTIONS. *Molecules* or *ions* of a dissolved substance move freely through the *solvent*, the *solution* becoming uniform in *concentration*; the phenomenon is similar to *diffusion of gases*.

DIFFUSION PLANT. A plant for separating *isotopes*, based on their different rates of *diffusion* in the gaseous state through a membrane.

DIFFUSION PUMP. See *condensation pump*.

DIGIT (astr.). One twelfth of the diameter of the *Sun* or *Moon*; used to denote the extent of an *eclipse*.

DIGIT (math.). A single figure or numeral; e.g. 325 is a number of 3 digits.

DIGITAL COMPUTER. A *computer* which operates on data in the form of *digits*, rather than the physical quantities used in *analogue computers*. Originally mechanical devices employing cogs, gears, and levers, now depend upon *electronic* techniques which allow computers to be constructed capable of dealing automatically with a very wide range of problems at very high speeds.

DIGITALIS. A *mixture* of *glucosides* of vegetable origin (e.g. digitonin, *digitoxin*), used in the treatment of certain heart conditions.

DIGITOXIN. $C_{41}H_{64}O_{13}$. A white crystalline *glucoside*, m.p. 252–3°C., obtained from *digitalis* and used as a heart stimulant.

DIHEDRAL. Formed by two intersecting *planes*.

DILATION. Dilatation (phys.). A change in *volume*.

DILATOMETER. Apparatus used for measuring *volume* changes of substances. Generally consists of a bulb with a graduated stem.

DILUTE. Containing a large amount of *solvent*, generally *water*. 'Dilute' laboratory solutions of *reagents* are generally of twice *normal* strength, containing 2 *gram-equivalents* per *litre*.

DILUTION. 1. The further addition of *water* or other *solvent* to a *solution*. 2. The *reciprocal* of *concentration*; the *volume* of *solvent* in which unit quantity of *solute* is dissolved.

DIMENSIONS OF UNITS. The dimensions of a physical quantity are the *powers* to which the *fundamental units* (length l, mass m, time t, etc.) expressing that quantity are raised. E.g. *volume*, l^3, is of dimensions three in length; *velocity*, i.e. length per unit time, l/t, is of dimensions one in length and -1 in time.

DIMER. A substance composed of *molecules* each of which comprises two molecules of a *monomer*.

DIMETHOXYMETHANE. Methylal. $(CH_3O)_2CH_2$. A colourless inflammable *liquid*, b.p. 45·5°C., used as a *solvent* and in perfumes.

DIMORPHISM. The existence of a substance in two different crystalline forms.

DIMORPHOUS. Existing in two different crystalline forms.

DI-NEUTRON. An unstable system comprising two *neutrons*.

DINITROBENZENE. $C_6H_4(NO_2)_2$. A colourless *insoluble* crystalline substance which exists in three *isomeric* forms, the most important of which is the *meta-form*, m.p. 90°C., which is used in the manufacture of *dyes*.

DIODE. A *thermionic valve* containing two *electrodes*, *anode* and *cathode*. The diode is used chiefly for *rectification* and *demodulation*.

DIOLS. Glycols. Dihydric *alcohols* derived from *aliphatic hydrocarbons* by the substitution of *hydroxyl groups* for two of the hydrogen *atoms* in the *molecule*. General *formula* $C_nH_{2n}(OH)_2$. See also *ethanediol*.

DIOPTRE. Unit of power of a *lens*; the power of a lens in dioptres is the *reciprocal* of its *focal length* in *metres*. The power of a *converging lens* is usually taken to be positive, that of a *diverging lens* negative.

DIOXAN. Diethylene dioxide. $(C_2H_4)_2O_2$. A colourless inflammable *liquid* cyclic *ether*, b.p. 101°C., used as a *solvent* and a dehydrating agent.

DIP, MAGNETIC. See *magnetic dip*.

DIP CIRCLE. Inclinometer. An instrument for measuring the *angle* of *magnetic dip*. Consists of a magnetized needle mounted to rotate in a vertical plane, the angle being measured on a circular scale, marked in degrees.

DIPEPTIDE. A *peptide* which consists of two *amino acids*.

DIPHENYLAMINE. $(C_6H_5)_2NH$. A colourless crystalline substance, m.p. 52·8°C., used in the manufacture of *dyes* and in analytical chemistry as a detector of *oxidizing agents*.

DIPLOID. A *cell* in which the *nucleus* contains *chromosomes* in pairs is said to be diploid. Characteristic of nearly all animal cells except *gametes*. See *haploid*.

DIPOLE. 1. Two equal point *electric charges* (electric dipole) or *magnetic poles* (magnetic dipole) of opposite sign, separated by a small distance. The dipole moment is the product of either charge (or pole) and the distance between the two. May also be expressed as the *couple* which would be required to maintain the dipole at right angles to a *field* (electric or magnetic) of unit intensity. *Molecules* in which the centres of positive and negative *charge* are separated constitute dipoles, the dipole moments of which are measured in *Debye units* or *coulomb metres*. Dipole moments can often provide evidence as to the shape of molecules, e.g. *water* has a dipole moment of $1 \cdot 85$ Debye units ($6 \cdot 1 \times 10^{-30}$ C m), which indicates that it is triangular in shape with an angle of $105°$ between the two O-H bonds. 2. A *radio aerial* consisting of two rods.

DIPOLE MOMENT. See *dipole*.

DIPPEL'S OIL. See *bone oil*.

DI-PROTON. An unstable system comprising two *protons*.

DIRECT CURRENT. d.c. An *electric current* flowing always in the same direction.

DIRECT DYES. Cotton dyes, substantive dyes. A group of *dyes* which dye cotton, viscose *rayon*, and other *cellulose* fibres direct, without the use of *mordants*. Generally used with 'assistants' such as common *salt* or *sodium sulphate*, which assist absorption by the fibre.

DIRECT MOTION (astr.). 1. The motion of a *planet* or other celestial body round the *Sun* in the same direction as the *Earth*. All the planets have direct motion, but some *comets* and *satellites* do not, and they are said to have 'retrograde motion'. 2. Motion across the sky from west to east.

DIRECT VISION SPECTROSCOPE. A *spectroscope* designed for compactness and portability. In this instrument, the middle portion of the *spectrum* (the yellow) remains undeviated. The eye thus looks in the direction of the source when observing the spectrum.

DIRECTRIX. A fixed line used to describe and define a curve, by relating the distance of a point on the curve to this line and to the *focus* of the curve. See *parabola* and *hyperbola*.

DISACCHARIDES. A group of *sugars* the *molecules* of which are derived by the *condensation* of two *monosaccharide* molecules with the elimination of a molecule of *water*. On *hydrolysis* disaccharides yield the corresponding monosaccharides. E.g. *cane-sugar*, sucrose, $C_{12}H_{22}O_{11}$, is a disaccharide which, on hydrolysis with dilute *acids*, gives a *mixture* of *glucose* and *fructose*, both monosaccharides having the formula $C_6H_{12}O_6$. (See *inversion of cane-sugar*.) Other important disaccharides are *lactose* and *maltose*.

DISCHARGE, ELECTRICAL. 1. The release of the *electric charge* stored in a *capacitor* through an external circuit. 2. The conversion of the *chemical energy* stored in an electric *cell* into *electrical energy*.

DISCHARGE IN GASES. The passage of *electricity* through a tube containing a *gas* at low pressure. *Electrons* and *ions* present in the tube are accelerated towards their respective *electrodes* by the applied *potential difference*, the net transfer of *electric charge* constituting the current. The electrons are accelerated sufficiently to produce ions by collision with the gas *molecules*. Re-combination of oppositely charged ions gives rise to luminous glows at certain parts of the tube. The study of this pheno-menon has led to many important results, including the discovery of the electron and of *isotopes*.

DISCRIMINATOR. An *electronic* circuit which converts *frequency* or *phase modulation* into *amplitude modulation*.

DISINFECTANT. A substance capable of destroying disease *bacteria*.

DISINTEGRATION (phys.). Any process in which the *nucleus* of an *atom* emits one or more particles or *photons*, either due to spontaneous *radioactivity* or as the result of a collision.

DISINTEGRATION CONSTANT. Decay Constant. Transformation Con-stant. The *probability* of the *decay* of an atomic *nucleus* per unit time which characterizes a *radioactive isotope*. It determines the exponential decrease with time, *t*, of the *activity*, *A*, given by:

$$A = A_0 e^{-\lambda t}$$

where A_0 is the activity when $t = 0$, and λ is the disintegration constant.

DISLOCATION. A line *defect* in a *crystal*, the result of a slip along a surface of one or more *lattice* constants.

DISORDERING. The displacement of *atoms* from their position in a *crystal lattice* (e.g. as a result of the effect of *ionizing radiation*) to positions which are not part of the lattice.

DISPERSE PHASE. The dissolved or suspended substance in a *colloidal solution* or *suspension*.

DISPERSION (chem.). A *disperse phase* suspended in a *disperse medium*; a system of particles dispersed and suspended in a *solid, liquid,* or *gas.*

DISPERSION MEDIUM. A medium in which a substance in the *colloidal state* is dispersed; the *solvent* in a *colloidal solution.*

DISPERSION OF LIGHT. The splitting of *light* of mixed *wavelengths* into a *spectrum*. A beam of ordinary *white light*, e.g. sunlight, on passing through an optical *prism* or a *diffraction grating*, is divided up or dis-persed into light of the different wavelengths of which it is composed; if the beam which emerges after dispersion is allowed to fall upon a screen, a coloured band or spectrum is observed. Dispersion by a prism is due to the fact that lightwaves of different wavelengths are refracted (see *refraction*) or bent through different angles on passing through the prism, and are thus separated. See Fig. 13, page 115.

DISPERSIVE POWER of a medium. A measure of the *dispersion of light* produced by a *prism* or a particular medium with respect to light of two specified *wavelengths* ('1' and '2'); given by the ratio $\dfrac{n_1 - n_2}{n - 1}$, where n_1 is the *refractive index* of the medium for wavelength 1, n_2 that for wavelength 2, and *n* is the average of n_1 and n_2. When considering the dispersive power of media for ordinary *white light*, the dispersive power is often defined as $\dfrac{n_b - n_r}{n_y - 1}$ where n_b, n_r, and n_y are the refractive indices for blue, red, and yellow light respectively.

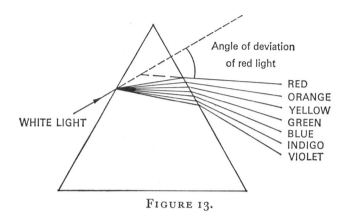

FIGURE 13.

DISSOCIATION (chem.). A temporary, reversible *decomposition* of the *molecules* of a *compound*, which occurs under some particular conditions. In *electrolytic dissociation*, the molecules are split into *ions* (see *ionic hypothesis*). In *thermal dissociation*, the effect of *heat* is to decompose a definite fraction of the molecules; e.g. *ammonium chloride*, NH_4Cl, dissociates into *ammonia*, NH_3, and *hydrogen chloride*, HCl, on heating. The products recombine on cooling, and the degree of dissociation depends on the *temperature*. The ratio of the product of the *active masses* of the molecules resulting from the dissociation, to the active mass of the undissociated molecules, when *chemical equilibrium* has been reached under a particular set of physical conditions, is called the 'dissociation constant'. See also *equilibrium constant*.

DISTILLATE. The *liquid* obtained by the *condensation* of the *vapour* in *distillation*.

DISTILLATION. The process of converting a *liquid* into *vapour*, condensing the vapour, and collecting the condensed liquid or *distillate*. Used for separating *mixtures* of liquids of different *boiling points* or for separating a pure liquid from a non-*volatile* constituent. (See *fractional distillation*.) Also used in the separation of *isotopes*. See *isotopes, separation of*.

DISTILLED WATER. *Water* which has been purified by *distillation* of the substances dissolved in it.

DIURNAL. Daily; performed or completed once every 24 hours.

DIVALENT. Bivalent. Having a *valency* of two.

DIVERGENT. Going away in different directions from a common path or point.

DIVERGING LENS. A *lens* which causes a parallel *beam* of *light* passing through it to diverge or spread out; *concave* lens. See Fig. 25, page 220.

DIVINYL ETHER. Vinyl ether. $H_2C:CHOCH:CH_2$. A colourless inflammable *liquid*, b.p. $39°C$., used as an *anaesthetic*.

DIVISION. An arithmetic operation in which a dividend is divided by a divisor to give a quotient and a remainder.

DNA. See *deoxyribonucleic acid*.

DOCOSANOIC ACID. Behenic acid. $CH_3(CH_2)_{20}COOH$. A crystalline *saturated fatty acid*, m.p. $80°C$., used in the manufacture of cosmetics and *waxes*, and as a *plasticizer*.

DODECAHEDRON. A *polyhedron* with twelve faces.

DODECANAL. Lauraldehyde. $CH_3(CH_2)_{10}CHO$. A colourless *insoluble* crystalline substance, m.p. $44·5°C$., used in perfumes.

DODECANOIC ACID. See *lauric acid*.

DOLOMITE. Pearl spar. Natural double *carbonate* of magnesium and calcium, $MgCO_3.CaCO_3$. A whitish solid which occurs naturally in vast amounts, comprising whole mountain ranges.

DONOR. An imperfection in a *semiconductor* which causes *electron* conduction.

DOPING. The addition of a small quantity of impurity to a *semiconductor* to achieve a particular characteristic.

DOPPLER BROADENING. The broadening of spectral emission or absorption lines (see *spectrum*) due to random motion of the emitting or absorbing *molecules*, *atoms*, or *nuclei*. See *Doppler effect*.

DOPPLER EFFECT. Doppler shift. Doppler's principle. The apparent change in the *frequency* of *sound* or *electromagnetic radiation* due to relative motion between the source and the observer. The *pitch* (*frequency*) of the sound emitted by a moving object (e.g. the whistle of a moving train) appears to a stationary observer to increase as the object approaches him and to decrease as it recedes from him. The *light* emitted by a moving object appears more red (red light being of lower frequency than the other colours) when it is receding from the observer (or the observer receding from it). Thus the fact that the light emitted by the *stars* of distant *galaxies* suffers a *red shift*, when observed from the Earth, is taken to mean that these distant galaxies are receding from our *Galaxy*. This is the principal evidence for the widely accepted hypothesis concerning the *expansion of the Universe*. The Doppler effect is also used in *radar*, to distinguish between stationary and moving targets and to provide information concerning their *velocity*, by measuring the frequency shift between the emitted and the reflected radiation. Named after C. J. Doppler (1803–53).

DOSE (phys.). The 'absorbed dose' is the *energy* imparted by *ionizing radiation* to unit *mass* of irradiated *matter*. Measured in *rads* (i.e. 100 *ergs* per gram or *joules* per *kilogramme*). The 'maximum permissible dose (or level)' is the recommended upper limit for the absorbed dose which a person should receive during a specified period.

DOUBLE BOND (chem.). Two *covalent bonds* linking two *atoms* in a chemical *compound*; characteristic of an *unsaturated compound*.

DOUBLE DECOMPOSITION (chem.). Metathesis. A *chemical reaction* between two *compounds* in which each of the original compounds is decomposed and two new compounds are formed. E.g. the action of *sodium chloride* on *silver nitrate* according to the equation $NaCl + AgNO_3 = AgCl + NaNO_3$.

DOUBLE REFRACTION. The formation of two refracted rays of *light* (see *refraction*) from a single incident ray; a property of certain *crystals*, notably *calcite*.

DOUBLE SALT. A compound of two *salts* formed by *crystallization* from a *solution* containing both of them. When redissolved the double salt *ionizes* as two salts. For example, *potassium sulphate* and *aluminium sulphate* in solution together will crystallize as the double salt K_2SO_4. $Al_2(SO_4)_3 . 24H_2O$.

DOUBLE STAR. Two *stars* which are held very close to each other as a result of their mutual gravitational attraction, and which move through *space* together giving the appearance, to the naked eye, of being one star.

DOUBLET. A pair of associated lines in a *spectrum* characteristic of the *alkali metals*.

DRACHM, FLUID. British unit of *volume*; 60 *minims*; 3·55 cc.

DRUG. 1. Any chemical substance used in medicine to cure or prevent disease. 2. A habit-forming *narcotic*; any substance which causes physiological or emotional dependence.

DRY CELL. Dry battery. A type of small *Leclanché cell* containing no free *liquid*. The *electrolyte* of *ammonium chloride* is in the form of a paste, and the negative zinc pole forms the outer container of the cell. Used for torch batteries, *radio* batteries, etc.

DRY ICE. Solid *carbon dioxide*, CO_2, used as a *refrigerant*.

DRYING OIL. An animal or vegetable *oil* which will harden to a tough film when a thin layer is exposed to the air. The hardening is due to *oxidation* or *polymerization* of the *unsaturated fatty acids* of which these oils partially consist. Used in *paints* and varnishes (e.g. *linseed oil*, dehydrated *castor oil*, and certain fish oils).

DUCTILITY. A property, especially of *metals*, of being capable of being drawn out into a wire.

DUCTLESS GLANDS. Endocrine glands. Glands or organs producing *hormones* in the body.

DULONG AND PETIT'S LAW. For a *solid element*, the product of the *atomic weight* and the *specific heat capacity*, i.e. the *atomic heat*, is a constant, approximately equal to 6·4 *calories* per *mole*. For validity of this law, see *atomic heat*. Named after P. L. Dulong (1785–1838) and A. T. Petit (1791–1820).

DUPLET. A pair of *electrons* shared between two *atoms* forming a single covalent bond. See *valency, electronic theory of*.

DURALUMIN*. A light hard aluminium *alloy* containing about 4% copper, and small amounts of magnesium, manganese, and silicon.

DUST CORE. A core for magnetic devices made of powdered *metal* (often molybdenum) held together with a suitable binder. Particularly suitable for *high frequency* equipment.

DUTCH LIQUID. See *dichloroethane.*

DUTCH METAL. An *alloy* of copper and zinc; a variety of *brass.*

DWARF STAR. A *star* of small *volume*, high *density*, and usually low *luminosity*. See also *white dwarf star.*

DYAD (chem.). An *element* having a *valency* of two.

DYES. Coloured substances which can be fixed firmly to a material to be dyed, so as to be more or less 'fast' to *water, light,* and *soap.* Usually *organic compounds;* some which were originally extracted from plants are now made artificially from *coal-tar by-products;* most modern dyes are entirely artificial and do not occur in Nature. See *acid dyes, azo dyes, direct dyes, mordants, vat dyes.*

DYNAMIC EQUILIBRIUM. If two opposing processes are going on at the same rate in a system, thus keeping the system unchanged, the system is said to be in dynamic equilibrium. E.g. a *liquid* in equilibrium with its *saturated vapour;* the rate of *evaporation* from the liquid surface is equal to the rate of *condensation* of the *vapour.*

DYNAMICS. A branch of *mechanics;* the mathematical and physical study of the behaviour of bodies under the action of *forces* which produce changes of motion in them.

DYNAMITE. An *explosive* consisting of *nitroglycerine* absorbed in *kieselguhr.*

DYNAMO. A device for converting *mechanical energy* into *electrical energy,* depending on the fact that if an electrical *conductor* moves across a *magnetic field,* an *electric current* flows in the conductor. (See *induction.*) The simplest form of dynamo consists of a powerful *electromagnet,* called the *field magnet,* between the *poles* of which a suitable conductor, usually in the form of a coil or coils, called the *armature,* is rotated. The mechanical energy of the rotation is thus converted into electrical energy in the form of a current in the armature.

DYNAMOMETER. Any instrument designed for the measurement of *power.*

DYNATRON OSCILLATOR. An oscillator, using a *tetrode* (screen grid valve) in such a way that the *anode* current increases as the anode *voltage* is reduced.

DYNE. *C.G.S. system unit* of *force;* the force which, acting upon a *mass* of 1 g, will impart to it an *acceleration* of 1 cm per second per second. 1 dyne $= 10^{-5}$ *newton* $= 7 \cdot 233 \times 10^{-5}$ *poundal.*

DYSPROSIUM. Dy. Element. A.W. 162·50. At. No. 66. S.G. 8·556, m.p. 1407° C. See *lanthanides.*

DYSTETIC MIXTURE. A *mixture* which has a constant maximum *melting point.*

E

EARTH. A *planet* having its *orbit* between those of *Venus* and *Mars*. Sphere, slightly flattened towards the poles (i.e. approximating to an oblate *spheroid* in shape). Equatorial radius 6378·388 kilometres (3963·34 miles); polar radius 6356·912 kilometres (3949·99 miles). Mean *density* 5·52 g per cc; mass 5·976 × 10²⁴ kg.

EARTHING a conductor. Making an electrical connection between the *conductor* and the Earth; the Earth is assumed to have zero *potential*.

EARTH'S CRUST. Lithosphere. The Earth's outer layer of surface soil of varying thickness lying upon a mass of hard rock several miles thick. The approximate estimated percentages by *weight* of the chief chemical *elements* composing the Earth's crust are: oxygen 47%, silicon 28%, aluminium 8%, iron 4·5%, calcium 3·5%, sodium and potassium 2·5% each, magnesium 2·2%, titanium 0·5%, hydrogen 0·2%, carbon 0·2%, phosphorus and sulphur 0·1% each.

EARTHSHINE. A faint illumination of the dark side of the *Moon* during a crescent *phase*, due to sunlight reflected from the *Earth's* surface.

EARTH'S MAGNETISM. See *magnetism, terrestrial*.

EAST-WEST ASYMMETRY OF COSMIC RAYS. The observed intensity of *cosmic ray* particles coming from the West is greater than that coming from the East at any given *latitude*. This asymmetry is due to the deflection of the primary charged cosmic ray particles by the *magnetic field* of the Earth, and indicates a preponderance of positively charged particles in the incoming radiation.

EBONITE. Vulcanite. A hard black insulating material made by vulcanizing *rubber* with high proportions of sulphur. Contains about 30% combined sulphur.

EBULLITION. See *boiling*.

ECCENTRICITY. 1. (math.) A *constant* used to describe a *conic*, equal to the distance from a point on the curve to the *focus* divided by the distance from that point to the *directrix*. 2. (astr.) A measure of the extent to which an *ellipse* is elongated, equal to the distance between the foci divided by the length of the *major axis*. This value is used to express the eccentricity of a *planet's orbit* round the *Sun*: e.g. the eccentricity of the *Earth's* orbit is 0·0167.

ECHELON (phys.). The type of grating which replaces the ordinary *diffraction grating* in *spectroscopy* when very high resolution is required. Consists essentially of a pile of plates of exactly equal thickness arranged in stepwise formation with a constant offset. The echelon can be used either as a transmission or as a reflection grating.

ECHO. The effect produced when *sound* or other *radiation* is reflected or thrown back on meeting a solid obstacle or a reflecting medium.

ECHO SOUNDER. A device for estimating the depth of the sea beneath a ship by measuring the time taken for a *sound* pulse to reach the sea bed and for its *echo* to return.

ECHOLOCATION. The location of an object by determining the direction of an *echo* reflected from it, or the time taken for the echo to return. E.g. *radar*, *echo sounding*, etc.

ECLIPSE. The passage of a non-luminous body into the *shadow* of another. An 'eclipse of the *Moon*', or lunar eclipse, occurs when the *Sun*, the *Earth*, and the Moon are in line so that the shadow of the Earth falls upon the Moon. An 'eclipse of the Sun', or solar eclipse, is said to occur when the shadow of the Moon falls on the Earth. See Fig. 14, which also illustrates the areas of partial and total eclipse.

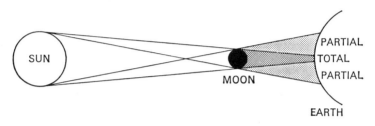

FIGURE 14.

ECLIPTIC. The *Sun's* apparent path in the sky relative to the *stars*; the circle described by the Sun on the *celestial sphere* in the course of a year.

ECOLOGY. The study of the relation of plants and animals to their environment.

ECOSPHERE. 1. The part of the Earth's *atmosphere* in which life can exist: also called the 'biosphere' or 'physiological atmosphere'. 2. The part of the atmosphere surrounding any *planet* on which life could exist. 3. The part of *space* surrounding any *star* in which life could be possible.

ECTOPLASM. The outer layer of the *cytoplasm* of a living *cell*. Usually a semi-solid *gel* containing relatively few granules.

EDDY CURRENT HEATING. See *induction heating*.

EDDY CURRENTS. Foucault currents. Induced (see *induction*) *electric currents* set up in the iron cores of *electromagnets* and other electrical apparatus. These currents cause considerable waste of *energy* in the cores of *armatures* of *dynamos* and in *transformers*.

EDISON ACCUMULATOR*. A nickel-iron *accumulator*. Named after T. A. Edison (1847–1931).

EFFECTIVE RESISTANCE. The *resistance* of a *conductor* of electricity to *alternating currents*; in addition to the *direct current* resistance it includes the effect of any losses caused by the current (e.g. *eddy currents*). Measured by the ratio of the total loss to the square of the *root mean square* of the current.

EFFECTIVE VALUE. See *root mean square of an alternating quantity*.

EFFERVESCENCE. The escape of small *gas* bubbles from a *liquid*, usually as the result of chemical action.

EFFICIENCY OF A MACHINE. The ratio of the output *energy* to the input energy. The efficiency of a machine can never be greater than unity. Often expressed as a percentage.

EFFLORESCENCE (chem.). The property of some crystalline *salts* of losing a part of their *water of crystallization*, and becoming powdery on the surface. E.g. crystals of *sodium carbonate*, $Na_2CO_3.10H_2O$.

EFFUSION (chem.) of gases. The passage of *gases* through small apertures under pressure. The relative rates of effusion of different gases under the same conditions are inversely proportional to the square roots of their *densities*.

EINSTEIN SHIFT. A slight displacement towards the red of the lines of the solar *spectrum* due to the *Sun's gravitational field*. Predicted by Einstein's general theory of *relativity* and subsequently verified experimentally. Named after Albert Einstein (1879–1955).

EINSTEINIUM. Es. *Transuranic element*, At. No. 99. Most stable *isotope*, $^{254}_{99}Es$, has a *half-life* of 276 days.

ELASTANCE. The *reciprocal* of *capacitance*; measured in reciprocal *farads* or *darafs*.

ELASTIC COLLISION. A collision between bodies under ideal conditions, such that their total *kinetic energy* before collision equals their total kinetic energy after collision. Referred to *nuclear physics*, an elastic collision is one in which an incoming particle is scattered without causing the *excitation* or breaking up of the struck *nucleus*.

ELASTIC CROSS-SECTION. See *cross-section*.

ELASTIC LIMIT. The limit of *stress* within which the *strain* in a material completely disappears when the stress is removed.

ELASTIC MODULUS. Modulus of elasticity. The ratio of *stress* to *strain* in a given material. The strain may be a change in length (see *Young's modulus*), a twist or *shear* (see *rigidity modulus*), or a change in volume (see *bulk modulus*); the stress required to produce unit strain being in each case expressed in *newtons* per square *metre* or *dynes* per sq cm.

ELASTICITY. The property of a body or material of resuming its original form and dimensions when the *forces* acting upon it are removed. If the forces are sufficiently large for the deformation to cause a break in the molecular structure of the body or material, it loses its elasticity and the *elastic limit* is said to have been reached. *Hooke's law* applies only within the elastic limit. See also *elastic modulus*.

ELASTIN. Elastic fibrous *protein* found in the connective *tissues* of vertebrates.

ELASTOMER. A material which after being stretched, will return to approximately its original length. Includes *natural rubber, synthetic rubbers*, and rubberlike *plastics*.

ELECTRET. A *dielectric* possessing a permanent electric *moment*.

ELECTRIC ARC. See *arc*.

ELECTRIC BELL. See *bell, electric*.

ELECTRIC CHARGE. Science is unable to offer any explanation regarding the nature of an electric charge, but it is able to describe in some detail the properties of *matter* that is so charged. The *elementary particle* called an *electron* is said to be negatively charged with electricity, and the *proton* is said to be positively charged to an equal but opposite extent. These entities represent the basic units of electrically charged matter. Therefore, matter which contains an equal number of protons and electrons is electrically neutral, but matter which contains an excess of electrons possesses an overall negative charge; similarly matter which has a deficiency of electrons (i.e. an excess of protons) possesses an overall positive charge. These positive and negative conventions are purely arbitrary, but much of science is based upon them. It is an observed fact that a *force* of repulsion acts between like charges and a force of attraction acts between unlike charges: the region in which these forces act is called an *electric field*. Electric charges are also acted upon by forces when they move in a *magnetic field* which possesses a component at right angles to their direction of motion. The size of an electric charge is measured in *electrostatic units* or in *electromagnetic units*, the derived *SI unit* being the *coulomb*. Symbol Q.

ELECTRIC CURRENT. An electric current is said to flow through a *conductor* when there is an overall movement of *electrons* through it. The *SI unit* of current is the *ampere*. Symbol I.

ELECTRIC CURRENT, HEATING EFFECT OF. When an *electric current* flows through a *conductor* of finite *resistance, heat energy* is continuously generated at the expense of *electrical energy*. The quantity of heat produced is proportional to the resistance of the conductor, and is equal to VI or I^2R *watts* (*joules* per *second*), V being the *potential difference* in *volts*, I the current in *amperes*, and R the resistance in *ohms*.

ELECTRIC DISPLACEMENT. Consider a uniform *electric field* of strength E in free *space*; i.e. the electric *flux* through unit area perpendicular to the field is E. Now suppose a *dielectric* medium is introduced into the field. The electric flux at any point in the medium becomes modified owing to the interaction between E and the *atoms* of the dielectric, and assumes a new value D, called the electric displacement.

ELECTRIC FIELD. The region near an *electric charge*, in which a *force* is exerted on a charged particle; completely defined in magnitude and direction at any point by the force upon unit positive charge situated at that point. The field strength E, or *force* exerted upon a unit charge at a distance r m from a charge Q, is given by:

$$E = \frac{Q}{4\pi r^2 \epsilon}$$

where ϵ is the *permittivity*; for a vacuum (ϵ_0) it is $8 \cdot 8542 \times 10^{-12}$ F m^{-1}. E is in N C^{-1}.

ELECTRIC INTENSITY. The strength of an *electric field* at a point.

ELECTRIC LIGHT. Illumination produced by the use of *electricity*; may be produced by virtue of the heating effect of an *electric current* on a wire or *filament* (see *electric-light bulb*), by an electric arc (see *arc lamp*), or by the passage of electricity through a *vapour*, as in the *mercury vapour lamp* or *fluorescent lamps*.

ELECTRIC-LIGHT BULB. A glass bulb, often filled with nitrogen or some other chemically inactive *gas*, containing a wire or *filament*, usually made of tungsten. The passage of an *electric current* through the filament heats it to a white heat.

ELECTRIC MOTOR. A device for converting *electrical energy* into *mechanical energy*, depending on the fact that when an *electric current* flows through a *conductor* placed in a *magnetic field* possessing a component at right angles to the conductor, a mechanical *force* acts upon the conductor. In its simplest form, consists of a coil or *armature* through which the current flows, placed between the poles of a powerful *electromagnet*, the *field magnet*; the mechanical force upon the conductor causes the armature to rotate.

ELECTRIC POLARIZATION. When an *electric field* is applied to an electrically neutral *atom*, a displacement of the *electrons* with respect to the positive *nucleus* occurs. (See *atom, structure of.*) This gives rise to a small electric *dipole* possessing an electric *moment* in the direction of the field. This effect occurs when a *dielectric* is placed in an electric field, the electric field acting upon each individual atom of the dielectric. The *resultant* total electric moment per unit volume is called the electric polarization.

ELECTRIC POTENTIAL AT A POINT. The *work* necessary to bring unit positive *electric charge* from an infinite distance to that point. Analogous to a level; a positive electric charge would be driven from the points of higher to lower potential. The derived *SI unit* of electric potential is the *volt*. See also *potential difference*.

ELECTRIC POWER. The rate of doing work, measured in *watts*. A power of 1 watt does 1 *joule* of work per second. The power in watts is given by the product of the *potential difference* in *volts* and the *current* in *amperes*.

ELECTRIC SPARK. A discharge of *electricity*, accompanied by *light* and *sound*, through a *dielectric* or *insulator*.

ELECTRICAL CAPACITY. See *capacitance*.

ELECTRICAL CONDENSER. See *capacitor*.

ELECTRICAL ENERGY. *The energy* associated with *electric charges* and their movements. Measured in *watt seconds* (*joules*) or *kilowatt-hours*. One kilowatt-hour equals $3 \cdot 6 \times 10^6$ joules or $8 \cdot 59845 \times 10^5$ *calories*.

ELECTRICAL IMAGE. A set of point charges on one side of a conducting surface which would produce the same *electric field* on the other side of the surface (in its absence) as the actual electrification of that surface.

ELECTRICAL INDUCTION. See *induction*.

ELECTRICAL LINE OF FORCE. A line in an *electric field* whose direction is everywhere that of the field.

ELECTRICITY. A general term used for all phenomena caused by *electric charge* whether static or in motion.

ELECTRICITY, FRICTIONAL. Triboelectricity. A separation of *electric charge* which results from the rubbing together of different materials; e.g. on rubbing *celluloid* with rabbit's fur, the fur is found to possess a positive charge, and the celluloid receives an equal negative charge. The rubbing motion strips some of the *electrons* from the *atoms* or *molecules* of the fur, which collect on the surface of the celluloid.

ELECTRICITY, STATIC. *Electricity* at rest, in contradistinction to dynamic or current electricity. In the static case its effects are due purely to the *electrostatic field* produced by the charge, whereas in the case of current electricity other effects, in particular a *magnetic field*, are added.

ELECTROCARDIOGRAPH. ECG. An instrument for recording the *current* and *voltage* waveforms associated with the contraction of the heart muscle.

ELECTROCHEMICAL EQUIVALENT of an ion. The *mass* of the *ion* liberated or deposited by 1 *coulomb* of *electricity*. Expressed in grams, this is numerically equal to 1/96487 of the *chemical equivalent*, which is therefore liberated or deposited by 96487 coulombs, or one *faraday*. See *electrolysis*.

ELECTROCHEMICAL SERIES. See *electromotive series*.

ELECTROCHEMISTRY. The study of the processes involved in the interconversion of *electrical energy* and *chemical energy*.

ELECTRODE. 1. A *conductor* by which an *electric current* enters or leaves an *electrolyte* in *electrolysis*, an electric *arc*, or a vacuum tube (see *discharge in gases* and *thermionic valve*): the positive electrode is the *anode*, the negative one the *cathode*. 2. In a *semiconductor* device, an element which emits or collects *electrons* or *holes*, or controls their movement by an *electric field*.

ELECTRODEPOSITION. The process of depositing by *electrolysis*, especially the deposition of one *metal* on another as in *electroplating*.

ELECTRODYNAMICS. The study of the relationship between electric and magnetic *forces* and their mechanical causes and effects.

ELECTRODYNAMOMETER. An instrument for measuring *current*, *voltage*, or *power*, in both *direct current* and *alternating current* circuits. Depends upon the interaction of the *magnetic fields* of fixed and movable coils.

ELECTROENCEPHALOGRAPH. EEG. An instrument used for recording the rhythmical *electric currents* which pass through the brain. The pattern obtained can be correlated with certain human physiological states (e.g. sleep) and pathological states (e.g. epilepsy).

ELECTROFORMING. The production, or reproduction, of *metal* articles by the deposition of a metal upon an *electrode* during *electrolysis*.

ELECTROKINETICS. The study of *electric charges* in motion and their behaviour in *electric* and *magnetic fields*, as opposed to *electrostatics*.

ELECTROLYSIS. The chemical *decomposition* of certain substances (*electrolytes*) by an *electric current* passed through the substance in a dissolved or molten state. Such substances are ionized (see *ionic hypothesis*) into electrically charged *ions*, and when an electric current is passed through them by means of conducting *electrodes*, the ions move towards the oppositely charged electrodes, there give up their electric charges, become uncharged *atoms* or groups, and are either liberated or deposited at the electrode, or react chemically with the electrode, the *solvent*, or each other, according to their chemical nature.

ELECTROLYSIS, FARADAY'S LAWS OF. 1. The chemical action of a current of *electricity* is proportional to the quantity of electricity which passes. 2. The *weights* of substances liberated or deposited by the same quantity of electricity are proportional to their *chemical equivalents*. See *electrochemical equivalent*. Named after Michael Faraday (1791–1867).

ELECTROLYTE. A *compound* which, in *solution* or in the molten state, conducts an *electric current* and is simultaneously decomposed by it. The current is carried not by *electrons* as in *metals*, but by *ions* (see *electrolysis*). Electrolytes may be *acids*, *bases*, or *salts*.

ELECTROLYTIC CAPACITOR (CONDENSER). A fixed electrical *capacitor* in which one *electrode* is a *metal* (usually aluminium) foil coated with a thin layer of the metal *oxide*, and the other electrode is a non-corrosive *salt solution* or paste. The metal foil is maintained positive to prevent the removal of the oxide film by the hydrogen liberated. Tantalum sheets are also used as electrodes, immersed in an *electrolyte* of *sulphuric acid*. The advantage of electrolytic capacitors is that they provide a high *capacitance* in a limited space.

ELECTROLYTIC DISSOCIATION, THEORY OF. Explanation of the phenomena of *electrolysis* on the supposition that *molecules* of *electrolytes* are dissociated into electrically charged *ions* in solution. See *ionization*.

ELECTROLYTIC GAS. Detonating gas. A mixture of hydrogen and oxygen, in a ratio of 2 to 1 by *volume*, formed by the *electrolysis* of *water*.

ELECTROLYTIC RECTIFIER. A *rectifier* consisting of two *electrodes* immersed in an *electrolyte*, which is used to convert an *alternating current* into a *direct current*. Depends on the properties of certain *metals* and *solutions* to allow current to flow in one direction only.

ELECTROMAGNET. A temporary *magnet* formed by winding a coil of wire round a piece of soft iron; when an *electric current* flows through the wire, the iron becomes a magnet.

ELECTROMAGNETIC PUMP. A device used for pumping *liquid metals*. A current is passed through the liquid metal which is contained in a flattened pipe placed between the poles of an *electromagnet*. The liquid metal is thus subjected to a *force* which acts along the axis of the pipe.

ELECTROMAGNETIC RADIATION. *Radiation* consisting of waves of *energy* associated with *electric* and *magnetic fields*, resulting from the acceleration of an *electric charge*. These electric and magnetic fields, which require no supporting medium and can be propagated through *space*, are at right angles to each other and to the direction of propagation. Electromagnetic waves travel through space with a uniform *velocity* of $2 \cdot 9979 \times 10^8$ *metres* per *second*, or 186 282 miles per second. The nature of electromagnetic radiations depends upon their *frequency* (see *electromagnetic spectrum*). Electromagnetic radiation is emitted by *matter* in discontinuous units called *photons*.

ELECTROMAGNETIC SPECTRUM. The range of *frequencies* over which *electromagnetic radiations* are propagated. The lowest frequencies are *radio* waves, increases of frequency produce *infrared radiation*, *light*, *ultraviolet radiation*, *X-rays*, *gamma-rays*, and finally the radiation associated with *cosmic rays*. See Table 10, page 442.

ELECTROMAGNETIC UNITS. E.M.U. A system of electrical *units*, within the *C.G.S. system*, based on the unit *magnetic pole*, which repels a similar pole, placed 1 cm away, with a *force* of 1 *dyne*. The E.M.U. of *electric current* is that current which, flowing in an arc of a *circle* of unit length and radius (i.e. 1 cm), exerts a force of 1 dyne on a unit magnetic pole placed at the centre. The E.M.U. of *resistance* is that resistance in which *energy* is dissipated at the rate of 1 *erg* per second by the flow of 1 E.M.U. of current. The E.M.U. of *electromotive force* or *potential* is that potential which, applied across the ends of a *conductor* of 1 E.M.U. resistance, causes 1 E.M.U. of current to flow.

ELECTROMAGNETIC WAVES. See *electromagnetic radiation* and *electromagnetic spectrum*.

ELECTROMETALLURGY. The study of electrical processes used in separating a *metal* from its *ore*; or refining or shaping metals by electrical means.

ELECTROMETER. An instrument for measuring *voltage* differences, which draws no current from the source. Essential for measuring *electrostatic* voltage differences.

ELECTROMOTIVE FORCE. E.M.F. The source of *electrical energy* required to produce an *electric current* in a circuit; a measure of its intensity. Defined as the rate at which electrical energy is drawn from the source and dissipated in a circuit when unit current is flowing in the circuit. The *SI unit* is the *volt*. See *potential difference*.

ELECTROMOTIVE SERIES. Electrochemical series. Potential series of the *metals*. A list of metals arranged in order of the magnitudes of their molar electrode potentials, i.e. the *potential difference* between the metal and a *normal solution* of one of its *salts*. Metals with high negative electrode potentials stand at the head of the electromotive series. The list represents the order in which the metals replace one another from their salts, a metal higher in the series replacing one lower down; similarly, metals placed above hydrogen will liberate it from *acids*. The chief metals in order are sodium, magnesium, aluminium, manganese, zinc, cadmium, iron, cobalt, nickel, tin, lead, hydrogen, copper, mercury, silver, platinum, gold.

ELECTRON. An *elementary particle* having a *rest mass* of 9.1091×10^{-31} *kilogrammes*, approximately $1/1836$ that of a hydrogen *atom*, and bearing a negative *electric charge* of 1.6021×10^{-19} *coulombs*. The radius of the electron is 2.81777×10^{-15} *metres*. The electron is a constituent of all atoms (see *atom, structure of*). The positively charged *anti-particle* of the electron is the *positron*, and the word 'electron' is sometimes used to include both negative electrons (negatrons or negatons) and positive electrons (positrons or positons). A *free electron* is one which has been detached from its atomic *orbit*.

ELECTRON AFFINITY. In general, the tendency of an *atom* or *molecule* to accept an *electron* and form a negative *ion*. In particular, the *energy* liberated when one *mole* of an *element* in the form of gaseous atoms is converted into negative ions. The *halogens* have high electron affinities.

ELECTRON CAPTURE. 1. The formation of a negative *ion* when a *free electron* is captured by an *atom* or *molecule* (also referred to as 'electron attachment'). 2. A *radioactive transformation* as a result of which a *nucleus* captures one of its *orbital electrons*.

ELECTRON DIFFRACTION. A *diffraction* effect resulting from the passage of *electrons* through *matter*, analogous to the *diffraction* of visible *light* or *X-rays*. The phenomenon of electron diffraction is the principal evidence for the existence of waves associated with electrons (see *de Broglie wavelength*). The diffraction of electrons when passed through *crystals* or thin *metal* foils is used as a method of investigating crystal structure.

ELECTRON GUN. The source of *electrons* in a *cathode ray tube* or *electron microscope*. Consists of a *cathode* emitter of electrons, an *anode* with an aperture through which the beam of electrons can pass, and one or more focusing and control *electrodes*.

ELECTRON LENS. A system of *electric* or *magnetic fields* used to focus a beam of *electrons* in a manner analogous to an optical *lens*. Used in *electron microscopes*, etc.

ELECTRON MICROGRAPH. A photograph of an object obtained with an *electron microscope*.

ELECTRON MICROSCOPE. An instrument similar in purpose to the ordinary *light microscope*, but with a much greater *resolving power*. Instead of a beam of light to illuminate the object, a parallel beam of *electrons* from an *electron gun* is used. The object, which must be in the form of a very thin film of the material, allows the electron beam to pass through it; but, owing to differential *scattering* in the film, an image of the object is carried forward in the electron beam. The latter then passes through a magnetic or *electrostatic* focusing system (see *electron lens*) which is equivalent to the optical lens system in an ordinary microscope, i.e. it produces a much magnified image. This is received on a fluorescent screen and recorded by a camera.

ELECTRON MULTIPLIER. See *photomultiplier*.

ELECTRON PROBE MICROANALYSIS. A method of analysing a very small quantity of a substance by directing a finely focused *electron* beam on to it so that an *X-ray* emission is produced characteristic of the *elements* present in the sample. The diameter of the beam is usually about 1 μm and quantities as small as 10^{-13} g can be detected by this means. The method may be used quantitatively for elements whose *atomic numbers* exceed 11.

ELECTRON SPIN RESONANCE. A phenomenon exhibited by paramagnetic substances (see *paramagnetism*) due to their unpaired *electrons*. The *spin* of an unpaired electron is associated with a *magnetic moment* which may align itself in one of two ways with respect to an applied *magnetic field*, each possible alignment corresponding to a different *energy level*. By applying an alternating magnetic field at right angles to the first unvarying magnetic field transitions between these two energy levels can be made, falling in the *microwave* region of the *electromagnetic spectrum*, thus producing the phenomenon known as electron spin resonance. If, however, the paramagnetic *molecule* includes magnetic nuclei, these transitions will interact with the nuclear spin (see *nuclear magnetic resonance*) producing a series of lines rather than a single resonance. Electron spin resonance spectroscopy consists of analysing this *hyperfine structure* so that the electron can be located within the molecule, thus providing information about the molecule's structure.

ELECTRON-VOLT. eV. A unit of *energy* widely used in *nuclear physics*. The increase in energy or the *work* done on an *electron* when passing through a *potential* rise of 1 *volt*. 1 electron-volt $= 1 \cdot 602 \cdot 10 \times 10^{-19}$ *joules*. 1 MeV $= 10^6$ electron-volts; 1 GeV $= 10^9$ electron-volts.

ELECTRONEGATIVE elements and groups. *Radicals* which behave as negative *ions*; radicals taking up *electrons*, thus acquiring a negative *electric charge*, when united with other radicals by electrovalent bonds (see *valency, electronic theory of*). The *halogens*, oxygen, sulphur, and other *non-metallic elements* are generally electronegative.

ELECTRONIC CHARGE. The negative *electric charge* of the *electron*, $1 \cdot 6021 \times 10^{-19}$ *coulombs*, $4 \cdot 80298 \times 10^{-10}$ *electrostatic units*.

ELECTRONICS. An applied physical science concerned with the development of electrical circuits using *thermionic valves, semiconductors*, and other devices in which the motion of *electrons* is controlled.

ELECTROPHILIC REAGENTS. Cationoid reagents. *Reagents* which react at centres of high *electron* density. Essentially electron acceptors (e.g. *halogens*) which gain or share electrons from an outside *atom* or *ion*.

ELECTROPHORESIS. Cataphoresis. The migration of the electrically charged *solute* particles present in a *colloidal solution* towards the oppositely charged *electrode*, when two electrodes are placed in the solution and connected externally to a source of *E.M.F.*

ELECTROPHORUS. A laboratory demonstration apparatus for showing electrostatic charging by *induction*.

ELECTROPLATING. Depositing a layer of *metal* by *electrolysis*, the object to be plated forming the *cathode* in an electrolytic tank or bath containing a *solution* of a *salt* of the metal which is to be deposited.

ELECTROPOSITIVE elements and groups. *Radicals* which behave as positive *ions*; radicals which give up *electrons*, thus acquiring a positive *electric charge*, when united with other radicals by electrovalent bonds (see *valency, electronic theory of*). The *metals* and *acidic hydrogen* are generally electropositive.

ELECTROSCOPE. An instrument for detecting the presence of an *electric charge*. The gold-leaf electroscope consists of two rectangular leaves of gold foil attached to a conducting rod of *metal* held by an insulating plug; when the rod and leaves acquire an electric charge, the leaves diverge owing to the mutual repulsion of charges of like sign.

ELECTROSTATIC FIELD. A region in which a stationary electrically charged particle would be subjected to a *force* of attraction or repulsion as a result of the presence of another stationary *electric charge*.

ELECTROSTATIC GENERATOR. A machine designed for the continuous separation of *electric charge*. Examples include the *Wimshurst machine* and the *Van der Graaf generator*.

ELECTROSTATIC PRECIPITATION. A widely used method of controlling the pollution of air (or other *gases*). The gas, containing *solid* or *liquid* particles suspended in it, is subjected to a uni-directional *electrostatic field*, so that the particles are attracted to, and deposited upon, the positive *electrode*.

ELECTROSTATIC UNITS. ESU. A system of electrical *units* based upon the electrostatic unit of *electric charge*. The electrostatic unit of charge (called the *statcoulomb*) is that quantity of electricity which will repel an equal quantity, 1 cm distant from it in a *vacuum*, with a *force* of 1 *dyne*.

ELECTROSTATICS. The study of static *electricity*.

ELECTROSTRICTION. The change in the dimensions of a *dielectric* when placed in an electric *field*.

ELECTROTYPING. The production of copies of plates of type, etc., by the electrolytic deposition of a layer of *metal* on a previously prepared mould. This is a cast of the object to be copied, made of *plastic* material and coated with a layer of *graphite* which acts as a *conductor* of electricity. It is then suspended to act as a *cathode* in an electrolytic bath (see *electroplating*) containing a *solution* of a *salt* of the metal required, usually copper. The passage of an *electric current* will deposit a layer of any required thickness of metal upon the cathode, the layer being a replica of the original type.

ELECTROVALENCY. See *valency, electronic theory of*.

ELECTROVALENT CRYSTAL. Ionic crystal. The type of *crystal* in which the component *ions* are held in their positions in the *lattice* by electrovalent bonds (see *valency, electronic theory of*). *Sodium chloride* is a typical example.

ELECTRUM. A natural *alloy* of gold (55%–85%) and silver.

ELEMENT (chem.). A substance consisting entirely of *atoms* of the same *atomic number*. The elements are listed in Table 3, pages 432–4.

ELEMENTARY PARTICLES. Fundamental particles. The basic units of which all *matter* is composed. The stable particles *protons, electrons*, and *neutrinos* combine with *neutrons* to form stable *atoms*. But many other short-lived particles and *resonances* have been detected which play an essential part in the structure of matter. For every particle which exists there is a corresponding *anti-particle* which has the same *mass* and *spin* but opposite *electric charge*. Some electrically *neutral* particles have anti-particles in which some other property is reversed (e.g. *strangeness*) and some neutral particles are regarded as their own anti-particles. There are several systems for classifying particles: one way is to divide them into *fermions* (with spin *quantum number* $\frac{1}{2}$) and *bosons* (with integral spin quantum number). Fermions are sub-divided into *baryons* and *leptons*, while bosons are sub-divided into *mesons* and *photons*. Some of the most important particles are listed in Table 6 on pages 436–7. The concept of elementarity is still somewhat vague, recent work having suggested that protons and neutrons are not indivisible units, but composite entities consisting of a core of unknown origin surrounded by a cloud of mesons. The hypothetical particles called *quarks* have also been suggested as the basic units out of which the known particles are constructed. They have, however, yet to be detected.

ELEMENTS (astr.). The numerical values required to define the elliptical *orbit* of a *planet* or *satellite*, such as the semi-*major axis* of the *ellipse*, and its *eccentricity*. The *plane* of the orbit is defined by the angle its plane makes with the plane of the *ecliptic*.

ELEMENTS, MAGNETIC. See *magnetic elements*.

ELEVATION, ANGLE OF. If C is a point above the level of another point A, the angle of elevation of C from A is the *angle* which C makes with the horizontal plane AX through A. See Fig. 11, page 105.

ELEVATION OF BOILING POINT. The rise in the *boiling point* of a *solution* produced by a non-volatile substance dissolved in a *solvent*. For a *dilute* solution the elevation is proportional to the number of *molecules* or *ions* present, and the elevation produced by the same *molecular concentration* (or ionic concentration in the case of an *electrolyte*) is a constant for a particular solvent. This forms the principle of the boiling point method (ebullioscopic method) for the determination of *molecular weights*.

ELEVEN-YEAR PERIOD. A periodic change in occurrence of *sunspots*, the cycle being complete in approximately eleven years; associated with this is a cyclic variation in the magnitude of the *daily variation*.

ELINVAR*. A variety of *steel* containing 36% nickel and 12% chromium. The *elasticity* is almost unaffected by changes of *temperature*; used for hair-springs of watches.

ELLIPSE. A closed *plane* figure formed by cutting a right circular *cone* by a *plane* obliquely through its *axis* (see *conic sections*). The sum of the distances from any point on the *perimeter* of an ellipse to its two *foci* is constant. In Fig. 15, page 130, X_1X_2 is the *major axis*, F_1 and F_2 are the foci, and A and B are any points on the perimeter such that $AF_1 + AF_2 = BF_1 + BF_2$.

ELLIPSOID. A solid figure traced out by an *ellipse* rotating about one of its *axes*.

ELLIPTICALLY POLARIZED LIGHT. *Light* which can be resolved into two vibrations lying in *planes* at right angles, and of equal *frequency*. The electric *vector* at any point in the path of the wave describes an *ellipse* about the direction of propagation of the light. The form of this ellipse is determined by the *amplitudes* of these two vibrations and by the difference of *phase* between them. (See also *polarization of light*.)

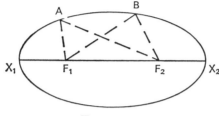

FIGURE 15.

ELUTION. The removal of an *adsorbate* from an adsorbent by dissolving it in a *liquid* (the eluent). The resulting solution is called the eluate.

ELUTRIATION. The washing, separation, or sizing of fine particles of different *weight* by suspending them in a current of air or *water*.

EMANATION. Radium emanation. The *gas* formed by the *radioactive disintegration* of certain substances, consisting principally of *radon, thoron,* and *actinon*.

EMBRYOLOGY. The branch of *biology* concerned with the study of the growth and development of embryos.

EMERY. A mixture of *corundum* and iron oxide, usually *magnetite*, Fe_3O_4. Used as an *abrasive*.

EMETINE. $C_{29}H_{40}O_4N_2$. An *alkaloid* obtained from the roots of Brazilian ipecacuanha, m.p. 68°C. Used as an emetic and as a remedy for amoebic dysentery.

EMF. See *electromotive force*.

EMISSION OF RADIATION. The net rate at which a body emits *heat radiation* to its surroundings depends on the *temperature* of the body, the temperature of its surroundings, and the nature of the surface of the body. Dull black surfaces have the greatest *emissive power* while brightly polished reflecting surfaces have least. See *Stefan's law*.

EMISSION SPECTRUM. The *spectrum* observed when *light* coming directly from a source is examined with a *spectroscope*.

EMISSIVE POWER, total. The total *energy* emitted from unit area of a surface of a body per second. The total emissive power depends upon the *temperature* of the body and the nature of its surface.

EMISSIVITY. The ratio of the total *emissive power* of a body to the total emissive power of a perfect black body at the same *temperature* (see *black body radiation*). The emissivity is a pure numeric, equal to the *absorptivity*. Symbol ϵ.

EMITTER. One of the three *electrodes* in a *transistor*.

EMPIRICAL. Based upon the results of experiment and observation only.

EMPIRICAL FORMULA. The simplest type of chemical *formula*, giving only the proportion of each *element* present, but no indication of the *molecular weight* or the molecular structure, e.g. $(C_4H_3O_2N)_n$.

EMULSIFYING AGENT. A substance, small quantities of which help to form or stabilize an *emulsion*.

EMULSION. A two-phase system in which the *disperse phase* consists of minute droplets of *liquid*.

EMULSION, PHOTOGRAPHIC. The light-sensitive coating on a *film* or plate (see *photography*). A 'nuclear emulsion' is a photographic emulsion specially prepared to record the tracks of *elementary particles* and nuclear fragments which pass through it.

EMULSOID SOL. See *colloidal solutions*.

ENAMEL. 1. A class of substances having similar composition to *glass* with the addition of *stannic oxide*, SnO_2, or other *infusible* substances to render the enamel *opaque*. 2. A finely ground oil *paint* containing a *resin*. 3. The external layer of teeth consisting mainly of calcium phosphate carbonate *salts*.

ENANTIOMORPHISM. The occurrence of substances in two crystalline forms, one being a mirror image of the other.

ENANTIOTROPIC substances. Substances which exist in two different physical forms, one being *stable* below a certain *temperature* (the *transition* temperature), the other above it. E.g. sulphur exists as alpha-sulphur at all temperatures below $96°$ C.; above this, the stable form is beta-sulphur.

ENDOCRINE GLANDS. See *ductless glands*.

ENDOENZYME. An *enzyme* which remains within a living *cell* and does not diffuse through the cell wall into the surrounding medium.

ENDOERGIC PROCESS. An *endothermic process* (often applied in the context of a *nuclear reaction*).

ENDOPLASM. The central part of the *cytoplasm* of living *cells*, usually distinct from the *ectoplasm* in that it is of greater fluidity and contains more granules.

ENDOPLASMIC RETICULUM. A system of membranes within the *cytoplasm* of many types of living *cell*. It appears to be connected with *protein* synthesis as these membranes are often covered with *ribosomes* in cells which make large quantities of protein.

ENDOSMOSIS. The inward flow of *water* into a cell containing an *aqueous solution*, through a *semipermeable membrane*, due to *osmosis*.

ENDOTHERMIC PROCESS. A process accompanied by the absorption of *heat*.

END POINT. The point in a *titration*, usually indicated by a change of colour of an *indicator*, at which a particular *reaction* is completed.

ENERGY. The capacity for doing *work*. The various forms of energy, interconvertible by suitable means, include *potential, kinetic, electrical, heat, chemical, nuclear,* and *radiant energy.* Interconversion between these forms of energy can only occur in the presence of *matter.* Energy can only exist in the absence of matter in the form of radiant energy. The derived *SI unit* of energy is the *joule.* Symbol *E.*

ENERGY BANDS. *Orbital electrons* are associated with specific amounts of *energy,* the change from one *energy level* to another taking place in *quantized* steps. In a crystalline *solid* the energies of all the electrons and *atoms* fall into several 'possible' energy bands between which lie 'forbidden' bands. These bands may be depicted on an 'energy level diagram'. The range of energies corresponding to states in which the electrons can be made to flow, by an applied *electric field,* is called the *conduction band.* The range of energies corresponding to states which can be occupied by *valency electrons,* binding the *crystal* together, is called the *valency band.* The valency band in an ideal crystal is completely occupied at the *absolute zero* of temperature, but in real crystals above absolute zero some electrons are missing from the valency band, and it is these electrons which give rise to *holes.*

ENERGY LEVELS. An *atom* as a whole, or an individual *nucleus,* can exist only in certain definite states characterized by the *energy* of the state. Thus, for each different atom or nucleus, there exists a series of energy levels corresponding to these permissible states. The lowest stable energy level of an atom or nucleus is referred to as the *ground state;* atoms or nuclei at higher energy levels than the ground state are said to be excited. See *excitation.*

ENERGY-RICH BONDS. A term used in *biochemistry* to distinguish between chemical *bonds* which when broken yield a large amount of *free energy* and those which give only a small yield of free energy ('energy-poor bonds'). The energy referred to in this context is the free energy liberated on *hydrolysis.* Energy-rich bonds usually involve *phosphate* groups and in this respect *adenosine triphosphate (ATP)* is of particular significance.

ENERGY VALUE of a food. A measure of the *heat* energy available by the complete combustion of a stated *weight* of the food; often given in large *Calories* per lb. It takes no account of the value of the food from any other point of view, or sometimes even of the suitability of the food for use by the human *organism.*

ENGINE. A device for converting one form of *energy* into another, especially for converting other forms of energy into *mechanical* (i.e. *kinetic*) *energy.*

ENRICH. In general, to increase the *abundance* of a particular *isotope* in a mixture of isotopes. In particular, to increase the abundance of the *fissile* isotope of a *nuclear fuel.*

ENTHALPY. Heat Content. *H.* A *thermodynamic* property of a substance given by $H = U + pV$, where U is the internal *energy,* p the *pressure,* and V the *volume.*

ENTROPY. *S.* A quantity introduced in the first place to facilitate the calculations, and to give clear expression to the results of *thermodynamics*. Changes of entropy (ΔS) can be calculated only for a *reversible process*, and may then be defined as the ratio of the amount of *heat* taken up (ΔQ) to the *absolute temperature* (T) at which the heat is absorbed, i.e. $\Delta S = \Delta Q / T$. Entropy changes for actual irreversible processes are calculated by postulating equivalent theoretical reversible changes. The entropy of a system is a measure of its degree of disorder. The total entropy of any isolated system can never decrease in any change; it must either increase (irreversible process) or remain constant (reversible process). The total entropy of the *Universe* therefore is increasing, tending towards a maximum, corresponding to complete disorder of the particles in it (assuming that it may be regarded as an isolated system). See *heat death of the Universe*.

ENZYME. A large group of *proteins* produced by living *cells*, which act as *catalysts* in the *chemical reactions* upon which life depends. The exact mechanism by which enzymes act is not fully understood; but it appears that certain parts of the enzyme *molecule* (called the 'active centres') combine with the *substrate* molecule in such a way that the substrate undergoes chemical changes very much more rapidly than it would in the absence of the enzyme, while the enzyme itself remains unchanged. As enzymes are not consumed in these reactions they are effective in only minute quantities. Nearly all enzymes are highly specific in their action and therefore enormous numbers of them are found in nature. Many enzymes require the assistance of certain accessory substances (e.g. *coenzymes*) for their proper functioning and some require precisely defined conditions of *temperature* and *pH* for their optimum performance.

Enzymes have an important bearing upon heredity; the characteristics which cells, and therefore *organisms*, possess is directly related to the enzymes which they contain: e.g. the person who inherits red hair has inherited a particular configuration of *nucleotides* in the *DNA* of his *chromosomes*, which is capable of producing a specific enzyme in the *cytoplasm* of his hair-producing cells, whose function it is to catalyse the synthesis of a red dye.

Enzymes are usually named by adding the suffix -ase to a word indicating the nature of the substrate (e.g. *amylase*) or the type of reaction involved (e.g. *dehydrogenase*). A few enzymes retain old names which relate to neither of these rules (e.g. *pepsin, trypsin*).

ENZYMOLYSIS. The *decomposition* of a substance catalyzed by an *enzyme*.

EOSIN. Tetrabromofluorescein. $C_{20}H_8Br_4O_5$. A red crystalline *insoluble* substance obtained from *fluorescein*, m.p. 295–6°C., used as a red *dye*.

EPACT. 1. The difference in days between the length of a solar *year* and a lunar year. 2. The *Moon*'s age in days at the start of the calendar year.

EPHEDRINE. $C_6H_5CHOHCH(CH_3)NHCH_3$. A white crystalline *optically active alkaloid*, m.p. 40°C., used in medicine to treat asthma, colds, etc.

EPHEMERIS. A table which gives the predicted positions and the movements of a celestial body such as a *planet* or *comet*. Also an annual publication containing astronomical data.

EPHEMERIS TIME. Time measured on the basis of the orbital movements of the *planets* and the *Moon*.

EPICENTRE. The point on the surface of the Earth which lies directly above the focus of an earthquake.

EPICYCLE. I. (math.) a *circle* whose centre rolls round the circumference of a larger circle without slipping. 2. (astr.) Ptolemy (A.D. 127–151) based his *astronomy* on the theory that the *planets* moved in epicycles round a larger circle, called the deferent, at the centre of which lay the *Earth*.

EPICYCLIC GEARS. A system of gears in which one or more wheels move around the outside, or the inside, of another wheel whose *axis* is fixed.

EPIDIASCOPE. An optical projector for throwing an enlarged image of either an *opaque* object or a transparency upon a screen. Used for illustrating lectures.

EPINEPHRINE. See *adrenaline*.

EPITHERMAL NEUTRONS. *Neutrons* which have *energies* in excess of the energy associated with thermal agitation. Neutrons which have speeds and energies intermediate between *fast* and *thermal neutrons* (i.e. between about 0·1 and 100 *electron-volts*).

EPOXY. Term used to describe a *compound* in which an oxygen *atom* is bound to two carbon atoms, forming a three-membered ring.

EPOXY (EPOXIDE) RESINS. *Thermosetting resins* derived from 1-chloro-2, 3-epoxypropane $(O.CH_2.CH.CH_2Cl)$ and bis-phenol-A $(HO.C_6H_4.$

$C(CH_3)_2.C_6H_4OH)$. Used as structural *plastics*, in surface coatings, and *adhesives*.

EPSOM SALTS. See *magnesium sulphate*. $MgSO_4.7H_2O$.

EQUATION, CHEMICAL. A representation of a *chemical reaction*, using the *symbols* of the *elements* to represent the actual *atoms* and *molecules* taking part in the reaction; the re-arrangement of the various atoms of the substances taking part is thus shown. E.g. the chemical equation $H_2+Cl_2=2HCl$ represents the reaction between hydrogen and chlorine to form *hydrogen chloride*, and states that a hydrogen molecule, consisting of two atoms of hydrogen (H_2), reacts with a similarly constituted chlorine molecule, to give two molecules of hydrogen chloride, each consisting of one hydrogen and one chlorine atom $(2HCl)$. From a knowledge of the equation for any chemical reaction, and of the *atomic weights* of all the elements taking part, it is thus possible to calculate the proportions by *weight* in which the substances react, since the whole bulk of the reaction consists merely of the repetition, a vast number of times, of the process depicted by the equation.

EQUATION, MATHEMATICAL. A statement of equality between known and unknown quantities, true only for certain values of the unknown quantities. Thus the equation $3x = 15$ is true only when $x = 5$.

EQUATION OF STATE of a substance. Any equation connecting the *pressure p, volume V,* and *temperature T* of the substance. Some equations of state attempt to cover more than one *phase* of the substance, e.g. *van der Waals' equation of state,* and are approximate. Others are intended to be applied to one particular phase of the substance, e.g. the gaseous phase, and then only within certain limits of *p, V,* and *T*. With these limitations, these latter equations can represent the actual behaviour of the substance with greater accuracy.

EQUATION OF TIME. The difference between mean solar time, as given by a clock, and apparent solar time, i.e. sundial time. The time of rotation of the *Earth* upon its axis is not exactly equal to the time from noon to noon, the difference being caused by the motion of the Earth relative to the *Sun* to complete a circuit in one *year,* and also by the inclination of the *ecliptic* to the *Equator*.

EQUATOR, CELESTIAL. See *celestial equator*.

EQUATOR, MAGNETIC. See *magnetic equator*.

EQUATOR, TERRESTRIAL. The *great circle* of the Earth, lying in a *plane* perpendicular to the *axis* of the Earth, which is equidistant from the two Poles.

EQUILATERAL FIGURE. A figure having all its sides equal in length. E.g. an equilateral *triangle*.

EQUILIBRIUM. A state of balance between opposing *forces* or effects.

EQUILIBRIUM, CHEMICAL. See *chemical equilibrium*.

EQUILIBRIUM CONSTANT. In any *chemical reaction* there is always a state of *chemical equilibrium,* at a given *temperature* and *pressure,* between the *concentration* of the reactants and the concentration of the products. The position of this equilibrium, under specific conditions, is expressed by the equilibrium constant, K, such that in the reaction $aA + bB = cC + dD$, K is given by:

$$\frac{(C_C)^c.(C_D)^d}{(C_A)^a.(C_B)^b}$$

where C_A is the concentration of the substance A, 'a' *molecules* of which take part in the reaction.

EQUIMOLECULAR MIXTURE. A *mixture* containing substances in equal molecular proportions; i.e. in the ratio of their *molecular weights*. E.g. *invert sugar,* formed by the *hydrolysis* of *cane-sugar*. Each *molecule* of the cane-sugar is split into a molecule of *glucose* and a molecule of *fructose,* thus forming an equimolecular mixture of the two latter.

EQUINOX. The moment (or, astronomically, the point) at which the *Sun* apparently crosses the *celestial equator;* the point of intersection of the *ecliptic* and the celestial equator.

EQUIPARTITION OF ENERGY. In any physical system in thermal equilibrium the average *energy* per *degree of freedom* is the same, and equals $kT/2$, where $k = Boltzmann's$ *constant* and $T =$ the *absolute temperature* of the system. This provides a means of calculating the total thermal energy of a system. Thus, in 1 *mole* of a monatomic *gas*, each *atom* possesses three degrees of freedom (due to its *translatory motion*), and the total number of atoms is L (*Avogadro's constant*). Hence the total energy per mole of the gas is $3LkT/2$ or $3RT/2$, since $k=R/L$, where R is the *gas constant*.

EQUIPOTENTIAL LINES AND SURFACES. Lines and surfaces having the same *electric potential*.

EQUIVALENT, CHEMICAL. See *chemical equivalents*.

EQUIVALENT, ELECTROCHEMICAL. See *electrochemical equivalent*.

EQUIVALENT WEIGHT. See *chemical equivalents*.

EQUIVOCATION. A term used in *information theory* to indicate the rate of loss of information (per second or per symbol) at the receiving end of a *channel* of information due to *noise*.

ERBIUM. Er. Element. A.W. 167·26. At. No. 68. S.G. 9·164, m.p. 1497°C. See *lanthanides*.

ERECTING PRISM. A right-angled optical *prism* used in optical instruments to render an inverted image upright.

ERG. A unit of *work* or *energy* in the *c.g.s. system* of units; the work done by a *force* of 1 *dyne* acting through a distance of 1 cm. 1 erg $= 10^{-7}$ *joules*.

ERGOMETRINE. Ergonovine. $C_{19}H_{23}N_3O_2$. A colourless crystalline *alkaloid*, obtained from ergot, and used in medicine to prevent haemorrhage.

ERGONOMICS. The engineering aspects of the study of the relation between human workers and their working environment.

ERGOSTEROL. $C_{28}H_{43}OH$. A white crystalline *sterol*, m.p. 163°C., which occurs in small amounts in the *fats* of animals; it is converted into *vitamin* D_2 (*calciferol*) by the action of *ultraviolet radiation*.

ERGOTAMINE. $C_{33}H_{35}N_5O_5$. A crystalline *insoluble polypeptide*, m.p. 212·4°C., obtained from ergot, and used in the form of its *tartrate* in medicine as a uterine stimulant.

ERGOTOXINE. $C_{35}H_{41}N_5O_6$. A white crystalline *insoluble alkaloid*, obtained from ergot, and used in medicine as a uterine stimulant.

ERINOID*. A *thermoplastic* material prepared from *casein* and *formaldehyde*.

ERLENMEYER FLASK. A flat-bottomed conical laboratory flask with a narrow neck. Named after E. Erlenmeyer (born 1909).

ERYTHRITOL. Erythrite. $CH_2OH(CHOH)_2CH_2OH$. An *optically active* white crystalline substance, m.p. 88–91°C., used in medicine in the treatment of heart disease and high blood pressure.

ERYTHROCYTES. Red blood cells. The cells of the *blood* which contain *haemoglobin* and whose function it is to transport oxygen through the body. Erythrocytes have no means of propulsion, and in mammals the cells have no *nuclei*. Human blood contains approximately five million erythrocytes per cubic millimetre.

ERYTHROMYCIN*. $C_{37}H_{67}NO_{13}$. An *antibiotic* produced by the Actinomycete mould, used to combat a variety of bacterial infections.

ESCAPE VELOCITY. The *velocity* which a projectile or *space probe* would need to attain in order to escape from a particular *gravitational field*. The escape velocity from the surface of a *planet* (or *moon*) depends on the planet's (or moon's) *mass* and diameter. The escape velocity from the *Earth's* surface is about 11 200 *metres/s* (25 000 m.p.h.) and from the *Moon's* surface about 2370 metres/s (5300 m.p.h.).

ESSENTIAL OILS. Natural *oils* obtained from plants, mostly *benzene derivatives* or *terpenes*. Used for their flavour or odour.

ESTER GUM. Rosin ester. A *compound* obtained by the *esterification* of *rosin* (colophony) or other natural gums, with a *polyhydric alcohol* (usually *glycerin*).

ESTERIFICATION. The formation of an *ester* by the *chemical reaction* of an *acid* with an *alcohol*; e.g. the action of *ethanol* on *acetic acid* to form *ethyl acetate* and *water*.

ESTERS. *Organic compounds* corresponding to *inorganic salts*, derived by replacing hydrogen of an *acid* by an organic *radical* or group. E.g. *ethyl acetate*, $CH_3COOC_2H_5$, is the ethyl ester of *acetic acid*, CH_3COOH. Many esters are pleasant-smelling *liquids* used for flavouring essences. Many vegetable and animal *fats and oils* also belong to this class.

ETALON. An *interferometer* used for studying fine *spectrum* lines. Depends upon the interference effects produced by multiple reflection between fixed, parallel, half-silvered *glass* or *quartz* plates.

ETHANE. C_2H_6. The second member of the *paraffin series* of *hydrocarbons*. A colourless odourless *gas*. B.p. $-88°C$. Used chiefly in organic synthesis.

ETHANEDIOL. Ethylene glycol, glycol. $(CH_2OH)_2$. A colourless *viscous liquid* with a sweet taste, b.p. $197°C$. Used as an *anti-freeze*, in the manufacture of *plasticizers*, and as a *solvent*.

ETHANETHIOL. Ethyl mercaptan. C_2H_5SH. A colourless inflammable *liquid*, b.p. $37°C$., used in the manufacture of *rubber accelerators*.

ETHANOL. Ethyl alcohol, spirits of wine. C_2H_5OH. A colourless inflammable *liquid*, b.p. $78.5°C$. Prepared by the *fermentation* of *sugars*. The active constituent of alcoholic drinks; used as a *fuel* and in the manufacture of other *organic compounds*. See *proof spirit* and *absolute alcohol*.

ETHANOLAMINES. *Organic compounds* derived from *ethanol* and *amino groups*: monoethanolamine, $NH_2CH_2CH_2OH$, has a m.p. of $10°C$.; diethanolamine, $NH(CH_2CH_2OH)_2$ a m.p. of $28°C$. and triethanolamine, $N(CH_2CH_2OH)_3$ a m.p. of $21°C$. Used as *solvents* and in combination with *fatty acids* in the manufacture of *detergents* and cosmetics.

ETHENOID PLASTICS. A class of *thermoplastic resins* made from substances containing a *double bond*, e.g. *acrylic*, *styrene*, and *vinyl resins*.

ETHER (AETHER). The hypothetical medium which was supposed to fill all *space*: postulated as a medium to support the propagation of *electromagnetic radiations*. Once the subject of controversy, now regarded as an unnecessary assumption.

ETHERS. A group of *organic compounds* with the general formula R-O-R' formed by the *condensation* of two *alcohol molecules*. The compound commonly called 'ether' is diethyl ether, $C_2H_5.O.C_2H_5$, b.p. 34·6° C., made by dehydrating *ethanol* by means of concentrated *sulphuric acid*. Diethyl ether is used as an *anaesthetic* and as a *solvent*.

ETHYL ACETATE. Acetic ether. $CH_3COOC_2H_5$. A colourless *liquid* with a pleasant fruity smell, b.p. 77° C. Used as a *solvent* and in medicine.

ETHYL ALCOHOL. See *ethanol*.

ETHYL BUTYRATE. Butyric ether. $C_3H_7COOC_2H_5$. A *volatile liquid*, b.p. 120° C., used in flavouring and in perfumes.

ETHYL CARBAMATE. Urethane. $NH_2COOC_2H_5$. A white crystalline powder, m.p. 48° C., used as a *fungicide* and in the manufacture of *urethane resins*.

ETHYL FLUID. A *solution* of *tetraethyl lead*, $Pb(C_2H_5)_4$, and *dibromoethane*, $C_2H_4Br_2$, used as an anti-*knock* compound in motor *fuel*.

ETHYL GROUP. The *univalent alkyl radical* $—C_2H_5$.

ETHYL NITRITE. Nitrous ether. $C_2H_5NO_2$. A *volatile liquid* with a sweet smell, b.p. 17° C., used in medicine.

ETHYLENE. Ethene. C_2H_4. The first member of the *olefine* series of *hydrocarbons*. A colourless inflammable *gas* with a sweetish smell, b.p. $-103·9°$ C., used as an *anaesthetic* and in the manufacture of *polythene*.

ETHYLENE DIBROMIDE. See *dibromoethane*.

ETHYLENE DICHLORIDE. See *dichloroethane*.

ETHYLENE GLYCOL. See *ethanediol*.

ETHYLENE OXIDE. C_2H_4O. An odourless toxic *gas*, b.p. 13° C., obtained by the *oxidation* of *ethylene*. Used in the manufacture of *ethanediol*.

ETHYLENE-PROPYLENE RUBBER. EPR. A fully *saturated, stereo regular, synthetic rubber* prepared by the solution *polymerization* of approximately equal proportions of *ethylene* and *propylene*. It cannot be cured by sulphur vulcanization but satisfactory vulcanization can be achieved by using peroxide curing systems.

ETHYNE. See *acetylene*.

EUCHLORINE. A gaseous *mixture* of chlorine, Cl_2, and explosive chlorine peroxide, ClO_2.

EUDIOMETER. A glass tube for measuring volume changes in *chemical reactions* between *gases*.

EUGENICS. The study of the genetic control of human populations, with a view to improving their constitution, by selectively encouraging breeding among those people considered by eugenicists to be the most desirable.

EUGENOL. $C_{10}H_{12}O_2$. A colourless oily *liquid*, m.p. 9·2° C., b.p. 255° C., extracted from oil of cloves. Used in perfumes and as an *antiseptic*.

EUROPIUM. Eu. Element. A.W. 151·96. At. No. 63. S.G. 5·24, m.p. 826° C. See *lanthanides*.

EUTECTIC MIXTURE. A *solid solution* of two or more substances, having the lowest *freezing point* of all the possible mixtures of the components.

This is taken advantage of in *alloys* of low *melting point,* which are generally eutectic mixtures.

EUTECTIC POINT. Two or more substances capable of forming *solid solutions* with each other have the property of lowering each other's *freezing point*; the minimum freezing point attainable, corresponding to the *eutectic mixture,* is termed the eutectic point.

EVAPORATION. The conversion of a *liquid* into *vapour,* without necessarily reaching the *boiling point*; used in concentrating *solutions* by evaporating off the *solvent.* As it is the fastest moving *molecules* that escape from the surface of a liquid during evaporation, the average *kinetic energy* of the remaining molecules is reduced, and therefore evaporation causes cooling.

EVAPOROMETER. See *atmometer.*

EVEN-EVEN NUCLEUS. A *nucleus* that contains both an even number of *protons* and an even number of *neutrons.*

EVEN-ODD NUCLEUS. A *nucleus* that contains an even number of *protons* but an odd number of *neutrons.*

EVOLUTE. A curve that is formed from the *locus* of the *centres of curvature* of another curve (the *involute*). The end of a stretched string from the evolute traces the involute.

EVOLUTION. See *Darwin's theory of evolution.*

EXCESS (chem.). A greater quantity of one substance or *reagent* than is necessary to react with a given quantity of another.

EXCESS ELECTRON. An *electron* in a *semiconductor* donated by an impurity, which is not required in the bonding system of the *crystal* and which is therefore available for *conduction* ('excess conduction').

EXCHANGE FORCE. 1. The type of *force* which holds *nucleons* together in the *nucleus* of an *atom.* Believed to result from the exchange of *mesons* between the nucleons. 2. A force occurring in ferromagnetic materials. See *ferromagnetism.*

EXCHANGES, PREVOST'S THEORY OF. Bodies at all *temperatures* are constantly radiating *energy* to each other, those at constant temperature receiving in a given time as much energy as they emit.

EXCIMER. An excited *dimer,* formed by the association of excited and unexcited *molecules* (see *excitation*) which in the *ground state* would remain dissociated. Excimer *fluorescence* occurs in many *polycyclic hydrocarbons.*

EXCITATION. The addition of *energy* to a *nucleus,* an *atom,* or a *molecule,* transferring it from its *ground state* to a higher *energy level.* The 'excitation energy' is the difference in energy between the ground state and the excited state.

EXCITON. A non-conducting, non-localized, excited *electron* state in a *semiconductor.* It may be regarded as a bound *electron-hole* pair, or alternatively as an atomic *excitation* which is passed from *atom* to atom.

EXCLUSION PRINCIPLE. See *Pauli exclusion principle.*

EXOCRINE GLANDS. Glands which discharge their secretions into ducts, such as tear and salivary glands.

EXOENZYME. An *enzyme* that functions outside the *cell* that produces it, e.g. *pepsin*.

EXOERGIC PROCESS. An *exothermic process* (often applied in the context of a *nuclear reaction*).

EXOSMOSIS. Outward osmotic flow. See *osmosis*.

EXOSPHERE. The outermost layer of the *Earth's atmosphere*, in which the *density* is such that an air *molecule* moving directly outwards has a 50% chance of escaping rather than colliding with another molecule. The exosphere lies beyond the *ionosphere* and starts some 400 kilometres above the Earth's surface. See Fig. 44, page 402.

EXOTHERMIC PROCESS. A process in which *energy* in the form of *heat* is released.

EXPANSION, COEFFICIENT OF. 1. Linear. The increase in length per unit length, caused by a rise in *temperature* of 1°C. 2. Area (superficial expansion). The increase in area per unit area caused by a rise in temperature of 1°C. 3. Volume. The increase in *volume* per unit volume caused by a rise in temperature of 1°C. For *isotropic* media, the area and volume coefficients are approximately double and treble the linear coefficients respectively, for the same substance.

EXPANSION OF GASES. A *perfect gas* expands by 1/273 of its volume at 0°C. for each degree rise in *temperature*, the *pressure* being constant (*Charles' Law*). Real gases obey this law only approximately at ordinary pressures, but the approximation becomes more and more valid as the pressure is reduced, i.e. as the gas tends towards a *perfect gas*.

EXPANSION OF LIQUIDS. The directly observed expansion is the *apparent expansion*, since the vessel containing the *liquid* also expands. The coefficient of true expansion is the sum of the coefficient of apparent expansion, and the coefficient of volume expansion of the containing vessel.

EXPANSION OF THE UNIVERSE. The widely accepted theory that the Universe is expanding, i.e. that clusters of *galaxies* are receding from each other. It is based upon the evidence of the *red shift* (see also *Doppler effect*) and the theory of *relativity*. See *Hubble's constant*.

EXPLICIT FUNCTION (math.). A variable quantity, x, is said to be an explicit function of y, when x is directly expressed in terms of y.

EXPLOSION. A violent and rapid increase of *pressure* in a confined space. May be caused by an external source of *energy* (e.g. *heat*) or by an internal *exothermic chemical reaction* in which relatively large *volumes* of *gases* are produced. Explosions may also occur as the result of the release of internal energy during an uncontrolled *nuclear reaction* (either *fission* or *fusion* or both).

EXPLOSIVES. Substances which undergo a rapid chemical change, with production of *gas*, on being heated or struck. The *volume* of gas produced being very great relative to the bulk of the *solid* explosive, great *pressures* are set up when the action takes place in a confined space.

EXPONENT (math.). The number indicating the *power* of a quantity. Thus the exponent of x in x^4 is 4.

EXPONENTIAL. The mathematical *series*,

$e^x = 1 + x + \dfrac{x^2}{2!} + \dfrac{x^3}{3!} + \ldots \dfrac{x^n}{n!}$ is called an exponential series.

When $x = 1$,

$e = 1 + 1 + \frac{1}{2} + \frac{1}{6} + \frac{1}{24} + \ldots = 2 \cdot 71828$ (approx).

The function of x, defined by $y = e^x$ is called an exponential function and e^x is the exponential of x. The constant e is the base of natural or Naperian *logarithms*.

EXPOSURE METER (phot.). A *photo-electric cell* operating a suitable indicating meter, used in *photography* to assess the amount of *light* available, so that the correct shutter speed and *aperture* may be chosen for a given 'speed' of *film*.

EXPRESSION (math.). A representation of a value, or relationship, in symbols.

EXTENDER. An *inorganic* powder added to *paints* to improve such properties as *film* formation, and to avoid settlement on storage. Also used in the *plastics* industry with reference to substances added to *glues* or synthetic *rubbers* which reduce their cost or to some extent modify their properties (e.g. *viscosity*).

EXTENSOMETER. An instrument for measuring the extension produced in a body under an applied *stress*.

EXTINCTION COEFFICIENT. A measure of the amount of *light* absorbed by a substance in *solution*. If light of intensity I_0 is passed through d m of a solution containing a *molecular concentration* c of the dissolved substance, so that its intensity is reduced to I_T, then the extinction coefficient is given by:

$$\frac{1}{cd} . \log_{10} \frac{I_0}{I_T}$$

EXTRACTION. The process of separating a desired constituent from a *mixture*, by means of selective *solubility* in an appropriate *solvent*. Also used to describe any process by which a pure *metal* is obtained from *ore*.

EXTRAORDINARY RAY. See *ordinary ray*.

EXTRAPOLATION. The process of filling in values or terms of a series on either side of the known values, thus extending the range of values.

EXTREMELY HIGH FREQUENCIES. EHF. *Radio frequencies* in the range 30,000 to 300,000 *megahertz*.

EXTRINSIC SEMICONDUCTOR. A *semiconductor* in which the *carrier* density results mainly from the presence of impurities or other imperfections, as opposed to an intrinsic semiconductor in which the electrical properties are characteristic of the *ideal crystal*.

EYE-PIECE. In optical instruments, the *lens* or system of lenses nearest the observer's eye; generally used to view the image formed by the *objective*.

F

FACE-CENTRED. See *body-centred*.

FACTOR (math.). A number or quantity is exactly divisible by its factors; thus the factors of 12 (i.e. the *integral* or whole-number factors) are 1, 2, 3, 4, 6, 12.

FACTOR, PRIME. The prime factors of a quantity are the *prime numbers* which, when multiplied together, give the quantity. Thus, the prime factors of 165 are 3, 5, and 11.

FACTORIAL. The *product* of a number and all the consecutive positive whole numbers below it down to 1. Thus, factorial 5, written 5! or $\lfloor 5 = 5 \times 4 \times 3 \times 2 \times 1 = 120$.

FACULAE. Large bright areas of the *photosphere* of the *Sun*, whose *temperatures* are higher than the average of the Sun's surface.

FAHRENHEIT SCALE of temperature. The *temperature* scale in which the *melting point* of *ice* is taken as 32°F. and the *boiling point* of *water* under standard atmospheric pressure (760 mm) as 212°F. 9 Fahrenheit degrees = 5 Celsius degrees. To convert degrees F. to degrees C., subtract 32 from the F. value, multiply by 5, and divide by 9; to convert degrees C. to degrees F., multiply by 9, divide by 5, then add 32 to the result. Named after G. D. Fahrenheit (1686–1736).

FAJANS' RULES. See *rules of Fajans*.

FALL-OUT. *Radioactive* substances deposited upon the surface of the Earth from the *atmosphere*. Three types of fall-out, subsequent to the *explosion* of a *nuclear weapon*, are recognized. 'Local fall-out' as a result of which large particles from the fire ball are deposited within a range of approximately 100 miles during the first few hours after the explosion. 'Tropospheric fall-out', during which fine particles are deposited around the globe, in the approximate *latitude* of the explosion, within a week or so. 'Stratospheric fall-out' consisting of the ultimate world-wide deposition, over a period of years, of the particles which were carried by the explosion into the *stratosphere*.

FARAD. The derived *SI unit* of *capacitance* defined as the capacitance of a *capacitor* between the plates of which there appears a *potential difference* of 1 *volt* when it is charged with one *coulomb* of electricity. Symbol F (equal to ampere seconds per volt). Equivalent to 10^9 *electromagnetic units* and 8.99×10^{11} *electrostatic units*. The practical unit is the microfarad, which is 10^{-6} farad. Named after M. Faraday (1791–1867).

FARADAY CONSTANT. *F*. The quantity of *electricity* required to liberate or deposit 1 *mole* of an *ion*. 96 487 *coulombs* per mole. See *electrochemical equivalent*. Named after M. Faraday (1791–1867).

FARADAY EFFECT. Faraday rotation. The rotation of the plane of vibration (see *polarization of light*) of polarized light on traversing an *isotropic* transparent medium placed in a *magnetic field* possessing a component in the direction of the light ray. Although originally restricted to light, the Faraday effect is now known to apply to other *electromagnetic radiations*. Thus, the plane of polarization of a *radar pulse* travelling through the *ionosphere* is rotated by the combined effects of the *ionization* and the Earth's magnetic field (see *magnetism, terrestrial*). By reflecting radar pulses from the *Moon*, or other Earth *satellites*, and measuring the total rotation, the extent of the ionization in the ionosphere can be calculated.

FAST FISSION. See *fast neutrons*.

FAST NEUTRONS. *Neutrons* resulting from *nuclear fission* that have lost little of their *energy* by collision and therefore travel at high speeds. It is usual to describe neutrons with energies in excess of $0 \cdot 1$ *MeV* as 'fast'. However, fission induced by fast neutrons is often described as 'fast fission' and in this context the neutrons are so described if they have energies in excess of the fission threshold of $^{238}_{92}U$, i.e. above $1 \cdot 5$ *MeV*.

FAST REACTOR. A *nuclear reactor* in which little or no *moderator* is used and in which, therefore, the *nuclear fissions* are caused by *fast neutrons*.

FATHOM. 6 feet. Used as a unit of marine depth.

FATHOMETER. A depth-sounding instrument. The depth of water is measured by noting the time the *echo* of a *sound* takes to return from the sea bed.

FATIGUE OF METALS. The deterioration of *metals* owing to repeated *stresses* above a certain critical value; it is accompanied by changes in the crystalline structure of the metal.

FATS AND OILS. Simple *lipids* consisting of mixtures of various *glycerides* of *fatty acids*. Natural *organic compounds* which occur in plants and animals and serve as storage materials. The distinction between fats and oils (as distinct from *mineral oils*, which are *hydrocarbons*) is one of *melting point*; the term oil is usually applied to glycerides *liquid* at 20° C., the others being termed fats.

FATTY ACIDS. *Monobasic organic acids* having the general formula R.COOH, where R is hydrogen or a group of carbon and hydrogen atoms. The *saturated* fatty acids have the general formula $C_nH_{2n+1}COOH$. Many fatty acids occur in living things, usually in the form of *glycerides* in *fats and oils*.

FEBRIFUGE. See *antipyretic*.

FEEDBACK. In general, the coupling of the output of a process to the input. In 'negative feedback' a rise in the output *energy* is arranged to cause a decrease in the input energy (e.g. a *governor*). In 'positive feedback' a rise in the output energy is caused to reinforce the input energy. In particular, these terms are applied to electronic *amplifiers*, in which a portion of the output energy is used to reduce or increase the amplification, by reacting on an earlier stage according to the relative *phase* of the return.

FEHLING'S SOLUTION. A solution of *cupric sulphate*, $CuSO_4$, *sodium hydroxide*, NaOH, and *potassium sodium tartrate (Rochelle salt)*. Used for the detection and estimation of certain *sugars* and other *reducing agents*, which act upon the solution with the formation of a red precipitate of *cuprous oxide*, Cu_2O. Named after Herman Fehling (1812–85).

FELSPAR. Feldspar. A large group of rock-forming *minerals* consisting chiefly of alumino-silicates of potassium and sodium. Constituents of *granite* and other primary rocks.

FEMTO-. Prefix denoting one thousand million millionth; 10^{-15}. Symbol f.

FERMAT'S PRINCIPLE OF LEAST TIME. The path taken by a ray of *light* or other *wave motion* in traversing the distance between any two points is such that the time taken is a minimum. Named after Pierre de Fermat (1601–65).

FERMENT. *Enzyme.* Any substance which will produce *fermentation*.

FERMENTATION. A chemical change brought about in organic substances by living *organisms* (*yeast, bacteria,* etc.) by *enzyme* action. Usually applied to the alcoholic fermentation produced by the action of *zymase* on certain *sugars*, giving *ethanol* and *carbon dioxide* according to the equation $C_6H_{12}O_6 = 2C_2H_5OH + 2CO_2$.

FERMI. A unit of length, used in *nuclear physics*, equal to 10^{-13} cm. Named after Enrico Fermi (1901–54).

FERMI-DIRAC STATISTICS. The branch of *statistical mechanics* used with systems of identical particles which have the property that their *wave function* changes sign if any two particles are interchanged. See *fermions*. Named after Enrico Fermi (1901–54) and P. A. M. Dirac (b. 1902).

FERMIONS. Particles which conform to *Fermi-Dirac statistics*. The numbers of fermions are conserved throughout all nuclear interactions, but they are divided into two groups, *baryons* and *leptons*, which are distinguished from each other in that members of one group cannot transform into members of the other group. All fermions have *spin* $\frac{1}{2}$. See Table 6, page 436.

FERMIUM. Fm. *Transuranic element.* At. No. 100. The most stable *isotope*, $^{257}_{100}Fm$, has a *half-life* of only 80 days.

FERRATE. A *salt* of the hypothetical ferric acid, H_2FeO_4.

FERRIC. Containing *tervalent* (trivalent) iron. Ferric *salts* are usually yellow or brown in colour.

FERRIC ALUM. Iron alum. See *ferric potassium sulphate*.

FERRIC CHLORIDE. $FeCl_3.6H_2O$. A brown-yellow *deliquescent* crystalline *salt*. Used as a *mordant* and in medicine.

FERRIC OXIDE. Fe_2O_3. A red *insoluble* substance that occurs naturally as *haematite*. M.p. $1565°C$., used as a *mordant* and a *pigment*.

FERRIC POTASSIUM SULPHATE. Ferric alum. $Fe_2(SO_4)_3.K_2SO_4.24H_2O$. A violet *soluble* crystalline *double salt* used in chemical *analysis*.

FERRICYANIDE. A *salt* of the unstable ferricyanic acid, $H_3Fe(CN)_6$, e.g. *potassium ferricyanide*.

FERRIMAGNETISM. The type of *magnetism* occurring in materials in which the *magnetic moments* of adjacent *atoms* are anti-parallel, but of unequal strength, or in which the number of magnetic moments orientated in one direction outnumber those in the reverse direction.

Ferrimagnetic materials therefore have a resultant magnetization similar to that of *ferromagnetism.* Typical ferrimagnetic materials are the *ferrites.*

FERRITE. 1. The name applied to several types of iron *ore.* 2. A *salt* of the hypothetical 'ferrous acid', derived from *ferric oxide,* Fe_2O_3. 3. Pure *alpha-iron,* or *solid solutions* of which *alpha-iron* is the *solvent.*

FERRITES. A group of *ceramic* materials which exhibit the property of *ferrimagnetism.* Consist of iron oxide to which small quantities of *transition metal* oxides (e.g. cobalt and nickel oxides) have been added. The *spinel* ferrites have the formula $MO.Fe_2O_3$ where M is a *divalent* transition metal ion. More complex barium-containing ferrites have also been manufactured. By suitable combinations of metallic oxides, ferrites can be made which exhibit *ferromagnetism,* but as they are electrical *insulators* and therefore do not suffer from the effects of *eddy currents,* they can be used as cores in coils and *transformers* in *electronic* equipment at *frequencies* which would be impossible with ordinary ferromagnetic materials. Ferrites are also used in the construction of memory circuits in *computers* and, on account of their light weight, in the electrical equipment of aircraft.

FERRITIN. A *protein* found in the liver and spleen which contains iron. Acts as a reservoir of iron for the whole body.

FERRO-. Prefix denoting iron, especially in names of *alloys;* e.g. *ferromanganese.*

FERROALUMINIUM. An *alloy* of aluminium (up to 80%) and iron.

FERROCHROME. An *alloy* of chromium with 30%–40% iron, obtained by the reduction of *chromite* with carbon in an electric furnace.

FERROCYANIDE. A *salt* of the *unstable* ferrocyanic acid, $H_4Fe(CN)_6$, e.g. *potassium ferrocyanide.*

FERROELECTRICS. *Dielectric* materials which have electrical properties analogous to certain magnetic properties such as *hysteresis,* e.g. *barium titanate* and *potassium sodium tartrate (Rochelle salt).* Ferroelectric materials usually also have piezo-electric properties (see *piezo-electric effect*).

FERROMAGNETIC SUBSTANCES. See *ferromagnetism.*

FERROMAGNETISM. The *metals* iron, cobalt, nickel, and certain *alloys* are vastly more magnetic than any other known substance: these metals are said to be ferromagnetic. Ferromagnetism is due to unbalanced *electron spin* in the inner electron *orbits* of the *elements* concerned (see *atom, structure of*) which gives the *atom* a resultant *magnetic moment.* The ionic spacing in ferromagnetic *crystals* is such that very large *forces,* called *exchange forces,* cause the alignment of all the individual magnetic moments of large groups of atoms to give highly *magnetic domains.* In an unmagnetized piece of iron, these domains are oriented at random, their magnetic axes pointing in all directions. The application of an external field serves to line up the domain axes, giving rise to the observed magnetism. Ferromagnetic substances have very large *magnetic permeabilities* which vary with the strength of the applied field. A given ferromagnetic substance loses its ferromagnetic properties at a certain critical temperature, the *Curie temperature* for that substance.

FERROMANGANESE. An *alloy* of manganese (70%–80%) and iron.

FERROSILICON. An *alloy* of silicon (15%) and iron, used in special *steels*.

FERROTUNGSTEN. An *alloy* of tungsten (up to 80%) and iron.

FERROUS. Containing *bivalent* (divalent) iron; more loosely, pertaining to iron. Ferrous *salts* are generally pale green in colour.

FERROUS SULPHATE. Green vitriol, copperas. $FeSO_4.7H_2O$. A pale green crystalline *soluble salt*. Made by dissolving scrap iron in dilute *sulphuric acid*. Used in *dyeing*, *tanning*, and *ink* manufacture.

FERTILE MATERIAL. *Isotopes* which can be transformed into *fissile material* by the absorption of *neutrons* (e.g. $^{238}_{92}U$, $^{232}_{90}Th$).

FERTILIZATION. The union of two sexually dissimilar *gametes* to form a *zygote*.

FERTILIZERS. Materials put into the *soil* to provide *compounds* of *elements* essential to plant life; more particularly nitrogen, phosphorus, and potassium. Nitrogen is provided in the form of *nitrates*, *ammonium salts*, *calcium cyanamide*, etc. (see *fixation of atmospheric nitrogen*); phosphorus is added in the form of *superphosphate*, *basic slag*, various *phosphates*, etc. Potassium is obtained from natural potassium salts. Products of organic *decomposition* and waste, manure, etc., contain these and other necessary elements and form valuable fertilizers.

FIBREGLASS*. See *glass fibre materials*.

FIBRIN. An *insoluble* substance precipitated in the *blood* of vertebrates in the form of a meshwork of fibres during the process of clotting. Fibrin is formed when *thrombin* acts upon *fibrogen*.

FIBROGEN. A *soluble protein* found in the *blood* of vertebrates which causes clotting of the blood by the action of the *enzyme thrombin* as a result of which *fibrin* is formed.

FIDELITY. A measure of the *frequency* response of a *sound*-producing system. 'High fidelity' systems are usually taken to be those which are capable of reproducing frequencies up to 12,000 *hertz* without distortion.

FIELD. The region in which an electrically charged body (see *electric field*), a magnetized body (see *magnetic field*), or a massive body (see *gravitational field*) exerts its influence. There may also be said to be a field between *nucleons* in extremely close proximity (less than 10^{-13} cm) as a result of *exchange forces*. A field is thus a model for representing the way in which a *force* can exist between bodies not in contact.

FIELD COIL. A coil of wire used for magnetizing an *electromagnet*, e.g. in a *dynamo*.

FIELD EMISSION. The emission of *electrons* from an unheated surface as a result of a strong *electric field* existing at that surface.

FIELD GUIDANCE. A method of guiding a missile to a point within a *field* by means of the properties of that field. The field may be natural (e.g. a *gravitational field*) or artificial (e.g. an *electromagnetic* or *radio* field).

FIELD LENS. The *lens* in the *eye-piece* system of optical instruments farthest from the eye.

FIELD MAGNET. A *magnet* which provides a *magnetic field* in the *dynamo*, *electric motor*, or other electrical machine.

FILAMENT. A thin thread. In incandescent *electric light bulbs* and *thermionic valves*, a wire of tungsten or other *metal* of high *melting point*, which is heated by the passage of an *electric current*.

FILE (*computers*). A body of information which has a describable structure, allowing all, or part, of it to be retrieved from the *store* (or *backing storage*) on demand.

FILLER. A *solid* substance added to synthetic *resins*, *paints*, and *rubbers*, either to modify their properties or to reduce their cost.

FILM. 1. (chem.). A thin layer of a substance formed on the surface of a *liquid* or at the interface between two immiscible liquids, usually only a few *molecules* thick. 2. (phot.). A flexible strip (usually *celluloid*) coated with a light-sensitive *emulsion*. See *photography*.

FILM BADGE. A badge containing a masked photographic *film* worn by workers in contact with *ionizing radiations* to indicate the extent of their exposure to these radiations.

FILTER. 1. (chem.). A device for separating *solids* or suspended particles from *liquids*. Consists of a porous material (e.g. filter-paper) through the pores of which only liquids and dissolved substances can penetrate. 2. (phys.). A material or device inserted in the path of an *electromagnetic radiation* to alter its *frequency* distribution.

FILTER PRESS. An apparatus used for carrying out *filtration*; consists of a series of frames (metal or wooden) the two sides of which are covered with filter cloth. The frames are clamped together and the *liquid* to be filtered is pumped into them so that the *solid* residue forms a cake between the cloths while the *filtrate* is drained off.

FILTRATE. A clear *liquid* after *filtration*; a substance which has been filtered, and contains no suspended matter.

FILTRATION. The process of separating *solids* from *liquids* by passing through a *filter*.

FINDER. A small low-powered *telescope* fixed parallel to the axis of a large telescope (usually astronomical) so that the object to be observed may be located and set in the field of vision of the large telescope.

FINENESS OF GOLD. The quantity of gold in an *alloy* expressed as parts per thousand. Thus gold with a fineness of 900 is an alloy containing 90% gold. See also *carat*.

FIRE. A *chemical reaction* accompanied by the evolution of *heat, light,* and *flame* (i.e. a glowing mass of *gas*). Generally applied to the chemical combination with oxygen of carbon and other *elements* constituting the substance which is being burnt. See *combustion*.

FIRECLAY. *Clay* consisting principally of *aluminium oxide*, Al_2O_3, and *silica*, SiO_2, which will only soften at high *temperatures* and which is therefore used as a *refractory* material. Fireclays often occur beneath *coal* seams.

FIRE-DAMP. An explosive mixture of *methane* (CH_4) and air, formed in coal mines.

FIRE EXTINGUISHERS. Hand devices for extinguishing *fires* in their early stages. They are usually classified according to the type of fire they are intended to combat, i.e. Class A fires (*paper*, wood, furnishings, and other common solid combustibles) and Class B fires (inflammable *liquids*, e.g. *petrol*, *paraffin*, etc.). Class A fires (which do not involve electrical equipment) are best combated with *water* under pressure delivered from extinguishers in which the water is expelled by stored pressure or by *carbon dioxide* produced by the action of *sulphuric acid* on *sodium hydrogen carbonate* (the 'soda-acid' type). Also in use are dry powder extinguishers (consisting of finely ground sodium or potassium hydrogen carbonate), and the *halogenated hydrocarbon* type, e.g., bromochlorodifluoromethane (BCF) or chlorobromomethane (CB). These halogenated hydrocarbons, however, like the fires themselves, produce *toxic* products of *combustion*, but BCF and CB are less toxic than *carbon tetrachloride* (CTC), as used in the older extinguishers.

Class B fires are best extinguished by the dry powder extinguishers, halogenated hydrocarbon extinguishers, or by carbon dioxide extinguishers. Also used are air-foam extinguishers (based on slaughterhouse products high in *protein*) or chemical foam extinguishers (based on solutions of *aluminium sulphate* and sodium hydrogen carbonate which react together on mixing, evolving carbon dioxide and producing a *foam*).

FISCHER-TROPSCH PROCESS. A process for the manufacture of *hydrocarbon oils* from *coal*, *lignite*, or *natural gas*. The process essentially consists of the *hydrogenation* of *carbon monoxide*, CO, in the presence of *catalysts*; this results in the formation of hydrocarbons and *steam*. Named after F. Fischer (d. 1948) and H. Tropsch (d. 1935).

FISSILE MATERIAL. *Isotopes* which are capable of undergoing *nuclear fission*. Sometimes the term is restricted to apply only to isotopes which are capable of undergoing fission upon impact with a slow *neutron* (e.g. $^{233}_{92}U$, $^{235}_{92}U$, $^{239}_{94}Pu$).

FISSION, NUCLEAR. See *nuclear fission*.

FISSION PRODUCTS. Both the stable and the unstable *isotopes* produced as the result of *nuclear fission*.

FISSION SPECTRUM. The *energy* distribution of the *neutrons* produced by the *nuclear fission* of a particular *fissile material*.

FITTIG'S SYNTHESIS. The preparation of *aromatic benzene derivatives* by the action of metallic sodium on a mixture of an *alkyl halide* and a brominated benzene *hydrocarbon*.

FITZGERALD-LORENTZ CONTRACTION. The explanation put forward independently by Fitzgerald (1893) and Lorentz (1895) to explain the result of the *Michelson-Morley experiment* on the supposition that a body moving with high *velocity* through the *ether* would experience a contraction in length in the direction of the motion. This contraction was later shown to be a direct consequence of the *relativity* theory. Named after G. F. Fitzgerald (1851–1901) and H. A. Lorentz (1853–1928).

FIXATION OF ATMOSPHERIC NITROGEN. The manufacture of *compounds* of nitrogen for use as *fertilizers*, from the free nitrogen in the air; made necessary by the increasing shortage of natural nitrogen compounds in the *nitrogen cycle*. This shortage is caused partly by increased cultivation of the *soil* due to increase of populations, and partly by the loss of nitrogen compounds from animal waste products by sewage disposal into the sea. The first practical process was the *Birkeland and Eyde process*; the *Haber* and *Serpek processes* are now the main ones used. In addition, certain *bacteria* in the soil fix atmospheric nitrogen.

FIXED AIR. Former name for *carbon dioxide*, CO_2.

FIXED ALKALI. Former name for *potassium* or *sodium carbonate*, to distinguish them from volatile alkali, ammonium carbonate.

FIXED POINT. Any accurately reproducible equilibrium *temperature*. Examples include the *ice point*, the *steam point*, and the *sulphur point*. See *International Practical Temperature Scale*.

FIXED STARS. True *stars*; heavenly bodies termed fixed because they do not appear to alter their relative positions on the *celestial sphere*.

FIXING, PHOTOGRAPHIC. Rendering that portion of the sensitive *film*, plate, or paper which has not been affected by *light*, insensitive to exposure, after *developing*. Usually carried out by the action of *sodium thiosulphate*, $Na_2S_2O_3$ (*hypo*), which reacts with the unaffected *silver bromide* to give a *soluble double salt*, silver sodium thiosulphate, which is then washed away. See *photography*.

FLAME. The glowing mass of *gas* produced during *combustion*.

FLASH PHOTOGRAPHY. See *spark photography*.

FLASH PHOTOLYSIS. See *photolysis*.

FLASH POINT. The lowest *temperature* at which a substance gives off sufficient inflammable *vapour* to produce a momentary flash when a small flame is applied.

FLAVOPROTEINS. Yellow conjugated *proteins* in which the *prosthetic group* is either flavine mononucleotide (FMN) or adenine dinucleotide (FAD). Flavoproteins are *enzymes* of the *dehydrogenase* type.

FLEMING'S RULES. Mnemonics for relating the direction of motion, *flux*, and *E.M.F.* in electric machines. If the forefinger, second finger, and thumb of the right hand are extended at right angles to each other, the forefinger indicates the direction of the flux, the second finger the direction of the E.M.F., and the thumb the direction of motion in an electric *generator*. If the left hand is used the digits indicate the conditions obtaining in an *electric motor*. Named after Sir John Ambrose Fleming (1849–1945).

FLINT. Natural variety of impure *silica*, SiO_2. 'Flints' of automatic lighters are composed of *pyrophoric alloys* of *metals* such as cerium and iron.

FLINT GLASS. A variety of *glass* containing lead silicate; used for optical purposes.

FLOCCULATION. The coagulation of finely divided particles into particles of greater mass.

FLOTATION, PRINCIPLE OF. The *weight* of *liquid* displaced by a floating body is equal to the weight of the body. A particular case of *Archimedes' principle*.

FLOTATION PROCESS. The separation of a *mixture*, e.g. of *zinc blende*, ZnS, and *galena*, PbS, making use of the *surface tension* of *water*. Zinc blende is not easily wetted by water and floats, supported by the surface film of water, while galena sinks. In modern practice, special materials are added to the water which cause one of the constituents to float in the froth produced by aerating and agitating the water. See *froth flotation*.

FLOWERS OF SULPHUR. A fine powder, consisting of very small *crystals* of *sulphur* obtained by the *condensation* of sulphur *vapour* during *distillation* of crude sulphur.

FLUE GAS. The gaseous products of *combustion* from a boiler furnace consisting predominantly of *carbon dioxide, carbon monoxide*, oxygen, nitrogen, and *steam*. Analysis of the flue gases is used to check the efficiency of the furnace. See *Orsat apparatus*.

FLUID. A substance which takes the shape of the vessel containing it; a *liquid* or *gas*.

FLUID DRACHM. See *drachm*.

FLUID MEASURE. See *apothecaries' fluid measure*.

FLUID OUNCE. British measure of *volume* of *liquids*. 28·41 cc. See *apothecaries' fluid measure*.

FLUIDICS. Fluidic logic. The study, design, and use of jets of fluid to carry out *amplification* and *logic* to perform tasks usually carried out by *electronics*. Fluidic systems, which depend on the flow of *fluids* instead of *electrons*, are about 10^6 times slower than electronics, but they can operate at higher *temperatures*. They are also unaffected by *ionizing radiations* and they are often cheaper and more reliable than corresponding electronic systems. They have therefore found use in *nuclear reactors* and space *rockets*.

FLUIDITY. The *reciprocal* of *viscosity*. The *c.g.s. unit* is the reciprocal of the *poise* known as the *rhe*.

FLUON*. See *fluorocarbons*.

FLUORENE. *Ortho*-diphenylene methane. $C_{13}H_{10}$. A white crystalline *aromatic solid hydrocarbon*, m.p. 116° C. Used in the manufacture of *dyes* and *resins*.

FLUORESCEIN. $C_{20}H_{12}O_5$. A dark red crystalline *organic compound*, m.p. 314° C. Dissolves in *alkaline solutions* to give a *liquid* of intense green *fluorescence*. Used as an *indicator* and in *dyes*.

FLUORESCENCE. The property of many substances (e.g. *quinine* sulphate solutions, *paraffin oil*, *fluorescein* solutions) of absorbing *light* of one *wavelength* (i.e. *colour*, when in the visible region of the *spectrum*) and in its place emitting light of another wavelength or colour. Unlike *phosphorescence*, the phenomenon ceases immediately the source of light is cut off.

FLUORESCENT LAMP. A *light* source consisting of a glass tube the inside of which is coated with a fluorescent substance (see *fluorescence*). The tube contains mercury *vapour* and is fitted with a *cathode* and *anode* between which a stream of *electrons* can be made to flow by the application of a suitable *voltage*. When the mercury *atoms* are struck by the electrons they emit *ultraviolet radiation* which is converted to visible radiation by the fluorescent substance on the tube walls.

FLUORIDATION. The addition of minute quantities of *fluorides* to drinking water supplies to give protection against caries (decay) in the teeth of growing children. 1 part per million of fluoride *ion* is usually added.

FLUORIDE. A *salt* of *hydrofluoric acid*. See *fluoridation*.

FLUORINE. F. Element. A.W. 18·9984. At. No. 9. A pale yellowish-green *gas*, resembling chlorine but more *reactive*. Occurs combined as *fluorspar* and as *cryolite*. Made by the *electrolysis* of a *solution* of *potassium hydrogen difluoride* in *anhydrous hydrogen fluoride*. The fluorine *organic compounds*, made by replacing hydrogen in organic compounds by fluorine, are assuming considerable industrial importance. See *fluorocarbons*.

FLUORITE. See *fluorspar*.

FLUOROCARBONS. A group of *synthetic organic compounds* (both *aliphatic* and *aromatic*) in which some or all of the hydrogen *atoms* have been substituted by fluorine atoms. Such compounds are usually non-inflammable, chemically resistant, and immiscible with *water* or *oil*. Polytetrafluoroethylene (Teflon* and Fluon*) is a *polymer* used as a *plastic*, while the Freons* are *monomers* used as *refrigerants* and *solvents*.

FLUOROSCOPE. A fluorescent screen (see *fluorescence*) for the direct visual observation of *X-ray* images; used diagnostically in medicine.

FLUOROSILICIC ACID. Hydrofluosilicic acid. H_2SiF_6. An *acid* which is only stable in the form of its fuming *aqueous solution*. Used as a *disinfectant* and wood preservative.

FLUORSPAR. Natural calcium fluoride, CaF_2, consisting of colourless *crystals*, often coloured by impurities. Used as a source of fluorine and its *compounds*.

FLUX (chem.). A substance added to assist fusion.

FLUX (phys.). The flux of any *vector* quantity (*electric intensity*, *magnetic intensity*, etc.) through an area is the product of the area and the component of the vector at right angles to the area. In *nuclear physics*, the *product* of the number of particles (including *photons*) per unit *volume* and their average *velocity*. See *luminous flux* and *magnetic flux*.

FLUX DENSITY. The *magnetic flux* or *luminous flux* per unit of cross-sectional area. The *S.I. unit* of magnetic flux density is the *tesla*.

FLUXMETER. An instrument for the measurement of *magnetic flux*. Essentially a moving coil *galvanometer* so designed that the coil experiences negligible restoring *torque* from its suspension system. A change in the magnetic flux through a flux coil connected to the galvanometer induces a current in the coil, thus causing a deflection of the galvanometer.

f-**NUMBER OF A LENS.** The ratio of the *focal length* to the *diameter* of a *lens*, especially a *camera* lens, e.g. *f*8 indicates that the focal length is eight times the diameter. For any particular lens, the smaller the *f*-number the larger the *aperture*. The reciprocal of the *f*-number is called the 'relative aperture'.

FOAM. A *colloidal* suspension of a *gas* in a *liquid*.

FOCAL LENGTH. The distance from the *optical centre* or pole to the principal *focus* of a *lens* (see Fig. 25, page 220), or *spherical mirror* (see Fig. 27, page 246). The focal length of a spherical mirror is half its *radius of curvature*.

FOCUS. 1. (Phys.) The point at which converging rays, usually of *light*, meet (real focus); or a point from which diverging rays are considered to be directed (virtual focus). The 'principal focus' of a *lens* (see Fig. 25, page 220) or *spherical mirror* (see Fig. 27, page 246) is the point on the principal axis through which rays of light parallel to the *principal axis* will be refracted or reflected. 2. (math.) One of the fixed points used to define a curve, by a linear relationship with the distance from one of these fixed points to any point on the curve. See *ellipse*, *parabola*, *hyperbola*.

FOG. The effect caused by the *condensation* of *water vapour* upon particles of dust, soot, etc.

FOLIC ACID. Pteroylglutamic acid, P.G.A., vitamin B_c. $C_{19}H_{19}N_7O_6$. A yellow crystalline substance forming part of the *vitamin* B complex, used in the treatment of anaemia. Also known as vitamin M.

FOOD PRESERVATION. The prevention of chemical *decomposition* and of the development of harmful *bacteria* in foods. Generally effected by the sterilization of the food (i.e. by the destruction of bacteria in it) by heating in sealed vessels, i.e. canning; or by making the conditions unfavourable for the development of bacteria, by pickling, drying, freezing, smoking, etc.

FOOT. British unit of length; one-third of a *yard*; 0·3048 *metres*.

FOOT-CANDLE. Unit of *illumination*. One *lumen* per square foot.

FOOT-LAMBERT. A unit of *luminance*. The luminance of a uniform diffuser emitting one *lumen* per square foot.

FOOT-POUND. A practical unit of *work*. The work done by a *force* of 1 pound weight acting through a distance of 1 foot.

FOOT-POUNDAL. A unit of *work* in the *f.p.s. system*; the work done by a *force* of 1 *poundal* acting through a distance of 1 foot.

FORBIDDEN BAND. See *energy band*.

FORCE. An external agency capable of altering the state of rest or motion in a body; measured in *newtons* (*SI units*), *dynes* (*c.g.s. units*), or *poundals* (*f.p.s. units*). The force, *F*, required to produce an *acceleration*, *a*, in a *mass*, *m*, is given by $F = ma$. If *m* is in *kilograms*, *a* in *metres* per sec. per sec., *F* will be in *newtons*.

FORCES, PARALLELOGRAM OF. See *parallelogram of forces*.

FORCES, TRIANGLE OF. See *triangle of forces*.

FORMALDEHYDE. HCHO. A *gas* with an irritating smell, very *soluble* in *water*. 40% *solution* is known as *formalin*. Made by the *oxidation* of *methanol*. Used in the manufacture of *plastics* and *dyes*, in the textile industry, in medicine, and as a *disinfectant*.

FORMALIN. A 40% *solution* of *formaldehyde*, used as a *disinfectant*.

FORMATE. A *salt* or *ester* of *formic acid*.

FORMIC ACID. HCOOH. A colourless, corrosive fuming *liquid* with a pungent smell. M.p. 8·4°, b.p. 100·5°C. Occurs in various plants and in ants. Made industrially from sodium formate, HCOONa, which is produced by the action of *carbon monoxide*, CO, on *sodium hydroxide*, NaOH. Used in dyeing, *tanning*, and *electroplating*.

FORMULA (chem.). The representation of a *molecule* or smallest portion of a *compound*, using *symbols* for the *atoms* of the *elements* which go to make up the molecule. E.g. the formula of *water*, H_2O, implies that the smallest portion of water that can exist independently consists of 2 hydrogen atoms chemically united with 1 oxygen atom. The *structural formula* represents the way in which the atoms in a molecule are actually believed to be joined by *valency bonds*. E.g. the structural formula of water is written H—O—H, indicating that 2 hydrogen atoms, having 1 valency each, are both attached to the *bivalent* oxygen atom. The *empirical formula* of a compound is its simplest formula, indicating only the numerical ratio of the atoms present in a molecule, but not necessarily their actual number. Thus the empirical formula of *hydrogen peroxide* is HO while its actual or *molecular formula* is H_2O_2.

FORMULA (math. and phys.). A statement of facts in a symbolical or general form, by substitution in which a result applicable to particular data may be obtained. Thus the time of swing of a *pendulum* (T) is given

by the formula $T = 2\pi \sqrt{\dfrac{l}{g}}$, showing the connection between length (l)

and time of swing. (g is the *acceleration due to gravity*.)

FORMYL GROUP. The *univalent radical* O:CH—, derived from *formic acid*.

FORTIN BAROMETER. A mercury *barometer* which, used in conjunction with various correction tables, enables accurate measurements of atmospheric pressure to be made. Named after J. Fortin (1750–1831).

FOSSIL. The remains of an *organism* preserved in rocks in the *Earth's crust*. Usually only the hard parts (bones, shells, etc.) are so preserved, but occasionally remains of organisms having no hard parts have been recognized.

FOSSIL FUELS. The remains of *organisms* embedded in the surface of the Earth, with high carbon and/or hydrogen contents, which are used by man as *fuels* (e.g. *coal, oil, natural gas*). Most of the *energy* obtained from the *combustion* of fossil fuels derives from the *exothermic* conversion of carbon into *carbon dioxide* and of hydrogen into *water (steam)*.

FOUCAULT PENDULUM. A *pendulum* consisting of a heavy weight attached to a long wire, which is free to swing in any direction. The slow turning of the *plane* of the pendulum's swing is a demonstration of the *Earth's* rotation. Named after its inventor, J. B. L. Foucault (1819–68).

FOURIER ANALYSIS. The expansion of a mathematical *function* or of an experimentally obtained curve in the form of a trigonometric series. Used as a method of determining the harmonic components of a complex periodic wave. Named after J. B. J. Fourier (1768–1830).

FOURTH DIMENSION. Ordinary *space* has three dimensions, i.e. length, breadth, and thickness, each one at right angles to both the others. Mathematically it is possible to write down equations, similar to those governing relations between points in ordinary three-dimensional space, but connecting any number of imaginary dimensions. These are sometimes said to refer to a 'hyperspace' of many dimensions. In dealing with a material particle, it is necessary to state not only where it is, but when it is there. Thus time is somewhat analogous to a dimension of space. *Relativity* has shown in particular in what manner time may be regarded as a fourth dimension, so that all real events take place in a four dimensional *space-time continuum*.

FOWLER'S SOLUTION. A *solution* containing potassium arsenite; used in medicine.

F.P.S. SYSTEM. The foot-pound-second system of units. The British system of physical *units* derived from the three *fundamental units* of length, *mass*, and time, i.e. the *foot, pound* mass, and the *second*.

FRACTIONAL CRYSTALLIZATION. The separation of a *mixture* of dissolved substances by making use of their different *solubilities*. The *solution* containing the mixture is evaporated until the least *soluble* component crystallizes out.

FRACTIONAL DISTILLATION. Fractionation. The separation of a *mixture* of several *liquids* which have different *boiling points*, by collecting separately 'fractions' boiling at different *temperatures*.

FRACTIONATING COLUMN. A long vertical column, containing rings, plates, or bubble caps, which is attached to a *still*. As a result of internal *reflux* a gradual separation takes place between high and low boiling 'fractions' of a liquid *mixture*.

FRACTIONATION. The separation of a *mixture*, usually of chemically related or otherwise similar components, into fractions of different properties. The term is usually applied to *fractional distillation*.

FRAME OF REFERENCE. A set of reference axes for defining the position of a point or body in *space*. A frame of reference in a four-dimensional *continuum* consists of an observer, a *coordinate* system and a clock to correlate positions with times.

FRANCIUM. Fr. Element. At. No. 87. No known stable *isotope* and only one natural *radioactive* isotope, $^{223}_{87}Fr$ (*half-life* 21 mins.). Belongs to *alkali metal* group of *elements*.

FRASCH PROCESS. A process for extracting sulphur from deposits deep down under sand. A series of concentric pipes is sunk down to the level of the sulphur deposit, *superheated steam* is forced down to melt the sulphur, which is then forced to the surface by compressed air blown down the centre pipe.

FRAUNHOFER DIFFRACTION. The class of *diffraction* phenomena in which both the *light* source and the receiving screen are effectively at an infinite distance from the diffracting system. Compare *Fresnel diffraction*. Named after J. von Fraunhofer (1787–1826).

FRAUNHOFER LINES. Dark lines in the continuous *spectrum* of the *Sun*, caused by the absorption of certain *wavelengths* of the *white light* from the hotter regions of the Sun by chemical *elements* present in the cooler *chromosphere* surrounding the Sun.

FREE (chem.). Uncombined; applied to *elements* which occur as such.

FREE ELECTRON. An *electron* which is not attached to an *atom, molecule,* or *ion*, but is free to move under the influence of an *electric field*.

FREE ENERGY. Gibbs Function. G. A *thermodynamic* quantity representing the *energy* that would be liberated or absorbed during a *reversible process*. Defined, under conditions of constant *temperature* and *pressure*, by $G = H - TS$, where H is the heat content (*enthalpy*), T the *absolute temperature*, and S the *entropy*. Referred to chemical processes, the important quantity is not the absolute magnitude of G, but the change in free energy, ΔG (also called the chemical *affinity*), during a reaction, which is given by $\Delta G = \Delta H - T.\Delta S$. By convention, if a reaction gives out *heat* ΔH will be negative (as the system is losing heat to the surroundings). Therefore, if $T.\Delta S$ is not large compared to ΔH, ΔG will also be negative indicating that the reaction will proceed to *chemical equilibrium*. When equilibrium has been attained, $\Delta G = O$, and if ΔG is positive the reaction will only occur if energy is supplied in some way to force it away from equilibrium. As the entropy, S, is a measure of the molecular disorder of a system, and as a change of state involves a change of molecular orderliness, the term $T.\Delta S$ is dependent upon changes of state.

The Helmholtz Free Energy, F, is defined as $U - TS$, where U is the *internal energy*. Also, $\Delta F = \Delta U - T.\Delta S$ and for a reversible *isothermal* process ΔF represents the maximum work available. ΔF is sometimes called the 'work function'.

FREE RADICAL. A group of *atoms* (see *radical*), which usually exists in combination with other atoms, but which may exist independently for short periods (short-lived free radicals) during the course of a *chemical reaction*, or for longer periods (free radical of long life) under special conditions.

FREEZE DRYING. A process for drying heat-sensitive substances, such as food or *blood plasma*, by *freezing* and then removing the frozen water by volatilization at low *pressure* and *temperature*.

FREEZING. Change of state from *liquid* to *solid*; takes place at a constant *temperature* (*freezing point*) for any given substance under a given *pressure*. The freezing point normally quoted is that for standard atmospheric pressure.

FREEZING MIXTURES. Certain *salts* which, when dissolved in *water* or mixed with crushed *ice*, produce a considerable lowering of *temperature*. The action depends upon absorption of *heat of solution* by the dissolving salt; in the case of mixtures in contact with ice, the *melting point* of ice is lowered in the presence of a dissolved substance; *latent heat* of fusion of ice is absorbed, and the salt dissolves in the melting ice.

FREEZING POINT. The *temperature* of equilibrium between *solid* and *liquid* substance at a pressure of one standard atmosphere (760 mm mercury).

FREEZING-POINT DEPRESSION. See *depression of freezing point*.

FRENCH CHALK. Powdered *talc*.

FRENKEL DEFECT. A *defect* in a *crystal lattice* caused by an *atom* or *ion* being removed from its normal position in the lattice (thus causing a *vacancy*) and taking up an *interstitial* position.

FREONS. See *fluorocarbons*.

FREQUENCY. The number of cycles, oscillations, or vibrations of a *wave motion* or oscillation in unit time, usually one second. In a wave motion the frequency is equal to the *velocity* of propagation divided by the *wavelength*. Symbol v or f. The derived *SI unit* of frequency is the *hertz*.

FREQUENCY BAND. A range of *frequencies* of *electromagnetic radiations* falling within prescribed limits. See Table 10, page 442, for internationally agreed *radio frequency* bands.

FREQUENCY MODULATION. FM. The type of *radio* transmission system in which the *frequency* of a *carrier wave* is modulated rather than its *amplitude* (as in *amplitude modulation*). Provides a method of transmission free from 'static' interference.

FREQUENCY OF A VIBRATING STRING. The fundamental *frequency, f*, of a stretched string of length l, under tension T, is given by:

$$f = \frac{1}{2rl}\sqrt{\frac{T}{\pi\rho}}$$

where r is the radius of the string and ρ its *density*.

FRESNEL. A unit of *frequency* equal to 10^{12} *hertz*. Named after A. J. Fresnel (1788–1827).

FRESNEL DIFFRACTION. A class of *diffraction* phenomena in which the *light* source or the receiving screen, or both, are at a finite distance from the diffracting system. Compare *Fraunhofer diffraction*.

FRESNEL LENS. An optical *lens* whose surface consists of a number of smaller lenses so arranged that they give a short *focal length*. Used in headlights, searchlights, etc. Named after A. J. Fresnel (1788–1827).

FRIABLE. Easily crumbled.

FRICTION. Name given to *forces* offering resistance to relative motion between surfaces in contact. See *tribology*.

FRICTION, COEFFICIENTS OF. If F_s = the frictional resistance when a body is on the point of sliding along a specified surface, F_k = the frictional resistance when steady sliding has been attained, and R = the perpendicular *force* between the surfaces in contact, the static coefficient of friction = F_s/R; the kinetic coefficient = F_k/R.

FRIEDEL-CRAFTS REACTION. Originally the *synthesis* of *aromatic hydrocarbons* by reacting *alkyl halides* with *benzene derivatives* in the presence of *anhydrous* aluminium chloride as a *catalyst*. Now extended to include the addition of *olefines* to, and the *condensation* of *alcohols* with, aromatic hydrocarbons in the presence of such catalysts as *anhydrous ferric chloride*, gallium chloride, boron trifluoride, and *hydrogen fluoride*.

FROTH FLOTATION. The separation of a *mixture* of finely divided minerals by agitating them in a froth of *water* and *oil*, so that some float and others sink. The process can be made selective by adjusting the nature of the froth with suitable *surface active agents*.

FRUCTOSE. Fruit sugar, laevulose. $C_6H_{12}O_6$. A sweet *soluble* crystalline *monosaccharide sugar*, m.p. 102°–104° C. Occurs in sweet ripe fruits, in the nectar of flowers, and in honey.

FRUSTUM. Any part of a solid figure cut off by a *plane* parallel to the base, or lying between two parallel planes.

FUEL. A substance which is used for producing *heat energy*, either by means of the release of its *chemical energy* by combustion (see *fossil fuels*) or its *nuclear energy* by *nuclear fission*.

FUEL CELL. A *cell* for producing *electricity* by *oxidation* of a *fuel*, thus converting *chemical energy* directly into *electrical energy*. The fuel cell is similar to an *accumulator* but instead of needing recharging with electrical energy, it has to be fed with fresh fuel. The simplest fuel cell consists of supplies of gaseous oxygen and hydrogen brought together over catalytic *electrodes*. Other cells use *hydrazine, ammonia*, or *methanol* to provide the hydrogen. Interest in electric cars has stimulated fuel cell development. Although hydrogen-oxygen fuel cells can provide higher energy densities than zinc-air accumulators, because they are very bulky their energy per volume is little better than that of a lead accumulator.

FUEL ELEMENT. An element of *nuclear fuel* for use in a *nuclear reactor*, usually uranium encased in a can.

FULLER'S EARTH. A variety of *clay*-like materials which absorb *oil* and *grease*. Chemical composition varies; consists of *hydrated silicates* of magnesium, calcium, aluminium, and sometimes other *metals*. Used in scouring textiles and in refining *fats and oils*.

FULMINATE. A *salt* of the *unstable* fulminic acid, HONC, which is *isomeric* with *cyanic acid*; e.g. *mercuric fulminate*.

FULMINATE OF MERCURY. See *mercuric fulminate*.

FUMARIC ACID. HOOCCH:CHCOOH. A colourless crystalline substance, m.p. $287°C$., *isomeric* with *maleic acid*. Used in the manufacture of synthetic *resins* and in *baking powders*.

FUMIGATION. The destruction of *bacteria*, insects, and other pests by exposure to poisonous *gas* or *smoke*.

FUMING NITRIC ACID. A brown fuming highly corrosive *liquid* consisting of *nitric acid* containing an excess of *nitrogen peroxide*. Used as an *oxidant* in *rockets* and in organic synthesis.

FUNCTION (math.). One quantity y is said to be a function of another quantity x, written $y=f(x)$, if a change in one produces a change in the other. Thus, in the statement $y=3x^2+5x$ (i.e. $f(x) = 3x^2+5x$), y is a function of x, and a change in the value of x produces a change in the value of y.

FUNDAMENTAL CONSTANTS. See Table 2, pages 430–31.

FUNDAMENTAL NOTE (phys.). See *quality of sound*.

FUNDAMENTAL UNITS. The *units* in which physical quantities (e.g. *viscosity, surface tension,* etc.) are measured are not all independent; many of them are derived from a small number of fundamental or basic units. *SI units* have seven fundamental or basic units. See also *c.g.s. system, f.p.s. system,* and *m.k.s. system.*

FUNGI. Simple plants which contain no *chlorophyll*. May consist of one *cell* or of many cellular filaments. Cause diseases of plants and of some animals, also cause decay of food, fabrics, and timber. Certain fungi are used in *brewing* and baking and for the production of *antibiotics.*

FUNGICIDE. A substance capable of destroying harmful *fungi*, such as moulds and mildews.

FUR IN KETTLES. An *insoluble* gritty deposit, consisting mainly of the *carbonates* of calcium, magnesium, and iron; formed by the *decomposition* of the *soluble bicarbonates* of these metals when *hard water* is boiled.

FURAN. Furfuran. C_4H_4O. A five-membered *heterocyclic compound* consisting of a colourless *liquid*, b.p. $32°C$. Used in organic synthesis and in the form of its *derivatives* in the manufacture of synthetic *resins*.

FURAN RESINS. A group of synthetic *resins* obtained by the partial *polymerization* of *furfuryl alcohol* or by the *condensation* of furfuryl alcohol with *furfuraldehyde* or *formaldehyde*. Used as *adhesives*, metal coatings, etc.

FURFURALDEHYDE. Furfural. C_4H_3OCHO. A *liquid organic compound*, b.p. $161·7°C$.; used as a *solvent* and in synthetic *resins*. See *furfural resins*, and *furan resins*.

FURFURAL RESINS. *Thermosetting* resins obtained by the condensation of *furfuraldehyde* and *phenol* or its homologues. Used as an *adhesive* and in the manufacture of moulding materials, varnishes, etc.

FURFURYL ALCOHOL. $C_4H_3OCH_2OH$. A yellowish *liquid*, b.p. $171°C$., used in the manufacture of *furan resins*.

FUSE, ELECTRICAL. A device to prevent an unduly high *electric current* from passing through a *circuit*. Consists of a piece of wire made of *metal* of low *melting point*, e.g. tin, placed in series in the circuit. An excessive current will raise the *temperature* of the fuse wire sufficiently to melt it and thus break the circuit.

FUSED (chem.). In the molten state, usually applied to *solids* of relatively high *melting point*; or, having previously been melted and allowed to solidify.

FUSEL OIL. A *mixture* of *butanol* and *iso-amyl alcohol* together with other organic substances; a *liquid* of unpleasant smell and taste; *by-product* of the *distillation* of alcohol produced by *fermentation*.

FUSIBLE ALLOYS. *Alloys* of low *melting point*; generally *eutectic mixtures* of *metals* of low melting point such as bismuth, lead, tin, and cadmium. *Wood's metal* and *Lipowitz alloy* both contain all four and melt below the *boiling point* of *water*. Fusible alloys having a melting point a little above the boiling point of water are used in the construction of automatic sprinklers, *heat* from a fire melting the metal and releasing a spray of water.

FUSION. Melting; melting together.

FUSION BOMB. See *nuclear weapons*.

FUSION, LATENT HEAT OF. See *latent heat*.

FUSION, NUCLEAR. See *nuclear fusion*.

FUSION MIXTURE. A *mixture* of *anhydrous sodium* and *potassium carbonates*, Na_2CO_3 and K_2CO_3.

G

g. Symbol for the value of the *acceleration due to gravity*.

GADOLINIUM. Gd. Element. A.W. 157·25. At. No. 64. S.G. 7·948, m.p. 1312° C. See *lanthanides*.

GAIN. A term used in *electronics* with reference to an increase in signal power; usually expressed as the ratio of the output power (for example, of an *amplifier*) to the input power in *decibels*.

GALACTOSE. $CH_2OH(CHOH)_4.CHO$. A *hexose sugar*, m.p. 166° C.; constituent of *lactose* and certain plant *polysaccharides*.

GALAXIES. Extra-galactic nebulae. The *stars* of the *Universe* are not evenly distributed throughout *space*, but are collected by gravitational attraction (see *gravitation*) into some 10^9 giant clusters called galaxies. Each galaxy contains about 10^{11} stars. The *Sun* is one of such a number of stars in our own *Galaxy* (the *Milky Way*) which is itself a member of a *Local Group of galaxies*. (See also *expansion of the Universe*.) The galaxies are separated from each other by enormous distances, the nearest galaxy to the Milky Way being some 16×10^5 *light years* away. Galaxies are either elliptical or spiral shaped (see *spiral galaxies*); a very few however appear to have no regular shape.

GALAXY, THE. The *Milky Way*. A cluster of some 10^{11} *stars*, one of which is the *Sun*. The Galaxy is a flat disc-shaped spiral structure, approximately 10^5 *light-years* across, with a slight bulge at the centre. The *solar system* is situated quite close to the central plane of this disc at a distance of about three fifths of its radius from the centre.

GALENA. Natural lead sulphide, PbS. A heavy crystalline *mineral* of metallic appearance; principal *ore* of lead. Used as a *semiconductor* in *crystal rectifiers*.

GALILEAN TELESCOPE. A type of refracting *telescope* invented by Galileo Galilei (1564–1642) but no longer used in *astronomy* although it is still used in principle in opera glasses. Consists of a *bi-convex objective* of long *focal length* and a *bi-concave eye-piece* of short focal length, producing an erect image.

GALLIC ACID. See *trihydroxybenzoic acid*.

GALLIUM. Ga. Element. A.W. 69·72. At. No. 31. A silvery-white *metal*, S.G. 5·9, m.p. 29·78° C. *Compounds* are very rare; the metal is used in high-temperature *thermometers* and gallium arsenide is used as a *semiconductor*.

GALLON. Unit of volume or capacity. The British Imperial gallon is the *volume* occupied by ten pounds of *distilled water* under conditions precisely defined by the 1963 Weights and Measures Act. Equal to 4·54609 cubic decimetres (*litres*). The U.S. gallon is 0·83268 British gallons.

GALVANIZED IRON. Sheet iron coated with a layer of zinc to prevent *corrosion*, usually made by dipping into the molten metal.

161

GALVANOMETER. An instrument for detecting, comparing, or measuring small *electric currents*, but not usually calibrated in *amperes*; requires calibration when an actual current measurement is needed. Usually depends upon the magnetic effect produced by an electric current. See *ammeter*, and *ballistic galvanometer*.

GAMBOGE. A yellow substance obtained from the hardened gum-resin of the tree Garcinia Hanburii. Used as a *pigment* and for colouring varnishes.

GAMETE. Germ cell. A reproductive *cell*, usually *haploid* and sexually differentiated. The female gamete (or *ovum*) unites with the male gamete (or *spermatozoon*) during *fertilization* to produce a *zygote*, which develops into a new individual. Some animal and plant gametes are *diploid* and these cells are capable of developing into new individuals without fertilization, by the process of *parthenogenesis*.

GAMETOCYTE. A *cell* which undergoes *meiosis* to form *gametes*.

GAMMA-IRON. An allotropic form (see *allotropy*) of iron, which is non-magnetic and exists between 900°C. and 1400°C. See *austenite*.

GAMMA RAYS. Gamma radiation. γ-rays. *Electromagnetic radiation* of the same nature, but shorter *wavelength* than *X-rays*. Emitted by the *nuclei* of *radioactive atoms* during *decay*. Gamma rays are emitted in *quantized* units called *photons*.

GANGUE. The useless stony minerals that occur with a metallic *ore*.

GARNET. A group of *minerals* of varying composition, mainly double *silicates* of calcium or aluminium with other *metals*. Several varieties are red in colour, and are used as gems.

GAS. A substance whose *physical state* (the gaseous state) is such that it always occupies the whole of the space in which it is contained. Consists of *atoms* or *molecules* which would move freely in a *perfect gas*, but which in a real gas are subject to small inter-molecular *forces* (*Van der Waals' forces*). See also *kinetic theory of gases*.

GAS CARBON. Retort carbon. A hard deposit consisting of fairly pure carbon, found on the walls of the *retorts* used for the *destructive distillation* of *coal* in the manufacture of *coal-gas*. Good *conductor* of *electricity*, used for making carbon *electrodes*.

GAS CHROMATOGRAPHY. Gas-liquid chromatography. A very sensitive method of analysing the components of a complex *mixture* of *volatile* substances. The apparatus consists of a long narrow tube, packed with an inert support material of uniform particle size (e.g. *diatomaceous earth*) that has been coated with a non-volatile *liquid* called the 'stationary phase', the whole tube and its contents being maintained in a thermostatically controlled oven. The sample to be analysed is carried through the tube by an *inert gas* (e.g. argon) so that the progress through the tube of various components of the mixture is selectively interfered with by the stationary phase, some components passing through the tube more rapidly than others. A detector measures the electrical *conductivity* of the gas leaving the column, differences being recorded on a strip chart which indicates peaks corresponding to the various components. The instrument is calibrated by analysing samples of known composition.

GAS-COOLED REACTOR. A *nuclear reactor* in which the *coolant* is a *gas*. In the Mark I, or *magnox* type, natural uranium *fuel* is used with a *graphite moderator*, the *fuel elements* being cased in magnox. The coolant used is *carbon dioxide* and the outlet *temperature* is about 350°C., the hot gas being used to raise *steam*. In the Mark II, or advanced gas-cooled reactor (A.G.R.), the moderator is also graphite and the coolant is carbon dioxide, but in this type the outlet temperature is much higher (about 600°C.) and the fuel is *ceramic uranium dioxide* in a *stainless steel* casing.

GAS CONSTANT. *R*. In the *gas equation*, $pV = RT$, the gas constant, *R*, equals 8·3143 *joules* per *kelvin* per *mole* or 1·9858 *calories* per degree *celsius* per mole.

GAS EQUATION. An *equation* connecting the *pressure* and *volume* of a quantity of *gas* with the *absolute temperature*. For one *mole* of a *perfect gas*, $pV = RT$, where $p =$ pressure, $V =$ volume, $T =$ absolute temperature, and $R =$ the *gas constant*.

GAS LAWS. Statements as to the *volume* changes of *gases* under the effect of alterations of *pressure* and *temperature*. *Boyle's law* states that at constant temperature the volume of a given mass of gas is inversely proportional to the pressure; i.e. $pV =$ constant. *Charles' law* states that at constant pressure all gases expand by 1/273 of their volume at 0°C. for a rise in temperature of 1°C.; i.e. the volume of a given mass of gas at constant pressure is directly proportional to the *absolute temperature*. The two laws may be combined in the expression $pV \propto T$, where *T* is the absolute temperature; or, for a *mole* of a gas, $pV = RT$ (see *gas equation*). This gives the behaviour of a gas when both temperature and pressure are altered. The gas laws are not perfectly obeyed by ordinary gases, being strictly true only for the *perfect gas*. See *gas laws, deviations from*.

GAS LAWS, DEVIATIONS FROM. *Gases* do not strictly obey the *gas laws*, but follow them more and more closely as the *pressure* of the gas is reduced. Various *equations* have been derived which attempt to give a better approximation to the behaviour of actual gases. The best known of these is *Van der Waals' equation*.

GAS MANTLE. A structure composed of the *oxides* of thorium (99%) and cerium (1%), made by impregnating a combustible fabric with a *solution* of the *nitrates* of the metals, and decomposing the nitrates by heat.

GAS MASER. A *maser* in which *microwave radiation* interacts with *gas molecules*.

GAS MASK. Respirator. A device for protecting the face and breathing organs against poisonous 'gases'. (These include poisonous *smokes*, etc., used in chemical warfare.) The air is drawn through a layer of *activated carbon* which adsorbs *vapours*, and also through a filter-pad which retains solid particles of smokes. Such an arrangement is effective against war 'gases' and smokes, but not against gases of low *molecular weight* such as *carbon monoxide* or *coal-gas*.

GAS OIL. Diesel oil. The *oil* left after *petrol* and *kerosene* have been distilled from crude *petroleum*. Used as a *fuel* for *diesel engines* and for carburetting *water gas*.

GAS THERMOMETER. An apparatus for measuring *temperature* by the alteration in *pressure* produced by temperature changes in a *gas* kept at constant *volume*, or by the alteration in volume of a gas kept at constant pressure. For practical purposes, other more convenient forms of thermometer are used whenever possible. However, the gas thermometer, operated at low pressure, gives the only direct means of determining the *thermodynamic temperature*.

GAS TURBINE. An *engine* which converts the *chemical energy* of a *liquid fuel* into *mechanical energy* by internal *combustion*, the gaseous products of which are expanded through a *turbine*. Used as the power plant in aeroplanes (both turbo-propeller and turbo-jet driven), locomotives, and experimentally in motor-cars. Also used as an auxiliary power plant in electrical generating stations.

GASEOUS COMBINATION, LAW OF. See *Gay-Lussac's law*.

GASOLINE. Gasolene, petrol. Mixture of *hydrocarbons* obtained from *petroleum*. See *petrol*.

GATE. 1. A *circuit* with only one output, but which has more than one input and which can be activated by various combinations of input signals. 2. A signal which activates a circuit for a predetermined time or until another signal is received. 3. A device for selecting portions of a *wave*, either on a time or *amplitude* basis.

GAUSS. The *c.g.s. system* unit of *magnetic flux density*. If a *magnetic field* of 1 *oersted* intensity exists in a medium of unit *magnetic permeability*, e.g. air, then the induction will be 1 gauss. Equal to 1 *maxwell* per square centimetre or 10^{-4} *weber* per square *metre* (i.e. 1 *telsa*). Named after K. F. Gauss (1777–1855).

GAUSS'S LAW. The total electric *flux* of a closed surface in an *electric field* is 4π times the *electric charge* within that surface.

GAUSSMETER. A *magnetometer* calibrated in *gauss*, for measuring *magnetic intensity*.

GAY-LUSSAC'S LAW OF GASEOUS COMBINATION. When *gases* combine, they do so in a simple ratio by *volume* to each other, and to the gaseous product, measured under the same conditions of *temperature* and *pressure*. Explained by *Avogadro's law*. Named after Joseph Louis Gay-Lussac (1778–1850).

GEGENSCHEIN. Counter glow. A faint elliptical patch of *light* in the sky which may be observed at night directly opposite the *Sun*, though it is rarely seen in Britain. Due to a reflection of sunlight by meteoric particles in *space*.

GEIGER COUNTER. Geiger-Muller counter. An instrument for the detection of *ionizing radiations* (chiefly *alpha, beta,* and *gamma rays*), capable of registering individual particles or *photons.* Consists normally of a fine wire *anode* surrounded by a *coaxial* cylindrical *metal cathode,* mounted in a glass envelope containing *gas* at low *pressure.* A large *potential difference,* usually about 1000 *volts,* is maintained between the anode and the cathode. The *ions* produced in the counter by an incoming ionizing particle are accelerated by the applied potential difference towards their appropriate *electrodes,* causing a momentary drop in the potential between the latter. This voltage *pulse* is then passed on to various *electronic* circuits by means of which it can, if desired, be made to work a counter. See Fig. 16. Named after Hans Geiger (1882–1947).

CATHODE CYLINDER

ANODE WIRE   LOW PRESSURE GAS   −ve   +ve

COUNTER   AMPLIFIER

HT SOURCE

FIGURE 16.

GEISSLER TUBE. A tube for showing the luminous effects of a *discharge* of *electricity* through various rarefied *gases.* Consists of a sealed glass tube containing platinum electrodes. Named after H. Geissler (1814–79).

GEL. A *colloidal solution* which has set to a jelly, the *viscosity* being so great that the solution has the *elasticity* of a *solid.* Formation attributed to a mesh-like structure of the *disperse phase* or *colloid,* with the *dispersion medium* circulating through the meshwork.

GELATIN. Gelatine. A complex *protein* formed by the *hydrolysis* of *collagen* in animal cartilages and bones, by boiling with *water. Soluble* in water; *solution* has the property of setting to a jelly. Used in foods, *photography,* as an *adhesive,* textile size, and in a variety of other arts and industries.

GELATION. The process of *freezing.* See also *regelation of ice.*

GELIGNITE. An *explosive* consisting of a *mixture* of *nitroglycerin, cellulose nitrate,* saltpetre (*potassium nitrate,* KNO_3), and wood pulp.

GENE. A hypothetical unit, comprising part of a *chromosome,* which controls an individual inherited characteristic of an *organism* and which is capable of *mutation* as a unit. (See also *cistron.*) The gene is regarded as being a particular molecular configuration of the *nucleic acids* (which partially constitute a chromosome) at a particular point on the length of a chromosome. There is considerable evidence to support the belief that genes function by controlling the manufacture of *enzymes* in *cells*; each gene being responsible for the manufacture of one enzyme. See *operon* and *genetic code*.

GENERAL THEORY OF RELATIVITY. See *relativity, theory of*.

GENERATION TIME. The average lapse of time between the creation of a *neutron* by *nuclear fission* and a subsequent fission produced by that neutron.

GENERATOR. A machine for producing *electrical energy* from *mechanical energy*. See *dynamo*.

GENERATRIX (math.). A point, line, or *plane* the movement of which produces a line, surface, or solid.

GENETIC CODE. The code by which inherited characteristics are handed from generation to generation. The code is expressed by the molecular configuration of the *chromosomes* of *cells*. Chromosomes consist of *deoxyribonucleic acid* (DNA) and *protein*, the code-bearing material being the DNA. Four different nitrogenous bases (*adenine, cytosine, guanine,* and *thymine*) occur in the *nucleotides* of DNA, and it appears that the sequence of three of these bases constitutes a unit of the genetic code, in that each sequence of three bases codes for one of the twenty different *amino acids* that go to make up the *enzymes* which control the characteristics of a cell. Chromosomes, which almost always exist in the *nuclei* of cells, transfer their coded information to the *cytoplasm* of these cells (where the enzyme proteins are assembled in units called *ribosomes*) by way of a 'messenger' nucleic acid (*ribonucleic acid*).

GENETICS. The study of heredity, variation, development, and *evolution*.

GENOTYPE. 1. The genetic constitution of an individual *organism* or of a well defined group of organisms. 2. A group of organisms which have the same genetic constitution. 3. A typical species of a genus. See also *phenotype*.

GENTIAN VIOLET. A purple dye derived from *aniline*, used as an *indicator*, an *antiseptic*, and a *dye*.

GEOCENTRIC. Having the *Earth* as a centre; measured from the centre of the Earth.

GEOCHEMISTRY. The study of the chemical composition of the *Earth's crust* and the changes which take place within it.

GEODESIC. Pertaining to the *geometry* of curved surfaces. A 'geodesic line', also called a 'geodesic', is the shortest distance between two points on a curved surface.

GEODESY. Surveying on a scale which involves making allowance for the curvature of the *Earth*.

GEOLOGICAL TIME SCALE. Geological periods. A scale of time which serves as a reference for correlating various events in the history of the *Earth*; it has been built up by studying the various strata of rocks which comprise the *Earth's crust* with special reference to the *fossils* found in them. The time scale is divided into three main 'eras', based upon the general character of the life which they contain, each era being sub-divided into 'periods'. The Table below gives the names of these eras and periods, together with their approximate ages.

GEOLOGICAL TIME SCALE

Era		Period	Time Scale millions of years
CENOZOIC	QUATERNARY	Holocene	0·01
		Pleistocene (Glacial)	1
	TERTIARY	Pliocene	10
		Miocene	25
		Oligocene	40
		Eocene	60
		Paleocene	70
MESOZOIC (SECONDARY)		Cretacious	135
		Jurassic	180
		Triassic	225
PALAEOZOIC (PRIMARY)		Permian	270
		Carboniferous	350
		Devonian	400
		Silurian	440
		Ordovician	500
		Cambrian	600
PRE-CAMBRIAN			2000

GEOLOGY. The scientific study of the *Earth's crust*.

GEOMETRIC MEAN. The geometric *mean* of n positive numbers, a, b, c ... is $\sqrt[n]{abc....}$ E.g. the geometric mean of 3 and 12 is 6.

GEOMETRICAL PROGRESSION. A series of quantities in which each term is obtained by multiplying the preceding term by some constant factor, termed the 'common ratio'. E.g. 1, 3, 9, 27, 81 ..., each term being three times the preceding. For a series of n terms, having common ratio r and the first term a, the sum, $S=a(r^n-1)/(r-1)$; or, if r is less than 1, a more convenient expression is $S=a(1-r^n)/(1-r)$.

GEOMETRY. The mathematical study of the properties and relations of lines, surfaces, and solids in space.

GEOPHYSICS. The study of the *Earth* and its *atmosphere* by physical methods. This includes *seismology, meteorology, hydrology, terrestrial magnetism,* etc.

GERANIOL. $C_{10}H_{17}OH$. A *liquid alcohol,* b.p. $107°C$., present either free, or as an *ester,* in many *essential oils.*

GERMAN SILVER. An *alloy* of copper, zinc, and nickel in varying proportions, approximating to 5 parts Cu, 2 of Zn, and 2 of Ni.

GERMANIUM. Ge. Element. A.W. 72·59. At. No. 32. A brittle white *metal.* S.G. 5·35, m.p. $937·4°C$. *Compounds* are rare. Used in the *transistor.*

GERMICIDE. A substance capable of destroying *bacteria.*

GETTER. Vacuum getter. A substance used for removing the last traces of air or other *gases* in attaining a high *vacuum.* E.g. magnesium metal is used in *thermionic valves*; after exhausting and sealing the valve a small amount of magnesium which is left in the valve is vaporized by *heat* and combines chemically with any remaining oxygen and nitrogen.

GeV. Abbreviation for *giga electron-volt,* i.e. 10^9 electron-volts. In America this is usually written BeV where the 'B' represents the American *billion.*

GHOSTS (phys.). False lines appearing in a *line spectrum* due to imperfections in the ruling of the *diffraction grating* used.

GIANT STAR. A *star* possessing high *luminosity,* low *density,* and a diameter 10 to 100 times that of the *Sun.*

GIBBERELLIC ACID. $C_{18}H_{21}O_4COOH$. A white crystalline substance which occurs in certain *fungi* and which is used to stimulate plant growth.

GIBBOUS. The shape of the *Moon* or a *planet* when it is more than half-phase, but less than full phase. (See *phases of the Moon.*)

GIBBS FUNCTION. See *free energy.* Named after Josiah Willard Gibbs (1839–1903).

GIGA-. Prefix denoting a thousand million (10^9). Symbol G.

GILBERT. The *c.g.s. unit* of *magnetomotive force* in *electromagnetic units.* Equal to $\dfrac{10}{4\pi}$ *ampere-turns.* Named after William Gilbert (1540–1603).

GILDING. Covering with a thin layer of metallic gold, often by *electrolysis* (see *electroplating*).

GILL. A unit of capacity equal to one quarter of a *pint.*

GILLION. 10^9, one thousand million.

GILSONITE. A pure form of *asphalt* which occurs in North America; used in *paints* and *varnishes.*

GLACIAL ACETIC ACID. Pure *acetic acid*; *solid* crystalline acetic acid below its *freezing point* ($16·6°C$.).

GLASS. A hard brittle *amorphous mixture,* usually *transparent* or *translucent,* of the *silicates* of calcium, sodium, or other *metals.* Ordinary soda glass is made by melting together sand (*silica*), *sodium carbonate,* and *lime.* Glass for special purposes may contain lead, potassium, barium or other metals in place of the sodium, and *boric oxide* in place of the silica. See *crown glass, flint glass.*

GLASS FIBRE MATERIALS. Fibreglass*. Fine *glass* fibres, usually less than a thousandth of an inch in diameter, which are woven into a cloth and impregnated with various *resins*. Owing to their high *tensile strength* and *corrosion* resistance these materials are used in small-boat building and for some motor-car body parts.

GLASS WOOL. A material consisting of very fine *glass* threads, resembling cotton wool. Used for filtering and absorbing corrosive *liquids*.

GLAUBER'S SALT. Crystalline *sodium sulphate*, $Na_2SO_4.10H_2O$. Named after J. R. Glauber (1604–68).

GLAZE. A *vitreous* covering for pottery, chemically related to *glass*.

GLOBULAR CLUSTERS. Self-contained, approximately spherical clusters of about one hundred thousand *stars*; some hundred of these clusters are known to be distributed about the centre of the *Milky Way*, and although they appear to be outside the *Galaxy*, they are believed to be gravitationally associated with it.

GLOBULINS. Groups of *proteins soluble* in dilute *solutions* of mineral *salts*, such as *sodium chloride*, NaCl; *magnesium sulphate*, $MgSO_4$, etc. Occur in many animal and vegetable *tissues* and fluids; e.g. lactoglobulin in milk, serum globulin in *blood*, vegetable globulins in seeds. Globulins are the main proteins of *antibodies*.

GLOVE BOX. A metal box which provides protection to workers who have to manipulate *radioactive* materials or which enables the manipulation of substances requiring a dust-free, *sterile*, or *inert* atmosphere. Manipulation is carried out by means of gloves fitted to ports in the walls of the box.

GLOW DISCHARGE. A silent discharge of electricity through a *gas* at low *pressure*, usually luminous. See *discharge in gases*.

GLUCINUM. See *beryllium*.

GLUCONIC ACID. $CH_2OH(CHOH)_4COOH$. A colourless *soluble* crystalline substance, m.p. $125°C$., obtained by the *oxidation* of *glucose*. Used for cleaning *metals*.

GLUCOSE. Dextrose, grape-sugar. $C_6H_{12}O_6$. A colourless crystalline *soluble hexose sugar*. M.p. $146°C$. Occurs in honey and sweet fruits. Other sugars and *carbohydrates* are converted into glucose in the human body before being utilized to provide *energy*. Glucose is an *optically active* substance, the naturally occurring sugar invariably being *dextrorotatory* (d-glucose). Commercially prepared from *starch* and other carbohydrates by *hydrolysis*; used in brewing, jam-making, confectionery, etc. The *laevorotatory* form (l-glucose) is rare and does not occur in nature.

GLUCOSIDES. Derivatives of *glucose* in which one hydrogen *atom* in the *molecule* is replaced by an organic *radical*. The term *glycoside* is applied generally to such *compounds* of all *sugars*.

GLUE. A general name for *adhesives*, particularly those made by extracting hides, bones, cartilages, etc., of animals with *water*.

GLUTAMATE. A *salt* or *ester* of *glutamic acid*.

169

GLUTAMIC ACID. A colourless crystalline *amino acid*, m.p. 206°C., used in the form of its sodium *salt* as a flavouring. See Table 5, page 435.

GLUTAMINE. A colourless *soluble amino acid*, m.p. 184–5°C. See Table 5, page 435.

GLUTEN. *Protein* contained in wheat flour (8%–15%).

GLYCERIC ACID. CH₂OH.CHOH.COOH. A colourless syrupy *liquid* obtained by the *oxidation of glycerol*.

GLYCERIDES. *Esters* of *glycerol* with *organic acids*. Animal and vegetable *fats* are mainly composed of triglycerides of *fatty acids*, such as *stearic*, *palmitic*, and *oleic*, a *molecule* of such a triglyceride being derived by the combination of one molecule of glycerol with three fatty acid molecules.

GLYCERIN(E). See *glycerol*.

GLYCEROL. Glycerin(e). CH₂OH.CHOH.CH₂OH. A thick syrupy sweetish *liquid triol soluble* in *water*. B.p. 290°C. Occurs combined with *fatty acids* in *fats and oils*; obtained by the *saponification* of fats in the manufacture of *soap*. Used in the manufacture of *explosives* (see *nitroglycerin*), *plastics*, in pharmacy, and as an *anti-freeze*.

GLYCEROL MONOACETATE. Acetin. CH₃COOC₃H₅(OH)₂. A colourless viscous *hygroscopic liquid*, b.p. 158°C., used in the manufacture of *explosives*.

GLYCERYL GROUP. The *trivalent radical* —CH₂(CH—)CH₂—, derived from *glycerol*.

GLYCINE. Aminoacetic acid, glycocoll. A colourless *soluble* crystalline *amino acid*, m.p. 232°C., used in organic synthesis. See Table 5, page 435.

GLYCOGEN. Animal starch. A complex *carbohydrate* formed from *glucose* and *starch* in the liver and other organs of animals, serving as a *sugar* reserve.

GLYCOL. See *ethanediol*.

GLYCOLIPIDS. Complex *lipids* which consist of *compounds* of *fatty acids* with *carbohydrates*, and which contain nitrogen but no *phosphoric acid*. Found in brain tissues.

GLYCOLS. See *diols*.

GLYCOLYSIS. The conversion of *glucose* into *lactic acid* by a series of *enzyme* catalyzed reactions which occur in living *organisms*.

GLYCOPROTEINS. Glucoproteins. Complex *proteins* which contain *carbohydrates*.

GLYCOSIDES. See *glucosides*.

GLYOXAL. Diformyl. (CHO)₂. A yellow crystalline substance, m.p. 15°C., b.p. 51°C. Used in the manufacture of *plastics*, and in textile finishing.

GLYPTAL RESINS. Alkyd resins. A class of synthetic *resins* obtained by the reaction of *polyhydric alcohols* with *polybasic organic acids* or their *anhydrides*; e.g. *glycerol* and *phthalic anhydride*. Used chiefly for surface coatings.

GNOTOBIOTICS. The study of germ-free life, especially in experimental conditions in which animals are inoculated with specific strains of *micro-organisms*.

GOLD. Au. Element. A.W. 196·967. At. No. 79. A bright yellow rather soft *metal*; m.p. 1063°C. S.G. 19·3. Extremely malleable and ductile. Not corroded by air or *water*; unattacked by most *acids*, but dissolves in *aqua regia*. Occurs mainly as the free metal; most *compounds* are unstable and easily reduced to gold. Extracted from ore and sand by the *amalgamation process* and the *cyanide process*. *Alloys* with copper or silver to give hardness are used for coinage, jewellery, and dentistry. Comp unds are used in *photography* and medicine.

GOLD CHLORIDE. See *auric chloride*.

GOLD LEAF. Gold is the most malleable of *metals*, and can be beaten into leaves 0·0001 mm thick (i.e. 254 000 thicknesses to the inch). The leaf has the appearance of metallic gold, but transmits green *light*; i.e. appears green when held up to the light.

GOLD-LEAF ELECTROSCOPE. See *electroscope*.

GOLDSCHMIDT PROCESS. The preparation of *metals* from their *oxides* by the *thermit* method.

GONIOMETER. An instrument for the measurement of *angles* (of *crystals*).

GOOCH CRUCIBLE. A laboratory *filter* consisting of a shallow *porcelain* cup, the flat bottom of which is perforated with small holes over which a layer of *asbestos* fibres is placed.

GOVERNOR. A device for regulating the speed of an *engine* or machine, on the principle of negative *feedback*, so that its speed is kept constant under all conditions of loading. Often achieved by controlling the *fuel* consumption, so that a rise in speed is arranged to reduce the fuel intake and a fall in speed to increase it.

GRADIENT. The degree of inclination of a slope, usually expressed as unit rise in height per number of units covered along the slope; i.e. the sine of the angle of rise (see *trigonometrical ratios*). Mathematically, the gradient is the ratio of the vertical distance to horizontal distance, i.e. the tangent of the angle. For small gradients the difference between the sine and the tangent is small.

GRADUATION. The marking that indicates the scale of an instrument, e.g. the stem of a *thermometer* is graduated in *degrees*.

GRAHAM'S LAW of gaseous diffusion. The velocity of *diffusion* of a *gas* is inversely proportional to the square root of its *density*. Named after Thomas Graham (1805–69).

GRAIN. British unit of *weight*. 1/7000 of a pound; 0·0648 g.

GRAM. GRAMME. One of the *fundamental units* of measurement in the *c.g.s. system* of units. Unit of *mass*, 1/1000 of the mass of the International Prototype *Kilogramme*, a platinum-iridium standard preserved in Paris. Symbol g.

GRAM WEIGHT. A unit of *force*, the pull of the Earth on the *gram* mass, varies slightly in different localities, depending on the value of *g*, the *acceleration due to gravity* at the given place. Force expressed in grams weight = force in *dynes* divided by the appropriate value of *g* at the place under consideration. A force of 1 gram weight = approx. 981 dynes. 1 g = 0·0353 oz; 453·6 g = 1 lb.

GRAM-ATOM. The *atomic weight* of an *element* expressed in *grams*; e.g. 32 g of sulphur. See *mole*.

GRAM-EQUIVALENT. The equivalent weight in *grams*. See *chemical equivalents*.

GRAM-ION. The sum of the *atomic weights* of the *atoms* in an *ion* (see *electrolysis*) expressed in *grams*.

GRAM-MOLECULAR VOLUME. The *volume* occupied by one *gram-molecule* of a gas. Approximately the same for all gases under the same conditions of *temperature* and *pressure*; at a pressure of 760 mm and 0°C., equal to 22·415 *litres* for a *perfect gas*.

GRAM-MOLECULE. Gram-molecular weight, mole, mol. The *molecular weight* of a *compound* expressed in *grams*. E.g. 18 g of *water*.

GRAM'S METHOD. A method of staining and classifying *bacteria* in which *gentian violet* is used to stain a bacterial smear. If the bacteria retain the violet dye, after washing with a *solution* of iodine and *potassium iodide* in water (Gram's solution) and counterstaining with safranine, they are said to be 'gram positive'. If they do not retain the dye they are said to be 'gram negative'. Named after Hans Gram (1853–1938).

GRANITE. A heterogenous *mixture* of *felspar*, *quartz*, and *mica*.

GRAPE SUGAR. See *glucose*.

GRAPH. A diagram, generally plotted between axes at right angles to each other, showing the relation of one *variable* quantity to another. E.g. the variation of rainfall with time, or the variation in the value of a mathematical *function* as different values are assigned to one of the variables in the function.

-GRAPH. A suffix applied to instruments which automatically record or write down observations; e.g. *barograph*.

GRAPHITE. Blacklead, plumbago. A natural *allotropic form* of carbon, used for pencil leads, in electrical apparatus, and as a lubricant for heavy machinery. Also used as a *moderator* in *nuclear reactors*.

GRAPHITE-MODERATED REACTOR. See *nuclear reactor*.

GRATICULE. 1. A scale, or network of fine wires, in the *eye-piece* of a *telescope* or *microscope*. 2. A network of parallel lines (longitudinal and latitudinal) on a map.

GRATING. See *diffraction grating*.

GRAVIMETRIC ANALYSIS. A branch of *quantitative chemical analysis*. The amount of a substance present is determined by converting it, by a suitable *chemical reaction*, into some other substance of known chemical composition, which can be readily isolated, purified, and weighed.

GRAVITATION, NEWTON'S LAW OF. Every particle in the *Universe* attracts every other particle with a *force* which is directly proportional to the product of the *masses* of the particles and inversely proportional to the square of the distance between them. Thus, the force of attraction between two masses m_1 and m_2, in *kilograms* separated by a distance of s *metres*, is given by $F = \dfrac{Gm_1m_2}{s^2}$ *newtons*, where G is the gravitational constant, $6\cdot670 \times 10^{-11}$ newton metre^2/kilograms^2.

GRAVITATIONAL FIELD. The region in which one massive body (i.e. a body which possesses the attribute of *mass*) exerts a *force* of attraction on another massive body.

GRAVITATIONAL MASS. See *inertial mass*.

GRAVITON. A hypothetical particle or *quantum* of gravitational *energy* (see *gravitation*) which has not yet been observed. If it exists it is expected to have zero *rest mass* and *charge*, and *spin* 2.

GRAVITY. The gravitational *force* (see *gravitation*) between the *Earth* (or other *planet* or *satellite*) and a body on its surface, or within its *gravitational field*. As gravity is proportional to the *mass* of the planet or satellite and inversely proportional to the square of the distance from its centre, the gravity on a planet or satellite in terms of the Earth's gravity is given by: $\dfrac{1}{M_p} \cdot \dfrac{d_p^2}{d_e^2}$, where M_p is the mass of the planet in Earth masses, and d_p and d_e are the diameters of the planet and Earth respectively. Substituting the relevant figures from Table 4, page 434, will show that gravity on the surface of the *Moon* is $\frac{1}{6}$ that on the surface of the Earth.

Gravity is responsible for the *weight* of a body; the weight of a body is the gravitational force of attraction which the Earth exerts on that body. It is equal to the mass of the body multiplied by the *acceleration due to gravity*. Gravity causes bodies to fall to Earth with a uniform acceleration, but the magnitude of the acceleration due to gravity varies with geographical location and altitude. Gravity is reduced to a very small extent by the *centrifugal force* caused by the Earth's rotation (for an object at rest on its surface). In order to stay in *orbit* round the Earth (or other planet or satellite), an orbiting body has to achieve a *velocity* which will produce a centrifugal force which exactly balances the force of gravity.

GREASE. A semi-solid lubricant composed of emulsified *petroleum* oils and *soluble hydrocarbon soaps*.

GREAT CIRCLE. A circle obtained by cutting a *sphere* by a *plane* passing through the centre. E.g. regarding the Earth as a sphere, the *Equator* is a great circle, as are all the *meridians* of longitude. On the Earth's surface, an apparent straight line joining any two points is an arc of a great circle, i.e. a *geodesic*.

GREEK FIRE. A mixture of materials which caught fire when wetted; used by the ancient Greeks in naval warfare. Probably composed of sulphur, *naphtha*, and *calcium oxide* or similar materials.

GREENOCKITE. See *cadmium sulphide*.

GREEN VITRIOL. Copperas. *Ferrous sulphate crystals*, $FeSO_4.7H_2O$.

GREGORIAN TELESCOPE. A form of astronomical reflecting *telescope* similar to a *Cassegranian telescope* in that a hole in the centre of the parabolic primary *mirror* allows *light* to pass to the *eye-piece*, but in the Gregorian telescope the secondary mirror is *concave* rather than *convex*. Although this type of telescope gives an erect image it is not now widely used as it is difficult to adjust. Named after James Gregory (1638–75). See Fig. 17.

GREGORIAN TELESCOPE

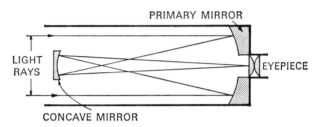

FIGURE 17.

GRID. 1. See *control grid*. 2. A system of *high tension* cables (overhead or underground) by which electrical power is distributed throughout a country. 3. A network of horizontal and vertical lines superimposed on a map to enable references to be given.

GRID BIAS. A fixed *voltage* applied between the *cathode* and the *control grid* of a *thermionic valve* which determines its operating conditions.

GRIGNARD REAGENTS. *Alkyl* magnesium *halides*, prepared by the action of magnesium metal on alkyl halides in *ether* solution; e.g. C_2H_5MgI. Used in organic *synthesis*. Named after François A. V. Grignard (1871–1935).

GROUND STATE. The most stable *energy* state of a *nucleus, atom,* or *molecule*. The normal state of an atom when its circum-nuclear *electrons* move in *orbits* such that the energy of the atom is a minimum. See *atom, structure of*.

GROUND WAVES. Direct waves. *Electromagnetic radiations* of *radio frequencies* which travel more or less directly from transmitting *aerial* to receiving aerial, that is without reflection from the *ionosphere*. See *sky waves*.

GRÜNEISEN'S LAW. The ratio of the coefficient of *expansion* of a *metal* to its *specific heat capacity* at constant pressure is a constant at all *temperatures*.

GUAIACOL. Methyl catechol. $CH_3OC_6H_4OH$. A yellowish crystalline substance, m.p. 28·6°C., b.p. 205°C., used in medicine as a local *anaesthetic*.

GUANIDINE. $HN:C(NH_2)_2$. A strongly *basic, water soluble,* crystalline *organic compound*, used in the manufacture of *plastics, explosives*, and rubber *accelerators*.

GUANINE. 2-aminohypoxanthine. $C_5H_5N_5O$. A colourless *insoluble* crystalline substance; one of the four nitrogenous bases occurring in the *nucleotides* of *nucleic acids* which plays a part in the formulation of the *genetic code*.

GUANO. Large deposits formed from the excrement and bodies of seabirds. Found on islands off the coast of Peru. Very rich in nitrogen and phosphorus *compounds*; valuable *fertilizer*.

GUIDED MISSILE. A missile (usually *rocket* propelled) whose flight path can be controlled during flight either by *radio* signals from an external source or by internal homing devices (pre-set or self-actuating). See *beam riding, command guidance, field guidance, homing guidance, inertial guidance, terrestrial guidance*.

GUM ARABIC. Gum Acacia. A *water soluble*, yellowish *gum* obtained from certain varieties of acacia. Used in food and pharmaceutical products and as an *adhesive*.

GUMS. A general name applied to a large class of substances of vegetable origin, usually exuded from plants.

GUN-COTTON. *Cellulose nitrate*, nitrocellulose. A powerful *explosive* formed by the action of *nitric acid* on *cellulose*.

GUN-METAL. A variety of *bronze* containing about 90% copper, 8%–10% tin, and up to 4% zinc.

GUNPOWDER. A *mixture* of *potassium nitrate*, KNO_3, powdered *charcoal*, and sulphur. When ignited, a number of *chemical reactions* take place, evolving *gases*, thus producing an *explosion* in a confined space.

GUTTA-PERCHA. A material very similar to *rubber*, obtained from the *latex* of certain Malayan trees; chemically, the *trans-form* of *polyisoprene*. A horny substance at ordinary temperatures; it is *thermoplastic* and at about 70° C. resembles unvulcanized rubber. Used for golf ball covers.

GYPSUM. Natural *hydrated calcium sulphate*, $CaSO_4.2H_2O$, which loses three quarters of its *water of crystallization* when heated to 120° C., becoming *Plaster of Paris*.

GYRATION. Motion round a fixed *axis* or centre.

GYRO-COMPASS. Gyroscopic compass. A compass which does not make use of *magnetism*, and is therefore not affected by magnetic storms, etc.; consists of a universally-mounted spinning wheel which has a rigidity of direction of axis and plane of rotation relative to space; the rotation being electrically maintained. See *gyroscope*.

GYROMAGNETIC RATIO. The ratio of the *magnetic moment* of an *atom* or *nucleus* to its *angular momentum*.

GYROSCOPE. A spinning wheel which is mounted in such a way that it is free to rotate about any axis; i.e. 'universally mounted'. Such a wheel has two properties upon which applications of the gyroscope depend – namely, 1. Rigidity in space (gyroscopic inertia); the support of the wheel may be turned in any direction without altering the direction of the wheel relative to space. 2. Precession. When a gyroscope is subjected to a *force* tending to alter the direction of its axis, the wheel will turn about an axis at right angles to the axis about which the force was applied.

H

HABER PROCESS. An industrial preparation of *ammonia*, for use in *fertilizers*, from atmospheric nitrogen. See *fixation of atmospheric nitrogen*. A heated mixture of nitrogen and hydrogen is passed over a *catalyst* under *pressure*; the *gases* combine to form ammonia gas according to the equation $N_2 + 3H_2 = 2NH_3$. Named after Fritz Haber (1868–1934).

HAEMATITE. Natural *ferric oxide*, Fe_2O_3. A valuable *ore* of iron.

HAEMATOLOGY. The study of *blood*, its constituents, and the diseases connected with it.

HAEMOCYTE. A *blood cell*.

HAEMOGLOBIN. Red colouring matter (respiratory pigment) present in the red *blood cells*; consists of a *protein*, *globin*, combined with a *prosthetic group*, *haem*, the latter being a highly complex *organic compound* containing iron, nitrogen, carbon, hydrogen, and oxygen. Serves to carry oxygen, which is breathed in, round the body in the form of an easily decomposed compound, *oxy-haemoglobin*.

HAFNIUM. Celtium. Hf. Element. A.W. 178·49. At. No. 72. A rare *metal*, S.G. 13·3, m.p. 2150° C. Used in the manufacture of tungsten *filaments*.

HAIR SALT. Natural *aluminium sulphate*, $Al_2(SO_4)_3.18H_2O$.

HALF-LIFE. Half-value period. The time taken for the *activity* of a *radioactive isotope* to *decay* to half of its original value, that is for half of the *atoms* present to disintegrate. Half-lives vary from isotope to isotope, some being less than a millionth of a second and some more than a million years. Symbol $t_\frac{1}{2}$.

HALF-PERIOD ZONES. The division of a *wave front* into elements of area or zones such that secondary wavelets (see *Huygens' construction*) reaching a given point ahead of the wave from adjacent zones differ in *phase* by half a period, or π. This construction is used in theoretical investigations of *Fresnel diffraction* in simple cases.

HALF-THICKNESS. Half value layer. The thickness of a specified material which, when introduced into the path of a given beam of *radiation*, reduces its intensity to one half of its original value.

HALF-WAVE PLATE. A plate of double refracting material (see *double refraction*) cut parallel to the *optic axis* and of such a thickness that a *phase* difference of π or 180° is introduced between the *ordinary ray* and the extraordinary ray for *light* of a particular *wavelength* (usually sodium light). The half-wave plate is chiefly used to alter the plane of vibration of plane-polarized light. See *polarization of light*.

HALIDE. A *binary compound* of one of the *halogen elements* (fluorine, chlorine, bromine, or iodine); a *salt* of the *hydride* of one of these elements.

HALL EFFECT. If an *electric current* flows in a wire placed in a strong transverse *magnetic field*, a *potential difference* is developed across the wire, at right angles to both the magnetic field and the wire. Named after Edwin H. Hall (1855–1938).

HALL MOBILITY. Drift mobility. The mobility of *carriers* in a *semiconductor*; numerically the *velocity* of the carriers under the influence of an *electric field* of 1 *volt* per *metre*.

HALLEY'S COMET. A bright *comet* that takes about 76 years to *orbit* the *Sun*; last seen in 1910 it is next due to be visible in 1986. Named after Edmund Halley (1656–1742) who first calculated its orbit.

HALO. A luminous ring sometimes observed surrounding the *Sun* or the *Moon*. Caused by the *refraction* of *light* by *ice crystals* in the *atmosphere*.

HALOGENATION. The introduction of *halogen atoms* into a *compound* by addition or substitution.

HALOGENS. The four *elements* fluorine, chlorine, bromine, and iodine, having closely related and graded properties. (Astatine is also a member of the halogen group, but it has no stable *isotopes*.)

HAPLOID. Having a set of single (unpaired) *chromosomes*; e.g. *gametes*.

HARD RADIATION. See *soft radiation*.

HARD WATER. *Water* which does not form an immediate lather with *soap*, owing to the presence of calcium, magnesium, and iron *compounds* dissolved in the water. The addition of soap produces an *insoluble* scum consisting of *salts* of these *metals* with the *fatty acids* of the soap, until no more is left in *solution*. Removal of these salts from solution renders the water soft. Hardness is divided into two types: 1. Temporary hardness, due to hydrogen carbonates (*bicarbonates*) of the metals. These enter the water by the passage of the water, containing dissolved *carbon dioxide*, over *solid carbonates* (*chalk* or *limestone* deposits, etc.). Such hardness is removed by *boiling*, the soluble bicarbonates being decomposed into the insoluble carbonates (see *fur in kettles*), carbon dioxide and water. 2. Permanent hardness, due to *sulphates* of the metals. This is destroyed by the addition of washing-soda, *sodium carbonate*, which precipitates the insoluble carbonates. All hardness may be destroyed by the use of *zeolites*.

HARDENING OF FATS. The conversion of *liquid fats* (oils) consisting mainly of *triolen* into hard fats by the action of hydrogen in the presence of a *catalyst*. See *hydrogenation of oils*.

HARDWARE. See *software*.

HARMONIC MOTION. See *simple harmonic motion*.

HARMONIC SERIES (math.). A *series* in which the *reciprocals* of the terms are in *arithmetical progression*. E.g. $1 + \frac{1}{2} + \frac{1}{3} + \frac{1}{4} \ldots$

HARMONICS OF A WAVE MOTION. Waves superimposed on a fundamental wave, having a *frequency* which is a whole multiple of the fundamental frequency. The second harmonic has a frequency twice that of the fundamental, the third harmonic three times, and so on.

HARTSHORN, SPIRITS OF. A *solution* of *ammonia* in *water*.

HEALTH PHYSICS. The branch of *physics* which deals with the effects of *ionizing radiation* on living *organisms*, with particular reference to the protection of humans from the ill-effects caused thereby.

HEAT. *Energy* possessed by a substance in the form of *kinetic energy* of atomic or molecular translation, rotation, or vibration. The heat contained by a body is the product of its *mass*, its *temperature*, and its *specific heat capacity*; it is expressed in *joules* (*SI units*), *calories* (*c.g.s. units*) or *British Thermal Units* (*f.p.s. units*). Heat is transmitted by *conduction*, *convection*, and *radiation*. The chief observable physical effects of a change in the heat content of a body may include rise in temperature; change of state from *solid* to *liquid* (melting), solid to *gas* (sublimation) and liquid to gas (*evaporation* and *boiling*); *expansion*; and electrical effects such as the *Peltier* and *Seebeck effects*.

HEAT CAPACITY. *C*. When the *temperature* of a system is increased by an amount dT as a consequence of the addition of a small quantity of *heat* dQ, the quantity dQ/dT is called the heat capacity. In practice, the heat in *joules* required to raise the temperature of a body or system by 1 K. See *specific heat capacity* and *molar heat capacity*.

HEAT DEATH OF THE UNIVERSE. The second law of thermodynamics (see *thermodynamics, laws of*) can be interpreted to mean that the *entropy* of a closed system tends towards a maximum and that its available *energy* tends towards a minimum. It has been held that the *Universe* constitutes a thermodynamically closed system, and if this were true it would mean that a time must finally come when the Universe 'unwinds' itself, no energy being available for use. This state is referred to as the 'heat death of the Universe'. It is by no means certain, however, that the Universe can be considered as a closed system in this sense.

HEAT EXCHANGER. Any device which transfers *heat* from one *fluid* to another without allowing the fluids to come into contact with each other. The simplest type consists of a cylinder within which a coiled tube is mounted. One fluid passes through the coiled tube in one direction, while the other fluid passes through the cylinder, outside the tube, in the other direction.

HEAT OF COMBUSTION. The amount of *heat* evolved by 1 *mole* of a substance when it is burned in oxygen.

HEAT OF FORMATION. The quantity of *heat* (usually expressed in *joules* or *calories*) liberated or absorbed when 1 *mole* of a *compound* is formed from its *elements* in their normal state. The heat of formation of elements is, for the purpose of thermochemical calculations, taken as zero. See *Hess's law*.

HEAT OF NEUTRALIZATION. The quantity of *heat* evolved when 1 *mole* of an *acid* or *base* is exactly neutralized. For all strong acids or bases, its value is approximately 57 500 *joules* (13 700 *calories*).

HEAT OF REACTION. The quantity of *heat* given out or absorbed in a *chemical reaction*, usually per *mole* of reacting substances. See *Hess's law*.

HEAT OF SOLUTION. The quantity of *heat* evolved or absorbed when 1 *mole* of a substance is dissolved in a large volume of *water*.

HEAT PUMP. A machine for extracting *heat* from a *fluid* which is at a slightly higher *temperature* than its surroundings. For example, the rivers flowing through industrial towns are often slightly warmer than the ambient temperature as a result of the disposal of hot effluents in them. A heat pump can be used to raise the temperature of this 'low temperature heat', so that it can be usefully employed.

HEAT RADIATION. See *infrared radiation*.

HEAT SHIELD. The shielding surface or structure which protects a *spacecraft* from excessive heating on re-entering the *Earth's* atmosphere. (See *re-entry*.)

HEAVISIDE-KENNELLY LAYER. A region of the *ionosphere*, between 90 and 150 kilometres above the surface of the *Earth* (for more recent designation of layers see *ionosphere*) which reflects *electromagnetic radiation* of *radio frequencies*. Inter-continental radio transmission, round the curved surface of the Earth, is possible because of the reflection of *sky-waves* by the Heaviside-Kennelly layer. Named after Oliver Heaviside (1850–1925) and Arthur Kennelly (1861–1939).

HEAVY HYDROGEN. See *deuterium*.

HEAVY SPAR. See *barytes*.

HEAVY WATER. Deuterium Oxide. D_2O. *Water* in which the hydrogen is replaced by *deuterium*. Present in natural water to the extent of about 1 part in 5000. Pure heavy water has S.G. 1·1, f.p. 3·82°C., b.p. 101·42°C. The term is also used when referring to water which contains appreciably more D_2O or HDO than natural water. Heavy water is used as a *moderator* in some *nuclear reactors*.

HECTARE. Metric unit of area; 10 000 square *metres*, 2·47105 *acres*.

HECTO-. Prefix denoting one hundred times. Symbol h.

HEISENBERG'S UNCERTAINTY PRINCIPLE. See *uncertainty principle*.

HELIOCENTRIC. Having the *Sun* as a centre; measured from the centre of the Sun.

HELIUM. He. Element. A.W. 4·0026. At. No. 2. An *inert gas* which occurs in certain *natural gases* in the U.S.A., occluded in *radioactive ores* (e.g. *monazite*, *pitchblende*) and in the *atmosphere* (1 part in 200,000). Non-inflammable, very light, valuable for filling airships and balloons.

HELIX. A spiral. Many large natural *molecules* (e.g. *proteins* and *nucleic acids*) are helical in shape.

HELMHOLTZ FREE ENERGY. See *free energy*. Named after Hermann von Helmholtz (1821–94).

HEMICELLULOSES. A group of *carbohydrates* which on *hydrolysis* with dilute mineral *acids* yield *monosaccharides*. Found in *cell* walls of plants where they function as reserve food materials, especially in seeds.

HEMIMORPHITE. Natural *zinc silicate*, $2ZnO.SiO_2.H_2O$.

HENRY. The derived *SI unit* of self- and mutual inductance (see *self-induction, mutual induction*). An inductance in a closed *circuit* such that a rate of change of current of 1 *ampere* per second produces an induced *E.M.F.* of 1 *volt*. Symbol H. Named after Joseph Henry (1797–1878).

HENRY'S LAW. The *weight* of a *gas* dissolved by a definite *volume* of *liquid* at constant *temperature* is directly proportional to the *pressure*. From this it follows that the volume of a gas absorbed by a given volume of liquid at constant temperature is independent of the pressure. The law holds only for sparingly *soluble* gases at low pressures. Named after William Henry (1774–1836).

HEPARIN. A complex *organic acid* related to the *polysaccharides* but containing sulphur and nitrogen, which prevents the clotting of *blood* by interfering with the formation, and action, of *thrombin*. Used as an anti-coagulent.

HEPTA-. Prefix meaning seven.

HEPTANE. C_7H_{16}. The seventh member of the *paraffin series*, which exists in nine isomeric forms (see *isomerism*). Contained in light *petroleum*; normal-heptane has b.p. 98·4°C. and S.G. 0·68.

HEPTAVALENT. Septivalent. Having a *valency* of seven.

HERTZ. The derived *SI unit* of *frequency* defined as the frequency of a periodic phenomenon of which the periodic time is one *second*; equal to 1 *cycle* per second. Symbol Hz. 1 kilohertz (kHz) = 10^3 cycles per second; 1 megahertz (MHz) = 10^6 cycles per second. Named after Heinrich Hertz (1857–94).

HERTZIAN WAVES. Wireless waves, *radio* waves. *Electromagnetic radiation* covering a range of *frequency* from above 3×10^{10} *hertz*, corresponding to the shortest *radar* waves of 1 cm, to below $1·5 \times 10^5$ *hertz*, corresponding to long radio waves of 2000 metres.

HERTZPRUNG-RUSSELL DIAGRAM. H-R diagram. A method of correlating data concerning *stars*. Consists of a *graph* in which the absolute *luminosity* of a star is plotted against its spectral type (obtained by examining the *spectra* of stars and arranging them in a sequence which reflects increasing *temperature*). This graph is thus essentially a plot of total *energy* output against surface temperature. The outstanding feature of this type of diagram is that most stars are concentrated in a narrow band running across the diagram: the stars at the upper end of the band are hot, bright, and bluish-white, while those at the lower end are cooler, dimmer, and reddish in colour. This band is called the 'main sequence' and stars which fall on it are called main sequence stars. It is mainly from H-R diagrams that the theory of *stellar evolution* has been derived. Named after Ejnar Hertzprung (b. 1873) and Henry N. Russell (1897–1957).

HESS'S LAW. If a *chemical reaction* is carried out in stages, the algebraic sum of the amounts of *heat* evolved in the separate stages is equal to the total amount of heat evolved when the reaction occurs directly; a consequence of the law of *conservation of energy* as applied to *thermochemistry*. Named after G. H. Hess (1802–50).

HETERO-. Prefix denoting other, different.

HETEROCYCLIC COMPOUNDS. *Organic compounds* containing a ring structure of *atoms* in the *molecule*, the ring including atoms of *elements* other than carbon. E.g. pyridine, C_5H_5N, having a *molecule* consisting of 5 carbon atoms and 1 nitrogen atom in a closed ring, with a hydrogen atom attached to each carbon atom.

HETERODYNE. A beat effect (see *beats*) produced by superimposing two waves of different *frequency*. Used extensively in *radio* receivers in which the received wave is combined with a wave (of slightly different frequency to the *carrier wave*) generated within the receiver. The two combining waves produce an *intermediate frequency* which is amplified and then *demodulated*. See *superheterodyne*.

HETEROGENEOUS. Not of a uniform composition; showing different properties in different portions.

HETERO-POLAR BOND. An electrovalent bond. See *valency, electronic theory of*.

HEURISTIC. Adjective describing the method of solving mathematical problems for which no *algorithm* exists: involves the narrowing down of the field of search for a solution by inductive reasoning from past experience of similar problems.

HEUSLER'S ALLOYS. *Alloys* containing neither iron, nickel, nor cobalt which exhibit strong *ferromagnetism*. Composed of copper, manganese, and aluminium. Named after Conrad Heusler.

HEXA-. Prefix denoting six; six times.

HEXADECANE. Cetane. $C_{16}H_{34}$. A colourless *liquid paraffin hydrocarbon*, m.p. 18°C., b.p. 287°C. Used as a *solvent* and in the determination of *cetane numbers*.

HEXADECANOL. Cetyl alcohol. $C_{16}H_{33}OH$. A white crystalline *insoluble solid*, m.p. 50°C., used in cosmetics and in pharmaceutical products.

HEXAMINE. Hexamethylenetetramine, urotropine. $(CH_2)_6N_4$. A white crystalline substance obtained by the *condensation* of *ammonia* with *formaldehyde*. Used in medicine, in the manufacture of vulcanized *rubber*, and in the manufacture of *cyclonite*.

HEXANE. C_6H_{14}. The sixth member of the *paraffin series* which exists in five isomeric forms (see *isomerism*). Contained in light *petroleum*; normal-hexane has b.p. 69°C. and S.G. 0·66.

HEXANOIC ACID. Caproic acid. $CH_3(CH_2)_4COOH$. An oily *liquid*, b.p. 205°C., with a cheese-like odour. Used in flavouring agents.

HEXAVALENT. Sexivalent. Having a *valency* of six.

HEXOGEN. See *cyclonite*.

HEXOSE. A *monosaccharide carbohydrate* whose *molecule* contains six carbon *atoms*, e.g. the *sugars glucose, fructose*, and *galactose*. Naturally occurring *polysaccharides* are usually made up of hexose units.

HEXYL GROUP. Any of the five *isomeric univalent radicals* C_6H_{13}—.

HEXYLRESORCINOL. $C_6H_{13}C_6H_3(OH)_2$. A yellow crystalline *solid*, m.p. 60°C., used as an *antiseptic* and in medicine.

HIGH FIDELITY. See *fidelity*.

HIGH FREQUENCY. HF. *Radio frequencies* between 3000 and 30 000 kilo*hertz*. See Table 10, page 442.

HIGH-FREQUENCY WELDING. Radio-frequency welding. A method of welding *thermoplastic* materials in which the *heat* required to fuse the surfaces together is generated by the application of *radio frequency electromagnetic radiation.*

HIGH-SPEED STEEL. A very hard *steel* containing 12%–22% tungsten, with chromium, vanadium, molybdenum, and small amounts of other *elements*; used for tools which remain hard even at red heat.

HIGH TENSION. High *voltage.*

HISTAMINE. $C_3H_3N_2.(CH_2)_2NH_2$. A white crystalline substance, m.p. 86°C., which occurs in animal *tissues* when they are injured and as part of the allergic reaction, causing dilation of blood vessels; also stimulates gastric secretion of *hydrochloric acid.*

HISTIDINE. A crystalline *soluble amino acid*, which occurs in fish and from which *histamine* is manufactured. See Table 5, page 435.

HISTOGRAM. A type of graphical representation, used in *statistics*, in which frequency distributions are illustrated by rectangles.

HISTOLOGY. The study of the structure of the *tissues* and organs of living creatures.

HODOSCOPE. An apparatus for tracing the path of a charged particle (usually a *cosmic-ray* particle).

HOLE. The absence of an *electron* in the *valency* structure (see *energy bands*) of a crystalline *semiconductor*. The filling of these vacancies by electrons, which thereby creates new holes, gives rise to 'hole conduction'. A hole may, therefore, be regarded as a mobile vacancy with a positive *electronic charge* and a positive *mass*; it is thus mathematically equivalent to a *positron.*

HOLMIUM. Ho. Element. A.W. 164·93. At. No. 67. S.G. 8·803, m.p. 1461°C. See *lanthanides.*

HOLO-. Prefix denoting whole-; e.g. holohedral *crystal*, a crystal having the full number of faces for perfect symmetry.

HOLOGRAM. The intermediate photographic record which contains the information for reproducing a three-dimensional image by *holography.*

HOLOGRAPHY. A method of reproducing three-dimensional images without *cameras* or *lenses* using photographic *film* and *coherent light*. A beam of coherent light from a *laser* is split in two by a semi-transparent mirror, so that one beam (the signal beam) can be *diffracted* by the object to be reproduced onto a photographic film or plate. The other beam (the reference beam) falls directly onto the film or plate (see Fig. 18a). The two beams form *interference* patterns on the plate thus forming the *hologram*. The fine speckled pattern on the plate contains information characteristic of the *wave fronts* themselves, rather than of the light intensities as in normal *photography*. To reproduce the image the hologram is illuminated by coherent light (usually of the same *wavelength* as the original beam). The hologram acts as a *diffraction grating* and produces two sets of diffracted waves which form equal angles with the plate (see Fig. 18b). One set of waves forms a *real image* on a screen or photographic plate, while the other forms a three-dimensional *virtual image*.

FIGURE 18a.

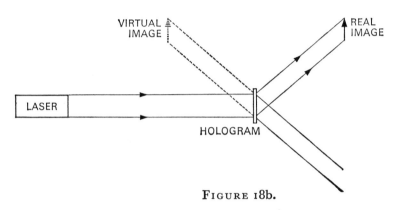

FIGURE 18b.

HOMEOMORPHOUS. Having the same crystalline form but different chemical composition.

HOMING GUIDANCE. A method of missile or *rocket* guidance in which the missile contains equipment enabling it to detect and steer itself onto its target.

HOMO-. Prefix denoting same-; e.g. *homogeneous*.

HOMOCYCLIC COMPOUNDS. *Organic compounds* the *molecules* of which contain a ring structure of *atoms* of the same kind (usually carbon). E.g. *benzene*, C_6H_6.

HOMOGENEOUS. Of uniform composition throughout.

HOMOLOGOUS PAIR. In *spectrographic analysis* an homologous pair consists of the particular spectral line (see *line spectrum*) utilized in the determination of the *concentration* of an *element* and an *internal standard line*, such that the ratio of the intensities of the *radiations* producing the lines remains unchanged with variations in the conditions of *excitation*.

HOMOLOGOUS SERIES. A series of chemical *compounds* of uniform chemical type, showing a regular gradation in physical properties, and capable of being represented by a general *molecular formula*, the *molecule* of each member of the series differing from the preceding one by a definite constant group of *atoms*. E.g. the *paraffin series*.

HOMOLOGUES. Members of the same *homologous series*; e.g. methane, CH_4, and *ethane*, C_2H_6.

HOMO-POLAR BOND. A covalent bond. See *valency, electronic theory of*.

HOOKE'S LAW. Within the *elastic limit*, a *strain* is proportional to the *stress* producing it. 'Ut tensio, sic vis.' See *elasticity, elastic modulus*. Named after Robert Hooke (1635–1703).

HORIZONTAL INTENSITY of the Earth's magnetic field (see *magnetism, terrestrial*). The total *magnetic intensity* of the Earth's field may be resolved into two components, the horizontal and the vertical. If $I=$ total intensity and θ the angle of dip (see *magnetic dip*) the horizontal intensity, $H = I \cos \theta$.

HORMONES. Specific substances produced by the *endocrine glands* of higher animals, which are secreted into the *blood* and which are thus carried to all parts of the body where they regulate many metabolic functions of the *organism*. They are quick-acting and only a minute amount may have a profound effect on *metabolism*. Hormones are either *proteins* (e.g. *insulin*), *steroids* (e.g. *cortisone*), or relatively simple *organic compounds* (e.g. *adrenaline*).

HORN SILVER. Cerargyrite, chlorargyrite. Natural *silver chloride*, AgCl. An important *ore* of silver.

HORNBLENDE. A rock-forming *mineral* consisting mainly of *silicates* of calcium, magnesium, and iron.

HORSEPOWER. h.p. British unit of *power*; *work* done at the rate of 550 *foot-pounds* per second. 1 h.p. = 745·7 *watts*.

HOT-WIRE INSTRUMENT. An electrical measuring instrument (*ammeter* or *voltmeter*) which depends upon the expansion, or change in *resistance*, of a wire which is heated by the passage of an *electric current*.

HUBBLE'S CONSTANT. The ratio of the distance between the *Local Group of galaxies* and a receding cluster of galaxies (see *expansion of the Universe*) to the rate at which the distant cluster recedes. The Hubble Constant therefore represents the hypothetical period of time since all the matter in the Universe was located in one 'super-dense' agglomeration, if it is assumed that its rate of expansion has been constant over this period. The value of Hubble's Constant is variously estimated as being between 5 and 10 thousand million years. Named after Edwin Hubble (1889–1953).

HUMIDITY OF THE ATMOSPHERE. A measure of the *water vapour* present in the air. It may be given in terms of *relative humidity*, or the *absolute humidity*.

HUMUS. Dark brown *colloidal* matter present in *soil* as the result of animal and vegetable *decomposition*. Important source of mineral nutrients for plants.

HUYGENS' CONSTRUCTION. Each point of a *wave front* may be regarded as a new source of secondary wavelets. Knowing the position of the wave front at any given time, the construction enables its position to be determined at any subsequent time. Named after Christian Huygens (1629–95).

HUYGENS' PRINCIPLE OF SUPERPOSITION. The resultant displacement at any point due to the superposition of any system of waves is equal to the sum of the displacements of the individual waves at that point. This principle forms the basis of the theory of *light interference*.

HYDRARGYRUM. See *mercury*.

HYDRATE. A *compound* containing combined *water*. Generally applied to *salts* containing *water of crystallization*.

HYDRATED. The opposite of *anhydrous*; containing chemically combined *water*; (*salt*) containing *water of crystallization*.

HYDRAULIC CEMENT. *Cement* which hardens in contact with *water*.

HYDRAULIC PRESS. An application of *Pascal's law*; a device whereby a *force* applied by a piston over a small area is transmitted through *water* to another piston having a large area; by this means very great forces may be obtained. See Fig. 19.

1 NEWTON

50 cm²

50 N

UNIFORM PRESSURE
1 N per cm²

1 cm²

FIGURE 19.

HYDRAULICS. The practical application of *hydrodynamics* to engineering.

HYDRAZINE. $H_2N.NH_2$. A fuming strongly *basic liquid*, b.p. 113° C., a powerful *reducing agent*. Used as a *rocket propellant*, either alone or mixed with the dimethyl *derivative*.

HYDRAZO GROUP. The *bivalent radical* —HNNH—.

HYDRAZOIC ACID. Azoimide. HN_3. A colourless poisonous *explosive liquid*, b.p. 37° C., which forms explosive *salts* with heavy *metals*. The salts are called *azides*.

HYDRIDE. A *binary compound* with hydrogen.

HYDRIODIC ACID. HI. A *solution* of the colourless *gas*, hydrogen iodide, in *water*.

HYDRO-. Prefix denoting *water-*; e.g. *hydrogen*, water producer. In chemical nomenclature, it often denotes a *compound* of hydrogen; e.g. *hydrochloric acid*.

HYDROBROMIC ACID. HBr. A *solution* of the pale yellow *gas*, hydrogen bromide, in *water*.

HYDROBROMIDE. A *salt* formed when an *organic base* (e.g. an *alkaloid*) combines with *hydrobromic acid*. The salt so formed is usually more *soluble* than the base.

HYDROCARBONS. *Organic compounds* which contain only carbon and hydrogen. Classified as either *aliphatic* or *aromatic compounds* (or a combination of both). Hydrocarbons may be either *saturated* or *unsaturated compounds*.

HYDROCHLORIC ACID. Muriatic acid, spirits of salts. A *solution* of the colourless pungent *gas* hydrogen chloride, HCl, in *water*. The concentrated *acid* contains 35%–40% HCl by weight, and is a colourless, fuming, corrosive *liquid*. Manufactured by the action of *sulphuric acid*, H_2SO_4, on *sodium chloride*, or by the direct chemical combination of hydrogen and chlorine obtained by the *electrolysis* of brine. Used in chemical industry.

HYDROCHLORIDE. A *salt* formed when an *organic base* (e.g. an *alkaloid*) combines with *hydrochloric acid*. The salt so formed is usually more *soluble* than the base.

HYDROCYANIC ACID. Prussic acid, hydrogen cyanide. HCN. A colourless, intensely poisonous *liquid* with a smell of bitter almonds. B.p. 26·5° C.

HYDRODYNAMICS. The mathematical study of the *forces, energy*, and *pressure* of *liquids* in motion.

HYDROELECTRIC POWER. *Electrical energy* obtained from water-power, the latter being used to drive a *dynamo*.

HYDROFLUORIC ACID. A *solution* of hydrogen fluoride, HF, in *water*. The term is also applied to the compound HF itself, a colourless, corrosive fuming *liquid*, b.p. 19·5° C. which attacks *glass* and is used for etching glass.

HYDROGEL. A *colloidal gel* in which *water* is the *solvent*.

HYDROGEN. H. Element. A.W. 1·00797. At. No. 1. A colourless, odourless, tasteless *gas*. The lightest substance known. It is inflammable, and combines with oxygen to form *water*. *Molecule* is *diatomic*; i.e. contains two *atoms*, written H_2. Occurs as water, H_2O, in *organic compounds*, and in all living things. Manufactured by the *Bosch process* and by *electrolysis*. Used in the *oxy-hydrogen burner*, as a *reducing agent*, in the manufacture of synthetic *ammonia* (see *fixation of atmospheric nitrogen*) and of synthetic oil (see *Fischer-Tropsch process*) and for *hydrogenation of oils*. Three *isotopes* of hydrogen are known; the two 'heavy' isotopes, *deuterium* and *tritium*, are of importance in *nuclear physics*.

HYDROGEN ARSENIDE. See *arsine*.

HYDROGEN BOMB. See *nuclear weapons*.

HYDROGEN BOND. A weak *electrostatic* chemical *bond* which forms between covalently bonded (see *valency, electronic theory of*) hydrogen *atoms* and a strongly *electronegative* atom with a *lone pair of electrons* (e.g. oxygen, nitrogen, fluorine). *Ice crystals* are held together by this type of bond, a *tetrahedral* structure being built up as in Fig. 20 (where the dotted lines represent hydrogen bonds). When ice melts this structure breaks down but some hydrogen bonds continue to exist, and liquid *water* consists of groups of water *molecules* held together by hydrogen bonds. The hydrogen bond is of enormous importance in biochemical processes, especially the N—H - - - N bond which enables complex *proteins* to be built up. Life would be impossible without this type of linkage.

1nm = 10^{-9} metre

FIGURE 20.

HYDROGEN BROMIDE. See *hydrobromic acid*.

HYDROGEN CHLORIDE. See *hydrochloric acid*.

HYDROGEN CYANIDE. See *hydrocyanic acid*.

HYDROGEN ELECTRODE. See *redox reactions*.

HYDROGEN FLUORIDE. See *hydrofluoric acid*.

HYDROGEN IODIDE. See *hydriodic acid*.

HYDROGEN ION. A positively charged hydrogen *atom*; a *proton*. The general properties of *acids* in *solution* are due to the presence of hydrogen ions.

HYDROGEN ION CONCENTRATION. The number of grams of *hydrogen ions* per *litre* of *solution*. Useful as a measure of the *acidity* of a solution and in this context is usually expressed in terms of $_pH = \log_{10} \dfrac{1}{[H^+]}$, where $[H^+]$ is the hydrogen ion concentration. As pure *water* at ordinary *temperatures* dissociates slightly into hydrogen ions and *hydroxyl ions* ($H_2O \leftrightharpoons H^+ + OH^-$), the concentration of each type of ion being 10^{-7} *mole* per litre, the pH of pure water will be $\log_{10} \dfrac{1}{10^{-7}} = 7$: this figure is accordingly taken to represent neutrality on the pH scale. If *acid* is added to water its hydrogen ion concentration will increase and its pH will therefore decrease. Thus a pH below 7 indicates acidity and similarly a pH in excess of 7 indicates alkalinity.

HYDROGEN PEROXIDE. Peroxide of hydrogen. H_2O_2. A thick syrupy *liquid*, b.p. $150 \cdot 2°C$.; as usually sold, a *solution* of the pure compound in *water*. Gives off oxygen readily, used as a *disinfectant* and *bleaching agent*. Strength of solution usually given in terms of 'volume strength'; thus, 10 volume hydrogen peroxide will evolve 10 times its own volume of oxygen *gas*.

HYDROGEN PHOSPHIDE. See *phosphine*.

HYDROGEN SULPHIDE. Sulphuretted hydrogen. H_2S. A colourless poisonous *gas* with a smell of bad eggs. Formed by the *decomposition* of organic matter containing sulphur; occurs naturally in some mineral waters. Prepared by the action of dilute *acids* on *sulphides* of *metals*; used in chemical analysis.

HYDROGENATION. Subjecting to the chemical action of, or causing to combine with, hydrogen.

HYDROGENATION OF COAL. The manufacture of artificial mineral *oil* from *coal* by the action of hydrogen; causing the carbon in coal to combine with hydrogen to form *hydrocarbons*. See *Bergius process, Fischer-Tropsch process*.

HYDROGENATION OF OILS. Artificial hardening of *liquid* animal and *vegetable oils* by the action of hydrogen. Liquid *fats and oils* contain a high percentage of liquid *triolein*, $C_{57}H_{104}O_6$, which may be converted into a solid *tristearin*, $C_{57}H_{110}O_6$, by the action of hydrogen in the presence of finely divided nickel which acts as a *catalyst*; the result being a hard fat of higher *melting point*.

HYDROLASE. An *enzyme* which catalyzes *hydrolysis*.

HYDROLITH. Calcium hydride. CaH_2. A substance which is *decomposed* by *water* and used for the production of hydrogen, according to the equation $CaH_2 + 2H_2O = Ca(OH)_2 + 2H_2$.

HYDROLOGY. The study of *water* with reference to its occurrence and properties in the *hydrosphere* and *atmosphere*.

HYDROLYSIS. The chemical *decomposition* of a substance by *water*, the water itself being also decomposed; the reaction is of the type $AB + H_2O = A(OH) + HB$. *Salts* of weak *acids*, weak *bases*, or both, are partially hydrolyzed in *solution*; *esters* may be hydrolyzed to form an *alcohol* and acid. See *saponification*.

HYDROMETER. An instrument for measuring the *density* or *specific gravity* of *liquids*. The common type consists of a weighted bulb with a graduated, slender stem; the apparatus floats vertically in the liquid being tested. In liquids of high density a greater length of stem is exposed than in liquids of low density.

HYDROPHILIC. Having an affinity for *water*. A hydrophilic *colloid* is one which readily forms a *stable solution* in *water*.

HYDROPHOBIC. Having no affinity for *water*; water-repellent. A hydrophobic *colloid* is one which will only form a *solution* in *water* with difficulty.

HYDROPONICS. Cultivation of plants without the use of *soil*, using instead *solutions* of those mineral *salts* which a plant normally extracts from the soil.

HYDROSOL. A *colloidal solution*, as distinct from a *hydrogel*, *water* being the solvent.

HYDROSPHERE. The watery portion of the *Earth's crust*, comprising the oceans, seas, and all other waters. Composition by *weight* is given as oxygen 85·8%, hydrogen 10·7%, chlorine 2·1%, sodium 1·1%, magnesium 0·14%, not more than 0·05% of any other *element* being present. The chief constituents are *water*, H_2O, *sodium chloride*, NaCl, and *magnesium chloride*, $MgCl_2$.

HYDROSTATICS. The mathematical study of *forces* and *pressures* in *liquids* or at rest.

HYDROSULPHATE. A *salt* formed when an *organic base* (e.g. an *alkaloid*) combines with *sulphuric acid*. The salt so formed is usually more *soluble* than the base.

HYDROSULPHIDE. A *compound* containing the *univalent* group —HS.

HYDROUS. Containing *water*.

HYDROXIDE. A *compound* derived from *water*, H_2O, by the replacement of one of the hydrogen *atoms* in the *molecule* by some other atom or group; compound containing the *hydroxyl group*. E.g. *sodium hydroxide*, NaOH.

HYDROXYL GROUP. The *univalent radical* or group consisting of one hydrogen and one oxygen *atom*, forming a part of a *molecule* of a *compound*. The —OH group. *Inorganic* compounds containing electro-valently bonded (see *valency, electronic theory of*) hydroxyl groups are *alkalis*; organic compounds containing covalently bonded hydroxyl groups are *alcohols*.

HYDROXYL ION. A negatively charged *ion*; a free *hydroxyl group* bearing a negative *electric charge*. The presence of hydroxyl ions is the cause of the characteristic properties of *alkaline solutions*.

HYGRO-. Prefix denoting moisture, humidity. E.g. *hygrometer*.

HYGRODEIK. A *wet and dry bulb hygrometer* with a chart attached which enables the *relative humidity* to be obtained directly from the readings of the two *thermometers*.

HYGROMETER. Any instrument designed to measure the *relative humidity* of the *atmosphere*.

HYGROSCOPE. An instrument for showing variations of *relative humidity* of the air.

HYGROSCOPIC. Having a tendency to absorb moisture.

HYOSCINE. Scopolamine. $C_{17}H_{21}NO_4$. A colourless crystalline *alkaloid*, m.p. 82° C., used in the form of its *hydrobromide* as a *sedative* and *narcotic*.

HYOSCYAMINE. $C_{17}H_{23}NO_3$. A poisonous crystalline *alkaloid*, m.p. 106° C., obtained from henbane, and used in the form of its *hydrobromide* or *hydrosulphate* as a *sedative* and antispasmodic.

HYPER-. Prefix denoting over, above, beyond.

HYPERBOLA. A curve traced out by a point which moves so that its distance from a fixed point, the *focus*, always bears a constant ratio greater than unity to its distance from a fixed straight line, the *directrix*. The curve has two branches and is formed by a *plane* cutting a right circular *cone* when the angle the plane makes with the base is greater than the angle formed by the cone's side (see *conic sections*).

HYPERBOLIC FUNCTIONS. Six mathematical functions analogous to the *trigonometrical ratios*. The hyperbolic functions are sinh, cosh, tanh, cosech, sech, and coth. Sinh x is defined as $\frac{1}{2}$ $(e^x - e^{-x})$ and cosh x as $\frac{1}{2}$ $(e^x + e^{-x})$. (See *exponential*.) The remaining functions are derived from sinh and cosh, on the same basis as the related trigonometrical ratios.

HYPERFINE STRUCTURE OF SPECTRUM LINES. The very fine structure of certain *spectrum* lines observed when they are examined under very high resolution. The lines are caused either (a) by the presence of different *isotopes* of the *element* emitting the spectrum, or (b) if the atomic *nuclei* of the element possess a *spin*, and therefore a resultant *magnetic moment*.

HYPERGOLIC. Term used to describe constituents of *rocket fuels* which ignite spontaneously upon contact with some other specific constituent.

HYPERMETROPIA. Long sight. A defect of vision in which the subject is unable to see near objects distinctly. Corrected by the use of *convex* spectacle *lenses*.

HYPEROL*. Trade name of a crystalline *compound* of *urea* and *hydrogen peroxide*; $CO(NH_2)_2.H_2O_2$. Evolves *hydrogen peroxide* by the action of *water*.

HYPERONS. A group of *elementary particles*, belonging to the class called *baryons*, which have greater *mass* than the *neutron* but very short lives. All baryons which are not *nucleons* are known as hyperons, but as all hyperons *decay* into nucleons they can be regarded as *excited* nucleons. For each hyperon there is a corresponding *anti-particle*. Hyperons are listed in Table 6 on pages 436–7.

HYPERSONIC. Having a speed in excess of Mach 5. See *Mach number*.

HYPERTONIC. A *solution* is said to be hypertonic with respect to another if it has a greater *osmotic pressure*.

HYPNOTIC (chem.). A substance producing sleep. A *sedative*.

HYPO-. Prefix denoting under, below.

HYPO (phot.). *Sodium thiosulphate*, $Na_2S_2O_3.5H_2O$. Formerly incorrectly called 'sodium hyposulphite'. Used in *photography*. See *fixing*.

HYPOCHLORITE. A *salt* of *hypochlorous acid*. Hypochlorites of sodium, potassium, and calcium are used as *disinfectants* and for *bleaching*, by virtue of their oxidizing properties.

HYPOCHLOROUS ACID. HClO. An *acid* which only exists in *solution*, but whose *salts*, the *hypochlorites*, are used in *bleaching*.

HYPOCYCLOID. The figure traced by a point on the circumference of a *circle* which rolls, without slipping, round the inside of a larger fixed circle.

HYPOPHOSPHOROUS ACID. $H(H_2PO_2)$. A colourless *deliquescent* crystalline substance, m.p. $26\cdot5°$ C., used as a *reducing agent*.

HYPOTENUSE. The side opposite the right angle (i.e. the longest side) in a right-angled *triangle*.

HYPOTHESIS. A supposition put forward in explanation of observed facts.

HYPOTONIC. A *solution* is said to be hypotonic with respect to another if it has a smaller *osmotic pressure*.

HYPSOMETER. 'Height-measurer'. An apparatus for the determination of the *boiling point* of a *liquid*. Since the boiling points of liquids depend upon the *pressure*, and the atmospheric pressure varies with the altitude, the apparatus may be used for the determination of altitude above sea-level.

HYSTERESIS. A physical phenomenon chiefly met in the elastic and magnetic behaviour of materials. When a body is stressed, the *strain* produced is a function of the *stress*. On releasing the stress, the strain lags behind; i.e. the strain for a given value of stress is greater when the stress is decreasing than when it is increasing. On removing the stress completely, a residual strain remains. This lagging of effect behind cause is called *hysteresis*. It also occurs in induced *magnetism*. See *hysteresis cycle*.

HYSTERESIS CYCLE. A cycle of magnetizing field variations to which an

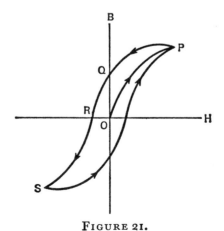

FIGURE 21.

initially demagnetized *ferromagnetic* substance is subjected. The magne-tizing field is periodically reversed in direction until a steady state is reached in which the *magnetic induction* in the specimen at any instant is a *function* only of the magnitude of the magnetizing field and the sign of its rate of change at that instant. When this condition has been reached, a plot of induction (B) against magnetizing field (H) gives a 'hysteresis loop' or curve. See Fig. 21. When H is reduced to zero along PQ, there is a residual magnetic induction in the substance, OQ, which is called the *remanence*. Reversing the *polarity* of H along QRS reduces the value of B to zero at R. The strength of field, OR, required to reduce B to zero is called the *coercive force*. Rapidly reversing the field of an *electromagnet* causes *energy* to be lost by heating up the core. This 'hysteresis loss' is proportional to the area of the hysteresis loop, which should therefore be as small as possible.

I

IATROCHEMISTRY. Medieval medical *chemistry*; early attempts at the application of drugs to medicine.

ICE. *Water*, H_2O, in the *solid* state. Formed at the *freezing point* of water, $0°$ C. As it is less dense than water, water expands (See *Water, expansion of*) on freezing, and ice floats on water. See *hydrogen bond*.

ICE POINT. The *temperature* of equilibrium between *ice* and *water* under normal atmospheric pressure (see *atmosphere*); i.e. the *melting point* of ice. The ice point is assigned the value of $0°$ C., in the *Celsius temperature* scale.

ICONOSCOPE. A form of camera tube (see *camera, television*) in which an *electron* beam scans a *mosaic*, thus converting an optical image into an electrical signal.

ICOSAHEDRON. A *polyhedron* with twenty faces.

-IDE. A chemical suffix denoting a *binary compound* of the two named *elements* or *radicals*; e.g. *hydrogen sulphide*, a compound of hydrogen and sulphur only.

IDEAL CRYSTAL. A *crystal* whose *lattice* is perfectly regular and which contains no foreign *atoms* or *ions* or other *defects* or imperfections.

IDEAL GAS. See *perfect gas*.

IDENTITY (math.). A statement of equality between known or unknown quantities, which holds true for all values of the unknown quantities. E.g. $3x \equiv 2x + x$ irrespective of what value is assigned to x.

IGNIS FATUUS. Will-o'-the-wisp. A pale *flame* sometimes seen over marshy ground, probably caused by the *spontaneous combustion* of *methane*, CH_4, or other inflammable *gases*.

IGNITION. The action of setting fire to something. Initiating *combustion* by raising the *temperature* of the reactants to the *ignition temperature*; particularly the process or means of firing the explosive mixture in an *internal-combustion engine* by an *electric spark*.

IGNITION TEMPERATURE OR POINT. The *temperature* to which a substance must be heated before *combustion* can take place.

ILLUMINATION of a surface. The amount of *light* falling on unit area of the surface per second. The derived *SI unit* of illumination is the *lux* (*lumen* per square *metre*).

ILMENITE. Natural ferrous titanate, $FeTiO_3$. An *ore* of *titanium*.

IMAGE, REAL (phys.). An image formed by a *mirror* or *lens* at a point through which the *rays* of *light* entering the observer's eye actually pass. Such an image can be obtained on a screen. See Fig. 25, page 220.

IMAGE, VIRTUAL (phys.). An image seen at a point from which the *rays* of *light* appear to come to the observer, but do not actually do so; e.g. the image seen in a plane *mirror* or through a *diverging lens*. Such an image cannot be obtained on a screen placed at its apparent position, since the rays of light do not pass through that point. See Fig. 25, page 220.

IMAGINARY NUMBERS. Numbers with negative *squares*; thus $\sqrt{-1}$ is an imaginary number, denoted by i; $i^2 = -1$.

IMIDAZOLE. Iminazole, glyoxaline. $C_3H_4N_2$. A colourless *soluble heterocyclic* crystalline substance, m.p. 90°C., used in organic synthesis.

IMIDE. Imido compound. A *compound*, derived from *ammonia*, containing the imido group, NH= , in which the two hydrogen *atoms* of ammonia are replaced by *metal* atoms or *acid radicals*.

IMINE. Imino compound. A *compound*, derived from *ammonia*, containing the imino group, NH= , in which the two hydrogen *atoms* of ammonia are replaced by non-acidic *organic radicals*.

IMMERSION OBJECTIVE. Oil-immersion lens. A type of *objective* used in high-power *microscopes*, the lowest *lens* of the objective lens system being immersed in a drop of cedar-wood oil placed upon the slide to be examined. Such an arrangement causes more *light* to enter the system than if the oil were absent.

IMMISCIBLE. Incapable of being mixed to form a *homogeneous* substance; usually applied to *liquids*; e.g. *oil* and *water* are immiscible.

IMPACT. The collision of bodies. See *conservation of momentum*.

IMPEDANCE. Z. The quantity which determines the *amplitude* of the current for a given *voltage* in an *alternating current* circuit. For a circuit containing *resistance R, self-inductance L*, and *capacitance C* connected in series, the impedance of the circuit is given by the expression

$$Z = \left[R^2 + \left[L\omega - \frac{1}{C\omega} \right)^2 \right]^{\frac{1}{2}},$$ where ω is a constant, the *angular frequency*

equal to $2\pi f$, f being the *frequency* of the alternating current.

IMPERMEABLE. Not permitting the passage of *fluids*.

IMPFING. 'Seeding' a *liquid* with a small *crystal* in order to induce crystallization.

IMPLICIT FUNCTION. A variable quantity, x, is said to be an implicit function of y, when x and y are connected by a relation which is not explicit. See *explicit function*.

IMPLOSION. The inward collapse of an evacuated vessel.

IMPROPER FRACTION. See *proper fraction*.

IMPULSE (phys.). The concept of a *force* acting during a very short time; given (for a constant force) by the product of the magnitude of the force and the time during which the force acts; equal to the total change of *momentum* produced by it.

IN VITRO. Said of experiments involving biological or biochemical processes which are carried out in 'glass' (i.e. after the *cells* or *tissues* in which the processes occur have been removed from the *organism* to which they belong) rather than in the living organism, when they are said to take place 'in vivo'.

IN VIVO. See *in vitro*.

INCANDESCENCE. The emission of *light* caused by high *temperatures*; white or bright-red heat.

INCIDENCE, ANGLE OF. The angle between a *ray* of *light* meeting a surface and the *normal* to the surface at that point. See Fig. 35, page 326.

INCLINATION. See *magnetic dip*.

INCLINOMETER. 1. See *dip circle*. 2. An instrument for measuring the angle of inclination which an aircraft makes with the horizontal.

INCUBATOR. A box designed to maintain a constant internal *temperature* by the use of a *thermostat*; used for rearing chickens and prematurely-born infants, and in *bacteriology*.

INDENE. $C_6H_4.C_3H_4$. A colourless *liquid hydrocarbon*, b.p. $182.2°C.$, obtained from *coal-tar* and used in organic synthesis.

INDETERMINANCY PRINCIPLE. See *uncertainty principle*.

INDEX (math.). The *exponent* of a quantity raised to a *power*; the number indicating the power to which the quantity is raised. E.g. the index of a in $4a^5$ is 5.

INDIAN INK. Chinese ink. Black *ink* containing a *suspension* of carbon.

INDICATOR (chem.). A substance which, by a sharp *colour* change, indicates the completion of a *chemical reaction*. Frequently used in *volumetric analysis*. Indicators for *titrations* of *acids* and *alkalis* are usually weak *organic acids* or *bases*, yielding *ions* of a different colour from the un-ionized *molecules*. (See *ionization*.) E.g. *litmus* is red with acids and blue with alkalis, a change in colour indicating that *neutralization* is complete. See *end point*.

INDIGO. $C_{16}H_{10}N_2O_2$. An important blue *vat dye*, formerly extracted from plants of the genus Indigofera, in which it occurs as indican, a *glucoside*. Now manufactured artificially on a large scale.

INDIUM. In. Element. A.W. 114.82. At. No. 49. A soft silvery-white *metal*, S.G. 7.31, m.p. $156.4°C.$ *Compounds* are rare. Used in electro-plating and in dental *alloys*.

INDOLE. C_8H_7N. A yellow *soluble* substance, m.p. $52.5°C.$, occurs in oil of jasmin, and is a *decomposition* product of *proteins* in animal intestines. Despite its unpleasant smell it is used in perfumes.

INDUCED CURRENT. See *induction, electromagnetic*.

INDUCED RADIOACTIVITY. Artificial radioactivity. *Radioactivity* induced in naturally stable *elements* by bombarding them with *neutrons* or other high *energy* particles (or *photons*).

INDUCTANCE. *L*. The property of an electric *circuit* as a result of which an *electromotive force* is generated by a change in the *current* flowing through the circuit (see *self-induction*), or by a change in the current of a neighbouring circuit with which it is magnetically linked (see *mutual induction*). The derived *SI unit* of inductance is the *henry*.

INDUCTION, CHARGING BY. A process of electrically charging an insulated *conductor*, using the *force* due to another nearby charge to separate the positive and negative charges existing on the conductor.

INDUCTION COIL. An instrument for producing a high *electromotive force* from a supply of low E.M.F. Essentially consists of a cylindrical soft-iron core, usually laminated to prevent losses due to *eddy currents*, round which are wound two coils, the primary and the secondary. The primary coil consists of a few hundred turns; rapid variation of an *electric current* in this coil, produced by a repeated interruption or break in the circuit by a mechanism similar to that in the electric *bell*, produces an induced E.M.F. (see *induction, electromagnetic*) in the secondary coil, which contains a very large number of turns of thin wire.

INDUCTION, ELECTROMAGNETIC. When the *magnetic flux* through a circuit changes, an *electromotive force* is induced in the circuit. This phenomenon is called electromagnetic induction. The induced E.M.F. is equal to the rate of decrease of magnetic flux through the circuit (*Faraday's Law*). If the circuit is closed, this E.M.F. gives rise to an induced current, and the phenomenon forms the basis of the *dynamo*, *transformer*, etc. The induced current is in such a direction that its *magnetic field* tends to neutralize the change in magnetic flux producing it (*Lenz's Law*).

INDUCTION HEATING. A form of heating in which electrically conducting material is heated as a result of the *electric current* induced in it by an alternating *magnetic field*.

INDUCTION, MAGNETIC. See *magnetic induction*.

INDUCTION MOTOR. A type of *electric motor* in which an *alternating current* supply fed to the primary winding sets up a flux causing *electrical currents* to be induced in the secondary winding of the *rotor*. The interaction between these currents and the flux causes the rotor to rotate.

INDUCTOMETER. A calibrated variable *inductance*.

INELASTIC COLLISION. A collision between bodies in which there is a loss of total *kinetic energy*. Referring to *nuclear physics*, an inelastic collision is one in which an incoming particle causes *excitation* or breaking up of the struck *nucleus*.

INELASTIC CROSS-SECTION. See *cross-section*.

INERT. Not easily changed by *chemical reaction*.

INERT GASES. Noble gases, rare gases. The *elements* helium, neon, argon, krypton, xenon, radon. They are all chemically inactive, although some *compounds* have been reported (e.g. XeF_2, XeO_3, $XePtF_6$, KrF_2). Argon occurs in appreciable amounts (0.8%) in the air; the others, with the exception of radon, occur in the air in very minute amounts.

INERTIA (phys.). The tendency of a body to preserve its state of rest or uniform motion in a straight line.

INERTIAL GUIDANCE. A method of automatic control used in *guided missiles* which depends upon the *forces* of *inertia*. The *velocities* or distances covered, computed from the *acceleration* measured within the missile, are compared with data stored before launching.

INERTIAL MASS. The *mass* of a body as determined by its *momentum* (in accordance with the law of *conservation of momentum*), as opposed to 'gravitational mass' which is determined by the extent to which it responds to the *force* of *gravity*. The *acceleration* of a falling body increases in proportion to its gravitational mass and decreases in proportion to its inertial mass. Since all falling bodies have the same constant acceleration it follows that the two types of mass must be equal.

INERTIAL SYSTEM. A *frame of reference* in which bodies are not accelerated, i.e. remain at rest or move with constant *velocity*, unless acted upon by external *forces*. *Newtonian mechanics* is valid in such a system.

INFINITESIMAL. A quantity smaller than any assignable quantity; the concept is obtained by imagining a quantity decreasing indefinitely without actually becoming zero.

INFINITY. ∞. That quantity which is greater than any assignable quantity.

INFORMATION THEORY. A branch of *cybernetics* which attempts to define the amount of information required to control a process of given complexity. See *bit, noise, redundancy, equivocation, channel capacity.*

INFRARED RADIATION. Invisible heat radiation, radiant heat. *Electromagnetic radiation* possessing *wavelengths* between those of visible *light* and those of *radio* waves, i.e. from approximately 0·8 μm (*microns*) to 1 mm. Infrared radiation has the power of penetrating *fog* or haze which would scatter ordinary visible light; thus photographs taken on a plate made sensitive to infrared radiation may often disclose detail invisible on an ordinary plate or to the naked eye.

INFRARED STARS. Celestial bodies whose principal emission is *infrared radiation*. Believed to consist of *stars* surrounded by dust clouds. In some cases the *light* from the central star penetrates the dust so that it can be seen with *optical telescopes*.

INFUSIBLE. Difficult to melt; having a very high *melting point*.

INFUSORIAL EARTH. See *kieselguhr.*

INJECTION MOULDING. A process by which *thermoplastic* articles are moulded. The thermoplastic material is softened in a heated chamber and then injected under pressure through an orifice into a cool closed mould.

INKS. Deeply coloured *liquids* of varied composition; many black and blue-black inks owe their colour to *organic compounds* of iron.

INORGANIC (chem.). Of *mineral* origin; not belonging to the large class of carbon *compounds* which are termed *organic*.

INORGANIC CHEMISTRY. The study of the *elements* and their *compounds*. Inorganic chemistry usually includes the study of elemental carbon, its *oxides, metal carbonates*, and *sulphides*, while all other carbon compounds belong to the study of *organic chemistry*.

INOSITOL. Hexahydroxycyclohexane. $C_6H_6(OH)_6$. An *optically active* white crystalline solid, m.p. 228–248° C., which occurs in the *vitamin* B complex and is an essential component of animal diets. Used in medicine.

INSECTICIDE. A substance used for killing insect pests.

INSOLATION. Exposure to the *rays* of the *Sun*.

INSOLUBLE. Not capable of forming a *solution* (in *water*, unless some other *solvent* is specified). It is a relative term, since most substances have been shown to dissolve in water to some extent.

INSTANTANEOUS FREQUENCY. The rate of change of *phase* of an oscillation, expressed in *radians* per second divided by 2π.

INSULATION. The prevention of the passage of *electricity*, or *heat*, by *conduction*.

INSULATOR. A non-conductor of *electricity* or *heat*.

INSULIN. A *hormone* produced in the pancreas which controls *sugar metabolism* in the body. When injected, it lowers the *blood* sugar content and so relieves the symptoms of diabetes mellitus. Insulin is one of the few *proteins* the detailed structure of which is known.

INTEGER. A whole number.

INTEGRAL. 1. Consisting of whole numbers or *integers*. 2. A mathematical *function* obtained by the process of *integration*. See Table 9, page 441.

INTEGRAL CALCULUS. The branch of the *calculus* making use of the processes of *integration*.

INTEGRAND. A mathematical *expression* which is to be subjected to *integration*.

INTEGRATED CIRCUIT. Microcircuit. A *microelectronic* circuit incorporated into a chip of *semiconductor*, usually crystalline silicon (a silicon chip). Integrated circuits consist of whole systems rather than single components, and are replacing separate *transistors* in modern *computers*. They are also expected to be used in other industries (e.g. cars, radios, etc.) in which small reliable electronic control circuits are required.

INTEGRATION. A mathematical process used in the *calculus*; the inverse process of *differentiation*. It gives a method of finding the areas enclosed by curves, and of finding solutions to other problems involving the summation of *infinitesimals*. See Table 9, page 441.

INTENSIFIER (phot.). A substance used to increase the *density* or contrast of an image on a photographic *film* or plate. Usually a *compound* from which a *metal* (e.g. silver, lead, uranium, etc.) can be deposited.

INTENSITY, ELECTRICAL. See *electric intensity*.

INTENSITY, MAGNETIC. See *magnetic field strength*.

INTENSITY OF ILLUMINATION. See *illumination*.

INTER-. Prefix denoting between, among.

INTERACTION. Mutual action between bodies, particles or systems. In *nuclear physics* the word is often used to mean the *force* between interacting particles. See *strong* and *weak nuclear interactions*.

INTERFACE. The surface which separates two chemical *phases*.

INTERFERENCE OF WAVE MOTIONS (phys.). The addition or combination of waves; if the crest of one wave meets the trough of another of equal *amplitude*, the wave is destroyed at that point; conversely, the superposition of one crest upon another leads to an increased effect (see also *Huygens' principle of superposition*). The *colour* effects of thin films are due to interference of *light* waves; *beats* produced by two notes of similar *frequency* are the result of the interference of *sound* waves.

199

INTERFEROMETER. Any instrument which divides a *beam* of *light* into a number of beams and re-unites them to produce *interference*. Uses include the accurate determination of *wavelengths* of light, the testing of *prisms* and *lenses*, the examination of the *hyperfine structure of spectrum lines*, measurement of the diameters of *stars* and the determination of the number of light waves of a certain wavelength in the standard *metre*. See also *radio interferometer*.

INTERFERON. A *protein* which is produced in many animal *cells* as the result of the presence of *viruses* (either active or inactive) in the cell, and which acts as a form of protection against these viruses.

INTERGALACTIC SPACE. The *space* between *galaxies*, in which intergalactic *matter* may occur.

INTERMEDIATE FREQUENCY. In *superheterodyne radio* receivers, the *carrier wave frequency* of the incoming radio wave is changed to a fixed intermediate frequency by *heterodyne* action, for ease of amplification before detection.

INTERMEDIATE NEUTRONS. *Neutrons* with *kinetic energies* between those of *epithermal* and *fast neutrons*, i.e. between 100 *electron-volts* and 0·1 *MeV*.

INTERNAL-COMBUSTION ENGINE. An *engine* in which *energy* supplied by a burning *fuel* is directly transformed into *mechanical energy* by the controlled *combustion* of the fuel in an enclosed cylinder behind a piston. Usually applied to the petrol-burning or oil-burning (*diesel*) engine.

INTERNAL ENERGY. Thermodynamic energy. U. The total *energy* associated with a system, which cannot itself usually be determined. However the change in the internal energy of a system, $\varDelta U$, is a useful *thermodynamic* quantity, and is defined by $\varDelta U = q - w$ where q is the *heat* abstracted by the system from its surroundings and w is the *work* done simultaneously on the surroundings.

INTERNAL STANDARD LINE. In *spectrographic analysis* an internal standard line is a line within the *line spectrum* of the material being analysed, due to a known amount of an *element* present in, or added to, the material. See also *homologous pair*.

INTERNAL STRESS. The *stress* within a solid material, e.g. *metal, glass*, etc., as a result of heat treatment, cold working, or non-uniform molecular structure.

INTERNATIONAL DATE LINE. An imaginary line on the surface of the *Earth* joining the North and South poles, approximately following the 180° *meridian* through the Pacific Ocean. This line is used to mark the internationally agreed start of a calendar day. Crossing from east to west a traveller changes the day to the next day, and crossing it from west to east goes one day back.

INTERNATIONAL CANDLE. The former unit of *luminous intensity*. A point source emitting *light* uniformly in all directions at one-tenth of the rate of the Harcourt pentane lamp burning under specified conditions. Now replaced by the *candela*.

INTERNATIONAL HYDROLOGICAL DECADE. The years 1965–1974 during which participating nations agree to cooperate in research in *hydrology*.

INTERNATIONAL PRACTICAL TEMPERATURE SCALE OF 1968. This temperature scale supersedes all previous practical scales. It consists of a practical scale of *temperature* defined so that it conforms as closely as possible to the *thermodynamic temperature*. The unit of temperature is the *kelvin* (symbol K). The eleven fixed points on the scale are given below. Between these points *interpolation* is made with a defining formula using a platinum *resistance thermometer*. Above the *freezing point* of gold a radiation *pyrometer* is used based on *Planck's Law of Radiation*.

	$T/\mathrm{K}.$	$t/^\circ\mathrm{C}.$
Triple point of equilibrium hydrogen	13·81	−259·34
Temperature of equilibrium hydrogen when its vapour pressure is 25/76 standard atmosphere	17·042	−256·108
B.p. of equilibrium hydrogen	20·28	−252·87
B.p. of neon	27·102	−246·048
Triple point of oxygen	54·361	−218·789
B.p. of oxygen	90·188	−182·962
Triple point of water	273·16	0·01
B.p. of water	373·15	100
F.p. of zinc	692·73	419·58
F.p. of silver	1235·08	961·93
F.p. of gold	1337·58	1064·43

INTERPLANETARY SPACE. The *space* between the *planets* within the *solar system*.

INTERPOLATION. The process of filling in intermediate values or terms of a series between known values or terms.

INTERRUPTED CONTINUOUS WAVES. ICW. A *continuous wave electromagnetic radiation* which is switched on and off at an *audio-frequency*.

INTERSTELLAR MATTER. Clouds of hydrogen *atoms* or *molecules*, mixed with a small proportion of dust, which exist between *stars*. The *density* of these clouds is very low, ranging between some 10^7 and 10^9 atoms per m³ (compared to about 10^{25} molecules per m³ for a *perfect gas* at *N.T.P.*).

INTERSTELLAR SPACE. The *space* between *stars* within a *galaxy*, in which *interstellar matter* may occur.

INTERSTITIAL. An additional *atom* or *ion* situated between the normal sites in a *crystal lattice*, causing a *defect*.

INTERSTITIAL COMPOUND. See *compound, interstitial*.

INTRA-. Prefix denoting within; e.g. intra-molecular *forces* are forces within the *molecule*, while *inter*-molecular forces are forces between molecules.

INTRINSIC ENERGY. It is assumed in calculations in *thermochemistry* that every substance possesses a definite quantity of intrinsic *energy*, i.e. energy which is inherent in the substance, and which may be in part released in the form of *heat* if the substance takes part in a *chemical reaction*. In a chemical action, no energy is gained or lost, and the sum of the intrinsic energies of the reacting substances is equal to the sum of the intrinsic energies of the final products plus or minus the energy given out or absorbed as heat during the reaction. See *Hess's law*. In *thermodynamics* the intrinsic energy of a material system is its total store of energy of all kinds. The absolute magnitude is not usually important, but changes in the intrinsic energy of a system, which depend only upon its initial and final conditions (and are therefore independent of the path of change), are used in thermodynamic calculations.

INTRINSIC SEMICONDUCTOR. See *extrinsic semiconductor*.

INULIN. $(C_6H_{10}O_5)_6.H_2O$. A *soluble polysaccharide* consisting of *fructose* units; occurs in many plants as a stored food. Used in making bread for diabetics.

INVAR*. An *alloy* containing 63·8% iron, 36% nickel, 0·2% carbon which has a very low coefficient of *expansion*. Used for balance wheels of watches and in other accurate instruments which would otherwise be affected by *temperature* changes.

INVERSE SQUARE LAW. A law which states that the intensity of an effect at a point B due to a source at A varies inversely as the *square* of the distance AB. Examples include the *illumination* of a surface, *gravitational field*, field due to an *electric charge*, etc. Thus, the illumination of a surface 1 *metre* away from a source will be 9 times as great as that of a surface 3 metres away.

INVERSE TRIGONOMETRICAL FUNCTIONS. If y=sin x (see *trigonometrical ratios*), then the inverse trigonometrical function of x is $\sin^{-1}y$ (or arc sin y), where $\sin^{-1}y$ is the *angle* whose sine is y. Similar inverse functions exist for the other trigonometrical and *hyperbolic* ratios.

INVERSE VARIATION. One quantity is said to vary inversely as another, or to be inversely proportional to another, if the *product* of the two is a constant.

INVERSION OF CANE-SUGAR. The conversion of *cane-sugar* (*sucrose*, $C_{12}H_{22}O_{11}$) into a mixture of equal amounts of *glucose* and *fructose*, two isomeric sugars (see *isomerism*) having the formula $C_6H_{12}O_6$. The action is one of *hydrolysis* and may be carried out by the action of the *enzyme invertase*, or by boiling with dilute *acids*. The resulting mixture is *laevorotatory*, while a solution of cane-sugar is *dextrorotatory*, inversion of the *optical rotation* being thus obtained.

INVERSION TEMPERATURE. See *Joule-Thomson effect*.

INVERT SUGAR. A *mixture* of *glucose* and *fructose* in equal proportions, obtained by the *inversion of cane-sugar*.

INVERTASE. Sucrase. An *enzyme* contained in *yeast* which converts *cane-sugar* into *glucose* and *fructose*. See *inversion of cane-sugar*.

INVERTER. A device for converting *direct current* into *alternating current*.

INVOLUTE. The curve formed when a piece of string is unwound from, or wound on to, another curve (the *evolute*). See Fig. 22.

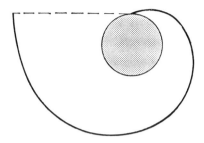

INVOLUTE OF A CIRCLE

FIGURE 22.

IODATE. A *salt* of *iodic acid*.

IODIC. Containing *pentavalent* iodine.

IODIC ACID. HIO_3. A colourless or yellow *soluble* powder formed by the *oxidation* of iodine with *nitric acid*.

IODIDE. A *binary compound* with iodine; *salt* of *hydriodic acid*, HI.

IODINE. I. Element. A.W. 126·90. At. No. 53. A blackish-grey, crystalline *solid*. S.G. 4·95. M.p. 114°C. B.p. 184°C. Very *volatile*, gives rise to a violet *vapour*. Very slightly *soluble* in *water*, readily soluble in *alcohol* (giving '*tincture* of iodine') and in *potassium iodide* solution, KI. *Compounds* occur in seaweed; sodium iodate, $NaIO_3$, occurs in crude *Chile saltpetre*. Essential to the functioning of the thyroid gland; lack of iodine in the diet is a cause of goitre. Used in medicine, chemical *analysis*, and *photography*. The *radioisotope* $^{131}_{53}I$, (*half-life* 8·6 days) is used in the treatment and diagnosis of disorders of the thyroid gland.

IODINE VALUE. A measure of the amount of *unsaturated fatty acid* present in a sample of *fat, oil, resin*, or other natural product. The *weight* of iodine absorbed by 100 g of the substance.

IODOFORM. CHI_3. A yellow, crystalline *solid* with a peculiar odour. M.p. 119°C. Used as an *antiseptic*.

IODOUS. Containing *trivalent* iodine.

ION. An electrically charged *atom* or group of atoms. Positively charged ions (*cations*) have fewer *electrons* than is necessary for the atom or group to be electrically neutral; negative ions (*anions*) have more. Thus, the *proton*, the hydrogen atom without its circum-nuclear electron, is a *hydrogen ion*; the *alpha-particle* is a helium ion. Gaseous ions can be produced in *gases* by *electric sparks*, the passage of energetic charged particles, *X-rays, gamma-rays, ultraviolet radiation*, etc. Ions in *solution* are due to the *ionization* of the dissolved substance (see *ionic hypothesis*).

ION ENGINE. A type of *reaction propulsion* engine for propelling *rockets* in *space*, the exhaust jet of which consists of a stream of positive *ions* accelerated to a high *velocity* by *electrostatic* repulsion from the engine body.

ION EXCHANGE. Certain substances have the power of acting on *solutions* containing *ions*, such as solutions of *salts*, and replacing some of the ions by others; e.g. in a typical *cation* exchange ('base exchange') action, when *hard water* is passed through a suitable ion exchange resin or a *zeolite*, the calcium ions in the water are replaced by sodium ions. In *anion* exchange *acid radicals* or anions are exchanged similarly. Ion exchange has many important industrial uses in addition to water softening.

ION MOBILITY. The *velocity* of an *ion* in a unit *electric field*.

IONIC BOND. An electrovalent bond. See *valency, electronic theory of*.

IONIC CRYSTAL. See *electrovalent crystal*.

IONIC HYPOTHESIS. Originally introduced to explain the phenomena of *electrolysis*, etc. Ionic *compounds* consist of oppositely charged *atoms* or groups of atoms termed *ions*. When an *electric current* is passed through such a compound in the dissolved or molten state, the ions are attracted to the oppositely charged *electrodes*.

IONIZATION. The formation of *ions*.

IONIZATION CHAMBER. A device for measuring the amount of *ionizing radiation*. Consists of a gas-filled chamber containing two *electrodes* (one of which may be the chamber wall) between which a *potential difference* is maintained. The radiation ionizes gas in the chamber and an instrument connected to one electrode measures the *ionization current* produced.

IONIZATION CURRENT. The *electric current* produced by the movement of *ions* or *electrons* in an *electric field* as a result of *ionizing radiation*.

IONIZATION POTENTIAL. Ionization energy. The *work* which must be done, measured in *electron-volts*, to remove an *electron* from an *atom*. (See *atom, structure of*.) More work is required to remove the second electron from an atom and each subsequent electron requires additional work. Table 7 on page 438 gives the first five ionization potentials for the commonest atoms.

IONIZING RADIATION. *Radiation* (either *electromagnetic* or corpuscular) which is capable of causing *ionization*, either directly or indirectly. *Electrons* and *alpha particles* are considerably more effective in this respect than *neutrons* or *gamma-rays*.

IONONE. $C_{13}H_{20}O$. A yellow *optically active soluble liquid ketone*, b.p. 140–146° C., used in perfumes.

IONOSPHERE. The region of the Earth's *upper atmosphere* in which *free electrons* arising from *ionization* occur, mainly as a result of *ultraviolet radiation* and *X-rays* from the *Sun*. The ionosphere is useful in that it enables inter-continental *radio* transmission round the curved surface of the Earth to be achieved, as a result of its property of reflecting *electromagnetic radiations* of *radio frequencies* (see *sky wave*); but it is an obstacle to *radio astronomy* because it reflects a large proportion of the radiation that arrives from extra-terrestrial sources. The ionosphere is usually divided into three regions: the D-region between 50 and 90 kilometres above the Earth, the E-region (the *Heaviside-Kennelly layer*) between 90 and 150 km, and the F-region (the *Appleton layer*) above 150 km. See Fig. 44, page 402. At night the electron concentration in the E-region falls off due to recombination with *ions*, but the F-region remains substantially ionized owing to the lower *density* of ions and their consequent infrequency of collisions with electrons. With the advent of artificial Earth *satellites* it is now possible to study the electron density of the different regions of the ionosphere from the top side.

IONOSPHERIC WAVE. See *sky wave*.

IRIDIUM. Ir. Element. A.W. 192·2. At. No. 77. A rare *metal* resembling, and occurring together with, platinum. S.G. 22·42, m.p. 2454°C. Extremely hard and resistant to chemical action. *Alloys* of platinum and iridium are used for fountain-pen nib-tips, *crucibles* for fine analytical work, and numerous other purposes where extreme hardness and a high *melting point* are required.

IRIS. 1. The coloured part of the eye of vertebrates. 2. A diaphragm forming an adjustable opening over a *lens* in an optical instrument.

IRON. Fe. (Ferrum.) Element. A.W. 55·847. At. No. 26. A white magnetic *metal*, S.G. 7·86, m.p. 1535°C. Physical properties are greatly modified by the presence of small amounts of other metals and of carbon. Occurs as *magnetite*, Fe_3O_4; *haematite*, Fe_2O_3; *siderite*, $FeCO_3$; *limonite*, *hydrated* Fe_2O_3; and as *pyrites* in combination with sulphur. Extracted by the *blast furnace* process. According to the method and conditions of working and cooling, the carbon in iron and *steel* may be present in various forms, upon which the particular properties of the metal depend. *Compounds* of iron are essential to the higher forms of life. See *pig iron, cast iron, wrought iron*.

IRON ALUM. See *ferric alum*.

IRON, COMPOUNDS OF. See under the required *ferric* or *ferrous* compound.

IRRADIATION. Exposure to *radiation* of any kind. Artificial *radioisotopes* are made by irradiation of stable isotopes with *neutrons* in a *nuclear reactor*. Intense irradiation can alter the physical and chemical properties of *solids*, but even small doses may be used for sterilization of food owing to the sensitivity of biological *cells* to irradiation by *ionizing radiation*.

IRREVERSIBLE PROCESS. A term of considerable importance in *thermodynamics*. Any but a completely *reversible process*.

IRREVERSIBLE REACTION. A *chemical reaction* which proceeds to completion, and in which the resulting products do not react to form the original substances. See *chemical equilibrium*.

IRRITABILITY. The property of living *organisms* which enables them to respond to external stimuli.

ISATIN. $C_8H_5NO_2$. An orange *soluble* crystalline substance, m.p. 203–5°C., used in the manufacture of *dyes*.

ISENTHALPIC. Of equal *enthalpy*.

ISENTROPIC. Of equal *entropy*.

ISINGLASS. A product containing about 90% *gelatin*, made from the swimming bladders of fish. Used for clarifying alcoholic beverages.

ISLAND UNIVERSES. Obsolete term for *galaxies*.

ISO-. 1. Prefix denoting equal. 2. (chem.). Prefix denoting an *isomer* with a branched chain.

ISOBAR. A line connecting points having equal (atmospheric) *pressure*.

ISOBARIC SURFACE. A surface of equal (atmospheric) *pressure*. An altimeter will record constant height when moving along such a surface. The intersection of an isobaric surface with the ground is along an *isobar*.

ISOBARS. *Isotopes* of different *elements*, which although having different *atomic numbers*, have identical *mass numbers*. E.g. the tin isotope, $^{115}_{50}Sn$, and the indium isotope, $^{115}_{49}In$, are isobars, 115 being the mass number and 50 and 49 the atomic numbers. Isobars have the same number of *nucleons*, but different numbers of *protons* in their *nuclei*.

ISOCHORE. A line which graphically represents the relationship between the *pressure* and the *temperature* of a *liquid* or *gas*, the *volume* of the system being kept constant.

ISOCHROMATIC FILM. See *orthochromatic film*.

ISOCLINAL. A line connecting points of equal angle of *magnetic dip*.

ISOCYANATE. A *salt* or *ester* of *isocyanic acid*; a *compound* containing the —NCO group.

ISOCYANIC ACID. $HN=C=O$. An unstable *tautomer* of *cyanic acid*, which forms stable *salts* called *isocyanates*.

ISODIAPHERES. *Nuclides* in which the difference between the number of *neutrons* and *protons* is the same, e.g. a nuclide and its *decay* product after it has emitted an *alpha-particle* are isodiapheres.

ISODIMORPHISM. The phenomenon of a *dimorphous* substance being isomorphous (see *isomorphism*) with another dimorphous substance in both its forms.

ISODYNAMIC LINE. A line passing through points of equal *horizontal intensity* of the Earth's magnetic field (see *magnetism, terrestrial*).

ISOELECTRIC POINT. The pH *value* at which a substance or system (e.g. a *protein solution*) is electrically *neutral*; at this value *electrophoresis* does not occur when a direct *electric current* is applied.

ISOGONAL LINE. A line passing through points of equal *magnetic declination*.

ISOGONISM (chem.). A type of *isomorphism* in which two substances having little or no chemical resemblance have the same crystalline form.

ISO-LEUCINE. A colourless crystalline *amino acid*. See Table 5, page 435

ISOMERIC. Exhibiting *isomerism*.

ISOMERISM. 1. The existence of two or more chemical *compounds* with the same *molecular formula* but having different properties owing to a different arrangement of *atoms* within the *molecule*. E.g. ammonium cyanate, NH_4CNO, and *urea* $CO(NH_2)_2$ are isomers. 2. In *nuclear physics*, *nuclei* having the same *atomic number* and the same *mass number*, but which exist in different *energy* states, are said to be isomeric. E.g. a nucleus in its *ground state* and a nucleus in a *metastable* excited state are isomers.

ISOMERS. See *isomerism*.

ISOMETRIC. 1. Referring to a system of *crystallization* in which the *axes* are at right angles to each other. 2. A method of projecting a drawing (isometric projection) in which the three axes are equally inclined to the surface of the drawing, and all lines are drawn to scale. 3. A line on a *graph* (isometric line) showing change of *temperature* with *pressure*, when the *volume* is kept constant.

ISOMORPHISM. Similarity or identity of crystalline form, usually indicating similar or analogous chemical composition; e.g. the *alums* are isomorphous.

ISO-OCTANE. $(CH_3)_3CCH_2CH(CH_3)_2$. The *isomer* of *octane* used in defining *octane numbers*.

ISOPHTHALIC ACID. $C_6H_4(COOH)_2$. The *meta-isomer* of *phthalic acid*, m.p. 345–7°C., used in the manufacture of synthetic *resins* and *plasticizers*.

ISOPRENE. $CH_2:CH.C(CH_3):CH_2$. A colourless *liquid*, b.p. 34°C. Natural *rubber* consists mainly of a polymer of isoprene. See *polymerization*.

ISOSCELES TRIANGLE. A *triangle* having two of its sides equal.

ISOSTERISM. The phenomenon of substances having *molecules* with the same number of *atoms* and the same total number of *electrons*; this leads to similarity in physical properties. E.g. *carbon dioxide*, CO_2, and *nitrous oxide*, N_2O.

ISOTHERM. Isothermal line. A line connecting points at an equal *temperature*.

ISOTHERMAL CHANGE. A change which takes place at constant *temperature*. E.g. the isothermal *expansion of a gas*. See *adiabatic*.

ISOTONES. *Atoms* whose *nuclei* contain the same number of *neutrons*, but which are of different *atomic number*.

ISOTONIC SOLUTIONS. *Solutions* having the same *osmotic pressure*, being of the same *molecular concentration*.

ISOTOPES. *Atoms* of the same *element* (i.e. having the same *atomic number*) which differ in *mass number* are called isotopes of that element. The isotopes of an element are identical in chemical properties, and in all physical properties except those determined by the *mass* of the atom. The different isotopes of an element contain different numbers of *neutrons* in their *nuclei*. Nearly all elements found in nature are mixtures of several isotopes. See *atom, structure of*.

ISOTOPES, SEPARATION OF. As the *isotopes* of an *element* have identical chemical properties but some slightly different physical properties, their separation depends upon physical operations. The following methods are used: *diffusion* (either *gaseous* or *thermal*); *distillation*; centrifuging of *gases* or *liquids*; *electrolysis* (depending upon different rates of discharge or *ionic mobility* of isotopic *ions*); electromagnetic or electrostatic methods (depending upon different mass-to-charge ratios between isotopic ions and their consequent separation in a steady *magnetic field* or an *electric field* varied at *radio frequencies*).

ISOTOPIC NUMBER. Neutron excess. The difference between the number of *neutrons* in an *isotope* and the number of *protons*.

ISOTOPIC SPIN. Isobaric spin. A *quantum number*, T, used to work out the properties of groups of *elementary particles* when the members of the group are identical in all respects except that of *electric charge*. E.g. the *nucleon* has isotopic spin, $T = \frac{1}{2}$, and its two states, the *proton* and the *neutron* are then described as different orientations of that spin in a fictitious 'isotopic space'. The word 'spin' is not intended to imply any conventional image of rotation in this context, it is used in analogy to *angular momentum* to which the concept of isotopic spin bears a close formal resemblance. Isotopic spin is conserved in all *strong nuclear interactions*.

ISOTOPIC WEIGHT. The *atomic weight* of an individual *isotope*. Isotopic weights are very nearly *integral* (whole numbers), the *integer* being called the *mass number* of the isotope concerned.

ISOTROPIC. Exhibiting uniform properties throughout, in all directions.

-ITE. A suffix denoting, in chemical nomenclature, a *salt* of the corresponding -ous *acid*; e.g. *sulphite* from sulphurous acid.

IVORY BLACK. A form of carbon obtained from *animal charcoal*, by dissolving out *inorganic compounds*, such as *calcium phosphate*, by means of *hydrochloric acid*.

J

JASPER. A coloured impure form of natural *silica*, SiO_2.

JAVELLE WATER. Eau de Javelle. A *solution* containing potassium hypochlorite, $KOCl$; made by the action of chlorine on a cold solution of *potassium hydroxide*, KOH. Used for *bleaching* and as a *disinfectant*.

JET. A very hard, lustrous form of natural carbon, allied to *coal*.

JET ENGINE. A *gas turbine* which produces a stream of hot *gas* enabling an aircraft to be propelled through the air by *reaction propulsion*. Air taken in at the front of the engine is compressed by a radial compressor. The compressed air then enters the combustion chambers providing the *oxidant* for the combustion of the *liquid fuel*. The *energy* released expands the gas and accelerates it rearwards, some of the energy of the gas being used to drive a *turbine* which in turn operates the compressor. After leaving the turbine the gas passes to the rear jet nozzle producing forward *thrust* by reaction on the structure of the jet tube.

JET PROPULSION. See *reaction propulsion*.

JOULE. The derived *SI unit* of *work* or *energy*. The work done when the point of application of a *force* of one *newton* is displaced through a distance of 1 *metre* in the direction of the force. The joule is also the work done per second by a *current* of 1 *ampere* flowing through a *resistance* of 1 *ohm*. Symbol J. 1 joule = 10^7 *ergs*. Named after James Prescott Joule (1818–89).

JOULE'S EQUIVALENT. See *mechanical equivalent of heat*.

JOULE'S LAWS. 1. The *intrinsic energy* of a *gas* at constant *temperature* is independent of its *volume*. Joule's law is obeyed strictly only by a *perfect gas*, real gases show deviations from it. 2. The *heat* produced by an *electric current I*, passing through a *conductor* of *resistance R*, for a time *t*, is equal to I^2Rt. If *I* is in *amperes*, *R* in *ohms*, and *t* in *seconds*, the heat produced will be in *joules*.

JOULE-THOMSON EFFECT. Joule-Kelvin effect. When a *gas* expands through a porous plug, a change of *temperature* occurs, proportional to the *pressure* difference across the plug. The temperature change is due partly to a departure of the gas from *Joule's law*, the gas performing internal work in overcoming the mutual attractions of its *molecules* and thus cooling itself; and partly to deviation of the gas from *Boyle's law*. The latter effect can give rise to either cooling or heating, depending upon the initial temperature and pressure difference used. For a given mean pressure, the temperature at which the two effects balance, resulting in no alteration of temperature, is called the 'inversion temperature'. Gases expanding through a porous plug below their inversion temperature are cooled, otherwise they are heated. Named after J. P. Joule and Sir William Thomson (Lord Kelvin) (1824–1907).

JUNCTION RECTIFIER. A *rectifier* based upon a *semiconductor junction*.

209

JUNCTION TRANSISTOR. A *transistor* having a *base electrode* and two or more electrodes connected to *semiconductor junctions*.

JUPITER (astr.). A *planet,* having twelve small *satellites,* with its *orbit* between those of *Mars* and *Saturn.* Largest of the planets, diameter 142 800 kilometres. Mean distance from the *Sun* 778·34 million kilometres. *Sidereal period* ('year') = 11·86 years. *Mass* approximately 317·89 times that of the *Earth.* Surface temperature probably about −150°C.

K

KAINITE. A double *salt* of *magnesium sulphate* and *potassium chloride*, $MgSO_4.KCl.3H_2O$ which occurs naturally in Poland and in the *Stassfurt Deposits*. A valuable source of potassium salts.

KALIUM. See *potassium*.

KAOLIN. See *china clay*.

KAON. A K-*meson*. See Table 6, page 437.

KARYO-. A prefix denoting the *nucleus* of a *cell* or its contents; e.g. 'karyotype', the sum of the morphological characteristics of the *chromosomes* of a cell.

KATABOLISM. See *catabolism*.

KEEPERS OF MAGNETS. Short bars of soft iron used to prevent permanent *magnets* from losing their *magnetism*.

KEKULÉ FORMULA. The graphic representation of *benzene* first suggested by F. A. Kekulé von Stradonitz (1829–96). See *benzene ring*.

KELP. Sea-weed or its *ash*, used as a source of iodine.

KELVIN. The *SI unit* of *thermodynamic temperature* defined as the fraction $1/273.16$ of thermodynamic temperature of the *triple point* of *water*, i.e. the triple point of water contains exactly 273.16 kelvins. The units of kelvin and *celsius (centigrade) temperature* interval are identical. A temperature expressed in degrees *celsius* is equal to the temperature in kelvins less $273.15°C$. This is true both for thermodynamic temperatures and on the *International Practical Temperature Scale*. Symbol K; the name 'degree kelvin' (symbol °K) was discontinued by international agreement in 1967. Named after Lord Kelvin (1824–1907).

KELVIN EFFECT. See *Thomson effect*.

KELVIN TEMPERATURE. *Temperature* expressed in *kelvins*. The same as the *absolute thermodynamic temperature*. See *thermodynamic temperature*. Symbol K.

KEPLER'S LAWS. 1. The *planets* move about the *Sun* in *ellipses*, at one focus of which the Sun is situated. 2. The *radius vector* joining each planet with the Sun describes equal areas in equal times. 3. The ratio of the *square* of the planet's year to the cube of the planet's mean distance from the Sun is the same for all planets. Named after Johann Kepler (1571–1630).

KERATIN. A *protein* forming the principal constituent of wool, hair, horns, and hoofs.

KEROSENE. Kerosine. See *paraffin oil*.

KERR EFFECT. When *plane-polarized light* is reflected from a highly polished *pole* of an *electromagnet* the light becomes *elliptically polarized*. Similarly, if a *beam* of light is passed through certain transparent *liquids* or *solids* to which a *potential difference* is applied, the plane of polarization of the light is rotated through an angle which depends upon the magnitude of the applied potential difference. This effect is made use of in the *Kerr cell*. Named after John Kerr (1824–1907).

KERR CELL. A transparent cell (based on the *Kerr effect*) filled with a *liquid*, such as *nitrobenzene*, which contains two *electrodes* placed between two polarizing mediums. *Light* can only pass through the cell if the two planes of *polarization* are parallel. As the Kerr effect occurs in time intervals as short as 10^{-8} *seconds*, the cell may be used as a high-speed shutter, and also as a means of modulating a *laser* beam.

KETEN. CH_2:CO. A colourless *gas*, b.p. $-56°$ C., used in the manufacture of *aspirin*: the first member of the keten series of the general formula CR_2:CO.

KETO-ENOL TAUTOMERISM. The type of *tautomerism* which occurs in *ketones* as the result of the migration of a hydrogen *atom* from an *alkyl group* to the *carbonyl group*. Thus, *acetone* contains in addition to ketone *molecules* (CH_3.CO.CH_3, the keto-form) a small proportion of molecules having the structure of an *unsaturated alcohol* (CH_2:COH.CH_3, the enol-form).

KETONES. A series of *organic compounds* having the general formula RR$'$ C:O, where R and R$'$ are *univalent hydrocarbon radicals*. E.g. *acetone*, dimethyl ketone, $(CH_3)_2CO$.

KETOSE. A *monosaccharide* which contains a *ketone* group.

keV. The symbol for 1000 *electron-volts*.

KICKSORTER. See *pulse height analyser*.

KIESELGUHR. Diatomaceous earth, infusorial earth. A mass of *hydrated silica* (SiO_2) formed from skeletons of minute plants known as diatoms. A very porous and absorbent material, used for filtering and absorbing various *liquids*, in the manufacture of *dynamite* and in other industries.

KILLED SPIRITS OF SALTS. A *solution* of *zinc chloride*, $ZnCl_2$, made by reacting zinc with *hydrochloric acid*. Used in soldering.

KILO-. Prefix denoting a thousand in the *metric system*. Symbol k.

KILOCYCLE. Measure of *frequency*. 1000 *cycles* per *second*. (Equal to 1 *kilohertz*.)

KILOGRAM. Kilogramme. 1000 *grams*. *SI unit* of *mass* defined in terms of the international prototype in the custody of the Bureau International des Poids et Mesures at Sèvres near Paris. Equal to 2·20462 lbs. Symbol kg.

KILOHERTZ. kHz. 1000 *hertz*. A measure of *frequency* equal to 1000 *cycles* per *second*.

KILOMETRE. 1000 *metres*. Equal to 1094 yards, 0·6214 mile.

KILOTON BOMB. A *nuclear weapon* with an explosive power equivalent to one thousand tons of *T.N.T.* (approximately 4×10^{12} *joules* or 10^{12} *calories*).

KILOWATT. kW. Unit of *power*. 1000 *watts*.

KILOWATT-HOUR. kWh. Board of Trade unit. A practical unit of *work*. Work done when a rate of work of 1000 *watts* is maintained for 1 hour.

KINEMATIC EQUATIONS. See *motion, equations of*.

KINEMATIC VISCOSITY. $\nu = \eta/\rho$. The ratio of the coefficient of *viscosity* to the *density* of a *fluid*. Measured in square *metres* per *second* (*SI units*) or *stokes*. 1 centistoke = 10^{-6} m^2/s.

KINEMATICS. The branch of *mechanics* which is concerned with the phenomena of motion without reference to *mass* or *force*. Kinematics deals with motion from the standpoint of measurement and precise description, while *dynamics* is concerned with the causes or laws of motion.

KINETIC ENERGY. The *energy* which a body possesses by virtue of its motion. The kinetic energy of a *mass m*, moving with *velocity v*, is $\frac{1}{2}mv^2$. The energy will be in *joules* if *m* is in *kilograms* and *v* is in *metres* per second. (In *c.g.s. units* it will be in *ergs*.) The kinetic energy of rotation of a body whose *moment of inertia* about an *axis* is *I*, and whose *angular velocity* about this axis is ω, is $\frac{1}{2}I\omega^2$. Again the energy will be in joules if *I* is in kg m^2 and ω is in *radians* per second. (In c.g.s. units it will be in ergs.)

KINETIC THEORY OF GASES. A mathematical explanation of the behaviour of *gases* on the assumption that gases consist of *molecules* which are in ceaseless motion in space, the *kinetic energy* of the molecules depending upon the *temperature* of the gas; the molecules are considered to be perfectly elastic particles which collide with each other and with the walls of the containing vessel (see *elastic collision*). The *pressure* exerted by a gas on the walls of the vessel is due to the collisions of the molecules with it. The *gas laws* may be shown to be in full agreement with this theory.

KINK INSTABILITY. In a *thermonuclear reaction* experiment, an instability in the magnetically confined *plasma* resulting from a local deformation of the plasma. The kink tends to grow because the *magnetic lines of forces* of the self-induced confining field are crowded on the *concave* side of the kink.

KIPP'S APPARATUS. A device used in laboratories for the production of a supply of any *gas* which can be evolved by the action of a *liquid* on a *solid* without heating. The simplest form is illustrated in Fig. 23 on page 214. Opening the tap T allows the liquid in C to reach the solid in B. A reaction occurs and gas is produced. When the tap is closed, gas production continues until the liquid is forced back into B. Named after Petrus Jacobus Kipp (1808–64).

KIRCHHOFF'S LAWS. 1. In any network of wires the algebraic sum of the *electric currents* which meet at a point is zero. 2. The algebraic sum of the *electromotive forces* in any closed circuit or mesh is equal to the algebraic sum of the products of the *resistances* of each portion of the circuit and the currents flowing through them. Named after Gustav Robert Kirchhoff (1824–87).

KISH. A variety of *graphite* occasionally formed in iron *smelting* furnaces.

KJELDAHL FLASK. A round-bottomed glass flask with a long wide neck, used in the estimation of nitrogen by the Kjeldahl method.

KLYSTRON. An *electron* tube used to generate or amplify *electromagnetic radiation* in the *microwave* region, by *velocity modulation*. Consists of two or more *resonant cavities* in which the electrons, from an *electron gun,* are concentrated into 'bunches'.

KNOCKING in the *internal-combustion* (petrol) *engine.* Violent *explosions* in the cylinder, often due to over-compression of the *mixture* of air and petrol vapour before sparking.

FIGURE 23.

KNOCK-ON COLLISION (phys.). A process in which an *elementary particle* or *nucleus* is set in motion by being struck by another high *energy* particle (or *photon*). The term is also used in relation to collisions as a result of which an *electron* is knocked out of its atomic *orbit* by some other particle. The 'knock-on' particle is the particle set in motion as the result of the collision.

KNOT. Unit of speed; 1 *nautical mile* per hour. (Approximately 1·15 statute miles per hour.)

KOLRAUSCH'S LAW. When *ionization* is complete, the *conductivity* of an *electrolyte* is equal to the sum of the conductivities of the *ions* into which the substance dissociates.

KOVAR*. An *alloy* of cobalt, iron, and nickel which has a coefficient of *expansion* similar to that of *glass.* Used for glass-to-metal seals, particularly in *thermionic valves* and *transistors.*

KREBS CYCLE. See *citric acid cycle.* Named after Hans Adolf Krebs (born 1900).

KRYPTOL*. A *mixture* of *graphite, carborundum,* and *clay,* used as an electrical *resistance* in electric furnaces.

KRYPTON. Kr. Element. A.W. 83·80. At. No. 36. An *inert gas,* which occurs in the *atmosphere* (1 part in 670 000).

KUPFER-NICKEL. Natural nickel arsenide, NiAs. An important *ore* of nickel.

L

LABELLED COMPOUND. A *compound* in which a stable *atom* is replaced by a *radioactive isotope* of that atom. The path taken through a mechanical or biological system by such a labelled compound can be traced by the *radiation* emitted by the 'labelled atom'. See also *radioactive tracing* and *tritiated compound*.

LABILE. Prone to undergo change or displacement; *unstable*.

LACHRYMATOR. See *tear-gas*.

LACTASE. An *enzyme* which catalyses the conversion of *lactose* into *glucose*. Present in the digestive juices of mammals.

LACTATE. 1. A *salt* or ester of *lactic acid*. 2. To produce milk.

LACTIC ACID. $CH_3CH(OH)COOH$. An *organic acid*, occurring in three stereoisomeric forms (see *stereoisomerism*). A colourless crystalline *solid*, m.p. 18° C. *dl*-lactic acid, a mixture of equal amounts of (*dextrorotatory*) *d*-acid and (*laevorotatory*) *l*-acid, is formed by the action of certain *bacteria* on the *lactose* of milk during souring. The *d*-form, sarcolactic acid, occurs in muscle tissue. The optically inactive *dl*-form is used in dyeing and *tanning*.

LACTOPROTEIN. Any of the *proteins* present in milk.

LACTOSE. Milk sugar. $C_{12}H_{22}O_{11}$. A hard, gritty, crystalline, *soluble*, *disaccharide sugar*, m.p. 203° C., less sweet than *cane-sugar*, which occurs in the milk of all mammals. *Hydrolysis* gives a mixture of *glucose* and *galactose*. In the action of certain *bacteria* on milk ('lactic acid fermentation') lactose is converted into *lactic acid*.

LAEVOROTATORY. Rotating or deviating the plane of vibration of *polarized light* to the left (observer looking against the oncoming light). See *optical activity*.

LAEVULIC ACID. Laevulinic acid. $CH_3CO(CH_2)_2COOH$. A white *soluble* substance, m.p. 37·2° C., produced by the *hydrolysis* of certain *carbohydrates*. Used in the manufacture of *plastics* and pharmaceutical products.

LAEVULOSE. Fructose, fruit sugar. $C_6H_{12}O_6$. See *fructose*.

LAKE. In dyeing, a coloured *insoluble* substance formed by the chemical combination of a *soluble dye* with a *mordant*.

LAMBERT. A unit of *luminance*. The luminance of a uniform diffuser of *light* which emits one *lumen* per sq cm. Named after J. H. Lambert (1728–77).

LAMBERT'S LAW OF ILLUMINATION. The *illumination* of a surface upon which the *light* falls normally from a *point source* is inversely proportional to the *square* of the distance between the surface and the source. If the *normal* to the surface makes an angle θ with the direction of the *rays*, then the illumination is proportional to $\cos \theta$.

LAMINA. A thin sheet.

LAMINAR FLOW. The flow of a *fluid* which closely follows the shape of a streamlined surface without turbulence.

LAMINATED IRON. Thin sheets of iron (or, more frequently *stalloy**) used for cores of *transformers* instead of solid iron cores, in order to reduce losses due to *eddy currents*.

LAMP-BLACK. Soot; an *allotropic* form of *carbon*.

LANOLINE. A *wax*-like material obtained from wool-grease, which contains *cholesterol*, $C_{27}H_{45}OH$, and other complex *organic* substances. Readily absorbed by the skin; used in ointments and cosmetics.

LANTHANIDES. Lanthanons. Rare earths. A group of rare metallic *elements* with *atomic numbers* from 57 to 71 inclusive. The properties of these *metals* are all very similar and resemble those of aluminium. The elements occur in *monazite* and other rare minerals. See Table 8, page 440.

LANTHANUM. La. Element. A.W. 138·91. At. No. 57. S.G. 6·2, m.p. 920° C. See *lanthanides*.

LAPIS LAZULI. Sodium aluminium silicate containing sulphur. A rare mineral of beautiful blue colour.

LAPLACE OPERATOR. Laplacian. ∇^2. The *differential* operator which gives the sum of the *partial derivatives* of second *order* with respect to each *variable*, i.e.

$$\nabla^2 u = \frac{\delta^2 u}{\delta x^2} + \frac{\delta^2 u}{\delta y^2} + \frac{\delta^2 u}{\delta z^2} = 0$$

This *equation* is known as the 'Laplace equation'. Named after Pierre Simon Laplace (1749–1827).

LARGE CALORIE. Kilogramme-calorie, Calorie. 1000 *calories*.

LARMOR PRECESSION. The orbital motion of the *electrons* about the *nucleus* of an *atom* is usually such as to give the atom a *resultant angular momentum* and a *magnetic moment*. These two properties cause the atom to precess (see *precessional motion*) about the direction of any applied *magnetic field*. This is Larmor precession; the *frequency* of this precession, known as the Larmor frequency, is equal to $eH/4\pi m$, where e and m are the electronic charge and mass, and H is the *magnetic field strength*. Named after Sir Joseph Larmor (1857–1942).

LASER. Light Amplification by Stimulated Emission of Radiation. An optical *maser*. The laser produces a powerful, highly directional, *monochromatic*, and *coherent* beam of *light*. It works on essentially the same principle as the maser, except that the 'active medium' consists of, or is contained in, an optically transparent cylinder with a reflecting surface at one end and a partially reflecting surface at the other. The stimulated waves make repeated passages up and down the cylinder, some of them emerging as light through the partially reflecting end. In the *ruby* laser, the chromium *atoms* of a cylindrical shaped ruby *crystal* are 'pumped' to an excited state (see *excitation*) by a flash lamp, and it can then be made to emit *pulses* of highly coherent light. Lasers have also been constructed using a mixture of *inert gases* (helium and neon) to produce a continuous beam. Another type of laser consists of a cube of specially treated gallium arsenide, which is capable of emitting *infrared radiation* when a current is passed through it.

LATENT HEAT. *L.* The quantity of *heat* absorbed or released in an *isothermal* transformation of *phase*. The *specific* latent heat of *fusion* is the *heat* required to convert unit *mass* of a *solid* to a *liquid* at the same *temperature*. The specific latent heat of *vaporization* is the heat required to convert unit mass of liquid to *vapour* at the same temperature. Measured in *joules* per *kilogramme*. The corresponding *molar* latent heats are measured in joules per *mole*. At the *melting* and *boiling points* of a substance, the addition of heat causes no rise in temperature until the change of state is complete.

LATERAL. In a sideways direction.

LATERAL INVERSION. The inversion produced by a plane *mirror*. Seen when the image of a printed page is observed in a mirror.

LATERAL VELOCITY. The component of a celestial body's *velocity* perpendicular to the *line of sight velocity*.

LATEX. A milky fluid produced by certain plants, which contains *proteins, carbohydrates, lipids, alkaloids, gums*, etc. The most important is the latex from *rubber* trees which yields natural rubber on coagulation.

LATITUDE. The *angular distance* of a point from the *equator* measured upon the curved surface of the Earth. In *astronomy* it is the *coordinate* of a celestial body from a fixed *plane*. The 'galactic latitude' is the *angular distance* from the plane of the *Milky Way*. The 'celestial latitude' is the angular distance between the celestial body and the *ecliptic*.

LATITUDE, LINES OF. Parallels of latitude. Circles parallel to the *equator*, joining points of equal *latitude*; the equator itself is latitude $0°$, while the poles are latitude $90°$.

LATTICE. 1. The regular network of fixed points about which *molecules, atoms*, or *ions* vibrate in a *crystal*. 2. In a *nuclear reactor*, a structure consisting of discrete bodies of *fissile* and non-fissile material (especially *moderator*), arranged in a regular geometrical pattern.

LATTICE ENERGY. The *energy* required to separate the *ions* of a *crystal* to an infinite distance from each other.

LAUDANUM. An alcoholic *tincture* of *opium*.

LAUGHING GAS. See *nitrous oxide*.

LAURALDEHYDE. Lauryl aldehyde. See *dodecanal*.

LAURIC ACID. Dodecanoic acid. $CH_3(CH_2)_{10}COOH$. A white crystalline *insoluble* substance, m.p. $44°C$., used in the manufacture of *soaps, detergents*, and cosmetics.

LAUROYL GROUP. The *univalent radical* $CH_3(CH_2)_{10}CO—$.

LAURYL ALCOHOL. Dodecanol. $CH_3(CH_2)_{11}OH$. A white crystalline *insoluble* substance, the commercial form of which consists of a mixture of *isomers* with m.p. in the range $20–30°C$. Used in the manufacture of *detergents*.

LAWRENCIUM. Lr. *Transuranic element*, At. No. 103. The only known isotope, $^{257}_{103}$Lw, has *half-life* of only 8 secs.

LD50. See *median lethal dose*.

LEACHING. Washing out a *soluble* constituent.

LEAD. Pb (Plumbum). Element. A.W. 207·19. At. No. 82. A soft, bluish-white *metal*, S.G. 11·34, m.p. 327·4°C. Occurs chiefly as *galena*, PbS. Extracted by roasting the *ore* in a *reverberatory furnace*. *Compounds* are poisonous. The metal is used in the lead *accumulator*, in *alloys* and in plumbing; compounds are used in *paint* manufacture.

LEAD ACCUMULATOR. See *accumulator*.

LEAD ACETATE. Sugar of lead. $(CH_3COO)_2Pb.3H_2O$. A white crystal-line *soluble salt*, m.p. 280°C., with a sweet taste. Used as a *mordant* and as a drier in *paints*.

LEAD ARSENATE. $Pb_3(AsO_4)_2$. A white crystalline substance, m.p. 1042°C., used as an *insecticide*.

LEAD CARBONATE. Normal lead carbonate, $PbCO_3$, is a white powder which occurs naturally as cerussite. Basic lead carbonate, $2PbCO_3$. $Pb(OH)_2$, is known as white lead and is widely used as a *pigment*.

LEAD-CHAMBER PROCESS. The manufacture of *sulphuric acid* by the action of *nitrogen dioxide*, NO_2, on *sulphur dioxide*, SO_2, to give *nitric oxide*, NO, and *sulphur trioxide*, SO_3. The former reacts with oxygen from the air to give NO_2 again; the SO_3 combines with *water* to give sulphuric acid, the process being carried out in large lead chambers.

LEAD DIOXIDE. Lead peroxide. PbO_2. An *amorphous*, dark brown powder.

LEAD MONOXIDE. Litharge. PbO. A yellow crystalline substance, m.p. 888°C., used in the manufacture of *glass*, *paints*, and *glazes*. See also *red lead*.

LEAD PEROXIDE. See *lead dioxide*.

LEAD TETRAETHYL. See *tetraethyl lead*.

LEBLANC PROCESS. Salt-cake process. An almost obsolete process for the manufacture of *sodium carbonate*, Na_2CO_3. *Common salt* is converted into *sodium sulphate*, Na_2SO_4 ('salt-cake') by heating with *sulphuric acid*. This is heated with *coal* and *limestone*; the sodium sulphate is reduced by the carbon to sodium sulphide, which then reacts with the lime-stone to give sodium carbonate and calcium sulphide. Named after Nicolas Leblanc (1742–1806).

LE CHATELIER PRINCIPLE. If a system in *equilibrium* is subjected to a *stress*, the system tends to react in such a way as to oppose the effect of the stress. Named after Henri-Louis Le Chatelier (1850–1936).

LECITHINS. A class of *organic compounds* occurring in living *organisms*. Chemically very similar to *fats*, but the *molecule* contains the *elements* nitrogen and phosphorus in addition to carbon, hydrogen, and oxygen.

LECLANCHÉ CELL. A *primary cell* with a positive *electrode* or pole of car-bon surrounded by a mixture of *manganese dioxide* and powdered carbon in a porous pot. This stands in a *solution* of *ammonium chloride*, the *electrolyte*, in a jar which also contains the negative electrode of zinc.

When the external circuit is completed, a current flows, chlorine *ions* in the electrolyte moving towards the zinc and ammonium ions toward the carbon electrode. The chlorine ions react with the zinc to form *zinc chloride*, and the ammonium ions decompose at the positive electrode to give *ammonia* and hydrogen. The hydrogen liberated tends to cause *polarization* of the cell. This tendency is partly counteracted by the manganese dioxide, which oxidizes the hydrogen. The *E.M.F.* is approximately 1·5 *volts*. Leclanché cells are widely used for many purposes which require an intermittent current. The common *dry cell* is a special form of Leclanché cell. Named after Georges Leclanché (1839–82).

LENGTH, BRITISH UNITS OF.

12 lines	= 1 inch
12 ins	= 1 foot
3 ft	= 1 yard
22 yds	= 1 chain
10 chains	= 1 furlong
8 fur	= 1 mile

For conversion to metric units see Table 1, page 425.

LENGTH, METRIC UNITS OF.

10 millimetres	= 1 centimetre
100 cm	= 1 metre
1000 m	= 1 kilometre

For conversion to British units see Table 1, page 425. The *SI unit* of length is the *metre*.

LENS. Any device which causes a *beam* of *rays* to converge or diverge on passing through it. The optical lens is a portion of a *transparent* refracting medium (see *refraction of light*), usually *glass*, bounded by two surfaces, generally curved. Such lenses are classified according to the nature of the surfaces into bi-*concave*, bi-*convex*, plano-convex, etc. (See

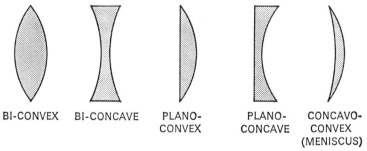

| BI-CONVEX | BI-CONCAVE | PLANO-CONVEX | PLANO-CONCAVE | CONCAVO-CONVEX (MENISCUS) |

FIGURE 24.

Fig. 24.) The centres of the *spheres* of which the lens surfaces are considered to form a part are termed the *centres of curvature*; the line joining these is the *optical axis*, the *optical centre* is a point on the axis within the lens; all rays passing through this point emerge without deviation. A parallel beam of *light* incident on a lens is made to converge (convex lens) or diverge (concave lens). The point of divergence or convergence is called a principal focus (see Fig. 25). Regarding all distances as being measured from the optical centre, and taking all distances as positive when measured in a direction opposite to that of the incident light, the distances of the object and image from the lens are given by the formula $1/v - 1/u = 1/f$, where u and v are the distances from the lens of object and image respectively, and f is the *focal length*, i.e. the distance of the focus from the lens (see Fig. 25.) Electrostatic and electromagnetic lenses, for converging beams of *electrons* and other elementary charged particles, are also of importance, e.g. in the *electron microscope*. See *electron lens*.

CONVERGING AND DIVERGING LENSES

FIGURE 25.

LENTICULAR. Pertaining to a *lens*, especially a *bi-convex* lens, or resembling such a lens in shape.

LENZ'S LAW. When a circuit and a *magnetic field* move relatively to each other, the *electric current* induced in the circuit will have a magnetic field opposing the motion. See *induction, electromagnetic*. Named after Heinrich Lenz (1804–65).

LEPTON. A collective name for *electrons*, *muons*, and *neutrinos*. The number of leptons minus the number of corresponding anti-leptons taking part in a process is called the 'lepton number'; a quantity which appears to be conserved in all processes. All leptons have *spin* $\frac{1}{2}$, but anti-leptons have spin in an opposite direction to that of their corresponding particles. See Table 6, page 436.

LEUCINE. A white *soluble amino acid*, m.p. 293–5° C., essential to mammals. See Table 5, page 435.

LEUCOCYTES. White *blood cells*. The cells of the *blood* which contain no *haemoglobin*. There are several types of leucocytes, the main function of which is the combating of infection. Human blood contains between 5000 and 10 000 leucocytes per cubic millimetre.

LEVER. A rigid bar which may be turned freely about a fixed point of support, the fulcrum. The *mechanical advantage* of a lever is given by the ratio of the perpendicular distance of the line of action of the effort from the fulcrum, to the perpendicular distance of the line of action of the resistance from the fulcrum.

LEWIS ACIDS AND BASES. A concept of *acids* and *bases* put forward by G. N. Lewis (1875–1946) in which an acid is defined as a substance which forms a covalent bond (see *valency, electronic theory of*) with a base by accepting from it a *lone pair of electrons*. A base is defined as a substance which forms a covalent bond with an acid by donating to it a lone pair of electrons.

LEWISITE. Chlorovinyl dichlorarsine. $ClCH:CHAsCl_2$. An oily liquid war 'gas' with lethal *vesicant* properties. Destroyed by *oxidizing agents*, e.g. *bleaching powder*.

LEYDEN JAR. A form of electrostatic *capacitor* of historical interest. Invented in 1745 in the Dutch town of Leyden.

LIBRATION. An oscillation of the *Moon's* face from side to side. Due to libration about 58% of the Moon's surface can be seen from the Earth.

LIEBIG CONDENSER. See *condenser* (chem.). Named after Baron von Liebig (1803–73).

LIGHT. The agency by means of which a viewed object influences the observer's eye. Consists of *electromagnetic radiation* within the *wavelength* range 4×10^{-7} *metres* to $7 \cdot 7 \times 10^{-7}$ metres approximately; variations in the wavelength produce different sensations in the eye, corresponding to different *colours*. See *colour vision*.

LIGHT PEN. An input/output *computer* device used with a *visual display unit*. When pointed at a *cathode ray tube* it can sense whether or not the spot is illuminated.

LIGHT QUANTUM. See *photon*.

LIGHT, VELOCITY OF. The mean value is $2 \cdot 997\,925 \times 10^{15}$ metres/sec. = 186 281 miles/sec. The special significance of the velocity of light in the *Universe* was revealed by the special theory of *relativity*. According to this now accepted theory, the velocity of light is absolute (i.e. independent of the velocity of the observer) and represents a limiting velocity in that the velocity of no body can exceed it. The special significance of the velocity of light is apparent from its presence in the *mass-energy equation* which follows from the special theory of relativity. In this equation the velocity of light appears as the 'connecting link' between *mass* and *energy*.

LIGHT-YEAR. An astronomical measure of distance; the distance travelled by *light* (see *light, velocity of*) in one year: equal to $9 \cdot 4605 \times 10^{15}$ *metres* or $5 \cdot 87848 \times 10^{12}$ miles.

LIGHTNING. An electric discharge in the form of a spark or flash between two charged clouds, or between a cloud and the *Earth*.

LIGHTNING CONDUCTOR. A *conductor* of *electricity* connected to earth and ending in one or more sharp points attached to a high part of a building. The effect of a passing *electric charge*, such as an electrically charged cloud, is to produce a discharge of electricity of opposite charge from the conductor; since the density of charge is greatest at the more pointed parts of the conductor, the strength of the *electric field* in the air near the sharp points will become so great as to make the air a conductor of electricity. Thus a stream of electricity of opposite charge to that of the cloud will proceed from the sharp points, causing a quiet neutralization of charges instead of an accumulation which may become great enough to break down the insulation of the air and thus cause a lightning discharge.

LIGNIN. A complex *organic* material which occurs in the woody *tissues* of plants, often combined with *cellulose*. The preparation of pure cellulose by removing the lignin is an important step in the manufacture of pulp for the *paper* and *rayon* industries.

LIGNITE. Brown coal. A brownish-black, natural deposit resembling *coal*, which contains a higher percentage of *hydrocarbons* than ordinary coal; it is probably of more recent origin.

LIGROIN. A *mixture* of *hydrocarbons* of the *paraffin series*; generally applied to a mixture having b.p. 70°–120° C.

LIME. Quicklime, see *calcium oxide*; or slaked lime, see *calcium hydroxide*. The term is sometimes loosely applied to calcium *salts* in general.

LIMESTONE. Natural *calcium carbonate*, $CaCO_3$.

LIME-WATER. A solution of *calcium hydroxide*, $Ca(OH)_2$, in *water*. Turns milky by the action of *carbon dioxide*, CO_2, owing to the formation of *insoluble calcium carbonate*, $CaCO_3$.

LIMIT. Limiting value (math.). A *function* of a variable quantity x, written $f(x)$, approaches a limiting value k as x approaches a value a, if the difference $k - f(a + \delta)$ may be made smaller than any assignable value by making δ sufficiently small.

LIMIT OF SPECTRAL SERIES. The lines appearing in the *line spectrum* of any *element* can be grouped into definite series. The shortest *wavelength* of any such series is called the limit of the series. At this series limit, the lines crowd closer and closer together from the long wavelength side.

LIMONENE. $C_{10}H_{16}$. An *optically active liquid terpene*, b.p. in the range 170–178° C., which occurs in certain *essential oils*.

LIMONITE. Natural *hydrated* form of *ferric oxide*, Fe_2O_3. An *ore* of iron.

LINALOL. $C_{10}H_{17}OH$. A colourless *liquid terpene alcohol*, b.p. 198–200°C., occurring in certain *essential oils* and used in perfumes.

LINALYL ACETATE. $C_{10}H_{17}COOCH_3$. A colourless *liquid*, b.p. 220°C., with a pleasant odour; used in perfumes and *soaps*.

LINE OF SIGHT VELOCITY. Radial velocity. The *velocity* at which a heavenly body approaches, or recedes from, the Earth. Measured spectroscopically by observing the shift of the spectral lines (see *spectrum*) of *elements* within the body, relative to those of the same elements on Earth. See *Doppler effect*.

LINE PAIR. In *spectrographic analysis* a line pair consists of the particular spectral line (see *line spectrum*) utilized in the determination of the *concentration* of an *element* and the *internal standard line* with which it is compared.

LINE PRINTER. An output device from a *computer* which prints a line of *characters* at a rate of between 300 and 1500 lines per minute.

LINE SPECTRUM. A *spectrum (emission* or *absorption)* consisting of definite single lines, each corresponding to a particular *wavelength*; characteristic of an *element* in the atomic state.

LINEAR. 1. Arranged in a line. 2. Having only one dimension. 3. (of a mathematical expression or *equation*) Having only first *degree* terms (see also *linear relationship*). 4. (of a component, *circuit* or piece of *electronic* equipment) Having an output directly proportional to the input.

LINEAR ACCELERATOR. Linac. An apparatus for accelerating *ions* to high energies. Consists of a row of cylindrical *electrodes* separated by small gaps and having a common axis. Alternate electrodes are connected to each other and a *high-frequency potential* is applied between the two sets of electrodes. The frequency, and the lengths of the different electrodes, are such that the ions are accelerated each time they cross a gap between two electrodes.

LINEAR MOTOR. A form of *induction motor*, in which the *stator* and *rotor* are linear instead of cylindrical, and parallel instead of *coaxial*.

LINEAR RELATIONSHIP. A relationship existing between two *variable* quantities which are directly proportional to each other. A *graph* representing the manner in which such quantities vary with each other will be a straight line.

LINES OF FORCE. See *electrical lines of force; magnetic lines of force*.

LINNAEAN SYSTEM. See *binomial nomenclature*. Named after Carolus Linnaeus (1707–78).

LINOLEIC ACID. $C_{17}H_{31}COOH$. A yellow oily liquid *unsaturated fatty acid*, b.p. 229°C., which occurs in various *vegetable oils*, particularly *linseed oil*. Once known as *vitamin F*, but its function in this capacity is now discredited.

LINSEED OIL. A *vegetable oil* extracted from the seeds of flax plants. Contains *glycerides* of *oleic acid* and other *unsaturated fatty acids*. Being easily oxidized and polymerized it is widely used in the *paint* and varnish industries and for manufacturing linoleum.

LIPASE. An *enzyme* with the power of hydrolyzing (see *hydrolysis*) *fats*.

LIPIDS. Lipoids. A group of *organic compounds* which are *esters* of *fatty acids* and which are characterized by being *insoluble* in *water* but *soluble* in many organic *solvents*. Usually divided into three groups: (1) 'Simple lipids' which include *fats and oils* as well as *waxes*; (2) 'Compound lipids' which include *phospholipids* and *glycolipids*; (3) 'Derived lipids' of which the most important are the *steroids*.

LIPOCLASTIC. Lipolytic. Fat-splitting; applied to *enzymes* having the power of hydrolyzing (see *hydrolysis*) *fats* into *fatty acid* and *glycerin*; e.g. *lipase*.

LIPOPROTEIN. A *protein* which includes a *lipid* in its structure.

LIPOWITZ' ALLOY. A fusible *alloy*, m.p. 65–70° C., which consists of 50% bismuth, 27% lead, 13% tin, 10% cadmium.

LIQUATION. The separation of a *solid mixture* by heating till one of the constituents melts and can be drained away.

LIQUEFACTION OF GASES. A *gas* possessing a *critical temperature* above room temperature may be liquefied merely by increasing the *pressure* on it. Otherwise, the gas must first be cooled to below its critical temperature and then compressed; or, if desired, cooled directly to its *boiling point* under normal pressure. The methods of cooling are (1) by *evaporation* under reduced pressure, as in the *cascade liquefier*; (2) by using the principle of the *Joule-Thomson effect* (the Linde process); (3) by causing the gas to expand against an external pressure; in so doing the gas does *work*, thereby cooling itself. This principle is used in the Claude process.

LIQUID. A state of *matter* intermediate between a *solid* and a *gas*, in which the *molecules* are relatively free to move with respect to each other but are restricted by cohesive *forces* to the extent that the liquid maintains a fixed *volume*. Liquids assume the shape of the vessel containing them, but are only slightly compressible.

LIQUID AIR. A pale blue *liquid*, containing mainly liquid oxygen, b.p. – 182·9° C., and liquid nitrogen, b.p. – 195·7° C.

LIQUID DROP MODEL OF THE NUCLEUS. A hypothetical model of the atomic *nucleus* in which its properties are compared to those of a drop of *liquid*.

LISSAJOUS FIGURE. The *locus* of the *resultant* displacement of a point on which two or more simple periodic motions are impressed. In the common case, two periodic motions are at right angles and are of the same *frequency*. The Lissajous figures then become, in general, a series of *ellipses* corresponding to the possible differences of *phase* between the two motions. Named after Jules Lissajous (1822–80).

LITHARGE. See *lead monoxide*.

LITHIUM. Li. Element. A.W. 6·939. At. No. 3. A light, silvery-white *alkali metal*, m.p.179° C., S.G. 0·534; the lightest *solid* known. Chemically resembles sodium, but is less active. Used in *alloys*.

LITHIUM CHLORIDE. LiCl. A white *soluble deliquescent* substance, m.p. 614° C., used as a *flux* and in mineral waters.

LOGIC

LITHOPONE. A *mixture* of *zinc sulphide*, ZnS, and *barium sulphate*, BaSO$_4$. Used in *paints* as a non-poisonous substitute for *white lead*.

LITHOSPHERE. See *Earth's crust*.

LITMUS. A *soluble* purple substance of vegetable origin; turned red by *acids* and blue by *alkalis*. Used as an *indicator*.

LITRE. Unit of *volume* in the *metric system*. Formerly defined as the volume of 1 *kilogramme* of pure *water* at 4°C. and 760 mm pressure (which is equivalent to 1000·028 cc). This definition still applies for purposes of the 1963 Weights and Measures Act. However, in *SI units* the litre is a special name for the cubic decimetre, but is not used for high precision measurements. For approximate purposes 1 litre = 1000 cc, and the symbol ml is often used synonomously with cc, though this practice is now deprecated.

LIVER OF SULPHUR. A *mixture* of *sulphides* and other sulphur *compounds* of potassium, obtained by fusing *potassium carbonate*, K$_2$CO$_3$, with sulphur. Used as an *insecticide* and *fungicide* in gardening.

LIXIVIATION. The extraction of *soluble* material from a *mixture* by washing with *water*.

LOADED CONCRETE. Normal *concrete* to which has been added some material containing *elements* of high *atomic number* (e.g. iron or lead shot). Used in the shielding of *nuclear reactors*.

LOCAL GROUP OF GALAXIES. The cluster of *galaxies* to which the *Galaxy* belongs. Distant clusters of galaxies are receding from the Local Group. See *expansion of the Universe*.

LOCAL OSCILLATOR. The *oscillator* in a *heterodyne* or *superheterodyne radio* receiver which produces the *radio frequency* oscillation with which the received wave is combined.

LOCUS (math.). The locus of a point is the line which can be drawn through adjacent positions of the point, thus tracing out the path of the point in space.

LODESTONE. A magnetic variety of natural iron oxide, Fe$_3$O$_4$, *magnetite*.

LOGARITHMIC SCALE. A scale of measurement in which an increase of one unit represents a tenfold increase in the quantity measured (for common *logarithms*).

LOGARITHMS. If a number, a, is expressed as a *power* of another number, b, i.e. if $a = b^n$, then n is said to be the logarithm of a to *base b*, written $\log_b a$. Common logarithms are to base 10. Multiplication, division, and other computations are shortened by the use of common logarithms; the addition of logarithms of numbers gives the logarithm of the *product* of the numbers; similarly *division* can be performed by subtraction of the logarithms. Logarithms corresponding to ordinary numbers have been tabulated, and calculations are carried out by the use of such tables. Natural or Napierian logarithms are to the base 'e' (which has the value 2·71828). $\log_e a = 2·303 \log_{10} a$. See also *characteristic, mantissa,* and *exponential*.

LOGIC. In an automatic data processing system, the systematic scheme

225

which defines the interactions of the physical entities representing data.

LONE PAIR OF ELECTRONS. A pair of unshared *valency electrons* which are responsible for the formation of coordinate bonds. See *valency, electronic theory of*.

LONG SIGHT. See *hypermetropia, presbyopia*.

LONGITUDE. The angle which the terrestrial *meridian* through the geographical poles and a point on the Earth's surface makes with a standard meridian (usually through Greenwich) is the longitude of the point. In astronomy, the 'celestial longitude' is the *angular distance* of a celestial body from the vernal *equinox* along the *ecliptic*, measured through 360° towards the East.

LONGITUDE, LINES OF. Imaginary *meridians* on the Earth's surface, referred to a standard meridian; *great circles* of the Earth intersecting at the poles.

LONGITUDINAL. Lengthwise; in a line with the length of the object under consideration.

LONGITUDINAL WAVES. Waves in which the vibration or displacement takes place in the direction of propagation of the waves; e.g. *sound* waves. See also *transverse waves*.

LORENTZ TRANSFORMATION. A set of *equations* for correlating *space* and *time coordinates* in two *frames of reference*, especially at *relativistic velocities*. Named after Hendrik Lorentz (1853–1928).

LOSCHMIDT'S CONSTANT. The number of *molecules* per cc of a *perfect gas* at $N.P.T.$; equal to $2 \cdot 68719 \times 10^{19}$ per cc (or $2 \cdot 68719 \times 10^{25}$ per cubic metre).

LOUDNESS OF SOUND. The magnitude of the physiological response of the ear to *sound*. As the ear responds differently to different *frequencies*, the loudness of a sound will depend to a certain extent on its frequency. However, loudness can be roughly correlated with the *cube root* of the intensity of sound, and different levels can be conveniently compared by the units *decibel* and *phon*.

LOUDSPEAKER. A device for converting *electric currents* into *sounds* loud enough to be heard at a distance. Commonest type consists of an *electromagnetically* vibrated paper cone.

LOVIBOND TINTOMETER*. A *colorimeter* in which the *colour* of a liquid, surface, powder, or light source is compared with a series of glass slides of standardized colours.

LOW FREQUENCY. LF. A *radio frequency* in the range 30–300 *kilohertz*.

LUMEN. The derived *SI unit* of *luminous flux*. The amount of *light* emitted per second in unit *solid angle* of one *steradian* by a uniform *point source* of one *candela* intensity; i.e. the amount of light falling per second on unit area placed at unit distance from such a source. Symbol lm.

LUMINANCE. The *luminous intensity* of any surface in a given direction per unit of orthogonally projected area of that surface, on a plane perpendicular to the given direction.

LUMINESCENCE. The emission of *light* from a body from any cause other than high *temperature*. *Fluorescence* and *phosphorescence* are particular cases of luminescence.

LUMINOSITY. 1. The property of emitting *light*. 2. The amount of light emitted by a *star*, irrespective of its distance from the *Earth*, usually expressed as a *magnitude*.

LUMINOUS FLUX. The luminous flux through an area is the amount of *light* passing through that area in one *second*. The derived *SI unit* of luminous flux is the *lumen*.

LUMINOUS INTENSITY. The amount of *light* emitted per second in unit *solid angle* by a *point source*, in a given direction. The *SI unit* of luminous intensity is the *candela*. The term is restricted to point sources.

LUMINOUS PAINT. *Paint* prepared from phosphorescent *compounds* such as *calcium sulphide*, etc., which glows after exposure to *light*. See *phosphorescence*.

LUNAR CAUSTIC. *Silver nitrate*, $AgNO_3$, usually fused and cast into sticks.

LUNATION. Synodic month. The time between one new moon (see *phases of the moon*) and the next; equal to 29 days 12 hours and 44 minutes.

LUTETIUM. Cassiopeium. Lu. Element. A.W. 174·97. At. No. 71. S.G. 9·842, m.p. 1652°C. See *lanthanides*.

LUX. Metre candle. The derived *SI unit* of *illumination*; one *lumen* per square *metre*. Symbol lx.

LYDDITE. An *explosive* consisting of *picric acid* (trinitrophenol, $C_6H_2OH\text{-}(NO_2)_3$, mixed with 10% *nitrobenzene* and 3% *Vaseline**.

LYMAN SERIES. A series of lines which occurs in the *ultraviolet* region of the *spectrum* of hydrogen. Named after T. Lyman.

LYOPHILIC COLLOID. 'Solvent-loving colloid'. See *colloidal solutions*.

LYOPHOBIC COLLOID. 'Solvent-hating colloid'. See *colloidal solutions*.

LYSERGIC ACID. $C_{15}H_{15}N_2COOH$. A crystalline substance obtained from ergot and used in the manufacture of the hallucinogen LSD (lysergic acid diethylamide).

LYSINE. An essential crystalline soluble *amimo acid*, m.p. 224°C. See Table 5, page 435.

LYSIS. The dissolution or destruction of *cells* (especially *blood cells* or *bacteria*) by a class of *antibodies* called lysins.

LYSOL*. A mixture of the *cresols* with a *solution* of *soft soap*. Used as a *disinfectant*.

M

MACH NUMBER. The ratio of the speed of a *fluid* or body to the local speed of *sound*. The speed of a fluid or body is therefore said to be *supersonic* if its Mach number is greater than unity. Named after Ernst Mach (1838–1916).

MACHINE. Defined mathematically as a device for overcoming resistance at one point by the application of a *force*, usually at some other point. Generally understood to be any arrangement for the purpose of taking in some definite form of *energy*, modifying it and delivering it in a form more suitable for the desired purpose.

MACHMETER. An instrument for measuring the speed of an aircraft relative to the speed of *sound*. See *Mach number*.

MACRO-. Prefix denoting large, in contrast to *micro-*, small.

MACROCYCLIC. Containing a ring structure consisting of more than twelve *atoms* in the *molecule*.

MACROMOLECULE. A very large *molecule*, generally of a *polymer*. See *polymerization*.

MAGELLANIC CLOUDS. Two small patches of *light* which appear, from the southern hemisphere, to be detached from the main bright band of *stars* which constitute the *Milky Way*. These objects are separate *galaxies*, being two of the smaller members of the *Local Group* to which our *Galaxy* belongs. Named after Ferdinand Magellan (1480–1521).

MAGENTA. Fuchsine. $C_{20}H_{22}N_3OCl$. A red dye, prepared from *aniline* and *toluidine*.

MAGIC NUMBERS. The numbers 2, 8, 20, 28, 50, 82, and 126. Atomic *nuclei* containing these numbers of *neutrons* or *protons* have exceptional stability.

MAGNADUR*. A *ferrite* used for making permanent *magnets*.

MAGNALIUM*. A light *alloy*, S.G. 2 to 2·5; consists of aluminium with from 5% to 30% magnesium.

MAGNESIA. See *magnesium oxide*, or *magnesium hydroxide*; 'magnesia alba' of pharmacy is *basic* magnesium carbonate; 'fluid magnesia' is a *solution* of magnesium hydrogen carbonate.

MAGNESITE. Natural magnesium carbonate, $MgCO_3$, which occurs in white masses; used in the manufacture of *refractories* and *fertilizers*.

MAGNESIUM. Mg. Element. A.W. 24·312. At. No. 12. A light, silvery-white *metal*, S.G. 1·74, m.p. 651°C., which tarnishes easily in air. Burns with an intense white *flame* to form *magnesium oxide*, MgO. Occurs as *magnesite*, $MgCO_3$; *dolomite*, $MgCO_3.CaCO_3$; *carnallite*, $KCl.MgCl_2.6H_2O$, and in many other *compounds*. Essential to life as it occurs in *chlorophyll*. Prepared by *electrolysis* of fused carnallite. Used in lightweight *alloys*, in *photography*, signalling, and incendiary bombs. Compounds used in medicine.

MAGNESIUM CHLORIDE. $MgCl_2$. A white *deliquescent* substance, m.p.

708°C., which occurs in *sea-water* and also as *carnallite*. A *concentrated solution* mixed to a paste with *magnesium oxide* sets to a stone-like mass owing to the formation of the oxychloride, Mg_2OCl_2 (Sorel's cement).

MAGNESIUM HYDROXIDE. Magnesia. $Mg(OH)_2$. A white crystalline substance, used as an *antacid* in 'milk of magnesia'.

MAGNESIUM OXIDE. Magnesia. MgO. A white tasteless substance, m.p. 2800°C., used as an *antacid* and a laxative.

MAGNESIUM SULPHATE. Epsom salts. $MgSO_4.7H_2O$. A white crystalline *soluble salt*, used in medicine and in leather processing.

MAGNESIUM TRISILICATE. Dimagnesium trisilicate. $2MgO.3SiO_2$. nH_2O. A white tasteless powder used as an *antacid* and to absorb odours.

MAGNET, PERMANENT. A *ferromagnetic substance* that has a permanent *magnetic field* and *magnetic moment* associated with it. See also *magnetic domains*.

MAGNETIC AMPLIFIER. A device for the amplification of small *direct currents* and of low *frequency alternating currents*. Depends upon the fact that the output from the secondary coil of a *transformer* due to an alternating current in the *primary coil* is also a function of a direct current (the signal to be amplified) in a third winding on the transformer core.

MAGNETIC BOTTLE. Any configuration of *magnetic fields* used in the *containment* of a *plasma* during controlled *thermonuclear reaction* experiments.

MAGNETIC CIRCUIT. A closed path following the *lines of force* of a *magnetic field*.

MAGNETIC DECLINATION. Magnetic variation, variation of the compass. The *angle* between the *planes* of the geographic and *magnetic meridian*. See *magnetism, terrestrial*.

MAGNETIC DIP. Angle of dip, inclination. The *angle* between the direction of the Earth's magnetic field (see *magnetism, terrestrial*) and the horizontal; i.e. the angle through which a magnetic needle will 'dip' from the horizontal when suspended free to swing in a vertical plane in the *magnetic meridian*. See *dip circle, magnetic equator*.

MAGNETIC DOMAINS. The fact that *ferromagnetic* substances are not necessarily always magnetized led to the theory that they consist of separate domains, each of which is spontaneously magnetized, but the *magnetic moments* of which may not be aligned. If an external *magnetic field* is applied to the substance the magnetic moments of the domains (not the domains themselves) are rotated so that they lie parallel to the field; the substance then acts as a permanent *magnet*.

MAGNETIC DRUM. A cylinder coated with magnetic material for storing information in a *computer*, especially in the *backing storage*. The information is stored in the magnetic coating in the form of magnetic *dipoles*, the orientation or polarity of which can be used to indicate one of the digits in a *binary notation*.

MAGNETIC ELEMENTS. The three quantities, *magnetic declination*, angle of dip (see *magnetic dip*), and *horizontal intensity*, which define completely the Earth's magnetic field (see *magnetism, terrestrial*) at any point.

MAGNETIC EQUATOR. Aclinic line. A line of zero *magnetic dip* lying fairly near the geographical *equator*, but passing North of it in Africa and the Indian Ocean, and South of it in America and the Eastern Pacific.

MAGNETIC FIELD. A *field* of *force* which is said to exist at any point if a small coil of wire carrying an *electric current* experiences a *couple* when placed at that point. A magnetic field may exist at a point as a result of the presence of either a permanent *magnet* or a circuit carrying an *electric current*, in the neighbourhood of the point.

MAGNETIC FIELD OF ELECTRIC CURRENT. A wire or coil carrying an *electric current* is surrounded by a *magnetic field*. The direction of the field relative to the current may be determined by the following corkscrew rule: If a corkscrew, held in the right hand, is turned along the conductor in the direction of the current, the movement of the thumb indicates the direction of the magnetic field produced. The strength of the magnetic field at the centre of a circular coil of wire of radius *r*, consisting of *n* turns, in which a current of *I* *amperes* is flowing, is $\frac{nI}{2\pi r}$ *amperes* per *metre* in *SI units* or $\frac{2\pi nI}{10r}$ *oersted* in *c.g.s. units*.

MAGNETIC FIELD STRENGTH. *H*. The strength of a magnetic field measured in *amperes* per *metre* (*SI units*) or *oersteds* (*c.g.s. units*). See *magnetic field of an electric current*.

MAGNETIC FLUX. *Φ*. The product of a given area and the component of the *magnetic field strength* at right angles to that area. The *c.g.s. unit* of magnetic flux is the *maxwell*. The derived *SI unit* of magnetic flux is the *weber*.

MAGNETIC FLUX DENSITY. Magnetic induction. *B*. The *magnetic flux* passing through unit area of a *magnetic field* in a direction at right angles to the *magnetic force*. The derived *SI unit* of magnetic flux density is the *telsa* (*weber* per square *metre*). The *c.g.s. unit* is the *gauss*.

MAGNETIC FORCE. The attractive or repulsive *force* exerted by a *magnetic field* on a *magnetic pole* or an *electric charge*.

MAGNETIC INDUCTION. 1. The induction of *magnetism* in a body by an external *magnetic field*. 2. *Magnetic flux density*.

MAGNETIC IRON ORE. See *magnetite*.

MAGNETIC LINE OF FORCE. Line of *magnetic force*. A line whose direction at each point is that of the *magnetic field* at that point; the path along which a free *magnetic pole* would travel.

MAGNETIC MERIDIAN. See *magnetism, terrestrial*.

MAGNETIC MIRRORS. The regions of high field strength at the end of an externally generated *magnetic field* used in the *containment* of a *plasma* in controlled *thermonuclear reaction* experiments. *Ions* which enter these regions of high field strength reverse their direction of motion (are reflected) and return to the central region of the plasma in which they become trapped.

MAGNETIC MOMENT. Moment of a magnet. The *couple* required to hold a *magnet* at right angles to a field of unit *magnetic intensity*; the product of the *magnetic pole strength* and the length of the magnet.

MAGNETIC MONOPOLE. A hypothetical unit of magnetic 'charge' analogous to *electric charge*. No evidence has been found for the existence of a separate *magnetic pole*, they are always found in pairs.

MAGNETIC PERMEABILITY. μ. The ratio of the *magnetic flux density* in a body to the external *magnetic field strength* which induces it. The 'relative permeability', μ_r, is the ratio of the permeability of a substance to the permeability of a *vacuum*, μ_0. μ_0 has the value $4\pi \times 10^{-7}$ *henry* per *metre*. For most substances μ_r has a constant small value. When μ_r is less than 1, the material is said to be *diamagnetic*; if μ_r is greater than 1, it is *paramagnetic*. A few substances, notably iron, have very large values of μ, which tend to fall as the field strength increases so that the magnetic flux density tends to a limiting value called the saturation value. Such substances are said to be *ferromagnetic*.

MAGNETIC POLE. A *magnet* appears to have its *magnetism* concentrated at two points termed the poles. If a bar magnet is suspended to swing freely, one of these, the North-seeking, North, or positive pole, will point North, and the other South. Unlike poles attract, and like poles repel each other. The *force* of attraction or repulsion between two poles varies inversely as the *square* of the distance between them (see *inverse square law*). The force between two poles of strength m_1 and m_2 (see *magnetic pole strength*) situated d centimetres apart in vacuum is $m_1 m_2 / d^2$ *dynes* in the *c.g.s. system*. In *SI units* it will be in *newtons* when d is in *metres*.

MAGNETIC POLE STRENGTH. The strength of a *magnetic pole* measured in terms of the unit magnetic pole; see *magnetic pole, unit*.

MAGNETIC POLE, UNIT. Unit *magnetic pole* in the *c.g.s. system* is one of such a strength that when situated 1 centimetre from an equal pole in *vacuum*, the *force* between the poles will be 1 *dyne*. In *SI units* the force will be 1 *newton* when the distance between the poles is 1 *metre*.

MAGNETIC POTENTIAL. Magnetomotive force. Concept analogous to *electric potential*; the difference of magnetic potential between two points is measured by the *work* done in carrying *unit magnetic pole* from one point to the other.

MAGNETIC STORM. A sudden disturbance in the Earth's magnetic field (see *magnetism, terrestrial*) associated with *sunspot* activity, which affects *compasses* and *radio* transmission.

MAGNETIC SUSCEPTIBILITY. The ratio of the intensity of *magnetization* produced in a substance to the strength of the *magnetic field* to which it is subjected.

MAGNETIC TAPE. *Plastic* tape coated with a *ferromagnetic* powder, used in tape recorders. The tape is passed over the gap in a *magnetic circuit* which is modulated in accordance with information to be recorded. The tape retains a record of the *modulation* which can be 'played back' through a suitable circuit. Magnetic tape is used in the *backing storage* of *computers*.

MAGNETIC VARIATION. See *magnetic declination*.

MAGNETISM. The branch of physics concerned with *magnets* and *magnetic fields*. See *diamagnetism, paramagnetism, ferromagnetism*, and *ferrimagnetism*.

MAGNETISM, TERRESTRIAL. The Earth's magnetism. The Earth possesses a *magnetic field*, the strength of which varies with time and locality. The field is similar to that which would be produced by a powerful *magnet* situated at the centre of the Earth and pointing approximately North and South. A magnetized needle suspended to swing freely in all planes will set itself pointing to the Earth's magnetic North and South poles, at an angle to the horizontal (see *magnetic dip*). The vertical plane through the *axis* of such a needle is termed the *magnetic meridian*, defined as the vertical plane which contains the direction of the Earth's magnetic field. The cause of the Earth's magnetism is not definitely known. The variations of the Earth's magnetic field with time are of two types, the 'secular' and the 'diurnal'. The secular variations are slow changes in the same sense, but at different rates, as a result of which the Earth's magnetic field has decreased by some 5% over the last hundred years. The cause of these variations is unknown. The diurnal variations are much smaller and more rapid variations which have been shown to be associated with changes in the *ionosphere* related to *sunspot* activity.

MAGNETITE. Magnetic iron ore. Natural black *oxide* of iron, Fe_3O_4.

MAGNETIZATION, INTENSITY OF. The *magnetic moment* per unit volume of a magnetized body.

MAGNETO. A small *dynamo* provided with a *spark-coil*, for *ignition* of *petrol* vapour in petrol *internal-combustion engines*.

MAGNETOHYDRODYNAMICS. MHD. A method of generating *electricity* by subjecting the *free electrons* in a high velocity *flame* or *plasma* to a strong *magnetic field*. The free electron concentration in the flame is increased by the thermal *ionization* of added substances of low *ionization potential* (e.g. containing sodium or potassium). These electrons constitute a current when they flow between *electrodes* within the flame, under the influence of the external magnetic field.

MAGNETOMETER. An instrument for comparing strengths of *magnetic fields*, and *magnetic moments*. Consists of a short *magnet* with a long, non-magnetic pointer at right angles across it, pivoted at the junction. The pointer swings along a circular scale, thus enabling deflections of the short magnet to be measured.

MAGNETOMOTIVE FORCE. MMF. See *magnetic potential* and *gilbert*.

MAGNETON. A *unit* for measuring the *magnetic moments* of atomic par-

232

ticles. The Bohr magneton, μ_B, is equal to $\dfrac{eh}{4\pi m_e} = 9 \cdot 2732 \times 10^{-24}$ *ampere metre*^{2}, where e and m_e are the charge and mass of the *electron* and h is *Planck's constant*. The nuclear magneton, μ_N, is equal to $\mu_B \cdot \dfrac{m_e}{m_p} =$ $5 \cdot 05 \times 10^{-27}$ ampere metre^2, where m_p is the mass of the *proton*.

MAGNETOSPHERE. The *space* surrounding the *Earth*, or any celestial body, in which there is a *magnetic field* associated with that body.

MAGNETOSTRICTION. A change in the dimensions of *ferromagnetic substances* on magnetization.

MAGNETRON. A *thermionic valve* capable of producing high power oscillations in the *microwave* region. Consists of a heater, a central *cathode*, and an *anode* with a number of radial segments, all enclosed in an evacuated container which is situated in the gap of an external *magnet*. The movement of the *electrons* is controlled by a combination of crossed *electric* and *magnetic fields*. Used extensively in *radar*.

MAGNIFICATION. (Of a *microscope* or other optical instrument.) The ratio of the linear dimensions of the final image to the linear dimensions of the object.

MAGNIFYING GLASS. A *convex lens*. See *microscope, simple*.

MAGNIFYING POWER OF A COMPOUND MICROSCOPE. The ratio of the *angle* subtended at the eye by the final image to the angle subtended by the object placed at the least distance of distinct vision (i.e. the shortest distance from the eye at which the object can be seen distinctly).

MAGNIFYING POWER OF A LENS. The ratio of the *angle* subtended at the eye by the *virtual image* to the angle subtended by the object when placed at the least distance of distinct vision; this latter is generally taken to be 25 cm.

MAGNITUDE OF STARS. The apparent magnitude is a measure of the relative apparent *brightness* of *stars*. A star of any one magnitude is approximately $2 \cdot 51$ times brighter than a star of the next magnitude. E.g. a star of the first magnitude is $(2 \cdot 51)^3$ times as bright as a star of the fourth magnitude. The absolute magnitude is defined as the apparent magnitude a given star would have at the standard distance of 10 *parsecs*.

MAGNOX. A magnesium *alloy* used for sheathing uranium *fuel elements* in certain types of *nuclear reactor*. See *gas-cooled reactor*.

MAIN SEQUENCE STARS. See *Hertzsprung-Russell diagram*.

MAJOR AXIS. The *axis* of an *ellipse* which passes through both *foci*. See Fig. 15, page 131.

MAJORITY CARRIERS. In a *semiconductor*, the type of *carrier* which constitutes more than half the total number of carriers.

MAKSUTOV TELESCOPE. An astronomical telescope developed by D. D. Maksutov in 1944. Consists of a *concave* spherical *mirror* the *aberration* of which is reduced by a *meniscus lens*.

MALACHITE. Natural *basic* copper carbonate, $CuCO_3.Cu(OH)_2$. A bright green *mineral*.

MALATE. A *salt* or *ester* of *malic acid*.

MALEATE. A *salt* or *ester* of *maleic acid*.

MALEIC ACID. $HOOCCH:CHCOOH$. A colourless crystalline *soluble unsaturated acid*, m.p. $137°$ C., *isomeric* with *fumaric acid*. Used in the manufacture of synthetic *resins, dyes*, and as a preservative.

MALIC ACID. Hydroxysuccinic acid. $COOH.CH_2.CH(OH).COOH$. A white crystalline *organic acid*, m.p. $98°-99°$ C. Occurs in unripe apples and other fruits.

MALLEABILITY. The ability to be hammered out into thin sheets.

MALONIC ACID. $CH_2(COOH)_2$. A white crystalline *soluble dibasic acid*, m.p. $135.6°$ C., used in the manufacture of *barbiturates*.

MALONYL GROUP. The *divalent radical* $—OCCH_2CO—$, derived from *malonic acid*.

MALONYL UREA. See *barbiturates*.

MALT. Grain (usually barley) which has been allowed to germinate and then heated and dried. See *brewing*.

MALT SUGAR. See *maltose*.

MALTASE. An *enzyme* occurring in *yeast* and other *organisms* which hydrolyzes (see *hydrolysis*) *maltose* into *glucose*.

MALTOSE. Malt sugar, maltobiose. $C_{12}H_{22}O_{11}$. A hard crystalline *soluble disaccharide sugar*, less sweet than *cane-sugar*. Formed in *malt* by the action of the *enzyme diastase* on *starch*.

MANDELIC ACID. $C_6H_5CHOHCOOH$. A white crystalline *optically active* substance, the *racemic form* of which has m.p. $120.5°$ C.; used as an *antiseptic*.

MANGANATE. A *salt* of *manganic acid*.

MANGANESE. Mn. Element. A.W. 54.938. At. No. 25. A reddish-white, hard brittle *metal*. S.G. 7.20, m.p. $1244°$ C. Occurs as *pyrolusite*, MnO_2, from which it is extracted by *reduction* with carbon or aluminium. Used in numerous *alloys*.

MANGANESE BRONZE. Manganese brass. A copper-zinc *alloy* containing up to 4% manganese.

MANGANESE DIOXIDE. Manganese peroxide, MnO_2. A heavy, black powder which occurs naturally as *pyrolusite*. Used as a source of manganese metal, as an *oxidizing agent*, in *glass* manufacture, in *Leclanché cells*, as a *catalyst* in the laboratory preparation of oxygen, etc.

MANGANESE STEEL. A very hard variety of *steel* containing up to 13% manganese.

MANGANIC ACID. H_2MnO_4. A hypothetical *acid* which exists only in *solution* or in the form of its *salts*, the *manganates*.

MANGANIN. An *alloy* containing 83% copper, 13% manganese, 4% nickel. As its electrical *resistance* is affected only slightly by change in *temperature* it is used for resistance coils.

MANNITOL. $HOCH_2(CHOH)_4CH_2OH$. A white crystalline *optically active carbohydrate alcohol*, the *racemic form* of which has m.p. 168° C.; used in the manufacture of synthetic *resins* and *plasticizers*.

MANNITOL HEXANITRATE. $C_6H_8(ONO_2)_6$. A colourless *insoluble* substance, m.p. 112° C., used as an *explosive* and in medicine.

MANOMETER. Any instrument used for measuring gaseous *pressure*.

MANTISSA. The decimal, always positive, portion of a common *logarithm*.

MARBLE. A form of natural *calcium carbonate*, $CaCO_3$.

MARGARINE. A butter substitute prepared from purified vegetable and animal *fats* and *oils*. Milk is added to a suitable blend of fats; bacterial action in the milk produces a butter-like flavour; vitamins A and D (see *vitamins*) and suitable colouring materials are added.

MARKOWNIKOFF'S RULE. When addition occurs between a hydrogen *halide* and an unsymmetrical *olefine*, the *halogen atom* becomes attached to the carbon *atom* with the least number of hydrogen atoms. Named after V. V. Markownikoff (1838–1904).

MARS (astr.). A *planet*, with two small *satellites*, having its *orbit* between those of the *Earth* and *Jupiter*. Mean distance from the *Sun* 227·94 million kilometres. *Sidereal period* ('year') = 686·98 days. Mass 0·107 that of the Earth, diameter 6790 kilometres. Probably possesses an atmosphere containing *carbon dioxide* and very small quantities of oxygen. Surface temperature ranges from about −70° C. to 30° C. No evidence of life on the planet is available.

MARSH GAS. See *methane*, CH_4.

MARSH'S TEST. A sensitive test for arsenic which depends upon the formation of *arsine* when arsenic or its *compounds* are present in a *solution* evolving hydrogen. When the arsine is passed through a narrow, heated tube, it is decomposed and leaves a deposit of metallic arsenic.

MARTENSITE. The hard and brittle constituent of *steel* produced when the material is cooled from its hardening *temperature* at a greater rate than its critical cooling rate.

MASCON. A local concentration of high *mass*, below the surface of the *Moon*, of unexplained origin.

MASER. Microwave Amplification by Stimulated Emission of Radiation. A class of *amplifiers* and *oscillators* which makes use of the internal *energy* of *atoms* and *molecules* to obtain low noise-level amplification and *microwave* oscillations of precisely determined *frequencies*. Stimulated emission, which is the basic principle on which these devices work, is the emission by an *atom* in an excited *quantum* state (see *excitation*) of a *photon*, as the result of the impact of a photon from outside of exactly equal energy. Thus the stimulating photon, or wave, is augmented by the one emitted by the excited atom. A maser consists of an 'active medium' (either in the gaseous or *solid state*), in which most of the atoms can be 'pumped' to an excited state by subjecting the system to *electromagnetic radiation* of frequencies which differ from that of the stimulating frequency. The active medium is enclosed in a *resonant cavity* so that a wave is built up with only one mode of oscillation, which is equivalent to a single output frequency. Masers can also be made to operate at optical frequencies, when they are referred to as optical masers or *lasers*.

MASS. *m.* It is a matter of observation that a *force* applied to a body produces an *acceleration* proportional to the force. The constant of proportionality is the mass of the body. In *SI units* the *kilogramme* is the unit of mass, in *c.g.s. units* it is the *gram*. The *f.p.s. system* uses the *pound* and the *slug*. See also *rest mass, relativistic mass, inertial mass*.

MASS ACTION LAW. The velocity of a chemical change is proportional to the *active masses* (*molecular concentrations*) of the reacting substances.

MASS DECREMENT. The difference between the *isotopic weight* of an *isotope* and its *mass number*.

MASS DEFECT. The difference between the *mass* of a *nucleus* and the sum of the masses of its constituent *nucleons*. The *energy* equivalent of the mass defect, on the basis of the *mass-energy equation*, must be supplied to a nucleus to split it into its component nucleons.

MASS-ENERGY EQUATION. *Mass* and *energy* are mutually convertible under certain conditions. The equation connecting the two quantities in any such transformation is $E = mc^2$, where c is the velocity of *light* in m/s and E is the energy, in *joules*, released when a mass of m *kilogrammes* is completely converted into energy. In *c.g.s. units*, if m is in *grams* and c is in cm per second, E will be in *ergs*. See *annihilation radiation, conservation of mass and energy*.

MASS NUMBER. Nucleon number. *A*. The *integer* which is nearest to the *atomic mass* of an *isotope*, i.e. the number of *nucleons* in the *nucleus* of an *atom*.

MASS SPECTROGRAPH. An apparatus for the determination of the exact *masses* of individual *atoms*, i.e. *isotopic weights*, by photographing the *mass spectrum* produced.

MASS SPECTROMETER. An apparatus for obtaining the *mass spectrum* of a *beam* of *ions* by means of suitably disposed *magnetic* and *electric fields*. The deflection of any individual ion in these fields depends on the ratio of its *mass* to its *electric charge, m/e*. Such a spectrum will appear as a number of lines on a photographic plate, each corresponding to a definite value of *m/e*. *Isotopes* were first discovered in this way. The method was formerly known as 'positive ray analysis'.

MASS SPECTRUM. A *spectrum* obtained with a *mass spectrometer* or *spectrograph* in which a *beam* of *ions* is arranged in order of increasing *charge* to *mass* ratio.

MASSICOT. Yellow powder form of unfused *lead monoxide*, PbO.

MASURIUM. Former name of *element* of At. No. 43; replaced in 1949 by the name *technetium*.

MATCHES. The heads of safety matches usually contain *antimony trisulphide, oxidizing agents* such as *potassium chlorate*, and some sulphur or *charcoal*; while the striking surface contains red phosphorus. Ordinary non-safety match-heads contain phosphorus sulphide, P_4S_3; very rarely red phosphorus.

MATRIX. 1. A mould for shaping a cast. 2. (math.) An arrangement of mathematical elements into rows and columns according to algebraic rules, in order to solve a set of *linear* equations. 3. (computers) An array of components for translating from one code to another. 4. (metallurgy) The crystalline *phase* in an *alloy*, in which the other phases are contained.

MATTE. A mixture of the *sulphides* of iron and copper obtained as an intermediate stage in the *smelting* of copper.

MATTER. A specialized form of *energy* which has the attributes of *mass* and extension in *space* and time.

MAUVE. Mauveine, aniline violet. A reddish-violet *dye*; a complex *organic compound*, the first organic dye to be prepared artificially.

MAXIMUM (math.). A *function* $y = f(x)$ has a maximum value at $x = a$ if $f(a)$ is greater than the values of the function immediately preceding and immediately following $x = a$. The function has a minimum value at $x = b$ if $f(b)$ is less than the value of the function immediately preceding and immediately following $x = b$.

MAXIMUM AND MINIMUM THERMOMETER. See *thermometer*.

MAXIMUM PERMISSIBLE DOSE (OR LEVEL). See *dose*.

MAXWELL, THE. The *c.g.s. unit* of *magnetic flux*. The flux through 1 square *centimetre normal* to a *magnetic field* of intensity of 1 *gauss*. 1 maxwell = 10^{-8} *webers*. Named after James Clerk Maxwell (1831–79).

MAXWELL-BOLTZMANN DISTRIBUTION. A statistical *equation* giving the distribution of *velocities* or positions of the *molecules* in a *gas*; based on the assumptions that all the particles are indistinguishable and each has an equal *probability* of appearing in a particular region. Named after James Clerk Maxwell (1831–79) and Ludwig Boltzmann (1844–1906).

MEAN (math.). Generally understood to be the arithmetic mean, i.e. the average. See also *geometric mean*.

MEAN FREE PATH. The average, or *mean*, distance travelled by a particle, *atom*, or *molecule* between collisions. In a *gas* the mean free path between molecules is inversely proportional to the *pressure*. See *kinetic theory of gases*.

MEAN FREE TIME. The average, or *mean*, time that elapses between two collisions of a particle, *atom*, or *molecule*.

MEAN SOLAR DAY. See *solar day*.

MECHANICAL ADVANTAGE. In a *machine*, the ratio of the actual load raised to the *force* required to maintain the machine at constant speed.

MECHANICAL EQUIVALENT OF HEAT. If H units of *heat* are completely converted into W units of *work* then $W = JH$, where J is a constant called the mechanical equivalent of heat, or Joule's equivalent. J represents the amount of work obtainable by the complete conversion of unit quantity of heat into mechanical work. 1 *calorie*

$(15°) = 4\cdot185 \times 10^7$ *ergs*; 1 *British Thermal Unit* = 778 ft-lb.; i.e. J has the values of $4\cdot185 \times 10^7$ ergs/calorie and 778 ft-lb./Btu respectively for these two sets of units. In *SI units*, W and H would both be measured in *joules*, and J would therefore equal 1.

MECHANICS. The branch of physical science dealing with the behaviour of *matter* under the action of *force*. See *dynamics*; *statistics*; *kinematics*.

MECHANISTIC THEORY. The view that all biological phenomena may be explained in mechanical, physical, and chemical terms; in opposition to the *vitalistic theory*.

MEDIAN. 1. A line joining a vertex of a *triangle* to the mid-point of the opposite side. 2. The middle number in a sequence of numbers.

MEDIAN LETHAL DOSE. (M)LD50. The *dose* of *ionizing radiation* which would kill 50% of a large batch of *organisms* within a specified period.

MEDIUM FREQUENCIES. M.F. *Radio frequencies* in the range 300–3000 *kilohertz*.

MEERSCHAUM. Natural *hydrated* magnesium silicate, $Mg_2Si_3O_8.2H_2O$. White *solid* used for tobacco pipes.

MEGA-. Prefix denoting one million times, in *metric units*; symbol M. More loosely, denoting 'very large'.

MEGAHERTZ. MHz. 1 million *hertz*. A measure of *frequency* equal to 10^6 *cycles* per *second*.

MEGATON BOMB. A *nuclear weapon* with an explosive power equivalent to one million tons of *T.N.T.* (approximately 10^{15} *calories* or 4×10^{15} *joules*).

MEGOHM. One million *ohms*.

MEIOSIS. A process of *cell* division as a result of which a *diploid* cell produces four *haploid cells*. Consists of two successive cell divisions, each of which resembles *mitosis*, but the *chromosomes* are duplicated only once in the process. Meiosis occurs in the life cycle of all sexually reproducing *organisms*. In animals it is the process by which *gametes* are formed from *gametocytes*.

MELAMINE. $C_3H_6N_6$. Triaminotriazine. A white crystalline substance, m.p. 354°C., which forms a *thermosetting* resin with *formaldehyde*.

MELANIN. $C_{17}H_{98}O_{33}N_{14}S$. A dark brown pigment produced in the skin *cells* called melanocytes. Skin and hair colours in many animals, including man, are due to melanin. People of different races have approximately the same number of melanocytes, colour differences being due to variations in the distribution of melanin in the skin. The *Sun* stimulates the production of melanin in melanocytes, and the function of the melanin is to absorb the Sun's harmful radiations.

MELTING POINT. The constant *temperature* at which the *solid* and *liquid phase* of a substance are in equilibrium at a given *pressure*. Melting points are normally quoted for standard atmospheric pressure, 760 mm. of mercury.

MENDELEEV'S LAW. See *periodic law*. Named after Dimitri Ivanovich Mendeleev (1834–1907).

MENDELEVIUM. Md. *Transuranic element*, At. No. 101. The most stable isotope, $^{258}_{101}$ Md, has *half-life* of 60 days.

MENISCUS. 1. The curved surface of a *liquid* in a vessel. If the *contact angle* between the liquid and the wall of the vessel is less than 90°, the meniscus is *concave*; if greater, the meniscus is *convex*. 2. A *concavo-convex lens*. See Fig. 24, page 219.

MENSURATION. The measurement of lengths, areas, and volumes.

MENTHOL. $C_{10}H_{20}O$. One of a series of *organic compounds* of the *camphor* group. A white crystalline substance which occurs in natural *oils*, m.p. 42° C., with a characteristic smell. Used in medicine.

MERCAPTANS. Thio-alcohols. *Organic compounds* with the general formula R.SH. For ethyl mercaptans see *ethanethiol*.

MERCAPTIDE. A metallic *salt* of a *mercaptan*.

MERCURIC. A *compound* of *bivalent* mercury.

MERCURIC CHLORIDE. Corrosive sublimate. $HgCl_2$. A white crystalline *soluble salt*, m.p. 276° C. Very poisonous, used as an *antiseptic*.

MERCURIC FULMINATE. Fulminate of mercury, mercuric isocyanate. $HS(ONC)_2$. A white crystalline substance which explodes on being struck, used in detonators to initiate *explosions*.

MERCURIC OXIDE. HgO. A *soluble* poisonous powder which occurs as yellow or red *crystals*; used as a *pigment* and an *antiseptic*.

MERCURIC SULPHIDE. HgS. An *insoluble* substance which occurs naturally as *cinnabar*. The pure *compound* consists of a red powder, m.p. 583·5° C., used as a *pigment*.

MERCUROUS. A *compound* of *univalent* mercury.

MERCUROUS CHLORIDE. Calomel. Hg_2Cl_2. A white *insoluble* powder used in medicine and as a *fungicide*.

MERCURY (astr.). A *planet* with its orbit nearest the *Sun*. Mean distance from the Sun 57·91 million kilometres. Sidereal period ('year') = 87·969 days. Mass 0·054 that of the *Earth*, diameter 4840 kilometres. Probably at a high *temperature* and without an atmosphere.

MERCURY. Quicksilver, Hydrargyrum. Hg. Element. A.W. 200·59. At. No. 80. A *liquid*, silvery-white *metal*, S.G. 13·6, m.p. −39° C., b.p. 357° C., which occurs as *cinnabar*, HgS. Extracted by roasting the *ore* in a current of air. Used in *thermometers, barometers, manometers*, and other scientific apparatus; *alloys* (called *amalgams*) used in dentistry. *Compounds* are poisonous; some are used in medicine.

MERCURY CELL. A *primary cell* consisting of a zinc *anode*, a *cathode* of *mercuric oxide* (HgO) mixed with *graphite* (about 5%), and an *electrolyte* of *potassium hydroxide* (KOH) saturated with *zinc oxide* (ZnO). The *E.M.F.* is about 1·3 *volts* and by suitable design the cell can be made to deliver about 0·3 *ampere-hours* per cubic cm.

MERCURY VAPOUR LAMP. A lamp emitting a strong bluish *light* by the passage of an *electric current* through mercury *vapour* in a bulb. The light is rich in *ultraviolet radiations*; used in artificial sun-ray treatment and in street lighting. See also *fluorescent lamp*.

MERIDIAN, CELESTIAL. The *great circle* of the *celestial sphere* passing through the *zenith* and the celestial poles, meeting the horizon at points called the North and South points.

MERIDIAN, MAGNETIC. See *magnetic meridian*.

MERIDIAN, TERRESTRIAL. Meridian of longitude. An imaginary *great circle* drawn round the *Earth*, which passes through both poles.

MESCALINE. $C_{11}H_{17}NO_3$. A white *soluble* crystalline powder, m.p. 35-6°C., obtained from the mescal cactus and used as a hallucinogen.

MESITYLENE. $C_6H_3(CH_3)_3$. A colourless *aromatic liquid hydrocarbon*, b.p. 164.7°C., which occurs in *coal-tar* and is used in organic synthesis.

MESITYL OXIDE. $(CH_3)_2C: CHCOCH_3$. A colourless oily *liquid*, b.p. 130°C., used as a *solvent* and in organic synthesis.

MESO-. A prefix indicating that a substance is optically inactive due to intra-molecular compensation.

MESONS. A group of unstable *elementary particles* with *rest masses* between those of the *electron* and the *proton*. Positive, negative, and neutral mesons exist; when charged the magnitude of the charge is equal to that of the electron. Mesons are found in *cosmic rays* and are emitted by *nuclei* under bombardment by high *energy* particles. They are believed to play a vital part in the cohesion of *nucleons* within nuclei, but no satisfactory explanation of the *exchange forces* with which they are associated has yet been given. Mesons belong to the class of particles called *bosons* and they all have zero *spin*. *Muons* were originally called μ-mesons, but they are now classified as *leptons* rather than mesons. See Table 6, page 437.

MESOPHERE. 1. The region of the Earth's *atmosphere* between the *ionosphere* and the *exosphere*, extending from about 400 kilometres to 1000 kilometres above the Earth's surface. Sometimes considered to be part of the exosphere. 2. The region of the Earth's atmosphere between the *stratosphere* and the *thermosphere*, extending from some 40 kilometres to 80 kilometres above the Earth's surface.

META-. 1. Prefix indicating that an *organic compound* contains a *benzene ring* substituted in the 1.3 positions. 2. Prefix indicating that an *acid* or *salt* is the least *hydrated* of several *compounds* of the same name.

METABOLISM. The chemical processes associated with living *organisms*. Usually divided into two parts: *catabolism*, as a result of which complex substances are decomposed into simple ones, with the release of *energy* which becomes available for the organism's activities; and *anabolism*, which comprises the building up of complex substances with the absorption or storage of energy. Metabolic reactions are usually under the control of *enzymes*, which are consequently of immense importance in the chemistry of life. Metabolic processes are very similar throughout the plant and animal kingdoms and there are therefore corresponding similarities between the enzymes which are manufactured by organisms.

METABOLITE. Any substance which takes part in the process of *metabolism*.

METAL. A substance having a 'metallic' lustre and being malleable, ductile, of high *specific gravity*, and a good *conductor* of *heat* and *electricity*. *Elements* having such physical properties to a greater or less degree are generally *electropositive*, combine with oxygen to give *bases*; their *chlorides* are stable towards *water*. A number of elements normally regarded as metals have only some of the above properties. See *metalloid*.

METALDEHYDE. Meta. A white, *volatile*, inflammable poisonous solid *polymer* of *acetaldehyde*, CH_3CHO. Used as *fuel* in small heaters.

METALLIC CRYSTALS. The type of *crystal* formed by most *metals*, in which the outer *electrons* of the metallic *atoms* are shared by the crystal as a whole. Thus, the positively charged metal *ions* in the crystal *lattice* are surrounded by a 'gas' of *free electrons*. These free electrons account for the fact that most metals are good conductors of *heat* and *electricity*.

METALLIC SOAP. An *insoluble salt* formed by a *metal* and a *fatty acid* (especially salts of lead and aluminium). Used for waterproofing textiles and as a drier for *paints*.

METALLOGRAPHY. The study of the crystalline structure of *metals* and *alloys*.

METALLOID. An *element* having some properties characteristic of *metals*, and others of non-metals. An element giving rise to an *amphoteric oxide*. E.g. arsenic, antimony.

METALLURGY. The science and technology of *metals*; in particular, the extraction of metals from their *ores*, their heat treatment, and the compounding of *alloys*.

METAMERISM. A type of *isomerism* exhibited by *organic compounds* of the same chemical class or type; caused by the attachment of different *radicals* to the same central *atom* or group. E.g. diethyl *ether* $(C_2H_5)_2O$, and methyl propyl ether, $CH_3OC_3H_7$.

METAMORPHISM. The transformation of the structure or constitution of rocks due to such natural factors as *heat* and *pressure*.

METAPHOSPHORIC ACID. HPO_3. An *acid* derived from *phosphorus pentoxide*, consisting of a colourless *deliquescent solid*.

METASTABLE STATE. (chem.). The state of supercooled *water* (see *supercooling*) or of supersaturated *solutions* (see *supersaturation*) in which the *phase* which is normally *stable* under the given conditions does not form unless a small amount of the normally stable phase is already present. Thus supercooled water will remain as *liquid* water below $0°C$. until a small *crystal* of *ice* is introduced.

METASTABLE STATE (phys.). An excited state (see *excitation*) of an *atom* or *nucleus* which has an appreciable life-time.

METATHESIS (chem.). See *double decomposition*.

METEOR. A *solid* body from outer *space*. A meteor becomes incandescent ('shooting star') on entering the Earth's *atmosphere* owing to the frictional *forces* set up at its surface. Small meteors burn up completely in the atmosphere, but some of the larger ones survive and fall to Earth as meteorites. Meteorites are of two kinds, those which are predominantly stone and those which are predominantly iron. The largest meteorites can weigh up to 100 tons. Every day some million meteors enter the Earth's atmosphere and some 10 tons of meteorite material are added to the planet's surface.

METEOR SHOWERS. Exceptionally heavy falls of *meteors* (about 20 times greater than the average) which enter the Earth's *atmosphere* when the Earth's *orbit* crosses the orbit of a *comet*, i.e. an orbit which contains either the material of which comets are made or into which they disintegrate.

METEORITE. See *meteor*.

METEOROLOGY. The science of the weather; the study of such conditions as atmospheric *pressure*, *temperature*, *wind* strength, *humidity*, etc., from which conclusions as to the forthcoming weather are drawn.

-METER. Suffix denoting measurer; e.g. *voltmeter*.

METHACRYLATE. A *salt* or *ester* of *methacrylic acid*.

METHACRYLIC ACID. $CH_2:C(CH_3)COOH$. A corrosive *liquid*, m.p. 15°C., b.p. 163°C. The *polymer* of its methyl *ester*, methyl methacrylate, is an important *plastic* (Perspex*).

METHANE. Marsh gas, fire-damp. CH_4. The first *hydrocarbon* of the *paraffin series*. An odourless, inflammable *gas*, b.p. $-161 \cdot 5°C$, which forms an explosive mixture with air. Formed from decaying *organic* matter and in coalmines; occurs in *coal-gas* and *natural gas*.

METHANOL. Methyl alcohol, wood spirit. CH_3OH. A colourless, poisonous *liquid* with a faint smell. B.p. 64·6°C. Obtained as wood naphtha by the *destructive distillation* of wood. Used to *denature methylated spirit*, as a *solvent*, and in chemical industry.

METHIONINE. An *amino acid* found in *casein*, wool, and other *proteins*, used in the treatment of certain liver diseases. See Table 5, page 435.

METHOXY GROUP. The *univalent radical*, CH_3O-.

METHYL ALCOHOL. See *methanol*.

METHYL CHLORIDE. See *chloromethane*.

METHYL CYANIDE. See *acetonitrile*.

METHYL GROUP. The *univalent* organic *radical* CH_3-.

METHYLAMINE. CH_3NH_2. A *gas* with an odour of *ammonia*, b.p. $-6\cdot3°C$.

METHYL SALICYLATE. Oil of wintergreen. $OH.C_6H_4COOCH_3$. A colourless oil, b.p. 223·3°C., used in flavours, perfumes, and medicine.

METHYLATED SPIRIT. A *liquid fuel* consisting, by *volume*, of 90% *ethanol*, 9·5% *methanol*, 0·5% *pyridine*, together with small amounts of *petroleum* and methyl violet dye.

METHYLATED SPIRIT, INDUSTRIAL. A variety of *methylated spirit* free from *pyridine*; consists of *ethanol* with 5% *methanol*.

METHYLCYCLOHEXANOL. $CH_3C_6H_{10}OH$. A colourless *viscous liquid* consisting of a mixture of *isomers* with b.p. in the range 167–174°C.; obtained from *cresol* and used as a *solvent* for *rubber* and *cellulose*.

METHYLENE BLUE. $C_{16}H_{18}N_{13}SCl$. A *soluble*, intense blue *dye*. Used as a dyestuff, in medicine, and as a stain in *biology*.

METHYLENE GROUP. The *bivalent radical* $CH_2 =$.

METOL. *p*-methylaminophenol. $CH_3NH.C_6H_4OH$. A white crystalline *compound*, m.p. 87°C. Used as a developer in *photography*. Term also often applied to the *sulphate* of the compound.

METRE. The *SI unit* of length. Redefined in 1960 as the length equal to 1 650 763·73 *wavelengths* in vacuo of the *radiation* corresponding to the transition between the levels $2p_{10}$ and $5d_5$ of the *isotope* $^{86}_{36}Kr$. This definition abrogated the platinum-iridium metre bar as the standard of length. One metre is equal to 39·3701 inches. Symbol m.

METRE BRIDGE. See *Wheatstone bridge*.

METRE-CANDLE. See *lux*.

METRIC SYSTEM (UNITS). A system of *weights* and measures originally based upon the *metre*. This was intended to be 1/10 000 000 of a quadrant of the Earth through Paris. See *weight, volume, length* (metric units of), *c.g.s system, m.k.s system*, and *SI units*.

METRIC TON. Tonne. 1000 *kilograms*; 2204·61 lb, 0·9842 ton.

METROLOGY. The scientific study of weights and measures.

MeV. Million *electron-volts*.

MHO. Reciprocal ohm. The unit of *conductance*; the ratio of the *electric current* flowing through a *conductor*, measured in *amperes*, to the *potential difference* between the ends of the conductor, measured in *volts*, gives the conductance in mhos. See also *siemens*.

MICA. A group of *minerals*, the most important of which are muscovite, $H_2KAl_3(SiO_4)_3$, and phlogopite, $H_2KMg_3Al(SiO_4)_3$. Naturally occurring mica can be split along its cleavages into small thick pieces ('blocks') or thin sheets ('splittings'). Being an excellent insulator and being resistant to high *temperatures*, mica is used as a *dielectric* in *capacitors*, as a support for *electrodes* in *thermionic valves*, and for heating elements in irons, etc. As mica is also transparent it is used for inspection windows of furnaces. Micanite* sheet is manufactured by bonding mica splittings with *shellac* or synthetic *resins*.

MICHELSON-MORLEY EXPERIMENT. An attempt to measure the *velocity* of the Earth through the *ether*, by measuring the effect which such a velocity would have upon the velocity of *light*. No such motion of the Earth relative to the ether was detected: a result of the greatest importance for the theory of *relativity*. Named after Albert A. Michelson (1852–1931) and Edward Morley (1838–1923).

MICRO-. 1. Prefix denoting one-millionth, in *metric units*. Symbol μ. 2. Prefix meaning 'very small'; on a small scale. See also *macro-*.

MICROBALANCE. A *balance* for weighing objects of very small *weight*, i.e. of the order of 10^{-3} to 10^{-6} g.

MICROBIOLOGY. The branch of *biology* concerned with the structure and function of *micro-organisms*.

MICROCOSMIC SALT. See *ammonium sodium hydrogen orthophosphate*.

MICROELECTRONICS. The design, manufacture, and use of *electronic* units using extremely small *solid-state* components, especially those based on *integrated circuits*.

MICROFARAD. μF. One-millionth of a *farad*.

MICROMETER. An instrument for the accurate measurement of small distances or *angles*.

MICROMINIATURIZATION. The techniques or the devices used in *microelectronics*.

MICRON. μm. Micrometre. One-millionth of a *metre*. 10 000 *Ångström units*.

MICRO-ORGANISM. A *unicellular organism* which can only be seen with the aid of a *microscope*.

MICROPHONE. A device for converting *sound* waves into *electrical energy* which may then be reconverted into sound after transmission by wire or *radio*. One common type consists of a diaphragm in contact with, or close to, loosely packed carbon granules. The vibration of the diaphragm which is set up by sound disturbs the packing of the carbon granules and alters the electrical *resistance* of the carbon. Thus an *electric current* flowing through the carbon will vary in a manner which depends upon the *frequency* and intensity of the vibrations produced by the sound on the diaphragm. See also *condenser microphone*.

MICROPHOTOMETER. A special form of *densitometer* enabling density variations over a very small area of the image to be measured.

MICROSCOPE, COMPOUND. An instrument consisting essentially of two *converging lenses* or systems of lenses called the *objective* and the *eye-piece* respectively. The objective, which is nearest the viewed object, forms a real inverted magnified *image* of the object just inside the focal distance (see *focal length*) of the eye-piece. This image is viewed through the eye-piece, which then acts as a *simple microscope* producing an inverted further magnified *virtual image*. See Fig. 26, page 245. The useful *magnification* obtainable with an optical microscope is limited by the *wavelength* of visible *light* as two points on a microscopic specimen cannot be distinguished from each other if they are not as far apart as half the wavelength of the light used to illuminate them. Thus for magnifications in excess of about 1500, an *ultraviolet microscope* or an *electron microscope* must be used.

MICROSCOPE, SIMPLE. Magnifying glass. A *convex lens* which is used to produce a virtual *image* larger than the viewed object. In Fig. 26, page 245, the *eye-piece* is used as a simple microscope.

MICROTOME. An apparatus for cutting thin sections of material, for microscopical examination.

MICROWAVES. *Electromagnetic radiation* with *wavelengths* ranging from very short *radio* waves almost to the *infrared* region; i.e. wavelengths from 30 cm to 1 mm.

MICROWAVE SPECTROSCOPY. The measurement of the absorption or emission of *electromagnetic radiation* in the *waveband* 0·1 mm to 10 cm by atomic or molecular systems. See *electron spin resonance.*

MIL. One thousandth of an inch.

MILK OF LIME. A *suspension* of *lime* in *water.*

MILK SUGAR. See *lactose.*

PRINCIPLE OF COMPOUND MICROSCOPE

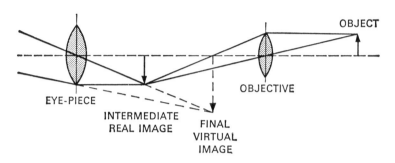

OBJECT

EYE-PIECE

OBJECTIVE

INTERMEDIATE
REAL IMAGE

FINAL
VIRTUAL
IMAGE

FIGURE 26

MILKY WAY. Originally a description of the luminous band of *stars* encircling the heavens. It is now known that these stars are members of the *Galaxy* to which the *Solar system* belongs, and the Galaxy is therefore often referred to as the Milky Way.

MILLI-. Prefix denoting one thousandth, in *metric units.* Symbol m.

MILLIAMMETER. A sensitive *ammeter* graduated to measure *milliamperes.*

MILLIAMPERE. mA. One thousandth of an *ampere.*

MILLIBAR. A unit of atmospheric pressure, used in *meteorology.* 1000 *dynes* per square centimetre or 100 *newtons* per square *metre*; approximately equal to 1/32 inch of mercury. See *pressure, units of.*

MILLICURIE. One thousandth of a *curie*; that quantity of a *radioactive isotope* which decays at the rate of $3·7 \times 10^7$ disintegrations per second.

MILLIGRAM. mg. 1/1000 *gram*; ·0154 *grain.*

MILLILITRE. ml. See *litre.*

MILLIMETRE. mm. 1/1000 *metre*; 0·0393701 inch. See *length, metric units.*

MINERAL. A substance which occurs naturally in the earth. The term, although applying mainly to *inorganic compounds,* also includes *mineral oil,* which consists chiefly of organic *hydrocarbons.*

MINERAL OIL. See *paraffin oil.*

MINIM. British fluid measure; 1/60 of a fluid drachm; 0·0591 cc. See *apothecaries' fluid measure.*

MINIMUM (math.). See *maximum.*

MINIUM. See *red lead.*

MINOR PLANETS. See *asteroids*.

MINORITY CARRIERS. In a *semiconductor*, the type of *carrier* which constitutes less than half the total number of carriers.

MIRROR. A surface which reflects regularly most of the *light* falling upon it, thus forming *images*. See *reflection*.

MIRROR IMAGE. An *image* of an object as viewed in a *mirror*; reversed in such a way that the image bears to the object the same relation as a right hand to a left.

MIRRORS, SPHERICAL. *Mirrors* the reflecting surfaces of which form a portion of a *sphere*. The surface of such a mirror may be regarded as being made up of an infinitely large number of very small plane mirrors, each at a *tangent to the curve* of the mirror. Thus a *ray* of incident *light* would be reflected at any point as if from such a small plane mirror. Spherical mirrors may be *convex*, with the reflecting surface on the outside of the sphere, or *concave*. The centre and radius of the sphere of which the mirror is considered to form a part, are termed the *centre* and *radius of curvature*; the centre of the mirror is the pole, and the line joining the centre of curvature to the pole is the axis. The principal focus (see *focus*) is at a point half-way between the pole and the centre of curvature. Regarding all distances as measured from the mirror and taking all distances in the direction opposite to that of the incident light as positive, the following relationship holds for spherical mirrors: $1/v + 1/u = 1/f = 2/r$, where u and v are the distances of object and image from the mirror, r the radius of curvature, and f the focal length. See Fig. 27.

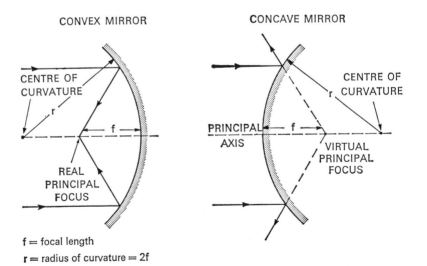

CONVEX MIRROR

CONCAVE MIRROR

CENTRE OF CURVATURE

CENTRE OF CURVATURE

PRINCIPAL AXIS

VIRTUAL PRINCIPAL FOCUS

REAL PRINCIPAL FOCUS

f = focal length

r = radius of curvature = 2f

FIGURE 27

MISCH METAL. An *alloy* of cerium with small amounts of other *rare earth metals*. Used for 'flints' in automatic lighters.

MISCIBLE. Capable of being mixed to form a *homogeneous* substance; usually applied to *liquids*; e.g. *water* and *alcohol* are completely miscible.

MISPICKEL. Arsenical pyrites. A natural *sulphide* of iron and arsenic, FeAsS.

MIST. Droplets of *water*, formed by the *condensation* of *water-vapour* on dust particles.

MITOCHONDRIA. Minute rod-shaped or granular bodies, about $\frac{1}{4}$–1 μm in diameter or length, which occur in the *cytoplasm* of most *cells*. Mitochondria contain many of the *enzymes* of the cell, particularly those required by the *citric acid cycle*.

MITOSIS. The process by which the *nuclei* of *diploid cells* reproduce. After the *chromosomes* in the nucleus have duplicated the process of mitosis is divided into four stages. 1. Prophase, during which the chromosomes appear, shorten, and thicken. 2. Metaphase, during which the nuclear membrane dissolves and a spindle forms, to the centre of which the chromosomes attach themselves. 3. Anaphase, during which the duplicates of the chromosomes separate and migrate to the ends of the spindle. 4. Telophase, during which two nuclear membranes form, each enclosing one set of chromosomes. The *cytoplasm* also divides in this stage, so that two new diploid cells are formed, each containing a set of chromosomes identical to that of the parent cell.

MIXED CRYSTALS. See *solid solutions*.

MIXTURES. Mechanical mixtures. Mixtures differ from chemical *compounds* in the following respects: 1. The constituents may be separated by suitable physical or mechanical means. 2. Most mixtures may be made in all proportions; in the case of *solutions* which may be regarded as molecular mixtures, there are often limits of *solubility*. 3. No *heat* effect (except in the case of solutions) is produced on formation; the formation of chemical compounds is invariably accompanied by the evolution or absorption of *energy* in the form of heat. 4. The properties of a mixture are an aggregate of the properties of the constituents, whereas a compound has individual properties, often quite unlike those of the component *elements*.

M.K.S. SYSTEM. A system of *units* derived from the *metre, kilogramme,* and *second*. Now superseded for scientific purposes by the *SI units*, which are based on the m.k.s. system.

MODERATOR. A substance used in *nuclear reactors* to reduce the speed of *fast neutrons* produced by *nuclear fission*. These substances consist of *atoms* of light *elements* (e.g. *deuterium* in *heavy water*, graphite, beryllium) to which the neutrons are able to impart some of their *energy* on collision, without being captured. Neutrons which have been slowed down in this way are much more likely to cause new fissions of $^{235}_{92}U$ than they are to be captured by $^{238}_{92}U$.

MODULATION. The process of varying some characteristic of one wave (usually a *radio frequency carrier wave*) in accordance with some characteristic of another wave. The main types are *amplitude, frequency,* and *phase modulation.* See also *velocity modulation.*

MODULE. 1. A *unit* used as a standard, especially in architecture. 2. A detachable section of a *spacecraft.* 3. A detachable unit in a *computer* system.

MODULUS. A constant *factor* or multiplier for the conversion of *units* from one system to another. See also *elastic modulus.*

MOEBIUS STRIP. A rectangular ribbon-shaped strip of paper or material one end of which has been twisted through 180 degrees before attaching it to the other end. This forms a single continuous surface, bounded by a continuous curve. Named after A. F. Moebius (1790–1868).

MOHO. Mohorovicic discontinuity. The discontinuity between the *Earth's crust* and its underlying mantle. It lies some 30–40 kilometres below the surface of the land and some 5–9 kilometres below the ocean floor. Earthquake waves suffer an abrupt change of velocity at this discontinuity. A 'mohole' is a hole drilled through the Earth's crust into the discontinuity for research purposes. Named after Andrija Mohorovicic (1857–1936).

MOHS SCALE OF HARDNESS. A scale in which each *mineral* listed is softer than (i.e. is scratched by) all those below it. 1. *Talc.* 2. *Gypsum.* 3. *Calcite.* 4. *Fluorite.* 5. *Apatite.* 6. *Orthoclase.* 7. *Quartz.* 8. *Topaz.* 9. *Corundum.* 10. *Diamond.*

MOLALITY. A method of expressing the strength of a *solution* (see also *concentration*): the number of *moles* of *solute* per *kilogramme* of *solvent.*

MOLAR. When the adjective 'molar' is used before the name of an extensive physical property, it implies 'divided by the amount of substance'. This usually, but not always, means 'per *mole*'. Often denoted by the use of the subscript m, e.g. V_m for *molar volume.* In some exceptional cases 'molar' is used to mean 'divided by *concentration*'.

MOLAR ELECTRODE POTENTIAL. See *electromotive series.*

MOLAR HEAT CAPACITY. C_m. The *heat capacity* of a substance, divided by the amount of substance. The amount of *heat* required to raise the *temperature* of 1 *mole* of a substance by 1 *kelvin.* Expressed in *joules* per mole per kelvin (*SI units*), or *calories* per *gram-molecule* per °C. (*c.g.s. units*).

MOLAR SOLUTION. An obsolete expression for a *solution* with a *concentration* of 1 *mole* per dm³.

MOLAR VOLUME. V_m. Gram-molecular volume. The volume occupied by 1 *mole* of a substance. All gases have approximately equal molar volumes under the same conditions of *temperature* and *pressure.* At 760 mmHg and 0°C, the molar volume of a *perfect gas* is 22·415 dm³ per mole.

MOLARITY. A word sometimes used for *concentration* expressed in *moles* of *solute* per cubic decimetre of *solvent*. However, owing to its confusion with *molality* its use for this purpose is deprecated.

MOLE. The basic *SI unit* of amount of substance. The amount of substance which contains as many elementary units as there are *atoms* in 0·012 kg of carbon-12. The elementary units must be specified and may be an atom, *molecule, ion, radical, electron*, etc., or a specified group of such entities. For example, 1 mole of HCl has a mass of 36·46 g: i.e. 1 mole of a compound has a mass equal to its *molecular weight* in grams. 1 mole of electrons has a mass of $5\cdot486 \times 10^{-4}$ g, i.e. $m_e \times N_A$ (see Table 2, page 430).

The mole replaces such former units as the *gram-atom, gram-molecule, gram-ion*, and *gram equivalent*. Symbol *mol*.

MOLE FRACTION. Mol fraction. The ratio of the number of *moles* of a particular component of a *mixture*, to the total number of moles present in the mixture.

MOLECULAR BIOLOGY. The study of the structure of the *molecules* which are of importance in *biology*.

MOLECULAR COMPOUNDS. Chemical *compounds* formed by the chemical combination of two or more complete *molecules*. E.g. the *hydrates* of *salts*.

MOLECULAR CONCENTRATION. The *concentration* of a *solution* expressed in terms of *mols* in a given *volume*.

MOLECULAR DISTILLATION. The *evaporation* of *molecules* from a surface, at *pressures* of about 10^{-3} cm of mercury, and their subsequent *condensation* under such conditions that their *mean free path* is of the same order as the distance between the heated and cooled surfaces. Used for *isotope separation* and distilling heat-sensitive *organic compounds*.

MOLECULAR FORMULA. A *formula* of a chemical *compound*, showing the kind and the number of *atoms* present in the *molecule*, but not their arrangement. See *structural formula*.

MOLECULAR ORBITAL. When two *atomic orbitals* overlap they coalesce to produce a single 'molecular orbital'.

MOLECULAR SPECTRUM. The *spectrum* emitted by *molecules*. Caused by transitions between different states of molecular rotation, vibration, etc.

MOLECULAR VOLUME. The *volume* occupied by one *mol* of a substance; equal to its *molecular weight* divided by its *density*.

MOLECULAR WEIGHT. Relative molecular mass. The ratio of the average *mass* per *molecule* of a specified isotopic composition of a substance to 1/12 of the mass of an *atom* of $^{12}_{6}C$. The sum of the *atomic weights* of all the atoms which comprise a molecule.

MOLECULAR WEIGHT DETERMINATION. The following are amongst the available methods: Determination of the *vapour density*; applicable to *gases* and *volatile liquids*. Measurement of the *depression of freezing point, elevation of boiling point*, and *osmotic pressure* produced by a definite *concentration* of the substance in *solution*; used for *soluble* substances which do not dissociate or associate in solution. (See *dissociation, association.*) Determination of the *chemical equivalent* of the substance, with a knowledge of the *equation* for the reaction.

MOLECULE. The smallest portion of a substance capable of existing independently and retaining the properties of the original substance.

MOLYBDATE. A *salt* of *molybdic acid.*

MOLYBDENUM. Mo. Element. A.W. 95·94, At. No. 42. A hard white *metal* resembling iron, S.G. 10·2, m.p. 2620°C, which occurs as molybdenite, MoS_2. Extracted by roasting the *ore* and reducing the *oxide* so formed in an electric furnace with carbon. Used for special *steels* and *alloys.*

MOLYBDENUM TRIOXIDE. Molybdic anhydride. MoO_3. A yellow crystalline substance, m.p. 795°C., used in the manufacture of molybdenum *compounds.*

MOLYBDIC ACID. H_2MoO_4. A yellow crystalline substance which loses a *molecule* of *water* at 70°C. to form *molybdic trioxide* (molybdic anhydride).

MOMENT, MAGNETIC. See *magnetic moment.*

MOMENT OF FORCE. A measure of the tendency of a *force* to rotate the body to which it is applied. Measured by multiplying the magnitude of the force by the perpendicular distance from the line of action of the force to the *axis* of rotation.

MOMENT OF INERTIA. The moment of inertia I of a body about any *axis* is the sum of the products of the *mass, dm,* of each element of the body and the *square* of r, its distance from the axis. $I = \Sigma r^2 dm$.

MOMENTUM. The product of the *mass* and the *velocity* of a body. For speeds approaching that of *light,* the variation of mass with velocity must be taken into account, and the value of m appropriate to the velocity of the body must be used in the expression for the momentum. See *relativistic mass.*

MOMENTUM, CONSERVATION OF. See *conservation of momentum.*

MONAD. An *element* having a *valency* of one.

MONATOMIC MOLECULE. A *molecule* of an *element,* consisting of a single *atom* of the element. E.g. the molecules of the *inert gases.*

MONAZITE. A *mineral* containing *phosphates* of cerium, thorium, and other *rare earths,* with some occluded helium.

MOND PROCESS. The extraction of nickel by the action of *carbon monoxide,* CO, on the impure *metal.* This gives *nickel carbonyl,* $Ni(CO)_4$, a *gas* which decomposes when heated to 200°C. into pure nickel and carbon monoxide, the latter being used again. Named after Ludwig Mond (1839–1909).

MONEL METAL*. An *alloy* of copper (25%–35%), nickel (60%–70%) and small amounts of iron, manganese, silicon, and carbon. Used as an *acid*-resisting material in chemical industry.

MONO-. Prefix denoting one, single.

MONOBASIC ACID. An *acid* having one *atom* of *acidic* hydrogen in a *molecule*; an acid giving rise to only one series of *salts*. E.g. *nitric acid*, HNO_3.

MONOCHROMATIC LIGHT. *Light* consisting of vibrations of the same or nearly the same *frequency*; light of one *colour*.

MONOCLINIC. Relating to *crystals* which have three unequal axes with one oblique intersection.

MONOHYDRATE. Containing one *molecule* of *water*.

MONOHYDRIC. Containing one *hydroxyl group* in a *molecule*.

MONOMER. A chemical *compound* consisting of single *molecules*; as opposed to a *polymer*, the molecules of which are built up by the repeated union of monomer molecules. See *polymerization*.

MONOSACCHARIDES. Simple sugars. A group of *carbohydrates* consisting chiefly of *sugars* having a *molecular formula*, $C_6H_{12}O_6$ (*hexoses*) or $C_5H_{10}O_5$ (*pentoses*); unlike the *polysaccharides*, they cannot be hydrolyzed to give simple sugars.

MONOSODIUM GLUTAMATE. See *sodium hydrogen glutamate*.

MONOTROPIC. Existing in only one *stable* physical form, any other form obtainable being unstable under all conditions.

MONOVALENT. Univalent. Having a *valency* of one.

MONTH. The 'solar month' is one twelfth of a solar *year*. The 'calendar month' is any of the twelve divisions of the year according to the Gregorian calendar. The 'lunar month' is the time taken for the *Moon* to complete one *orbit* of the *Earth*. This may be measured in various ways. The 'synodic month' is the period between two successive *phases of the Moon*, equal to 29·5306 days. The 'sidereal month' is the Moon's period with respect to successive conjunctions with a *star*, equal to 27·3217 days. The 'anomolistic month' is the Moon's period between two successive *perigees*, equal to 27·5546 days. The 'Draconic month' is the Moon's period with respect to two successive similar *nodes*, equal to 27·2122 days.

MOON. The only *satellite* of the *Earth*. Mean distance from the Earth, 384 400 kilometres; synodic *month* 29·5306 days, sidereal month 27·3217 days. Mass 0·0123 that of the Earth; diameter 3476 kilometres. Devoid of *water* or an *atmosphere*. Man first set foot on the Moon in July 1969.

MORDANTS. Substances used in dyeing, especially fabrics of plant origin. The fabric is first impregnated with the mordant, which is generally a *basic metal hydroxide* for *acidic dyes*, or an acidic substance for basic dyes. The dye then reacts chemically with the mordant forming an insoluble *lake* which is firmly attached to the fabric.

MORPHIA. See *morphine*.

MORPHINE. $C_{17}H_{19}O_3N$. A white crystalline *alkaloid* which occurs in *opium*, m.p. 253°C. Powerful *narcotic*, used medically in the form of its *sulphate* or *hydrochloride* for relieving pain. Dangerous habit-forming drug.

251

MORPHOLINE. $O(CH_2CH_2)_2NH$. A colourless *hygroscopic liquid*, b.p. 128° C., used as a *solvent* for *resins* and *waxes*.

MORPHOLOGY. The study of the form and structure of *organisms*.

MORTAR. A building material consisting mainly of *lime* and *sand* which hardens on exposure through chemical action between the ingredients and atmospheric *carbon dioxide*.

MOSAIC. 1. In television cameras (see *camera, television*), a device for the electrical storage of the optical image. Usually consists of a sheet of *mica* one side of which is covered with mutually insulated particles of a *photo-emissive* material, each of which is capacitively coupled through the mica to a conducting coating on the reverse side. This conducting coating, called the signal plate, is the output *electrode* from which the electrical signal representing the optical image is obtained. 2. In *nuclear physics*, a *photomicrograph* of a track in an *emulsion*, prepared from a number of photographs of consecutive fields of view and reconstructed as though the track lay in one *plane*.

MOSAIC GOLD. Crystalline *stannic sulphide*, SnS_2, consisting of shining, golden-yellow scales.

MÖSSBAUER EFFECT. The discovery by R. L. Mössbauer (born 1929) in 1957 that in certain cases appreciable fractions of the *gamma-ray spectrum* emitted by some excited (see *excitation*) *nuclei* may be undisturbed by nuclear recoil or *lattice* vibrations and the consequent *Doppler effects*. The Mössbauer effect has been used to test the predictions of the theory of *relativity*, to investigate the properties of the *solid state* and the nature of *magnetism*.

MOTHER-LIQUOR. A *solution* from which substances are crystallized.

MOTION, EQUATIONS OF. Kinematic equations, which apply to bodies moving with uniform *acceleration*, a; the equations numbered (1)–(4) below. In the velocity-time *graph* (Fig. 28, page 253):

Gradient of $AB = \tan a = a$

$\therefore BC = t.\tan a = at$

and $BD = v = $ final *velocity*

hence $v = u + at \ldots$(1) where u is the initial velocity.

The area under AB equals the distance covered, s,

$\therefore s = $ area $ACDO + $ area ABC

i.e. $s = ut + \frac{1}{2}at^2 \ldots$(2)

Also, using (1); $s = ut + \frac{1}{2}(v - u)t$

$$or \ s = \frac{u+v}{2}.t \ldots(3)$$

Combining (1) & (2), $v^2 = u^2 + 2as \ldots$(4).

MOTION, LAWS OF. See *Newton's laws of motion*.

MOTOR. A device for converting other forms of *energy* into mechanical energy. Generally applied to the *internal-combustion engine* and the *electric motor*.

MUCIC ACID. $HOOC.(CHOH)_4COOH$. A white crystalline powder obtained by the *oxidation* of *gums* or *galactose*; used in organic synthesis.

MUCOPROTEINS. Glycoproteins. *Proteins* which contain a *carbohydrate* group.

MULTICELLULAR. Said of an *organism* that consists of more than one *cell*.

MULTIPLE PROPORTIONS, LAW OF. See *chemical combination, laws of*.

MULTIPLE STAR. A system of *stars* consisting of three or more components held together by *gravitation*.

MULTIPLICATION CONSTANT (FACTOR). The 'effective' multiplication constant of a *nuclear reactor* is the ratio of the average number of

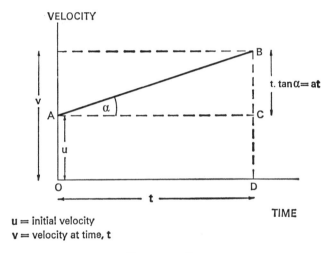

VELOCITY

u = initial velocity
v = velocity at time, t

FIGURE 28

neutrons produced by *nuclear fission* per unit time, to the total number of neutrons absorbed or leaking out in the same time. See *subcritical* and *supercritical*.

MUMETAL*. An *alloy* of high *magnetic permeability* containing up to 78% nickel in addition to iron, copper, and manganese.

MUNTZ METAL*. An *alloy* containing 3 parts of copper and 2 parts of zinc.

MUON. μ-meson. An *elementary particle* with a *mass* 207 times that of an *electron*, which exists in negatively and positively charged forms. Originally so called as it was classified as a *meson*. However as these particles have *spin* $\frac{1}{2}$, they are now classified as *leptons*. See Table 6, page 436.

MURIATE. *Chloride*; a *salt of hydrochloric acid*.

MURIATIC ACID. See *hydrochloric acid*.

MUSTARD GAS. Dichlorodiethyl sulphide. $(CH_2CH_2Cl)_2S$. An oily *liquid* which has been used as a 'war gas'. Destroyed by *oxidizing agents*, e.g. *bleaching powder*.

253

MUTAGEN. A substance which produces *mutations*.

MUTAROTATION. A change in the *optical rotation* of a substance.

MUTATION. A change in the chemical constitution of the *chromosomes* of an *organism*: the changes are normally restricted to individual *genes*, but occasionally involve serious alteration to whole chromosomes. When a mutation occurs in *gametes* or *gametocytes* an inherited change may be produced in the characteristics of the organisms which develop from them. It is due to the *natural selection* of strains of organisms which have become better adapted to their environment, as a consequence of genetic mutations, that the *evolution* of species has taken place. A *somatic* mutation is one which occurs to a body *cell*, and which is consequently passed on to all the cells which are derived from it by *mitosis*. Natural mutations are relatively rare events, and at this stage of biological evolution, when they occur in the cells of higher animals, almost always produce deleterious characteristics. Artificial mutations can be brought about by *ionizing radiations* (hence the genetic and *carcinogenetic* dangers of *nuclear weapons*) and by certain chemical substances.

MUTUAL CONDUCTANCE. The ratio of the change of *anode current* to the change in *control grid voltage*, when a small change is made to the control grid voltage in a *thermionic valve*. Used as a measure of the valve's performance. See also *transconductance*.

MUTUAL INDUCTION. The induction of an *E.M.F.* in a *circuit* due to a changing current in a separate circuit with which it is magnetically linked. The induced E.M.F. is proportional to the rate of change of the current in the second circuit, the constant of proportionality being called the coefficient of mutual induction, or the mutual inductance. The derived *SI unit* of mutual inductance is the *henry*.

MYCOLOGY. The branch of *botany* concerned with *fungi*.

MYDRIATIC. A substance used to dilate the pupil of the eye.

MYOGLOBIN. A form of *haemoglobin* which occurs in muscle fibres.

MYOPIA. Short sight. A defect of vision in which the subject is unable to see distant objects distinctly. Corrected by the use of *concave* spectacle *lenses*.

N

NADIR (astr.). The lowest point; the point opposite the *zenith* on the *celestial sphere*. See Fig. 2, page 36.

NANO-. Prefix indicating one thousand millionth. E.g. a nanosecond is 10^{-9} seconds and a nanometre is 10^{-9} metres. Symbol n.

NAPHTHA. A general name for *mixtures* of *hydrocarbons* in various proportions, obtained from *paraffin oil*, *coal-tar*, etc. Wood naphtha is impure *methanol*, CH_3OH, produced by the *destructive distillation* of wood.

NAPHTHALENE. $C_{10}H_8$. A white crystalline *cyclic hydrocarbon* with a penetrating odour which occurs in *coal-tar*. M.p. $80 \cdot 2°$ C., b.p. $218°$ C. Used in the manufacture of organic *dyes* and in moth-balls.

NAPHTHOL. $C_{10}H_7OH$. Two *isomeric derivatives* of *naphthalene*, both of which darken in colour on exposure to *light*: 1-naphthol (α-naphthol) is a yellow crystalline substance, m.p. $93 \cdot 3°$ C., used in the manufacture of *dyes* and perfumes; 2-naphthol (β-naphthol) is a white crystalline substance, m.p. $122°$ C., used as an *antiseptic* and in the manufacture of dyes, *drugs*, and perfumes.

NAPHTHYL GROUP. The *univalent radical*, $C_{10}H_7 -$.

NAPIERIAN LOGARITHM. See *logarithm*. Named after John Napier (1550–1617).

NARCEINE. $C_{23}H_{27}NO_8.3H_2O$. A white crystalline *alkaloid* which occurs in *opium*, m.p. $176°$ C.; used as a muscle relaxant.

NARCOTIC. Producing sleep, stupor, or insensibility.

NASCENT STATE. Certain *elements*, notably hydrogen, are more active when being set free in a *chemical reaction* than in their ordinary state; such 'nascent' elements are supposed to owe their activity to being composed of single *atoms* instead of *molecules*, or alternatively to some of the *chemical energy* liberated on the reaction being associated with the hydrogen instead of being released in the form of *heat*.

NATRIUM. See *sodium*.

NATRON. Natural sodium sesquicarbonate, $Na_2CO_3.NaHCO_3.2H_2O$.

NATURAL (chem.). Occurring in nature; not artificially prepared.

NATURAL ABUNDANCE. The *abundance* of each different *isotope* in an *element* as it is normally found in nature.

NATURAL FREQUENCY. The *frequency* of free oscillation of any system.

NATURAL GAS. A mixture of gaseous *hydrocarbons*, predominantly *methane*, often containing other *gases*, issuing from the earth in some localities, more particularly near deposits of *mineral oil*. Mixed with *coal-gas*, or alone, it is used as a *fuel*.

NATURAL LOGARITHM. See *logarithm*.

NATURAL SELECTION. The theory, first proposed by Charles Darwin, which explains the mechanism of biological evolution (see *Darwin's theory of evolution*). According to this theory, the life-forms best adapted to their environment will survive and reproduce in the greatest numbers. As new characteristics arise as small uncontrolled variations (resulting from genetic *mutations*) nature selects for survival those strains of *organisms* which inherit distinctive characteristics best fitting them for their environment.

NAUTICAL MILE. Defined in the U.K. as 6080 ft, but internationally as 1852 *metres*, 1 U.K. nautical mile therefore equals 1.00064 international nautical miles. 1 international nautical mile equals 1·15078 miles.

NEAR INFRARED or ULTRAVIOLET. The shortest *infrared* or the longest *ultraviolet wavelengths*; i.e. those wavelengths of these two types of *radiation* which are 'nearest' in magnitude to those of visible *light*.

NEBULA (astr.). A cloudy, luminous patch in the heavens which consists of a *galaxy* of *stars*, or of materials from which such galaxies are being formed.

NEGATIVE (math. and phys.). In any convention of signs, regarded as being counted in the minus, or negative direction, as opposed to positive.

NEGATIVE FEEDBACK. See *feedback*.

NEGATIVE, PHOTOGRAPHIC. See *photography*.

NEGATIVE POLE. The south-seeking pole of a *magnet*. See *magnetic pole*.

NEGATRON. Negaton. See *electron*.

NEODYMIUM. Nd. Element. A.W. 144·24. At. No. 60. S.G 6·9, m.p. 1024°C. See *lanthanides*.

NEON. Ne. Element. A.W. 20·183. At. No. 10. A colourless odourless invisible *inert gas* which occurs in the *atmosphere* (1 part in 55,000). Obtained by the *fractional distillation of liquid air*. A discharge of *electricity* through neon at low *pressures* produces an intense orange-red glow; used for neon signs.

NEOPLASM. New growth of abnormal *tissue* in plants or animals; a tumour which may be either benign or malignant.

NEOPRENE*. *Trans*-polychloroprene. $(CH_2.CH.CCl.CH_2)_n$. A synthetic *rubber* having a high *tensile strength* and better heat and *ozone* resistance than natural rubber.

NEPER. A unit for expressing the *ratio* of two values (e.g. *currents*, *voltages*, etc.) equal to the natural *logarithm* of the ratio of the quantities. 1 neper = 8·686 *decibels*. Named after John Napier (1550–1617).

NEPHOSCOPE. A grid-like instrument for determining speed of celestial objects (including clouds) by observation of time of transit.

NEPTUNE (astr.). A *planet* with two *satellites*. *Orbit* lies between those of *Uranus* and *Pluto*. Mean distance from the *Sun*, 4496·7 million kilometres. *Sidereal period* ('year'), 164·8 years. Mass 17·46 times that of the *Earth*, diameter 44 800 kilometres. Surface temperature probably below −200°C.

NEPTUNIUM. Np. *Transuranic element*, At. No. 93. Most stable *isotope*, $^{237}_{93}$Np, has a *half-life* of 2·2 × 10⁶ years. A *metal* of silvery appearance,

5

S.G. 20·45, m.p. 640°C., produced as a *by-product* by *nuclear reactors* in the manufacture of plutonium.

NERNST EFFECT. If a *temperature* gradient is maintained across an electrical *conductor* (or *semiconductor*) which is placed in a transverse *magnetic field*, a *potential difference* will be produced across the conductor. Named after Walter Nernst (1864–1941).

NERNST HEAT THEOREM. The *entropy* change for *chemical reactions* involving crystalline *solids*, is zero at the *absolute zero* of temperature. See also *thermodynamics, laws of*.

NEROL. $C_{10}H_{17}OH$. A colourless *liquid unsaturated alcohol, isomeric* with *geraniol*, b.p. 224°C., used in perfumes and obtained from *neroli oil*.

NEROLI OIL. An *essential oil* obtained from the flowers of orange trees.

NERVE CELL. See *neurone*.

NERVE FIBRE. An *axon* or *dendrite*.

NERVE GAS. A war-gas which attacks the nervous system especially the nerves controlling respiration. Most nerve gases are *derivatives* of *phosphoric acid*.

NESSLER'S SOLUTION. A *solution* of potassium mercuric iodide, $KHgI_3$, in *potassium hydroxide* solution. Used as a test for *ammonia*, with which it forms a brown coloration or precipitate. Named after Julius Nessler (1827–1905).

NEURON (E). Nerve cell. A special type of biological *cell*, being the unit of which the nervous systems of animals are composed. Consists of a *nucleus* surrounded by a *cytoplasm* from which thread-like fibres project. In most neurones impulses are received by numerous short fibres called *dendrites* and carried away from the cell by a single long fibre called an *axon*. Transfer of impulses from neurone to neurone takes place at junctions between axons and dendrites which are called *synapses*.

NEUROTOXIN. A poison which attacks the nervous system.

NEUTRAL (chem.). Neither *acid* nor *alkaline*. Containing equal numbers of *hydroxyl* and *hydrogen ions* and having a pH of 7.

NEUTRAL (phys.). Having neither negative nor positive net *electric charge*.

NEUTRAL TEMPERATURE. The temperature of the hot junction of a *thermocouple* at which the *electromotive force* round the circuit is a maximum and the rate of change of E.M.F. with *temperature* is a minimum.

NEUTRALIZATION (chem.). The addition of *acid* to *alkali*, or vice versa, till neither is in excess and the *solution* is neutral.

NEUTRETTO. A *meson* with zero *electric charge*.

NEUTRINO. A stable *elementary particle* with no *electric charge* or *rest mass*, but with *spin* ½. Originally postulated to preserve the laws of *conservation of mass and energy* and *conservation of momentum*. The existence of the particle has since been established experimentally, and it is known to exist in two forms; the neutrino, which is emitted with *positrons*, and the anti-neutrino, which is emitted with negative *electrons* (e.g.

in *neutron* decay). Both forms also appear in the decay of some *mesons*. See Table 6, page 436.

NEUTRON. An *elementary particle* which is a constituent of all atomic *nuclei* except that of normal hydrogen. The neutron has no *electric charge* and a *mass* only very slightly greater than that of the *proton* ($1 \cdot 67482 \times 10^{-27}$ *kilogrammes*). Outside a nucleus a neutron decays, with a *half-life* of 12 minutes, into a proton, an *electron*, and an anti-*neutrino*. Neutrons and protons may be considered as different aspects of the same particles and the name *nucleon* is used to describe both of them.

NEUTRON EXCESS. See *isotropic number*.

NEUTRON FLUX. A measure of the number of *neutrons* passing through 1 sq cm in any direction in 1 second.

NEUTRON NUMBER. N. The number of *neutrons* in an atomic *nucleus*; equal to the *mass number* minus the *atomic number*.

NEUTRON STAR. A hypothetical state of a *star* at the end of its evolutionary process (see *stellar evolution*) when it has consumed all its *nuclear fuel* and no longer has a source of internal *energy*. The star would then become highly compressed by *gravitational forces* and apart from a thin outer shell would consist only of *neutrons*. Such a star would be expected to have a density some 10^7 times greater than a *white dwarf*. No neutron stars have been identified with certainty, although it is thought that *pulsars* may be this type of star.

NEUTRON TEMPERATURE. The *energies* possessed by *neutrons* in thermal equilibrium with their surroundings may be expressed in terms of a *temperature*, if it is assumed that they behave as a *monatomic gas*. Under these conditions, the neutron temperature on the *Kelvin scale*, T, is given by: $E = \dfrac{3kT}{2}$, where E is the neutron energy and k is *Boltzmann's constant*.

NEW CANDLE. See *candela*.

NEWTON. The derived *SI unit* of *force*. The force required to give a *mass* of one *kilogram* an *acceleration* of one *metre* per second per second. Symbol N. Named after Sir Isaac Newton (1642–1727).

NEWTON'S LAW OF COOLING. The rate at which a body loses *heat* to its surroundings is proportional to the *temperature* difference between the body and its surroundings (an *empirical* law, true only for small differences of temperature).

NEWTON'S LAWS OF MOTION. The fundamental laws on which classical *dynamics* is based. 1. Every body continues in its state of rest or uniform motion in a straight line except in so far as it is compelled by external *forces* to change that state. 2. Rate of change of *momentum* is proportional to the applied force, and takes place in the direction in which the force acts. 3. To every action there is an equal and opposite reaction.

NEWTON'S RINGS. Coloured rings which may be observed round the point of contact of a *convex lens* and a *plane* reflecting surface. Caused by the *interference* effects which occur between *light* waves reflected at the upper and lower surfaces of the air film separating the lens and the flat surface.

NEWTONIAN MECHANICS. A system of *mechanics* developed from *Newton's laws of motion.* Provides an accurate means of determining the motions of bodies possessing ordinary *velocities.* The motions of particles having very high velocities must be treated by relativistic mechanics, i.e. a system of mechanics based on the theory of *relativity,* as the change of *mass* of a particle with its velocity becomes important under such conditions.

NEWTONIAN TELESCOPE. Newtonian Reflector. A form of astronomical reflecting *telescope* consisting of a large *concave* focussing *mirror* on the *axis* of which is mounted a small plane mirror or reflecting *prism,* enabling the image to be viewed through an *eye-piece* which is perpendicular to the axis of the main mirror. See Fig. 29.

NEWTONIAN TELESCOPE

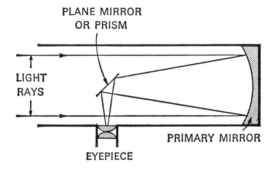

FIGURE 29.

NIACIN. See *nicotinic acid.*

NICHROME*. Trade name for a nickel-chromium *alloy* used for wire in electrical devices, owing to its high *resistance* and its ability to withstand high *temperatures.*

NICKEL. Ni. Element. A.W. 58·71. At. No. 28. A silvery-white magnetic *metal,* resembling iron, which resists corrosion. S.G. 8·90, m.p. 1455°C. Occurs combined with sulphur or arsenic in pentlandite, *kupfer-nickel,* smaltite and other *ores.* The ore is roasted to form the *oxide,* which is reduced to the metal by hydrogen, and the metal is then purified by the *Mond process.* Used for *nickel-plating,* in coinage, for *alloys* such as *nickel steel, nickel silver, platinoid, constantan, nichrome*,* and as a *catalyst.*

NICKEL ACETATE. $(CH_3COO)_2Ni.4H_2O$. A green crystalline *soluble* substance, used in *nickel plating*.

NICKEL CARBONYL. $Ni(CO)_4$. A colourless *volatile liquid*, b.p. $43°C$., which decomposes at $200°C$. into nickel and *carbon monoxide*. See *Mond process*.

NICKEL-IRON ACCUMULATOR. See *accumulator*.

NICKEL MONOXIDE. Nickelous oxide. NiO. A green *insoluble* powder, m.p. $1990°C$., used as a *pigment* and in the manufacture of nickel *compounds*. See also *nickel oxide*.

NICKEL OXIDE. Nickelic oxide. Ni_2O_3. A black *insoluble* powder, which decomposes into *nickel monoxide* at $600°C$., used in nickel-iron *accumulators*.

NICKEL PLATING. Depositing a thin layer of metallic nickel by an electrolytic process. See *electrolysis*.

NICKEL SILVER. A group of *alloys* of copper, nickel, and zinc in varying proportions, containing up to 30% nickel. A typical composition is 60% copper, 20% nickel, 20% zinc.

NICKEL STEEL. *Steel* containing up to 6% nickel.

NICOL PRISM. An optical device, constructed from a crystal of *calcite*, used for obtaining plane polarized light. Named after William Nicol ($1768–1851$). See *polarization of light*.

NICOTINAMIDE. Niacinamide. $C_5H_4NCONH_2$. *Vitamin* of the B complex. A colourless *soluble* substance, m.p. $124°C$., used in medicine to treat pellagra.

NICOTINE. $C_{10}H_{14}N_2$. A colourless, intensely poisonous oily *liquid*, *alkaloid*, b.p. $247·3°C$., which occurs in tobacco leaves.

NICOTINIC ACID. Pyridine-3-carboxylic acid, niacin. $C_5H_4N.COOH$. *Vitamin* of the B complex. A colourless crystalline *solid*, m.p. $235°C$. Occurs in meat and *yeast*; deficiency causes pellagra.

NIOBIUM. Columbium. Nb. Element. A.W. $92·906$. At. No. 41. A rare grey *metal*, S.G. $8·4$, m.p. $2500°C$. Small quantites in *stainless steel*, preserve the steel's *corrosion* resistance at high *temperatures*.

NIT. A unit of *luminance* equal to one *candela* per square *metre*.

NITON. An obsolete name for *radon*.

NITRAMINES. *Nitro derivatives* of *amines* with the general formula $R.NH.NO_2$.

NITRATE. A *salt* or *ester* of *nitric acid*.

NITRATION. Introduction of the *nitro group*, $-NO_2$, into *organic compounds* by the use of *nitric acid*. Of importance in the production of *explosives*, many nitro derivatives of organic compounds being chemically *unstable*.

NITRE. Saltpetre. See *potassium nitrate*.

NITRIC ACID. Aqua fortis. HNO_3. A colourless, corrosive, *acid liquid*, b.p. $86°C$., which is a powerful *oxidizing agent*. Attacks most *metals* and many other substances with evolution of brown fumes of *nitrogen dioxide*, NO_2. Manufactured by the action of concentrated *sulphuric acid*,

H_2SO_4, on *sodium* or *potassium nitrate*, and by the *oxidation* of *ammonia*, NH_3, by passing a mixture of ammonia and air over heated platinum which acts as a *catalyst*. Widely used in chemical industry.

NITRIC OXIDE. NO. A colourless *gas* which reacts with oxygen on contact to form *nitrogen dioxide*, NO_2.

NITRIDES. *Compounds* of *trivalent* nitrogen and *metals* (e.g. magnesium nitride, Mg_3N_2), formed by passing nitrogen over the red-hot metal. Some non-metallic *elements* (e.g. boron and silicon) also form nitrides.

NITRIFICATION. 1. The treatment of a substance with *nitric acid*. 2. The process of conversion, by the action of *bacteria*, of nitrogen *compounds* from animal and plant waste and decay, into *nitrates* in the *soil*.

NITRILE RUBBERS. A group of synthetic *rubbers* which are copolymers (see *polymerization*) of *butadiene* and *acrylonitrile*. These materials, which can be vulcanized in a similar manner to natural rubber, have a high resistance to *oil*, *fuels*, and *aromatic solvents*. Their properties can be modified by varying the proportions of the constituents; increasing the acrylonitrile content results in greater oil resistance.

NITRITE. A *salt* or *ester* of nitrous acid, HNO_2.

NITRO GROUP. The *univalent radical* $NO_2 -$.

NITROBENZENE. $C_6H_5NO_2$. A pale yellow, oily, poisonous *liquid*, b.p. 211°C., with an odour of bitter almonds. Produced by the action of *nitric acid* on *benzene*; reduction of nitrobenzene yields *aniline*.

NITROCELLULOSE. See *cellulose nitrate*. Although the term nitrocellulose is chemically incorrect for this compound, it is extensively used.

NITROCHALK. A *mixture* of *calcium carbonate*, $CaCO_3$, and *ammonium nitrate*, NH_4NO_3, used as a *fertilizer*.

NITROGEN. N. Element. A.W. 14·0067. At. No. 7. An odourless, invisible, chemically inactive *gas*, forming approximately 4/5 of the *atmosphere*. The chief natural *compound* is *Chile saltpetre*. Compounds are used as *fertilizers* and in the manufacture of *nitric acid*. The element is vital to living *organisms*, forming an essential part of *proteins* and *nucleic acids*. See *fixation of atmospheric nitrogen; nitrogen cycle*.

NITROGEN CYCLE. The circulation of nitrogen *compounds* in nature through the various *organisms* to which nitrogen is essential. *Inorganic* nitrogen compounds in the *soil* are taken in by plants, and are combined by the plants with other *elements* to form *nucleic acids* and *proteins*, the latter being the form in which nitrogen can be utilized by the higher animals. The result of animal waste and decay is to bring the nitrogen which the animals had absorbed back into the soil in the form of simpler nitrogen compounds. Bacterial action of various kinds converts these into compounds suitable for use by plants again. In addition to this main circulation, a certain amount of atmospheric nitrogen is 'fixed' (i.e. combined) by the action of *bacteria* associated with the roots of leguminous plants, and by the action of atmospheric *electricity*; while some combined nitrogen is set free by the action of *denitrifying bacteria*. See Fig. 30, page 262.

NITROGEN DIOXIDE. Nitrogen peroxide, NO_2. A dark brown *gas* with a pungent smell, formed by the *reduction* of *nitric acid* and in the decomposition, by *heat*, of some *nitrates*. On cooling to a low *temperature* becomes paler in colour, owing to the *association* of the *molecules* to form *nitrogen tetroxide*.

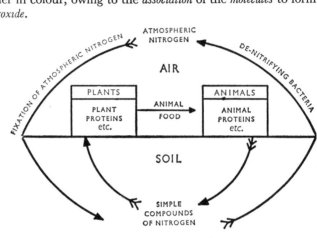

FIGURE 30.

NITROGEN TETROXIDE. N_2O_4. A colourless *solid*, yellow *liquid*, or brown *gas*, used as an *oxidant* in *rocket fuels* and as a nitrating agent.

NITROGLYCERIN. Glyceryl trinitrate. $C_3H_5(NO_3)_3$. A pale yellow, heavy, oily *liquid* which explodes with great violence when subjected to sudden shock or detonation. Used as an *explosive*, either alone or in the form of *dynamite*.

NITROLIME. See *calcium cyanamide*.

NITROMETHANE. CH_3NO_2. A colourless oily *liquid*, b.p. 100·8° C., used as a *solvent* and in organic synthesis.

NITROSO GROUP. The *univalent radical* $O=N-$.

NITROUS ETHER. See *ethyl nitrite*.

NITROUS OXIDE. Laughing gas. N_2O. A colourless *gas* used as a mild *anaesthetic* in dentistry, etc.

NOBELIUM. No. *Transuranic element*. At. No. 102. Most stable *isotope*, $^{255}_{102}$No, has *half-life* of 3 minutes.

NOBLE METALS. *Metals* such as silver, gold, and platinum, which do not corrode or tarnish in air or *water*, and are not easily attacked by *acids*. From the chemical point of view, unreactive metals are low in the *electromotive series*.

NODAL POINTS. Two points on the axis of a *lens* system, such that if the incident *ray* passes through one, travelling in a given direction, the emergent ray passes through the other in a parallel direction.

NODES. 1. Points of zero displacement in a system of *standing waves*. See also *antinodes*. 2. (astr.) Two points at which the *orbit* of a celestial body intersects the *ecliptic*. 3. (math.) Points on a curve or surface which can have more than one *tangent*.

NOISE (elec.). 1. An effect observed in amplifying circuits due to the amplification, together with the input signal, of spurious *voltages* arising from such causes as the vibration of certain components, the random motion of the *electrons* constituting the *current* in the *conductors*, etc. 2. A term used in *information theory* to indicate a disturbance which does not represent any part of a message from a specified source.

NOMOGRAM. Nomograph. An alignment chart arranged so that the value of a *variable* can be found, without calculation, from the values of one or two other variables which are known.

NONANOIC ACID. Pelargonic acid, $CH_3(CH_2)_7COOH$. A colourless oily *liquid*, b.p. 253–5°C., used in the manufacture of *lacquers* and *plastics*.

NON-CONSERVATION OF PARITY. See *parity*.

NON-ELECTROLYTES. Substances which do not yield *ions* in *solution* and which therefore form solutions of low electrical *conductivity*. See *electrolysis*.

NON-FERROUS METAL. Any *metal* other than *iron* or *steel*.

NON-METALLIC ELEMENTS. Chemical *elements* not possessing the properties of the *metals*.

NOR-. (chem.). A combining form of *normal*. The prefix is also used to indicate the loss of a *methyl group*, e.g. noradrenaline, or the loss of a *methylene group* from a chain.

NORMAL. 1. (math.) A line *perpendicular* to a surface. 2. (chem.) A prefix denoting either a *normal solution* (abbrev. N–) or an *isomer* with an unbranched chain (abbrev. *n*–).

NORMAL SOLUTION (chem.). A *solution* containing 1 *gram-equivalent of solute* per *litre* of solution. See *normality*.

NORMAL STATE of atom. See *ground state*.

NORMALITY (chem.). An obsolescent method of expressing *concentrations of solutions*; number of *gram-equivalents* of *reagent* per *litre* of solution. Thus, a solution containing 2 gram-equivalents per litre is a twice-*normal* or 2N solution.

NORMALIZING. A *heat* treatment applied to *steel* in order to relieve internal *stresses*. Involves heating above a critical *temperature* and cooling in air.

NOTATION. The representation of numbers, quantities, or other entities by symbols; a system of symbols for such a purpose.

NOVA. A *star* which ejects a small part of its material in the form of a *gas* cloud. During the process the star becomes 5000 to 10 000 times more luminous than it was before the outburst. 'Dwarf' novae increase their *luminosity* by a factor of only 10–100. Novae appear to be one of a pair of *binary stars*. See also *supernovae*.

N-P-N TRANSISTOR. See *transistor*.

N.T.P.; S.T.P. Normal (standard) *temperature* and *pressure*. A pressure of 760 mm of mercury and a temperature of 0° C.; standard conditions under which *volumes* of *gases* are compared.

N-TYPE CONDUCTIVITY. The *conductivity* in a *semiconductor* caused by a flow of *electrons*, whereas p-type conductivity is caused by a flow of *holes*.

NUCLEAR BARRIER. Potential Barrier. The region of high *potential energy* through which a charged particle must pass on entering or leaving an atomic *nucleus*.

NUCLEAR CHARGE. The positive *electric charge* on the *nucleus* of an *atom*. When expressed in units equal to the charge on the *electron*, this is numerically equal to the *atomic number* of the *element*, to the number of *protons* in the nucleus, and to the number of electrons surrounding the nucleus in the *neutral* atom. See *atom, structure of*.

NUCLEAR ENERGY. Atomic energy. *Energy* released during a *nuclear reaction* as the result of the conversion of *mass* into *energy* (see *mass-energy equation*). Nuclear energy is released in *nuclear reactors* and *nuclear weapons*.

NUCLEAR FISSION. A *nuclear reaction* in which a heavy atomic *nucleus* (e.g. uranium) splits into two approximately equal parts, at the same time emitting *neutrons* and releasing very large amounts of *nuclear energy*. Fission can be spontaneous or it may be caused by the impact of a neutron (see *chain reaction*), an energetic charged particle or a *photon* (*photofission*). See also *nuclear reactor* and *nuclear weapon*.

NUCLEAR FORCE. The attractive *force* which acts between *nucleons* when they are extremely close together (closer than 10^{-13} cm.). The nuclear force replaces the repulsive electromagnetic interaction between *protons* at such proximities and holds the nucleons together in the atomic *nucleus* (see *exchange forces*). The precise nature of the nuclear force is not known.

NUCLEAR FUEL. A substance which undergoes *nuclear fission* or *nuclear fusion* in a *nuclear reactor*, a *nuclear weapon*, or a *star*.

NUCLEAR FUSION. A *nuclear reaction* between light atomic *nuclei* as a result of which a heavier nucleus is formed and a large quantity of *nuclear energy* is released. E.g. the fusion of two *deuterium* nuclei to form a *tritium* nucleus and a *proton* is accompanied by an energy release of $4 MeV$ $(D+D=T+p+4 MeV)$. For fusion to be possible the reacting nuclei must possess sufficient *kinetic energy* to overcome the *electrostatic field* which surrounds them. The *temperatures* associated with fusion reactions are therefore extremely high. Fusion reactions occur on *Earth* during the explosion of a hydrogen bomb (see *nuclear weapons*) and during controlled *thermonuclear reactions*. Fusion reactions are believed to be the source of the energy of the *stars* (including the *Sun*).

NUCLEAR ISOMERS. *Atoms* of an *element* of the same *mass* but possessing different rates of *radioactive decay*.

NUCLEAR MAGNETIC RESONANCE. NMR. All atomic *nuclei*, except *even-even nuclei*, have *magnetic moments* associated with them, which tend to be aligned by an externally applied *magnetic field*, but because nuclei possess *angular momentum*, they precess (see *precessional motion*) about the direction of the applied field. The *energy* of the interaction between the applied and the nuclear magnetic fields is *quantized* (see *quantum mechanics*), so that only certain orientations of the nucleus relative to the applied field are permitted: a transition from one orientation to another involves the absorption or emission of a *quantum* of *electromagnetic radiation*, the *frequency* of which can be shown to equal the precessional frequency. With the magnetic field strengths customarily used (up to about 2 *tesla* or 20 kilo*gauss*) the energies involved are small, and the radiations fall in the *radio frequency* band, i.e. 1–100 *megahertz*. Transitions from one *energy level* to another can be induced by applying a second magnetic field, at right angles to the first, which rotates in *phase* with the nuclear precession. NMR spectroscopy (also called 'radio frequency spectroscopy') consists of observing the point of *resonance* at which such transitions are induced. Data obtained in this way provide valuable information concerning nuclear properties. As the *orbital electrons* 'shield' the nucleus to a certain extent from the applied magnetic field, at a given frequency nuclei in different electronic (i.e. chemical) environments will resonate at slightly different values of the applied field. This phenomenon, known as the 'chemical shift' enables NMR spectroscopy to be of great value in working out the configuration of complex *molecules*.

NUCLEAR PHYSICS. The study of the *physics* of the atomic *nucleus* and of sub-atomic particles.

NUCLEAR POWER. Electric or motive power produced from a unit in which the primary *energy* source is a *nuclear reactor*.

NUCLEAR REACTION. Any reaction which involves a change in the *nucleus* of an *atom*, as distinct from a *chemical reaction* which only involves the *orbital electrons*. Such reactions occur naturally, on the *Earth* in *radioactive elements*, and in *stars* as *thermonuclear reactions*. They are also produced artificially in *nuclear reactors*, *nuclear weapons*, and controlled thermonuclear reactions. See also *nuclear fission* and *nuclear fusion*.

Nuclear reactions are represented by enclosing within a bracket the symbols for the incoming and outgoing particles or *quanta* (separated by a comma), the initial and final *nuclides* being shown outside the bracket. Thus the reaction:

$$^{14}_{7}N + ^{4}_{2}He \rightarrow ^{17}_{8}O + ^{1}_{1}H$$

is represented: $^{14}N(\alpha, p)^{17}O$.

NUCLEAR REACTOR. Atomic pile. An assembly in which a *nuclear fission chain reaction* is maintained and controlled for the production of *nuclear energy*, *radioactive isotopes*, or artificial *elements*. The *nuclear fuel* used in a reactor consists of a *fissile* material (e.g. $^{235}_{92}U$) which undergoes fission, as a consequence of which two *nuclides* of approximately

265

equal *mass* are produced together with between two and three *neutrons* and a considerable quantity of *energy*. These neutrons cause further fissions so that a chain reaction develops; in order that the reaction should not get out of control, its progress is regulated by neutron absorbers (see *control rods*), only sufficient free neutrons being allowed to exist in the reactor to maintain the reaction at a constant level. The fissile material is usually mixed with a *moderator* which slows down (see *thermalize*) the *fast neutrons* emitted during fission, so that they are more likely to cause further fissions of the fissile material than they are to be captured by the $^{235}_{92}U$ *isotope*. In a 'heterogeneous reactor' the fuel and the moderator are separated in a geometric pattern called a *lattice*. In a 'homogeneous reactor' the fuel and the moderator are mixed so that they present a uniform medium to the neutrons (e.g. the fuel, in the form of a uranium *salt*, may be dissolved in the moderator).

Besides this classification, reactors may be described in a number of ways. They may be described in terms of neutron energy (see *fast reactor*, *thermal reactor*) or in terms of function, e.g. a 'power reactor' for generating useful *electric power*, a 'production reactor' for manufacturing fissile material (see also *breeder reactor* and *converter reactor*) and a 'propulsion reactor' for supplying motive power to ships or submarines. Reactors are also described in terms of their fuel (e.g. 'graphite-moderated reactor') or their coolant (e.g. *boiling-water reactor*, *gas-cooled reactor*).

The term nuclear reactor may also be applied to a device in which a controlled *thermonuclear reaction* takes place, in this case it is referred to as a 'fusion reactor'.

NUCLEAR TRANSMUTATIONS. The changing of *atoms* of one *element* into those of another by suitable *nuclear reactions*.

NUCLEAR WEAPONS. Weapons in which the explosive power is derived from *nuclear fission* or a combination of nuclear fission and *nuclear fusion*. The fission bomb (atom[ic] bomb or A-bomb) consists essentially of two or more *masses* of a suitable *fissile* material (e.g. $^{235}_{92}U$ or $^{239}_{94}Pu$) each of which is less than the *critical mass*. When the bomb is detonated the subcritical masses are brought rapidly together to form a supercritical assembly, so that a single fission at the instant of contact sets off an uncontrolled *chain reaction*. The resulting release of *nuclear energy* produces a devastating *explosion* the effect of which is comparable to the explosion of tens of *kilotons* of *T.N.T.* The fusion bomb (thermonuclear bomb, hydrogen bomb, or H-bomb) consists of a fission bomb surrounded by a layer of hydrogenous material (e.g. lithium deuteride). At the *temperature* resulting from the explosion of the fission bomb, fusion of the hydrogen nuclei to form helium nuclei takes place (see *thermonuclear reaction*) with the evolution of even greater quantities of energy. The explosive effect of a fusion bomb (or fission-fusion bomb) is comparable to the explosion of tens of *megatons* of T.N.T. See also *fall-out*.

NUCLEASES. A group of *enzymes* which break down *nucleic acids*.

NUCLEIC ACIDS. Large *molecules* consisting of chains of *nucleotides*. Present in all living matter in which they are responsible for storing and transferring the *genetic code*. See *deoxyribonucleic acid* and *ribonucleic acid*.

NUCLEOLUS. A small dense body containing *nucleoprotein*, one or more of which occur in the *nucleus* of biological *cells*.

NUCLEON. A constituent of the atomic *nucleus*, i.e. a *proton* or a *neutron*.

NUCLEON NUMBER. See *mass number*.

NUCLEONICS. The practical applications of *nuclear physics*, and the techniques associated with these applications.

NUCLEOPHILIC REAGENTS. *Reagents* which react at centres of low *electron* density (e.g. *hydroxyl ions*). Nucleophilic reagents behave as electron donors, either transferring electrons or sharing their electrons with outside *atoms* or *ions*. *Molecules* or ions containing an atom with an unshared electron pair often act as nucleophilic reagents.

NUCLEOPROTEIN. Compounds of *nucleic acids* and *proteins* which are found in *cell nuclei* principally in the form of *chromosomes*. *Viruses* consist almost entirely of nucleoproteins. Life is based on the self-replicating properties of nucleoproteins.

NUCLEOR. The 'core' of a *nucleon*, which according to recent views consists of a nucleor surrounded by a cloud of *pions*.

NUCLEOSIDE. A *compound* formed from a nitrogenous base (*purine* or *pyrimidine*) and a *pentose sugar*, e.g. adenosine which consists of *adenine* and D-ribofuranose. The phosphorylated *derivative* of a nucleoside is called a *nucleotide*.

NUCLEOTIDE. A most important type of *compound* found in all living matter. Nucleotides consist of a nitrogenous base (*purine* or *pyrimidine*), a *pentose sugar* and a phosphate group. Found free in *cells* as *adenosine triphosphate* and as part of various *coenzymes*; found in the form of *polynucleotide* chains as *nucleic acids*.

NUCLEUS. Vital central point; particle of *matter* acting as centre; e.g. a particle of dust will act as a nucleus for the *condensation* of *water vapour* in *mist*.

NUCLEUS, ATOMIC. The positively charged core of an *atom*, consisting of one or more *protons* and, except in the case of hydrogen, one or more *neutrons*. The number of protons in the nucleus is given by the *atomic number* and the number of neutrons by the difference between the *mass number* and the *atomic number* (i.e. the *neutron number*). Nearly the whole of the *mass* of an atom is concentrated in its nucleus, which occupies only a tiny fraction of its *volume*. See *atom, structure of*.

NUCLEUS OF CELL. A membrane-bounded body found within the *cytoplasm* of most biological *cells* of both plants and animals. The nucleus contains the *chromosomes* which become visible under a *microscope* during *mitosis* or *meiosis*. The nucleus is therefore the repository of the substances which control the characteristics of cells and their progeny.

NUCLIDE. Nucleide. The *nucleus* of an *atom* of a specific *isotope*, characterized by its *atomic number, mass number,* and its *energy* state. An 'isotope' refers to a type of atom while a 'nuclide' refers to its nucleus.

NUMERATOR. The number above the line in a *vulgar fraction.* E.g. 3 in $\frac{3}{16}$.

NUTATION. An oscillation of the *Earth's* poles about the mean position.

NYLON. Officially defined as 'a generic term applied to any long-chain synthetic *polyamide* which has recurring *amide* groups as an integral part of the main *polymer* chain, and which is capable of being formed into a filament in which the structural elements are oriented in the direction of the axis'. The familiar commercial form of nylon is a substance formed by the *condensation polymerization* of *adipic acid* with *diaminohexane.* The *solid* polymer is melted and forced through fine jets to make filaments which are then collected in the form of yarn.

NYSTATIN. $C_{46}H_{77}NO_{19}$. A yellow *insoluble antibiotic* obtained from 'streptomyces nousei' and 'aureus'. Used to treat infections caused by *fungi.*

O

OBJECTIVE (phys.). A *lens* or system of lenses nearest the object in a *telescope* or compound *microscope*.

OBLATE SPHEROID. See *spheroid*.

OBTUSE ANGLE. An *angle* greater than 90°.

OCCLUSION. Certain *solids* have the property of absorbing or occluding some *gases*, either by the formation of a chemical *compound*, or by forming a *solid solution*, or by the *condensation* of the gas on the surface of the solid.

OCCULTATION. The cutting off of the *light* or *radio* emission from one celestial body when another is interposed between it and the observer. E.g. a *star* may become invisible to an *optical* or *radio telescope* when it is hidden behind the *Moon*.

OCHRE. A natural *hydrated* form of *ferric oxide*, Fe_2O_3, containing various impurities. Used as a red or yellow *pigment*.

OCTA-, OCTO-. Prefix denoting eight, eightfold.

OCTACALCIUM PHOSPHATE. OCP. $Ca_2H(PO_4)_3 . 2 \cdot 5H_2O$. A crystalline substance of importance in the chemistry of bones, teeth, and precipitated *calcium phosphates*.

OCTAGON. An eight-sided *polygon*. The angle between the sides of a regular octagon is 135°.

OCTAHEDRON. A *polyhedron* having eight faces.

OCTANE. C_8H_{18}. A *hydrocarbon* of the *paraffin series* which exists in several isomeric forms (see *isomerism*). A colourless *liquid*, b.p. 126°C., S.G. 0·704.

OCTANE NUMBER OF A FUEL. Defined as the percentage by *volume* of *iso-octane*, C_8H_{18} (2.2.4-trimethylpentane) in a mixture of *iso*-octane and *normal heptane*, C_7H_{16}, which is equal to the *fuel* in knock characteristics (see *knocking*) under specified test conditions.

OCTANOL. Octyl alcohol. $C_8H_{17}OH$. A group of *isomeric alcohols* of which the most important is octan-1-ol, a colourless *liquid*, m.p. 16·7°C., b.p. 194–5°C., used as a *solvent*.

OCTANT. The portion of a *circle* cut off by an arc and two radii at 45°; one eighth of the area of a circle.

OCTAVE. The interval between two musical notes, the fundamental components (see *quality of sound*) of which have *frequencies* in the ratio two to one. This use of the word has been extended to include the interval between two frequencies of any type of oscillation which are in the ratio two to one.

OCTAVES, LAW OF. An incomplete statement of the *Periodic Law* made by Newlands independently of Mendeleev.

OCTET. A stable group of eight *electrons* which constitutes the outer electron *shell* of an *atom* of an *inert gas* (except helium whose only electron shell contains two electrons). When the atoms of the *elements* (except hydrogen) combine to form *compounds*, they do so by donating or sharing electrons so that each combining atom has a completed octet in its outer shell. See *valency, electronic theory of*.

OCTYL GROUP. The *univalent radical*, C_8H_{17}—.

ODD-EVEN NUCLEUS. A *nucleus* which contains an odd number of *protons* and an even number of *neutrons*.

ODD-ODD NUCLEUS. A *nucleus* which contains an odd number of both *protons* and *neutrons*.

OERSTED. The unit of *magnetic field strength* or *magnetic intensity* in *c.g.s. electromagnetic units*, defined as the strength of a magnetic field which would cause a unit *magnetic pole* to experience a *force* of 1 *dyne* in a vacuum. Equivalent to $1/4\pi \times 10^3$ *amperes* per *metre*. Named after Hans Christian Oersted (1777–1851).

OESTROGENS. Female sex *hormones* of which the most important are the *sterols* oestradiol ($C_{18}H_{24}O_2$), oestrone ($C_{18}H_{22}O_2$), and oestriol ($C_{18}H_{24}O_3$).

OHM. The derived *SI unit* of *resistance* defined as the resistance between two points of a *conductor* when a constant difference of potential of 1 *volt*, applied between these two points, produces in the conductor a *current* of 1 *ampere*. The former 'international ohm' was defined as the resistance, at 0° C, of a column of mercury 106·3 cm in length, of *mass* 14·4521 g, and of uniform cross-sectional area. 1 'international ohm' = 1·00049 'absolute' SI ohms. Symbol Ω. Named after Georg Ohm (1787–1854).

OHM'S LAW. The ratio of the *potential difference* between the ends of a *conductor* and the *current* flowing in the conductor is constant. This ratio is termed the *resistance* of the conductor. For a potential difference of *V volts* and a current of *I amperes*, the resistance, *R*, in *ohms* is equal to V/I.

OHMMETER. An instrument for measuring *resistance* in *ohms*, e.g. a *Wheatstone bridge*.

OIL CAKE. A mass of oilseeds (e.g. linseed, cottonseed) from which the *oil* has been expelled in a press (expellers) or extracted by a *solvent* (extractions); used as cattle food.

OIL OF VITRIOL. Concentrated *sulphuric acid*.

OIL OF WINTERGREEN. See *methyl salicylate*.

OIL, SYNTHETIC. Natural *mineral oils* are composed of various *hydrocarbons*. It is possible to make similar products artificially from *coal*, etc., by combining carbon or *carbon monoxide* with hydrogen. See *Bergius process; Fischer-Tropsch process*.

OIL-IMMERSION LENS. See *immersion objective*.

OILS. See *fats and oils*.

OLEATE. A *salt* or *ester* of *oleic acid*.

OLEFIANT GAS. See *ethylene*.

OLEFINES. Olefins, alkenes. The *ethylene* series of *unsaturated hydrocarbons*, having the general formula C_nH_{2n}.

OLEIC ACID. $C_{17}H_{33}COOH$. An *unsaturated liquid organic acid*, m.p. 15°C., which occurs in the form of *glycerides* in many *fats and oils*. A high proportion of *triolein*, the glyceride of oleic acid, in a fat or oil makes it more liquid.

OLEIN. See *triolein*.

OLEUM. Fuming sulphuric acid. Pyrosulphuric acid. $H_2S_2O_7$. Concentrated *sulphuric acid* containing extra *sulphur trioxide*. A *hygroscopic* substance, m.p. 35°C., used as a dehydrating agent and in *explosives*.

OLEYL ALCOHOL. $CH_3(CH_2)_7CH:CH(CH_2)_7CH_2OH$. An *unsaturated liquid alcohol*, b.p. 205°C., used in organic synthesis.

OLFACTORY. Pertaining to the sense of smell.

OLIVINE. $(Mg,Fe)_2SiO_4$. A mineral *silicate* of magnesium and iron. The transparent form is used as a gem.

OMEGATRON. An instrument in which *ions* are caused to move in spiral paths by the application of an *electric field* at right angles to a constant *magnetic field*. As the *angular frequency* of rotation of the ions depends upon their *charge* to *mass* ratio, it is possible by this means to separate ions of different *isotopes*. The instrument may be used for the absolute determination of atomic *masses* and for isotopic and chemical analysis.

ON-LINE WORKING. The use of a device which is connected directly to a *computer* so that is becomes a *peripheral* device. In 'off-line working', the device produces information in readable form for subsequent processing by a computer.

ONTOGENY (bio.). The history of the development of an individual member of a species, as opposed to 'phylogeny' which is the history of the evolution of the species (or other biological group).

OOCYTE. A female *gametocyte* which undergoes *meiosis* to form an *ovum*.

OPACITY. The extent to which a medium is *opaque*. Numerically the *reciprocal* of the *transmittance*.

OPAQUE. Not permitting a *wave motion* (e.g. *light*, *sound*, *X-rays*) to pass. Usually applied to light; not *transparent* or *translucent*. See *opacity*.

OPEN-CHAIN COMPOUNDS. *Organic compounds* not derived from ring compounds; *aliphatic compounds*.

OPEN CLUSTERS. Clusters of *stars* which have a common motion through *space*. The open clusters are much less densely populated with stars than the *globular clusters*, containing only some hundreds of stars interspersed with *gas* and dust clouds.

OPEN-HEARTH PROCESS. Siemens-Martin process. A process for *steel* manufacture. *Pig-iron* and steel scrap or iron *ore* in calculated amounts are heated together by *producer gas* on a hearth in a furnace.

OPERON. A group of *genes* whose function is to control the *synthesis* of the individual *enzymes* which act together as one enzyme system. One of the genes in an operon, known as the 'operator gene', starts and stops the activity of the complete operon.

OPIUM. The dried, milky juice from unripe fruits of the opium poppy,

Papaver somniferum. **Contains** several *alkaloids,* including *morphine,* *narceine,* and *codeine.*

OPPOSITION (astr.). A *planet* having its *orbit* outside that of the *Earth* is in opposition when the Earth is in a line between the *Sun* and the planet.

OPTIC AXIS. The direction in a doubly refracting *crystal* in which *light* is propagated without *double refraction.*

OPTICAL ACTIVITY. Optical rotation. The property possessed by some substances and their *solutions* of rotating the plane of vibration of polarized light (see *polarization of light*). The amount of this rotation is proportional to the distance the light travels in the medium, and to the *concentration* of the solution. The amount of rotation also depends upon the *wavelength* (i.e. the *colour*) of the light used. This last phenomenon is termed 'rotary dispersion'.

OPTICAL AXIS. Principal axis. The line passing through the *optical centre* and the *centre of curvature* of a spherical *mirror* or *lens.*

OPTICAL CENTRE. A point, situated for all practical purposes at the geometrical centre of a thin *lens,* through which an incident *ray* passes without being deviated.

OPTICAL ISOMERISM. A form of *isomerism* in which the isomers differ in their *optical activity.* See *stereoisomerism.*

OPTICAL MASER. See *laser.*

OPTICAL ROTATION. See *optical activity.*

OPTICAL TELESCOPE. An astronomical *telescope* which is used to observe celestial bodies by the *light* which they emit, as compared to a *radio telescope* which is used to observe their *radio frequency* emissions.

OPTICAL TEMPERATURE. The *temperature* of a celestial body as calculated from its *light radiation.*

OPTICS. The study of *light.*

OPTICS, GEOMETRICAL. The branch of *optics* built up on the laws of *reflection* and *refraction,* and assuming the *rectilinear propagation of light;* it involves no consideration of the physical nature of light. Mainly concerned with the formation of images by *mirrors* and *lenses.*

ORBIT. 1. The path of one heavenly body around another as a result of their mutual gravitational attraction. Particularly the path of the *planets* around the *Sun,* or the *Moon* (or *artificial satellites*) around the *Earth.* 2. The path of an *electron* around the *nucleus* of an *atom.* See *orbital electron* and *atom, structure of.*

ORBITAL. See *atomic orbital* and *molecular orbital.*

ORBITAL ELECTRON. Planetary electron. An *electron* contained within an *atom* which may be thought of as orbiting around the *nucleus,* in a manner analogous to the *orbit* of a *planet* around the *Sun.* See *atom, structure of,* and *Bohr theory.*

ORBITAL VELOCITY. The *velocity* of a *satellite* or spacecraft which enables it to *orbit* round the *Earth* or other celestial body. A *synchronous orbit* round the Earth requires an orbital velocity of about 3200 *metres* per *second* (7200 miles per hour).

ORCINOL. $CH_3C_6H_3(OH)_2.H_2O$. A white crystalline substance, m.p. 107–8° C., which reddens on exposure to *air*. Used in the analytical detection of *carbohydrates*.

ORDER (math.). The number of times a *function* has been differentiated to give a particular *derivative*: the *degree* of the highest derivative in a *differential equation*.

ORDINARY RAY. When a *ray* of *light* is incident upon a *crystal* which exhibits *double refraction* so that the direction of the ray makes an angle with the *optic axis* of the crystal, the ray splits into two rays. One of these obeys the ordinary laws of *refraction* and is called the ordinary ray. The other is the 'extraordinary ray'.

ORDINATE. In *analytical geometry*, the ordinate of a point is the perpendicular distance of the point from the x-axis. See Fig. 5, page 65.

ORE. A *mineral* containing a *metal* (or in some instances a *non-metal*, e.g. sulphur) which is used as a source of that metal (or non-metal).

ORGANIC ACID. An *organic compound* which is able to give up a *proton* to a *base*; i.e. one which contains one or more *carboxyl groups* or in some cases *hydroxyl groups* (e.g. *phenol*).

ORGANIC BASE. A *molecule* or *ion* possessing a *lone pair of electrons* which can be used for coordination (see *valency, electronic theory of*) with a *proton*. The common *organic compounds* which fulfil this condition owe their basic character to an oxygen or nitrogen *atom*.

ORGANIC CHEMISTRY. The *chemistry* of the *organic compounds*; the chemistry of carbon compounds excluding the *metal carbonates* and the *oxides* and *sulphides* of carbon. Originally, the chemistry of substances produced by living *organisms*, as distinct from the *inorganic chemistry* of substances of *mineral* origin.

ORGANIC COMPOUNDS. Chemical *compounds* containing carbon combined with hydrogen, and often also with oxygen, nitrogen, and other *elements*. The *molecules* of organic compounds are often very complex, and contain a large number of *atoms*. They are not usually ionized in *solution* (see *dissociation*), and frequently show the phenomenon of *isomerism*.

ORGANISM. A living animal or plant.

ORGANOMETALLIC COMPOUND. A *compound* in which one or more organic *radicals* are attached to an *atom* of a *metal*; e.g. $Na(CH_3)$.

ORIGIN (math.). The point of intersection of two or more axes (*see coordinates, cartesian*, and *polar coordinates*).

ORMULU. An *alloy* of copper, zinc, and tin in various proportions; generally containing at least 50% copper.

ORPIMENT. Natural *arsenic trisulphide*, As_2S_3. A yellow mineral.

ORSAT APPARATUS. A portable apparatus for determining the amount of *carbon dioxide*, oxygen, and *carbon monoxide* in flue or exhaust *gases*. A measured *volume* of the gas is successively passed through three tubes,

273

the first of which contains *potassium hydroxide* to absorb the CO_2, the second alkaline *pyrogallol* to absorb oxygen, and the third cuprous chloride in *hydrochloric acid* to absorb the CO. The diminution of volume after the gas has been passed through each tube indicates the quantity of each constituent gas.

ORTHO-. 1. Prefix denoting right, straight, correct. 2. Prefix indicating that an *organic compound* contains a *benzene ring* substituted in the 1.2 positions. 3. Prefix indicating that an *acid* or *salt* is the most *hydrated* of several compounds of the same name.

ORTHOCHROMATIC FILM. A photographic *film* sensitive to green in addition to blue and violet *light*, thus giving a more accurate representation of *colours* in monochrome than ordinary film. See *photography*.

ORTHOCLASE FELSPAR. Natural potassium aluminium silicate, $K_2O.Al_2O_3.6SiO_2$. A constituent of *granite*.

ORTHOGONAL. 1. (math.) Rectangular, or involving right angles. 2. (of *crystals*) Having a set of mutually *perpendicular axes*.

ORTHO-HYDROGEN. Hydrogen *molecules* in which the *spins* of the two constituent *atoms* are parallel.

ORTHOPHOSPHORIC ACID. H_3PO_4. A colourless *deliquescent* substance, m.p. 42·5° C., used in *fertilizers* and as a flavouring agent in drinks.

OSCILLATOR. 1. A device for producing sonic or *ultrasonic* pressure waves in a medium. 2. A device with no rotating parts for converting *direct current* into *alternating current*; usually consists of *thermionic valves* or *transistors* coupled with a suitable *resonant circuit*.

OSCILLOSCOPE. See *cathode ray oscilloscope*.

OSMIC ACID. Osmium tetroxide, OsO_4. A colourless crystalline *solid*, m.p. 40° C.: *solution* used as a stain for *fat* globules in microscopy.

OSMIRIDIUM. A natural *alloy* of osmium and iridium, with smaller amounts of platinum, rhodium, and ruthenium. Hard and resistant to *corrosion*; used for tipping pen-nibs.

OSMIUM. Os. Element. A.W. 190·2. At. No. 76. A hard white crystalline *metal*. S.G. 22·48, m.p. 3045° C. Heaviest substance known. Occurs together with platinum (see *osmiridium*); used in *alloys* with platinum and iridium.

OSMOMETER. An instrument for measuring *osmotic pressures*.

OSMOSIS. The flow of *water* (or other *solvent*) through a *semipermeable membrane*; i.e. a membrane which will permit the passage of the solvent but not of dissolved substances. There is a tendency for *solutions* separated by such a membrane to become equal in *molecular concentration*; thus water will flow from a weaker to a stronger solution, the solutions tending to become more nearly equal in concentration.

OSMOTIC PRESSURE of a solution. The *pressure* which must be applied to a *solution* in order to prevent the flow of *solvent* through a *semipermeable membrane* separating the solution and the pure solvent. When a solvent is allowed to flow through such a membrane into a vessel or cell containing a solution, the solvent will flow into the cell (see *osmosis*) until such a pressure is set up as to balance the pressure of the solvent flowing in. The osmotic pressure of a dilute solution is analogous to gaseous pressure; a substance in solution, if not dissociated (see *dissociation*), exerts the same osmotic pressure as the gaseous pressure it would exert if it were a *gas* at the same *temperature*, and occupying the same *volume*. The osmotic pressure, temperature, and volume of a dilute solution of a *non-electrolyte* are connected by laws exactly similar to the *gas laws*.

OSTWALD'S DILUTION LAW. A law relating the dissociation constant, K (see *dissociation*), and the degree of dissociation (or *ionization*), a, of a weak *electrolyte* of *concentration* c *moles* per *litre*. This law states that for a binary electrolyte $K = \dfrac{ca^2}{1-a}$, an equation which applies with a fair degree of accuracy to weak *organic acids* and *bases*. Named after Wilhelm Ostwald (1853–1932).

OUABAIN. $C_{29}H_{44}O_{12}$. A white crystalline *glycoside*, m.p. 200°C., obtained from wood; used as a heart stimulant.

OUNCE, AVOIRDUPOIS. $437\frac{1}{2}$ *grains*; 28·3 *grams*.

OUNCE, FLUID. 8 fluid *drachms*; 28·41 cc.

OUNCE, TROY. 480 *grains*; 31·1 *grams*.

OVERTONES. Notes of lesser intensity and higher *pitch* (i.e. of higher *frequency*) than the *fundamental note*, and superimposed upon the latter to give a note of characteristic *quality*.

OVSHINSKY DEVICE. Ovonic device. A device consisting of a special *glass*, which incorporates selenium and tellurium, the *resistance* of which drops rapidly when a suitable *voltage* is applied across it. These devices are used as special purpose switches in *electronic circuits*. The type which stays 'on' after the voltage has been removed is called a 'memory switch'.

OVUM. A female *gamete* produced by *meiosis* from an *oocyte*.

OXALATE. A *salt* or *ester* of *oxalic acid*.

OXALIC ACID. $(COOH)_2.2H_2O$. A white crystalline poisonous *soluble solid*, m.p. 101°C., whose *salts* occur in wood sorrel and other plants. Used in dyeing, *bleaching*, *ink* manufacture, metal polishes, and for removing ink stains.

OXIDANT. Oxydant. The substance which supplies the oxygen in an *oxidation* reaction. The term is frequently used with reference to the substance which supplies the oxygen in a *combustion* process, particularly in a *rocket*. The oxidant used in rockets is usually liquid oxygen, *hydrogen peroxide*, or *nitric acid*.

OXIDASE. An *enzyme* which catalyses *oxidation* of the *substrate*.

OXIDATION. The combination of oxygen with a *substance*, or the removal of hydrogen from it. The term is also used more generally to include any reaction in which an *atom* loses *electrons*; e.g. the change of a *ferrous ion*, Fe^{++}, to a *ferric* ion, Fe^{+++}.

275

OXIDATION NUMBER. Oxidation state. A measure of the extent of *oxidation* of an *atom* or *ion* expressed as a number which indicates the ionic *charge* of that atom or ion. The elemental state is indicated by an oxidation number of 0. In ionic compounds the oxidation number of monatomic ions is equal to their electric charge. In *covalently bonded* compounds the oxidation number is obtained by applying certain formal rules.

OXIDATION-REDUCTION REACTIONS. See *redox reactions*.

OXIDE. A *binary compound* with oxygen.

OXIDIZING AGENT. A substance which brings about an *oxidation* reaction.

OXO-. Prefix denoting the O= *radical* in a *compound*.

OXY-ACETYLENE BURNER. A device for obtaining a very high-*temperature flame* (3300°C.) for *welding*, by burning a mixture of oxygen and *acetylene* in a special jet.

OXYDIACETIC ACID. Diglycolic acid. $O(CH_2COOH)_2$. A white *soluble* substance, m.p. 148°C., used in the manufacture of *plastics* and *plasticizers*.

OXYGEN. O. Element. A.W. 15·9994, At. No. 8. An odourless, invisible *gas*; the most abundant of all the *elements* in the *Earth's crust* including the seas and the *atmosphere*; forms approximately one fifth of the atmosphere. Chemically very active; *combustion* and *respiration* both involve combination with oxygen. Essential to most forms of life. *Compounds* (*oxides*) are very widely distributed. The pure element is made by the *fractional distillation* of *liquid air*. Used for *welding* and metal-cutting.

OXY-HAEMOGLOBIN. An *unstable compound* formed by the action of oxygen on *haemoglobin* in *respiration*.

OXY-HYDROGEN BURNER. A device similar to the *oxy-acetylene burner* except that hydrogen instead of *acetylene* is burnt in oxygen; gives a *flame* temperature of about 2400°C.

OZOKERITE. Earth-wax. A natural *mixture* of *solid hydrocarbons*. A brownish or greyish mass, resembling *paraffin wax*.

OZONE. O_3. An *allotropic form* of oxygen, containing three *atoms* in the *molecule*. It is a bluish *gas*, very active chemically, and a powerful *oxidizing agent*. Formed when oxygen or air is subjected to a silent electric discharge. Occurs in ordinary air in very small amounts only; the health-giving effects sometimes attributed to it in sea-air are probably due to other causes. Ozone in the *atmosphere* is mainly present in the *ozone layer*. Used for purifying *air* and *water*, and in *bleaching*.

OZONE LAYER. Ozonosphere. The layer in the *upper atmosphere*, some 15 to 30 kilometres above the *Earth's* surface, in which most of the atmospheric *ozone* is concentrated. It is responsible for absorbing a large proportion of the *Sun's ultraviolet radiation*. Without this absorption the Earth would be subjected to a degree of ultraviolet radiation lethal to plants.

P

PACKING FRACTION. The difference between the *mass* of an *isotope* (on the physical scale of *atomic weights*) and its *mass number*, divided by the mass number. E.g. one chlorine isotope has a mass of 32·9860 and a mass number of 33, its packing fraction is therefore:

$$\frac{32 \cdot 9860 - 33 \cdot 000}{33} = -0 \cdot 00042$$

Packing fractions are often multiplied by 10^4 for convenience, and in this example the packing fraction would be given as $-4 \cdot 2$.

PAINT. A *liquid* containing a coloured material (*pigment*) in *suspension*. The application of the paint to a surface, and the *evaporation* or hardening of the liquid, covers the surface with the pigment in the form of a skin. The liquid generally consists of *linseed oil*, a 'thinner' of *turpentine* or other *volatile* liquid, and a 'drier' to accelerate drying or hardening of the linseed oil. Paints may also be based on *water* in the form of an *emulsion*, and are then called 'emulsion paints'. Such paints usually consist of an emulsion of *butadiene* and *styrene*, *polyvinyl acetate*, or *acrylic resins* in water.

PAIR PRODUCTION. The creation of a negative *electron* and *positron* as a result of the interaction between a *photon* or a fast particle (usually an electron) and the *field* of an atomic *nucleus* (see also *showers*). 'Internal pair production' occurs as the result of the de-*excitation* of an excited nucleus. Pair production, which is sometimes extended to mean the creation of any *elementary particle* and its *anti-particle*, is an example of the creation of *matter* from *energy* in accordance with the *mass-energy equation*.

PALAEONTOLOGY. The branch of *geology* that is concerned with the study of *fossils* and their relationship to the evolution of the *Earth's crust* and life upon Earth.

PALLADIUM. Pd. Element. A.W. 106·4. At. No. 46. A silvery-white *metal* which occurs with and resembles platinum. S.G. 11·97, m.p. 1549° C. Used in *alloys* and as a *catalyst*.

PALMITIC ACID. $C_{15}H_{31}COOH$. A wax-like *fatty acid*, m.p. 64° C., which occurs in the form of *tripalmitin* in palm oil and many natural *fats*. Used in the manufacture of *soap*.

PALMITIN. See *tripalmitin*.

PANCHROMATIC FILM. A photographic *film* sensitive to *light* of all *colours* including red, thus giving a more accurate representation of colours in monochrome than *orthochromatic film*. See *photography*.

PANTOTHENIC ACID. $C_9H_{17}NO_5$. A white *insoluble solid* member of the *vitamin* B complex, of importance to many *organisms*. Occurs in rice, bran, and plant and animal *tissues*. It is essential for the growth of *cells*.

PAPAIN. An *enzyme*, found in the fruit and leaves of the paw-paw tree, which is capable of digesting *proteins*. Used for softening meat for human consumption.

PAPAVERINE. $C_{20}H_{21}NO_4$. A white *insoluble alkaloid*, m.p. $147°C.$, obtained from *opium*; used in the form of its *hydrochloride* in medicine as an antispasmodic.

PAPER. Paper normally consists of sheets of *cellulose*, mainly obtained from wood pulp from which *lignin* and other non-cellulosic materials have been removed.

PAPER CHROMATOGRAPHY. A method of analysing *mixtures* of *compounds*, depending upon the different rates at which compounds in *solution* will migrate across a sheet of porous paper specially prepared with *indicators*.

PARA-. 1. Prefix denoting beside, beyond; or wrong, irregular. 2. Prefix indicating that an *organic compound* contains a *benzene ring* substituted in the 1.4 positions.

PARABOLA. A curve traced out by a point which moves so that its distance from a fixed point, the *focus*, is equal to its distance from a fixed straight line, the *directrix*.

PARABOLIC REFLECTOR. Paraboloid reflector. A *concave* reflector, the section of which is a *parabola*. Used for producing a parallel *beam* of *electromagnetic radiation* when a source is placed at its *focus*, or for collecting and focusing an incoming parallel beam of radiation. If the radiation is *light* the reflector is usually called a parabolic mirror, but with *microwave* or *radio frequency* radiation (see *radio telescope*) it may be called a 'dish aerial'.

PARABOLOID OF REVOLUTION. The surface obtained by rotating a *parabola* about its *axis of symmetry*.

PARACASEIN. See *caseinogen*.

PARACHOR. A relation showing the influence of *temperature* upon the *surface tension* of a *liquid*; interpreted as the *molecular volume* measured at a standard internal *pressure*. The value is composed, approximately, of a sum of terms for separate *atoms*, and of constants for various types of linkage between the atoms, thus giving a method for the determination of the constitution and structure of *molecules*.

PARAFFIN (chem.). *Alkane*. A *hydrocarbon* of the *paraffin series*.

PARAFFIN OIL. Kerosene. A mixture of *hydrocarbons* obtained in the *distillation of petroleum*. The boiling range of the kerosenes is $150°-300°C.$ Used for paraffin lamps, oil-burning engines, domestic heaters.

PARAFFIN SERIES. An *homologous series* of *hydrocarbons* having the general formula C_nH_{2n+2}. They are chemically inert, *stable*, and inflammable. The first four members of the series (*methane, ethane, propane, butane*) are *gases* at ordinary *temperatures*; the next eleven are *liquids*, and form the principal constituents of *paraffin oil*; the higher members are *solids*, forming the chief constituents of *paraffin wax*.

PARAFFIN WAX. A white translucent *solid* melting to a colourless *liquid* in the range $50°-60°C.$ Consists of a *mixture* of the higher *hydrocarbons*

278

of the *paraffin series*. Used for candles, waxed paper, and polishes.

PARAFORMALDEHYDE. Paraform. $(HCOH)_n$. A solid *polymer* of *formaldehyde*, readily converted into formaldehyde on heating. Used in fumigation.

PARA-HYDROGEN. Hydrogen *molecules* in which the *spins* of the two constituent *atoms* are anti-parallel.

PARALDEHYDE. $(CH_3CHO)_3$. A *liquid polymer of acetaldehyde*, b.p. $124°C$. Used in medicine as a *hypnotic*.

PARALLAX. 1. The difference in direction, or shift in the apparent position, of a body due to a change in position of the observer. 2. (astr.) The apparent displacement of a celestial body due to the point of observation being either on the *Earth's* surface rather than its centre (diurnal parallax), or on the Earth rather than the centre of the *Sun* (annual parallax). Annual parallax is expressed as the angle P in Fig. 31.

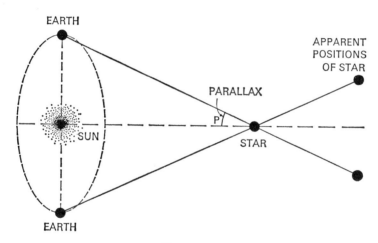

FIGURE 31.

PARALLEL BEAM OF LIGHT. A *beam* of *light* which neither converges nor diverges; theoretical concept of a beam of light from an infinitely great distance, so that the *rays* composing the beam may be considered to be parallel; e.g. light from the *Sun*.

PARALLEL, CONDUCTORS IN. Electrical *conductors* joined in parallel between two points A and B, so that each conductor joins A to B. If R_1, R_2, R_3, etc., are the *resistances* of the separate conductors, the total resistance R between A and B is given by the formula:

$$\frac{1}{R} = \frac{1}{R_1} + \frac{1}{R_2} + \frac{1}{R_3} \ldots \text{ etc. See Fig. 32, page 280.}$$

FIGURE 32.

PARALLELEPIPED. A solid figure having six faces, all *parallelograms*; all opposite pairs of faces being similar and parallel.

PARALLELOGRAM. A plane four-sided *rectilinear* figure having its opposite sides parallel. It may be proved that in all parallelograms the opposite sides and *angles* are equal; the *diagonals* bisect each other; and the diagonals bisect the parallelogram. The *area* of a parallelogram is given by (*a*) the product of the base and the vertical height, and (*b*) the product of two adjacent sides and the *sine* of the angle between them.

PARALLELOGRAM OF FORCES. If a particle is under the action of two *forces* which are represented in direction and magnitude by the two sides of a *parallelogram* drawn from a point, the *resultant* of the two forces is represented by the *diagonal* of the parallelogram drawn from that point.

PARALLELOGRAM OF VELOCITIES. If a body has two component *velocities*, represented in magnitude and direction by two adjacent sides of a *parallelogram* drawn from a point, the *resultant* velocity of the body is represented by the *diagonal* of the parallelogram drawn from that point.

PARAMAGNETISM. Substances possessing a *magnetic permeability* slightly greater than unity, i.e. possessing a small positive *magnetic susceptibility*, are said to be paramagnetic. The *atoms* of a paramagnetic substance possess a permanent *magnetic moment* due to unbalanced *electron spins* or unbalanced orbital motions of the electrons around the *nucleus* (see *atom, structure of*). Application of a *magnetic field* to such a substance tends to align the magnetic axes of the atoms in the direction of the field, giving the substance a resultant magnetic moment.

PARAMETER. A *variable*; the term is used in at least two different senses. 1. In two-dimensional *analytical geometry* it is often convenient to express the variables (x,y) each in terms of a third variable t, such that x and y are functions of t; $x=f(t)$, $y=g(t)$. The equations are termed parametric equations, and t is a parameter. 2. A variable which may be kept constant while the effect of other variables is investigated.

PARAMETRIC AMPLIFIER. An *amplifier* of *microwaves* which depends on the periodic variation, by an alternating *voltage*, of the *reactance* of a *thermionic valve* or *semiconductor* device.

PARASITIC CAPTURE. The absorption of a *neutron* by a *nuclide*, which does not result in a *nuclear fission* or the production of a useful artificial *element*.

PARIS GREEN, Schweinfurt green. Cupric acetoarsenite. A double *salt* of copper arsenite and acetate, $Cu(CH_3COO)_2.3Cu(AsO_2)_2$. Used as a *pigment*, *insecticide*, and a wood preservative.

PARITY. Space-reflection symmetry. Mirror symmetry. The principle of space-reflection symmetry, or conservation of parity, states that no fundamental distinction can be made between left and right; that the laws of *physics* are the same in a right-handed system of coordinates as they are in a left-handed system. This law holds for all the phenomena described by *classical physics*, but in 1957 it was shown to be violated by certain interactions between *elementary particles*. Interactions between elementary particles are of three types: *strong nuclear interactions*, electromagnetic interactions, and *weak nuclear interactions*. For all strong nuclear interactions and electromagnetic interactions parity is conserved, that is to say, if a left-polarized particle exists (i.e. one which *spins* in an opposite sense to its direction of motion) there will be an approximately corresponding number of right-polarized particles. It has been found, however, that for weak nuclear interactions parity is not conserved. Thus, in a typical weak interaction, such as the *decay* of a *neutron*, the emitted *electron* is always left-polarized. As a result of non-conservation of parity in weak interactions it is now possible to make a fundamental distinction between left and right.

If parity is conserved, it is said to be even (or positive) when the *wave function* of a definite state of a system is left unchanged by reversing the sign of all the coordinates; it is said to be odd (or negative) if the sign of the wave function is thereby changed. If parity is not conserved the wave functions bear no simple relation to each other under these circumstances.

PARSEC. An astronomical unit of distance, corresponding to a *parallax* of one second of arc. 19×10^{12} miles, $3 \cdot 26$ *light-years*, $3 \cdot 084 \times 10^{16}$ *metres*.

PARTHENOGENESIS. The development of an *ovum* into a new individual without *fertilization* by a male *gamete*. Occurs naturally in some plants (e.g. dandelion) and some animals (e.g. aphids); can be induced artificially in others.

PARTIAL DERIVATIVE. The *derivative* of a *function* with respect to only one of its *variables*, all other variables in the function being taken as *constant*.

PARTIAL FRACTIONS. The fractions into which a particular fraction can be separated, so that the sum of partial fractions so obtained equals the original fraction. E.g. the partial fractions of $1/(x^2-1)$ are:

$$\frac{1}{2(x-1)} \text{ and } \frac{-1}{2(x+1)}.$$

PARTIAL PRESSURES. See *Dalton's law of partial pressures*.

PARTICLE ACCELERATOR. See *accelerator*.

PASCAL. The derived *SI* unit of *pressure*, equal to 1 *newton* per square metre. Symbol Pa. Named after Blaise Pascal (1623–62).

PASCAL'S LAW OF FLUID PRESSURES. *Pressure* applied anywhere to an enclosed body of *fluid* is transmitted equally in all directions. This pressure acts at right angles to every portion of the surface of the container, the *force* per unit *area* being uniform throughout.

PASCHEN SERIES. A series of lines which occurs in the *infrared* region of the *spectrum* of hydrogen. Named after Friedrich Paschen (1865–1947).

PASCHEN'S LAW. The breakdown or 'sparking potential' for a pair of parallel *electrodes* situated in a *gas*, i.e. the *potential* which must be applied between them for sparking to occur, is a *function* only of the product of the *pressure* of the gas and the separation of the electrodes.

PASSIVE IRON. Iron made chemically unreactive by the surface action of concentrated *nitric acid* or other powerful *oxidizing agent*, which produces a protective film of iron oxide on the surface of the metal.

PASTEURIZATION. Partial sterilization, especially of milk; heating to a *temperature* sufficiently high to kill *bacteria*, but not spores of bacteria. Named after Louis Pasteur (1822–95).

PATHOGENIC. Causing disease. A 'pathogen' is an *organism* which causes disease.

PAULI EXCLUSION PRINCIPLE. Each *electron* moving round the *nucleus* of a *neutral atom* can be characterized by values of four *quantum numbers*. The principle states that no two electrons in a neutral atom can have the same set of four quantum numbers. The principle is of great importance in the theoretical building-up of the *periodic table*. Named after Wolfgang Pauli (1900-1958).

PEARL. A secretion consisting mainly of *calcium carbonate*, $CaCO_3$, produced by various molluscs.

PEARL ASH. *Potassium carbonate*, K_2CO_3, made from wood *ashes*.

PEARL SPAR. See *dolomite*.

PEARLITE. A microconstituent of iron or *steel* consisting of alternate layers of *ferrite* and *cementite*.

PEAT. An early stage in the formation of *coal* from vegetable matter. An accumulation of partly decomposed plant material, used as *fuel*.

PECTINS. A class of complex *polysaccharides* occurring in plants, particularly fruits. *Solutions* have the power of setting to a jelly; this is probably responsible for the 'setting' of jams.

PELARGONIC ACID. See *nonanoic acid*.

PELTIER EFFECT. When an *electric current* flows across the junction between two different *metals* or *semiconductors*, a quantity of *heat*, proportional to the total *electric charge* crossing the junction, is evolved or absorbed, depending on the direction of the current. This effect is due to the existence of an *electromotive force* at the junction. Named after Jean Peltier (1785–1845).

PENCIL LEAD. A mixture of *graphite* with *clay* in various proportions, to give different degrees of hardness.

PENCIL OF LIGHT (phys.). A collection of *rays* proceeding from or towards a point.

PENDULUM, SIMPLE. A device consisting of a weight or 'bob' swinging on the end of a string or wire. In the case of an ideal pendulum, when the *angle* described by the pendulum is small, the string has negligible *weight*, and the *mass* of the pendulum is concentrated at one point, the time of one complete swing, T, is given by the formula $2\pi\sqrt{l/g}$, where l is the length of the string, and g the *acceleration due to gravity*.

PENETRATION FACTOR. The *probability* that an incident particle, in a *nuclear reaction*, will pass through the *nuclear barrier*.

PENICILLIN. A class of chemically related *antibiotics* produced by the Penicillium mould. A very powerful agent for preventing the growth of several types of disease *bacteria*.

PENNYWEIGHT. 24 grains, 1/20 troy ounce. See *troy weight*.

PENTA-. Prefix denoting five, fivefold.

PENTACHLOROPHENOL. C_6Cl_5OH. A white *insoluble derivative* of *phenol*, m.p. 174°C., used as a *fungicide*.

PENTAERYTHRITOL. $C(CH_2OH)_4$. A white *soluble* powder, m.p. 260°C., used in the manufacture of *plastics*, *plasticizers*, and *explosives*.

PENTAGON. A five-sided *polygon*: the angle between the sides in a regular pentagon is 108°.

PENTANE. C_5H_{12}. The fifth member of the *paraffin series* which exists in three isometic forms (see *isomerism*). Contained in light *petroleum*; *n*-pentane has b.p. 36°C. and S.G. 0·62. Used as a *solvent* and *anaesthetic*.

PENTAVALENT. Quinquevalent. Having a *valency* of five.

PENTODE. A *thermionic valve* containing five *electrodes*: a *cathode*, an *anode* or plate, a *control grid*, and (between the two latter) two other grids called the *screen grid* and the *suppressor grid*.

PENTOSE. A *monosaccharide sugar* containing five carbon *atoms* and having the general formula $C_5H_{10}O_5$. The most important pentose is *ribose* which is an essential constituent of the *nucleic acids*.

PENTYL ACETATE. Amyl acetate, banana oil. $CH_3COOC_5H_{11}$. An *ester* of *amyl alcohol* and *acetic acid*. A colourless liquid, b.p. 148°C., with an odour of pear drops. Used as a *solvent*, a flavour, and in perfumes.

PENTYL GROUP. The *univalent radical* C_5H_{11}—; also called *amyl group*.

PENUMBRA. Half-shadow, formed when an object in the path of *rays* from a large source of *light* cuts off a portion of the light. See *shadow*.

PEPSIN. A digestive *enzyme* produced in the stomach which converts *proteins* into *peptones*; it acts only in an *acid* medium.

PEPTIDASE. An *enzyme* which attacks *peptide* linkages and splits off *amino acids*. See also *proteinase*.

PEPTIDE. A *compound* of two or more (see *polypeptide*) *amino acids* formed by *condensation* of the -NH₂ group of one acid and the *carboxyl group* of another. The peptide linkage, —NH—CO—, results.

PEPTONES. Organic substances produced by the *hydrolysis* of *proteins* by the action of *pepsin* in the stomach. They are *soluble* in *water*, and are absorbed by the body.

283

PER-

PER-. Prefix denoting, in chemical nomenclature, an excess of the normal amount of an *element* in a *compound*; e.g. *peroxide*.

PERBORIC ACID. HBO_3. A hypothetical *acid* known only in the form of its *salts*, the *perborates*; e.g. *sodium perborate*.

PERBORATE. A *salt* of *perboric acid*, HBO_3.

PERCHLORATE. A *salt* of *perchloric acid*, $HClO_4$.

PERCHLORIC ACID. $HClO_4$. A colourless *hygroscopic liquid*, b.p. 390° C., which forms *salts* called *perchlorates*.

PERCUSSION CAP. A device used in fire-arms. A small copper cylinder containing *mercuric fulminate* or other violent *explosive* which will explode on being struck, thus initiating the explosion of the main charge.

PERFECT GAS. Ideal gas. A theoretical concept of a *gas* which would obey the *gas laws* exactly. Such a gas would consist of perfectly elastic *molecules*, the *volume* occupied by the actual molecules, and the *forces* of attraction between them, being zero or negligible.

PERI-. Prefix denoting around, about.

PERICLASE. Natural *magnesium oxide*, MgO.

PERICYNTHION. The time of, or the point of, the nearest approach of a *satellite* in lunar *orbit* to the *Moon's* surface. Opposite of *apocynthion*.

PERIGEE. The *Moon*, the *Sun*, or an artificial *Earth satellite*, are said to be in perigee when they are at their least distance from the Earth. Opposite of *apogee*.

PERIHELION. The time of, or the point of, the nearest approach of a *planet* to the *Sun*. Opposite of *aphelion*. See Fig. 1, page 25.

PERIMETER. The distance all round a *plane* figure; e.g. the perimeter of a *circle* is its circumference.

PERIOD (phys.). If any quantity is a *function* of the time, and this function repeats itself exactly after constant time intervals T, the quantity is said to be periodic, and T is called the period of the function.

PERIODATE. A *salt* of a *periodic acid*.

PERIODIC ACIDS. A series of *unstable acids* formed by the addition of *water* to the hypothetical iodine heptoxide, I_2O_7, e.g. HIO_4. Known in the form of their *salts*, the *periodates*.

PERIODIC LAW. The statement that 'the properties of the *elements* are in periodic dependence upon their *atomic weights*', published by Mendeleev in 1869. The law is brought out clearly when the elements are arranged in the *periodic table*.

PERIODIC SYSTEM. Arrangement of the chemical *elements* in the *periodic table*.

PERIODIC TABLE. An arrangement of the chemical *elements* in order of their *atomic numbers* in such a way as to demonstrate the *periodic law*. In such an arrangement elements having similar properties occur at regular intervals and fall into groups of related elements. From the position of an element in the periodic table its properties may be predicted with a fair measure of success; Mendeleev was able to forecast the existence and properties of then undiscovered elements by means of his original table. The periodic law has since been shown to reflect the grouping of *electrons* in the outer *shells* of the *atoms* of the elements. Elements with the same numbers of electrons in their outer shells have similar chemical properties, as these electrons determine the valencies (see *valency, electronic theory of*) of the atoms. See Table 8, page 440.

PERIPHERALS. Peripheral devices. Devices connected to the *C.P.U.* or the high-speed *store* of a *computer*. Forming part of the *hardware*, they include *backing storage*, input and output devices, *on-line* equipment, *visual display units*, etc.

PERIPHERY. The external surface or boundary of a body; the circumference or *perimeter* of any closed figure.

PERISCOPE. Device for viewing objects which are above the eye-level of the observer, or are placed so that direct vision is obstructed. Essentially consists of a long tube, at each end of which is a right-angled *prism*, so situated that, by *total internal reflection* at the longest faces, *light* is turned through an angle of 90° by each prism. Thus light from a viewed object enters the observer's eye in a direction parallel to, but below, the original direction of the object.

PERMALLOY*. Class of iron-nickel *alloys* with high *magnetic permeability*. Used in parts of electrical machinery which are subject to alternating *magnetic fields*; causes only low losses of *energy* due to *hysteresis*.

PERMANENT GAS. A *gas* which cannot be liquefied by *pressure* alone; a gas above its *critical temperature*.

PERMANENT HARDNESS OF WATER. Hardness which is not destroyed by *boiling* the *water*. See *hard water*.

PERMANENT MAGNETISM. Magnetic properties of substances (especially *steel*) possessed without the influence of an external *magnetic field*.

PERMANGANATE. A *salt* of *permanganic acid*, $HMnO_4$. Term commonly applied to *potassium permanganate*.

PERMANGANIC ACID. $HMnO_4$. A hypothetical *acid* known only in *solution* or in the form of its *salts*, the *permanganates*.

PERMEABILITY. A body is said to be permeable to a substance if it allows the passage of the substance through itself.

PERMEABILITY, MAGNETIC. See *magnetic permeability*.

PERMITTIVITY. ϵ. The 'absolute permittivity' of a *dielectric* medium is the ratio of the *electric displacement* to the strength of the *electric field* at the same point. In *SI units*, the permittivity of a vacuum ϵ_0, is $8.854\ 185 \times 10^{-12}$ F m^{-1}. The relative permittivity (also called *dielectric constant*), $\epsilon_r = \epsilon/\epsilon_0$.

PERMUTATION (math.). An arrangement of a specified number of different objects. E.g. the six possible permutations of the digits 123 are 123, 132, 213, 231, 312, 321. The number of possible permutations of n objects if all are taken each time, denoted by ^nP_n, is *factorial n*. The number of permutations of n different objects taken r at a time, ^nP_r, is $n!/(n-r)!$.

PEROXIDE. An *oxide* which yields *hydrogen peroxide* with an *acid*; term also applied to an oxide which contains more oxygen than the normal oxide of an *element*.

PERPENDICULAR. At right angles; a straight line making an *angle* of 90° with another line or *plane*.

PERPETUAL MOTION. The concept of a machine which, once set in motion, will go on for ever without receiving *energy*. It is impossible to make a machine which will go on for ever and be able to do *work*, i.e. create energy without receiving energy from outside. To do so would contravene the first two laws of *thermodynamics*.

PERSISTENCE OF VISION. The sensation of *light*, as interpreted by the brain, persists for a brief interval after the actual light stimulus is removed; successive images, if they follow one another sufficiently rapidly, produce a continuous impression. Use is made of this in the cine-projector and in *television*.

PERSONAL EQUATION. The time interval or lag peculiar to a person between the perception and recording of any event. In many physical observations an error is introduced by the time-lag between the actual occurrence of the observed event, its perception by the observer, and its recording.

PERSPEX*. See *polymethyl methacrylate*.

PERSULPHATE. A *salt* of a *persulphuric acid*.

PERSULPHURIC ACIDS. 1. Permonosulphuric acid, Caro's acid. H_2SO_5. A white crystalline substance which decomposes at 45°C., used as an *oxidizing* agent. 2. Perdisulphuric acid. $H_2S_2O_8$. A white crystalline substance which decomposes at 65°C., used in the manufacture of *hydrogen peroxide*.

PERTURBATIONS. Deviations in the motions of the *planets* from their true elliptical *orbits*, as a result of their gravitational attractions for each other.

PETRI DISH. A shallow flat-bottomed circular glass dish, which may have a fitting cover; used in laboratories for a variety of purposes, especially for cultivating *micro-organisms*. Named after J. R. Petri (died 1921).

PETRIFACTION. The change of an *organic* structure, such as a tree, into a stony or *mineral* structure. Generally caused by dissolved *hydrated silica*, SiO_2, penetrating into the pores and gradually losing its *water*.

PETROCHEMICALS. Chemical substances derived from *petroleum* (or *natural gas*).

PETROL. Gasoline. A complex *mixture* consisting mainly of *hydrocarbons*, such as *hexane, heptane,* and *octane*; other *fuels* and special ingredients are often added.

PETROLATUM. Petroleum jelly, Vaseline*. A purified mixture of *hydrocarbons* consisting of a semi-solid whitish or yellowish mass.

PETROLEUM. Mineral oil. A natural *mixture* of *hydrocarbons* and other *organic compounds*. Composition of various petroleums varies according to source; e.g. American petroleum contains a high proportion of *paraffins* while Russian petroleum is rich in *cyclic hydrocarbons*. *Fractional distillation* yields *petrol, paraffin oil,* lubricating oil, *petrolatum,* and *paraffin wax.*

PETROLEUM ETHER. A *mixture* of the lower *hydrocarbons* of the *paraffin series* consisting mainly of *pentane* and *hexane*. B.p. 30°–70°C.

PETROLOGY. The study of the origin, structure, and composition of rocks.

PEWTER. An *alloy* of approximately 4 parts of tin to 1 of lead, with small amounts of antimony.

pH VALUE. See *hydrogen ion concentration.*

PHAGE. See *bacteriophage.*

PHAGOCYTE. A *blood cell* (particularly a *leucocyte*) which can engulf a foreign particle or *bacterium.*

PHARMACOGNOSY. The knowledge or study of *drugs.*

PHARMACOLOGY. The study of the action of chemical substances upon animals and man.

PHARMACOPHORE. The portion of a *molecule* of a substance which is regarded as determining the special physiological action of the substance.

PHARMACY. The preparation and dispensing of *drugs* and medicines.

PHASE (chem.). A separate part of a *heterogeneous* body or system. E.g. a *mixture* of *ice* and *water* is a two-phase system, while a *solution* of *salt* in water is a system of one phase.

PHASE (phys.). 1. Points in the path of a *wave motion* are said to be points of equal phase if the displacements at those points at any instant are exactly similar; i.e. of the same magnitude and varying in the same manner. 2. One of the circuits in a system or apparatus in which there are two or more alternating *voltages* displaced in phase (meaning as 1) relative to one another. In a 'two-phase' system the displacement is one quarter of a *period,* in a 'three-phase' system it is one third of a period.

PHASE ANGLE. 1. (phys.) The *angle* between the *vectors* representing two harmonically varying quantities (e.g. *current* and *voltage*) which have the same *frequency.* 2. (astr.) The *angle,* seen from the *Moon* or a *planet,* between the *Earth* and the *Sun.*

PHASE CONTRAST MICROSCOPE. A *microscope* which uses the difference in *phase* of the *light* transmitted or reflected by an object to form an *image* by relative differences in *intensity.*

PHASE MODULATION. *Modulation* of the *phase angle* of a *sinusoidal carrier wave.* The *phase* of the modulated wave differs from that of the carrier by an amount proportional to the instantaneous value of the modulating wave.

PHASE RULE. $F+P=C+2$. For a *heterogeneous* system in equilibrium, the sum of the number of *phases* plus the number of *degrees of freedom* is equal to the number of *components,* plus two. E.g. with *ice, water,* and

287

water vapour in equilibrium, the number of phases is 3, the number of components 1, and hence the number of degrees of freedom is 0; the system is said to be invariant, since no single variable can be changed without causing the disappearance of one phase from the system.

PHASES OF THE MOON. The various shapes of the illuminated surface of the *Moon* as seen from the *Earth* (new moon, first quarter, full moon, third quarter); due to variations in the relative positions of Earth, *Sun*, and Moon.

PHENACETIN. $CH_3CONHC_6H_4OC_2H_5$. A white crystalline substance, m.p. $134 \cdot 7°C$., used to relieve pain and as an *antipyretic*.

PHENAZINE. $C_6H_4N_2C_6H_4$. A yellow crystalline substance, m.p. $171°C$., used in the manufacture of *dyes*.

PHENETOLE. $C_6H_5OC_2H_5$. Phenyl ethyl ether. A *volatile aromatic liquid*, b.p. $172°C$.

PHENOBARBITONE. Luminal. Phenylethylbarbituric acid. $C_6H_5.C_2H_5$. $C:(NHCO)_2:CO$. A white crystalline powder, m.p.$174°C$.; used as a sedative and *hypnotic* drug usually in the form of the *soluble* sodium *salt*.

PHENOL. Carbolic acid. C_6H_5OH. A white crystalline *solid*, m.p. $41°C$., with a characteristic 'carbolic' smell. It is *soluble* in *water*, corrosive, and poisonous. Used as a *disinfectant* and in the manufacture of *plastics* and *dyes*.

PHENOL-FORMALDEHYDE RESIN. Phenolic resin. A very widely used type of synthetic *resin* produced by the *condensation* of *phenols* with *formaldehyde*: forms the basis of *thermosetting* moulding materials, also used in *paints*, varnishes, and *adhesives*.

PHENOLPHTHALEIN. $C_{20}H_{14}O_4$. A colourless crystalline *solid*, m.p. $261°C$. A solution in *alcohol* turns a deep purple-red in the presence of *alkalis*, and is used as an *indicator*. Also used in *dye* manufacture and as a laxative.

PHENOLS. A class of *aromatic organic compounds* containing one or more *hydroxyl groups* attached directly to the *benzene* ring. They correspond to the *alcohols* in the *aliphatic* series, forming *esters* and *ethers*, but they also have weak *acidic* properties and form *salts*. See *phenol*.

PHENOTHIAZINE. Thiodiphenylamine. $C_6H_4NH.S.C_6H_4$. A green *insoluble* substance, m.p. $185 \cdot 5°C$., used as an *insecticide* and in the manufacture of drugs.

PHENOTYPE. 1. The characteristics possessed by an individual *organism* as a result of the interaction of its inherited characteristics (see *genotype*) with its environment. 2. A group of organisms having the same phenotype (meaning 1).

PHENYL GROUP. The *univalent radical* C_6H_5—.

PHENYLACETIC ACID. Phenyl acetate. $CH_3COOC_6H_5$. A colourless *liquid*, b.p. $195 \cdot 7°C$., used as a *solvent*.

PHENYLALANINE. A crystalline *soluble amino acid*, m.p. $283°C$., obtained from eggs and milk, essential to the diet of mammals. See Table 5, page 435.

PHENYLENE GROUP. The *divalent radical* $C_6H_4=$, which exists in three isomeric forms. See *benzene ring*.

PHEROMONES. Chemical substances secreted by an *organism* which elicit a behavioural response from other organisms of the same species, especially substances which act as sex attractants.

PHLOGISTON THEORY. A theory of *combustion* which was generally accepted during the eighteenth century until refuted by Lavoisier. All combustible substances were supposed to be composed of phlogiston, which escaped on burning, and a calx or ash, which remained. Replacement of phlogiston into the calx would restore the original substance.

PHON. A unit of loudness, used in measuring the intensity of *sounds*. The loudness, in phons, of any sound is equal to the intensity in *decibels* of a sound of *frequency* 1000 *hertz* which seems as loud to the ear as the given sound.

PHOSGENE. Carbonyl chloride. $COCl_2$. A colourless, poisonous *gas* with a penetrating smell resembling musty hay. Used extensively as a poison gas during 1915–18.

PHOSPHATE. A *salt* of *phosphoric acid*, H_3PO_4. Phosphates are used as *fertilizers* to rectify a deficiency of phosphorus in the *soil*.

PHOSPHINE. PH_3. A colourless, inflammable poisonous *gas* with an unpleasant smell.

PHOSPHITE. A *salt* of *phosphorous acid*, H_3PO_3.

PHOSPHOLIPIDS. Phosphatides. Compound *lipids* which contain *phosphoric acid* groups and nitrogenous *bases*. Found in brain tissue and in egg yolk.

PHOSPHOR. A substance which is capable of *luminescence*, i.e. storing *energy* (particularly from *ionizing radiation*) and later releasing it in the form of *light*. If the energy is released after only a short delay (between 10^{-10} and 10^{-4} seconds) the substance is called a 'scintillator'.

PHOSPHOR BRONZE. An *alloy* of copper (80%–95%), tin (5%–15%), and phosphorus (0·25%–2·5%) which is hard, tough, and elastic.

PHOSPHORESCENCE. A form of *luminescence* in which a substance emits *light* of one *wavelength* after having absorbed *electromagnetic radiation* of a shorter wavelength. Unlike *fluorescence*, phosphorescence may continue for a considerable time after *excitation*.

PHOSPHORIC ACID. See *orthophosphoric acid*, *metaphosphoric acid*, and *pyrophosphoric acid*.

PHOSPHOROUS ACID. H_3PO_3. A colourless *deliquescent* crystalline substance, m.p. 73·6° C., from which *phosphites* are obtained.

PHOSPHORUS. P. Element. A.W. 30·9738. At. No. 15. Occurs in several *allotropic forms*, white phosphorus and red phosphorus being the commonest. The former is a waxy white, very inflammable and poisonous *solid*, m.p. 44° C. Red phosphorus is a non-poisonous, dark red powder, not very inflammable. The *element* occurs only in the combined state, mainly as *calcium phosphate*, $Ca_3(PO_4)_2$. Extracted by heating with *coke* and *silica* (sand) in an electric furnace, and distilling off the phosphorus. Essential to life; calcium phosphate is the main constituent of animal bones. *Compounds* are used as *fertilizers* and *detergents*.

PHOSPHORUS PENTOXIDE. P_2O_5. A *deliquescent* colourless crystalline *solid*, m.p. 563° C. Used as a drying agent.

PHOSPHORUS TRICHLORIDE. PCl_3. A colourless fuming *liquid*, b.p. 75·5° C., used as a chlorinating agent.

PHOSPHORYL GROUP. The trivalent radical $\equiv PO$.

PHOT. Unit of *illumination*; an illumination of one *lumen* per square centimetre.

PHOTOCHEMICAL REACTIONS. *Chemical reactions* which are initiated, assisted, or accelerated by exposure to *light*. E.g. hydrogen and chlorine combine explosively on exposure to sunlight but only slowly in the dark.

PHOTOCHROMISM. Phototropism. The property of certain *dyes*, or other *compounds*, as a result of which they undergo a reversible change in the *colours* which they absorb when exposed to *light* of different *wavelengths*. Thus some photochromic materials will darken in bright light, but will revert to their original colour when the source of light is removed.

PHOTOCONDUCTIVE EFFECT. A *photo-electric effect* in which the electrical *conductivity* of certain substances, notably selenium, increases with the intensity of the *light* to which the substance is exposed.

PHOTODISINTEGRATION. 1. A *nuclear reaction* caused by a *photon* in which the *nucleus* emits charged fragments or *neutrons*. 2. See *photodissociation*.

PHOTODISSOCIATION. Photodisintegration. The *dissociation* of a chemical *compound* as the result of the absorption of *radiant energy*.

PHOTO-ELECTRIC CELL. Photocell. A device used for the detection and measurement of *light*. The cell may depend for its action upon (1) the normal *photo-electric effect*; the cell is then called a *photo-emissive* cell; (2) the *photovoltaic effect* (*rectifier* or *barrier layer* cell); or (3) the *photoconductive effect* (conductivity cell). Photo-emissive cells consist of two *electrodes*, a plane *cathode* coated with a suitable *photosensitive* material, and an *anode* which is maintained at a positive *potential* with respect to the cathode and which attracts the *photo-electrons* liberated by the latter. These electrodes are arranged in an envelope which is either evacuated, or, for greater sensitivity, contains a *gas* at low *pressure*. The *electric current* passing through the cell is a measure of the *light* intensity incident on the cathode. For rectifier or barrier cells, the *potential difference* developed across the boundary gives rise to a current when the faces of the cell are connected externally. This current can be measured directly by suitable means such as a *galvanometer*. Rectifier cells require no external source of *E.M.F.* and are very convenient for photographic *exposure meters*, etc. The conductivity cell is simply an arrangement for measuring the *resistance* of a layer of material, usually selenium, which shows the photoconductive effect.

PHOTO-ELECTRIC EFFECT. In general, any effect arising as a result of a transfer of *energy* from *light* incident on a substance to *electrons* in the substance. The term is normally restricted to one type of the effect, namely the emission of electrons by substances when irradiated with light of a *frequency* greater than a certain minimum *threshold frequency*. Electrons liberated in this way are called photo-electrons, and constitute a photo-electric current when the system is included in a suitable circuit.

PHOTO-ELECTRONS. See *photo-electric effect.*

PHOTO-EMISSIVE. A substance is described as being photo-emissive if it is capable of emitting *electrons* when it is subjected to *electromagnetic radiation*. The *wavelength* of the radiation which will provoke such emission depends upon the nature of the substance: *light* provokes some *metals* into photo-emission, other materials require *ultraviolet radiation* or *X-rays.*

PHOTOFISSION. *Nuclear fission* caused by *photons* (of *gamma-rays*).

PHOTOGRAPHY. By means of a system of *lenses* in the *camera* an image of the object to be photographed is thrown for a definite length of time on to a plate or *film* made of *glass, celluloid,* or other *transparent* material and covered with an *emulsion* containing *silver bromide,* AgBr, or *silver chloride,* AgCl. The effect of this exposure of the film is to make the silver compound easily reduced (see *reduction*) to metallic silver by the chemical action of *developing*; developers produce a black deposit of fine particles of metallic silver on those portions of the film which had been exposed to *light,* thus giving a negative image. *Fixing* consists of the chemical action of *sodium thiosulphate,* $Na_2S_2O_3$, ('hypo'), and other *reagents* on the unchanged silver *salts* to give a *soluble compound,* which is then washed out with *water,* leaving a negative which is free of light-sensitive silver salts. By placing the finished negative over a piece of sensitive paper similar to film, and exposing to light, the silver salts in the paper are affected in a similar way to those in the original film; those portions of the negative which were darkest let through least light, and thus give the whitest portions on the developed paper. The negative image is thus again reversed, and a correct image or photograph is obtained on the paper, which is then fixed and washed as before.

PHOTOLYSIS. The *decomposition* of a chemical *compound* as the result of irradiation by *light* or *ultraviolet radiation.* 'Flash photolysis' is a method of identifying the free *radicals* formed when the *vapour* of a compound at low *pressure* is exposed to an intense, but very brief, flash of radiation. A second flash, following shortly after the first, is used to photograph the *absorption spectrum* of the *gases* which records the free radicals present. Subsequent flashes at regular intervals may be used to calculate the lifetimes of the radicals so formed.

PHOTOMESON. A *meson* produced by the interaction between a *photon* and an atomic *nucleus.*

PHOTOMETER. An instrument for comparing the *luminous intensity* of sources of *light*. In *astronomy photo-electric* photometers are used to measure the intensity of *light* from distant *stars*.

PHOTOMICROGRAPH. A photograph obtained with the aid of a *microscope*.

PHOTOMULTIPLIER. Electron multiplier. A *photo-electric cell* of high sensitivity used for detecting very small quantities of *light* radiation. Consists of a system of *electrodes* suitably arranged in an evacuated envelope. Light falling on the first electrode ejects *electrons* from this surface (see *photo-electric effect*). These electrons are accelerated to the second electrode, where they each produce further electrons by the process of *secondary emission*. This process continues until the secondary emission from the final electrode is sufficient to produce a useful *electric current*, permitting measurement or the operation of a *relay*.

PHOTON. A *quantum* of *electromagnetic radiation* which has zero *rest mass*, and *energy* equal to the product of the *frequency* of the radiation and *Planck's constant*. Photons are generated when a particle possessing an *electric charge* changes its *momentum*, in collisions between *nuclei* or *electrons*, and in the *decay* of certain nuclei and particles. In some contexts it is convenient to regard a photon as an *elementary particle*.

PHOTOSENSITIVE. Substances are said to be photosensitive if they produce a *photoconductive, photo-electric*, or *photovoltaic effect* when subjected to suitable *electromagnetic radiation*.

PHOTOSPHERE. The visible, intensely luminous portion of the *Sun* which has an estimated *temperature* of 6000 K.

PHOTOSYNTHESIS. The process by which green plants manufacture their *carbohydrates* from atmospheric *carbon dioxide* and *water* in the presence of sunlight. The reaction, which is highly complex in detail, may be summarized by the equation:

$$6CO_2 + 6H_2O = C_6H_{12}O_6 + 6O_2.$$

When *light* falls upon green plants the greater part of the *energy* is absorbed by small particles called chloroplasts, which contain a variety of pigments, amongst them *compounds* called *chlorophylls*. The chlorophylls transform the energy of the light into *chemical energy* by a process which is not fully understood, but which is known to involve the *photolysis* of water and the activation of *adenosine triphosphate* (ATP). The energy-rich ATP subsequently energizes the fixation of the CO_2, after a series of reactions, so that *sugar molecules* are formed. As animals are unable to fix atmospheric CO_2 in this way, they depend for their carbon on the plants (or other animals) which they consume. Photosynthesis is therefore essential to all the higher life forms, either directly or indirectly.

PHOTOVOLTAIC EFFECT. A *photo-electric effect* in which *light* falling on a specially prepared boundary between certain pairs of substances (e.g. copper and *cuprous oxide*) produces a *potential difference* across the boundary.

PHTHALIC ACID. $C_6H_4(COOH)_2$. A white crystalline *soluble* substance, m.p. 207°C.; used in the manufacture of *dyes* and perfumes and in medicine.

PHTHALIC ANHYDRIDE. $C_6H_4(CO)_2O$. A white crystalline substance obtained by heating *phthalic acid*, m.p. 130·8°C., used in the manufacture of *glyptal resins* and *plasticizers*.

PHYLOGENY. See *ontogeny*.

PHYSICAL CHANGE. Any change in a body or substance which does not involve an alteration in its chemical composition.

PHYSICAL CHEMISTRY. The study of the *physical changes* associated with *chemical reactions* and the dependence of physical properties on chemical composition.

PHYSICAL STATES OF MATTER. The physical state in which *matter* exists, at a particular *temperature* and *pressure*, depends upon the *kinetic energy* of, and interaction between, its component *atoms, molecules*, or *ions*. In *gases* the distance between the fast moving atoms or molecules is such that the interaction between them is very small (see *Van der Waals' forces*); they are therefore free to move about the space which contains them almost independently of each other (see *kinetic theory of gases*). In the *solid state* the atoms, molecules, or ions have insufficient kinetic energy to overcome the strong *forces* which act between them, they therefore vibrate about the fixed positions of a *crystal lattice*. *Liquids* represent an intermediate state between gases and solids. Raising the temperature of a solid increases the kinetic energy of its components so that they are able to overcome the forces between them, the solid then becomes a liquid and eventually a gas. Increasing the pressure of a gas increases the number of collisions between the components and thus facilitates their interactions: for this reason increased pressure causes, or assists in, the *liquefaction of gases*. A hot ionized *plasma* has sometimes been referred to as the fourth state of matter.

PHYSICS. The study of the properties of *matter* and *energy*.

PHYSIOLOGICAL SALINE. An *isotonic solution* of *salts* in *distilled water* used for preserving *cells*. Such solutions contain no food for the cells and their survival in them is therefore restricted.

PHYSIOLOGY. The study of the functioning of the various organs of living beings.

PHYSOSTIGMINE. Eserine. $C_{15}H_{21}O_2N_3$. A colourless *alkaloid*, m.p. 105–6°C., used in the treatment of glaucoma.

PHYTAMINS. See *auxins*.

PHYTO-. Prefix denoting 'plant'; e.g. a phytocide is a substance which kills plants.

PI. π. Symbol for the ratio of the circumference of any *circle* to its diameter. 3·14159 ... (Approximately 22/7.)

PICO-. Prefix denoting one million millionth. E.g. a picofarad is 10^{-12} farad. Symbol p.

PICOLINE. $CH_3C_5H_4N$. Three *isomeric derivatives* of *pyridine* which occur in *coal-tar* and *bone oil*. The most important, 2-picoline, is a colourless oily *liquid*, b.p. 128° C., used as a *solvent* and in medicine as a *sedative*.

PICRATE. A *salt* or *ester* of *picric acid*.

PICRIC ACID. 2,4,6-trinitrophenol. $C_6H_2(NO_2)_3OH$. A bright yellow crystalline *solid*, m.p. 122° C. Formerly used as an explosive (see *lyddite*), as a *dye*, and (in *solution*) for treating burns.

PIEZO-ELECTRIC EFFECT. A property of certain *asymmetric crystals*. When such crystals are subjected to a *pressure*, positive and negative *electric charges* are produced on opposing faces; the signs of these charges are reversed if the pressure is replaced by a tension. The inverse piezo-electric effect occurs if such crystals are subjected to an *electric potential*, an alteration in size of the crystal taking place.

PIG-IRON. An impure form of iron obtained from iron *ores* by the *blast furnace* process. See *cast iron*.

PIGMENT. A coloured substance which, when applied to a surface, colours the surface. Distinct from a *dye*, which penetrates the fibres or tissues of the surface; in general, pigments are *insoluble* materials which may be removed by mechanical means.

PIGMENT COLOUR. Body colour. The *colour* of most natural objects is due to the differential absorption by the substance of the different *wavelengths* (i.e. colours) present in the incident white *light*. The incident light penetrates a small distance into the substance, undergoes this absorption and is then diffusely reflected out again. The colour the body appears is determined by the wavelengths absorbed the least. Thus, a substance which absorbs chiefly the red and yellow will appear blue. See also *surface colour*.

PILE, VOLTAIC. See *voltaic pile*.

PILOCARPINE. $C_{11}H_{16}N_2O_2$. A white crystalline *alkaloid*, m.p. 34° C., used in medicine.

PINCH EFFECT. 1. The constriction of a *liquid conductor* of *electricity* (e.g. mercury or molten *metal*) which occurs when a substantial *current* is passed through it. 2. The constriction of a *plasma* due to the *magnetic field* of a high current within the plasma. See *thermonuclear reactions*.

PINCHBECK. An *alloy* of copper and zinc used as an imitation gold.

PINENE. $C_{10}H_{16}$. A *liquid terpene*, b.p. 156·2° C., which is the principal constituent of *turpentine* and is found in other *essential oils*. Used in the manufacture of *camphor*.

PINK SALT. Ammonium chlorostannate, $(NH_4)_2SnCl_6$. Used as a *mordant* in dyeing.

PINKING. See *knocking*.

PINT. Unit of capacity equal to one eighth of a *gallon*.

PION. A pi-*meson*. See Table 6, page 437.

PIPERAZINE. $C_4H_8(NH_2)$. A colourless *deliquescent heterocyclic compound,* m.p. 104°C., used as an *insecticide* and in medicine.

PIPERIDENE. $C_5H_{10}NH$. A colourless *liquid,* b.p. 106°C., used as a *solvent.*

PIPERINE. $C_{17}H_{19}NO_3$. A white crystalline *alkaloid,* m.p. 129·5°C., the active constituent of pepper.

PIPETTE. A glass tube with the aid of which a definite *volume* of *liquid* may be transferred.

PITCH. Hard dark substances which melt to viscous tarry *liquids;* they may be the residue from the *destructive distillation* of wood, *coal-tar, asphalt,* or various *bitumens,* etc.

PITCH OF A NOTE. A measure of the *frequency* of vibration of the source producing the note; a high frequency produces a note of high pitch. See *sound.*

PITCH OF A SCREW. The distance between adjoining crests of the thread, measured parallel to the *axis* of the screw.

PITCHBLENDE. A natural *ore* consisting mainly of uranium oxide, U_3O_8. Occurs in Saxony, Bohemia, East Africa, and Colorado. Contains small amounts of radium, of which it is the principal source.

PITOT TUBE. An instrument for measuring the *velocity* of a *fluid;* consists of a tube with two openings, one facing the moving fluid and the other facing away from it. The difference in *pressure* created in the tube between the two openings, as measured by a *manometer,* allows the velocity of the fluid to be determined. Named after Henri Pitot (1695–1771).

PLANCK'S CONSTANT. h. The universal constant relating the *frequency* of a *radiation,* ν, with its *quantum* of *energy,* E; i.e. $E = h\nu$. Planck's constant has the dimensions of *action* (energy × time) and its value is $6·62559 \times 10^{-34}$ *joule seconds* or $6·62559 \times 10^{-27}$ *erg* seconds. The symbol $\hbar$ is often used for $\dfrac{h}{2\pi}$. Named after Max Planck (1858–1947).

PLANCK'S LAW OF RADIATION. The *energy* of *electromagnetic radiation* (including *light*) is composed of discrete *quanta,* the magnitude of which is given by the *product* of *Planck's constant* and the *frequency* of the radiation.

PLANE (math.). A flat surface; mathematically defined as a surface containing all the straight lines passing through a fixed point and also intersecting a straight line in space.

PLANE-POLARIZED LIGHT. See *polarization of light.*

PLANETARIUM. A complex system of optical projectors for representing the movements of the *planets* and *stars* on a domed ceiling; often extended to include the building in which they are contained.

PLANETOIDS. See *asteroids.*

PLANETS. Heavenly bodies revolving in definite *orbits* about the *Sun.* In order of increasing distance from the Sun they are *Mercury, Venus,* the *Earth, Mars, Jupiter, Saturn, Uranus, Neptune*, and *Pluto*. See Table 4, page 434.

PLANIMETER. A mechanical integrating instrument for measuring *plane* areas, consisting of a movable tracing arm the movements of which are recorded on a dial.

PLANO-. Prefix used in conjunction with the words *concave* and *convex* to describe the shape of a *lens*. See Fig. 24, page 219.

PLASMA (bio.). See *blood plasma*.

PLASMA (phys.). 1. The region in a *discharge in gases* in which the numbers of positive and negative *ions* are approximately equal. 2. The term has been extended to include the very hot ionized gas in which controlled *thermonuclear reaction* experiments are carried out. In such a plasma, which has been described as the fourth state of matter, the *ionization* is virtually complete. Again the numbers of positive ions and electrons are approximately equal and the plasma is therefore virtually electrically *neutral* and highly conducting. See also *containment*.

PLASMOLYSIS. The effect of *osmosis* on *cells* of living *organisms*. A cell placed in a *solution* which is of a greater *molecular concentration* than (i.e. is *hypertonic* to) the contents of the cell becomes plasmolyzed; the *water* in the cell flows out through the cell wall and the cell contents contract.

PLASTER OF PARIS. Powdered *calcium sulphate*, $CaSO_4.\frac{1}{2}H_2O$, obtained by heating *gypsum* to 120°C.–130°C. With *water*, sets and hardens.

PLASTICIZER. 1. A non-*volatile liquid* added to *paints* and varnishes to prevent brittleness of the dried film. 2. A liquid or *solid* substance added to synthetic or natural *resins* to modify their flow properties.

PLASTICS. Many different definitions have been given. In general, the term may be taken to cover materials which are *stable* in normal use, but which at some stage of their manufacture are plastic, and can be shaped or moulded by *heat, pressure*, or both. Most plastics are polymers (see *polymerization*), and are classified into *thermoplastic* and *thermosetting* materials.

PLATELET. See *blood platelet*.

PLATINIC. Containing *tetravalent* platinum.

PLATINIZED ASBESTOS. *Asbestos* in the fibres of which a black deposit of finely-divided platinum has been formed. Used as a *catalyst*.

PLATINOID. An *alloy* of 60% copper, 24% zinc, 14% nickel, and 2% tungsten.

PLATINOUS. Containing *divalent* platinum.

PLATINUM. Pt. Element. A.W. 195·09. At. No. 78. A hard silvery-white ductile and malleable *metal*. S.G. 21·45. M.p. 1773·5°C. Very resistant to *heat* and *acids*. Coefficient of *expansion* very nearly equal to that of *glass*. Occurs as the metal, alloyed with osmium, iridium, and similar metals. Used for electrical contacts, scientific apparatus, as a *catalyst* (see *platinized asbestos*), and in jewellery.

PLATINUM CHLORIDE SOLUTION. See *chloroplatinic acid.*

PLUMBAGO. Black-lead, *graphite.* A natural *allotropic form* of carbon.

PLUTO. A *planet* with its *orbit* outside that of *Neptune.* Discovered in 1930. Mean distance from the *Sun*, 5907 million kilometres. *Sidereal period* ('year') 248·4 years. *Mass* approximately one tenth that of the *Earth*, diameter approximately 5900 kilometres. Surface temperature probably below −200° C.

PLUTONIUM. Pu. At. No. 94. *Transuranic element.* Different *isotopes* of plutonium can be produced by suitable *nuclear reactions.* The isotope $^{239}_{94}$Pu is produced in *nuclear reactors* and is of considerable importance since it undergoes *nuclear fission* when bombarded by *slow neutrons.* This isotope, which has a *half-life* of 24 400 years, is also used in *nuclear weapons*, one *kilogram* having an *energy* equivalent of about 10^{14} *joules.*

PNEUMATIC. Operated by, or filled with, compressed air.

P-N-P TRANSISTOR. See *transistor.*

POINT SOURCE OF LIGHT. A theoretical concept of a source of *light* in which all the light is emitted from a single point.

POISE. A unit of *viscosity* in *c.g.s. units.* Defined as the tangential *force* per unit area (*dynes* per sq cm) required to maintain unit difference in *velocity* (cm per second) between two parallel *planes* separated by one centimetre of *fluid.* 1 centipoise = 10^{-3} *newton* seconds per square *metre* (the *SI unit* of viscosity).

POISEUILLE'S EQUATION. The *volume* V of a *liquid* flowing through a cylindrical tube per second is given by the equation $V = \dfrac{\pi p r^4}{8 l \eta}$, where *p* is the *pressure* difference between two points on the *axis* of the tube at a distance *l* apart, η is the coefficient of *viscosity* and *r* is the radius of the tube. The result assumes uniform *streamline* flow, and also that the liquid in contact with the walls of the tube is at rest. Named after Jean Louis Poiseuille (1799–1869).

POISON, NUCLEAR. Reactor poison. A substance which absorbs *neutrons* in a *nuclear reactor.* Poisons may be deliberately added to reduce the reactivity, or they may be *fission products*, such as xenon, which have to be periodically removed.

POISSON'S RATIO. The ratio of the *lateral strain* to the *longitudinal* strain in a stretched wire. Given by the ratio of d/D to l/L, where $D =$ original diameter, $L =$ original length, $d =$ decrease in diameter, and $l =$ increase in length. Named after Simeon Poisson (1781–1840).

POLAR BOND. An electrovalent bond. See *valency, electronic theory of.*

POLAR COORDINATES. The position of any point *P* lying in a *plane* can be completely determined by (1) its distance, *r*, from any selected point *O* in the plane, termed the *origin*, and (2) the *angle* θ which the line joining *P* and *O* (called the *radius vector*) makes with any *coplanar* reference line passing through *O*. The angle is taken as positive when measured anti-clockwise from the reference line. The polar co-

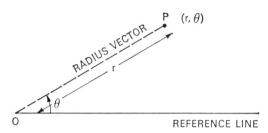

FIGURE 33.

ordinates of the point P are r and θ, denoted by $(r,\ \theta)$. See Fig. 33, above.

POLAR MOLECULE. A *molecule*, the configuration of *electric charge* in which constitutes a permanent electric *dipole*.

POLARIMETER. Polariscope. An apparatus for measuring the rotation of the plane of vibration of polarized light by optically active substances. See *polarization of light* and *optical activity*.

POLARISCOPE. See *polarimeter*.

POLARIZATION, ANGLE OF. The *angle* of reflection from a *dielectric* medium, e.g. *glass*, at which the reflected *ray* is completely polarized, the plane of vibration being at right angles to the plane of incidence. See *polarization of light*.

POLARIZATION, ELECTRIC. See *electric polarization*.

POLARIZATION, ELECTROLYTIC. An increase in the electrical *resistance* of an *electrolyte* due to various causes; chiefly associated with the accumulation of gaseous *molecules* on the *electrodes* at which they are liberated.

POLARIZATION OF LIGHT. Ordinary *light* consists of electric (E) and magnetic (H) vibrations taking place in all possible *planes* containing the *ray*, the vibrations themselves being at right angles to the direction of the light path; i.e. light is a *transverse wave* motion. For each E vibration the associated H vibration takes place in a plane at right angles to it. In plane-polarized light, the E vibrations are confined to one plane, called the plane of vibration, and hence the associated H vibrations are also confined to one plane, the plane at right angles to this, called the plane of polarization. See also *circularly* and *elliptically polarized light*.

POLAROID*. Trade name of thin *transparent films* which produce plane-polarized light (see *polarization of light*) on transmission. Consist of thin sheets of *cellulose nitrate* packed with ultramicroscopic doubly-refracting *crystals* (see *double refraction*) with their *optic axes* parallel. The crystals produce plane-polarized light by differential absorption of the *ordinary* and *extraordinary rays*.

POLARON. An *excitation* in a *solid* consisting of *polar molecules* resulting from the interaction between an *electron* and its *strain field*. The presence of a polaron can be detected by irregularities in the shape of the *conduction band*.

POLE, MAGNETIC. See *magnetic pole*.

POLE OF MIRROR. See *mirrors, spherical*.

POLE STRENGTH. See *magnetic pole strength*.

POLONIUM. Po. Radium-F. A *radioactive element* decaying by *alpha-particle* emission. At. No. 84. Forms a stage in the radioactive *disintegration* of radium. The principal *isotope* has a *mass number* of 209 and a *half-life* of 103 years.

POLY-. Prefix denoting many, several, numerous.

POLYAMIDE. A *polymer* in which the units are linked by *amide* or *thio-amide* groupings. See *nylon*.

POLYBASIC. An *acid* containing more than one *atom* of *acidic hydrogen* in a *molecule*.

POLYCYCLIC. Having more than one ring in a *molecule*.

POLYESTER. A *polymer* formed (usually) from a *polyhydric alcohol* and a *polybasic acid*. Used in the manufacture of synthetic *resins, fibres,* and *plastics*.

POLYETHYLENE. See *polythene*.

POLYGON. A *plane* figure bounded by straight lines.

POLYGON OF FORCES. If any number of *forces*, acting on a particle, can be represented in magnitude and direction by the sides of a *polygon* taken in order, the forces will be in *equilibrium*.

POLYHEDRON. A solid figure having *polygons* for its faces. A regular polyhedron has all its faces equal in all respects; the five possible types of regular polyhedra are: (1) *tetrahedron*, 4 triangular faces; (2) *cube*, 6 square faces; (3) *octahedron*, 8 triangular faces; (4) *dodecahedron*, 12 five-sided faces; (5) *icosahedron*, 20 triangular faces.

POLYHYDRIC ALCOHOLS. *Alcohols* containing two or more *hydroxyl groups* in the *molecule*. E.g. *diols* are dihydric alcohols and *triols* are trihydric alcohols.

POLYMER. A product of *polymerization*.

POLYMERIZATION. Originally understood to be the chemical union of two or more *molecules* of the same *compound* to form larger molecules, resulting in the formation of a new compound of the same *empirical formula* but of greater *molecular weight*. E.g. *paraldehyde*, $(CH_3CHO)_3$, is formed by the polymerization of *acetaldehyde*, CH_3CHO, and each molecule of the *polymer* is made up of three molecules of the acetaldehyde *monomer*. The meaning of the term has been extended to cover (1) 'addition polymerization', in which the molecule of the polymer is a multiple of the monomer molecule, as in the case of paraldehyde; (2) 'condensation polymerization', in which the monomer molecules are joined by *condensation* into a polymer molecule, which differs in empirical formula from the monomer; and (3) 'copolymerization', in which the polymer molecule is built up from two or more different kinds of monomer molecules. Many important products, such as *plastics* and textile fibres, consist of polymeric substances, either *natural* (e.g. *cellulose*), or *synthetic* (e.g. *nylon*).

POLYMETHYL METHACRYLATE. A colourless, *transparent, solid thermoplastic*, produced by the *polymerization* of methyl methacrylate (see *methacrylic acid*), which is widely used because of its optical properties in place of *glass*. (Trade name Perspex*.)

POLYMORPHISM. The existence of the same substance in more than two different crystalline forms.

POLYNOMIAL (math.). An expression consisting of three or more terms.

POLYNUCLEOTIDE. A chain of *nucleotides* linked together as in a *nucleic acid*. *Ribonucleic acid* consists of a single chain, while *deoxyribonucleic acid* usually consists of a double *helix* comprising two polynucleotide chains.

POLYPEPTIDE. A chain of three or more *amino acids* each of which is joined to its neighbours by the *peptide* linkage. Polypeptide chains may consist of up to several hundred amino acid units. *Proteins* consist of polypeptide chains cross-linked together in a variety of ways.

POLYPLOIDY. Having more than twice the normal *haploid* number of *chromosomes* in a *cell*. Artificial polyploidy can be induced (e.g. by *colchicine*) and is used to produce fertile hybrids with desired characteristics.

POLYPROPYLENE. A colourless *transparent thermoplastic* material produced by the *polymerization* of *propylene*. Used where a flexible *plastic* material is required. Similar to *polythene* but of greater strength.

POLYSACCHARIDES. A large class of natural *carbohydrates*. The *molecules* are derived from the *condensation* of several, frequently very many, molecules of simple *sugars* (*monosaccharides*). The class includes *cellulose* and *starch*.

POLYSTYRENE. A *thermoplastic* material, produced by the *polymerization* of *styrene* $(C_6H_5CH:CH_2)$, possessing good electrical insulating properties.

POLYTHENE. Polyethylene, Alkathene*. A tough waxy *thermoplastic* material, made by the addition *polymerization* of *ethylene*, C_2H_4. Used as an insulating material and for many other purposes where a flexible, chemically resistant *plastic* material is required.

POLYURETHANE. See *urethane resins*.

POLYVALENT. 1. Having more than one *valency*. 2. Having a valency of more than one. 3. (Of a *serum*). Containing more than one type of *antibody* and therefore effective against more than one type of *micro-organism*.

POLYVINYL ACETATE. PVA. A colourless *thermoplastic* material, produced by the *polymerization* of *vinyl acetate* $(CH_2:CHOOC.CH_3)$. Used in *adhesives, inks,* and lacquers for coating paper and fabric.

POLYVINYL CHLORIDE. PVC. A colourless *thermoplastic* material, produced by the *polymerization* of *vinyl chloride* $(CH_2:CHCL)$ with good resistance to *water, acids, alkalis,* and *alcohols*.

POLYVINYLIDENE CHLORIDE. A white *thermoplastic* material, produced by the *polymerization* of *vinylidene chloride* (CH_2 : CCl_2). Also used as a copolymer with *acrylonitrile* or *vinyl chloride* giving products with a wide range of flexibilities.

POLYWATER. Anomolous water. Name suggested for a form of *water* which can be prepared by condensing ordinary water in fine *quartz* or *glass capillary tubes*. Polywater has a *density* of about 1·4 grams per cc and remains stable up to 400–500° C. It also has a higher *viscosity* than ordinary water. It is believed to consist of hexagonally arranged water *molecules*, formed by the catalytic effect of the *silica* in the glass or quartz.

POPULATION TYPE. A classification of *stars* into two types: Population I consists of hot white young stars such as those which form the spiral arms of *spiral galaxies*; Population II consists of older stars, such as *red giants* which are found at the centres of spiral galaxies.

PORCELAIN. A hard white material made by the firing of a *mixture* of pure kaolin (*china clay*) with *felspar* and *quartz*, or with other materials containing *silica*.

POSITION CIRCLE. A *circle* with centre at an observed point and radius such that the circumference passes through the place of observation. The portion of the circumference near the place of observation approximates to a *position line* if the radius is large.

POSITION LINE. A line of position on which the observer is situated at a given time. The intersection of two position lines, determined at the same time, fixes the position of the observer.

POSITIVE (math., phys.). In any convention of signs, regarded as being counted in the plus, or positive direction, as opposed to *negative*.

POSITIVE COLUMN. A luminous region in a *discharge in gases* near to the positive *electrode*.

POSITIVE FEEDBACK. See *feedback*.

POSITIVE MAGNETIC POLE. The north-seeking pole of a *magnet*. See *magnetic pole*.

POSITIVE RAY ANALYSIS. See *mass spectrometer*.

POSITIVE RAYS. Streams of *ions* bearing positive *electric charges*. May be produced by means of an electric discharge in a rarefied gas. See *discharge in gases*.

POSITRON. Positive *electron*. An *elementary particle* with the same *mass* as the electron and an *electric charge* of equal magnitude but opposite sign. Positrons are produced during several *decay* processes and during *pair production*; they do not themselves decay spontaneously but on passing through matter they collide with negative electrons as a result of which both particles are annihilated. See *annihilation radiation*.

POSITRONIUM. An unstable unit, resembling an *atom* of hydrogen, which consists of a *positron* (instead of a *proton*) and an *electron*. Decays by annihilation in less than 10^{-7} seconds into two or three *photons*.

POTASH. *Potassium carbonate*, K_2CO_3. Term also applied to *potassium hydroxide*, KOH (caustic potash) and, loosely, to potassium *salts* in general.

POTASSIUM. Kalium. K. Element. A.W. 39·102. At. No. 19. A silvery-white soft highly reactive *metal*, strongly resembling sodium. S.G. 0·86, m.p. 62·3° C. Widely distributed in the form of various *salts* (e.g. *carnallite*); essential to life; found in all living matter. Salts used as *fertilizers*.

POTASSIUM ANTIMONATE. $KSb(OH)_6.\frac{1}{2}H_2O$. A white, crystalline substance, used as a *pigment*.

POTASSIUM BICARBONATE. See *potassium hydrogen carbonate*.

POTASSIUM BROMIDE. KBr. A white crystalline *salt*, m.p. 730° C., used in medicine and *photography*.

POTASSIUM CARBONATE. Potash, carbonate of potash. K_2CO_3. A white, very *soluble, deliquescent salt*, m.p. 891° C., used in the manufacture of *glass* and *soap*.

POTASSIUM CHLORATE. $KClO_3$. A white crystalline *soluble* substance, m.p. 356° C., used as an *oxidizing agent* and in the manufacture of fireworks.

POTASSIUM CHLORIDE. Potassium muriate. KCl. A white, crystalline *soluble* substance, m.p. 776° C., used in medicine and as a *fertilizer*.

POTASSIUM DICHROMATE. Dichromate or bichromate of potash. $K_2Cr_2O_7$. A red crystalline *soluble salt*, m.p. 398° C., prepared from *chrome iron ore*. Used as an *oxidizing agent*, and in the *paint* and *dye* industries.

POTASSIUM FERRICYANIDE. $K_3Fe(CN)_6$. A red *soluble* crystalline substance, used in the manufacture of *pigments* and *paper*.

POTASSIUM FERROCYANIDE. $K_4Fe(CN)_6.3H_2O$. A yellow *soluble* crystalline substance, used as a *dye* and in case-hardening.

POTASSIUM HYDROGEN CARBONATE. Potassium bicarbonate. $KHCO_3$. A white *soluble* substance, used in cooking and as an *antacid*.

POTASSIUM HYDROGEN DIFLUORIDE. Acid potassium fluoride. KHF_2. A *deliquescent* crystalline substance used in the manufacture of fluorine.

POTASSIUM HYDROGEN TARTRATE. Cream of Tartar. $C_4O_6H_5K$. A white crystalline powder obtained from *argol* (tartar), used in *baking powder*.

POTASSIUM HYDROXIDE. Caustic potash. KOH. A white *deliquescent solid*, m.p. 360·4° C., dissolves in *water* to give an *alkaline solution*. Used in medicine and in the manufacture of *soap*.

POTASSIUM IODIDE. KI. A white crystalline *soluble* substance, m.p. 686° C., used in *photography* and in medicine.

POTASSIUM NITRATE. Nitre, saltpetre. A white *soluble* crystalline *salt*, m.p. 336° C., which acts as an *oxidizing agent* when hot. Used in medicine, for pickling meat, and in *gunpowder*.

POTASSIUM PERMANGANATE. Permanganate of potash. $KMnO_4$. A deep purple, crystalline, *soluble salt*. Dissolved in *water* it gives a purple *solution* which acts as a powerful *oxidizing agent*. Used as a *disinfectant* and in *volumetric analysis*.

POTASSIUM SODIUM TARTRATE. Rochelle salt. $COOK.(CHOH)_2$ $COONa.4H_2O$. A white crystalline *soluble salt*, m.p. 70–80°C., used in the preparation of *baking powder*, Seidlitz powders, etc.

POTASSIUM SULPHATE. K_2SO_4. A white *soluble* crystalline substance, m.p. 1069°C., used in *fertilizers* and mineral waters.

POTASSIUM THIOCYANATE. KSCN. A colourless *hygroscopic* substance, m.p. 173·2°C., used in the manufacture of *dyes* and *drugs*.

POTENTIAL. See *electric potential*.

POTENTIAL BARRIER. See *nuclear barrier*.

POTENTIAL DIFFERENCE. If two points have a different *electric potential* there is said to be a potential difference (p.d.) between them; if the points are joined by an electric *conductor*, an *electric current* will flow between them. Defined as the *work* performed when a unit positive *electric charge* is moved from one of the points to the other. See also *electromotive force*, E.M.F. The practical unit of p.d. and E.M.F. is the *volt*.

POTENTIAL ENERGY. The *energy* which a body possesses by virtue of its position. E.g. a coiled spring, or a vehicle at the top of a hill, possesses potential energy. Measured by the amount of *work* the body performs in passing from that position to a standard position in which the potential energy is considered to be zero. The potential energy of a *mass, m,* raised through a height, *h*, is *mgh*, where *g* is the *acceleration due to gravity*.

POTENTIAL SERIES. See *electromotive series*.

POTENTIOMETER. 1. An instrument for measuring *direct current E.M.F.* or *potential differences*, which does not draw current from the circuit containing the E.M.F. to be measured. In its simplest form consists of a uniform *resistance AB* (see Fig. 34, page 304) in the form of a single wire, connected to a source of E.M.F., *E*. A slide wire contact *C* is connected, in series with a sensitive *galvanometer G*, to one terminal of the E.M.F. to be measured. The other terminal is connected to *A*, so that the E.M.F.s across *XY* and *AC* are in opposition through *G*. Contact *C* is then adjusted until no current flows through the galvanometer. The required E.M.F. is then given by El_1/L, where *L* is the total length of the resistance *AB*, and l_1 is the length *AC* for zero current through *G*. 2. A *voltage divider*.

POUND. British unit of *weight*. Formerly defined as the weight, in vacuo, of a platinum cylinder called the Imperial Standard Pound. Redefined by statute in 1963 as 0·453 592 37 *kilogram*. Used as a unit of *force*, i.e. the force of attraction of the *Earth* upon a *mass* of one pound, and as a unit of mass.

POUNDAL. Unit of *force* in the *f.p.s. system*. That force which, acting on a *mass* of 1 *pound*, will impart to it an *acceleration* of 1 foot per second per second. Approximately 1/32 of a force of 1 pound weight.

POWDER METALLURGY. The science or practice of manufacturing

small *metal* articles by sintering powdered metals under *heat* and *pressure*.

POWER (math.). A quantity successively multiplied by itself is said to be raised to a power, the magnitude of the power being the number of times that the quantity occurs in the multiplication. Thus $2 \times 2 \times 2 \times 2$ is 2 raised to the fourth power, 2 to the fourth, denoted as 2^4, 4 being the *index* or *exponent*.

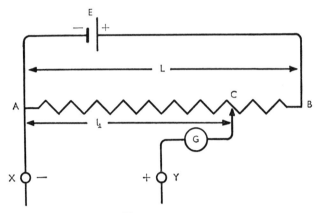

FIGURE 34.

POWER (phys.). Rate of doing *work*. Measured in units of work per unit time. The derived *SI unit* of power is the *watt*. See also *horsepower*.

POWER ALCOHOL. Industrial *ethanol* used as a *fuel*.

POWER FACTOR. In an electrical *circuit*, the ratio of the *power* dissipated, P, to the product of the *electromotive force*, E, and the *current*, I. In single-phase and three-phase circuits the power factor is given by cos ϕ, where ϕ is the *phase angle* between the E.M.F. and the current, i.e. $P = EI$ cos ϕ.

POWER REACTOR. See *nuclear reactor*.

PRASEODYMIUM. Pr. Element. A.W. 140·907. At. No. 59. S.G. 6·78, m.p. 935°C. See *lanthanides*.

PRECESSIONAL MOTION. A rotating body is said to precess when, as a result of an applied *couple*, the *axis* of which is at right angles to the rotation axis, the body turns about the third mutually perpendicular axis.

PRECIPITATE (chem.). An *insoluble* substance formed in a *solution* as the result of a *chemical reaction*.

PRECIPITATION (chem.). The formation of a *precipitate*. A common type of precipitation, much used in chemical analysis and preparations, occurs by *double decomposition* when two *solutions* are mixed if each of the solutions contains one *radical* of an *insoluble compound*.

PRESBYOPIA. Long sight. A defect of vision normally occurring in elderly people. Subject is able to see distant objects clearly, but is unable to accommodate the eye to see near objects distinctly. Corrected by the use of *convex* spectacle *lenses*.

PRESSURE. The *force* per unit *area* acting on a surface. 'Absolute pressure' is the pressure measured with respect to zero pressure. 'Gauge pressure' is the pressure measured by a gauge in excess of the pressure of the *atmosphere*. The *SI unit* of pressure is the *newton* per square *metre*, sometimes called the *pascal*. The *c.g.s. system* uses the *dyne* per square centimetre (1 Nm^{-2} = 10 dynes cm^{-2}). Other units are the *bar* ($= 10^5$ Nm^{-2}), the *atmosphere* ($= 101\ 325$ Nm^{-2}), the mm Hg ($= 133 \cdot 322$ Nm^{-2}). See also Table I, page 429

PRESSURIZED WATER REACTOR. PWR. A *nuclear reactor* in which *water* is the coolant and the *moderator*, but in which the water is maintained at a high *pressure* in order to prevent it *boiling*. The pressurized water is passed through a *heat exchanger* to generate *steam* which may be used for producing *electric power* in a conventional *turbo-generator*.

PRIMARY CELL. Voltaic cell. A device, usually irreversible, for producing an *electromotive force* and delivering an *electric current* as the result of a *chemical reaction*. See *Daniell cell, Leclanché cell, Weston cell, Mercury cell*.

PRIMARY COIL. The input coil of a *transformer* or *induction coil*.

PRIMARY COLOURS (phys.). Red, green, and a bluish-violet. Any *colour* may be obtained by suitably combining *light* producing these (see *colour vision*). Also the *pigment colours* red, yellow, and blue, which cannot be imitated by mixing any other pigment colours.

PRIME NUMBER (math.). A number possessing no *factors* (i.e. divisible by no whole number, other than itself and one).

PRINCIPAL AXIS. See *optical axis*.

PRINCIPAL FOCUS. See *mirrors, spherical; lens*.

PRINCIPAL PLANE (phys.). In a *crystal* exhibiting *double refraction*, a principal plane is a *plane* containing the *optic axis* and either the *ordinary ray* (principal plane of ordinary ray) or the *extraordinary ray* (principal plane of extraordinary ray).

PRINCIPAL POINTS (phys.). Two points on the *optical axis* of a thick *lens* or combination lens system, such that if the object distance is measured from one and the image distance from the other, the *equations* obtained relating object-image distance, etc., are similar to those obtained for a thin lens.

PRINCIPAL SECTION (phys.). A principal section of a *crystal* exhibiting *double refraction* is a *plane* passing through the *optic axis* and at right angles to one of the crystal surfaces.

PRINCIPLE OF SUPERPOSITION. See *Huygens' principle of superposition*.

PRINTED CIRCUIT. An *electronic circuit* in which the wiring between components, and certain fixed components themselves, are printed on to an insulating board. The board is coated with copper and the portion of the metal which represents the wiring or components is photographically covered with a protective film, the rest of the metal being etched away in an *acid* bath.

PRISM (math.). A solid figure having two identically equal faces (bases) consisting of *polygons* in parallel *planes*; the other faces being *parallelograms* equal in number to the number of sides of one of the bases.

PRISM, OPTICAL. A triangular *prism* made of material *transparent* to the *light* being used; e.g. *glass* for visible light, *quartz* for *ultraviolet* and near *infrared radiation*.

PRISMATIC. In the shape of a *prism*.

PRISMATIC OPTICAL INSTRUMENTS. Instruments (field-glasses, etc.) in which a right-angled *prism* is used to invert the inverted image produced by the *objective*.

PROBABILITY DISTRIBUTION OF ELECTRONS. The *probability* that an *electron* within an *atom* will be at a certain point in *space* at a given time; determined by the magnitude of the square of the *wave function*.

PROBABILITY, MATHEMATICAL. If an event can happen in a ways and fail in b ways, and, except for the numerical difference between a and b, is as likely to happen as to fail, the mathematical probability of its happening is $\dfrac{a}{a+b}$ and of its failing, $\dfrac{b}{a+b}$.

PROCESS CONTROL. The control of complex industrial or chemical processes by *electronic* means.

PRODUCER GAS. A *fuel gas* produced by the partial *combustion* of *coke* or *coal* in a restricted supply of air, to which *steam* may have been added. The principal constituents of the gas are *carbon monoxide* (25%–30%), nitrogen (50%–55%), and hydrogen (10%–15%). *Hydrocarbons* and *carbon dioxide* will also be present.

PRODUCT (math.). The product of two or more quantities is the result of multiplying them together.

PRODUCTION REACTOR. See *nuclear reactor*.

PROGESTERONE. $C_{21}H_{30}O_2$. A white crystalline *steroid hormone*, m.p. 128·5° C., responsible for preparing the reproductive organs of mammals for pregnancy and for protecting the embryo.

PROGRAM. Programme. The sequence of instructions fed into a *computer* in order to enable it to carry out a process.

PROJECTILE. A body which is thrown or projected. If the projectile is discharged with a *velocity v* at an *angle a* to the horizontal, the following formulae hold true if the resistance of the air is neglected (g being the *acceleration due to gravity*):

Time to reach highest point of flight $= \dfrac{v \sin a}{g}$

Total time of flight $= \dfrac{2v \sin a}{g}$

Maximum height $= \dfrac{v^2 \sin^2 a}{2g}$

Horizontal range $= \dfrac{v^2 \sin 2a}{g}$

PROLATE SPHEROID. See *spheroid*.

PROLINE. A white, crystalline *amino acid*, m.p. 220°C., which occurs in most *proteins*. See Table 5, page 435.

PROMETHIUM. Pm. A *radioactive element* of the *lanthanide* series. At. No. 61. M.p. 1035°C., b.p. 2460°C. Occurs as a fission product of uranium in *nuclear reactors*. The most stable *isotope*, $^{145}_{61}$Pm, has a *half-life* of about eighteen years.

PROMPT CRITICAL. Capable of sustaining a *nuclear fission chain reaction* on the *prompt neutrons* alone, without contribution from *delayed neutrons*.

PROMPT NEUTRONS. *Neutrons* resulting from *nuclear fission* (either during the fission process or from freshly formed fission fragments) which are emitted without measurable delay, i.e. in less than a millionth of a second. See *delayed neutrons*.

PROOF SPIRIT. *Ethanol* containing 49·28% alcohol by *weight*, or 57·10% by *volume*, and having a *specific gravity* of 0·91976 at 60°F. Formerly defined as the weakest solution of alcohol which would fire *gunpowder* when brought into contact with it and ignited.

PROOF SPIRIT, DEGREES. The number of degrees under proof is the *volume* percentage of *water* in a *solution* regarded as containing *proof spirit* and water; degrees over proof is the volume increase obtained when 100 volumes of the spirit are diluted with sufficient water to obtain proof spirit. Spirits are usually sold on the basis, '30° under proof' or '70° proof' both of which mean the same. Such spirit contains $57·1 \times 70/100 = 39·97\%$ alcohol by volume.

PROPANE. C_3H_8. The third *hydrocarbon* of the *paraffin series*. An inflammable *gas*. B.p. −42·17°C. Used as a *fuel*.

PROPANOL. Propyl alcohol. Two *isomeric liquid alcohols* used as *solvents*. Propan-1-ol (n-propyl alcohol), $CH_3CH_2CH_2OH$, has b.p. 97·1°C.; propan-2-ol (iso-propyl alcohol), $CH_3CHOHCH_3$, has b.p. 82·4°C.

PROPELLANT. 1. The explosive substance used to fill cartridges, shell cases, and *solid fuel rockets*. The term is also used to include the fuel and *oxidant* of rockets when these are separate. 2. A *gas* used in *aerosol* preparations to expel the *liquid* contents through an atomizer.

PROPENE. Propylene. $CH_2:CH.CH_3$. The second member of the *olefine* series of *hydrocarbons*. A colourless *gas*, b.p. −47°C. See also *polypropylene*.

PROPER FRACTION. A fraction in which the *numerator* is less than the *denominator*, e.g. $\frac{3}{4}$. In an 'improper fraction' the numerator is greater than the denominator, e.g. $\frac{4}{3}$.

PROPER MOTION OF A STAR. The component of a *star's* motion in *space* relative to the *Sun* that is perpendicular to the line of sight.

PROPIONALDEHYDE. Propanal. Propyl aldehyde. CH_3CH_2CHO. A colourless *liquid aldehyde*, b.p. 48·8°C., used in the manufacture of *plastics*.

PROPORTION (math.). An equality between two *ratios*. If $a/b = c/d$, the four quantities, a, b, c, d are in proportion.

PROPULSION REACTOR. See *nuclear reactor*.

PROPYL GROUP. The *univalent alkyl radical* C_3H_7—.

PROPYLENE. See *propene*.

PROSTHETIC GROUP. A non-*protein* group which is combined to a protein, e.g. the haem group in *haemoglobin* or the *nucleic acid* in *nucleoprotein*.

PROTARGOL. A powder containing finely divided silver and *protein*; with *water*, it forms a *colloidal solution* of silver.

PROTEASES. Proteinases. A group of *enzymes* capable of breaking up *proteins* into *amino acids*, of building up amino acids into proteins, and of substituting one amino acid for another in protein *molecules*. Occurring in all living tissues, they conduct the processes of protein *metabolism* in the living *organism*.

PROTEINS. A class of complex nitrogenous *organic compounds* of high *molecular weight* (18 000–10 000 000) which are of great importance to all living matter. Protein *molecules* consist of hundreds or thousands of *amino acids* joined together by the *peptide* linkage into one or more inter-linked *polypeptide* chains, which may be folded in a variety of different ways. Some twenty different amino acids occur in proteins and each protein molecule is likely to contain all of them arranged in a variety of sequences. It is the sequence of the different amino acids which give individual proteins their specific properties. The particular sequence of the amino acids in proteins, which are synthesized in the *cytoplasms* of *cells*, is determined by the sequence of the *nucleotides* in the *nucleic acids* of the *chromosomes*, three nucleotides coding for each amino acid. Most proteins form *colloidal solutions* in water or dilute *salt* solutions, but some (notably the fibrous proteins) are *insoluble*. Proteins may be simple, i.e. yielding only amino acids on *hydrolysis*, others are 'conjugated', i.e. combined with other substances (see *prosthetic groups*). *Enzymes* are a particularly important group of proteins as they determine the *chemical reactions* which will take place in a cell, and therefore the characteristics which it will have.

PROTEOLYTIC. Proteoclastic. Having the power of decomposing or *hydrolyzing proteins*.

PROTIUM. The hydrogen *isotope* with *mass number* of one.

PROT(O)ACTINIUM. Pa. *Radioactive* element. At. No. 91. The most abundant natural *isotope*; has a *mass number* of 231 and a *half-life* of 32 480 years.

PROTON. A stable *elementary particle* with *electric charge* equal in magnitude to that of the *electron* but of opposite sign, and with *mass* 1836·12 times greater than that of the electron (i.e. 1·00727663 *atomic mass units* or $1·67252 \times 10^{-27}$ *kilogramme*). The proton is a *hydrogen ion* (i.e. a normal hydrogen atomic *nucleus*) and is a constituent of all other atomic nuclei. See *atom, structure of*.

PROTON NUMBER. See *atomic number*.

PROTOPLASM. The *matter* of which biological *cells* consist. Usually divided into two parts, the *cytoplasm* and the *nucleus*.

PROTOSTAR. A developing *star* consisting of condensing interstellar *gas* and dust.

PRUSSIAN BLUE. Potassium *ferric* ferrocyanide, $KFe[Fe(CN)_6]$. A deep blue substance obtained by the action of a ferric *salt* on *potassium ferrocyanide*.

PRUSSIC ACID. An intensely poisonous solution of *hydrocyanic acid*, HCN.

PSEUDO-SCALAR. A *scalar quantity* which changes sign in the transition from a right-handed to a left-handed system of coordinates.

PSEUDO-VECTOR. Axial vector. A *vector* quantity which changes sign in the transition from a right-handed to a left-handed system of co-ordinates.

PSYCHROMETRY. The measurement of the *humidity of the atmosphere*.

PTOMAINES. A class of extremely poisonous *organic compounds* formed during the putrefaction of *proteins* of animal origin. Food poisoning, frequently misnamed ptomaine poisoning, is almost invariably due to causes other than the ptomaines.

PTYALIN. An *enzyme* which occurs in the saliva and serves to convert *starch* into *sugar*.

P-TYPE CONDUCTIVITY. See *N-type conductivity*.

PUDDLING PROCESS. The preparation of nearly pure *wrought iron* from *cast iron* which contains a high percentage of carbon. The cast iron is heated with *haematite*, Fe_2O_3, the oxygen in which oxidizes the carbon.

PULSARS. Pulsating stars. *Stars* which emit *radio frequency electromagnetic radiation* in brief *pulses* at extremely regular intervals. Many such objects have been located by *radio telescopes*, a few of them have also been observed to emit pulses of light. It has been suggested that pulsars are *neutron stars*, emitting pulses of radiation as they rotate.

PULSE. A brief increase in the magnitude of a quantity whose value is usually constant (e.g. *current* or *voltage*).

PULSE HEIGHT ANALYSER. An instrument incorporating an *electronic* circuit which permits only *voltage pulses* of predetermined *amplitudes* to be passed to succeeding circuits. The range of amplitudes which are passed through such circuits is referred to as the 'channel width' or 'window'. In a single-channel analyser the channel width is usually pre-set and the *threshold* varied to scan the amplitude spectrum of in-coming pulses. In a multi-channel instrument, often called a 'kick-sorter', the incoming pulses are sorted and recorded according to their amplitudes. The kicksorter is used for distinguishing between *isotopes* by sorting the characteristic 'kicks' which their *radiations* give.

PULSE-JET. A type of *ram-jet* in which the *combustion* process is not con-tinuous, but is arranged to occur at intervals between which the *pres-sure* in the combustion chamber is allowed to build up. The German 'flying bombs' of World War II were powered by pulse-jets fitted with air intake valves which opened when the pressure resulting from the passage of the projectile through the air exceeded the pressure in the combustion chamber: each new charge being separately fired.

PURINE. $C_5H_4N_4$. A white crystalline *organic base*, m.p. 216°C., related to *uric acid*. *Derivatives* are of great importance biologically as they occur in *adenosine triphosphate* and *nucleic acids*. *Adenine* and *guanine* are typical purines.

PURPLE OF CASSIUS. A purple *pigment*, consisting of a *mixture* of colloidal gold and *stannic acid*. Used for making ruby *glass*.

PUSH-PULL. A term used to describe an *electronic circuit* in which two components are out of phase by 180°. E.g. a push-pull *amplifier* has two *valves* arranged so that the *control grid* input signals are 180° out of phase, the output circuits being arranged to combine the two signals so that they are in phase.

PUTREFACTION. Chemical *decomposition*, by the action of *bacteria*, of the bodies of dead animals and plants; especially the *decomposition* of *proteins* with the production of offensive substances.

PUTTY. A material composed of powdered *chalk* mixed with *linseed oil*.

PUTTY POWDER. Impure tin oxide, SnO_2.

PYKNOMETER. An apparatus for determining the *density* and coefficient of *expansion* of a *liquid*. A glass vessel which is graduated to hold a definite *volume* of liquid at a given *temperature*. By weighing it full of liquid at different temperatures, the variations in density, and therefore the apparent expansion, may be found.

PYRAMID (math.). A solid figure having a *polygon* for one of its faces (termed the base), the other faces being *triangles* with a common *vertex*. The *volume* of a pyramid is one-third of the *product* of the area of the base and the vertical height.

PYRENE. 1. $C_{16}H_{10}$. A yellow, crystalline *hydrocarbon*, m.p. 149°C., found in *coal-tar*. 2. Trade name for a *fire extinguisher* consisting of *carbon tetrachloride*, CCl_4.

PYREX*. A type of *glass* which is resistant to heat and chemical attack; widely used in laboratory glassware.

PYRIDINE. C_5H_5N. A colourless *heterocyclic liquid* with an unpleasant smell. B.p. 115°C. Occurs in *bone-oil* and *coal-tar*. Used for making *methylated spirit* unpalatable; *compounds* derived from it are used in medicine.

PYRIDOXINE. Vitamin B_6. $C_8H_{11}NO_3$. A *pyridine derivative* which is a member of the *vitamin* B complex; believed to be of importance in the utilization of *unsaturated fatty acids* by many *organisms*.

PYRIMIDINE. $C_4H_4N_2$. An *organic base*, m.p. 22°C., b.p. 123·5°C., consisting of a *heterocyclic* six-membered ring. *Derivatives* are of great biological importance as they occur in *nucleic acids*. *Uracil*, *thymine*, and *cytosine* are typical pyrimidines.

PYRITES. Natural *sulphides* of certain *metals*. Iron pyrites is FeS_2; copper pyrites ('fools' gold') is $CuFeS_2$.

PYRO-. Prefix denoting fire, strong heat. In chemical nomenclature denotes a substance obtained by heating; e.g. pyroboric acid, obtained by heating *boric acid*. Also used to indicate that the *water* content of an *acid* or *salt* is intermediate between that of the *ortho-* and *meta- compounds* of the same name.

PYRO-ELECTRICITY. The property of certain *crystals*, e.g. *tourmaline*, of acquiring *electric charges* on opposite faces when the crystals are heated.

PYROGALLOL. Pyrogallic acid, 1, 2, 3-trihydroxybenzene. $C_6H_3(OH)_3$. A white crystalline *soluble solid*, m.p. 132°C., which is a powerful *reducing agent*; *alkaline solution* rapidly absorbs oxygen. Used in photographic *developing* and in gas analysis for the estimation of oxygen. See *Orsat apparatus*.

PYROLIGNEOUS ACID. A watery *liquid* obtained by the *destructive distillation* of wood. Contains *acetic acid*, CH_3COOH, *methanol*, CH_3OH, *acetone* $(CH_3)_2CO$, and small amounts of other *organic compounds*.

PYROLUSITE. Natural *manganese dioxide*, MnO_2. A black crystalline *solid*, S.G. 4·8; the principal *ore* of manganese.

PYROLYSIS. Chemical *decomposition* by the action of *heat*.

PYROMETERS. Instruments for measuring high *temperatures*. The four main types are: (1) platinum resistance *thermometers*, which make use of the increased electrical *resistance* of platinum wire with rise in temperature; (2) thermo-electric thermometers, using the principle of the *thermocouple*; (3) optical pyrometers, in which the temperature is estimated by the intensity of the *light* emitted by the body in a narrow *wavelength* range; and (4) *radiation* pyrometers, which detect the *heat* radiation from the hot body (see *radiomicrometer*).

PYROPHORIC ALLOYS. *Alloys* which emit sparks when scraped or struck, and are therefore used as 'flints' in lighters. See *misch metal; Auer metal*.

PYROPHOSPHORIC ACID. $H_4P_2O_7$. A crystalline *soluble* substance, m.p. 61°C., formed from *phosphorus pentoxide* and two *molecules* of *water*.

PYROSULPHURIC ACID. See *oleum*.

PYROTECHNICS. Fireworks.

PYROXINE. A group of *minerals* consisting principally of *silicates* of magnesium, iron, and calcium.

PYRUVIC ACID. $CH_3.CO.COOH$. A *liquid organic acid*, m.p. 13°C., of importance in the metabolic (see *metabolism*) breakdown of *glucose*. Pyruvic acid is itself broken down in the *citric acid cycle*.

PYTHAGORAS, THEOREM OF. In a right-angled *triangle* the square on the *hypotenuse* is equal to the sum of the squares on the other two sides. Named after the Greek mathematician (*c.* 582–500 B.C.).

Q

Q-VALUE. Nuclear energy change, nuclear heat of reaction. The net amount of *energy* released in a *nuclear reaction*; usually expressed in million *electron-volts*, *MeV*, per individual reaction.

Q.S.G. Quasi stellar galaxy. A *quasar* which is not a radio source.

QUADRANT. Quarter-circle. A *sector* of a *circle* bounded by an arc and two radii at right angles.

QUADRATIC EQUATION. An *equation* involving the *square* or second *power* of the unknown quantity; satisfied by two values (known as *roots*) of the unknown quantity. Any quadratic equation may be written in the form $ax^2 + bx + c = 0$; the roots of this equation are given by the expression $x = \dfrac{-b \pm \sqrt{b^2 - 4ac}}{2a}$. The sum of the roots is $\dfrac{-b}{a}$ and their product is $\dfrac{c}{a}$.

Thus any quadratic equation may be solved by substitution of the appropriate values in the above expressions.

QUADRATURE. The position of the *Moon* or outer *planet* such that a line between it and the *Earth* makes a right angle with a line joining the Earth to the *Sun*.

QUADRILATERAL. A *plane* figure bounded by four straight lines.

QUADRIVALENT. Tetravalent. Having a *valency* of four.

QUALITATIVE. Dealing only with the nature, and not the amounts, of the substances under consideration.

QUALITATIVE CHEMICAL ANALYSIS. The determination of the chemical nature of substances; identification of substances present in a *mixture*.

QUALITY CONTROL. The application of the theory of mathematical *probability* to sampling the output of an industrial process, with the object of detecting and controlling any variations in quality.

QUALITY OF SOUND. Most sounds are not 'pure'; i.e. they are composed of vibrations of more than one *frequency*. A note consists of a 'fundamental', of greatest intensity and lowest *pitch*; and several *overtones*, of much lesser intensity and of frequencies which are simple multiples of that of the fundamental. The various overtones produce a characteristic quality or timbre in the note.

QUANTITATIVE. Dealing with quantities as well as the nature of the substances under consideration.

QUANTITATIVE CHEMICAL ANALYSIS. The determination of the amounts of substances present, by chemical means.

QUANTIZED. A quantity is said to be quantized if, in accordance with *quantum mechanics*, it can only have certain discrete values (each of which is called a *quantum*). Such a quantity cannot vary continuously, differences in value being separated by 'jumps'.

QUANTUM. According to the *quantum theory*, *energy* exists in discrete units, only whole numbers of which can exist: each unit is called a quantum (plural 'quanta'). The quantum of *electromagnetic radiation* is the *photon*; in certain contexts the quantum of energy associated with *nuclear forces* may be taken as the *meson*.

QUANTUM ELECTRONICS. The study of the generation or amplification of *microwave power* in *solid crystals*, in accordance with the laws of *quantum mechanics*.

QUANTUM MECHANICS. The system of mechanics which, during the present century, has replaced *Newtonian mechanics* as a method of interpreting physical phenomena occurring on a very small scale (e.g. the motion of *electrons* and *nuclei* within *atoms*; see *atom, structure of*). Quantum theory originated with the discovery by Max Planck that the *heat radiation* from a black-body (see *black-body radiation*) is *quantized*, i.e. emitted in discrete *quanta* of *energy*, the magnitudes of which are given by the product of the *frequency* of the radiation and a universal constant, now known as *Planck's constant*. It was soon realized that all *electromagnetic radiations* are quantized (see *photon*) and the theory was developed by Niels Bohr so that the *spectrum* of hydrogen could be accounted for *quantitatively* (see *Bohr theory*). This early version of quantum mechanics was refined by Sommerfeld to take into account the elliptical *orbits* of electrons. More recently quantum mechanics has been developed in a specialized form, known as *wave mechanics*, which is more versatile and involves fewer arbitrary assumptions than the original theory.

QUANTUM NUMBERS. *Integral* or half-integral numbers which specify the state of a system or its components in *quantum mechanics*. An *electron* within an *atom* is specified by four quantum numbers: (1) the principal quantum number, n, defining the *energy level* or *shell* in which the electron occurs; (2) the azimuthal quantum number, l, defining the shape and multiplicity of the orbit within that shell; (3) the magnetic orbital quantum number, m_l, which determines the orientation of the orbit with reference to a strong magnetic field; and (4) the magnetic *spin* quantum number, m_s, which determines the direction of spin of an electron in a magnetic field. See also *Pauli's exclusion principle*.

QUANTUM THEORY. The theory which grew up around Planck's introduction into *physics* of the concept of the discontinuity of *energy*. The system of *quantum mechanics* evolved from this theory during the first half of the twentieth century.

QUARKS. Three hypothetical *elementary particles*, with three corresponding *antiparticles*, which have been postulated by Murray Gell-Mann as the basis of all *matter*. When *unitary symmetry* had provided a means of classifying the properties of most of the known 'elementary' particles, it was observed that different arrangements of only three truly fundamental particles could provide all the properties of all the others.

These properties, which include fractional *electric charge*, are given in the following table:

QUARK	ρ	η	λ	
CHARGE	2/3	$-1/3$	$-1/3$	(fractions of *electronic charge*)
STRANGENESS	0	0	-1	
SPIN	$\frac{1}{2}$	$\frac{1}{2}$	$\frac{1}{2}$	

The *masses* and lifetimes are uncertain. On this theory a *neutron* would consist of $\rho + 2\eta$; a *proton* would consist of $\eta + 2\rho$. No quarks have yet been identified with certainty.

QUART. Unit of capacity equal to one quarter of a *gallon*.

QUARTER-WAVE PLATE. A plate of doubly refracting material (see *double refraction*) cut parallel to the *optic axis* of the *crystal*, and of such a thickness that a *phase* difference of $\pi/2$ or $90°$ is introduced between the *ordinary* and *extraordinary rays* for *light* of a particular *wavelength* (usually sodium light). Plane-polarized light (see *polarization* of *light*) incident normally upon such a plate, with its plane of vibration making an angle of $45°$ with the optic axis, emerges from the plate *circularly polarized*. A quarter-wave plate is often used in the analysis of polarized light.

QUARTZ. Natural crystalline *silica*, SiO_2, which sometimes occurs in clear, colourless *crystals* (*rock crystal*); more frequently as a white, *opaque* mass. Quartz crystals exhibit the *piezo-electric effect* to a marked extent.

QUARTZ CLOCK. A clock regulated by a *quartz crystal* which vibrates with a definite constant *frequency* under the effect of an alternating *electric field* tuned to this *resonance* frequency of the crystal. (See *piezo-electric effect*.) Being much more accurate than a pendulum-regulated clock, it is used for astronomical and other very precise work.

QUASARS. Quasi stellar radio sources. Recently discovered extra-galactic sources of high energy *electromagnetic radiation*. Originally located by radio astronomers (see *radio astronomy*) because of their powerful *radio frequency* emissions. Several hundred of these objects have now been observed, some of them are also visible with *optical telescopes* as they emit *light*. If their observed *red-shifts* are interpreted as high *velocities* of recession, their enormous *energy* outputs cannot be explained by any known process.

QUATERNARY AMMONIUM COMPOUNDS. *Compounds* of the general formula NR_4OH; theoretically derived from *ammonium hydroxide*, NH_4OH, by replacement of the hydrogen *atoms* by *organic radicals*.

QUENCHING. The process of terminating the discharge in a *Geiger counter* by preventing re-ignition.

QUENCHING OF STEEL. Rapid cooling by immersion into *water* or *oil*, to harden the *steel*.

QUICKLIME. See *calcium oxide*, CaO.

QUICKSILVER. See *mercury*.

QUIET SUN. The *Sun's* condition when no *sunspots, solar flares* or *solar prominences* are taking place. *Radio frequency* emission (see *radio astronomy*) from the Sun, which has to be observed during the rare periods of the quiet Sun, has enabled temperature measurements of the various layers of the solar atmosphere to be made.

QUINHYDRONE. $C_6H_4O_2C_6H_4(OH)_2$. A green crystalline substance, m.p. 171°C.

QUINIDINE. $C_{20}H_{24}N_2O_2$. A colourless crystalline *alkaloid, isomeric* with *quinine*, m.p. 174–5°C., used in medicine.

QUININE. $C_{20}H_{24}O_2N_2.3H_2O$. A colourless bitter-tasting crystalline *alkaloid* which occurs in Cinchona bark, m.p. 57°C. Used in the treatment of malaria.

QUINOL. Hydroquinone. Para-dihydroxybenzene. $C_6H_4(OH)_2$. An *aromatic organic compound* obtained by the *reduction* of *quinone*; m.p. 170°C. Being a powerful *reducing agent*, it is widely used in photographic *developing*.

QUINOLINE. C_9H_7N. A colourless *liquid base*, b.p. 237°C., which occurs in *coal-tar*. Used as a *solvent* and in the manufacture of *dyes*.

QUINONES. *Aromatic organic compounds* containing a *benzene* ring in which two *atoms* of hydrogen are replaced by two atoms of oxygen. Quinones are used in *photography* and in *dye* manufacture, they are also widely distributed in plants. *Para*-quinone, or para-benzoquinone, $O:C_6H_4:O$ is a crystalline *solid*, m.p. 116°C., with a pungent odour.

QUINQUEVALENT. Pentavalent. Having a *valency* of five.

QUOTIENT. See *division*.

R

RACEMIC ACID. Racemic tartaric acid, *dl*-tartaric acid. The *racemic form* of *tartaric acid*.

RACEMIC FORM. An isomeric form of a substance which exhibits *stereoisomerism*. Consists of an *equimolecular mixture* of the two *optically active* forms. Such a racemic form is denoted by the letters *dl.*, e.g. *dl-tartaric acid*; it is optically inactive and is said to be externally compensated.

RAD. The unit of absorbed *dose* of *ionizing radiation*. One rad is equal to the *energy* absorption of 100 *ergs* per gram of *irradiated* material.

RADAR. An abbreviation of the words RAdio Detection And Ranging. A general term now used to include any system employing *microwaves* for the purpose of locating, identifying, navigating, or guiding such moving objects as ships, aircraft, missiles, or artificial *satellites*. The system consists essentially of a generator of *electromagnetic radiation* of centimetric *wavelengths*, the output of which is *pulse* modulated (see *modulation*) at a *radio frequency* and fed to a movable *aerial* whence it is radiated as a *beam*. Distant objects which cross the path of the beam reflect the pulses back to the transmitter, which also acts as a receiver. A *cathode-ray tube* indicator displays the received signal in the correct time sequence so that the time taken for a pulse to travel to the object and back can be measured. Thus the distance of the object from the transmitter can be calculated, and its direction can be ascertained from a knowledge of the direction of the aerial. This fundamental technique has been extended so that automatic guidance and navigation can be effected by *computers* without the necessity of a display.

RADIAL VELOCITY. See *line of sight velocity*.

RADIAN. The supplementary *SI unit* of plane *angle* defined as the angle subtended at the centre of a *circle* by an arc equal in length to the radius of the circle. 2π radians $= 360°$, 1 radian $= 57 \cdot 296°$. Symbol rad.

RADIANT ENERGY. *Energy* that is transmitted in the form of *radiation*, particularly *electromagnetic radiation*. Radiant energy is the only form in which energy can exist in the absence of *matter*.

RADIANT HEAT. See *infrared radiation*.

RADIATION. In general, the emission of any *rays*, *wave motion*, or particles (e.g. *alpha particles*, *beta particles*, *neutrons*) from a source; usually applied to the emission of *electromagnetic radiation*.

RADIATION BELTS. See *Van Allen radiation belts*.

RADIATION HAZARD. The potential danger to health resulting from exposure to *ionizing radiation* or the consumption of *radioactive* substances.

RADIATION POTENTIAL. Resonance potential. The *energy* (expressed in *electron-volts*) necessary to transfer an *electron* from its normal position in an *atom* to some other possible position; i.e. to an *energy level* of greater energy.

RADIATION SICKNESS. Illness caused by exposure to *ionizing radiation*. Initial symptoms are vomiting and diarrhoea, followed in some cases by leukaemia.

RADIATIVE CAPTURE. See *capture*.

RADIATIVE COLLISION. A collision between charged particles in which part of the *kinetic energy* is converted into *electromagnetic radiation*.

RADICAL. Radicle. 1. (chem.). A group of *atoms*, present in a series of *compounds*, which maintains its identity through chemical changes which affect the rest of the *molecule*, but which is usually incapable of independent existence. E.g. the *ammonium* radical, NH₄—; *ethyl group*, C_2H_5—. See also *free radical*. 2. (math.). Relating to a *root*. The symbol $\sqrt{}$ is called the 'radical sign'.

RADIO. The use of *electromagnetic radiation* to communicate electrical signals without wires ('wireless' transmission). In the widest sense the term incorporates sound broadcasting (including *radio telephony* and *radio telegraphy*), television, and *radar*. Transmission by radio involves a transmitter feeding a transmitting *aerial*, from which electromagnetic energy is broadcast, either as *ground waves* or *sky waves*, to a receiving aerial which feeds a receiver. The transmitter in sound broadcasting consists of a generator of a *radio frequency carrier wave* which is modulated (see *modulation*) in accordance with the *electric currents* provided by the amplified output of a *microphone*. The modulated carrier wave is fed to the transmitting aerial and if the receiving aerial is tuned to the *frequency* of the carrier wave (see *resonant circuit*) it will enable the receiver selectively to amplify and demodulate the transmitted signal. *Demodulation* is achieved by *rectification* of the signal by a *thermionic valve* or *transistor*. In this way a current is produced in the output stage of the receiver which varies in *amplitude* in accordance with the frequency of the sound wave fed to the microphone at the transmitter. This current may then be used to operate a loudspeaker which reproduces the original sound.

RADIO-. See *radioactive*.

RADIO ASTRONOMY. The study of heavenly bodies by the reception and analysis of the *radio frequency electromagnetic radiation* which they emit or reflect. In general, electromagnetic radiations from extra-terrestrial sources are either absorbed by the Earth's *atmosphere* or reflected away from the Earth by the *ionosphere*. The two exceptions, which allow us to experience the rest of the *Universe*, are the optical *wavelengths* which are able to penetrate the atmosphere, and the radio wavelengths in the band 1 cm–10 *metres* which are too long to be absorbed by the atmosphere and too short to be reflected by the ionosphere. The radiations which pass through this 'radio window' onto the Universe come from a variety of sources, ranging from objects within the *solar system* (e.g. the *Sun* and the *planet Jupiter*) to *galaxies* which are too distant to be observed by *optical telescopes*. In general radio frequency emission may be due to thermal, or non-thermal causes: emission from the *quiet Sun* is of thermal origin for example, whereas the radiation from *sunspots* is of unexplained non-thermal origin. The method by which radio astronomy attempts to make sense out of the apparently incoherent radio 'noise' from the Universe, is to construct maps of the sky in terms of radio emission, at several different *frequencies*. The intensities of the sources thus located are then compared with optical observations. In this way *radio sources* and *radio galaxies* have been identified. See also *radio telescope*.

RADIO-FREQUENCY. The *frequency* of an *electromagnetic radiation* which falls within the range used in *radio*, i.e. 10 *kilohertz* to 100 000 *megahertz*.

RADIO FREQUENCY HEATING. A general term which includes industrial *induction* or *dielectric heating*, particularly when the *frequency* of the alternating field is above about 25 *kilohertz*.

RADIO-FREQUENCY WELDING. See *high frequency welding*.

RADIO GALAXIES. *Galaxies* which emit *electromagnetic radiation* of *radio frequencies* as observed by the techniques of *radio astronomy*. The exact source of this galactic radiation is not always understood, but radiation has been received from galaxies which have been observed optically to be in collision. See also *radio sources, quasars, pulsars*, and *synchrotron radiation*.

RADIO INTERFEROMETER. A type of *radio telescope* which consists of two or more separate *aerials*, each receiving *electromagnetic radiation* of *radio frequencies* from the same source, and each joined to the same receiver. The instrument works on the same principle as the optical *interferometer*, but as the *wavelengths* of the incident radiation are much greater, the distance between aerials has to be correspondingly increased. The chief advantage of radio interferometers, over single aerial *parabolic reflectors*, is that they can be made more sensitive to radiation from sources of small angular diameter. See also *radio astronomy*.

RADIO SOURCE. Formerly known as a 'radio star', a term which is no longer used. A discrete source of *electromagnetic radiation* of *radio frequencies* outside the *solar system*. Such sources have been discovered by the techniques of *radio astronomy*, both within the *Galaxy* and outside it, but only a small number have been identified with *stars* which can be located with *optical telescopes*. Other sources are *supernovae* explosions and remnants, colliding *galaxies* and gas clouds, *quasars*, and *pulsars*; some sources, however, remain unexplained.

RADIO STAR. See *radio source*.

RADIO TELEGRAPHY. The transmission of coded messages (e.g. in Morse code) by *radio*.

RADIO TELEPHONY. The use of *radio*, rather than wires or cables, for all or part of a *telephone* system.

RADIO TELESCOPE. An instrument used in *radio astronomy* to pick up and analyse the *radio frequency electromagnetic radiations* of extra-terrestrial sources. The two principal types of radio telescope are: (1) *parabolic reflectors*, which are usually steerable so that they can be pointed at any part of the sky, and which reflect the incoming radiation on to a small *aerial* at the *focus* of the *paraboloid*; and (2) fixed *radio interferometers*. The latter have greater position-finding accuracy and greater ability to distinguish a small source against an intense background, while the former are more versatile owing to their mobility.

RADIO WINDOW. See *radio astronomy*.

RADIOACTIVE. Possessing, or pertaining to, *radioactivity*. Sometimes only the prefix 'radio-' is used to describe radioactive *nuclides* or the substances containing them, e.g. radiocarbon is an abbreviation for radioactive carbon.

RADIOACTIVE AGE. The age of a *mineral, fossil,* or wooden object as estimated from its content of *radioisotopes*. This method assumes that the content of *radioisotopes* has remained unchanged except for radioactive *decay*. See also *dating* and *radiocarbon dating*.

RADIOACTIVE EQUILIBRIUM. A state ultimately reached when a *radioactive* substance of slow *decay* (see *radioactivity*) yields a radioactive product on *disintegration*. This product may also decay to give a further radioactive substance, and so on. The amount of any of the daughter radioactive products present after equilibrium has been reached remains constant, the loss due to decay being counterbalanced by gain from the decay of the immediate parent.

RADIOACTIVE SERIES. Radioactive family. A series of *radioisotopes*, each except the first being the *decay* product of the previous one. The final member of the series, usually an isotope of lead, is stable. See *radioactivity*.

RADIOACTIVE STANDARD. A specimen of a material containing a *radioisotope* of precisely known rate of *decay*, which is used for the calibration of instruments measuring *radiation*.

RADIOACTIVE TRACING. Any two *isotopes* of an *element* are chemically identical. Thus, by introducing a small amount of a *radioisotope*, called a tracer, the course taken by the stable isotope of the same element can be followed or traced by detecting the course of the accompanying *radioisotope* by suitable means. This can be done in various ways; e.g. *Geiger counter*. See *labelled compound*.

RADIOACTIVITY. The property of spontaneous *disintegration* possessed by certain unstable types of atomic *nuclei*. The disintegration is accompanied by the emission of either *alpha-* or *beta-particles* and/or *gamma rays*. The most common type of disintegration involves beta-particle emission and occurs either: (1) when a *neutron* present in the unstable nucleus is converted into a *proton* with the emission of an *electron* and an anti-*neutrino*, or more rarely (2) when a proton is converted into a neutron with the emission of a *positron* and a neutrino. These *beta transformations* are accompanied by unit change of *atomic number* but no change in *mass number*. Alpha particles are only emitted by certain *radioisotopes* of the heavier *elements*; when this occurs the atomic number of the daughter nucleus is two less than that of the parent and its mass number is reduced by four units. Gamma-ray emission accompanies alpha or beta emission when the daughter nucleus is formed in an excited state (see *excitation*).

Natural radioactivity is due to the disintegration of naturally occurring *radioisotopes*, which may be arranged in three *radioactive series*. The rate at which *radioisotopes* disintegrate is uninfluenced by any chemical changes, any normal changes of *temperature* or *pressure*, or by the effects of *electric* or *magnetic fields*. However 'induced' or 'artificial' *radioisotopes* of most elements can be formed by bombardment with particles (e.g. neutrons) or *photons* in a *nuclear reactor* or *accelerator*.

Radiations emitted by *radioisotopes* are used in the treatment of disease (see *radiotherapy*) and in *radioactive tracing*.

RADIOBIOLOGY. The branch of *biology* which is concerned with the effects of *radiation* on living *organisms* and the behaviour of *radioactive* materials, or the use of *radioactive tracing*, in biological systems.

RADIOCARBON DATING. The estimation of the age of wooden archaeological objects by measuring their content of the *radioisotope* of carbon, $^{14}_{6}C$. The impact of *cosmic rays* on the Earth's *atmosphere* causes a very small proportion of nitrogen *atoms* to transform into $^{14}_{6}C$ atoms. Some of these radioactive carbon atoms find their way, via *carbon dioxide* and *photosynthesis*, into living trees. When a tree is cut down, however, it ceases to acquire further $^{14}_{6}C$ atoms. Therefore by comparing the *radioactivity* of a modern piece of wood with that of a specimen of unknown age, the length of time that has elapsed since the latter ceased to be living can be estimated (provided that it is not more than about 6000 years). This method has been checked by comparison with specimens of wood of known age from the tombs of the Pharaohs and has been found to be fairly reliable.

RADIOCHEMISTRY. The study and application of chemical techniques to the purification of *radioactive* materials, and the formation of *compounds* containing radioactive *elements*.

RADIODIAGNOSIS. The branch of medical *radiology* which is concerned with the application of *X-rays* to diagnosis.

RADIOGENIC. Resulting from *radioactive decay*.

RADIOGRAPH. A photographic record of an image produced by short *wavelength radiation*, such as *X-rays* and *gamma rays*.

RADIOGRAPHY. The formation of images on *fluorescent* screens or photographic material by short *wavelength radiation*, such as *X-rays* and *gamma rays*.

RADIOISOTOPE. An *isotope* of an *element* which is *radioactive*.

RADIOLOCATION. The location of distant objects, such as ships or aircraft, by *radar*.

RADIOLOGY. The science of *X-rays* and *radioactivity*, including *radiodiagnosis* and *radiotherapy*.

RADIOLUCENT. Almost *transparent* to *radiation*, especially *X-rays* and *gamma rays*, but not entirely so. An object or material which allows these radiations to pass with little or no alteration is said to be 'radio-transparent'. Objects and materials which are *opaque* to them are said to be 'radio-opaque'.

RADIOLYSIS. The chemical *decomposition* of substances as a result of *irradiation*.

RADIOMICROMETER. An extremely sensitive instrument for measuring *heat radiations*. Consists of a *thermocouple* connected directly into a single copper loop forming the coil of a sensitive *galvanometer*.

RADIONUCLIDE. A *nuclide* of an *atom* which is *radioactive*.

RADIO-OPAQUE. See *radiolucent*.

RADIOSONDE. A small balloon which is used to carry meteorological instruments into the *Earth's atmosphere*. Measurements of *temperature, pressure*, etc. are transmitted by these instruments back to Earth by *radio*.

RADIOTHERAPY. The treatment of disease by means of *radiation*, particularly *X-rays* and techniques involving *radioactivity*.

RADIOTRANSPARENT. See *radiolucent*.

RADIUM. Ra. Naturally occurring *radioactive element*. At. No. 88. The most stable *isotope*, $^{226}_{88}Ra$, has a *half-life* of 1620 years. Very rare *metal*, chemically resembling barium; m.p. 700°C., S.G. 5. See *radioactivity*.

RADIUM EMANATION. See *radon*.

RADIUS. See *circle*.

RADIUS OF CURVATURE. Consider any point P on a curve S lying in a *plane*. A *circle* can be drawn with centre at a unique point O on the *normal* to S at P, such that the curve and the circle are tangential at P. The radius of this circle, OP, is the radius of curvature of the curve at P. The concept may be extended to a point on a three-dimensional curved surface. In this case, an infinite number of radii of curvature exist, corresponding to the infinite number of plane curves which can form the line of intersection of the curved surface and the plane containing the normal at P. Of these curves, two are unique, one having a maximum radius of curvature at P and the other a minimum. These two are called the principal radii of curvature at P.

RADIUS OF GYRATION. The *moment of inertia I*, of a body of *mass m* about a given *axis* can be expressed in the form $I = mk^2$. k is called the radius of *gyration* about that axis.

RADIUS VECTOR (astr.). A line drawn from a central body (the focus) to a *planet* in any position in its *orbit*.

RADIUS VECTOR (math.). The position of any point P in space with respect to a given *origin O* may be completely defined by the direction and length of the line OP. This line is called the radius vector of the point P. See *polar coordinates*.

RADIX. A number which forms the *base* of a system of numbers, *logarithms*, etc., e.g. the radix of the *binary notation* is 2.

RADON. Rn. Radium emanation, niton. Element. At. No. 86. The most stable *isotope*, $^{222}_{86}Rn$, has a *half-life* of 3·825 days. Naturally occurring *radioactive* gas, the immediate *disintegration* product of radium; chemically belongs to the *inert gases*.

RAFFINATE. A *refined liquid*, especially an *oil* after its *soluble* components have been removed by *solvent extraction*.

RAFFINOSE. Melitose. $C_{18}H_{32}O_{16}.5H_2O$. A colourless crystalline *trisaccharide*, m.p. 80° C., which occurs in *beet sugar* but does not have a sweet flavour.

RAINBOW. A colour effect produced by the *refraction* and internal *reflection* of sunlight in minute droplets of *water* in the air; the effect is visible only when the observer has his back to the *Sun*.

RAM JET. Atherodyde, athodyd. A simple type of aerodynamic *reaction propulsion* system in which *thrust* is obtained by the *combustion* of *fuel* in air, compressed only by the forward *velocity* of the vehicle. A ram jet is also known as a 'flying drainpipe' as it consists essentially of a long duct into which fuel is fed at a controlled rate. However, the air intake and exhaust gas outlet need to be correctly designed in order to achieve maximum efficiency of the combustion process in that part of the duct which serves as a combustion chamber. The shape of the duct will depend upon whether or not the velocity of the vehicle is intended to be *supersonic*. See also *pulse-jet*.

RAMAN EFFECT. When *monochromatic light* passes through a *transparent* medium, some of the light is scattered. If the *spectrum* of this scattered light is examined, it is found to contain, apart from light of the original *wavelength*, weaker lines differing from this by constant amounts. Such lines are called Raman lines, and they are due to the loss or gain of *energy* experienced by the *photons* of light as a result of interaction with the vibrating *molecules* of the medium through which they pass. The Raman effect is therefore useful in the study of molecular *energy levels*. Named after Sir C. V. Raman (b. 1888).

RAMSDEN EYE-PIECE. An *eye-piece* consisting of two *plano-convex lenses* (curved surfaces inwards) of equal *focal length f*, and separated by a distance of $2/3f$. The eye-piece has low spherical *aberration*, is fairly *achromatic* and is very useful when cross-wires or a scale are desired in the eye-piece. Named after Jesse Ramsden (1735–1820).

RANDOM SAMPLE. A sample taken in such a way that every individual, object, or component comprising the group, set, or mass to be sampled, has an equal *probability* of forming part of the sample.

RANKINE TEMPERATURE.°R. The absolute *Fahrenheit scale*. Zero degrees Rankine is $-459.67°$F. and therefore $°F+459.67=°R.$ Named after W. J. M. Rankine (1820–70).

RAOULT'S LAW. When a *solute* which does not dissociate (see *ionic hypothesis*) in *solution* is dissolved in a *solvent* to form a *dilute* solution, then (1) the ratio of the decrease in *vapour pressure* to the original vapour pressure is equal to N_1/N_2, N_1 and N_2 being the total numbers of *molecules* present of solute and solvent respectively; or, alternatively (2) the *elevation of the boiling point* of the solution above that of the pure solvent is proportional to N_1/N_2; or (3) the *depression of the freezing point* of the solution below that of the pure solvent is proportional to N_1/N_2. Named after Francois Raoult (1830–1901).

RAPESEED OIL. See *colza oil*.

RARE EARTH ELEMENTS. See *lanthanides*.

RARE GASES. See *inert gases*.

RAREFACTION. A reduction in *pressure*. The opposite of compression.

RASTER. The pattern of lines which scan the fluorescent screen of a *cathode ray tube* in a *television* receiver.

RATIO. The numerical relation one quantity bears to another of the same kind. E.g. 6 tons and 4 tons, and 30 and 20, are both in the ratio of 3:2.

RATIONAL NUMBER. (math.). A whole number, or a number which can be expressed as the *ratio* of two whole numbers.

RAY. The *rectilinear* path along which any *radiation*, e.g. *light*, travels in any direction from a point in the source of the radiation. Loosely used to denote radiation of any kind.

RAYON. Formerly 'artificial silk', the term has been used to describe all types of man-made textile fibres, as distinct from those produced directly by plants (e.g. cotton) or animals (wool, silk). The use of the term 'rayon' to include fibres not made from *cellulose* and its derivatives has not, however, been universally accepted. The two most important types of rayon from cellulose are (1) *viscose* rayon, made by forcing a solution of viscose through fine holes into a *solution* which decomposes the viscose to give threads of cellulose, and (2) *cellulose acetate* rayon, made by forcing a solution of cellulose acetate through fine holes into warm air and allowing the *solvent* to *evaporate*, thus leaving threads of cellulose acetate.

R.D.X.* See *cyclonite*.

REACTANCE. *X*. A property of *alternating current* circuits which together with the *resistance*, *R*, makes up the *impedance* *Z*, according to the relation, $Z = (R^2 + X^2)^{\frac{1}{2}}$. If the circuit comprises the resistance, an *inductance L*, and *capacitance C* all in series, the reactance is given by:
$$X = \omega L - 1/\omega C$$
where ω is the angular frequency ($\omega = 2\pi f$, f being the *frequency* of the *alternating current*).

REACTANT. A substance which takes part in a *chemical reaction*.

REACTION, CHEMICAL. See *chemical reaction*.

REACTION PROPULSION. Jet propulsion. A form of aerodynamic propulsion in which a high *velocity* stream of *gas* (usually produced by *combustion*) reacts upon the vehicle in which it was produced, in accordance with *Newton's* (third) *law of motion*, so that the vehicle is propelled through the medium in which it is travelling. The lower the *density* of the medium, the higher the *efficiency* of the propulsion. Reaction propulsion is the only known method of propulsion through *space* where there is no supporting medium, and it is upon this principle that *rockets* are propelled. See also *jet engine, ion engine.*

REACTIVE (chem.). Readily entering into *chemical reactions*; chemically active.

REACTOR. 1. A device for introducing *reactance* into an electrical circuit (e.g. a *capacitor*). 2. See *nuclear reactor.*

REAGENT. A chemical substance used to produce a *chemical reaction.*

REALGAR. Natural red *arsenic disulphide,* As_2S_2.

REAL-TIME WORKING. A method of operating a *computer* as part of a larger system, in which information from the computer output is available at the time it is required by the rest of the system.

RÉAUMUR SCALE. A *temperature* scale in which the *melting point* of *ice* is taken as $0°R$. and the *boiling point* of *water* as $80°R$. Named after Rene Antoine Réaumur (1683–1757).

RECIPROCAL OF A QUANTITY. 1 divided by the quantity; e.g. the reciprocal of 5 is $\frac{1}{5}$.

RECIPROCAL OHM. See *mho* and *siemens.*

RECIPROCAL PROPORTIONS, LAW OF. See *chemical combination, laws of.*

RECOIL ELECTRON. See *Compton effect.*

RECTANGLE. A *quadrilateral* with right angles between all four sides.

RECTIFICATION (chem.). The purification of a *liquid* by *distillation.*

RECTIFICATION (math.). The process of determining the length of a curve.

RECTIFICATION (phys.). The conversion of an *alternating* into a *direct current.* See *rectifier.*

RECTIFIED SPIRIT. *Ethanol,* usually obtained by *fermentation* on an industrial scale, and purified by *fractional distillation.*

RECTIFIER (phys.). The device for transforming an *alternating current* into a *direct current*; consists of an arrangement which presents a much higher *resistance* to an *electric current* flowing in one direction than in the other. See *rectifying valve*; *crystal rectifier*; *barrier-layer rectifier*; *junction rectifier*; *semiconductor.*

RECTIFYING VALVE. The *thermionic valve* commonly used for *rectification* is the *diode.* The valve will pass current only when the *anode* is at a positive *potential* with respect to the *cathode.* Hence if an alternating potential is applied to a circuit containing such a valve, a *direct current* will flow through the circuit.

RECTILINEAR. In a straight line; consisting of straight lines.

RECTILINEAR PROPAGATION OF LIGHT. To a first approximation *light* travels in straight lines, as is evident from the formation of *shadows* and other everyday experience; see, however, *diffraction.*

RED GIANT. A type of *star*; see *stellar evolution.*

RED LEAD. Minium. Pb_3O_4. A bright scarlet powder, used as a *pigment,* in *glass* manufacture, and as an *oxidizing agent.*

RED SHIFT. See *Doppler effect.*

REDOX REACTION. Oxidation-reduction reaction. A *chemical reaction* in which an *oxidizing agent* is reduced and a *reducing agent* is oxidized, thus involving the transfer of *electrons* from one *atom, ion,* or *molecule* to another. The 'redox potential', is the *potential* required in a *cell* to produce *oxidation* at the *anode* and *reduction* at the *cathode*. This potential is measured relative to a standard 'hydrogen electrode' which is taken as zero. The hydrogen electrode consists of platinum, over which hydrogen is bubbled, to produce a standard *concentration* of hydrogen ions.

REDUCED TEMPERATURE, PRESSURE, AND VOLUME. Ratios of the *temperature,* the *pressure,* and the *volume* to the *critical temperature, critical pressure,* and *critical volume* respectively.

REDUCING AGENT. A substance which removes oxygen from, or adds hydrogen to, another substance: in the more general sense, one which donates *electrons.* See *reduction.*

REDUCTASE. An *enzyme* which promotes a *reduction* reaction.

REDUCTION. The removal of oxygen from a substance, or the addition of hydrogen to it. The term is also used more generally to include any reaction in which an *atom* gains *electrons.*

REDUNDANCY. A term used in *information theory* to indicate that the information rate from a source is less than a hypothetical maximum value. Defined as the amount by which the *ratio* of the information rate to its hypothetical maximum value falls below unity; usually expressed as a percentage.

RE-ENTRY. The position, time, or act of re-entering the *Earth's* atmosphere after a journey into *space.* The 'angle of re-entry' is critical because of the enormous quantity of *heat* generated by a *spacecraft* as it enters the atmosphere. This heat is generated by *friction* between the *atoms* and *molecules* of the atmosphere and the great speed of the moving spacecraft; it is normally absorbed by the *heat shield.* Too sharp an angle of re-entry would cause the spacecraft to burn up, too oblique an angle would cause the spacecraft to bounce off the atmosphere.

REFINE. Purify: remove the impurities from (*sugar, metals, oil,* etc.).

REFLECTANCE. A measure of the extent to which a surface is capable of reflecting *radiation,* defined as the *ratio* of the intensity of the reflected radiation to the intensity of the incident radiation.

REFLECTION, ANGLE OF. The angle between a *ray* of *light* reflected from a surface, and the *normal* to the surface at that point.

REFLECTION OF LIGHT. Certain surfaces have the property of reflecting or returning *rays* of *light* which fall upon them, according to definite laws (see *reflectance, reflection of light, laws of*).

REFLECTION OF LIGHT, LAWS OF. 1. The incident *ray,* the reflected ray, and the *normal* to the reflecting surface at the point of incidence lie in the same *plane.* 2. The *angle* between the incident ray and the normal (i.e. the angle of *incidence*) is equal to the angle between the reflected ray and the normal (i.e. the angle of *reflection*).

REFLECTION, TOTAL INTERNAL. See *total internal reflection.*

REFLECTOR. 1. Any surface which reflects *radiation,* particularly *electromagnetic radiation.* (See also *parabolic reflector.*) 2. A layer **of** material (which may contain *moderator*) surrounding the core of **a** *nuclear reactor* which reflects back into the core some of the *neutrons* which would otherwise escape.

REFLEX ANGLE. An *angle* greater than 180° and less than 360°.

REFLEX CAMERA. A *camera* which allows the photographer to view the exact scene which he is photographing. It incorporates a movable plane *mirror* to reflect the scene viewed by the camera *lens* on to **a** groundglass screen. Some reflex cameras use a similar principle but have a separate lens for viewfinding.

REFLUX. Flow back; e.g. a reflux condenser is a *condenser* used so **that** the *vapour* over a *boiling liquid* is condensed to a liquid which flows back into the vessel, so preventing its contents from boiling dry.

REFRACTION, ANGLE OF. The angle between the refracted *ray* and **the** *normal* to the surface at the point of *refraction*. See Fig. 35.

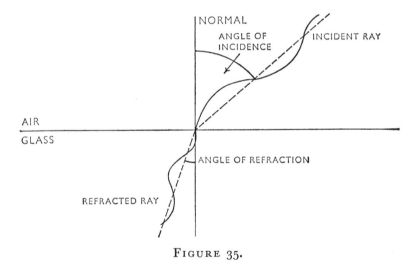

FIGURE 35.

REFRACTION, LAWS OF. 1. The incident *ray*, the refracted ray, and the *normal* to the surface of separation of the two media at the point of incidence lie in the same *plane*. 2. Snell's law. The ratio of the sine of the *angle* of *incidence* to the sine of the angle of *refraction* is a constant for any pair of media. See *refractive index*. Named after Willebrord Snell (1591–1626).

REFRACTION CORRECTION. The small correction which has to be made to the observed *altitude* of a heavenly body due to the *refraction* of the *light*, which it emits or reflects, by the Earth's *atmosphere*. All bodies appear to be slightly higher than they actually are.

REFRACTION OF LIGHT. When a *ray* of *light* travels obliquely from one medium to another, it is bent or refracted at the surface separating the two media. The refraction occurs because light travels at slightly different *velocities* in different media; thus at the interface between media there is a slight change of *wavelength*. See Fig. 35. The ray before refraction is termed the incident ray; on being refracted it becomes the refracted ray. A line perpendicular to the refracting medium at the point where the incident ray enters it is the *normal*. *Glass, water*, etc., cause the incident ray to be turned towards the normal when the ray enters from a medium less optically dense, such as air. Similar considerations apply to *wave motions* other than light.

REFRACTIVE INDEX OF A MEDIUM. *n*. The ratio of the sine (see *trigonometrical ratios*) of the angle of *incidence* to the sine of the angle of *refraction* when *light* is refracted from a *vacuum* (or, to a very close approximation, from air) into the medium. This is equivalent to the fundamental definition: the ratio of the *velocity* of *light* in free space to that in the medium. See *refraction of light*. Some typical values are given in the following table:

		Refractive indices
Diamond		2·4173
Glass		1·5–1·7
Quartz (fused)		1·458
Ethanol (at 25° C.)		1·359
Water (at 25° C.)		1·332
Carbon Dioxide	(at 0° C. and 760 mm)	1·000450
Air	(at 0° C. and 760 mm)	1·000293
Oxygen	(at 0° C. and 760 mm)	1·000272

REFRACTIVITY. If the *refractive index* of a medium is *n*, its refractivity is defined as $n-1$. The 'specific refractivity' is given by $\dfrac{n-1}{\rho}$ where ρ is the *density* of the medium; the 'molecular refractivity' is defined as the specific refractivity multiplied by the *molecular weight*.

REFRACTOMETER. An apparatus for the measurement of the *refractive index* of a substance.

REFRACTORY (chem.). A material not damaged by heating to high *temperatures*. Such materials are made into bricks and used for lining furnaces, etc.

REFRIGERANT. A *fluid* used in the *refrigerating cycle* of a refrigerator, usually consisting of a *liquid* which will vaporize at a low *temperature* (e.g. *freon* or *ammonia*).

REFRIGERATING CYCLE. The cycle of operations which takes place in a refrigerator. The *refrigerant* absorbs *heat* from the cold chamber and its contents, which causes it to vaporize; it is then pumped to a compressor where it gives up heat and condenses back to a *liquid*; it again passes to the cold chamber, thus constituting a continuous cycle.

REGELATION OF ICE. The *melting point* of *ice* is lowered by increased *pressure*; therefore ice near its melting point is melted by sufficient pressure, and solidification or regelation takes place again when the pressure is removed.

REGENERATOR. A *heat exchanger* usually consisting of a chamber filled with bricks arranged in checkerwork. The exhaust gases from a furnace, and the cold air to be used in the *combustion*, are passed alternately through the chamber for specified periods. *Heat* from the exhaust gases is stored in the brickwork and transferred to the cold air, thus increasing the efficiency of the combustion process.

RELATIVE APERTURE. See *f-number*.

RELATIVE ATOMIC MASS. See *atomic weight*.

RELATIVE DENSITY. See *specific gravity*.

RELATIVE HUMIDITY. The hygrometric state of the atmosphere can be defined either as: (1) the ratio of the *pressure* of the *water vapour* actually present in the atmosphere to the pressure of the vapour which would be present if the vapour were *saturated* at the same *temperature*; or (2) the ratio of the *mass* of water vapour per unit *volume* of the air to the mass of water vapour per unit volume of saturated air at the same temperature. The numerical difference between the two is very small and can normally be neglected. The relative humidity is usually expressed as a percentage. Its value may be determined from a knowledge of the *dew-point*, since the *saturated vapour pressure* at the dew-point is equal to the aqueous vapour pressure at the temperature of the experiment. The result is then obtained by reference to tables which give the saturated vapour pressure at different temperatures.

RELATIVE MOLECULAR MASS. See *molecular weight*.

RELATIVE PERMEABILITY. See *magnetic permeability*.

RELATIVISTIC MASS. The *mass* of a body which is travelling at a speed comparable to the *velocity* of *light*. The relativistic mass, m, of a body travelling at a velocity, v, is given by:
$$m = m_0 \left(1 - v^2/c^2\right)^{-\frac{1}{2}}$$
where m_0 is the *rest mass* and c is the velocity of light.

RELATIVISTIC PARTICLE. A particle which has a speed comparable to the *velocity* of *light*; i.e. a particle with a *relativistic mass* substantially in excess of its *rest mass*.

RELATIVISTIC VELOCITY. A *velocity*, approaching the *velocity* of *light*, at which the effect of the theory of *relativity* is significant.

RELATIVITY, THEORY OF. A theory, formulated by Einstein, which recognizes the impossibility of determining absolute motion and leads to the concept of a four-dimensional *space-time continuum*. The special theory, which is limited to the description of events as they appear to observers in a state of uniform motion relative to one another, is developed from two axioms: (1) the laws of natural phenomena are the same for all observers, and (2) the velocity of *light* is the same for all observers irrespective of their own *velocity*. The more important consequences of this theory are (a) the *mass* of a body is a function of its velocity (see *relativistic mass*); (b) the *mass-energy equation* for the inter-conversion of mass and *energy*; (c) the *Fitzgerald-Lorentz contraction* appears as a natural consequence of the theory. The general theory, applicable to observers not in uniform relative motion, leads to a novel concept of the theory of *gravitation*. In this theory the presence of *matter* in *space* causes space to 'curve' in such a manner that the *gravitational field* is set up. Thus gravitation becomes a property of space itself. The validity of the theory of relativity has been amply confirmed in modern *physics*.

RELAY, ELECTRICAL. A device by which the *electric current* flowing in one circuit can open or close a second circuit and thus control the switching on and off of a current in the second circuit. Electrical relays may be mechanical switches operated by *electromagnets*, or they may be *electronic* switches based upon mercury or gas-filled *thermionic valves* e.g. a *thyratron*.

RELUCTANCE. The ratio of the *magnetomotive force* acting in a *magnetic circuit* to the *magnetic flux*.

RELUCTIVITY. The *reciprocal* of *magnetic permeability*.

REM. Roentgen equivalent man. The unit dose of *ionizing radiation* which gives the same biological effect as that due to one *roentgen* of *X-rays*.

REMANENCE. The residual magnetization of a *ferromagnetic substance* subjected to a *hysteresis cycle* when the magnetizing field is reduced to zero.

RENNET. An extract of the fourth stomach of the calf, containing *rennin*.

RENNIN. An *enzyme* having the power of coagulating the *protein* in milk.

RESINS. Natural resins are *amorphous organic compounds* which are secreted by certain plants and insects; usually *insoluble* in *water* but *soluble* in various *organic solvents*. Typical natural resins are *rosin* and *shellac*. *Synthetic* resins were originally described as a group of synthetic substances whose properties resembled natural resins. The term is now applied more generally to any synthetic *plastic* material produced by *polymerization*, although chemically modified natural *polymers*, such as those based on *cellulose* or *casein*, are not usually classed as synthetic resins.

RESISTANCE, ELECTRICAL. *R.* The ratio of the *potential difference* between the ends of a conductor to the *electrical current* flowing in the conductor. See *Ohm's law*. All materials except *superconductors* resist the flow of an electric current, converting a proportion of the *electrical energy* into *heat*. The extent to which a conductor resists the flow of a given current depends upon its physical dimensions, the nature of the material of which it is made, its *temperature*, and in some cases the extent to which it is illuminated. See *photoconductive effect*. The derived *SI unit* of resistance is the *ohm*.

RESISTANCE THERMOMETER. The electrical *resistance* of a *conductor* varies with *temperature*, normally increasing with rise in temperature.

This forms the basis of a convenient and accurate *thermometer*, in which the temperature is deduced from the measurement of the resistance of a spiral of a metal (usually platinum) in the form of a wire.

RESISTIVITY. Specific resistance. A constant for any material equal to the *reciprocal* of its *conductivity*. The resistivity is defined as the *resistance* offered by a cube of the material at $0°C$. Thus the resistivity, ρ equals $\dfrac{RA}{l}$ where R is the resistance of a uniform *conductor* of length l and cross-sectional area A. Usually expressed in *ohm metres*.

RESISTOR. A device used in *electronic* circuits primarily for its *resistance*. The most common types are either 'wire-wound', or made of finely ground carbon particles mixed with a *ceramic* binder.

RESOLUTION OF FORCES. The division of *forces* into components which act in specified directions.

RESOLVING POWER. The ability of an optical system (e.g. *microscope*, *telescope*, the eye, etc.) to produce separate images of objects very close together.

RESONANCE (chem.). The oscillation of *electrons* between *atoms* within an *ion* or *molecule*, as a consequence of which no single description can be given of the *valency bonds* between the atoms (see *valency, electronic theory of*). For example, if a *molecule* AB consists of *atoms* A and B joined by a covalent bond, at any instant the two electrons forming the bond may be; (1) both under the influence of *nucleus* A, i.e. A^-B^+, (2) both under the influence of nucleus B, i.e. $A^+ B^-$, or (3) equally under the influence of both nuclei, i.e. $A-B$. In practice the 'average' structure of the molecule will be somewhere between these 'pure' structures, and is called a 'resonance hybrid'.

RESONANCE (phys.). If, to a system capable of oscillation, a small periodic *force* is applied, the system is in general set into forced oscillations of small *amplitude*. As the *frequency*, f, of the exciting force approaches the *natural frequency* of the system, f_0, the amplitude of the oscillations builds up, becoming a maximum when $f=f_0$. The system is then said to be in resonance with the exciting force, or simply in resonance.

RESONANCE NEUTRON. See *resonance, nuclear*.

RESONANCE, NUCLEAR. Resonance is said to occur in *nuclear reactions* if the *energy* of an incident particle or *photon* is equal, or near to, the value of an appropriate *energy level* of the compound *nucleus*. Thus a resonance *neutron* is one whose energy corresponds to a particular energy level of a nucleus which will readily absorb it.

RESONANT CAVITY. A space enclosed by electrically conducting surfaces, in which electromagnetic *energy* may be stored or excited. The *frequency* of the oscillations within a resonant cavity will depend upon its physical dimensions.

RESONANT CIRCUIT. An *electronic* circuit containing both an *inductance* and a *capacitance* which is capable of *resonance*. When the *capacitor* discharges through the inductor an induced *E.M.F.* is produced which charges the capacitor again in the opposite sense, this again discharges through the inductor and the circuit will continue to oscillate in this way provided that it is supplied with *energy* from an external source. The *frequency* of the oscillation will depend upon the values of the capacitance and the inductance, and the circuit can therefore be tuned to resonate at any desired frequency by suitable alteration of the value of its components. Coupled with a *thermionic valve* or *transistor* to supply energy, a resonant circuit is used in *radio* transmitters to generate *radio frequency* oscillations, and in receivers for their selective detection.

RESORCINOL. *Meta*-dihydroxy*benzene*. $C_6H_4(OH)_2$. A white *soluble* crystalline substance obtained from *phenol*, m.p. $110°C$. Used in the manufacture of synthetic *resins* and *drugs*.

RESPIRATION. *Aerobic* respiration is the process by which living *organisms*, or their components, take oxygen from the *atmosphere* and give off *carbon dioxide*. *Anaerobic* respiration is the process by which organisms, or their components, obtain *energy* from chemically combined oxygen when they do not have access to free oxygen. Many organisms can respire anaerobically for a short time only, but certain *bacteria* depend entirely on anaerobic respiration.

RESPIRATORY PIGMENT. A substance formed in *blood cells* or *blood plasma* which is capable of combining loosely and reversibly with oxygen, e.g. *haemoglobin*.

RESPIRATORY QUOTIENT. RQ. The ratio of the *volume* of *carbon dioxide* expired by an *organism* or tissue to the volume of oxygen consumed by it over the same period.

REST MASS. The *mass* of a body when at rest relative to the observer. The mass of a body varies with its *velocity* (see *relativity, theory of*), a result of great importance when velocities approaching those of *light* are considered, e.g. in *nuclear physics*. See *relativistic mass*.

RESTITUTION, COEFFICIENT OF. *e*. A measure of the *elasticity* of bodies upon impact. For two smooth spheres of a given material colliding, *e* is equal to the ratio of the relative *velocity* of the spheres along their line of centres immediately after impact to their relative velocity before impact.

RESULTANT (phys.). A single *force* or *velocity* which produces the same effect as the two or more forces or velocities acting together.

RETARDATION (phys.). Deceleration. Negative *acceleration*; the rate of decrease of *velocity*.

RETORT (chem.). 1. A *glass* vessel consisting of a large bulb with a long neck narrowing somewhat towards the end. 2. In industrial processes, any vessel in which a *chemical reaction* or process takes place, especially *distillation*. 3. In the canning industry, a large *autoclave* for heating sealed cans by *superheated steam* under pressure.

RETORT CARBON. See *gas carbon*.

RETROGRADE MOTION. See *direct motion*.

RETRO-ROCKET. A small *rocket*, forming part of a larger one, which produces *thrust* in the opposite direction to that of the main rocket with the object of decelerating it; e.g. to enable a lunar *module* to make a 'soft' landing on the *Moon*.

REVERBERATORY FURNACE. A furnace designed for operations in which it is not desirable to mix the material with the *fuel*; the roof is heated by *flames*, and the *heat* is radiated down on to the material off the roof.

REVERSIBLE PROCESS (in *thermodynamics*). A process which can be performed in the reverse direction, the whole series of changes constituting the process being exactly reversed. A reversible process can take place only in infinitesimal steps about equilibrium states of the system.

REVERSIBLE REACTION. A *chemical reaction* which may be made, under suitable conditions, to proceed in either direction. See *chemical equilibrium*.

REYNOLDS NUMBER. (Re). A dimensionless quantity applied to a *liquid* flowing through a cylindrical tube, given by $(Re) = \dfrac{u \rho l}{\eta}$, where $u =$ *velocity* of flow, $\rho = density$ of the liquid, l is the diameter of the tube, and η the coefficient of *viscosity* of the liquid. At low velocities, the flow of the liquid is *streamline*. At a certain value of (Re), corresponding to a critical velocity u_c, the flow becomes *turbulent*. Named after Osborne Reynolds (1842–1912).

r_H SCALE. A scale of hydrogen pressures which gives a measure of the strength of a *reducing agent*. The r_H value is defined as $\log_{10} 1/[H]$, where $[H]$ is the hydrogen pressure which would produce the same electrode potential as that of a given *redox reaction* at the same *pH value*.

RHE. The unit of *fluidity*. The *reciprocal* of the *poise*.

RHENIUM. Re. Element. A.W. 186·20. At. No. 75. A hard heavy grey *metal*, S.G. 20·53, m.p. 3167°C. Used in *thermocouples* and as a *catalyst*.

RHEOLOGY. The study of the deformation and flow of *matter*.

RHEOSTAN. An *alloy* of 52% copper, 25% nickel, 18% zinc, and 5% iron which is used for electrical resistance wire.

RHEOSTAT. A variable electrical *resistor*.

RHESUS FACTOR. Rh factor. A group of *antigens* in the red *blood cells* of some humans (said to be Rh positive) but absent in some individuals (Rh negative). If a Rh negative mother conceives a Rh positive foetus, a severe reaction may in some circumstances occur. The chief danger is to second and subsequent children born to a Rh negative mother.

RHODIUM. Rh. Element. A.W. 102·905. At. No. 45. A silvery-white hard *metal*, S.G. 12·5, m.p. 1966°C. Occurs with and resembles platinum. Used in *alloys*, *catalysts*, and *thermocouples*.

RHODOPSIN. Visual purple. A complex *organic compound* formed in the retina of the eye. Makes the eye more sensitive in very dim light;

lack of it causes night blindness. Formed with the aid of *vitamin* A.

RHOMBUS. A *quadrilateral* having all its sides equal.

RIBOFLAVIN. Lactoflavin. Vitamin B_2. $C_{17}H_{20}N_4O_6$. A *water soluble* substance which is a member of the *vitamin* B complex. Forms part of various *enzymes* concerned with cellular *respiration*, it promotes growth in the young, and plays an important part in the health of the skin. Also known as vitamin G.

RIBONUCLEASE. An *enzyme* which *catalyzes* the *hydrolysis* of *ribonucleic acid*.

RIBONUCLEIC ACID. RNA. Long thread-like *molecules* consisting of single *polynucleotide* chains. The *sugar* of the *nucleotides* is *ribose*, and the four nitrogenous bases which occur in them are the same as those found in *deoxyribonucleic* acid, except that *uracil* replaces *thymine*. RNA is the chief constituent, together with *protein*, of many types of *virus*, and it appears to be responsible for the self-replication of the virus. 'Messenger' RNA transmits the coded information contained by the *chromosomes* of the *nucleus* of a *cell* to the *protein*-making *ribosomes* of the *cytoplasm*. 'Transfer', soluble or s-RNA transfers the activated *amino acids* on to the messenger RNA.

RIBOSE. $C_5H_{10}O_5$. A *pentose monosaccharide sugar*, m.p. $95°C$.; the *dextrorotatory* form is of great biological importance as it occurs in the *nucleotides* of *ribonucleic acid*.

RIBOSOMES. Small granules (about 10^{-8} *metres* in diameter) which occur in the *cytoplasms* of *cells* and which appear to be the sites of *protein* synthesis.

RICINOLEIC ACID. $C_{17}H_{32}OHCOOH$. A yellow *liquid*, b.p. $227°C$., which occurs in *castor oil* and is used in the manufacture of *soap*.

RIGIDITY MODULUS. *Elastic modulus* applied to a body under a shearing *strain*.

RING COMPOUND (chem.). A chemical *compound* in the *molecule* of which some or all of the *atoms* are linked in a closed ring. See *carbocyclic*, *heterocyclic compounds*.

RINGER'S FLUID. *Physiological saline* containing sodium, potassium, and calcium *chlorides*; widely used for sustaining *cells* or tissues during *in vitro* biochemical experiments. Named after Sydney Ringer (1835–1910).

RNA. See *ribonucleic acid*.

ROCHELLE SALT. $COOK.(CH.OH)_2.COONa.4H_2O$. See *potassium sodium tartrate*.

ROCHON PRISM. A *prism* used for obtaining plane-polarized light (see *polarization of light*) and in other related problems. Such a prism, made of *quartz*, may be used for work with *ultraviolet radiation*.

ROCK CRYSTAL. A pure natural crystalline form of *silica*, SiO_2.

ROCK SALT. Natural crystalline *sodium chloride*, NaCl.

ROCKET. A projectile driven by *reaction propulsion* which contains its own *propellants*. A rocket is therefore independent of the Earth's *atmosphere* both with respect to *thrust* and *oxidant* and provides the only known practicable means of propulsion in *space*. 'Chemical' rockets may be powered by either *solid* or *liquid fuels* which burn in oxygen, while 'nuclear' rockets would be powered by a propulsion reactor (see *nuclear reactor*). 'Multistage' or 'step' rockets are rockets built up of several separate sections, each stage being jettisoned when it has burnt out. The 'booster', or first stage, of a space rocket accelerates the projectile up to the thinner regions of the atmosphere, when subsequent stages take over the propulsion. Thus the necessarily high *escape velocity* is not achieved in denser parts of the atmosphere (which would introduce *friction* heating problems), moreover as each stage is jettisoned the projectile becomes substantially lighter, and higher velocities can be achieved with less thrust (see *specific impulse*). Deceleration of rockets is obtained by the use of *retro-rockets*. 'Rocket motors' are also used on certain types of aircraft for take-off, or when a high thrust is required for a short period.

RODINAL*. A photographic *developer* consisting of an *alkaline solution* of *para*-aminophenol, $NH_2C_6H_4OH$, with sodium bisulphite, $NaHSO_3$.

ROENTGEN. The amount of *X-* or *gamma-radiation* which will produce *ions* carrying 1 *electrostatic unit* of electricity of either sign in 1 cc of dry air. Named after Wilhelm Konrad Roentgen (1845–1923).

ROENTGEN RAYS. See *X-rays*.

RONGALITE. A *compound* of sodium sulphoxylate and *formaldehyde*, $NaHSO_2.HCHO$. Used as a *reducing agent* in dyeing.

ROOT (math.). 1. One of the equal *factors* of a number or quantity. The square root, $\sqrt[2]{}$ or $\sqrt{}$, is one of two equal factors; e.g. $9 = 3 \times 3$ or -3×-3; hence $\sqrt[2]{9} = \pm 3$. Similarly the *cube* or third *root* is denoted by $\sqrt[3]{}$, etc. May also be denoted by a fractional *index*; thus $\sqrt[2]{x} = x^{\frac{1}{2}}$; $\sqrt[5]{x} = x^{\frac{1}{5}}$. 2. The root of an *equation* is a value of the unknown quantity which satisfies the equation.

ROOT MEAN SQUARE VALUE OF ALTERNATING QUANTITY. If y is a periodic *function* of t, of *period* T, the root mean square (R.M.S.) value of y is the square *root* of the mean of the square of y taken over a period. The R.M.S. value I of an *alternating current* is important since it determines the *heat* generated (RI^2) in a *resistance* R (see *electric current*, *heating effect of*). All ordinary A.C. measuring instruments give R.M.S. values of current, etc. If the alternating quantity can be represented by a pure *sine wave*, the R.M.S. value of the quantity A is related to the maximum value a of the quantity (i.e. *amplitude*) by the expression $A = a/\sqrt{2}$. The R.M.S. value of a current is also known as the 'effective value of the current'. Similarly, the R.M.S. value of an alternating *E.M.F.* is known as the 'effective E.M.F.'.

ROOT MEAN SQUARE VALUE OF VARIABLE. R.M.S. Given by the expression

$$\text{R.M.S.} = \sqrt{\frac{\text{(Sum of squares of the individual values of the variable)}}{\text{(total number of values)}}}$$

ROSE'S METAL. An *alloy* of 50% bismuth, 25% lead, and 25% tin; m.p· 94°C.

ROSIN. Colophony. A yellowish *amorphous resin* obtained as a residue from the *distillation* of *turpentine*. S.G. 1·08, m.p. 120°–150°C. Used in varnishes, *soaps*, and *soldering* fluxes. See also *ester gum*.

ROTAMETER*. A device for measuring the rate of flow of *fluids*; consists of a small float which is suspended by the fluid in a vertical calibrated tube. The height of the float gives a measure of the rate of flow.

ROTARY CONVERTER. An *alternating current electric motor* mechanically coupled to a *direct current generator*. Used for converting an AC supply into DC.

ROTARY DISPERSION. See *optical activity*.

ROTOR. The rotating part of a *turbine, electric motor,* or *generator*.

RUBBER. An elastic *solid* obtained from the *latex* of the Hevea brasiliensis tree. Raw natural rubber consists mainly of the *cis*-form of poly*isoprene*, $(CH_2.CH:C(CH_3):CH_2)n$, a *hydrocarbon polymer*, with *molecular weight* of about 300,000. Nearly all rubber articles are made by 'compounding' raw rubber, i.e. mixing it with other ingredients and then vulcanizing it in moulds by heating with sulphur and *accelerators*.

RUBBER, SYNTHETIC. A class of synthetic *elastomers* made from *polymers* or copolymers (see *polymerization*) of simple *molecules*. See *butyl rubber, neoprene, nitrile rubber, styrene-butadiene rubber* (SBR), *silicone rubber,* and *stereo-regular rubbers*.

RUBIDIUM. Rb. Element. A.W. 85·47. At. No. 37. A soft, extremely *reactive,* white *metal* resembling sodium. S.G. 1·53, m.p. 38·9° C. Occurs in a few rare *minerals*.

RUBY. A red form of *corundum,* Al_2O_3, which owes its colour to traces of chromium. Used in *lasers* and as a gem stone.

RULES OF FAJANS. Rules which describe the conditions determining whether an electrovalent or a covalent bond (see *valency, electronic theory of*) will be formed between *atoms*. Fajans' rules state that an electrovalent bond will be replaced by a covalent bond if: (1) the charge on either of the *ions* resulting from an electrovalent donation of *electrons* is large (i.e. if more than 1 or 2 electrons are donated); or (2) the volume of the *cation* is small or that of the *anion* is large.

RUST. An *hydrated oxide* of iron, mainly $Fe_2O_3.H_2O$, formed on the surface of iron when it is exposed to moisture and air.

RUTHENIUM. Ru. Element. A.W. 101·07. At. No. 44. A hard brittle *metal,* S.G. 12·2, m.p. 2450°C. Occurs together with platinum; used in *alloys* and as a *catalyst*.

RUTILE. A crystalline form of natural *titanium dioxide,* TiO_2.

RYDBERG CONSTANT. A constant relating to those atomic *spectra* which are similar to the hydrogen *atom* spectrum (see *Balmer series*). The Rydberg constant for hydrogen is $1·09677 \times 10^7 \, m^{-1}$. The general

Rydberg formula is:

$$\frac{1}{\lambda} = R \left(\frac{1}{n^2} - \frac{1}{m^2} \right)$$

where R is the Rydberg constant and n and m are positive *integers.* The quantity $R_\infty hc$, where h is *Planck's constant* and c is the *velocity of light*, is sometimes treated as a unit of *energy* called the rydberg, symbol Ry, such that Ry $= 2 \cdot 17972 \times 10^{-18}$ *joule.* R_∞ is defined as

$$\frac{m_e e^4}{8 \epsilon_0^2 h^3 c}$$

where m_e is the *mass* of an *electron* and e its charge; ϵ_0 is the *permittivity* of a vacuum. Named after J. R. Rydberg.

S

SACCHARIDE. A simple *sugar*; a *monosaccharide*.

SACCHARIMETER. An apparatus for determining the *concentration* of a *sugar solution* by measuring the *angle* of rotation of the plane of vibration of polarized light passing through a tube containing the solution. See *optical activity*; *polarization of light*.

SACCHARIN. $C_6H_4SO_2CONH$. A white, crystalline, sparingly *soluble solid*; m.p. 227°C. When pure, it has about 550 times the sweetening power of *sugar*, but has no food value, and may have harmful effects if used to excess. Manufactured from *toluene*, $C_6H_5CH_3$. Also used in the form of a sodium *salt* called 'saccharin sodium', $C_6H_4COSO_2NNa$. $2H_2O$.

SACCHAROMETER. A type of *hydrometer* used for finding the *concentration* of *sugar solutions* by determining their *density*; usually graduated to read the percentage of sugar direct.

SACCHAROSE. See *sucrose*.

SAFETY LAMP. Davy lamp. An oil-lamp which will not ignite inflammable *gases*, e.g. *methane* (fire-damp). Has a cylinder of wire gauze acting as a chimney; the *heat* of the *flame* is conducted away by the gauze, and while fire-damp will burn inside the gauze, the *temperature* of the gauze does not rise sufficiently high to ignite the gas outside.

SAFROLE. $CH_2{:}CHCH_2C_6H_3O_2CH_2$. A yellowish crystalline substance, m.p. 11·2°C., b.p. 234·5°C., used in the manufacture of perfumes, flavours, and *soaps*.

SAL AMMONIAC. See *ammonium chloride*, NH_4Cl.

SAL VOLATILE. Commercial 'ammonium carbonate', actually consisting of a mixture of ammonium bicarbonate, NH_4HCO_3, ammonium carbamate, $NH_4O.CO.NH_2$, and ammonium carbonate, $(NH_4)_2CO_3$.

SALICIN. $CH_2OHC_6H_4OC_6H_{11}O_5$. A colourless *soluble glucoside*, m.p. 200°C., used as an *antipyretic* and *analgesic*.

SALICYLATE. A *salt* or *ester* of *salicylic acid*.

SALICYLIC ACID. $OH.C_6H_4COOH$. A white crystalline solid, m.p. 159°C. Used as an antiseptic and in the form of a derivative as *aspirin*.

SALINE. Containing *salt*, especially the salts of *alkaline metals* and magnesium. A 'saline solution' is a solution of salts in *water*, especially one which is *isotonic* with body fluids.

SALINOMETER. A type of *hydrometer* used for determining of *concentration* of *salt solutions* by measuring their *density*.

SALT (chem.). A chemical *compound* formed when the hydrogen of an *acid* has been replaced by a *metal*. A salt is produced, together with *water*, when an acid reacts with a *base*. Salts are named according to the acid and the metal from which the salt is derived; thus *sodium sulphate* is a salt derived from sodium and *sulphuric acid*.

SALT, COMMON. See *sodium chloride*, $NaCl$.

SALTCAKE. See *sodium sulphate*, $Na_2SO_4.10H_2O$.

SALTPETRE. Nitre. See *potassium nitrate*.

SALTS OF LEMON. Potassium quadroxalate, $KH_3C_4O_8.2H_2O$. A white, *soluble*, poisonous, crystalline *salt*. Used for removing ink-stains.

SAMARIUM. Sm. Element. A.W. 150·35. At. No. 62. S.G. 7·536, m.p. 1072°C. See *lanthanides*.

SAND. Hard, granular powder, generally composed of granules of impure *silica*, SiO_2.

SANDSTONE. Rock formed from *sand* or *quartz* particles cemented together with *clay, calcium carbonate*, and iron oxide.

SAPONIFICATION. The *hydrolysis* of an *ester*; the term is often confined to the hydrolysis of an ester using an *alkali*, thus forming a *salt* (a *soap* in the case of some of the higher *fatty acids*) and the free *alcohol*.

SAPONIFICATION NUMBER. One of the characteristics of a *fat or oil*; the number of *milligrams* of *potassium hydroxide* required for the complete *saponification* of one gram of the fat or oil.

SAPONINS. *Glucosides*, derived from plants, that form a lather with water. Used as foaming agents and *detergents*.

SAPPHIRE. A natural crystalline form of blue, *transparent corundum* (*alumina*, Al_2O_3); the colour being due to traces of cobalt or other *metals*.

SATELLITES. Bodies which rotate in *orbits* round other bodies of greater *mass* under the influence of their mutual *gravitational field*. Particularly bodies, or moons, which rotate around *planets*. E.g. the *Moon* is a satellite of the *Earth*. See also *satellites, artificial*.

SATELLITES, ARTIFICIAL. In 1957 the first man-made artificial *satellite* was launched by Russia into *orbit* around the *Earth*. This, and subsequent Russian and American artificial satellites, have been used to obtain, and *radio* back to Earth, information concerning conditions prevailing in the *upper atmosphere* and the *ionosphere*. Valuable information has also been obtained relating to *cosmic rays*, the *density* of *matter* and the frequency of *meteors* in *space*, the shape and *magnetic fields* of the Earth, and the nature of solar *radiations*. As a result of the earlier American satellites the *Van Allen radiation belts* were discovered.

'Communication' satellites are artificial Earth satellites used for relaying radio (and *television*) signals around the curved surface of the Earth. 'Passive' satellites merely reflect the transmissions from their surfaces, while 'active' satellites are equipped to receive and retransmit signals. See also *synchronous orbit*.

SATURATED COMPOUND (chem.). A *compound* which does not form *additional compounds*; a compound the *molecule* of which contains no double or multiple *valency bonds* between the *atoms*.

SATURATED SOLUTION. A *solution* which can exist in *equilibrium* with excess of *solute*. The saturation *concentration* is a function of the temperature.

SATURATED VAPOUR. A *vapour* which can exist in *equilibrium* with its *liquid*.

SATURATED VAPOUR PRESSURE. The *pressure* exerted by a *saturated vapour*. This pressure is a function of the *temperature*.

SATURN (astr.). A *planet*, with ten small *satellites*, and surrounded by characteristic rings (see *Saturn's rings*). *Orbit* lies between those of *Jupiter* and *Uranus*. Mean distance from the *Sun*, 1427·01 million kilometres. *Sidereal period* ('year'), 29·46 years. Mass, approximately 95·14 times that of the *Earth*, diameter 119 300 kilometres. Surface temperature, about −150°C.

SATURN'S RINGS. Three concentric rings, probably composed of the remains of a broken-up *satellite*, which are seen round the *planet Saturn*.

SBR. See *styrene-butadiene rubber*.

SCALAR QUANTITY. Any quantity which is sufficiently defined when the magnitude is given in appropriate units. Compare *vector*.

SCALENE. (Of a *triangle*) having three unequal angles and sides. (Of a *cone*) having its *axis* inclined to its *base*.

SCALER. Scaling circuit. An *electronic* device or circuit which produces an output *pulse* when a prescribed number of input pulses has been received. If the prescribed number is two (or ten) the circuit is referred to as a binary (or decade) scaling circuit or scaler.

SCANDIUM. Sc. Element. A.W. 44·956. At. No. 21. S.G. 2·99, m.p. 1539°C. A rare *metal* which occurs in small quantities as the oxide Sc_2O_3.

SCANNING. The repeated and controlled traversing of: (1) a *mosaic* in a television *camera*, or a screen in a *cathode-ray tube*, with an *electron* beam; (2) an airspace with a *radar aerial*; or more generally (3) any area or volume with a moving detector in order to measure some quantity or detect some object.

SCATTERING. The deflection of any *radiation* as a result of its interaction with *matter*. E.g. the change in direction of a particle or *photon* on interacting with a *nucleus* or *electron*. If the scattered particle or photon loses *energy* by causing *excitation* of the struck nucleus the scattering is said to be 'inelastic'; if energy is not lost in this way the scattering is 'elastic'. See also *scattering of light*.

SCATTERING OF LIGHT. When a *beam* of *light* traverses a material medium, scattering of the beam takes place. Two types of scattering occur: (1) by random *reflection*; i.e. small particles suspended in the medium act as tiny *mirrors* and, being randomly orientated with respect to the beam, produce random reflections. This type occurs when the size of the particles is large in comparison with the *wavelength* of the light: (2) by *diffraction*; this occurs when particles which are small compared with the wavelength of the light are present in the medium. Owing to diffraction phenomena, the particles act as centres of radiation and each particle scatters the light in all directions. In this type, the degree of scattering is proportional to the inverse fourth *power* of the wavelength of the light. Thus, blue light is scattered to a greater extent than red. The blue colour of the sky is due to scattering by the actual *molecules* of the *atmosphere*.

SCHEELE'S GREEN. A bright green *precipitate*, probably consisting of cupric arsenite, $Cu_3(AsO_3)_2.2H_2O$. Used as a *pigment* and *insecticide*. Named after Karl Wilhelm Scheele (1742–86).

SCHLIEREN PHOTOGRAPHY. In a fast moving *fluid* in which there is *turbulent flow*, streaks (German, 'Schliere') become visible because they have a different *density* and *refractive index* from the bulk of the fluid. These streaks can be photographed using *spark photography*, or other high speed photographic methods.

SCHMIDT TELESCOPE (CAMERA). A type of astronomical reflecting *telescope* consisting of a primary spherical *mirror* with a correcting plate at, or near, its *centre of curvature*. This plate corrects for *aberration, coma,* and *astigmatism*, enabling a wide area of the sky to be photographed with good *definition*. The instrument is not used visually but *images* are photographed on a curved surface. See Fig. 36. Named after Bernhard Schmidt (1879–1935).

SCHMIDT TELESCOPE

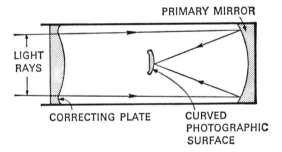

FIGURE 36.

SCHOTTKY DEFECT. See *vacancy*.

SCHWEITZER'S REAGENT. A deep blue *solution* formed by the action of *ammonia* solution on cupric hydroxide, $Cu(OH)_2$. Dissolves *cellulose*, which is re-precipitated by the action of dilute *acids*; this is the basis of the cuprammonium process of *rayon* manufacture. Named after Mathias Schweitzer.

SCINTILLATION COUNTER. A device in which *light* flashes, produced by a scintillator (see *phosphor*) when exposed to *ionizing radiation*, are converted into electrical *pulses* by a *photomultiplier*, thus enabling the number of ionizing events to be counted.

SCINTILLATION SPECTROMETER. A device for determining the *energy* distribution of a given *radiation*. Consists of a *scintillation counter* which incorporates a *pulse height analyser*.

SCINTILLATOR. See *phosphor*.

SCLEROMETER. An instrument for measuring the hardness of a material, usually by measuring the pressure required to scratch it, or by measuring the height to which a standard ball will rebound from it when dropped from a fixed height. See *Mohs Scale* and *Brinell test*.

SCLEROPROTEIN. A class of complex, *insoluble*, fibrous *proteins*, (e.g. *keratin, collagen, elastin*) which occur in the surface coatings of animals and which form the framework binding *cells* together in animal tissues.

-SCOPE. Suffix applied to names of instruments for observing or watching, usually as distinct from measuring. E.g. *telescope*.

SCOPOLAMINE. See *hyoscine*.

SCREEN GRID. A grid placed between the *anode* and *control grid* of a *thermionic valve*, usually held at a fixed positive *potential*.

SCRUPLE. 1/24 ounce Troy. See *troy weight*.

SEA-WATER. The approximate composition (not including inland seas such as the Dead Sea) is water, 96·4%; common *salt*, NaCl, 2·8%; *magnesium chloride*, $MgCl_2$, 0·4%; *magnesium sulphate*, $MgSO_4$, 0·2%; *calcium sulphate*, $CaSO_4$, and *potassium chloride*, KCl, 0·1% each.

SEBACIC ACID. $HOOC(CH_2)_8COOH$. A *dibasic* crystalline *fatty acid*, m.p. 134·5°C., used in the manufacture of *plasticizers* and *resins*.

SECANT. A straight line cutting a *circle* or other curve.

SECANT (trig.). See *trigonometrical ratios*.

SECOND. 1. The *SI unit* of time defined as the duration of 9 192 631 770 *periods* of the *radiation* corresponding to the transition between two hyperfine levels of the *ground state* of the caesium – 133 atom. Symbol s. 2. A measure of *angle*: 1/60 of a minute.

SECOND DERIVATIVE. (math.). The *derivative* of a derivative, written d^2x/dy^2. E.g. *acceleration* (*a*) is the second derivative of distance (*s*) with respect to time (*t*), or the first derivative of *velocity* (*v*) with respect to time i.e., $a = \dfrac{d^2s}{dt^2} = \dfrac{dv}{dt}$.

SECONDARY CELL. See *accumulator*.

SECONDARY COLOUR. A colour obtained by mixing two *primary colours*, e.g., green and orange.

SECONDARY EMISSION OF ELECTRONS. When a primary *beam* of rapidly-moving *electrons* strikes a *metal* surface, secondary electrons are emitted from the surface. The effect is of importance in the *thermionic valve*, the *photomultiplier*, etc. In the thermionic valve, the emission occurs when the electrons strike the *anode*, and may be suppressed or controlled in multi-electrode tubes (*tetrode, pentode*) by various grids called the *suppressor* and *screen grids*.

SECTOR. See *circle*.

SECULAR VARIATION OF MAGNETIC DECLINATION. If the *Earth*'s magnetic North Pole is considered to rotate round the geographical North Pole, completing a cycle in about 930 years, a representation of a steady variation of *magnetic declination*, known as the secular variation, will be seen. Thus, the magnetic declination in London is at present westerly, and decreasing until it is due to become zero at the beginning of the twenty-second century.

SEDATIVE. A *drug* which reduces nervousness and excitement.

SEDIMENTATION. The process of separating an *insoluble solid* from a *liquid* in which it is suspended by allowing it to fall to the bottom of the containing vessel, with or without agitation or *centrifuging*.

SEEBECK EFFECT. If two wires of different *metals* are joined at their ends to form a *circuit* and the two junctions are maintained at different *temperatures*, an *electric current* flows round the circuit. Named after T. J. Seebeck (1770–1831).

SEGER CONE. A device for estimating the approximate *temperature* of a furnace; the cones are made of material softening at a definite temperature. Named after Hermann Seger (d. 1893).

SEGMENT. See *circle* and *sphere*.

SEISMOGRAPH. An instrument for recording earthquake shocks.

SEISMOLOGY. The scientific study of earthquakes and the phenomena associated with them.

SELENATE. A *salt* or *ester* of *selenic acid*.

SELENIC ACID. H_2SeO_4. A strongly corrosive crystalline *acid*, m.p. 58°C., with properties resembling those of *sulphuric acid*.

SELENIDE. A *compound* containing *divalent* selenium with a *metal* or other group.

SELENIUM. Se. Element. A.W. 78·96. At. No. 34. A non-metal resembling sulphur in its chemical properties. S.G. 4·81, m.p. 217°C. Exists in several *allotropic forms*. The so-called 'metallic' selenium, a silvery-grey crystalline *solid*, varies in electrical *resistance* on exposure to *light* and is used in *photo-electric cells*. Occurs as *selenides* of metals, together with their *sulphides*; used in the manufacture of *rubber* and of ruby *glass*.

SELENIUM CELL. A *photo-electric cell* depending for its action on the *photo-conductive effect*, or the *photovoltaic effect*.

SELENIUM RECTIFIER. A *rectifier* which consists of alternate layers of iron and selenium in contact.

SELENOLOGY. The scientific study of the *Moon*, its nature, origin, and movements. Now that samples of the Moon's surface are available for study on Earth, selenology will become a branch of *chemistry* as well as *astronomy*.

SELF-ABSORPTION. The decrease in the *radiation* from a *radioactive* material caused by the absorption of a part of the radiation by the material itself.

SELF-EXCITING. (Of a *generator*.) Having *magnets* which are excited by *current* drawn from the output of the generator.

SELF-INDUCTANCE. The coefficient of *self-induction*.

SELF-INDUCTION. The *magnetic field* associated with an *electric current* cuts the *conductor* carrying the current. When the current changes, so does the magnetic field, resulting in an induced *E.M.F.* (See *induction*, *electromagnetic.*) This phenomenon is called self-induction. The induced E.M.F. is proportional to the rate of change of the current, the constant of proportionality being called the coefficient of self-induction, or the self-inductance. The magnitude of the self-inductance is a function only of the geometry of the electrical circuit and can be calculated in a few simple cases. The derived *SI unit* of inductance is the *henry*. Symbol L.

SEMICONDUCTOR. An electrical *conductor* whose *resistance* decreases with rising *temperature* and the presence of impurities, in contrast to normal metallic conductors for which the reverse is true. Semiconductors, which may be *elements* or *compounds*, include germanium, silicon, selenium, and lead-telluride. In general, semiconductors consist of *covalent crystals*, 'ideal' examples of which at the *absolute zero* of temperature would pass no *electric current* as all the *valency electrons* would be held by the covalent bonds. At normal temperatures, however, some of the electrons have sufficient thermal *energy* to break free from the bonds leaving *holes*. Electrons liberated in this way will have random thermal motions, but in an imposed *electric field* there will be a net drift against the field resulting in so called *N-type conductivity*. The behaviour of the holes is more complex, but they may be regarded as positive charges free to move about the crystal giving rise to *P-type conductivity*. The total current passed by such an *intrinsic semiconductor* is therefore the sum of the electron current and the hole current in the direction of the field. A rise in temperature will create more *carriers*, due to more bonds being broken by thermal energy, and thus lower resistance. The foregoing refers to 'ideal' crystals, but real crystals will have inherent *defects, dislocations,* and impurities which will produce additional carriers (see *extrinsic semiconductor*). In practical semiconductors impurities are added in controlled quantities during crystal growth, the number of *valency electrons* of the impurity *atoms* determining whether the *majority carriers* will be P- or N-type. A P-N *semiconductor junction* is formed when there is a change along the length of a crystal from one type of impurity to the other. At a P-N junction an internal electric field is created between the charged impurity *ions* of the two types. This field is sufficient to prevent the drift of electrons from the N-side to the P-side of the junction, and the drift of holes in the opposite direction. If an external positive *voltage* is applied to the P-side and a negative voltage to the N-side, the internal field can be overcome and a substantial current will flow as a result of the tendency of the majority carriers on each side to migrate to the other side: the magnitude of the current will depend upon the applied voltage. Reversing the voltage increases the effect of the internal field and the only current to flow will be the small number of *minority carrier* electrons on the P-side carried over to the N-side; similarly minority carrier holes will be carried from the N- to the P- regions. The reverse current is therefore small and does not depend upon the applied voltage. The P-N junction is thus a very efficient

343

rectifier and is widely used for this purpose; it is also the basis of the *transistor*.

SEMICONDUCTOR DIODE. See *crystal rectifier*.

SEMICONDUCTOR JUNCTION. A plane which separates two layers of a *semiconductor* each of which have different electrical characteristics. For example, a P-N junction separates the P- region (in which *holes* are the *majority carriers*) from the N- region (in which *electrons* are the majority carriers).

SEMIPERMEABLE MEMBRANE. A membrane allowing the passage of some substances and not of others; a partition which permits the passage of pure *solvent molecules* more readily than those of the dissolved substance. E.g. copper ferrocyanide, $Cu_2Fe(CN)_6$, is permeable to *water*, but only very slightly permeable to dissolved substances. Used as a partition between *solution* and solvent in osmotic measurements (see *osmotic pressure*) and in *dialysis*.

SEMIPOLAR BOND. A *valency bond* in which two *electrons* are donated by one *atom* (usually nitrogen or oxygen) to another atom which requires both of them to complete its *octet*. This is equivalent to one electrovalent bond and one covalent bond (see *valency, electronic theory of*) and is therefore called a semipolar bond.

SENSITOMETER. An instrument for measuring the sensitivity of a photographic plate or film (see *photography*).

SEPARATION ENERGY. The *energy* required to remove a particle (a *proton* or a *neutron*) from a particular atomic *nucleus*.

SEPTIVALENT. Heptavalent. Having a *valency* of seven.

SERIES (math.). A sequence of numbers or mathematical expressions such that the nth term may be written down in general form, and any particular term (say, the rth) may be obtained by substituting r for n; e.g. x^n is the general term of the series $1, x, x^2, x^3 \ldots x^n$.

SERIES, RESISTANCES IN. If a number of *conductors* of electricity are connected in series, i.e. one after the other, so that the current flows through each in turn, the total *resistance* is the sum of the separate resistances of the conductors. See Fig. 37.

FIGURE 37.

SERINE. A white crystalline *amino acid*, m.p. 246°C., that occurs in many *proteins*. See Table 5, page 435.

SERPEK PROCESS. A process for the *fixation of atmospheric nitrogen*. Aluminium is made to react with nitrogen to form aluminium nitride, which is then decomposed by *steam* to give *ammonia*.

SERUM. The *liquid* which remains after the clotting and removal of *blood cells* and *fibrin* from the *blood*; any similar body liquid.

SERVOMECHANISM. A mechanism that converts a small low-powered mechanical motion into a mechanical motion requiring considerably greater power. The output power is always proportional to the input power, and the system may include a negative *feedback* device (usually *electronic*).

SESAME OIL. A yellow oil obtained from sesame seeds, m.p. $-6°$ C., S.G. 0·919, used in the manufacture of *margarine* and cosmetics.

SETS. A set is a group of objects or elements which have at least one common characteristic. If these objects or elements are represented by m_1, m_2, m_3, etc., then $\{m_1, m_2, m_3 \ldots\} = M$ is the way of writing that m_1, m_2, m_3, etc. belong to the set M.

$m_1 \in M$ means that m_1 is a member of set M. If some of the objects or elements m_1, m_2, m_3 etc. can be classified into a subset A, and some others into subset B, then $A \subset M$ (read as subset A is contained in set M) and $B \subset M$ (read as subset B is contained in set M). If, for example, m_2 belongs to both subsets A and B, then $m_2 \in A \cap B$, means that m_2 is a member of subsets A and B, or m_2 belongs to the intersection of subsets A and B. The mathematical theory dealing with relationships between sets is known as 'set theory'.

SEXIVALENT. Hexivalent. Having a *valency* of six.

SEXTANT. An instrument for determining the *angle* between two objects (e.g. horizon and *star*). Commonly employed for determining the radius of a *position circle*.

SHADOW. A dark patch formed by a body which obstructs *rays* of *light*. A shadow cast by an object in front of a *point source* of light is a sharply defined area; a source of light of appreciable size produces two distinct regions, the *umbra* or full shadow, and the *penumbra* or half-shadow. See Fig. 38.

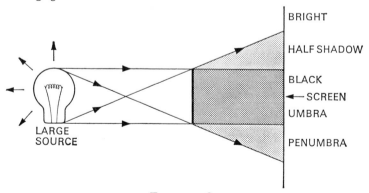

BRIGHT

HALF SHADOW

BLACK

←—SCREEN

UMBRA

PENUMBRA

LARGE
SOURCE

FIGURE 38.

SHADOW BANDS. A series of wavy *shadow* bands which fall across the

Earth just before and after *totality* in a solar *eclipse*. Due to differences in *density* of the *atmosphere*.

SHEAR. A *stress* applied to a body in the *plane* of one of its faces.

SHELLAC. A yellowish natural *resin* secreted by the lac insect (Laccifer lacca) which is parasitic on certain trees native to India and Thailand. Consists of several *polyhydroxy organic acids* (predominantly aleuritic acid, $C_{16}H_{32}O_5$, and shellolic acid, $C_{15}H_{20}O_6$) together with 3%–5% of *wax*. Shellac produces smooth, durable *films* from alcoholic *solutions* and *alkaline* dispersions, which adhere to a variety of surfaces: used in varnishes, polishes, leather dressings, and sealing wax. Owing to its electrical insulation properties it is used in insulating varnishes and in micanite* (see *mica*).

SHELLS, ELECTRON. According to the interpretation of *quantum mechanics*, the *electrons* contained within an *atom* circle round the *nucleus* in *orbits* at various distances from the nucleus. These orbital electrons may be visualized as forming a series of concentric shells: electrons in the same shell having the same principal *quantum number, n*. The shells are designated by the letters K-P (equivalent to values of *n* from 1–6) in order of increasing distance from the nucleus. The number of electrons in each shell is restricted (see *Pauli's exclusion principle*), but each shell is capable of containing $2n^2$ electrons. Table 7, page 438, gives the electronic configuration of the commoner *elements*. Within each shell, electrons are further classified into sub-shells (or *energy* sub-levels) according to their orbital *angular momentum*, which is represented by their azimuthal quantum number, *l*. The separate sub-shells are distinguished by the letters s, p, d, and f (corresponding to values of *l* of 0, 1, 2, and 3). E.g. an electron designated 4f, has a principal quantum number of 4 (N shell) and an azimuthal quantum number of 3 (f sub-shell).

SHERARDIZING. A method of plating iron or *steel* with zinc, to form a *corrosion* resistant coating. The iron or steel is heated in contact with zinc powder to a *temperature* slightly below the *melting point* of zinc. At this temperature the two metals amalgamate forming internal layers of zinc-iron *alloys* and an external layer of pure zinc.

SHOCK WAVE. A very narrow region of high *pressure* and *temperature* in which air flow changes from *subsonic* to *supersonic*. See also *sonic boom*.

SHOOTING STAR. See *meteor*.

SHORT CIRCUIT. If a *potential difference* exists between two points *A* and *B* (e.g. the terminals of an electrical supply), a system of *conductors* connecting *A* and *B* constitutes a *circuit*. If now *A* and *B* are placed in contact, or joined by a conductor of much lower *resistance* than the rest of the circuit, most of the current will flow direct between *A* and *B*, which are then said to be short-circuited or 'shorted'.

SHORT SIGHT. See *myopia*.

SHOWER. The production by one high *energy* particle, originating from *cosmic rays* or *accelerators*, of several fast particles. 'Cascade' showers (or soft showers) consist of *electrons, positrons,* or *photons* formed by successive *pair productions* or *radiative collisions.* 'Penetrating' showers contain *nucleons* and *muons* capable of penetrating up to about 20 cm of lead. 'Auger' showers (or extensive showers) extend over areas of up to 1000 square metres.

SHUNT, ELECTRICAL. A device for altering the amount of *electric current* flowing through a piece of apparatus, such as a *galvanometer.* Consists of a *conductor* connected in *parallel* with the apparatus.

SIDEBAND. The band of *frequencies* lying on either side of a *modulated carrier wave;* the width of each sideband is equal to the highest modulating frequency.

SIDE-CHAIN (chem.). An *aliphatic radical* or group attached to a *benzene ring* or other cyclic group in the *molecule* of an *organic compound.* E.g. in *toluene,* $C_6H_5.CH_3,$ the *methyl group,* $CH_3,$ is a side-chain attached to a benzene ring.

SIDEREAL DAY. The period of a complete rotation of the *Earth* upon its *axis,* with respect to the *fixed stars.* It is 4·09 minutes shorter than a mean *solar day.*

SIDEREAL PERIOD OF A PLANET. The 'year' of a *planet.* The actual period of its revolution round the *Sun.* See Table 4, page 434.

SIDEREAL YEAR. See *year.*

SIDERITE. 1. Natural ferrous carbonate, $FeCO_3.$ An important *ore* of iron. 2. A *meteorite* consisting of *metals* (principally iron) and metallic *compounds.*

SIEMENS. A unit of electric *conductance* equivalent to one reciprocal ohm, or *mho.* Symbol S. Named after Sir William Siemens (1823–83).

SIEMENS-MARTIN PROCESS. See *open-hearth process.*

SIGMA PILE. An assembly consisting of a *neutron* source and a *moderator,* without any *fissile* material, which is used to study the properties of moderators.

SIGN, ALGEBRAICAL. The plus or minus sign, $+$ or $-$, indicating opposite senses or directions; thus $+5$ is numerically equal, but opposite in sign, to -5.

SILAGE. A stored form of cattle-fodder produced by a limited *fermentation* of green fodder pressed down and stored in a pit. *Lactic acid* is formed during the process.

SILANES. A class of silicon *hydrides* of the general formula $Si_nH_{2n+2},$ forming a *homologous series* analogous to the *hydrocarbons.*

SILICA. Silicon dioxide. $SiO_2.$ A hard, *insoluble,* white or colourless *solid* with a high *melting point* (1610–1713°C.). Very abundant in nature in the forms of *quartz, rock-crystal, flint,* and as *silicates* in rocks. Used in the form of a white powder in the manufacture of *glass, ceramics,* and *abrasives.*

SILICA GEL. A form of *silica,* $SiO_2,$ with a highly porous structure capable of adsorbing (see *adsorption*) 40% of its *weight* of *water* from a *saturated vapour.* Used in *gas* drying and as a *catalyst* support.

SILICATE. A *salt* of *silicic acid,* $H_2SiO_3.$ A very large number of rocks,

347

earths, and other *minerals* consist of silicates of calcium, aluminium, magnesium, and other *metals*. Such silicates are conveniently considered as being *compounds* of *silica* and the *oxide* of the metal in question.

SILICIC ACIDS. A *mixture* of gelatinous substances obtained by treating *silicates* with *acids*. Meta-silicic acid is $H_2SiO_3(SiO_2.H_2O)$ and *ortho*-silicic acid is $H_4SiO_4(SiO_2.2H_2O)$.

SILICOL PROCESS. The manufacture of hydrogen by the action of *sodium hydroxide* (caustic soda, $NaOH$) *solution* on silicon.

SILICON. Si. Element. A.W. 28·086. At. No. 14. A non-metal similar to carbon in its chemical properties. Occurs in two *allotropic forms*; a brown *amorphous* powder and dark grey *crystals*; S.G. 2·42, m.p. 1420°C. Occurs in nature as *silica* and as various *silicates*. Used in *alloys* and in the form of *silicates* in *glass*. *Silicones* are also widely used.

SILICON CARBIDE. SiC. A hard black *insoluble* substance, m.p. 2700°C., used as an *abrasive* and in *resistors* required to withstand high *temperatures*.

SILICON CHIP. See *integrated circuit*.

SILICON TETRACHLORIDE. $SiCl_4$. A colourless fuming *liquid*, b.p. 57·57°C., used in making silicon *compounds* and smokescreens.

SILICONE RUBBERS. Dimethyl *siloxane polymers*. A group of synthetic *rubbers* with high and low *temperature* resistance superior to that of natural rubbers.

SILICONES. A term originally applied to *compounds* of the general formula R_2SiO, where R stands for *hydrocarbon radicals*. Now defined as polymeric (see *polymerization*) *organic siloxanes* of the general type $(R_2SiO)_n$. Used as lubricants, for water-repellent finishes, high-*temperature* resisting *resins*, and lacquers.

SILK. A thread-like substance produced by the silkworm. Consists mainly of the *proteins* sericin and fibroin.

SILOXANES. A group of *compounds* with the general *formula* R_2SiO, where R stands for an *organic* group or hydrogen. See also *silicones*.

SILVER. Ag. Element. A.W. 107·87. At. No. 47. A white, rather soft *metal*; S.G. 10·5, m.p. 960·5°C. Extremely malleable and ductile; the best known *conductor* of electricity. Occurs as the metal, and as *argentite* or silver glance, Ag_2S; *horn silver*, $AgCl$; and other *compounds*. Extracted by alloying with lead, and then separating the lead by *cupellation* and other methods. Used in coinage and jewellery; *compounds* used in *photography*.

SILVER BROMIDE. AgBr. A pale yellow, *insoluble salt*, m.p. 434°C., used in *photography*.

SILVER CHLORIDE. AgCl. A white *insoluble salt*, m.p. 455°C., which occurs naturally as *horn silver* (cerargyrite), used in *photography* and *antiseptics*.

SILVER GLANCE. See *argentite*.

SILVER IODIDE. AgI. A yellow *insoluble salt*, m.p. 558°C., which occurs naturally as iodyrite, used in *photography*, medicine, and in seeding clouds to produce artificial rain.

348

SILVER NITRATE. Lunar caustic. $AgNO_3$. A white *soluble* crystalline *salt*, m.p. 209°C. Used in marking-inks, medicine, and chemical analysis.

SILVER PLATING. Depositing a layer of metallic silver, generally by *electrolysis*. See *electroplating*.

SIMPLE HARMONIC MOTION. S.H.M. A point is said to move in simple harmonic motion when it oscillates along a line about a central point,

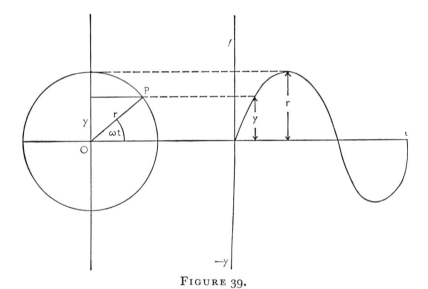

FIGURE 39.

O, so that its *acceleration* towards O is always proportional to its distance from O. Thus, if a point P moves in a *circle*, centre O and radius *r*, with a constant *angular velocity* ω, the projection of P on any diameter will move in S.H.M. If the distance from O of the projection of P on a vertical diameter is *y*, at time *t*, then a *graph* of *y* against *t* will give a 'sine wave' of *amplitude r* and *equation* $y = r\sin\omega t$. (See Fig. 39.) This equation may be rewritten in the more general form:

$$y = r\sin 2\pi \left(\frac{t}{T} - \frac{x}{\lambda} \right)$$

where *T* is the *period* of the wave, λ its *wavelength* and *x* the distance it has travelled from O in time *t*.

SIMULTANEOUS EQUATIONS. A set of *equations* in which the values of the *variables* will satisfy all the equations; if the equations contain *n* variables, then to obtain a *solution* there must be at least *n* equations.

SINE. See *trigonometrical ratios*.

SINE WAVE. Sinusoidal wave. See *simple harmonic motion*.

SINTERING. Compressing *metal* particles into a coherent *solid* body. The process is carried out under *heat*, but at a *temperature* below the *melting point* of the metal. Certain non-metals such as *ceramics* and *glass* may also be sintered.

SINUSOIDAL. Having the characteristics of a sine wave. See *simple harmonic motion.*

SIPHON. A bent tube used for transferring *liquid* from one level to a lower level via a third level higher than either. If the shorter arm of an inverted U-tube filled with liquid is immersed below the liquid surface in A (see Fig. 40), liquid will flow from A to C through the tube. The siphon depends for its action on the fact that the *pressure* at A tending to force the liquid up the tube is $P - P_{ab}$ and the pressure acting upwards on the liquid at C is $P - P_{bc}$, where $P =$ external atmospheric pressure, and P_{ab} and P_{ac} are the pressures due to the *weights* of the liquid columns AB and AC respectively. Hence flow from A to B will occur provided BC is greater than AB.

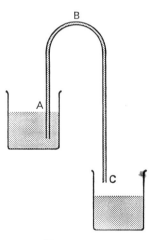

FIGURE 40.

SI UNITS. Système International d'Unités. An internationally agreed *coherent* system of *units*, derived from the *M.K.S. system*, now in use for all scientific purposes and thereby replacing the *c.g.s. system* and the *f.p.s. system*. The seven basic units are; the *metre* (symbol m), *kilogram* (kg), *second* (s), *ampere* (A), *kelvin* (K), *mole* (mol), and *candela* (cd). The *radian* (rad) and *steradian* (sr) are supplementary units. Derived units include the *hertz* (Hz), *newton* (N), *joule* (J), *watt* (W), *coulomb* (C), *volt* (V), *farad* (F), *ohm* (Ω), *weber* (Wb), *telsa* (T), *henry* (H), *lumen* (lm) and *lux* (lx). Decimal multiples are given in the following table (where possible a prefix representing 10 raised to a *power* which is a multiple of three should be used). See conversion tables on pages 425–9.

Factor	Name of Prefix	Symbol	Factor	Name of Prefix	Symbol
10	deca-	da	10^{-1}	deci-	d
10^2	hecto-	h	10^{-2}	centi-	c
10^3	kilo-	k	10^{-3}	milli-	m
10^6	mega-	M	10^{-6}	micro-	μ
10^9	giga-	G	10^{-9}	nano-	n
10^{12}	tera-	T	10^{-12}	pico-	p
			10^{-15}	femto-	f
			10^{-18}	atto-	a

SKATOLE. C_9H_9N. A white *soluble* crystalline substance, m.p. $265°C.$, with a strong odour, used in the manufacture of perfumes.

SKIP DISTANCE. There is a minimum angle of *incidence* at the *ionosphere* below which a *sky wave* of a given *frequency* cannot be reflected, but is transmitted through to outer *space*. Consequently there is a region surrounding a *radio* transmitter within which no sky wave can be received. The minimum distance at which reception of the sky wave is possible is called the skip distance.

SKY WAVE. Ionospheric wave. A *radio* wave may travel from transmitting *aerial* to receiving aerial by one of two paths: either directly along the ground (see *ground wave*), or by reflection from the *ionosphere*. In the latter case it is called a sky wave or ionospheric wave.

SLAG. Non-metallic material obtained during the *smelting* of metallic *ores*; generally formed as a molten mass floating on the molten *metal*.

SLAKED LIME. See *calcium hydroxide*.

SLAKING. The addition of *water*.

SLATE. Natural form of aluminium silicate formed from *clay* hardened by *pressure*.

SLIDE RULE. Mathematical instrument used for rapid calculations; in principle consists of a grooved ruler with a scale, with another similarly marked ruler sliding inside the groove. Multiplication and division are carried out by adding or subtracting lengths on the two rulers, the divisions on which are in a logarithmic scale, by a process analogous to addition and subtraction which could be carried out on two rulers by adding or subtracting lengths.

SLOW NEUTRON. A *neutron* whose *kinetic energy* does not exceed about 10 *electron-volts*.

SLUG. A *unit* of *mass* in the *f.p.s. system* defined as the mass which will acquire an *acceleration* of 1 ft/sec² when acted upon by a *force* of 1 lb. Equal to 32·174 lbs.

SMELTING. Extraction of a *metal* from its *ores* by a process involving *heat*. Generally the process is one of chemical *reduction* of the *oxide* of the metal with carbon in a suitable furnace.

351

SMOG. A dark, thick, dust- and soot-laden, sulphurous *fog* which, under certain meteorological conditions, pollutes the atmosphere of some industrial cities and the lungs of their inhabitants.

SMOKE. A suspension of fine particles of a *solid* in a *gas*; smoke from *coal* consists mainly of fine particles of carbon.

SNELL'S LAW. See *refraction, laws of*.

SOAP. A mixture of the sodium *salts* of *stearic acid*, $C_{17}H_{35}COOH$, *palmitic acid*, $C_{15}H_{31}COOH$, and *oleic acid*, $C_{17}H_{33}COOH$; or of the potassium salts of these acids ('soft soap'). Made by the action of *sodium* or *potassium hydroxide* on *fats*, the process of *hydrolysis* or *saponification* giving the soap, with *glycerol* as a by-product. The term soap is also applied to *fatty acid* salts of *metals* other than sodium or potassium, although such compounds are unlike the ordinary soaps.

SODA. Term applied to various sodium *compounds*; *washing soda, sodium carbonate*, $Na_2CO_3,10H_2O$; *baking soda, sodium hydrogen carbonate*, $NaHCO_3$; *caustic soda, sodium hydroxide*, $NaOH$.

SODA-LIME. A *solid mixture* of *sodium hydroxide*, $NaOH$, and *calcium hydroxide*, $Ca(OH)_2$, made by slaking quicklime (see *calcium oxide*) with a *solution* of *sodium hydroxide* and drying by *heat*.

SODA NITRE. *Caliche*. Impure natural *sodium nitrate*.

SODA WATER. *Water* containing *carbon dioxide*, CO_2, under *pressure*; releasing the pressure lowers the *solubility* of the gas, and thus causes *effervescence*.

SODIUM. Na. (Natrium.) Element. A.W. 22·9898. At. No. 11. A soft silvery-white *metal*, S.G. 0·971, m.p. 97·5°C. Very *reactive*, tarnishes rapidly in air; reacts violently with *water* to form *sodium hydroxide*, $NaOH$, and hydrogen *gas*. *Compounds* are very abundant and widely distributed; the commonest is *sodium chloride*, NaCl (common salt). Essential to life. The metal is used in the preparation of *organic compounds*.

SODIUM AZIDE. NaN_3. A colourless crystalline substance, used in the manufacture of *explosives*.

SODIUM BENZOATE. C_6H_5COONa. A white *soluble* powder, used as an *antiseptic* and a food preservative.

SODIUM BICARBONATE. $NaHCO_3$. See *sodium hydrogen carbonate*.

SODIUM CARBONATE. Washing soda. $Na_2CO_3.10H_2O$. A white crystalline *soluble salt*, m.p. 850°C. Used in the household, in the manufacture of *glass, soap, paper*, and for *bleaching*.

SODIUM CHLORATE. $NaClO_3$. A colourless *soluble* crystalline substance, m.p. 248–261°C., used in the manufacture of *explosives*, as a *mordant, oxidizing agent*, and an *antiseptic*.

SODIUM CHLORIDE. Common salt, salt. NaCl. A white crystalline *soluble salt*, m.p. 801°C. Occurs extensively in *sea water* and as halite.

SODIUM CYANIDE. NaCN. A white *soluble deliquescent* substance, m.p. 563·7°C., used in *electroplating*, case-hardening, and fumigation.

SODIUM CYCLAMATE. $C_6H_{11}NHSO_3Na$. A white crystalline *soluble* powder, formerly used as a sweetening agent in soft drinks and for diabetics, but now banned from such use owing to possible side-effects.

SODIUM DICHROMATE (BICHROMATE). $Na_2Cr_2O_7.2H_2O$. An orange *soluble* crystalline substance, m.p. 356·7°C. (after losing its *water of crystallization* at 100°C.), used as a *mordant, corrosion* inhibitor, *oxidizing agent*, and in *electroplating*.

SODIUM DITHIONITE. Sodium hydrosulphite. $Na_2S_2O_4$. A white crystalline *soluble* powder, used as a *reducing agent* and in *bleaching*.

SODIUM ETHOXIDE. Sodium ethylate. C_2H_5ONa. A white *hygroscopic* substance, used in organic synthesis.

SODIUM FLUORIDE. NaF. A colourless crystalline substance, m.p. 988°C., used in the *fluoridation* of *water* and as an *insecticide*.

SODIUM HYDROGEN CARBONATE. Sodium bicarbonate. $NaHCO_3$. A white *soluble* powder, used in *baking powder, fire extinguishers*, and in medicine as an *antacid*.

SODIUM HYDROGEN GLUTAMATE. Monosodium glutamate. MSG. $HOOC.(CH_2)_2CH(NH_2)COONa$. A white *soluble* crystalline substance, used to intensify the flavour of foods.

SODIUM HYDROXIDE. Caustic soda. NaOH. A white *deliquescent solid*, m.p. 318·4°C. Dissolves in *water* to give an *alkaline solution*. Used in the manufacture of *soap, rayon*, and other chemicals.

SODIUM NITRATE. $NaNO_3$. A white *soluble* crystalline *salt*, m.p. 306·8°C.; occurs naturally as *Chile saltpetre*; used as a *fertilizer* and in the manufacture of *nitric acid* and *explosives*.

SODIUM PERBORATE. $NaBO_3.4H_2O$. A white *soluble* crystalline substance, m.p. 63°C., used in *bleaching* and as a disinfectant.

SODIUM PEROXIDE. Na_2O_2. A yellow powder, formed when sodium *metal* burns in air. Reacts with *water* to give *sodium hydroxide* and oxygen *gas*. Used in *bleaching* and as an *oxidizing agent*.

SODIUM PHOSPHATE. Three principal *compounds* are called by this name. 1. Sodium dihydrogen orthophosphate (monobasic), NaH_2PO_4, a white *soluble* crystalline substance used in *electroplating* and dyeing. 2. Disodium hydrogen orthophosphate (dibasic), Na_2HPO_4, a white soluble crystalline substance used in *dyes, fertilizers, detergents, baking powder*, and medicine. 3. Trisodium orthophosphate (tribasic), Na_3PO_4. $12H_2O$, a colourless soluble crystalline substance used in detergents, and in the manufacture of *paper* and water softeners.

SODIUM SILICATE. Na_2SiO_3. A white *soluble* crystalline *salt*, used in the household as 'water-glass', in fireproofing textiles, and in the manufacture of *paper* and *cement*.

SODIUM SULPHATE. Glauber's salt. Saltcake. $Na_2SO_4.10H_2O$. A white *soluble* crystalline *salt*. Used in the manufacture of *soap, detergents*, and *dyes*.

SODIUM SULPHIDE. Na_2S. An orange *soluble deliquescent* substance, m.p. 1180°C., used in the manufacture of *soaps* and *dyes*.

SODIUM SULPHITE. Na_2SO_3. A white crystalline *soluble* powder, used as a food preservative, in *bleaching*, and in *photography*.

353

SODIUM TETRABORATE (correctly disodium tetraborate). Borax sodium biborate, sodium pyroborate. $Na_2B_4O_7.10H_2O$. A white, *soluble* crystalline *salt,* occurring naturally as *tincal.* On heating it loses *water of crystallization* and melts to a clear glass-like solid (see *borax bead test*). Used as an *antiseptic,* in fireproofing, as a *flux,* and in the manufacture of *glass* and *ceramics.*

SODIUM THIOCYANATE. NaSCN. A colourless *deliquescent* crystalline substance, m.p. $287°$ C., used in medicine.

SODIUM THIOSULPHATE. Sodium hyposulphite, *hypo.* $Na_2S_2O_3.5H_2O$. A white crystalline very *soluble salt,* used in *photography* for fixing.

SODIUM VAPOUR LAMP. A luminous *discharge* obtained by passing an *electric current* between two *electrodes* in a tube containing sodium *vapour* at low *pressure.* Used in street lighting as the characteristic yellow light is less absorbed by fog and mist than *white light.*

SOFT IRON. Iron containing little carbon, as distinct from *steel*; iron which does not retain *magnetism* permanently, but loses most of it when the magnetizing field is removed.

SOFT RADIATION. *Ionizing radiation* of relatively long *wavelength* and low penetrating power, as opposed to 'hard' radiation which is of shorter wavelength and high penetrating power.

SOFT SOAP. See *soap.*

SOFT WATER. *Water* which forms an immediate lather with *soap.* See *hard water.*

SOFTWARE. The *programs* used in a *computer,* especially the general programs supplied by the computer manufacturer. The 'hardware' is the actual equipment of the computer itself.

SOIL. Soils vary enormously in their chemical composition. The *inorganic* portion of a soil is composed of *silicates* of various *metals,* mainly of aluminium, but also of iron, calcium, magnesium, etc., free *silica* (sand) and other *inorganic* matter, depending on the source. *Organic* matter in the soil is mainly derived from decomposed plants; much of it is in the form of a class of black, sticky substances known collectively as *humus.*

SOL. See *colloidal solution.*

SOLAR CELL (BATTERY). An electric *cell* which converts *energy* from the *Sun* into *electrical energy.* Usually a *semiconductor* device sensitive to the *photovoltaic effect*; e.g. a P-N *semiconductor junction* in a *crystal* of silicon. Used in artificial *satellites* and *space probes* to power *electronic* equipment.

SOLAR CONSTANT. The *energy* which would (in the absence of the *atmosphere*) be received per minute by an area of 1 sq. cm. placed at the mean distance of the *Earth* from the *Sun* and at right angles to the incident *radiation*; approximately 2 *calories* per minute per square centimetre. Equal to about 14,000 *joules* per *second* per square *metre.*

SOLAR DAY. The variable interval between two successive returns of the *Sun* to the *meridian.* The mean solar day is the average value of this. See *time measurement.*

SOLAR FLARES. Short high *temperature* outbursts seen as bright areas in the *chromosphere* of the Sun. Jets of particles (known as the *solar wind*) and strong *radio frequency electromagnetic radiations* (see *radio astronomy*) are emitted during solar flares. Solar flares are associated with *sunspots* and usually cause magnetic and *radio* disturbances on *Earth*.

SOLAR PARALLAX. The *angle* subtended by the mean equatorial radius of the *Earth* at a distance of one *astronomical unit*.

SOLAR PROMINENCES. Large eruptions of luminous *gas* which rise several thousands of kilometres above the *Sun's chromosphere*.

SOLAR SYSTEM, THE. The system of nine *planets* – *Mercury, Venus,* the *Earth, Mars, Jupiter, Saturn, Uranus, Neptune* and *Pluto* – and of the belt of *asteroids* revolving in elliptical *orbits* round the *Sun*. The orbits are nearly circular, and lie very nearly in the same *plane*. See Table 4, page 434.

SOLAR WIND. Streams of electrically charged particles (*protons* and *electrons*) emitted by the *Sun*, predominantly during *solar flares* and *sunspot* activity. Some of these particles become trapped in the Earth's magnetic field (see *magnetism, terrestrial*) forming the outer *Van Allen radiation belt*, but some penetrate to the *upper atmosphere* where they congregate in narrow zones in the region of the Earth's *magnetic poles* producing auroral displays (see *aurora borealis*).

SOLAR YEAR. See *year*.

SOLDER. An *alloy* for joining *metals*. Soft solders are alloys of tin and lead in varying proportions; brazing solders are usually composed of copper and zinc.

SOLENOID. A coil of wire wound uniformly on a cylindrical former, having a length which is large compared with its radius. When a current of I *electromagnetic units* is passed through the solenoid, a uniform *magnetic field H* is produced inside the coil parallel to its *axis*. The magnitude of H in *oersteds* is given by $H = 4\pi nI$, where n is the number of turns per unit length of the solenoid. In *SI units*, if I is in *amperes* and n is the number of turns per *metre*, $H = nI$ amperes per metre.

SOLID (math.). A three-dimensional figure, having length, breadth, and thickness; a figure occupying *space* or having a measurable *volume*.

SOLID ANGLE. The ratio of the area of the surface of the portion of a *sphere* enclosed by the conical surface forming the angle, to the square of the radius of the sphere. See *steradian*.

SOLID SOLUTION. A solid *homogeneous mixture* of two or more substances. E.g. some *alloys* are solid solutions of the *metals* in each other, the process of *solution* having taken place in the molten state.

SOLID STATE. The *physical state of matter* in which the constituent *molecules, atoms,* or *ions* have no *translatory motion* although they vibrate about the fixed positions which they occupy in a *crystal lattice*. A solid is said to possess *cohesion*, remaining the same shape unless changed by external *forces*. Certain solids are not crystalline, they are then said to be *amorphous*. A crystalline solid has a definite *melting point* at which it becomes a *liquid*; amorphous solids have no precise melting point, but when heated become increasingly pliable until they assume the properties usually associated with liquids, they may therefore be thought of as 'supercooled' liquids.

SOLID STATE PHYSICS. The branch of *physics* which deals with the nature and properties of *matter* in the *solid state*. The term is often used to refer especially to the study of the properties of *semiconductors* and 'solid state devices', i.e. *electronic* devices consisting entirely of solids, without moving parts, *gases*, or heated *filaments*, e.g. semiconductors, *transistors*, *integrated circuits*, etc.

SOLIDIFYING POINT. The constant *temperature* at which a *liquid* solidifies under a given *pressure*, usually the standard *atmosphere*.

SOLSTICE. The time (or, more accurately, the point) at which the *Sun* reaches its greatest *declination* North or South. The points are situated upon the *ecliptic* half-way between the *equinoxes*; the times are approximately 21 June and 21 December.

SOLUBILITY. The extent to which a *solute* will dissolve in a *solvent*. Usually expressed in grams per 100 g of solvent at a specified *temperature*.

SOLUBILITY PRODUCT. The product of the *concentrations* of the *ions* of a dissolved *electrolyte* when in *equilibrium* with undissolved substance. For sparingly *soluble* electrolytes, the solubility product is a constant for a given substance at a given *temperature*. When the solubility product for a given compound is exceeded in a *solution*, some of it is precipitated until the product of the ionic concentrations falls to the constant value.

SOLUBLE. Capable of being dissolved (usually in *water*).

SOLUTE. A substance which is dissolved in a *solvent* to form a *solution*.

SOLUTION. A *homogeneous* molecular *mixture* of two or more substances of dissimilar molecular structure; term commonly applied to solutions of *solids* in *liquids*. Other types of solutions include *gases* in liquids, the *solubility* of gases decreasing with rise in *temperature*; gases in solids; liquids in liquids; and solids in solids (e.g. some *alloys*), see *solid solutions*.

SOLVATION. The combination of *solvent molecules* with *molecules* or *ions* of the *solute*. The *compound* so formed is called a 'solvate'.

SOLVAY PROCESS. Ammonia-soda process. An industrial preparation of *sodium carbonate* or *washing-soda*, $Na_2CO_3.10H_2O$, from common *salt*, NaCl, and *calcium carbonate*, $CaCO_3$. By the action of *ammonia*, NH_3, and *carbon dioxide* (obtained by heating $CaCO_3$) on salt *solution*, the less soluble *sodium hydrogen carbonate*, $NaHCO_3$, is precipitated. The action of *heat* on this gives the required sodium carbonate, while the ammonia is recovered from solution by the action of the *lime* (*calcium oxide*) which remains when the calcium carbonate is heated. Named after Ernest Solvay (1833–1922).

SOLVENT. A substance (usually *liquid*) having the power of dissolving other substances in it; that component of a *solution* which has the same *physical state* as the solution itself. E.g. in a solution of *sugar* in *water*, water is the solvent, while sugar is the *solute*.

SOLVENT EXTRACTION. See *extraction*.

SOMATIC. Pertaining to the body. Somatic *cells* are the cells of which the body of an *organism* is constructed, as opposed to the reproductive or germ cells. See also *mutation*. In another sense the word refers to the body as opposed to the mind: e.g. psychosomatic medicine is the study of the influence of psychological factors upon physiological illness.

SONAR. SOund NAvigation Ranging. An apparatus for locating submerged objects by transmitting a high *frequency sound* wave and collecting the reflected wave. The time for the wave to travel to the object and return gives an indication of the depth.

SONIC BOOM. The loud noise created by the *shock wave* set up by an aircraft or missile travelling at *supersonic speeds*. A subsonic aircraft produces pressure waves ahead of itself, which travel at the speed of *sound*, and 'clear a path' for the oncoming aircraft. In supersonic flight the aircraft overtakes the pressure waves so that a shock wave *cone* is created with the nose of the aircraft at its *vertex*. In level flight the intersection of the shock wave cone with the ground produces a *hyperbola*, at all points along which the sonic boom is simultaneously experienced; subsequently the boom will be experienced at all points within the hyperbola's path over the ground.

SORBITE. 1. The constituent of *steel* produced when *martensite* is *tempered* above 450°C., consisting of *ferrite* and finely divided *cementite*. 2. Sorbitic pearlite. The constituent of steel produced by the decomposition of *austenite* when cooled at a slower rate than will yield *troostite* and a faster rate than will yield *pearlite*.

SORBITOL. $CH_2OH(CHOH)_4CH_2OH$. A white crystalline sweet *soluble* substance, m.p. 110°C. (for the *dextrorotatory compound*), obtained from *dextrose*; used as a *sugar* substitute and in the manufacture of synthetic *resins*.

SOUND. A physiological sensation received by the ear. It is caused by a vibrating source and transmitted as a longitudinal pressure *wave motion* (see *longitudinal waves*) through a material medium such as air.

SOUND, VELOCITY OF. The *velocity* of propagation of *sound* waves (see *wave motion*). This velocity is a function of the *temperature* and of the nature of the propagating medium. In *gases* it is independent of the *pressure*. In air at 0°C. it is 1120 feet or 332 metres per second, approximately 760 miles per hour.

SOXHLET EXTRACTION APPARATUS. A device for extracting the *soluble* portion of any substance by a continuous circulation of the boiling *solvent* through it.

SPACE. That part of the boundless four-dimensional *continuum* in which *matter* can be physically (rather than temporally) extended. (See *space-time*.) More colloquially, space (or 'outer' space) is that part of the *Universe* which lies beyond the Earth's *atmosphere* and in which the density of matter is very low.

SPACECRAFT. A vehicle capable of travelling in *space*.

SPACE PROBE. A *rocket*-propelled missile which has sufficient *velocity* to escape from the Earth's *atmosphere*. Space probes are used for making measurements of conditions within the *solar system* which cannot be made by terrestrial observation. The measurements are made by miniaturized *electronic* equipment within the probe, the results of which are signalled back to earth by *radio*. A Moon-probe, or Lunar-probe, is one intended to study the *Moon* and its environment.

SPACE-REFLECTION SYMMETRY. See *parity*.

SPACE-TIME. The development of the theory of *relativity* has led to the disappearance of a clear-cut distinction between a three-dimensional *space* and an independent *time*; in the modern view, space and time are considered as being welded together in a four-dimensional space-time *continuum*.

SPALLATION. A *nuclear reaction* in which a high *energy* incident particle, or *photon*, causes several particles or fragments to be emitted by the target *nucleus*. The *mass number* and *atomic number* of the target nucleus may thus be reduced by several units.

SPARK. See *electric spark*.

SPARK COIL. See *induction coil*.

SPARK PHOTOGRAPHY. Flash photography. *Photography* in which the source of *light* is an *electric spark* usually of predetermined duration. Photographs are taken in the dark (or low light) and the *camera lens* is left open, thus the exposure time can be made very short and rapidly moving objects can be photographed.

SPARKING-PLUG. A device for providing an *electric spark* for exploding the *mixture* of air and *petrol vapour* in the cylinder of the *internal-combustion engine*.

SPARKING POTENTIAL. Sparking voltage. The difference in *potential* (i.e. the *voltage*) required for an *electric spark* to pass across a given gap. See *Paschen's law*.

SPARTEINE. $C_{15}H_{26}N_2$. A bitter colourless *alkaloid*, m.p. 30° C., used in medicine.

SPECIAL THEORY OF RELATIVITY. See *relativity, theory of*.

SPECIFIC. When the adjective 'specific' is used before the name of an extensive physical quantity, it implies 'divided by *mass*'. E.g. *specific heat capacity* is *heat capacity* per unit mass. When the extensive quantity is denoted by a capital letter (e.g. V for *volume*), the specific quantity is usually denoted by the corresponding small letter ($v = V/m$ for *specific volume*). In some older physical quantities the word has had other meanings (e.g. *specific resistance*), but such uses are now deprecated.

SPECIFIC ACTIVITY. *a*. The *activity* per unit *mass* of a pure *radioisotope*; or the activity of a radioisotope in a material per unit mass of that material. Expressed in *curies* per g or *disintegrations* per second per kg.

SPECIFIC CHARGE. The *electric charge* to *mass* ratio of an *elementary particle*.

SPECIFIC GRAVITY, S.G. Relative density. The *ratio* of the *density* of a substance at the *temperature* under consideration to the density of *water* at the temperature of its maximum density (4°C.). Numerically equal to the density in grams per cubic centimetre, but is stated as a pure number, while the density is stated as *mass* per unit *volume*. The table below gives the S.G. of some common materials.

THE SPECIFIC GRAVITY OF SOME COMMON MATERIALS

Material	S.G.	Material	S.G.
Cork	0·24	Aluminium	2·7
Pine	0·45	Diamond	3·5
Oak	0·80	Titanium	4·5
Water	1·00	Iron (cast)	6·9–7·5
Brick	1·6	Steel	7·6–7·8
Earth	1·9–2·1	Brass (cast)	8·1
Cement (set)	2·2	Lead	11·3
Granite	2·6	Mercury	13·6
Marble	2·7	Gold	19·3

SPECIFIC HEAT CAPACITY. Specific heat. *c*. *Heat capacity* divided by *mass*. The quantity of *heat* required to raise the *temperature* of unit mass of a substance by one degree. Expressed in *joules* per kg per *kelvin* (*SI units*), *calories* per gram per °C. (*c.g.s. units*), or *British thermal units* per lb per °F (*f.p.s. units*).

The two most important specific heat capacities of a *gas* are (1) that measured at constant pressure, c_p, and (2) that measured at constant volume, c_v. c_p is greater than c_v because when a gas is heated at constant pressure it has to do work against the surroundings in expanding. The ratio c_p/c_v, usually denoted by γ (gamma) varies from 1·66 for *monatomic* gases to just over 1 for more complex *molecules*. The value of gamma therefore gives some indication of the number of atoms in the molecules of a gas.

SPECIFIC IMPULSE. A term used in connexion with *rockets*. The ratio of the *thrust* produced (in lbs) to the rate of *fuel* consumption (lbs per sec.). The specific impulse therefore has the dimension of 'seconds', and may be thought of as the length of time one pound of *propellant* would last if expended at a rate which would continuously produce one pound of thrust.

SPECIFIC RESISTANCE. See *resistivity*.

SPECIFIC VOLUME. The *volume*, at a specified *temperature* and *pressure*, occupied by 1 unit mass (usually 1 kg) of the substance. The *reciprocal* of the *density*.

SPECTRAL LINES. See *line spectrum*.

SPECTRAL SERIES. The emission *spectrum* of any substance may be analysed into one or more groups of *frequencies* (or *wavelengths*), the frequencies in each group forming a series. For example, the spectrum of the hydrogen *atom* possesses series given by the expression

$$\nu = \text{constant} \left(\frac{1}{n_o{}^2} - \frac{1}{n^2} \right),$$

where v is the frequency of the spectral *lines*. For the different series, n_0 takes the values 1, 2, 3, 4, etc. For any one value of n_0, n may have all *integral* values from $n_0 + 1$ upwards, the expression then giving the frequencies of all the lines in that particular series. See also *Balmer series* and *Rydberg constant*.

SPECTRAL TYPES. Spectral classes. The classification of *stars* based on the *spectrum* of the *light* which they emit. The system now used is the Harvard classification which comprises ten types of star.

SPECTROGRAPH. An instrument by which *spectra* may be photographed; a photograph taken by means of such an instrument. See *spectrographic analysis*.

SPECTROGRAPHIC ANALYSIS. Investigation of the chemical nature of a substance by the examination of its *spectrum*, using the fact that the position of emission and absorption *lines* and *bands* in the spectrum of a substance is characteristic of it.

SPECTROHELIOGRAPH. An instrument used to photograph the *Sun* with *light* of a particular *wavelength*.

SPECTROMETER. 1. A type of *spectroscope* so calibrated that it is suitable for the precise measurements of *refractive indices*. 2. An instrument for measuring the *energy* distribution of a particular type of *radiation*, e.g. a *scintillation spectrometer*.

SPECTROPHOTOMETER. A *photometer* for comparing two *light* radiations wavelength by wavelength.

SPECTROSCOPE. An instrument for *spectrographic analysis* or the observation of *spectra*.

SPECTROSCOPIC BINARY. A *binary star* system that cannot be seen as two stars by a *telescope*, but which show a *Doppler effect* in their *line spectrum* as these stars revolve about each other. See *visual binary*.

SPECTROSCOPY. The study of *matter* and *energy* by the use of a *spectroscope*. See *spectrographic analysis*.

SPECTRUM. The result obtained when *electromagnetic radiations* are resolved into their constituent *wavelengths* or *frequencies*. In the visible region (i.e. *light* waves) a well-known example is provided by the coloured bands produced when white light is passed through a *prism* or *diffraction grating*. (See *spectrum colours*.) Spectra formed from bodies emitting radiations are termed *emission spectra*. When white light is passed through a semi-transparent medium, selective absorption of radiations of certain wavelengths or bands of wavelengths takes place; the spectrum of the transmitted light is called an *absorption spectrum*. A continuous spectrum is one in which all wavelengths, between certain limits, are present. A *line spectrum* is one in which only certain wavelengths or 'lines' appear. The emission and absorption spectra of a substance are fundamental characteristics of it and are often used as a means of identification. Such spectra arise as a result of transitions between different *stationary states* of the *atoms* or *molecules* of the substance, electromagnetic waves being emitted or absorbed simultaneously with the transition. The frequency ν of the emitted or absorbed radiation is given by $E_1 - E_2 = h\nu$, where E_1 and E_2 are the *energies* of the first and second states respectively between which the transition takes place, and h is *Planck's constant*. When E_1 is greater than E_2, electromagnetic waves are emitted; in the converse case, they are absorbed.

SPECTRUM COLOURS. The *colours* visible in the continuous *spectrum* of *white light*. These colours, their *wavelengths* and *frequencies* are given in the following Table:

Colour of Light	Wavelength/ 10^{-7} metres	Frequency/ 10^{14} hertz
Red	6·470–7·000	4·634–4·284
Orange	5·850–6·470	5·125–4·634
Yellow	5·750–5·850	5·215–5·125
Green	4·912–5·750	6·104–5·215
Blue	4·240–4·912	7·115–6·104
Violet	4·000–4·240	7·495–7·115

SPECULAR REFLECTION. Perfect or regular reflection of *electromagnetic radiation*, e.g. *light*. Occurs whenever the reflecting surface is flat to approximately $1/8$ of a *wavelength* of the radiation incident upon it.

SPECULUM. A reflecting *mirror*, especially a metallic mirror (see *speculum metal*) used in a reflecting *telescope*.

SPECULUM METAL. An *alloy* of $2/3$ copper and $1/3$ tin; used for *mirrors* and *reflectors*. See *speculum*.

SPEED. The ratio of the distance covered to the time taken by a moving body. Speed in a specified direction is *velocity*.

SPELTER. Commercial zinc, about 97% pure, containing lead and other impurities.

SPERMACETI. A white, waxy *solid* consisting mainly of cetyl palmitate, $C_{15}H_{31}COOC_{16}H_{33}$. M.p. 40°–50° C. Obtained from the head of the sperm whale. Used in the manufacture of *soaps* and cosmetics.

SPERMATOCYTE. A male *gametocyte* which undergoes *meiosis* to form spermatids which change into *spermatozoa*.

SPERMATOZOON. Sperm. A male *gamete*, four of which are derived by *meiosis* from a single *spermatocyte*.

SPHERE (math.). A *solid* figure generated by the revolution of a semicircle about a diameter as *axis*. The flat surface of a section cut by a *plane* passing through the centre is a *great circle*; surface of a section cut off by any other plane is a small circle. The solid cut off by a plane of a great circle is a hemisphere; that cut off by a small circle is a segment. The *volume* of a sphere having radius $r = \frac{4}{3}\pi r^3$; surface area $= 4\pi r^2$.

SPHERICAL ABERRATION. See *aberration, spherical.*

SPHERICAL COORDINATES. Three-dimensional *polar coordinates.* A point in *space* is defined by the length of its *radius vector* and the *angle* which this vector makes with two perpendicular *planes.*

SPHERICAL MIRROR. See *mirrors, spherical.*

SPHERICAL TRIANGLE. A *triangle* drawn on a spherical surface, bounded by the arcs of three *great circles.* The properties of such triangles differ from those of *plane* triangles; calculations relating to them form the purpose of spherical trigonometry.

SPHERICAL TRIGONOMETRY. *Trigonometry* which deals with *spherical triangles.*

SPHEROID. A *solid* figure generated by an *ellipse* rotating about its minor axis (oblate spheroid, a 'flattened sphere') or about its major axis (prolate spheroid, an 'elongated sphere').

SPHEROMETER. An instrument for the accurate measurement of small thicknesses, or curvature of spherical surfaces.

SPIEGEL. Spiegeleisen. An *alloy* of iron, manganese, and carbon, used in the manufacture of *steel* by the *Bessemer process.*

SPIN. A term of special significance in *nuclear physics.* Sub-atomic particles (*electrons, neutrons, nuclei, mesons,* etc.) may possess, in addition to other forms of *energy* such as energy of translation, energy due to the spinning of the particle about an *axis* within itself. This gives rise to a spin energy term in the quantum analysis (see *quantum mechanics*) of permissible *energy levels.* Quantum considerations limit the magnitude of the spin *angular momentum* of *orbital electrons* to two values, given by $J \dfrac{h}{2\pi}$ or

$J\hbar$ (see *Planck's constant*) where J is the spin *quantum number* which can have the values $\pm\frac{1}{2}$. The plus and minus signs indicate that the spin can be clockwise or anti-clockwise. For all *baryons* and *leptons* J is half integral ($\frac{1}{2}$, $\frac{3}{2}$), but for *mesons* and *photons* it is integral (0, 1, 2). See Table 6, page 436.

SPINELS. A group of *minerals* having the general composition $MO.R_2O_3$, M being a *bivalent metal* (magnesium, ferrous iron, manganese, zinc) and R a *tervalent* metal (aluminium, chromium, ferric iron). See *ferrites.*

SPIRAL GALAXIES. Spiral nebulae. *Galaxies* in which the *stars,* dust, and *gas* clouds are concentrated in the arms of a spiral. Spiral galaxies are believed to have evolved from 'elliptical' galaxies. The *Galaxy* to which the *solar system* belongs is also spiral in form.

SPIRILLUM. A spiral-shaped *bacterium.*

SPIRITS OF SALT. A *solution* of *hydrochloric acid.*

SPIRITS OF WINE. See *ethanol.*

SPONTANEOUS COMBUSTION. The *combustion* of a substance of low *ignition point*, which results from the *heat* produced within the substance by slow *oxidation*.

SPUTTERING. A process for depositing a thin uniform film of a *metal* on to a surface. A disc of the metal to be 'sputtered' is made the *cathode* of a low-pressure discharge system (see *discharge in gases*). The material to be coated is placed between cathode and *anode*, the whole arrangement being enclosed and evacuated to a *pressure* of between 1 and 0·01 mm. A discharge is set up by applying a *voltage* (1,000–20,000 volts) between anode and cathode. Metallic *atoms* are ejected from the cathode and are deposited on the surface to be coated.

SQUARE. 1. A *quadrilateral* having all its sides equal and all its *angles* right angles. 2. The square of a quantity is that quantity raised to the second *power*, i.e. multiplied by itself.

SQUARE ROOT. See *root*.

SQUARE WAVE. A *wave motion* which alternates between two fixed values for equal lengths of time, the time of transition between the two values being negligible compared to the duration of each fixed value.

SQUARING THE CIRCLE. The problem of constructing a *square* exactly equal in area to a given *circle*. The exact area of a circle cannot be determined, except in terms of π, which cannot be expressed as an exact fraction or decimal, although any required degree of approximation can be obtained. The problem, therefore, appears to be impossible of solution.

STABILIZATION (chem.). The prevention of chemical *decomposition* of a substance by the addition of a 'stabilizer' or 'negative *catalyst*'.

STABLE (chem.). Not readily decomposed.

STABLE EQUILIBRIUM (phys.). A body at rest is in stable *equilibrium* if, when slightly displaced, it tends to return to its original position of equilibrium. If the displacement tends to increase, the body is said to be in unstable equilibrium. Positions of stable equilibrium are positions of minimum *potential energy*; those of unstable equilibrium are of maximum potential energy.

STAINLESS STEEL. A class of chromium *steels* containing 70%–90% iron, 12%–20% chromium, 0·1%–0·7% carbon.

STALACTITE. The downward growth of *calcium carbonate*, $CaCO_3$, formed on the roof of a cave by the trickling of *water* containing calcium *compounds*.

STALAGMITE. The upward growth from the floor of a cave; of the same nature and origin as a *stalactite*.

STALAGMOMETRY. The measurement of *surface tension* by determining the *weight* (or *volume*) of a drop of the *liquid* hanging from the end of a tube.

STALLOY*. *Steel* containing 3·5% silicon, having low *energy* losses due to *hysteresis*. Used in portions of electrical apparatus which are subjected to alternating *magnetic fields*.

STAND OIL. A *drying oil* which has been thickened by heating in an inert atmosphere (without the addition of driers). The thickening is due to *polymerization* of some of the constituents.

STANDARD ATMOSPHERE. See *atmosphere*.

STANDARD CELL. A specially prepared *primary cell*, e.g. the *Weston cell*, characterized by a high constancy of *E.M.F.* over long periods of time. The E.M.F. is a function of the *temperature*, and in the Weston cell it decreases by about 1 part in 10^5 per $1°$ rise.

STANDARD DEVIATION. A measure, used in *statistics*, of the scatter of a series of numbers or measurements about their *mean* value. Defined as the *square root* of the average value of the *squares* of the deviations from their mean value.

STANDARD TEMPERATURE AND PRESSURE. S.T.P. See *N.T.P.*

STANDING WAVE. Stationary wave. A wave produced by the simultaneous transmission of two similar *wave motions* in opposite directions. In *acoustics*, standing waves are caused by *interference* between waves of the same *frequency* in such a way that the combined intensity varies between maxima and minima over the region of interference.

STANNATE. A *salt* of a *stannic acid*.

STANNIC. Containing *quadrivalent* tin.

STANNIC ACID. $SnO_2.xH_2O$. A series of *amorphous insoluble compounds*. In a-stannic acid $x=1$, in β-stannic acid $x=2$.

STANNIC CHLORIDE. $SnCl_4$. A colourless fuming *liquid*, b.p. $114\cdot1°C.$, used in the manufacture of *mordants*.

STANNIC OXIDE. SnO_2. Tin ash. A white *amorphous insoluble* powder, m.p. $1127°C.$, used in the manufacture of *glass* and polishes.

STANNIC SULPHIDE. Mosaic gold. SnS_2. A golden *insoluble* powder used in the manufacture of gold *paint*.

STANNOUS. Containing *bivalent* tin.

STANNOUS CHLORIDE. $SnCl_2$. A white crystalline substance, m.p. $246°C.$, which forms a dihydrate known as 'tin salt', m.p. $37\cdot7°C.$ Used as a *reducing agent*, a *mordant*, and a tinning agent.

STANNUM. See *tin*.

STARCH. Amylum. *Polysaccharide carbohydrates* consisting of chains of *glucose* units arranged in one of two forms: *amylose* and *amylopectin*. Most *natural* starches are mixtures of these two forms (e.g. potato and cereal starches are 20%–30% amylose and 70%–80% amylopectin). Starch is a white tasteless *insoluble* powder which on *hydrolysis* (by boiling with *dilute acids*, or by reacting with *amylases*) gives first *dextrin* and finally glucose. Starch is stored by plants in the form of granules and occurs in most seeds.

STARCH GUM. See *dextrin*.

STARS. Heavenly bodies of a similar nature to the *Sun*, i.e. intensely hot, glowing masses which produce their *energy* by *thermonuclear reactions*. The nearest star to the Sun is over 4 *light-years* away; the other *fixed stars* visible to the naked eye are all members of the *Galaxy* and many of them are members of *binary star* systems. The stars are not uniformly distributed throughout the *Universe*, being grouped into enormous clusters called *galaxies*. The nearest galaxy to ours is some 16×10^5 *light-years* away. See also *stellar evolution*.

STASSFURT DEPOSITS. Natural deposits of several *inorganic salts*. The deposit consists of several strata, of a total estimated thickness of 800 *metres*. They are a source of potassium and sodium *compounds* in the form of *carnallite*; also of magnesium bromide, $MgBr_2.6H_2O$, and *rock-salt*.

STAT-. Prefix attached to the name of electrical *units* to indicate the corresponding *electrostatic unit* (e.g. *statcoulomb*).

STATCOULOMB. The *electrostatic unit* of *electric charge* in the *c.g.s.* *system* equal to 3.3356×10^{-10} *coulombs*.

STATES OF MATTER. See *physical states of matter*.

STATIC ELECTRICITY. See *electricity, static*.

STATICS. A branch of *mechanics*; the mathematical and physical study of the behaviour of *matter* under the action of *forces*, dealing with cases where no motion is produced.

STATIONARY ORBIT. See *synchronous orbit*.

STATIONARY STATES. A term used in *quantum mechanics*. If only certain energy values or *energy levels* for the total energy of a system are permissible, the energy is said to be *quantized*. These levels are characteristic of the state of the system; such states are called stationary states. A transition from one stationary state to another can occur only with the emission or absorption of energy in the form of *photons*; i.e. *electromagnetic radiation* is emitted or absorbed.

STATIONARY WAVE. See *standing wave*.

STATISTICAL MECHANICS. The study of the mechanical properties of large assemblies of particles or components in terms of *statistics*. E.g. the *kinetic theory of gases* treats the *molecules* of a *gas* in terms of statistical mechanics.

STATISTICS. The collection and study of numerical facts or data and their interpretation in mathematical terms, with special reference to the theory of *probability*.

STATOR. The fixed part of any *electric motor* or *generator* which contains the stationary magnetic circuits.

STEADY STATE THEORY. A theory in *cosmology* which postulates that the *Universe* has always existed in a steady state, that the *expansion of the Universe* is compensated by the continuous creation of *matter* which is viewed as a property of *space*, and that despite local evolutionary processes, the Universe as a whole is not evolving. The rate at which matter would have to be spontaneously created to compensate for the Universe's expansion (about 10^{-43}kg m^{-3} s^{-1}) is far too low to be measurable and therefore evidence to support this theory has to be sought in other directions. If it could be established that the *density* of matter throughout the Universe does not vary with distance or time, this would support the steady state theory rather than its main competitor the *superdense theory*. *Radio astronomy* is being used to assess the density of matter at the most distant parts of the observable Universe in order to decide between these two theories.

STEAM. *Water*, H_2O, in the gaseous state; water above its *boiling point*. An invisible *gas*; the white clouds which are frequently termed 'steam' consist of droplets of *liquid* water formed by the *condensation* of steam.

STEAM ENGINE. A machine utilizing *steam* power; either a steam turbine (see *turbine*) or a reciprocating steam engine, consisting essentially of a cylinder in which a piston is moved backwards and forwards by the expansion of steam under pressure.

STEAM POINT. The *temperature* at which the maximum *vapour pressure* of *water* is equal to standard atmospheric pressure (see *atmosphere*), i.e. the normal *boiling point*. In the *Celsius temperature* scale the steam point is given the value of $100°$ C.

STEARATE. A *salt* or *ester* of *stearic acid*.

STEARIC ACID. $C_{17}H_{35}COOH$. A white *solid fatty acid*, m.p. $69°$C., which occurs as *tristearin* in many *fats*. Used in the manufacture of *soaps*, candles, and cosmetics.

STEARIN. *Tristearin*; the term is also sometimes applied to a mixture of *palmitic* and *stearic acids* (see *stearine*).

STEARINE. A hard white waxy *solid* consisting mainly of *stearic* and *palmitic acids*. Made by the *saponification* of natural *fats*.

STEEL. Iron containing from $0·1\%$ to $1·5\%$ carbon in the form of *cementite* (iron carbide, Fe_3C). The properties of different steels vary according to the percentage of carbon and of *metals* other than iron present, and also according to the method of preparation. Prepared by the *open-hearth* and *Bessemer processes*. See also *stainless steel*.

STEELYARD. A weighing-machine for heavy loads. In principle it consists of a long, rigid bar, with a pan or hook at one end for taking the load to be weighed. The rod is pivoted about a fixed point or fulcrum near the *centre of gravity*, which is fairly near the end with the pan or hook. The other portion of the bar is graduated, and a movable weight slides along this, the weight balanced by it being proportional to its distance from the centre of gravity. See Fig. 41.

FIGURE 41.

STEFAN'S LAW. The total *energy* emitted in the form of *heat radiation* per unit time from unit area of a black body is proportional to the fourth power of its *absolute temperature* (see *black body radiation*). The constant of proportionality, Stefan's constant, $= 5·6697 \times 10^{-8}$ W m^{-2} K^{-4}. Also known as the Stefan-Boltzmann Law and constant. Named after Josef Stefan (1853–93). See Table 2, page 431.

STELLAR EVOLUTION. According to current views *stars* evolve during the course of their history. It is thought that they are born from *condensations* of *gas* (mostly hydrogen) which is compressed as a result of the *gravitational field* between the constituents. The compression is so great in the interior of the gas that *thermonuclear reactions* occur during which hydrogen is converted to helium (and possibly heavier *elements*) with the evolution of *energy*. On a *Hertzprung-Russell diagram* the stars remain on the 'main sequence' until they have consumed some 10% of their hydrogen. They then become *red giants* and consume their hydrogen at increased rates so that eventually they contract and become *white dwarfs*. See also *novae* and *supernovae*.

STELLITE*. An *alloy* of cobalt (35%–80%), chromium (15%–40%), tungsten (10%–25%), molybdenum (0%–40%), and iron (0%–5%), which is hard and non-corroding; used for surgical instruments.

STEP-ROCKET. See *rocket*.

STERADIAN. The supplementary *SI unit* of *solid angle*. That solid angle which encloses a surface on the *sphere* equal to the *square* of the radius. Symbol sr.

STERE. A metric unit of *volume*; 1 cubic *metre*.

STEREOCHEMISTRY. *Chemistry* involving consideration of the arrangement in *space* of the *atoms* in a *molecule*. If a molecule is considered as a three-dimensional entity in space, possibilities of *stereoisomerism* or space *isomerism* arise; thus, a molecule consisting of four different *radicals* or *atoms* attached to a central carbon atom can exist in two distinct space arrangements, one being a *mirror image* of the other. Such isomerism is associated with *optical activity*.

STEREOISOMERISM. *Isomerism* caused by possibilities of different arrangement in three-dimensional space of the *atoms* within a *molecule*, resulting in two isomers which are mirror images of each other. See also *cis-trans isomerism*, and *stereochemistry*.

STEREO-REGULAR RUBBERS. A group of synthetic *rubbers* manufactured by a solution *polymerization* process using special *catalysts* which control the stereoisomeric (see *stereoisomerism*) regularity of the products. These materials can therefore be made to resemble closely the structure of natural rubber. In *cis* – 1, 4 poly*isoprene*, the structure of natural rubber is substantially duplicated, and this *elastomer* can be used for many of the purposes which were the exclusive preserve of natural rubber. A similar product is *cis* – 1, 4 poly*butadiene* which is also used in place of natural rubber. See also *ethylene – propylene rubber*.

STEREOSCOPE. An optical device by which two-dimensional pictures are given the appearance of depth and solidity.

STEROIDS. Derived *lipids* which include *sterols*, the *bile acids*, certain *hormones* and *glucosides*, and *vitamin* D.

STEROLS. Derived *lipids* of the *steroid* group. *Cholesterol* and *ergosterol* are typical examples; present in many living *organisms* in which they play an essential part.

STIBINE. Antimony hydride. SbH_3. A poisonous *gas*.

STIBNITE. Natural *antimony trisulphide*, Sb_2S_3. The principal *ore* of antimony.

STILBENE. Diphenylethene. $C_6H_5CH{:}CHC_6H_5$. A colourless *insoluble* substance, m.p. 124°C., used in the manufacture of *dyes*.

STILBOESTROL. $(HO.C_6H_4.C.C_2H_5{:})_2$. A white crystalline *organic compound*, m.p. 171°C.; used in medicine as an *oestrogen*.

STILL. A *metal* or *glass* apparatus used for the *distillation* of *liquids*.

STIMULATED EMISSION. See *maser* and *laser*.

STOCHASTIC PROCESS. A process which has some element of *probability* in its structure.

STOICHIOMETRIC. A *compound* is said to be stoichiometric when it is pure, i.e. when its component *elements* are present in the exact proportions represented by its chemical *formula*. A stoichiometric *mixture* is one which will yield on reaction a stoichiometric compound (e.g. two *molecules* of hydrogen and one molecule of oxygen constitute a stoichiometric mixture because they yield exactly two molecules of *water* on *combustion*).

STOICHIOMETRY. The part of *chemistry* dealing with the composition of substances; more particularly with the determination of combining proportions or *chemical equivalents*.

STOKE. *C.g.s. system* unit of *kinematic viscosity* equal to the *viscosity* of a *fluid* in *poises* divided by the *density* in grams per cm^3. 1 centistoke $= 10^{-6}$ square *metres* per *second*. Named after Sir George Stokes (1819–1903).

STOKES' LAW. A small *sphere* falling under the action of *gravity* through a *viscous* medium ultimately reaches a constant *velocity* equal to $v = \dfrac{2gr^2(d_1 - d_2)}{9\eta}$ where $r =$ radius of the sphere, $d_1 = density$ of the sphere, $d_2 =$ density of the medium, and $\eta =$ the coefficient of *viscosity* of the medium.

STOPPING POWER. A measure of the ability of a substance to reduce the *kinetic energy* of a charged particle passing through it. The 'linear' stopping power is the energy lost per unit distance; the 'mass' stopping power is the linear stopping power divided by the *density* of the substance. Stopping power is often expressed relative to such standard substances as air or aluminium.

STORAGE BATTERY. See *accumulator*.

STORE. A part of the *hardware* of a *computer* in which information is stored. A 'random access' store is one in which the *access time* for any stored information is approximately the same. A 'high-speed' store is a random access store with an access time measured in *micro*seconds. If this high speed is not required, *backing storage* is used.

STRAIN (phys.). When a body is deformed by an applied *stress* the strain is the ratio of the dimensional change to the original or unstrained dimension. The strain may be a ratio of lengths, areas, or volumes.

STRAIN GAUGE, ELECTRICAL. A grid of fine resistance wire supported on a paper base which is attached by a suitable adhesive to the surface under test, so that any strains set up in the latter are accurately transferred to the gauge wire. The electrical *resistance* of the gauge is proportional to the *strain*, so that methods of measuring resistance may be used for measuring strain. The gauge is suitable for measuring strains of the order of 10^{-4} to 10^{-2}.

STRAIN HARDENING. Work hardening. An increase in the *hardness* and *tensile strength* of a *metal*, due to cold working, which causes a permanent alteration (distortion) of its crystalline structure.

STRANGENESS. Certain *elementary particles* (K-*mesons* and *hyperons*) *decay* about 10^{12} times more slowly than would be expected from the large amounts of *energy* released in the processes. These particles, which are called strange particles, have been arbitrarily assigned a *quantum number*, *s*, to account for this strangeness. For ordinary particles (*nucleons*, *pions*, *muons*, etc.) $s = 0$; each strange particle has a specific, *integral* value of *s* which is not equal to 0. See Table 6, page 436.

STRATOPAUSE. The boundary between the *stratosphere* and the *mesosphere*.

STRATOSPHERE. A layer of the *atmosphere* beginning approximately 11 kilometres (7 miles) above the surface of the *Earth*.

STRATUM. A layer.

STREAMLINE. A *streamline* is a line in a *fluid* such that the *tangent* to it at every point is in the direction of the *velocity* of the fluid particle at that point, at the instant under consideration. When the motion of the fluid is such that, at any instant, continuous streamlines can be drawn through the whole length of its course, the fluid is said to be in streamline flow.

STREPTOMYCIN. $C_{21}H_{39}N_7O_{12}$. An *antibiotic* substance produced by the Streptomyces fungus. Effective against several types of disease *bacteria*, including some against which *penicillin* is inactive. Used in the treatment of tuberculosis.

STRESS (phys.). A *force* per unit area. When a stress is applied to a body (within its *elastic limit*) a corresponding *strain* is produced, and the ratio of stress to strain is a characteristic constant of the body. See *elastic modulus*.

STROBOSCOPE. An instrument with the aid of which it is possible to view objects which are moving rapidly with a periodic motion (see *period*) and to see them as if they were at rest. For example, if a disc, rotating at *n* revolutions per second, is illuminated by a source which is flashing at the same *frequency*, then at any particular flash the eye will see the disc in exactly the same position as it was for the previous flash. The disc will therefore appear stationary. If the frequency of the motion is not quite equal to that of the flashing, the disc will appear to rotate slowly.

STRONG NUCLEAR INTERACTIONS. The *interactions* which give rise to the *exchange forces* between *nucleons, hyperons*, and some *mesons*, when they are less than 10^{-13} cm apart. These are the strongest forces known in nature, being 100 times more powerful than electromagnetic interactions and 10^{12} times more powerful than *weak nuclear interactions*.

STRONTIA. See *strontium oxide*. *Strontium hydroxide* is also sometimes known as strontia.

STRONTIUM. Sr. Element. A.W. 87·62. At. No. 38. A *reactive metal* resembling calcium. S.G. 2·6; m.p. 757° C. Occurs as celestine, $SrSO_4$, and strontianite, $SrCO_3$. *Compounds* colour a *flame* crimson; used in fireworks. The *radioisotope* strontium-90 is present in the *fall-out* from nuclear explosions. It presents a health hazard as it has a relatively long *half-life* of 28 years and, owing to its chemical similarity to calcium, can become incorporated into bone. See *strontium unit*.

STRONTIUM HYDROXIDE. Strontia. $Sr(OH)_2$. A white *deliquescent* crystalline powder, m.p. 375° C., used in *sugar* refining as it combines with the sugar to form an *insoluble saccharate*.

STRONTIUM OXIDE. Strontia. SrO. A grey *amorphous* powder, m.p. 2430° C., with similar properties to *calcium oxide*. Used in the manufacture of strontium *salts*.

STRONTIUM NITRATE. $Sr(NO_3)_2$. A colourless crystalline substance, m.p. 570° C., used in fireworks and flares to give a bright crimson colour.

STRONTIUM UNIT. SU. A measure of the *concentration* of strontium-90 in an *organic* medium (e.g. milk, bone, *soil*, etc.) relative to the concentration of calcium in the same medium. 1 SU $= 10^{-12}$ *curies* of strontium-90 per gram of calcium.

STRUCTURAL FORMULA. A chemical *formula* which in addition to showing the *atoms* present in a *molecule*, also gives an indication of its structure. E.g. the structural formula of *benzene* (C_6H_6) is given by the *benzene ring*.

STRYCHNINE. $C_{21}H_{22}N_2O_2$. An *alkaloid* which occurs in the seeds of nux vomica. A white crystalline substance, slightly *soluble* in *water*; m.p. 284° C. It has an intensely bitter taste and a powerful and very dangerous action on the nervous system. Used in medicine in minute doses.

STYRENE. Phenylethylene. $C_6H_5.CH:CH_2$. A colourless *aromatic liquid*, b.p. 146° C., which polymerizes to a *thermoplastic* material (see *polystyrene*) and is used in the manufacture of synthetic *rubber*. See *styrene-butadiene rubber*.

STYRENE-BUTADIENE RUBBER. SBR. A widely used, general purpose synthetic *rubber*. Copolymer (see *polymerization*) of *butadiene* and about 35% of *styrene*, which is *vulcanized* in a similar manner to natural rubber. Properties are in general inferior to natural rubber, except for abrasion resistance, but passenger car tyres are made very largely from SBR. This *elastomer* is not suitable, however, for incorporation into heavy duty tyres.

SUB-. Prefix denoting under, below. In *chemistry* it is used to indicate either that the *element* mentioned is present in a lower proportion than usual, e.g. sub-oxide, or that the *compound* is *basic*, e.g. subacetate.

SUBATOMIC. Consisting of particles smaller than, or forming a part of, the *atom*. See *atom, structure of*.

SUBERIC ACID. $HOOC(CH_2)_6COOH$. A white crystalline *dibasic acid*, m.p. $140°C$., obtained from *castor oil* and used in the manufacture of *plastics* and *plasticizers*.

SUBCRITICAL. Said of a *nuclear reactor* in which the effective *multiplication constant* is less than unity, and in which the nuclear *chain reaction* is therefore not self-sustaining.

SUBGIANT. A *giant star* with a lower absolute *magnitude* than an ordinary giant.

SUBLIMATE. A *solid* obtained by the direct *condensation* of a vaporized solid without passing through the *liquid* state.

SUBLIMATION (chem.). The conversion of a *solid* direct into *vapour*, and subsequent *condensation*, without melting.

SUBSONIC. Moving at, or relating to, a *speed* which is less than Mach 1. See *Mach number*.

SUBSTANTIVE DYES. See *direct dyes*.

SUBSTITUENT. See *substitution product*.

SUBSTITUTION PRODUCT. A *compound* obtained by replacing an *atom* or group by another atom or group in a *molecule*. The new atom or group is known as the 'substituent'.

SUBSTRATE. A substance whose reactivity is increased by a specific *enzyme*.

SUBTEND (math.). Two points, *A* and *B*, are said to subtend the *angle ACB* at the point *C*.

SUCCINATE. A *salt* or *ester* of *succinic acid*.

SUCCINIC ACID. $(CH_2COOH)_2$. A white crystalline *organic dibasic acid*, m.p. $185°C$. Used in the manufacture of *dyes*, lacquers, and other products.

SUCCINITE. See *amber*.

SUCRASE. See *invertase*.

SUCROCLASTIC. *Sugar*-splitting; applied to *enzymes* which have the power of hydrolyzing complex *carbohydrates*. E.g. *invertase*.

SUCROSE. Cane-sugar, beet sugar, saccharose. Common 'sugar' of the household. $C_{12}H_{22}O_{11}$. A white sweet crystalline *disaccharide*, m.p. $160°-186°C$. Found in numerous plants, particularly the sugar cane, sugar beet and maple tree sap.

SUCTION. This is not a positive *force* which 'draws' a *liquid* up; a liquid raised by so-called suction is actually pushed up by atmospheric *pressure*, which is greater than the pressure of the partial *vacuum* caused by the suction.

SUGAR. In general, any sweet, *soluble*, *monosaccharide* or *disaccharide* *carbohydrate*; term commonly applied to *sucrose*.

371

SUGAR OF LEAD. See *lead acetate.*

SULPHANILIC ACID. $NH_2C_6H_4SO_3H.H_2O$. A grey crystalline *soluble* substance, m.p. 288° C., used in the manufacture of *dyes.*

SULPHATE. A *salt* or *ester* of *sulphuric acid.*

SULPHATE OF AMMONIA. See *ammonium sulphate.*

SULPHIDE. A *binary compound* of an *element* or group with sulphur; a *salt* of hydrogen sulphide, H_2S.

SULPHITE. A *salt* or *ester* of *sulphurous acid,* H_2SO_3.

SULPHONAMIDE DRUGS. Sulpha drugs. A group of *organic compounds,* containing the sulphonamide group $SO_2.NH_2$ or its *derivatives;* includes sulphanilamide ($NH_2C_6H_4.SO_2NH_2$), sulphapyridine ($NH_2C_6H_4SO_2$-NHC_5H_4N), sulphathiazole ($NH_2C_6H_4SO_2NHC_3H_2NS$), sulpha-diazine ($NH_2C_6H_4SO_2NHC_4H_3N_2$), and many others. Of great value in the treatment of many diseases caused by *bacteria.*

SULPHONATE. A *salt* or *ester* of *sulphonic acid.*

SULPHONIC ACIDS. *Acid organic compounds* which contain the sulphonic acid group, $-SO_2.OH$.

SULPHUR. S. Element. A.W. 32·064. At. No. 16. A non-metallic *element* occurring in several *allotropic forms.* The stable form under ordinary conditions is rhombic or alpha-sulphur, a pale-yellow brittle crystal-line *solid,* S.G. 2·07, m.p. 112·8° C., b.p. 444·6° C. Burns with a blue *flame* to give *sulphur dioxide;* combines with many *metals* to form *sulphides.* Occurs as the element in many volcanic regions and as sulphides of many *metals.* Extracted in vast quantities in Texas by the *Frasch process.* Used in the manufacture of *sulphuric acid, carbon disulphide,* for *vulcanizing rubber,* in the manufacture of *dyes* and various chemicals, for killing moulds and pests, and in medicine. Essential to life.

SULPHUR DIOXIDE. SO_2. A colourless *gas* with a choking penetrating smell; *liquid* SO_2 is used in *bleaching,* fumigating, and as a *refrigerant.*

SULPHUR POINT. The *temperature* of equilibrium between *liquid* sulphur and its *vapour* at a *pressure* of one standard atmosphere; 444·6° C.

SULPHUR TRIOXIDE. Sulphuric anhydride. SO_3. A white crystalline *solid,* m.p. 16·8° C. Combines with *water* to form *sulphuric acid.*

SULPHURETTED HYDROGEN. See *hydrogen sulphide.*

SULPHURIC ACID. Vitriol, oil of vitriol. A colourless oily *liquid dibasic acid,* S.G. 1·84. Extremely corrosive, reacts violently with *water* with evolution of *heat,* chars *organic* matter. Prepared by the *lead chamber* and the *contact processes.* Used extensively in many processes in chemical industry, and in the lead *accumulator.*

SULPHURIC ACID, FUMING. See *oleum.*

SULPHURIC ANHYDRIDE. See *sulphur trioxide.*

SULPHURIC ETHER. Diethyl ether. See *ethers.*

SULPHUROUS ACID. H_2SO_3. A colourless *liquid* formed when *sulphur dioxide* dissolves in *water.* Used in the form of its *salts,* the *sulphites.*

SULPHURYL CHLORIDE. SO_2Cl_2. A colourless *liquid,* b.p. 69·1° C., used as a chlorinating agent.

SULPHURYL GROUP. The *divalent radical* = SO_2.

SUN, THE. The incandescent, approximately spherical heavenly body around which the *planets* rotate in elliptical *orbits* (see *solar system*). The Sun is a 'main sequence' *star* (see *Hertzprung-Russell diagram*), being one of some 10^{11} stars which constitute our *Galaxy*. Mean distance from the *Earth* approximately $149 \cdot 6 \times 10^6$ kilometres, distance to nearest star approximately 40×10^{12} km. The diameter of the Sun is about 1 392 000 kilometres, its *mass* is approximately 2×10^{30} kilogrammes, its average *density* $1 \cdot 4$ grams per cm^3. The visible surface of the Sun, called the *photosphere*, is at a *temperature* of about 6000°C.; its interior temperature is some 13 000 000°C. At this internal temperature *thermonuclear reactions* occur in which hydrogen is converted into helium, these reactions providing the Sun with its vast supply of *energy*. The Sun is composed of about 90% hydrogen, 8% helium, and only 2% of the heavier *elements*.

SUNSPOTS. Large patches, which appear black by contrast with their surroundings, visible upon the surface of the *Sun*. Owing to the rotation of the Sun, they appear to move across its surface. Their appearance is spasmodic, but their number reaches a maximum approximately every eleven years. (See *eleven year period*.) Connected with such phenomena as magnetic storms and the *Aurora Borealis*. See *solar flares*, *solar prominences*, and *solar wind*.

SUPER HIGH FREQUENCY. S.H.F. *Radio frequencies* in the range 3000 to 30 000 *megahertz*.

SUPER-. Prefix denoting over, above.

SUPERCONDUCTIVITY. The electrical *resistance* of a *metal* or *alloy* is a function of *temperature*, decreasing as the temperature falls and tending to zero at the *absolute zero*. It is found that for certain metals and alloys (e.g. lead, vanadium, tin) the resistance changes abruptly, becoming vanishingly small at a temperature in the neighbourhood of a few degrees above absolute zero. This phenomenon is termed superconductivity, and the temperature at which it sets in is the transition temperature. A current induced by a *magnetic field* in a ring of superconducting material will continue to circulate after the magnetic field has been removed. (See also *cryotron*.) This effect has been used to produce large magnetic fields without the expenditure of appreciable quantities of *electrical energy*.

SUPERCOOLING. The *metastable* state of a *liquid* cooled below its *freezing point*. A supercooled liquid will usually freeze on the addition of a small particle of the *solid* substance, and often on the addition of any solid particle or even on shaking; the *temperature* then rises to the freezing point.

SUPERCRITICAL. Said of a *nuclear reactor* in which the effective *multiplication factor* exceeds unity, and in which the nuclear *chain reaction* is therefore self-sustaining.

SUPERDENSE THEORY. The theory in *cosmology* that the *Universe* has evolved from one 'superdense' agglomeration of *matter* which suffered a cataclysmic explosion. The observed *expansion of the Universe* is regarded as a result of this explosion, the *galaxies* flying apart like fragments from an exploding bomb. This hypothesis, which presupposes a finite beginning and probably a finite end to the history of the Universe, is in opposition to the *steady state theory*.

SUPERFLUID. A *fluid* which flows without *friction* and which has an abnormally high thermal *conductivity*, e.g. helium below 2·186 K.

SUPERGIANT STAR. A *star* of exceptionally high *luminosity*, low *density*, and a diameter some hundreds of times greater than the *Sun*.

SUPERHEATED STEAM. *Steam* above a *temperature* of 100° C., which is obtained by heating *water* under a *pressure* greater than atmospheric.

SUPERHEATING. Heating a *liquid* above its *boiling point*, when the liquid is in a *metastable* state. See *supercooling*.

SUPERHETERODYNE. Superhet. Abbreviation of 'supersonic heterodyne'. A method of *radio* reception in which the *frequency* of the *carrier wave* is changed in the receiver to a 'supersonic' *intermediate frequency* (i.e. a frequency above the audible limit for *sound*) by a *heterodyne* process.

SUPERNOVAE. *Stars* which suffer an explosion becoming some 10^8 times brighter than the *Sun* during the process. Relatively rare events, only two having been recorded within our *Galaxy*, although they have been observed fairly regularly in other *galaxies*. Believed to be caused when a star runs out of hydrogen and contracts under its own *gravitational field*. The contraction causes a sufficiently high *temperature* in the interior for *thermonuclear reactions* to occur which produce heavy *elements*. The formation of heavy elements, with *atomic numbers* in excess of about 40, absorbs *energy* and the star collapses inwards, increasing its speed of rotation and ultimately flinging a large portion of its *matter* into *space*. It is believed that the *planets* of the *solar system* consist of matter thrown into space by a supernova, which was subsequently collected by the Sun's gravitational field. The residue of a supernova explosion is a *white dwarf* star.

SUPERPHOSPHATE. An artificial *fertilizer* consisting mainly of calcium hydrogen orthophosphate. See *calcium phosphate*.

SUPERPLASTICITY. The property, exhibited by certain metallic *alloys*, of stretching several hundred per cent before failing, e.g. zinc in aluminium.

SUPERSATURATION. The *metastable* state of a *solution* holding more dissolved *solute* than is required to *saturate* the solution.

SUPERSONIC. Moving at, or relating to, a *speed* in excess of Mach 1. See *Mach number*.

SUPERSONICS. See *ultrasonics*.

SUPPLEMENTARY ANGLES. *Angles* together totalling 180°, or two right angles.

SUPPRESSOR GRID. A grid, placed between the *screen grid* and the *anode* of a *thermionic valve*, to reduce the *secondary emission* of *electrons* between them.

SURD. An irrational quantity; a *root* which cannot be expressed as an exact number or fraction; e.g. $\sqrt{2}$.

SURFACE ACTIVE AGENT. Surfactant. A substance introduced into a *liquid* in order to affect (usually to increase) its spreading, wetting, and similar properties (i.e. properties which depend upon its *surface tension*). Many *detergents* fall into this class.

SURFACE COLOUR. Certain reflecting surfaces, e.g. *metal* surfaces, exhibit selective reflection of *light* waves; i.e. they reflect some *wavelengths* (*colours*) more readily than others. When illuminated by *white light*, such surfaces reflect light deficient in certain wavelengths, and the body appears coloured. The body is then said to show surface colour, as opposed to *pigment colour*. Bodies showing surface colour when viewed by transmitted light appear to be of the *complementary colour* to that observed when viewed by reflected light. Substances which show pigment colour appear the same colour whether viewed by reflected or transmitted light.

SURFACE TENSION. γ. An open surface of a *liquid* is under a state of tension, causing a tendency for the portions of the surface to separate from each other; the surface thus shows properties similar to those of a stretched elastic film over the liquid. The tension is an effect of the *forces* of attraction existing between the *molecules* of a liquid. Measured by the force per unit length (*newtons* per *metre*) acting in the surface at right angles to an element of any line drawn in the surface. A surface tension exists in any boundary surface of a liquid.

SURFACTANT. See *surface active agent*.

SUSCEPTIBILITY, MAGNETIC. See *magnetic susceptibility*.

SUSPENSION (chem.). A two-phase system (see *phase*) consisting of very small *solid* particles distributed in a *liquid dispersion medium*.

SUSPENSOID SOL. See *colloidal solutions*.

SYLVINE. Natural *potassium chloride*, KCl, usually containing *sodium chloride* as an impurity. An important source of potassium *compounds*.

SYMBIOSIS. A relationship between two different types of *organism* which live together for their mutual benefit. E.g. the relationship between *cellulose*-digesting *bacteria* and the herbivores whose alimentary tract they inhabit.

SYMBOL (chem.). A letter or letters representing an *atom* of an *element*; e.g. S = one atom of sulphur. Often loosely taken to mean the element in general, e.g. Fe = iron. See *formula*. The symbols of all the elements are given in Table 3, on pages 432–4.

SYMMETRY. The correspondence of parts of a figure with reference to a *plane*, line, or point of symmetry. Thus, a *circle* is symmetrical about any diameter; a *sphere* is symmetrical about a plane of any great circle.

SYNAPSE. A junction between *neurones* by which nerve impulses are transferred within the nervous systems of animals. A synapse is usually formed between the *axon* of one neurone and the cell body or *dendrite* of another.

SYNCHROCYCLOTRON. A type of *cyclotron* which enables *relativistic velocities* to be achieved by modulating the *frequency* of the accelerating *electric field*.

SYNCHRONOUS MOTOR. An *alternating current electric motor* whose speed of rotation is proportional to the *frequency* of its power supply.

SYNCHRONOUS ORBIT. Stationary orbit. The *orbit* of an artificial Earth *satellite* which has a *period* of 24 hours. The altitude corresponding to such an orbit is about 35 700 km; a satellite in a circular orbit parallel to the *equator* at this altitude would appear to be stationary in the sky. Communication satellites in synchronous orbits are used for relaying *radio* signals between widely separated points on the Earth's surface.

SYNCHROTRON. An *accelerator* of the *cyclotron* type in which the *magnetic field* is modulated but the *electric field* is maintained at a constant *frequency*.

SYNCHROTRON RADIATION. High *energy electrons* within a *synchrotron* emit *light* as a consequence of their *acceleration* in a strong *magnetic field*; this emission is known as synchrotron radiation. The term is also used to describe the emission of *radio frequency electromagnetic radiations* from interstellar gas clouds in *radio galaxies* (see *radio astronomy*) as this emission is believed to be an analogous phenomenon.

SYNERESIS. The separation of *liquid* from a *gel*.

SYNODIC MONTH. See *lunation*.

SYNODIC PERIOD OF A PLANET. The period between two successive *conjunctions* with the *Sun*, as observed from the *Earth*.

SYNTHESIS (chem.). 'Putting together'; the formation of a *compound* from its *elements* or simpler compounds.

SYNTHETIC (chem.). Artificially prepared from the component *elements* or simpler materials; not obtained directly from natural sources.

SYSTÈME INTERNATIONAL D'UNITÉS. See *SI units*.

SYZYGY. A point of *opposition* or *conjunction* of a *planet*, or the *Moon*, with the *Sun*.

T

TACHOMETER. An instrument for measuring the rate of revolution of a revolving shaft.

TACHYON. A hypothetical particle which travels faster than the *velocity of light*. To satisfy the *special theory of relativity* such a particle would have imaginary *energy* and *momentum* if it had a real *rest mass*, or imaginary rest mass if the energy was real. Its presence could be detected by the *Cerenkov radiation* it emits, but no such particle has yet been detected.

TACNODE. A point at which two branches of a curve touch each other and have a common *tangent*.

TALC. *Hydrated* magnesium silicate, $3MgO.4SiO_2.H_2O$. Used as a lubricant and in talcum powder.

TALL OIL. A resinous substance obtained as a *by-product* in the manufacture of wood-pulp, used in *soaps* and *paints*.

TALLOW. The rendered fat of animals, particularly cattle and sheep. Consists of various *glycerides*.

TANDEM GENERATOR. An *accelerator* of the *electrostatic generator* type. The name is derived from the fact that it consists essentially of two *Van der Graaff generators* in series, thus enabling twice as much *energy* to be obtained for a given accelerating *potential* as could be obtained from a single machine. Negative *ions* are accelerated from ground potential, the *electrons* are then 'stripped' off and the positive particles accelerated back to ground potential.

TANGENT GALVANOMETER. A *galvanometer* consisting of a coil of wire (n turns of radius r) held in a vertical plane parallel to the Earth's *magnetic field*, H, with a small magnetic needle pivoted at the centre of the coil which is free to rotate in a horizontal plane. A direct *electric current*, I, flowing through the coil produces a magnetic field at right angles to that of the Earth. The needle takes up the direction of the *resultant* of these two fields: if θ is the *angle* of deflection of the needle from its equilibrium position parallel to the Earth's field, then the current will be given by: $I = Hr \tan \theta / 2\pi n$.

TANGENT OF AN ANGLE. See *trigonometrical ratios*.

TANGENT TO A CURVE. A straight line touching the curve at a point. The tangent to a *circle* at any point is at right angles to the radius of the circle at that point.

TANNIC ACID. $C_{76}H_{52}O_4$. A white *amorphous soluble solid* extracted from gallnuts, m.p. approx. $210°C$.; also a class of similar *ester*-like substances widely distributed in plants. Used in *tanning* and in the manufacture of *ink*.

TANNING. The conversion of raw animal hide into leather by the action of substances containing *tannin, tannic acid*, or other agents.

TANNINS. A class of complex *organic compounds* of vegetable origin. Consists of *mixtures* of *derivatives* of poly-hydroxy *benzoic acids*; e.g. *tannic acid*.

377

TANTALUM. Ta. Element. A.W. 180·948. At. No. 73. A greyish-white *metal*, very ductile and malleable. S.G. 16·6, m.p. 2996°C. Occurs together with niobium in a few rare *minerals*; extracted by *reduction* of the *oxide* with carbon in an electric furnace. Used for electric lamp *filaments*, in *alloys*, in cemented *carbides* for very hard tools, and in electrolytic *rectifiers*.

TAPE RECORDING. See *magnetic tape*.

TAR. Various dark, viscous *organic* materials; e.g. *coal-tar*.

TARTAR. See *argol*.

TARTAR EMETIC. See *antimony potassium tartrate*.

TARTARIC ACID. COOH.(CH.OH)$_2$.COOH. An *organic acid* existing in four stereoisomeric forms (see *stereoisomerism*). The common form, *d*-tartaric acid, obtained from *argol*, is a white *soluble* crystalline *solid*, m.p. 170°C. Used in dyeing, calico-printing, and in making *baking-powder* and effervescent 'health salts'. *dl*-tartaric acid (*racemic acid*), m.p. 203–4°C., occurs in grapes.

TARTRATE. A *salt* or *ester* of *tartaric acid*.

TAURINE. NH$_2$(CH$_2$)$_2$SO$_3$H. A white crystalline substance, m.p. 328°C., obtained from the *bile* of mammals.

TAUTOMERISM. Dynamic isomerism. The existence of a *compound* as a mixture of two *isomers* in equilibrium. The two forms are convertible one into the other, and removal of one of the forms from the *mixture* results in the conversion of part of the other to restore the equilibrium; but each of the two forms may give rise to a stable series of *derivatives*. A substance exhibiting this property is called a 'tautomer'. See also *keto-enol tautomerism*.

TEAR GASES. Lachrymators. Substances which can be distributed in the form of a *vapour* or *smoke*, producing an irritating effect on the eyes.

TECHNETIUM. Masurium. Tc. Element. At. No. 43. The most stable *isotope*, $^{97}_{43}$Tc, has a *half-life* of 2·6 × 10^6 years. Not found in nature but formed as a *fission product* of uranium.

TEFLON*. See *tetrafluoroethylene* and *fluorocarbons*.

TEKTITES. Small glass-like bodies whose chemical composition is unrelated to the geological formations in which they are found: believed to be associated with *meteorites* of extra-terrestrial origin. 'Carbonaceous' tektites contain traces of carbon *compounds*.

TELECOMMUNICATIONS. The telegraphic or telephonic communication of signals, images, or sounds by line or *radio* transmission.

TELEGRAPH. A method of transmitting messages over a distance by means of electrical impulses sent through wires. By depressing a key at the transmitting end, a circuit is closed and an *electric current* flows through the conducting wire or cable to the receiver; the dots and dashes of the Morse code being obtained by varying the length of time for which the current flows. At the receiving end, the feeble electrical impulses are made to operate a *relay*, which then closes a local circuit, carrying a larger current. This current either sounds a *buzzer*, or a *tele-*

phone receiver, or causes the dots and dashes to be automatically recorded.

TELEMETER. Any apparatus for recording a physical event at a distance. E.g. an instrument in an artificial *satellite* which transmits measurements made in *space* back to *Earth* by *radio*.

TELEPHONE. The circuit, which is closed when the line is connected, consists essentially of a transmitter and a receiver connected by an electrical *conductor*. The transmitter is usually a carbon *microphone*, by means of which variable electrical impulses, depending on the nature of the *sounds* made into the microphone, are caused to flow through the circuit. In the telephone receiver these impulses flow through a pair of coils of wire wound upon soft iron pole-pieces attached to the poles of a *magnet*; an iron diaphragm near these coils experiences variable pulls, and thus vibrates so as to produce sounds corresponding to those made into the microphone.

TELEPHOTO LENS. A combination of a *convex* and a *concave lens*, used to replace the ordinary lens of a *camera* in order to magnify the normal image. The size of the image obtained on the photographic *film* varies as the *focal length* of the lens. The telephoto lens system increases the effective focal length without the necessity of increasing the distance between the film and the lens.

TELESCOPE. A device for viewing magnified images of distant objects. In the refracting telescope the *objective* is a large *convex lens* which produces a small, bright, real *image*; this is viewed through the *eye-piece*, which is another convex lens, serving to magnify the image. In the reflecting telescope a large *concave* mirror (see *speculum*) is used instead of the objective lens to produce the real image, which is then magnified by the eye-piece. For terrestrial needs, these types of telescope are unsuitable, since the images formed are inverted; for terrestrial purposes telescopes are equipped with a further lens or *prism* which causes the image to be seen erect. See also *Cassegranian, Galilean, Gregorian, Maksutov, Newtonian, Schmidt,* and *radio telescopes*.

TELETYPE*. Trade name for a *computer terminal* consisting of a device resembling a typewriter which can be combined with a paper-tape reader and punch.

TELEVISION. The transmission of visible, moving images by electrical means. In 'closed circuit' television the transmission is by line; in 'broadcast' television it is by *radio* waves. In either case *light* waves are converted into electrical impulses by a television *camera* and reconverted into a picture on the screen of a *cathode ray tube* in the receiver. In broadcast television the transmitter consists of equipment for broadcasting modulated *radio frequency electromagnetic radiations* representing a complete television signal, which includes *sound*, vision, and synchronizing signals. The receiver is based on the *superheterodyne* principle, the sound and vision signals being fed to separate *intermediate frequency* amplifiers, *detectors*, and output stages.

379

TELLURIC. 1. Pertaining to the *Earth* (as a *planet*), or the earth or *soil*.
2. Derived from or containing *hexavalent* tellurium.

TELLURIUM. Te. Element. A.W. 127·6. At. No. 52. A silvery-white brittle non-metal, resembling sulphur in its chemical properties. S.G. 6·24, m.p. 452° C. Exists in several *allotropic forms*. Used in *alloys* and for colouring *glass*.

TELLUROUS. Containing *tetravalent* tellurium.

TEMPERATURE. The temperature of a body is a measure of its 'hotness', which can be defined as a property determining the rate at which *heat* will be transferred to or from it. Temperature is thus a measure of the *kinetic energy* of the *molecules*, *atoms*, or *ions* of which *matter* is composed. The basic physical quantity, the *thermodynamic temperature*, is expressed in *kelvins*. These units are also used in the *International Practical Temperature Scale*. Other scales of temperature are the *Celsius* (*Centigrade*), *Fahrenheit*, and *Réaumur scales*.

TEMPERING OF STEEL. Imparting a definite degree of hardness to *steel* by heating to a definite *temperature* (which is sometimes determined by the *colour* which the steel assumes) and then *quenching*, i.e. cooling, in *oil* or *water*.

TEMPORARY HARDNESS OF WATER. Hardness of *water*, which is destroyed by *boiling*. See *hard water*.

TEMPORARY MAGNETISM. Induced magnetism. *Magnetism* which a body (e.g. soft iron) possesses only by virtue of being in a *magnetic field* and which largely disappears on removing the body from the field.

TENSILE STRENGTH. Tenacity. The tensile (pulling) *stress* which has to be applied to a material to break it. Measured as a *force* per unit area; e.g. *newtons* per square *metre*; *dynes* per square centimetre; pounds or tons per square inch.

TENSIMETER. An instrument for measuring *vapour pressure*.

TENSIOMETER. 1. An apparatus for measuring the *surface tension* of a *liquid*. 2. An apparatus for measuring the tension in a wire, fibre, or beam. 3. An apparatus for measuring the moisture content of *soil*.

TENSOR. A magnitude or set of *functions* by which the components of a system are transformed from one system of *coordinates* to another: a quantity expressing the ratio in which the length of a *vector* is increased.

TERA-. Prefix denoting one million million; 10^{12}. Symbol T.

TERBIUM. Tb. Element. A.W. 158·924. At. No. 65. S.G. 8·25, m.p. 1356° C. See *lanthanides*.

TEREPHTHALIC ACID. $C_6H_4(COOH)_2$. A white *insoluble* crystalline substance, the *para-isomer* of *phthalic acid*, used in the manufacture of synthetic *resins* and fibres (see *Terylene**).

TERMINAL. 1. (phys.) The point at which an electrical connection is made; the point, or the connecting device, at which *current* enters or leaves a piece of electric equipment. 2. An input or output device connected to a *computer*; it may be a *line printer*, a punched-card reader, a *teletype*, or a *visual display unit*.

TERMINAL VELOCITY. If a body free to move in a resisting medium is acted upon by a constant *force* (e.g. a body falling under the force of *gravity* through the atmosphere), the body accelerates until a certain terminal velocity is reached, after which the *velocity* remains constant.

TERMINATOR. The line on the surface of the *Moon*, or a *planet*, which separates the dark and light hemispheres.

TERMOLECULAR REACTION. A *chemical reaction* in which there are three *reactant molecules*. E.g. $2H_2 + O_2 \rightarrow 2H_2O$.

TERNARY COMPOUND. A chemical *compound* consisting of three *elements*. E.g. HNO_3 (*nitric acid*).

TERNARY FISSION. A very rare form of *nuclear fission* as a result of which a heavy *nucleus* breaks up into three fragments of comparable *mass*. The term is also used for the more frequent case in which one of the three fragments (e.g. an *alpha-particle*) is much lighter than the others.

TERPENES. A class of *hydrocarbons* occurring in many fragrant *essential oils* of plants. Colourless *liquids*, generally with a pleasant smell; include *pinene*, $C_{10}H_{16}$, the chief ingredient of *turpentine*; and *limonene*, $C_{10}H_{16}$, found in the essential oils of oranges and lemons.

TERPINEOL. $C_{10}H_{17}OH$. Several *isomeric unsaturated alcohols* which occur in *essential oils*. α-terpineol, m.p. 35°C., b.p. 220°C., is used as a *solvent* and in perfumes.

TERRAMYCIN*. Oxytetracycline. $C_{22}H_{30}N_2O_{11}$. An *antibiotic* powder obtained from 'streptomyces rimosus' *bacteria*, used to combat streptococci and staphylococci infections.

TERRESTRIAL GUIDANCE. A method of missile or *rocket* guidance in which the missile steers itself with reference to the strength and direction of the *Earth*'s *gravitational* or *magnetic field* (magnetic guidance).

TERRESTRIAL MAGNETISM. See *magnetism, terrestrial*.

TERTIARY COLOUR. A *colour* obtained by mixing two *secondary colours*. E.g. brown and grey.

TERVALENT. Trivalent. Having a *valency* of three.

TERYLENE*. Dacron*. Trade name for a widely used *synthetic* fibre consisting of a straight-chain *polyester*. Made by the *condensation* of the *diol ester* of *terephthalic acid, ethanediol* being eliminated.

TESLA. The derived *SI unit* of *magnetic flux density*, defined as the density of one *weber* of *magnetic flux* per square metre. Symbol T. Named after Nikola Tesla (1870–1943).

TESLA COIL. A *transformer* for producing high *voltages* at high *frequencies*, consisting of a coil the primary circuit of which has a small number of turns but includes a spark gap and a fixed *capacitor*. The secondary winding has a large number of turns and the secondary circuit is *tuned*, by means of a variable capacitor, to resonate with the primary.

TESTOSTERONE. $C_{19}H_{28}O_2$. A male sex *hormone* (*androgen*), which in the pure form consists of a white *insoluble* crystalline substance, m.p. 155°C, whose function is to promote the development of male characteristics.

TETRA-. Prefix denoting four, fourfold.

TETRACHLOROETHYLENE. Perchlorethylene. $Cl_2C:CCl_2$. A colourless non-inflammable *liquid*, b.p. 121°C., used as a *solvent* and in dry cleaning.

TETRAD. An *element* having a *valency* of four.

TETRAETHYL-LEAD. $(C_2H_5)_4Pb$. A colourless oily *liquid*, used as an anti-*knocking compound* in *petrol*.

TETRAETHYL PYROPHOSPHATE. T.E.P.P. $(C_2H_5)_4P_2O_7$. A colourless *hygroscopic liquid*, b.p. 155°C., used as an *insecticide* and rat poison.

TETRAFLUOROETHYLENE. $CF_2:CF_2$. A fluorinated *olefine gas*, b.p. −76·3°C., which polymerizes (see *polymerization*) into a *thermoplastic* material with good electrical insulation properties (trade names Teflon*, and Fluon*).

TETRAHEDRON. A four-faced, *solid* figure, contained by four *triangles*; a *pyramid* with a triangular base.

TETRANITROMETHANE. $C(NO_2)_4$. A colourless *volatile liquid*, b.p. 126°C., used as an *oxidant* in *rockets*.

TETRAVALENT. Quadrivalent. Having a *valency* of four.

TETRODE. A *thermionic valve* containing four *electrodes*; a *cathode*, an *anode* or plate, a *control grid*, and (between the two latter) a *screen grid*.

THALIDOMIDE. $C_{13}H_{10}N_2O_4$. A white crystalline substance, formerly used as a *tranquillizer* but found to be the cause of deformed children when taken by pregnant women.

THALLIC. Containing *trivalent* thallium.

THALLIUM. Tl. Element. A.W. 204·37. At. No. 81. A white malleable *metal* resembling lead. S.G. 11·85, m.p. 303·5°C. Used in *alloys*; its *salts* are used in *insecticides* and rat poisons.

THALLOUS. Containing *univalent* thallium.

THEBAINE. $C_{19}H_{21}NO_3$. A white *insoluble* substance, m.p. 193°C., present in *opium* in small quantities.

THEINE. See *caffeine*.

THEOBROMINE. $C_7H_8N_4O_2$. A white *insoluble* crystalline *alkaloid*, m.p. 337°C., which is *isomeric* with 'theophylline'; m.p. 272°C. Both occur in tea and are used in medicine.

THEODOLITE. An instrument for the measurement of *angles*, used in surveying. Consists essentially of a *telescope* moving along a circular scale graduated in *degrees*.

THEOPHYLLINE. See *theobromine*.

THEOREM. A statement or proposition which is proved by logical reasoning from given facts and justifiable assumptions.

THEORY OF GAMES. A mathematical treatment of competitive games with special reference to the strategic and tactical decisions which have to be made in situations involving conflicting interests, in the light of specific odds and *probabilities*. The theory is extended for use in military and commercial situations.

THERAPEUTICS. Healing; remedial treatment of diseases.

THERM. Practical unit of quantity of *heat*; 100 000 *British thermal units*, 25 200 000 *calories*, $1\cdot05506 \times 10^8$ *joules*.

THERMAL BARRIER. The limit to the *speed* with which an aircraft or *rocket* can travel in the Earth's *atmosphere* due to overheating caused by *friction* with the atmospheric *molecules*.

THERMAL CAPACITY. See *heat capacity*.

THERMAL CROSS-SECTION. A nuclear *cross-section* as measured with *thermal neutrons*.

THERMAL DIFFUSION. If a *temperature* gradient is maintained over a *volume* of *gas* containing *molecules* of different *masses*, the heavier molecules tend to diffuse down the temperature gradient, and the lighter molecules in the opposite direction. This forms the basis of a method of separating the different *isotopes* of an *element* in certain cases.

THERMAL DISSOCIATION. See *dissociation*.

THERMAL EQUILIBRIUM. The state of a system in which there is no net flow of *heat* between its components.

THERMAL NEUTRONS. *Neutrons* of very slow speed and consequently of low *energy*. Their energy is of the same order as the thermal energy of the *atoms* or *molecules* of the substance through which they are passing; i.e. about 0·025 *electron-volts* which is equivalent to an average *velocity* of about 2200 *metres* per second. Thermal neutrons are responsible for numerous types of *nuclear reactions*, including *nuclear fission*.

THERMAL REACTOR. A *nuclear reactor* in which most of the *nuclear fissions* are caused by *thermal neutrons*.

THERMAL SPIKE. The zone of high *temperature* briefly produced in a substance along the path of a high *energy* particle or *nuclear fission* fragment.

THERMALIZE. To bring *neutrons* into *thermal equilibrium* with their surroundings: to reduce the *energy* of neutrons with a *moderator*: to produce *thermal neutrons*.

THERMION. An *ion* emitted by a hot body.

THERMIONIC EMISSION. The emission of *electrons* from a heated *metal*, especially in *thermionic valves*.

THERMIONIC VALVE or TUBE. A system of *electrodes* arranged in an evacuated *glass* or *metal* envelope. For special purposes a *gas* at low *pressure* may be introduced into the valve. The electrodes are: (1) a *cathode* which emits *electrons* when heated; (2) an *anode* or plate maintained at a positive *potential* with respect to the cathode; the electrons emitted by the latter are attracted to it. Most valves also contain a number of perforated electrodes or grids (see *control grid, screen grid, suppressor grid*) interposed between the cathode and anode, designed to control the flow of current through the valve. The cathode can be in the form of a *filament* heated by an *electric current* passing through it, or an electrode heated indirectly by a separate filament. See *diode, triode, tetrode, pentode*.

THERMIONICS. The branch of *electronics* dealing with the emission of *electrons* from substances under the action of *heat*, particularly the study and design of *thermionic valves*.

THERMISTOR. A *semiconductor*, the electrical *resistance* of which decreases rapidly with increase of *temperature*; e.g. the resistance may be of the order of 10^5 ohms at 20°C. and only 10 ohms at 100°C. Used as a sensitive temperature-measuring device and to compensate for temperature variations of other components in a circuit.

THERMIT. Thermite. A *mixture* of aluminium powder and the *oxide* of a *metal*, e.g. *ferric oxide*. When ignited by magnesium ribbon, a *chemical reaction* begins in which the aluminium combines with the oxygen of the oxide, forming *aluminium oxide* and the metal. A great quantity of *heat* is given out during the reaction, the reduced metal (see *reduction*) appearing in the molten state. The mixture is used for *welding* iron and *steel*, and in incendiary bombs; the principle is applied in the *extraction* of certain metals from their oxides (see *Goldschmidt process*).

THERMOBAROGRAPH. An instrument for measuring and recording atmospheric *temperature* and *pressure*, consisting of a *thermograph* and a *barograph*.

THERMOCHEMISTRY. The branch of *physical chemistry* dealing with the quantities of *heat* absorbed or evolved during *chemical reactions*. See *heat of reaction* and *Hess's law*.

THERMOCOUPLE. An instrument for the measurement of *temperature*. Consists of two wires of different *metals* joined at each end. One junction is at the point where the temperature is to be measured and the other is kept at a lower fixed temperature. Owing to this difference of temperature of the junctions, a thermo-electric *E.M.F.* is generated, causing an *electric current* to flow in the circuit (see *Seebeck effect*). This current can be measured by means of a *galvanometer* in the circuit, or the thermo-electric E.M.F. can be measured using a *potentiometer*.

THERMODYNAMIC ENERGY. *U*. See *internal energy*.

THERMODYNAMIC TEMPERATURE. *T*. Although formerly referred to as a scale of *temperature* (Kelvin scale of temperature, or absolute scale of temperature), the concept of a temperature scale is now restricted to the *International Practical Temperature Scale of 1968*. The thermodynamic temperature is a basic physical quantity, which depends on the concept of temperature as a measure of the thermal *energy* of random motion of the particles of a system in *thermal equilibrium*. Originally, thermodynamic temperature was defined in terms of the *ice point* and *steam point* of *water* using a *gas thermometer*. However, in 1954 this was replaced by a definition using only one fixed point, the *triple point* of water, which was fixed as 273·16 *kelvins* exactly. The magnitude of the unit of thermodynamic temperature, the kelvin, is the same as the *degree* on the International Practical Scale of Temperature.

THERMODYNAMICS. The study of the general laws governing processes which involve *heat* changes and the conservation of *energy*.

THERMODYNAMICS, LAWS OF. 1. The law of the conservation of *energy*.

In a system of constant *mass*, energy can be neither created nor destroyed. A special case of this general law is the principle of the *mechanical equivalent of heat*. 2. Heat cannot be transferred by any continuous, self-sustaining process from a colder to a hotter body. Or stated in terms of *entropy*; the entropy of a closed system increases with time. 3. See the *Nernst heat theorem*. The consequence of this law is that the *absolute zero* of temperature can never be attained.

THERMO-ELECTRIC EFFECT. See *Seebeck effect*.

THERMO-ELECTRICITY. *Electricity* produced by the direct conversion of *heat* energy into *electrical energy*. See *thermocouple*; *Thomson effect*; *Seebeck effect*.

THERMOGRAPH. A self-registering *thermometer*; an apparatus which records *temperature* variations during a period of time on a *graph*.

THERMOMETER. An instrument for the measurement of *temperature*. Any physical property of a substance which varies with temperature can be used to measure the latter; e.g. the *volume* of a *liquid* or gas maintained under a fixed *pressure*; the pressure of a gas at constant volume; the electrical *resistance* of a *conductor*; the *E.M.F.* produced at a *thermocouple* junction, etc. The property chosen depends on the temperature range, the accuracy required, and the ease with which the instrument can be made and used. The common mercury thermometer depends upon the expansion of mercury with rise in temperature. The mercury is contained in a bulb attached to a narrow graduated sealed tube; the expansion of the mercury in the bulb causes a thin thread of it to rise in the tube. See also *gas thermometer*; *pyrometers*; *resistance thermometer*; *thermocouple*; *Beckmann thermometer*; *thermometer, clinical*; *thermometer, maximum and minimum*.

THERMOMETER, CLINICAL. A mercury *thermometer* designed to measure the *temperature* of the human body, and graduated to cover a range of a few degrees on either side of the normal body temperature. A constriction in the tube near the bulb causes the mercury thread to break when the thermometer is taken away from the warm body, and the mercury in the bulb starts to contract. The thread thus remains in the tube to indicate the maximum temperature reached, until it is shaken down.

THERMOMETER, MAXIMUM AND MINIMUM. A thermometer which records the highest and lowest *temperatures* reached during a period of time. Consists of a bulb filled with *alcohol*, which, by expansion, pushes a mercury thread along a fine tube, graduated in degrees. At each end of the mercury thread is a small *steel* 'index' which is pushed by the mercury; one is thus left at the farthest point reached by the mercury thread, corresponding to the maximum temperature, and the other at the lowest point.

THERMO-MILLIAMMETER. An instrument for measuring small alternating *electric currents*. The current passes through a wire made of *constantan* or platinum, which is in contact with or very close to a *thermocouple*. The thermocouple is connected to a sensitive *milliammeter*, the heat of the constantan wire producing a thermo-electric current in the thermocouple; this current is recorded by the milliammeter. In a more sensitive instrument, the heater wire and thermocouple are arranged in an evacuated *quartz* envelope.

THERMONUCLEAR BOMB. See *nuclear weapons*.

THERMONUCLEAR REACTION. A *nuclear fusion* reaction in which the interacting particles or *nuclei* possess sufficient *kinetic energy*, as a result of their thermal agitation, to initiate and sustain the process. The hydrogen bomb (see *nuclear weapons*) makes use of thermonuclear reactions by employing a fission bomb to attain the required *temperature*, which is in excess of 20×10^6 °C. Controlled thermonuclear reactions attempt to make use of fusion reactions in *deuterium* and *tritium* gas, at a temperature in the range 50×10^7 to 5×10^9 °C., for the purpose of generating *electrical energy*. The central problem in achieving this end is that of *containment*, i.e. separating the *plasma* (or high temperature ionized gas) from the walls of the containing vessel. In general, the plasma may be contained either by the use of externally applied *magnetic fields*, or by the magnetic fields produced by currents flowing in the plasma itself (see *pinch effect*). The nature and instabilities of these magnetic fields are the subject of contemporary research. The machines in which these experiments are carried out may be classified according to whether the *magnetic lines of force* of the containing field are closed- or open-ended. The closed field group include *torus*-shaped machines such as $ZETA$, while the open-ended machines include those using *magnetic mirrors* or rotating plasmas.

THERMOPILE. An instrument for detecting and measuring *heat* radiations. Consists of a number of rods of antimony and bismuth, connected alternately in series. When the junctions are exposed to heat, the thermo-electric current produced (see *thermocouple*) may be detected or measured by a sensitive *galvanometer*.

THERMOPLASTIC. A substance which becomes plastic on being heated; a *plastic* material which can be repeatedly melted or softened by heat without change of properties.

THERMOSETTING PLASTICS. *Plastics* which, having once been subjected to *heat* (and *pressure*), lose their plasticity.

THERMOSPHERE. The region of the *upper atmosphere* in which the *temperature* increases with *altitude*. See Fig. 44, page 402.

THERMOSTAT. An instrument for maintaining a constant *temperature*, by the use of a device which cuts off the supply of *heat* when the required temperature is exceeded, and automatically restores the supply when the temperature falls below that required. Usually consists of a *bimetallic strip* so arranged that when it is heated (or cooled) the power supply contacts are opened (or closed).

THIAMIN(E). Aneurin. Vitamin B$_1$. $C_{12}H_{17}ON_4SCl$. A member of *vitamin* B complex; a white crystalline powder, *soluble* in *water* and *alcohol*.

Widely required by many living *organisms* for the *metabolism* of *carbohydrates*. Occurs in liver, milk, eggs, and fruit. Deficiency causes beriberi, and nervous disorders.

THIAZINES. A group of *compounds* consisting of a six-membered ring, four of which are carbon *atoms*, one of which is a sulphur atom, and one a nitrogen atom.

THIAZOLE. S.CH:N.CH:CH. A colourless *volatile liquid*, b.p. 116·8°C., whose *molecule* consists of a five-membered ring. *Derivatives* used in dyestuffs and in medicine.

THIO-. Prefix denoting sulphur, in the naming of chemical *compounds*.

THIOACETAMIDE. CH_3CSNH_2. A colourless *soluble* crystalline substance, m.p. 115–16°C., used as a source of *hydrogen sulphide*.

THIOCYANATE. A *salt* or *ester* of *thiocyanic acid*.

THIOCYANIC ACID. HSCN. An *unstable acid* which forms *salts* called *thiocyanates*.

THIOKOLS*. *Rubber*-like *polymer* materials of the general formula $(RS_x)n$, where R is an *organic bivalent radical*, and x is usually between 2 and 4. They are very resistant to the swelling action of *oils*, and undergo a form of *vulcanization* on being heated with certain metallic *oxides*.

THIONIN. $C_{12}H_9N_3S$. A dark brown *thiazine derivative*, used as a *dye* in miscroscopy.

THIONYL CHLORIDE. $SOCl_2$. A yellowish fuming *liquid*, b.p. 78°C., used in *organic synthesis*.

THIOPHEN. C_4H_4S. A colourless *liquid*, b.p. 84·12°C., which occurs in *coal-tar* and is used as a *solvent*.

THIOSULPHATE. A *salt* or *ester* of *thiosulphuric acid*.

THIOSULPHURIC ACID. $H_2S_2O_3$. An *unstable acid* formed by replacing one oxygen *atom* of *sulphuric acid* (H_2SO_4) by one sulphur atom. Known only in *solution* or in the form of its *salts* or *esters*, the *thiosulphates*.

THIOUREA. Thiocarbamide. $NH_2CS.NH_2$. A colourless *organic compound*, m.p. 180°C. Used in the manufacture of thiourea-aldehyde *plastics*.

THIXOTROPY. The rate of change of *viscosity* with time. Certain *liquids*, e.g. some *paints*, possess the property of increasing in viscosity with the passage of time when the liquid is left undisturbed. On shaking, the viscosity returns to its original value.

THOMSON EFFECT. Kelvin effect. A *temperature* gradient along a conducting wire gives rise to an *electric potential* gradient along the wire. Named after Sir William Thomson (Lord Kelvin) (1824–1907).

THOMSON SCATTERING. The scattering of *photons* of *electromagnetic radiations* by *electrons* according to J. J. Thomson's formula. Named after Sir Joseph John Thomson (1856–1940).

THORIDES. Natural *radioisotopes* which occur in the *radioactive series* containing thorium.

THORIUM. Th. Element. A.W. 232·038. At. No. 90. A dark grey *radio-*

active metal, S.G. 11·2, m.p. 1845°C. *Compounds* occur in *monazite*; the metal is used in *alloys* and *filaments*.

THORIUM DIOXIDE. Thoria. ThO_2. A white *insoluble* powder, m.p. 3050°C., used in *gas mantles*, *refractories* and special *glasses*.

THORON. A gaseous *radioisotope* of radon, $^{220}_{86}Rn$, produced by the *disintegration* of thorium. *Half-life* 51·5 *seconds*.

THREONINE. A colourless *soluble* crystalline *amino acid*, m.p. 230°C., which is essential to the diet of animals. See Table 5, page 435.

THRESHOLD. The lowest value of any stimulus, signal, or agency which will produce a specified effect. E.g. *threshold frequency*.

THRESHOLD FREQUENCY. *Light* incident on a *metal* surface will give rise to the emission of *electrons* (see *photo-electric effect*) only if the *frequency* of the light is greater than a certain *threshold* value which is characteristic of the metal used.

THROMBIN. An *enzyme* formed in the *blood* of vertebrates which acts upon *fibrogen* to form *fibrin*, therefore essential to the process of blood clotting. Thrombin is formed from a blood *protein*, prothrombin.

THROMBOCYTES. See *blood platelets*.

THRUST. The propulsive *force* produced by a *reaction propulsion* motor. See also *specific impulse*.

THULIUM. Tm. Element. A.W. 168·934. At. No. 69. S.G. 9·33, m.p. 1545°C. See *lanthanides*.

THYMINE. 5-methyluracil. $C_5H_6N_2O_2$. One of the two *pyrimidine* bases occurring in the *nucleotides* of *deoxyribonucleic acid*, which plays a part in the formulation of the *genetic code*.

THYMOL. 3-hydroxy-*p*-cymene. $C_{10}H_{14}O$. A white crystalline *phenol derivative*, m.p. 51·5°C., b.p. 233·5°C., which smells of thyme. Occurs in many *essential oils*; used as a mild *antiseptic*.

THYRATRON. A gas-filled *thermionic valve* (usually a *triode*) in which a *voltage* applied to the *control grid* initiates, but does not limit, the *anode* current. Used as an *electronic* switch.

THYROXIN(E). $C_{15}H_{11}I_4NO_4$. An iodine-containing *amino acid* produced by the thyroid gland. The pure form is a white crystalline substance, m.p. 236°C., used in cases of thyroid deficiency.

TIDES. Movement of the seas caused by the attraction exerted upon the seas by the *Moon*, and to a lesser extent by the *Sun*. At full and new moon the tidal force of the Sun is added to that of the Moon, causing high spring tides; while at half-moons the forces are opposed, causing low neap tides. See Fig. 42, page 389.

TIMBRE. See *quality of sound*.

TIME EXPOSURE. A long *photographic* exposure in which the *camera* shutter is operated manually, or by some device not normally part of the camera.

TIME-LAPSE PHOTOGRAPHY. *Photography* in which a slow process, such as the growth of a plant, is photographed by a series of single exposures on cinematic film at regular intervals. When the film is projected at normal speed, the process is seen in a greatly speeded up version.

TIME MEASUREMENT. The *SI unit* of time is the *second* to which all time-measuring devices are ultimately referred. Such devices include the *pendulum* and the *quartz clock*. See also *year*.

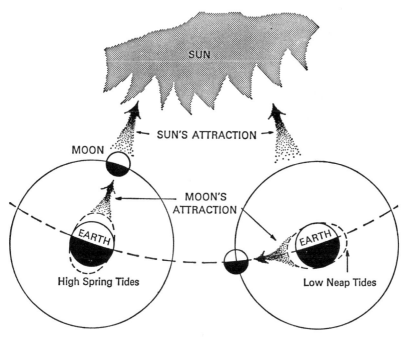

FIGURE 42.

TIME REFLECTION SYMMETRY. The proposition that any physical situation should be reversible in time. Known to hold for *strong nuclear interactions* and electromagnetic interactions, but some doubt remains as to its validity with respect to *weak nuclear interactions*. According to this principle, if time could be reversed (i.e. run backwards) the time reflection of a particular physical situation would correspond to what one would normally see by reflecting the situation in a space mirror, except that all the particles would be replaced by their *anti-particles*. Thus, if left-polarized (see *parity*) *neutrinos* exist, right-polarized anti-particles must also exist: experimental evidence appears to confirm this.

TIN. Sn. (Stannum.) Element. A.W. 118·69. At. No. 50. A silvery-white *metal*, S.G. 7·31, m.p. 231·85°C., which is soft, malleable, and ductile. Unaffected by air or *water* at ordinary *temperatures*. Occurs in three *allotropic forms*, below 18°C. passes into 'grey tin', causing *tin plague*. Occurs as *stannic oxide*, SnO_2, *cassiterite* or *tinstone*. The metal is

389

extracted by heating the *oxide* with powdered carbon in a *reverberatory furnace*. Used for tin-plating and in many *alloys*.

TIN PLAGUE. An allotropic change (see *allotropy*) in which white tin changes into a grey powdery form at low *temperatures*.

TIN PLATE. Iron coated with a thin layer of tin, by dipping it into the molten *metal*.

TIN SALT. See *stannous chloride*.

TINCAL. An impure form of *sodium tetraborate* (*borax*).

TINCTURE. An alcoholic extract or a *solution* in *alcohol*.

TINSTONE. See *cassiterite*.

TINTOMETER. An instrument for comparing the colour of *solutions* with a series of standard solutions or stained glass slides. See also *Lovibond* tintometer*.

TISSUE CULTURE. The preparation of fragments of the *tissues* or *cells* of *organisms* for biochemical examination *in vitro*. Tissue cultures are usually maintained in correctly balanced *physiological saline*.

TISSUES. A collection of similar *cells* and intercellular material which form the structural material of a plant or animal.

TITANIC. Containing *tetravalent* titanium.

TITANIUM. Ti. Element. A.W. 47·90, At. No. 22. A malleable and ductile *metal* resembling iron. S.G. 4·5, m.p. 1675°C. *Compounds* are fairly widely distributed in Nature, but the metal is difficult to extract. Used in *alloys*.

TITANIUM DIOXIDE. Titanic oxide, titania. TiO_2. A white *insoluble* powder, m.p. 1830–1850°C., used as a white *pigment*, in *plastics*, and *ceramics*.

TITANOUS. Containing *trivalent* titanium.

TITRATION. An operation forming the basis of *volumetric analysis*. The addition of measured amounts of a *solution* of one *reagent* from a *burette* (called the 'titrant') to a definite amount of another reagent until the action between them is complete, i.e. till the second reagent is completely used up. (See *end point*.)

T.N.T. See *trinitrotoluene*.

TOBACCO MOSAIC VIRUS. TMV. A simple *virus* widely used in biochemical and biological studies, particularly concerning the transference of the *genetic code*. The virus particle consists of a single helix of *ribonucleic acid* containing some 6400 *nucleotides*, coated with about 2200 *molecules* of a single *protein*, each molecule of which comprises a *polypeptide* chain of 158 *amino acids* in a known sequence.

TOCOPHEROL. Vitamin E. $C_{20}H_{50}O_2$. A yellow *insoluble* substance, m.p. 200–210°C. A *vitamin* which has been shown to prevent sterility in rats; deficiency in humans is associated with muscular dystrophy and vascular abnormalities. Occurs in vegetable leaves and wheat germ.

TOLUATE. A *salt* or *ester* of *toluic acid*.

TOLUIC ACID. $CH_3C_6H_4COOH$. Three *isomeric aromatic acids*. Ortho-toluic acid is a white crystalline substance, m.p. 107–8°C., used in *organic synthesis*.

TOLUENE. Toluol. $C_6H_5CH_3$. A *hydrocarbon* of the *benzene* series. A colourless inflammable *liquid* with a peculiar smell. B.p. 110°C. Occurs in *coal-tar*. Used as a starting-point in the preparation of *dyes*, *drugs*, *saccharin*, and *T.N.T.*

TOLUIDINE. $CH_3.C_6H_4.NH_2$. An *amine* derived from *toluene* which exists in three isomeric (see *isomerism*) forms. *Ortho*-toluidine is a colourless *liquid*, b.p. 199·7°C., used for making *dyes*.

TOLUOL. See *toluene*.

TOLUYL GROUP. Three *isomeric univalent radicals*, $CH_3C_6H_4CO—$, derived from *toluic acid*.

TOLYL GROUP. Three *isomeric univalent radicals*, $CH_3C_6H_4—$, derived from *toluene*.

TOMOGRAPHY. A technique for using *X-rays* for photographing one specific *plane* of the body, for diagnostic purposes.

TONE OF SOUND. See *quality of sound*.

TONNE. Metric ton; 1000 *kilogrammes*; 2204·62 lbs, 0·9842 ton.

TONOMETER. 1. An instrument for measuring the *pitch* of a *sound*, usually consisting of a set of calibrated *tuning forks*. 2. An instrument for measuring *vapour pressure*. 3. An instrument for measuring blood pressure, or the pressure within an eye-ball.

TOPAZ. Crystalline aluminium silicate and fluoride.

TOPOLOGY. A branch of *geometry* concerned with the way in which figures are 'connected', rather than with their shape or size. Topology is thus concerned with the geometrical factors which remain unchanged when an object undergoes a continuous deformation (e.g. by bending, stretching, or twisting) without tearing or breaking.

TOROIDAL. Having the shape of a toroid or *torus*.

TORQUE. A *force*, *moment* of a force, or system of forces which tends to produce rotation.

TORR. A unit of *pressure* used in the field of high vacuum: equivalent to 1 mm of mercury. Equal to 133·322 *newtons* per square metre.

TORRICELLIAN VACUUM. The space, containing mercury *vapour*, which is produced at the top of a column of mercury when a long tube sealed at one end is filled with mercury and inverted in a trough of the metal. The mercury sinks in the tube until it is balanced by the atmospheric pressure (see *barometer*), the Torricellian vacuum being the space above it. Named after Evangelista Torricelli (1608–47).

TORSION. 'Twisting' about an *axis*, produced by the action of two opposing *couples* acting in parallel *planes*.

TORSION BALANCE. If a wire is acted upon by a *couple* the *axis* of which coincides with the wire, the wire twists through an angle determined by the applied couple and the *rigidity modulus* of the wire. The amount of twist produced can thus be used to measure an applied *force*. In the

391

torsion balance, the force to be measured is applied at right angles to, and at the end of, an arm attached to the wire.

TORUS (phys.). A 'doughnut' or anchor-ring shaped *solid* of circular or elliptical cross-section.

TOTAL INTERNAL REFLECTION. When *light* passes from one medium to another which is optically less dense, e.g. from *glass* to air (see *refraction* and *density, optical*), the *ray* is bent away from the *normal*. If the incident ray meets the surface at such an angle that the refracted ray must be bent away at an angle of more than 90°, the light cannot emerge at all, and is totally internally reflected.

TOTALITY. The period in a total *eclipse* of the *Sun*, during which the bright surface of the Sun is totally obscured from view on *Earth* by the *Moon*.

TOURMALINE. A class of natural crystalline *minerals*, consisting of *silicates* of various *metals* and containing boron. The *crystals* show some interesting *pyro-electric*, *piezo-electric* and optical *effects*.

TOXIC. Poisonous.

TOXICOLOGY. The study of poisons.

TOXIN. Poison; the name is generally confined to intensely poisonous substances produced by certain *bacteria*, which cause dangerous effects when they attack food or the human body.

TRACE ELEMENT. An *element* required in very small quantities by an *organism*. Such elements often form essential constituents of *enzymes*, *vitamins*, or *hormones*.

TRACER. See *radioactive tracing*.

TRAJECTORY. The path of a *projectile*.

TRANQUILLIZER. A *drug* used to reduce tension and anxiety, without impairing alertness or causing drowsiness.

TRANSAMINATION. The transfer of an *amino group* from one *compound* (e.g. an *amino acid*) to another.

TRANSCENDENTAL (math.). 1. (Of a number or quantity) Not capable of being expressed as the *root* of an algebraic *equation* with *rational coefficients*, e.g. π or e. 2. (Of a function) Not capable of being expressed by a finite number of algebraic operations, e.g. $\sin x$, e^x. (See *exponential*.)

TRANSCONDUCTANCE. The *mutual conductance* between the *control grid* of a *thermionic valve* and its *anode*; usually expressed in *mhos* or *micromhos*.

TRANSDUCER. A device which receives waves (electrical, acoustical, or mechanical) from one or more media or transmission systems and supplies related waves (not necessarily of the same type as the input) to one or more other media or transmission systems. If the transducer derives *energy* from sources other than the input waves it is said to be 'active': if the input waves are the only source of energy it is said to be 'passive'.

TRANS-FORM. See *cis-trans isomerism*.

TRANSFORMATION CONSTANT. See *disintegration constant*.

TRANSFORMATION, NUCLEAR. The change of one *nuclide* into another.

TRANSFORMER. A device by which an *alternating current* of one *voltage* is changed to another voltage, without alteration in *frequency*. A step-up transformer, which increases the voltage and diminishes the current, consists in principle of an iron core on which is wound a *primary coil* of a small number of turns of thick, insulated wire; and, forming a separate circuit, a secondary coil of a larger number of turns of thin, insulated wire. When the low-voltage current is passed through the primary coil, it induces a current in the secondary (see *induction*) by producing an alternating *magnetic field* in the iron core. The ratio of the voltage in the primary to that in the secondary is very nearly equal to the ratio of the number of turns in the primary to that in the secondary. The step-down transformer works on the same principle, with the coils reversed.

TRANSIENT. 1. (math.). A *function* whose value tends to *zero* as the independant *variable* tends to *infinity*. 2. (phys.). A short-lived oscillation in a system caused by a sudden change of *voltage*, *current*, or load.

TRANSISTOR. A *semiconductor* device capable of amplification in a similar manner to *thermionic valves*. Consists of two P-N *semiconductor junctions* back to back forming either a P-N-P or N-P-N structure. In a P-N-P transistor the thin central N-region is called the *base*, one P-region is called the *emitter*, the other the *collector*. In an N-P-N transistor the P-region is the base. In order to obtain amplification an N-P-N transistor is included in a circuit which supplies a positive *voltage* to the collector (N-region) and a negative voltage to the emitter (the other N-region). The collector in this type of transistor therefore corresponds to the *anode* of a thermionic valve while the emitter corresponds to the *cathode*. The base (P-region) is also positively biased and is analogous to the *control grid*. With this arrangement the large number of *electrons* in the emitter region is attracted to the P-layer, which, if it is sufficiently thin, will allow the electrons to pass through it and be attracted into the positive collector. The magnitude of the collector current will depend on the extent of the positive bias on the P-layer base. By suitable design the device can be made to give a collector current some 20–100 times the base current. The advantages of a transistor over a valve are that it is less bulky and fragile, that it requires no heater current, and that the voltage at the collector need only be a few volts. A P-N-P transistor works in an exactly analogous manner to an N-P-N device, but the collector current consists mainly of *holes* instead of electrons. The device described here is a *junction transistor*, as this type has almost entirely replaced the earlier 'point contact' transistor.

TRANSITION ELEMENTS. *Elements* which have chemical properties resembling those of their horizontal neighbours in the *periodic table*. These elements have incomplete inner electron *shells* and are characterized by their variable *valencies*: they occur in the middle of the long periods of the periodic table.

TRANSITION, NUCLEAR. A change in the configuration of an atomic *nucleus*. It may involve a *transformation* (e.g. by *alpha-* or *beta-particle* emission) or a change in *energy level* by the emission of a *gamma-ray*.

TRANSITION TEMPERATURE. 1. Transition point. The *temperature* at which one form of a polymorphous substance (see *polymorphism*) changes into another; the temperature at which both forms can co-exist. 2. See *superconductivity*.

TRANSLATORY MOTION. A motion which involves a non-reciprocating movement of *matter* from one place to another.

TRANSLUCENT. Permitting the passage of *light* in such a way that an object cannot be seen clearly through the substance; e.g. frosted *glass*.

TRANSMISSION COEFFICIENT. Transmittance. *T*. When a *beam of light* (or other *electromagnetic radiation*) passes through a medium the radiation is absorbed to a greater or less extent (depending upon the medium and the *wavelength* of the radiation) and the intensity of the beam decreases. The ratio of the intensity after passing through unit distance of the medium to the original intensity is called the transmission coefficient.

TRANSMITTANCE. See *transmission coefficient*.

TRANSMITTER. 1. The equipment required to broadcast *electromagnetic radiation* of *radio frequencies*. The transmitter consists of devices for producing the *carrier wave*, *modulating* it, and feeding it to the *aerial* system. 2. The part of a *telephone* system which converts *sound* waves into *electric currents*, or the part of a *telegraph* system which converts mechanical movements into electrical currents.

TRANSMUTATION OF ELEMENTS. Changing one chemical *element* into another. Once the aim of *alchemy*; subsequently held to be impossible; with the present knowledge of *radioactivity* and atomic structure it is seen that the process goes on continuously in *radioactive* elements. Artificial transmutation by suitable *nuclear reactions* forms the basis of experimental *nuclear physics*. See also *transition, nuclear*, and *transformation, nuclear*.

TRANSPARENT. Permitting the passage of *light* in such a way that objects can be seen clearly through the substance.

TRANSPONDER. *Electronic* equipment designed to receive a specific signal and automatically transmit a reply.

TRANSPORT NUMBER. Transference number. The proportion of the total *electric current* passing through an *electrolyte* which is carried by a particular type of *ion*. The *anion* transport number plus the *cation* transport number equals unity.

TRANSURANIC ELEMENTS. *Elements* beyond uranium in the *periodic table*; i.e. elements of *atomic number* greater than 92. Such elements do not occur in Nature, but may be obtained by suitable *nuclear reactions*; they are all *radioactive* and members of the *actinide* group. See Table 8, page 440.

TRANSVERSE. Cross-wise; in a direction at right angles to the length of the body under consideration.

TRANSVERSE WAVES. Waves in which the vibration or displacement takes place in a *plane* at right angles to the direction of propagation of the wave; e.g. *electromagnetic radiation*. See also *longitudinal waves*.

TRAPEZIUM. A *quadrilateral* having two of its sides parallel. The area of a trapezium having parallel sides *a* and *b* units in length, and vertical height *h* units is given by $\dfrac{h(a+b)}{2}$.

TRIAD. An *element* having a *valency* of three.

TRIANGLE. A *plane* figure bounded by three straight lines. The three *angles* total 180°. The area of any triangle is given by the following expressions: 1. Half the *product* of one of the sides and the perpendicular upon it from the opposite vertex ($\frac{1}{2}$ × base × height). 2. Half the product of any two of the sides and the *sine* of the angle between them ($\frac{1}{2}$ *bc sin A*). 3. $\sqrt{s(s-a)\ (s-b)\ (s-c)}$, where *a*, *b*, and *c* are the lengths of the sides, and *s* is half the sum of *a*, *b*, and *c*.

TRIANGLE OF FORCES. If three *forces* acting at the same point can be represented in magnitude and direction by the sides of a *triangle* taken in order, they will be in *equilibrium*.

TRIANGLE OF VELOCITIES. If a body has three component *velocities* which can be represented in magnitude and direction by the sides of a *triangle* taken in order, the body will remain at rest.

TRIATOMIC. Having three *atoms* in the *molecule*, e.g. *ozone*, O_3; having three replaceable atoms or *radicals* in the molecule.

TRIAZINE. $C_3H_3N_3$. Three *isometric compounds* having three nitrogen and three carbon *atoms* forming a six-membered ring. *Cyclonite* is a *derivative* of triazine.

TRIAZOLE. $C_2H_3N_3$. Four *isomeric compounds* having three nitrogen and two carbon *atoms* forming a five-membered ring.

TRIBASIC ACID. An *acid* having three *atoms* of *acidic hydrogen* in the *molecule*, thus giving rise to three possible series of *salts*; e.g. *phosphoric acid*, H_3PO_4, can give rise to trisodium orthophosphate, Na_3PO_4, disodium hydrogen orthophosphate, Na_2HPO_4, and sodium dihydrogen orthophosphate, NaH_2PO_4. (See *sodium phosphate*.)

TRIBO-ELECTRICITY. See *electricity, frictional*.

TRIBOLOGY. The study of *friction* and lubrication.

TRIBOLUMINESCENCE. The emission of *light* when certain *crystals* (e.g. *cane-sugar*) are crushed.

TRIBROMOMETHANOL. CBr_3CH_2OH. A white crystalline powder, m.p. 79–82° C., used as an *anaesthetic*.

TRICHLOROETHYLENE. $CHCl:CCl_2$. A colourless *liquid*, b.p. 87° C.; widely used as industrial *solvent*, in dry cleaning, and as an *anaesthetic*.

TRIETHANOLAMINE. See *ethanolamines*.

TRIETHYLAMINE. $(C_2H_5)_3N$. A colourless *inflammable liquid*, b.p. 89–90° C., used as a *solvent*.

TRIGLYCERIDES. See *glycerides*.

TRIGONOMETRICAL RATIOS. If a perpendicular *AB* is drawn from any point on arm *OA* of an *angle AOB* to the other arm, the following ratios

395

are constant for the particular angle: AB/AO, sine (sin AOB); OB/AO, cosine (cos AOB); AB/OB, tangent (tan AOB); AO/AB, cosecant (cosec AOB); AO/OB, secant (sec AOB); and OB/AB, cotangent (cot AOB). See Fig. 43.

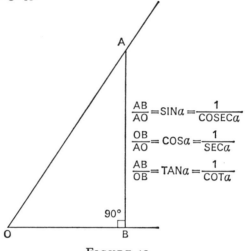

$$\frac{AB}{AO} = SIN\alpha = \frac{1}{COSEC\alpha}$$

$$\frac{OB}{AO} = COS\alpha = \frac{1}{SEC\alpha}$$

$$\frac{AB}{OB} = TAN\alpha = \frac{1}{COT\alpha}$$

FIGURE 43.

TRIGONOMETRY. A branch of mathematics using the fact that numerous problems may be solved by the calculation of unknown parts (i.e. sides and *angles*) of a *triangle* when three parts are known. The solution of such problems is greatly assisted by the use of the *trigonometrical ratios*.

TRIHYDROXYBENZOIC ACID. Gallic acid. $C_6H_2(OH)_3COOH$. A yellowish crystalline substance, used in *tanning* and the manufacture of *inks*.

TRILLION. 10^{18}, a million million million (British); 10^{12}, a million million (American).

TRIMER. A substance composed of *molecules* which are formed from three molecules of a *monomer*.

TRINITROBENZENE. T.N.B. $C_6H_3(NO_2)_3$. Three *isomeric* crystalline *compounds*, m.p. 121–127° C., used as high *explosives*, and having greater power than *T.N.T.*

TRINITROPHENOL. See *picric acid*.

TRINITROTOLUENE. T.N.T. Trotyl. $C_7H_5(NO_2)_3$. A pale yellow, crystalline *solid*, m.p. 82° C., made by the *nitration* of *toluene*. High *explosive*.

TRIODE. A *thermionic valve* containing three *electrodes*; an *anode* or plate, a *cathode*, and a *control grid*.

TRIOLEIN. Olein. $(C_{17}H_{33}COO)_3.C_3H_5$. A *glyceride* of *oleic acid*; b.p. 235–240° C., *liquid* oil which occurs in many natural *fats and oils*.

TRIOLS. Trihydric *alcohols* derived from *aliphatic hydrocarbons* by the substitution of *hydroxyl groups* for three of the hydrogen *atoms* in the *molecule*.

TRIPALMITIN. Palmitin. $(C_{15}H_{31}COO)_3.C_3H_5$. A *glyceride* of *palmitic acid*;

a *solid*, fat-like substance, m.p. 65·5°C., b.p. 310–320°C., which occurs in palm-oil and many other natural *fats and oils*.

TRIPLE BOND. Three *covalent bonds* linking two *atoms* in a chemical *compound*, e.g. *acetylene*, $CH \equiv CH$.

TRIPLE POINT. The point at which the gaseous, *liquid*, and *solid phases* of a substance are in *equilibrium*. For a given substance, the triple point occurs at a unique set of values of the *temperature, pressure*, and *volume*.

TRISACCHARIDES. A group of *sugars* the *molecules* of which consist of three *monosaccharides*.

TRISTEARIN. Stearin. $(C_{17}H_{35}COO)_3.C_3H_5$. A *glyceride* of *stearic acid*; a *solid*, fat-like substance, m.p. 53·5°C., which occurs in natural *fats*; formed by the hydrogenation of *triolein*. See *hydrogenation of oils*.

TRITIATED COMPOUND. A *compound* in which some hydrogen *atoms* have been replaced by *tritium*, so that it may be used in *radioactive tracing*.

TRITIUM. $T.{}^3_1H$. A *radioactive isotope* of hydrogen with *mass number* 3 and *atomic mass* 3·016. The *abundance* of tritium in natural hydrogen is only one *atom* in 10^{17}, and its half life is 12·5 years. It can, however, be made artificially in *nuclear reactors* and *tritiated compounds* are used in *radioactive tracing*.

TRITON. The *nucleus* of a *tritium atom*.

TRIVALENT. Tervalent. Having a *valency* of three.

TROCHOTRON. A multi-*electrode thermionic valve* used as a *scaler*.

TRONA. A natural crystalline *double salt* of *sodium carbonate* and *sodium hydrogen carbonate*, $Na_2CO_3.NaHCO_3.2H_2O$, found in dried lakes.

TROOSTITE. 1. The constituent of *steel* produced when *martensite* is *tempered* below 450°C., consisting of *ferrite* and finely divided *cementite*. 2. Troostitic pearlite. The constituent of steel produced by the decomposition of *austenite* when cooled at a slower rate than yields martensite and a faster rate than yields *sorbite*.

TROPICAL YEAR. See *year*.

TROPINE. $C_8H_{15}NO$. A white crystalline *hygroscopic soluble alkaloid*, m.p. 63°C.

TROPOPAUSE. The boundary between the *troposphere* and the *stratosphere*.

TROPOSPHERE. The lower part of the Earth's *atmosphere* in which *temperature* decreases with height, except for local areas of 'temperature inversion'. See Fig. 44, page 402.

TROTYL. See *trinitrotoluene*.

TROUTON'S RULE. The ratio of the *latent heat* of vaporization per *mole*, to the *boiling point* in degrees *kelvin* is a constant for all substances. The rule is only approximate.

TROY WEIGHT. 1 grain = 0·0648 gram.

20 grains = 1 scruple.

24 grains = 1 pennyweight.

3 scruples = 1 drachm.

8 drachms = 1 ounce troy = 1·1 ounce avoirdupois.

TRYPSIN. An *enzyme* produced by the pancreas. In the process of digestion it breaks up *proteins* into *amino-acids*.

TRYPTOPHAN. A colourless crystalline *amino acid*, m.p. 281–9° C., which is essential to the diet of animals and occurs in the seeds of some vegetables. See Table 5, page 435.

TUBE OF FORCE. A theoretical concept of a tube formed by the *lines of force* drawn out into space through every point on a small closed curve upon the surface of a charged *conductor*.

TUNGSTATE. A *salt* of *tungstic acid*.

TUNGSTEN. W. Wolfram. Element. A.W. 183·85. At. No. 74. A grey hard ductile malleable metal, which is resistant to *corrosion*; S.G. 19·3, m.p. 3410° C. Occurs as *wolframite*, $FeWO_4$, and scheelite, $CaWO_4$. Obtained by converting the *ore* to the *oxide* and then reducing the latter. Used in *alloys*, in cemented *carbides* for hard tools, and for electric lamp *filaments*. The names *tungsten* and *wolfram* for this element were both officially recognized in 1951.

TUNGSTEN TRIOXIDE. WO_3. A yellow *insoluble* powder, m.p. 1473° C., used in the manufacture of *tungstates*.

TUNGSTIC ACID. H_2WO_4. *Hydrated tungsten trioxide.* A white crystalline powder which loses a *molecule* of *water* at 100° C., used in the manufacture of lamp *filaments*.

TUNING FORK. A two-pronged *metal* fork which, when struck, produces a pure *tone* of constant specified *pitch*. Used in *acoustics* and for tuning musical instruments.

TUNING, RADIO. See *resonant circuit*.

TUNNEL DIODE. A *semiconductor* device which has negative *resistance* over a part of its operating range. Consists of a P-N *semiconductor junction* in which both the P- and N- regions contain very large numbers of impurity *atoms*, thus producing a high *potential* barrier at the junction. If a small *voltage* is applied to the device, positive at the P- region, an *electron* current will flow (despite the high potential barrier) as a result of the *tunnel effect*. After a certain voltage has been reached this effect is reduced and the current declines with increasing voltage, thus exhibiting the negative resistance characteristic. At higher voltages the normal *majority carrier* current flows and the current again increases with voltage. Used in switching circuits and where low noise amplification is required up to *frequencies* of about 1000 *megahertz*.

TUNNEL EFFECT. The passage of an *electron* through a narrow *potential* barrier in a *semiconductor*, despite the fact that, according to classical *mechanics*, the electron does not possess sufficient *energy* to surmount the barrier. Explained by *quantum mechanics* on the assumption that electrons are not completely localized in *space*, a part of the energy of the wave associated with the electron being able to 'tunnel' through the barrier.

TURBINE. Any motor in which a shaft is steadily rotated by the impact or reaction of a current of *steam*, air, *water*, or other *fluid* upon blades of a wheel. In an 'impulse' turbine the fluid is directed from jets or nozzles on to the *rotor* blades. In a 'reaction' turbine a ring of stationary blades replaces the nozzles and the rotor is driven by reaction between the fluid, the stationary blades, and the rotor blades. Many turbines work on a combination of the reaction and impulse principles. See also *gas turbine*.

TURBO-GENERATOR. A steam *turbine* coupled to an electric *generator* for the production of *electric power*. Usual arrangement in a 'conventional' power station.

TURBULENT FLOW. The type of *fluid* flow in which the motion at any point varies rapidly in direction and magnitude.

TURPENTINE. Oil of turpentine. A *liquid* extracted by *distillation* of the *resin* of pine trees. B.p. 155°–165°C. Composed chiefly of *pinene*. Used as a *solvent*.

TURQUOISE. Natural basic aluminium phosphate, coloured blue or green by traces of copper.

TWADDELL SCALE. A scale for measuring the *specific gravity* of *liquids*. Degrees Twaddell=200 (S.G. − 1); S.G.=1+Degrees Twaddell/200. Named after W. Twaddell (19th century).

TWEETER. A *loudspeaker* designed to reproduce the higher *audio-frequency* sounds, i.e. 5–15 *kilohertz*.

TYNDALL EFFECT. The *scattering of light* by particles of *matter* in the path of the light, thus making a visible 'beam', such as is caused by a *ray* of light illuminating particles of dust floating in the air of a room. Named after John Tyndall (1820–93).

TYPE METAL. An *alloy* of 60% lead, 30% antimony, and 10% tin. Owing to the presence of antimony it expands on solidifying and thus gives a sharp cast.

TYROSINE. A white crystalline *amino acid*, m.p. 310–320°C., obtained from most *proteins*. See Table 5, page 435.

U

UDOMETER. Pluviometer. A rain gauge.

ULTIMATE STRESS. Tenacity. The load required to fracture a material divided by its original area of cross-section at the point of fracture. The ultimate stress is divided by the 'factor of safety', in order to obtain the 'working stress'.

ULTRACENTRIFUGE. A high speed *centrifuge*. Used in the determination of the *molecular weights* of large *molecules* in high *polymers* and *proteins*.

ULTRA-HIGH FREQUENCIES. U.H.F. *Radio frequencies* in the range 300 to 3000 *megahertz*.

ULTRAMARINE. An artificial form of *lapis lazuli*, made by heating together *clay*, *sodium sulphate*, carbon, and sulphur.

ULTRAMICROBALANCE. A *balance* for weighing accurately to 10^{-8} grams.

ULTRAMICROSCOPE. An instrument, making use of the *Tyndall effect* for showing the presence of particles which are too small to be seen with the ordinary *microscope*. A powerful *beam* of *light* is brought to a focus in the *liquid* which is examined; suspended particles appear as bright specks by *scattering the light*.

ULTRASONIC FREQUENCY. A *frequency* in excess of about 20 000 *hertz*.

ULTRASONIC GENERATOR. A device for the production of pressure waves of *ultrasonic frequency*.

ULTRASONICS. Supersonics. The study of pressure waves which are of the same nature as *sound* waves, but which have frequencies above the audible limit.

ULTRAVIOLET MICROSCOPE. A *microscope* in which the object is illuminated by *ultraviolet radiation*. *Quartz* lenses are used and the image is recorded photographically. As ultraviolet radiation is of shorter *wavelength* than visible *light*, greater magnification can be obtained than with an optical microscope.

ULTRAVIOLET RADIATION. *Electromagnetic radiation* in the *wavelength* range of approximately 4×10^{-7} to 5×10^{-9} *metres*; i.e. between visible *light* waves and *X-rays*. The longest ultraviolet waves have wavelengths just shorter than those of violet light, the shortest perceptible by the human eye. They affect photographic *films* and plates; their action on *ergosterol* in the human body produces *vitamin* D. Radiation from the *Sun* is rich in such rays; they may be produced artificially by the *mercury vapour lamp*.

UMBRA. A region of complete *shadow*. See Fig. 38, page 345.

UNCERTAINTY PRINCIPLE. Indeterminancy principle. It is impossible to determine with accuracy both the position and the *momentum* of a particle (e.g. an *electron*) simultaneously. The more accurately the position is known, the less accurately can the momentum be determined. If the range of values for the position is Δp, and the range of values for the momentum Δm, then $\Delta p.\Delta m = h$, where h is *Planck's Constant*. The principle, which was first stated by Heisenberg, arises from the dual particle wave nature of *matter*. See *De Broglie wavelength*.

UNFILLED APERTURE. A method of constructing a *radio telescope* in which two *aerials* of different shapes are combined into one *radio interferometer* in such a way that only two perpendicular arms of the aerial system are built, giving the effect of two large apertures. The two arms may be spaced at varying distances apart, or they may be superimposed upon one another as in the 'Mills Cross' radio telescope. Unfilled aperture telescopes are suitable for use at long *wavelengths*.

UNGULA. A part of a *cylinder* or *cone* which is cut off by a *plane* not parallel to its base.

UNIAXIAL CRYSTAL. A doubly refracting *crystal* possessing only one *optic axis*.

UNICELLULAR. (Of an *organism*.) Consisting of only one *cell* (e.g. *bacteria*, protozoa, etc.).

UNIFIED FIELD THEORY. A theory which attempts to describe the electromagnetic and *gravitational fields* in one set of *equations*. No such satisfactory theory has yet been devised. To achieve complete unification the theory would also have to explain *strong* and *weak nuclear interactions*.

UNIT. A quantity or dimension adopted as a standard of measurement.

UNITARY SYMMETRY. SU3. A method of classifying *elementary particles* according to their properties in a similar manner to the classification of atomic properties in the *periodic table*. SU3 has successfully predicted the existence of particles which have subsequently been detected experimentally, e.g. omega-minus (see Table 6, page 436).

UNITY (math.). One.

UNIVALENT (chem.). Monovalent. Having a *valency* of one.

UNIVERSE. The total of all the *matter, energy*, and *space* that man is capable of experiencing, or whose existence he can deduce or has grounds for postulating. The universe is currently best described in terms of a four-dimensional curved *space-time continuum* (see *relativity*); it contains some 10^{41} *kilogrammes* of matter, collected in some 10^9 *galaxies*. See *heat death of the Universe, steady state theory, superdense theory*.

UNSATURATED COMPOUND (chem.). A *compound* having some of the *atoms* in its *molecule* linked by more than one *valency bond* (see *double bond* and *triple bond*); a compound which can form *addition compounds*.

UNSTABLE (chem.). Easily decomposed.

UNSTABLE EQUILIBRIUM. See *stable equilibrium*.

UPPER ATMOSPHERE. The upper *atmosphere* of the *Earth* is usually taken to include its gaseous envelope from 30 *kilometres* upwards (i.e. that part of the atmosphere which is inaccessible to direct observations by balloons). Information is obtained from *space probes* and artificial Earth *satellites*. See Fig. 44, page 402.

Up to about 100 km the composition of the upper atmosphere is

THE EARTH'S ATMOSPHERE

FIGURE 44.

similar to that at ground level (see *atmosphere*). Above this height the *dissociation* of oxygen into *atoms* is almost complete, and at above 150 km the nitrogen separates out owing to its greater *mass* so that monatomic oxygen predominates. There is considerable *ionization* in the upper atmosphere as a result of solar *ultraviolet radiation* and *X-rays*. See *ionosphere*.

URACIL. Pyrimidinedione. $C_4H_4N_2O_2$. A white crystalline *pyrimidine* base, m.p. 338° C., which occurs in the *nucleotides* of *ribonucleic acid*.

URANIC. Containing *tetravalent* uranium.

URANIUM. U. Naturally occurring *radioactive element*. A.W. 238·03, At. No. 92. A hard white *metal*, S.G. 19·05, m.p. 1150° C. The natural element consists of 99·28% $^{238}_{92}U$ (*half-life* 4·5 × 10⁹ years) and 0·71% $^{235}_{92}U$ (half-life 7·1 × 10⁸ years). The latter *isotope* is capable of sustaining a nuclear *chain reaction* and is of greater importance in *nuclear reactors* and *nuclear weapons*.

URANIUM DIOXIDE. UO_2. A black *insoluble* crystalline *radioactive* substance, m.p. 2500° C., used as a *fuel* in advanced *gas-cooled reactors*.

URANIUM TRIOXIDE. Uranic acid, uranyl oxide. UO_3. A red *insoluble radioactive* powder, which decomposes on heating.

URANOUS. Containing *trivalent* uranium.

URANUS (Astr.). A *planet* possessing five *satellites*, with its *orbit* lying between those of *Saturn* and *Neptune*. Mean distance from the *Sun*, 2869·6 million kilometres. *Sidereal period* ('year') 84 years. *Mass* approximately 14·52 times that of the *Earth*, diameter 47 100 kilometres. Surface temperature, about − 180° C.

URANYL GROUP. The *bivalent* group, = UO_2, which forms *salts* with *acids*.

UREA. Carbamide. $CO(NH_2)_2$. A white crystalline *organic compound*, m.p. 132° C., which occurs in urine. The first organic compound to be prepared artificially. Used as a *fertilizer*, in medicine, and in *urea-formaldehyde resins*.

UREA-FORMALDEHYDE RESINS. *Thermosetting resins* with good *oil* resistant properties, produced by the condensation *polymerization* of urea and *formaldehyde*.

UREASE. An *enzyme* capable of splitting *urea* into *ammonia* and *water*.

UREIDO GROUP. The *univalent radical*, $NH_2CONH—$, derived from *urea*.

URETHANE RESINS. A group of synthetic *resins* based on urethane (*ethyl carbamate*), $NH_2COOC_2H_2$. Used in lacquers, varnishes, and foams.

UREYLENE GROUP. The *divalent radical*, $—NHCONH—$, derived from *urea*.

URIC ACID. $C_5H_4N_3O_4$. An *organic acid*, belonging to the *purine* group; a colourless crystalline *solid*, slightly *soluble* in *water*. Occurs in very small amounts in the urine of some animals as a breakdown product of *amino acids* and *nucleic acids*. Sodium and potassium *salts* of the acid are deposited in the joints in cases of gout.

UROTROPINE. See *hexamethylene tetramine*.

V

VACANCY. Schottky defect. An irregularity which occurs in a *crystal lattice* when a site normally occupied by an *atom* or *ion* is unoccupied. See *defect*.

VACCINE. A preparation containing *viruses* or other *micro-organisms* (either killed or of attenuated virulence) which is introduced into the human system to stimulate the formation of *antibodies*. In this way immunity (partial or complete) to subsequent infection by this type of micro-organism is conferred.

VACUUM. A *space* in which there are no *molecules* or *atoms*. A perfect vacuum is unobtainable, since every material which surrounds a space has a definite *vapour pressure*. The term is generally taken to mean a space containing air or other *gas* at very low *pressure*. 'Ultra-high' vacua (i.e. vacua in which the pressure does not exceed 10^{-9} *torr* or 10^{-7} N m^{-2}) occur naturally at heights of more than 800 kilometres above the *Earth's* surface, and by special techniques pressures of 10^{-13} torr can be achieved in the laboratory.

VACUUM DISTILLATION. The process of *distillation* carried out at a reduced *pressure*. The reduction in pressure is accompanied by a depression in the *boiling point* of the substance to be distilled, thus lower *temperatures* can be employed. This process therefore enables substances to be distilled which at normal pressures would decompose.

VACUUM TUBE. See *thermionic valve*; *discharge in gases*.

VALENCY. The combining power of an *atom*; the number of hydrogen atoms which an atom will combine with or replace. E.g. the valency of oxygen in water, H_2O, is 2.

VALENCY BAND. The range of energies (see *energy bands*) in a *semiconductor* corresponding to states which can be occupied by the *valency electrons* which bind the *crystal* together. Electrons missing from the valency band give rise to *holes*.

VALENCY BOND. The link holding *atoms* together in a *molecule*. In the case of two *univalent* atoms joined together, a single valency bond holds them together; it is possible for an atom to satisfy two or three valency bonds of another atom, giving rise to a *double* or *triple bond*.

VALENCY ELECTRON. An outer *electron* of an *atom* which takes part in formation of a *valency bond*.

VALENCY, ELECTRONIC THEORY OF. An explanation of *valency* on the basis of atomic structure (see *atom, structure of*), and particularly on the assumption that certain arrangements of outer *electrons* in *atoms* (e.g. *octets* or outer *shells* of 8 electrons) are stable and tend to be formed by the transfer or sharing of electrons between atoms. The chief types of linkage are: (1) electrovalent bonds formed by the transfer of electrons from one atom to another; the atom which loses an electron becomes a positive *ion*, and the other a negative ion. This provides an explanation of the behaviour of *electrolytes*. (2) Covalent bonds. The sharing of a pair of electrons, one being provided by each atom. This applies to many non-ionizable bonds, e.g. those in *organic compounds*. If both electrons in a covalent bond are donated by the same atom, the bond is referred to as a coordinate or dative bond. Many bonds possess electronic configurations intermediate between the above forms. See *resonance* (chem.) and *hydrogen bond*.

VALERIC ACID. Pentanoic acid. C_4H_9COOH. A *fatty acid* which exists in several *isomeric* forms, the common form being a colourless *liquid* with a pungent odour, b.p. 186–7°C., used in perfumes.

VALINE. A white crystalline *soluble amino acid*, which occurs in most *proteins*. Used in medicine and *culture media*. See Table 5, page 435.

VALVE, WIRELESS. See *thermionic valve*.

VAN ALLEN RADIATION BELTS. Two belts of charged particles trapped within the Earth's *magnetic field* which were discovered by J. Van Allen (born 1914) in 1958 from the results of artificial *satellite* and *space probe* experiments. The inner belt, ranging from 2400 to 5600 km above the Earth's surface, is believed to consist of secondary charged particles emitted by the Earth's *atmosphere* as a consequence of the impact of *cosmic rays*. The outer belt lies between 13 000 and 19 000 km above the Earth, and it is believed that the particles it contains originate from the *Sun*.

VAN DE GRAAFF GENERATOR. An *electrostatic generator* used for accelerating charged particles of atomic magnitudes, e.g. *protons*, to high *energies*. Named after R. J. Van de Graaff (born 1901).

VAN DER WAALS' EQUATION OF STATE. $\left(p+\dfrac{a}{v^2}\right)(v-b)=RT$ for a *mole* of a substance in the gaseous and *liquid phases* where $p=pressure$, $v=volume$, $T=absolute\ temperature$, $R=$ the *gas constant*; $\dfrac{a}{v^2}$ is a correction for the mutual attraction of the *molecules*, and b is a correction for the actual volume of the molecules themselves. The equation represents the behaviour of ordinary *gases* more correctly than the *perfect gas* equation $pv=RT$. Named after J. D. Van der Waals (1837–1923).

VAN DER WAALS' FORCE. An attractive *force* existing between *atoms* or *molecules* of all substances. The force arises as a result of *electrons* in neighbouring atoms or molecules (see *atom, structure of*) moving in sympathy with one another. This force is responsible for the term a/v^2 in *van der Waals' equation of state*. In many substances this force is small compared with the other inter-atomic attractive and repulsive forces present.

VANADATE. A *salt* or *ester* of *vanadic acid*.

VANADIC ACID. HVO_3. A yellow *insoluble* crystalline substance. Other *acids* are formed by the addition of *water molecules*, e.g. H_3VO_4.

VANADIUM. V. Element. A.W. 50·942. At. No. 23. A very hard white *metal*, S.G. 5·966, m.p. 1890° C. Occurs in a few rather rare *minerals*. Used in *alloys*.

VANADYL GROUP. The *divalent* group $= VO_2$, which forms *salts* with *acids*.

VANILLIN. $CH_3O(OH)C_6H_3CHO$. A white *insoluble* crystalline substance, m.p. 80–81° C., obtained from vanilla beans; used as a flavour and in perfumes.

VAN'T HOFF'S LAW. The *osmotic pressure* of a dilute *solution* is equal to the *pressure* which the *solute* would exert in the gaseous state, if it occupied a *volume* equal to the volume of the solution, at the same *temperature*. Named after Jacobus Van't Hoff (1852–1911).

VAPOUR. A substance in the gaseous state, which may be liquefied by increasing the *pressure* without altering the *temperature*. A *gas* below its *critical temperature*.

VAPOUR DENSITY. A measure of the *density* of a *gas* or *vapour*; usually given relative to oxygen or hydrogen. The latter is the ratio of the *mass* of a certain *volume* of the gas to the *mass* of an equal volume of hydrogen, measured under the same conditions of *temperature* and *pressure*. Numerically this ratio is equal to half the *molecular weight* of the gas.

VAPOUR PRESSURE. All *liquids* and *solids* give off *vapour*, consisting of *molecules* of the substance. If the substance is in an enclosed space, the *pressure* of the vapour will reach a maximum which depends only upon the nature of the substance and the *temperature*; the vapour is then saturated and its pressure is the *saturated vapour pressure*.

VAREC. Kelp. The *ash* of seaweed, from which iodine is extracted.

VARIABLE (math.). 1. A symbol or term which assumes, or to which may be assigned, different numerical values. An 'independent variable' is a variable in a *function* which determines the value of other variables. A 'dependent variable' has its value determined by other variables. E.g. in $y = 5x^2 + 2$, x is the independent variable and y is the dependent variable. 2. Not *constant*.

VARIANCE. 1. (statistics). The *square* of the mean *deviation*. 2. (chem.). The number of *degrees of freedom* which a system can have.

VARIATE (statistics). A *variable* which may have any of a *set* of values according to specified *probabilities*.

VARIATION (math.). If a quantity y is some *function* of another quantity x, $(y = f(x))$, then, as x varies, y varies in a manner determined by the function. If $f(x) = x \times a$ (where a is a constant), then y is said to vary directly as x, or to be directly proportional to x, $y \propto x$. If $f(x) = a/x$, y is said to vary inversely as x, or to be inversely proportional to x; $y \propto 1/x$.

VARIOMETER. A *variable inductance* consisting of two coils in *series*, arranged so that one coil can rotate within the other. Also used as a means of measuring inductance.

VASELINE*. See *petrolatum*.

VAT DYES. A class of *insoluble dyes* which are applied by first reducing them to leuco-compounds which are *soluble* in *alkalis*. The *solution* is applied to the material, and the insoluble dye is regenerated in the fibres by *oxidation*. *Indigo* and many synthetic dyes belong to this class.

VECTOR. Any physical quantity which requires a direction to be stated in order to define it completely. E.g. *velocity*.

VECTORS, PARALLELOGRAM LAW OF. If a particle is under the action of two like *vector* quantities which are represented by the two sides of a *parallelogram* drawn from a point, the *resultant* of the two vectors is represented in magnitude and direction by the diagonal of the parallelogram drawn through the point.

VECTORS, TRIANGLE LAW OF. If a particle is acted upon by two *vector* quantities represented by two sides of a *triangle* taken in order, the *resultant* vector is represented by the third side of the triangle.

VEGETABLE OILS. Oils obtained from the leaves, fruit, or seeds of plants, consisting of *esters* of *fatty acids* and *glycerol*. See also *fats and oils*.

VELOCITIES, PARALLELOGRAM OF. A special case of the parallelogram of *vectors*. See *parallelogram of velocities*.

VELOCITIES, TRIANGLE OF. A special case of the triangle of *vectors*. See *triangle of velocities*.

VELOCITY. The rate of motion in a given direction; measured as length per unit time.

VELOCITY OF LIGHT. See *light, velocity of*.

VELOCITY MODULATION. The *modulation* of the *velocity* of a stream of *electrons* by alternately accelerating and decelerating them. See also *klystron*.

VELOCITY RATIO OF A MACHINE. The ratio of the distance through which the point of application of the applied *force* moves, to the distance through which the point of application of the resistance moves in the same time. For an 'ideal' machine which requires no *energy* to move its component parts, the velocity ratio is equal to the *mechanical advantage*.

VELOCITY, RELATIVE. The *velocity* of one body relative to another is the rate at which the first body is changing its position with respect to the second. If the velocities of two bodies are represented by two sides of a *triangle* taken in order, their relative velocity is represented by the third side.

VENETIAN WHITE. A mixture of *white lead* and *barium sulphate*, $BaSO_4$, in equal parts. Used in *paints*.

VENTURI TUBE. A device for measuring the rate of flow of a *fluid*, consisting of an open-ended tube flared at each end, so that the fluid *velocity* in the narrow central portion is higher than at the flared ends. The fluid velocity can be calculated from the difference in *pressure* between the centre and the ends. Named after G. B. Venturi (1746–1822).

VENUS (Astr.). A *planet* with its *orbit* between those of *Mercury* and the *Earth*. Mean distance from the *Sun*, 108·21 million kilometres. *Sidereal period* ('year'), 224·701 days. *Mass*, approximately 0·815 that of the

Earth, diameter 12 300 kilometres. There is no evidence of oxygen in the *atmosphere* of the planet, but the Mariner *space probe* indicated that its surface temperature is about 425°C. and that it is covered by a dense cloud layer with freezing temperatures high up in the atmosphere.

VERDIGRIS. A green deposit formed upon copper; consists of *basic* copper carbonate or *sulphate* of variable composition.

VERMICIDE. A substance used to kill worms.

VERMICULITE. A group of low-grade *micas* which expand and exfoliate on heating to a light water-absorbent material. Used in the exfoliated form as *heat* and *sound* insulating materials, and in special (potting) *soils.*

VERMILION. A scarlet form of *mercuric sulphide*, HgS; used as a *pigment.*

VERNIER. A device for measuring subdivisions of a scale. For a scale graduated in (say) centimetres and tenths, a vernier consists of a scale which slides alongside the main scale, and on which a length of nine-tenths of a cm is subdivided into ten equal parts. Each vernier division is thus 0·9 cm. If it is desired to measure a length *AB*, the main scale is placed with its zero mark at *A*, and the vernier scale is slid till its zero mark is at *B*. By noting which division on the vernier scale is exactly in line with a division on the main scale, the second decimal place of the length *AB* is obtained. Thus, if *B* falls between 4·6 and 4·7 cm on the main scale, and the fourth division on the vernier scale is just in line with a main scale division line, the length *AB* is 4·64 cm. See Fig. 45. Named after Pierre Vernier (1580–1637).

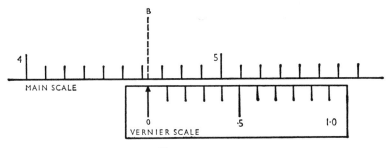

FIGURE 45.

VERNIER MOTOR (ENGINE). A small *rocket* motor used to correct the flight path or *velocity* of a missile or *spacecraft.*

VERONAL*. Diethylbarbituric acid, barbital. $C_8H_{12}N_2O_3$. A white crystalline *barbiturate*, m.p. 191°C., used as a *hypnotic.*

VERSED SINE. One minus the cosine of an angle (see *trigonometrical ratios*).

VERTEX. 1. (math.). The point on a geometrical figure furthest from the *base*. 2. (astr.). The point on the *celestial sphere* towards which, or from which, a *star* appears to move.

VERY HIGH FREQUENCIES. VHF. *Radio frequencies* in the range 30 to 300 *megahertz*.

VERY LOW FREQUENCIES. VLF. *Radio frequencies* below 30 *kilohertz*.

VESICANT. Blister-producing.

VIBRATION, PLANE OF. See *polarization of light*.

VIDEO FREQUENCY SIGNAL. The signal which transmits the picture and synchronizing information in a *television* system.

VINASSE. The residual *liquid* obtained after *fermentation* and *distillation* of beetroot molasses. Used as a source of *potassium carbonate*.

VINEGAR. A *liquid* containing 3%–6% *acetic acid*, obtained by the *oxidation* of *ethanol* by the action of *bacteria* on wine, beer, or fermented wort.

VINYL ACETATE. $CH_2:CHOOCCH_3$. A colourless *insoluble liquid*, b.p. 71–2° C., which *polymerizes* to form *polyvinyl acetate*.

VINYL CHLORIDE. $CH_2:CHCl$. A colourless *gas*, b.p. −13·9° C., which *polymerizes* to form *polyvinyl chloride*. Used as a *refrigerant* in the unpolymerized form.

VINYL ETHER. See *divinyl ether*.

VINYL GROUP. The *unsaturated univalent radical* $CH_2:CH —$.

VINYLIDENE CHLORIDE. $CH_2:CCl_2$. A colourless inflammable *liquid*, b.p. 32° C., which *polymerizes* to form *polyvinylidene chloride*.

VINYLIDENE GROUP. The *unsaturated bivalent radical* $CH_2:C=$.

VIRGIN NEUTRONS. *Neutrons*, produced by any means, before they have experienced a collision.

VIROLOGY. The study of *viruses* and the diseases they cause.

VIRTUAL IMAGE. See *image, virtual*.

VIRTUAL STATE. In *classical physics* a *force* between bodies not in contact (e.g. electrostatic repulsion) is represented by a *field*. In *quantum mechanics* this force may be represented by an exchange of particles between the interacting bodies. The exchanged particle is not in a 'real' state, however, although its properties can be calculated; such a particle is described as existing in the virtual state. E.g. electrically charged particles may be visualized as interacting as the result of the exchange of virtual *photons*. A virtual particle which is responsible for a force can, by the addition of *energy* to the system, be converted into a real particle. The virtual state depends upon the concept of indeterminism expressed in the *uncertainty principle*.

VIRTUAL WORK. If a body, acted upon by a system of *forces*, is imagined to undergo a small displacement, then in general the forces will do *work*, termed the virtual work of the forces. If the body is in *equilibrium*, the total virtual work done is zero. This principle of virtual work is used to determine the positions of equilibrium of a body or a system of bodies under the action of given forces, and to determine relations between the forces acting on such a system in a given equilibrium position.

VIRUS. A disease-producing particle, too small to be seen by an optical *microscope* but visible with an *electron microscope*. Viruses are only capable of multiplication within a living *cell*, each type of virus requiring a specific host cell. The simplest viruses consist of a single helical strand of *ribonucleic acid* coated with *protein molecules* (see *tobacco mosaic virus*). The active principle of these viruses resides in the RNA as it is only this part of the particle which enters the cell. Other viruses are considerably more complex and may be up to 0·2 *micrometre* in diameter. Viruses are considered to be on the borderline between the animate and the inanimate. See also *bacteriophage*.

VISCOMETER. An instrument for the measurement of *viscosity*.

VISCOSE. A thick treacly brownish *liquid*, consisting mainly of a *solution* of cellulose *xanthate* in dilute *sodium hydroxide*. It is made from *cellulose* by the action of sodium hydroxide and *carbon disulphide*. Used for the production of viscose *rayon* and of cellulose film, of the type used for transparent wrappings.

VISCOSE RAYON. See *rayon*.

VISCOSITY. η. The property of a *fluid* whereby it tends to resist relative motion within itself. If different layers of a fluid are moving with different *velocities*, *viscous forces* come into play, tending to slow down the faster-moving layers and to increase the velocity of the slower-moving layers. For two parallel layers in the direction of flow, a short distance apart, this viscous force is proportional to the velocity gradient between the layers. The constant of proportionality is called the coefficient of viscosity of the fluid. Measured in *newton seconds* per square *metre* (*SI units*) or *poise* (*c.g.s. units*). 1 centipoise $= 10^{-3}$ Ns/m². See also *kinematic viscosity*.

VISCOUS. Having high *viscosity*; a viscous *liquid* drags in a treacle-like manner.

VISIBLE SPECTRUM. The range of *electromagnetic radiations* which are visible to man. See *spectrum colours*.

VISUAL BINARY. A *binary star* system which can be resolved into two *stars* with an optical *telescope*. See also *spectroscopic binary*.

VISUAL DISPLAY UNIT. A *computer peripheral* device whose output is a *cathode ray tube* for displaying text or diagrams. It may have an input device consisting of a keyboard or it may be a *light pen*.

VISUAL PURPLE. See *rhodopsin*.

VITALISTIC THEORY. The view that life, and all consequent biological phenomena, are due to a 'vital force'.

VITAMINS. Accessory food factors. A group of organic substances, occurring in various foods, which are necessary for a normal diet. Absence or shortage leads to various deficiency diseases. Before the chemical nature of any of the vitamins was known, they were named by the letters of the alphabet. Vitamin A, $C_{20}H_{29}OH$, occurs in milk, butter, green vegetables, and in liver, especially of fish. Deficiency causes 'night-blindness' (see *rhodopsin*) and ultimately more serious eye troubles; the resistance of the mucous membranes to infection also decreases. This vitamin can be made in the body from *carotene*. Vitamin B, originally regarded as a single substance, has been shown to be a whole group of *compounds* termed the vitamin B complex; these occur in wheat-germ, *yeast*, and other sources. B_1 see *thiamin*; B_2 see *riboflavin* (also called vitamin G); B_6 see *pyridoxine*; B_{12} see *cyanocobaltamine*; B_c see *folic acid* (also called vitamin M). See also other members of the complex, *nicotinic acid, inositol, pantothenic acid, choline,* and *biotin* (also called vitamin H). Vitamin C see *ascorbic acid*. Vitamin D consists of several compounds, all of which are *sterols*. The most important is *calciferol*. Vitamin E see *tocopherol*. Vitamin F see *linoleic acid*. Vitamin G (B_2) see *riboflavin*. Vitamin H see *biotin*. Vitamin K consists of naphthoquinone compounds whose deficiency causes haemorrhage. Vitamin M (B_c) see *folic acid*.

VITREOSIL*. A translucent form of *silica*, SiO_2, prepared from sand. Used for making laboratory apparatus which is required to withstand large and sudden changes in *temperature*; does not crack at such changes owing to very low expansion.

VITREOUS. Pertaining to, composed of, or resembling *glass*.

VITRIOL. Concentrated *sulphuric acid*, H_2SO_4, oil of vitriol; *copper sulphate*, $CuSO_4.5H_2O$, blue vitriol; *ferrous sulphate*, $FeSO_4.7H_2O$, green vitriol; *zinc sulphate*, $ZnSO_4.7H_2O$, white vitriol.

VOLATILE. Passing readily into *vapour*; having a high *vapour pressure*.

VOLT. The derived *SI unit* of electric *potential* defined as the difference of potential between two points on a conducting wire carrying a constant *current* of one *ampere* when the *power* dissipated between these points is one *watt*. Also the unit of *potential difference* and *electromotive force*. 1 volt $= 10^8$ *electromagnetic units*. Symbol $V (= \frac{W}{A})$. Named after Alessandro Volta (1745–1827).

VOLTAGE. The *potential, potential difference* or *electromotive force* of a supply of electricity, measured in *volts*.

VOLTAGE DIVIDER. Potential divider, potentiometer. A *resistor* or series of resistors connected across a source of *voltage* (V) and tapped at a point to give a fraction (v) of the total voltage. In Fig. 46, page 412, $v/V = r_2/r_1 + r_2$.

VOLTAGE DOUBLER. An *electronic circuit* which delivers a *direct current voltage* approximately twice the peak *alternating current* voltage it feeds on. Usually consists of two *rectifiers* whose outputs are connected in *series*.

VOLTAIC CELL. See *cell* (phys.).

VOLTAIC PILE. The earliest electric *battery*, devised by Volta. A number of *cells* joined in series, each consisting of a sheet of zinc and copper separated by a piece of cloth moistened with dilute *sulphuric acid*.

VOLTAMETER. An electrolytic cell in which a *metal*, generally silver or copper, is deposited by *electrolysis* of a *salt* of the metal upon the *cathode*. From the increase in *weight* of the cathode and a knowledge of the *electrochemical equivalent* of the metal, the quantity of electricity which has passed through the circuit may be found.

VOLTMETER. An instrument for measuring the *potential difference* between two points. In principle consists of an arrangement similar to an *ammeter* with a high *resistance* in series incorporated in the instrument, the scale being calibrated in *volts*. When the instrument is connected in parallel between the points where the p.d. is being measured, very little current flows through it, and a correct reading of the *voltage* is obtained.

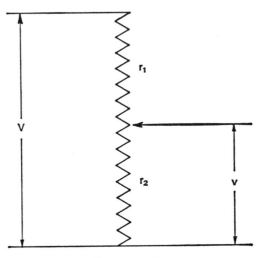

FIGURE 46.

VOLUME. *V*. The measure of bulk or space occupied by a body.

VOLUME, BRITISH UNITS OF.

Solids: 1728 cubic inches = 1 cubic foot.

27 cubic feet = 1 cubic yard.

(1 cubic inch = 16·3871 cm³.)

Liquids: 4 gills = 1 pint.

2 pints = 1 quart.

4 quarts = 1 gallon, 4546·09 cm³.

VOLUME, METRIC UNITS OF.

1000 cubic millimetres = 1 cubic centimetre.

1000 cm³ = 1 dm³ = 1 *litre*.

VOLUMETRIC ANALYSIS. A group of methods of *quantitative chemical analysis* involving the measurement of *volumes* of the reacting substances. The amount of a substance present is determined by finding the volume of a *solution* of another substance, of known *concentration*, which is required to react with it. The added volume is measured by adding the reacting solution from a *burette*; the *end point* of the reaction is often shown by a suitable *indicator*.

VULCANITE. A hard insulating material made by the action of *rubber* on sulphur.

VULCANIZED RUBBER. The product obtained by heating *rubber* with sulphur.

VULGAR FRACTION. Common fraction. A fraction expressed in terms of a *numerator* and a *denominator*, e.g. $\frac{3}{4}$.

W

WANKEL ROTARY ENGINE. Epitrochoidal engine. A type of *internal-combustion engine* employing a 4-stroke cycle, but without reciprocating parts. It consists essentially of an elliptical combustion chamber fitted with valve-less inlet and outlet ports, and a conventional *sparking-plug*. An epicyclically-driven roughly triangular-shaped piston rotates within this chamber dividing it into three gas-tight sections, the volume of each of which varies as the piston rotates. The explosive mixture sucked in through the inlet port is compressed by the rotating piston and exploded by the sparking-plug. The explosion provides the power to rotate the piston and sweep the exhaust gases round to the outlet port. The small number of moving parts and the absence of vibration are the chief advantages of this type of engine. Named after Felix Wankel (b. 1902).

WASHING-SODA. Crystalline *sodium carbonate*, $Na_2CO_3.10H_2O$.

WATER. H_2O. The normal *oxide* of hydrogen. Natural water (river, spring, rain, etc.) is never quite pure but contains dissolved substances. Pure water is a colourless, odourless *liquid*, m.p. 0°C., b.p. 100°C., which has a maximum *density* at 4°C. of 1·000 grams per cc. Liquid water consists of associated *molecules*, $(H_2O)_n$, due to *hydrogen bonds* between the molecules.

WATER EQUIVALENT (phys.). See *heat capacity*.

WATER, EXPANSION OF. *Water* on cooling reaches its maximum *density* at 3·98°C when its density is 0·999973 g/cm^3; it then expands as its temperature falls to 0°C, the density at 0° being 0·999841 g/cm^3; on freezing, it expands still further, giving *ice* with a density of 0·9168 g/cm^3 at 0°C. This accounts for the bursting of water-pipes in frosts.

WATER GAS. *Fuel gas* obtained by the action of *steam* on glowing hot *coke*, giving *carbon monoxide* and hydrogen. The formation of water gas is accompanied by absorption of *heat* (an *endothermic* reaction); thus the coke is rapidly cooled and has to be reheated at intervals by a blast of hot air, which causes partial *combustion* and makes the coke incandescent again.

WATER GLASS. *Sodium silicate*, Na_2SiO_3.

WATER OF CONSTITUTION. The portion of *water of crystallization* which, in some *hydrated salts*, is retained more tenaciously than the rest. Thus, *cupric sulphate*, $CuSO_4.5H_2O$, when heated to 100°C. loses 4 *molecules* of water of crystallization and becomes $CuSO_4.H_2O$, but the last molecule is retained till the temperature reaches 250°C.

WATER OF CRYSTALLIZATION. A definite molecular proportion of water chemically combined with certain substances in the crystalline state; e.g. the *crystals* of *cupric sulphate* contain 5 *molecules* of *water* with every molecule of cupric sulphate, $CuSO_4.5H_2O$.

WATER SOFTENING. The removal of the causes of hardness of water (see *hard water*). Generally depends on the *precipitation* or removal from *solution* of the *metals* the *salts* of which cause the hardness.

WATER VAPOUR. *Water* in the gaseous or *vapour* state; it is present in the *atmosphere* in varying amounts. See *humidity*.

WATT. The derived *SI unit* of *power*, equal to one *joule* per *second*. The *energy* expended per second by an unvarying *electric current* of 1 *ampere* flowing through a *conductor* the ends of which are maintained at a *potential difference* of 1 *volt*. Equivalent to 10^7 *ergs* per second. The power in watts is given by the product of the current in amperes and the potential difference in volts. 1000 watts = 1 *kilowatt*; 745·7 watts = 1 *horsepower*. Symbol W (=J/s). Named after James Watt (1736–1819).

WATTAGE. *Power* measured in *watts*.

WATTMETER. An instrument for the direct measurement of the *power*, in *watts*, of an electrical *circuit*.

WATT-SECOND. A unit of *work* or *energy* equivalent to one *joule*. See also *kilowatt-hour*.

WAVE. A periodic disturbance in a medium or in *space*, which may involve the elastic displacement of material particles or a periodic change in some physical quantity such as *temperature, pressure, electric potential, electromagnetic field* strength, etc. See *wave motion*.

WAVE EQUATION. The *equation* of *wave mechanics* which gives mathematical expression to *wave motion*:

$$\nabla^2 \psi = \frac{1}{c^2}\frac{\delta\psi}{\delta t^2}$$

where ∇^2 is the *Laplace operator*, ψ is the *wave function*, c is the *velocity of light*, and t is the time at any instant.

WAVE FORM. The shape of a *wave*, illustrated graphically by plotting the values of the periodic quantity against time.

WAVE FRONT. The locus of adjacent points in the path of a *wave motion* which possess the same *phase*.

WAVE FUNCTION. In *wave mechanics, orbital electrons* are not treated as particles moving in precisely defined *orbits*, but as 3-dimensional *standing wave* systems represented by a wave function, ψ, the magnitude of which represents the varying *amplitudes* of the wave system at various points around the *nucleus*. The volume containing all the points where ψ has an appreciable magnitude is called the *orbital* of the electron. Thus, according to wave mechanics, the precise position and *velocity* of an electron (which cannot be defined without error, see *uncertainty principle*) is replaced by a *probability* that an electron, visualized as a particle, will be at a certain point in *space* at a particular instant of time. The *probability distribution* of electrons is given by the magnitude of ψ^2. See also *wave equation*.

WAVE GUIDE. A hollow *metal conductor* through which *microwaves* may be propagated. Used extensively in *radar*.

WAVE MECHANICS. A development of *quantum mechanics*. Every particle

415

is considered to be associated with a kind of periodic *wave*, whose *frequency* and *amplitude* are determined by rules which are derived partly by analogy with the propagation of *light* waves, partly by ad hoc hypothesis from known quantum conditions, and partly from necessary conditions of continuity. These waves, however, are not conceived as having any real physical existence, the term 'wave' being really used only by analogy as a description of the mathematical relations employed, since in all but the simplest cases the waves would have to be imagined in a 'hyperspace' of very many dimensions. See also *wave function* and *wave equation*.

WAVE MOTION. The propagation of a periodic disturbance carrying *energy*. At any point along the path of a wave motion, a periodic displacement or vibration about a mean position takes place. This may take the form of a displacement of air *molecules* (e.g. *sound* waves in air), of water molecules (waves on water), a displacement of elements of a string or wire, displacement of electric and magnetic *vectors* (*electromagnetic waves*), etc. The locus of these displacements at any instant is called the *wave*. The wave motion moves forward a distance equal to its *wavelength* in the time taken for the displacement at any point to undergo a complete *cycle* about its mean position. See *longitudinal waves*; *transverse waves*.

WAVE NUMBER. $\sigma = \dfrac{1}{\lambda}$. The number of *waves* in unit length. Reciprocal of *wavelength*.

WAVE THEORY OF LIGHT. The theory that *light* is propagated as a *wave motion* (see *electromagnetic radiation*); formerly the existence of a medium, the *ether*, was postulated for the transmission of light waves. This hypothesis has been rejected as unnecessary, and the classical wave theory has been modified to include the dual particle (*photon*) wave concept which is required to explain all the observed phenomena.

WAVELENGTH. λ. The distance between successive points of equal *phase* of a *wave*; e.g. the wavelength of the waves on water could be measured as the distance from crest to crest. The wavelength is equal to the *velocity* of the *wave motion* divided by its *frequency*. For *electromagnetic radiation* $\lambda = c/\nu$, where c is the *velocity of light* and ν is the frequency.

WAVEMETER. An instrument for measuring the *wavelength* of a *radio frequency electromagnetic radiation*.

WAX. True waxes (e.g. *beeswax*) are simple *lipids* consisting of *esters* of higher *fatty acids* than are found in *fats and oils*, with *monohydric alcohols*. The term is often loosely applied to *solid*, non-greasy, *insoluble* substances which soften or melt at fairly low *temperatures*, e.g. *paraffin wax*.

WEAK NUCLEAR INTERACTIONS. Interactions which are responsible for the *decay* of all particles except *protons*, *electrons*, *neutrinos*, and *photons*. Weak nuclear interactions are some 10^{12} times weaker than *strong nuclear interactions*.

WEBER. The derived *SI unit* of *magnetic flux* defined as the flux which, linking a circuit of one turn, produces in it an *E.M.F.* of one *volt* as it reduces to zero at a uniform rate in one *second*. Symbol Wb(= Vs). 1 weber = 10^8 *maxwells*. Named after Wilhelm Weber (1804–91).

WEIGHT. The *force* of attraction of the *Earth* on a given *mass* is the weight of that mass.

WEIGHT, BRITISH UNITS OF. Avoirdupois weights.

$437\frac{1}{2}$ grains	= 1 ounce.
7000 grains = 16 ounces	= 1 *pound* = 0·453592 *kilogrammes*
14 pounds	= 1 stone.
2 stone	= 1 quarter.
4 quarters	= 1 hundredweight.
2240 pounds = 20 cwt	= 1 ton.
2000 pounds	= 1 short ton.

See Table 1, pages 428.

WEIGHT, METRIC UNITS OF.

1000 milligrams	= 1 gram	= 15·432 grains
1000 grams	= 1 *kilogramme*	= 2·20462 lb.
1000 kilogrammes	= 1 tonne	= 0·984207 ton.

See Table 1, page 428.

WELDING. Joining of two *metal* surfaces by raising their *temperature* sufficiently to melt and fuse them together.

WESTON CELL. Cadmium cell. A *primary cell* used as a standard of *E.M.F.* Produces 1·0186 *volts* at 20° C. Consists of a mercury *anode* covered with mercurous sulphate and a cadmium *amalgam cathode* coated with cadmium sulphate *crystals*. The *electrolyte* is a *saturated solution* of cadmium sulphate.

WET AND DRY BULB HYGROMETER. An instrument for determining the *relative humidity* of the *atmosphere*. Consists of a pair of *thermometers* side by side, the bulb of one being surrounded by moistened muslin. This one will indicate a lower temperature than the other, on account of loss of *heat* by *evaporation*; the difference in the readings will depend upon the relative humidity, which can be found by reference to special tables calculated for the purpose.

WETTING AGENT. A substance which lowers the *surface tension* of a *liquid*.

WHALE OIL. Animal *fat* obtained from the fatty layer of blubber of true whales. After extraction it is divided into various fractions and used for *soap* manufacture and other purposes; on *hydrogenation* a hard tasteless edible fat is obtained.

WHEATSTONE BRIDGE. A divided electrical *circuit* used for the measurement of *resistances*. When no current flows from C to D, as indicated by the absence of deflection on the *galvanometer G*, $R_1/R_2 = R_3/R_4$, where R_1, etc., are resistances. See Fig. 47, page 418. This principle is applied in the metre bridge. A wire, AB, of uniform resistance and generally 1 metre in length, corresponds to R_3 and R_4 in the Wheatstone bridge diagram; for R_1 a standard resistance is used, while R_2 is the resistance to be measured. By a sliding contact a point of no deflection in the galvanometer is found along *AB*, the resistances R_3 and R_4 being proportional to the lengths cut off. Named after Sir Charles Wheatstone (1802–75).

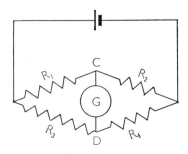

FIGURE 47.

WHISTLER. An *atmospheric* whistle of descending *pitch* which can be picked up under certain circumstances by a *radio* receiver. Caused by *electromagnetic radiations*, produced by *lightning* flashes, which follow the *lines of force* of the Earth's *magnetic field* and are reflected back to Earth by the *ionosphere*.

WHITE ARSENIC. See *arsenic trioxide*.

WHITE BRONZE. *Bronze* which contains a high proportion of tin.

WHITE DWARF. A class of small, highly dense *stars* of low *luminosity*. They are the remnants of stars that have consumed nearly all their available hydrogen. Owing to their small size they have high surface *temperatures* and therefore appear white. See *supernovae*.

WHITE LEAD. See *lead carbonate*.

WHITE LIGHT. *Light* which can be resolved into a continuous *spectrum* of *wavelengths* (i.e. *colours*); e.g. the light from an incandescent 'white-hot' *solid*.

WHITE SPIRIT. A *mixture* of *petroleum hydrocarbons* of boiling range 150°–200° C. Used as a *solvent* and in the *paint* and varnish industry.

WIDE-ANGLE LENS. A *camera lens* with a wide angle of view (up to 100°) and a short *focal length*.

WIEDEMANN-FRANZ LAW. The ratio of the thermal *conductivity* to the electrical conductivity is the same for all *metals* at a given *temperature*. This ratio is proportional to the *absolute temperature*. Most pure metals obey the law with reasonable accuracy at ordinary temperatures.

WIGNER EFFECT. The effect produced when the *atoms* in a *crystal* are displaced as a result of *irradiation*. If *graphite*, for example, is bombarded with *neutrons*, the shape of the crystal *lattice* is altered and the material suffers a change of physical dimensions. See also *Wigner energy*. Named after Eugene Paul Wigner (born 1902).

WIGNER ENERGY. *Energy* stored within a crystalline substance as a result of the *Wigner effect*. In a *nuclear reactor* in which *graphite* is used as the *moderator*, some of the energy lost by the *neutrons* is stored in the graphite; this is known as the Wigner energy.

WIGNER NUCLIDES. Pairs of *isobars* of odd *mass number* in which the *atomic number* and *neutron* number differ by one. E.g. $^3_1$H and $^3_2$He.

WILSON CLOUD CHAMBER. See *cloud chamber*. Named after C. T. R. Wilson (1869–1961).

WIMSHURST MACHINE. A laboratory apparatus for generating static *electricity*. Named after J. Wimshurst (1836–1903).

WIND. A large-scale movement of air, generally caused by a *convection* effect in the *atmosphere*.

WIRELESS. See *radio*.

WOLFRAM. W. See *tungsten*.

WOLFRAMITE. 'Wolfram'. Natural ferrous tungstate, $FeWO_4$.

WOLLASTON PRISM. A *prism* for obtaining plane-polarized light (see *polarization of light*). Constructed of *quartz*, this prism, like the *Rochon prism*, may be used for *ultraviolet radiation*. Named after W. H. Wollaston (1766–1828).

WOOD NAPHTHA. See *methanol*.

WOOD SUGAR. See *xylose*.

WOOD'S METAL. An *alloy* of 50% bismuth, 25% lead, 12·5% tin, 12·5% cadmium. M.p. 71°C.

WOOFER. A *loudspeaker* designed to reproduce the lower *audio-frequency* sounds.

WORD. The smallest number of *bits* of information which a particular *computer* can conveniently process as a single unit; usually 12 to 64 bits.

WORK (phys.). The work done by a *force f* when it moves its point of application through a distance *s* is equal to *fs cos θ*, where *θ* is the *angle* between the line of action of the force and the displacement. The derived *SI unit* of work is the *joule*; other units include *erg, foot-pound, foot-poundal*.

WORK FUNCTION. 1. At the *absolute zero* of temperature, the *free electrons* present in a *metal* are distributed amongst a large number of discrete *energy* states E_1, E_2, etc., up to a state of maximum energy *E*. At higher temperatures a small proportion of the electrons have energies greater than *E*. The work function of a metal is the energy which must be supplied to free electrons possessing energy *E*, to enable them to escape from the metal. 2. Helmholtz *free energy*.

WORK HARDENING. See *strain hardening*.

WORKING STRESS. See *ultimate stress*.

WORT. See *brewing*.

WROUGHT IRON. The purest commercial form of iron; iron nearly free from carbon. It is very tough and fibrous and can be welded.

X

XANTHATES. *Salts* or *esters* of the series of xanthic acids which have the general formula ROCSSH. Cellulose xanthate is the important intermediate product in the manufacture of *viscose*.

XANTHEN(E). $C_6H_4O.CH_2C_6H_4$. A yellow crystalline substance, m.p. 100·5°C., which forms the basis of the xanthene *dyes*.

XANTHINE. $C_5H_4N_4O_2$. A yellow *soluble* crystalline substance, found in urine, *blood*, and certain animal *tissues*.

XANTHONE. $C_6H_4.CO.O.C_6H_4$. A yellow *insoluble* crystalline *ketone*, m.p. 174°C., which occurs in several natural yellow *pigments*.

XENON. Xe. Element. A.W. 131·3. At. No. 54. An *inert gas* occurring in exceedingly minute amounts in the air (about 0·006 parts per million by volume). Used in filling certain types of *thermionic valve*.

XEROGRAPHY. A method of photographic copying in which an electrostatic image is formed on a surface coated with selenium when it is exposed to an optical image. A dark powder (consisting of *graphite* and a *thermoplastic resin*), oppositely charged to the electrostatic image, is dusted on to the surface after exposure so that particles adhere to the charged regions; the image thus formed is then transferred to a sheet of charged paper and fixed by heating.

X-RADIATION. *Electromagnetic radiation* consisting of *X-rays*.

X-RAY CRYSTALLOGRAPHY. The study of crystalline substances by observation of the *diffraction* patterns which occur when a *beam* of *X-rays* is passed through a *crystal*. It is principally as a result of the use of X-ray crystallography that the structure of certain *proteins* (e.g. *haemoglobin*) and *nucleic acids* has been analysed.

X-RAY SPECTRUM. Each *element*, when bombarded by *electrons*, emits *X-rays* of a characteristic *frequency* which depends upon the *atomic number*; a photograph of the *line spectrum* corresponding to various elements may thus be obtained from the X-rays emitted.

X-RAY STARS. *Stars* which emit *X-rays*: they have recently been discovered by instruments carried outside the *Earth's atmosphere* by *space probes*. The nature of the stars, or their mechanism of X-ray emission, is not known.

X-RAY TUBE. An evacuated tube for producing *X-rays*, which contains an *electron gun* and a heavy *metal* target forming part of a massive *anode*. The metal emits X-rays when it is bombarded by high energy *electrons*. The *wavelength* of the radiation depends on the *voltage* between the *cathode* and the anode, the *temperature* of the cathode, and the metal of the target.

X-RAYS. Röntgen rays. *Electromagnetic radiations* of the same type as *light*, but of much shorter *wavelength*, in the range of 5×10^{-9} *metres* to 6×10^{-12} metres approximately. Produced when a stream of *electrons* strikes a material object. X-rays affect a photographic plate in a way similar to light. The absorption of the rays by *matter* depends upon the *density* and the *atomic weights* of the material. The lower the A.W. and density, the more *transparent* is the material to X-rays. Thus, bones are more opaque than the surrounding flesh; this makes it possible to take an X-ray photograph (*radiograph*) of the bones of a living person.

X UNIT. X.U. Unit of length, 10^{-11} cm. Used mainly for expressing *X-ray wavelengths*.

XYLAN. A complex *polysaccharide* which occurs closely associated with *cellulose* in plants.

XYLENE. Xylol, dimethylbenzene. $C_6H_4(CH_3)_2$. A *liquid* resembling *toluene* which occurs in *coal-tar*. It exists in three *isomeric* forms, a *mixture* of which boils at 137°–140°C. Used in the manufacture of *dyes*.

XYLIDINE. $(CH_3)_2C_6H_3NH_2$. A colourless *liquid* which exists in six *isomeric* forms, a *mixture* of isomers has b.p. between 214° and 224°C. Used in the manufacture of *dyes*.

XYLOL. See *xylene*.

XYLONITE*. Trade name for a *plastic* material of the *cellulose nitrate* type. See also *celluloid*.

XYLOSE. Wood sugar. $C_5H_{10}O_5$. A colourless crystalline *pentose*, m.p. 144°C., found in *xylan*.

XYLYL GROUP. The *univalent radical* $CH_3C_6H_4CH_2$—.

Y

YAGI AERIAL. A directional *aerial* consisting of one or two *dipoles*, a parallel reflector, and a series of directors in front of the dipole, all so arranged that *radiation* is focused on to the dipole. Used in *television* and *radio astronomy*. Named after Hidetsuga Yagi (b. 1886).

YARD. British unit of length. The Imperial standard yard used to be defined as the distance, at 62° F., between the central traverse lines on two gold plugs in a certain *bronze* bar. The yard was redefined by the 1963 Weights and Measures Act as 0·9144 *metres*.

YEAR. A measure of time, commonly understood to be the time taken by the *Earth* to complete its *orbit* round the *Sun*. The civil year has an average value of 365·2425 mean *solar days*; 3 successive years consisting of 365 days, the fourth or leap year of 366. Century years do not count as leap years unless divisible by 400. The tropical, astronomical, or solar year, the average interval between two successive returns of the Sun to the first point of Aries, is 365·2422 mean solar days; the sidereal year, the interval in which the Sun appears to perform a complete revolution with reference to the fixed *stars*, is 365·2564 mean solar days. The anomolistic year, the average period of revolution of the Earth round the Sun from *perihelion* to perihelion, is 365·2596 mean solar days.

YEASTS. *Unicellular micro-organisms* producing *zymase*, which converts *sugars* into *alcohol* and *carbon dioxide*. Used in *brewing* for the production of alcohol, and in baking because the carbon dioxide produced causes the dough to 'rise'.

YIELD POINT. If a wire or rod of a material such as *steel* is subjected to a slowly increasing tension, the elongation produced is at first proportional to the tension (*Hooke's law*). If the tension is increased beyond the *elastic limit*, a point is reached at which a sudden increase in elongation occurs with only a small increase in tension; this is the yield point.

YOUNG'S MODULUS. *Elastic modulus* applied to a stretched wire or to a rod under tension or compression; the ratio of the *stress* on a cross-section of the wire or rod to the longitudinal *strain*. Named after Thomas Young (1773-1829).

YPERITE. See *mustard gas*.

YTTERBIUM. Yb. Element. A.W. 173·04. At. No. 70. S.G. 6·97, m.p. 824° C. See *lanthanides*.

YTTRIUM. Y. Element. A.W. 88·905. At. No. 39. S.G. 4·34, m.p. 1495° C.

Z

ZEEMAN EFFECT. When a substance which emits a *line spectrum* is placed in a strong *magnetic field*, the single lines are split up into groups of closely spaced lines. From the separation of the lines in these groups information on atomic structure can be deduced. Named after Pieter Zeeman (1865–1943).

ZENER CURRENT. The current in a *semiconductor*, consisting of *electrons* which have escaped from the *valency band* into the *conduction band* under the influence of a strong *electric field*. Named after C. M. Zener (b. 1905).

ZENITH (astr.). The highest point; the point on the *celestial sphere* directly overhead. See Fig. 2, page 36, which also illustrates the 'zenith angle'.

ZEOLITE. Natural *hydrated silicate* of calcium and aluminium. The term is also now applied to artificial substances used in softening *hard water* by the 'base-exchange' method (see *ion exchange*). The calcium in the water replaces sodium in the zeolite; the process may be reversed and the zeolite restored by washing it with a *solution* of common *salt*.

ZERO. Nought; the starting-point of any scale of measurement.

ZERO POINT ENERGY. The *energy* possessed by the *atoms* or *molecules* of a substance at the *absolute zero* of temperature.

ZETA. Zero Energy Thermonuclear Apparatus. A *torus*-shaped apparatus used for studying controlled *thermonuclear reactions* at Harwell.

ZIEGLER CATALYSTS. *Catalysts* capable of initiating the *polymerization* of *ethylene* and *propylene* at normal *temperatures* and *pressures*, e.g. titanium trichloride and aluminium alkyl. Named after Carl Ziegler (b. 1897).

ZINC. Zn. Element. A.W. 65·37. At. No. 30. A hard, bluish-white *metal*; m.p. 419°C.; b.p. 907°C.; S.G. 7·14. Occurs as *calamine*, $ZnCO_3$, *zincite*, ZnO, and *zinc blende*, ZnS. Extracted by roasting the ore to form the *oxide*, which is then reduced with carbon and the resulting zinc distilled. Used in *alloys*, especially *brass*, and in *galvanized iron*.

ZINC BLENDE. Natural *zinc sulphide*, ZnS. An important *ore* of zinc.

ZINC CARBONATE. *Calamine*. $ZnCO_3$. A white *insoluble* crystalline substance, used in medicine in the treatment of skins.

ZINC CHLORIDE. $ZnCl_2$. A white *deliquescent soluble* substance, m.p. 283°C., used as an *antiseptic*, a wood preservative, and as a *flux*.

ZINC-COPPER COUPLE. Metallic zinc coated with a thin film of copper by immersing zinc in *copper sulphate solution*. Evolves hydrogen with hot *water*.

ZINC OXIDE. ZnO. A white *amorphous* powder, m.p. 1975°C., widely used as a *pigment*, in *glass* manufacture, in cosmetics, and in medicine.

ZINC PHOSPHIDE. Zn_3P_2. A grey *insoluble* crystalline substance, used as a rat poison.

ZINC SULPHATE. White vitriol. $ZnSO_4.7H_2O$. A white *soluble* crystalline powder, m.p. 100°C., used as a *mordant*, in zinc plating, in the manufacture of *paper*, and in medicine.

ZINC SULPHIDE. ZnS. A white or yellowish *insoluble* crystalline substance, which occurs naturally as *zinc blende*. Used as a *pigment*.

ZINC SILICATE. Several silicates of zinc exist. Natural zinc silicate, hemimorphite, is $2ZnO.SiO_2.H_2O$ (see also *calamine*). Zinc *meta*silicate, $ZnSiO_3$, has m.p. $1437°C$. Zinc *ortho*silicate, Zn_2SiO_4, has m.p. $1509°C$.

ZINCITE. Natural *zinc oxide*, ZnO. An important *ore* of zinc.

ZIRCON. Zirconium silicate. $ZrSiO_4$. A colourless or yellowish *insoluble* substance, m.p. $2550°C$. Used as a gemstone when *transparent* and a *refractory* when coloured.

ZIRCONIA. See *zirconium dioxide*.

ZIRCONIUM. Zr. Element. A.W. 91·22. At. No. 40. A rare *metal*, S.G. 6·4, m.p. $1852°C$. Used in *alloys*, *abrasives*, and flame proofing *compounds*.

ZIRCONIUM DIOXIDE. Zirconia. ZrO_2. A white crystalline *insoluble* substance, m.p. $2715°C$., used as a *pigment* and a *refractory*. The *hydrated* form, $ZrO_2.xH_2O$, also known as 'zirconium hydroxide' and 'zirconic acid', is a white *amorphous* powder.

ZIRCONYL GROUP. The *univalent* group ZrO—.

ZODIAC. Zone of *celestial sphere* containing paths of *Sun, Moon,* and *planets*. Bounded by two circles, equidistant from the *ecliptic* and about $18°$ apart; divided into 12 signs of the zodiac, named after 12 constellations.

ZODIACAL LIGHT. A faint luminous patch seen in the sky, on the western horizon after sunset, or on the eastern horizon before sunrise, believed to be due to the *scattering* of sunlight by meteoric matter revolving round the *Sun*.

ZONE OF SPHERE. A portion of the surface of a *sphere* cut off by two parallel *planes*. Area is given by $2\pi rd$, where r is the radius of the sphere and d the distance between the two planes.

ZONES OF AUDIBILITY. An intense *sound*, e.g. due to an *explosion*, can usually be heard or detected at all points in a large area around the source of the sound, and also in distant zones of audibility separated from that area by regions in which the sound cannot be detected. Sound waves can reach these zones by reflection down from the *upper atmosphere*.

ZONES, FRESNEL. See *half-period zones*.

ZOOLOGY. The scientific study of animals.

ZOOM LENS. A cinematic or television *camera lens* whose *focal length* can be adjusted continuously to vary the *magnification* without loss of focus.

ZWITTERION. An *ion* carrying both a positive and negative *electric charge*.

ZYGOTE. A fertilized *ovum*; the product of the union of two *gametes*.

ZYMASE. An *enzyme* present in *yeast* which acts on *sugar* with the formation of *alcohol* and *carbon dioxide*. See *fermentation*.

ZYMOLOGY. Enzymology. The study of *fermentation* and the action of *enzymes*.

ZYMOTIC. Relating to, or caused by, *fermentation*.

TABLE I

6-FIGURE CONVERSION FACTORS
SI, CGS, AND FPS UNITS

Length

	m	cm	in	ft	yd
1 metre	1	100	39·3701	3·28084	1·09361
1 centimetre	0·01	1	0·393701	0·0328084	0·0109361
1 inch	0·0254	2·54	1	0·0833333	0·0277778
1 foot	0·3048	30·48	12	1	0·333333
1 yard	0·9144	91·44	36	3	1

	km	mi	n.mi
1 kilometre	1	0·621371	0·539957
1 mile	1·60934	1	0·868976
1 nautical mile	1·85200	1·15078	1

1 light year $= 9 \cdot 4607 \times 10^{15}$ metres $= 5 \cdot 87848 \times 10^{12}$ miles.
1 Astronomical Unit $= 1 \cdot 495 \times 10^{11}$ metres.
1 parsec $= 3 \cdot 0857 \times 10^{16}$ metres $= 3 \cdot 2616$ light years.

TABLE I — *cont.*

6-FIGURE CONVERSION FACTORS
SI, CGS AND FPS UNITS

Area

	m²	cm²	in²	ft²
1 square metre	1	10⁴	1550	10·7639
1 square centimetre	10⁻⁴	1	0·155	1·07639 × 10⁻³
1 square inch	6·4516 × 10⁻⁴	6·4516	1	6·94444 × 10⁻³
1 square foot	9·2903 × 10⁻²	929·03	144	1

	m²	km²	yd²	mi²	acre
1 square metre	1	10⁻⁶	1·19599	3·86019 × 10⁻⁷	2·47105 × 10⁻⁴
1 square kilometre	10⁶	1	1·19599 × 10⁶	0·386019	247·105
1 square yard	0·836127	8·36127 × 10⁻⁷	1	3·22831 × 10⁻⁷	2·06612 × 10⁻⁴
1 square mile	2·58999 × 10⁶	2·58999	3·0976 × 10⁶	1	640
1 acre	4·04686 × 10³	4·04686 × 10⁻³	4840	1·5625 × 10⁻³	1

1 are = 100 square metres.
1 hectare = 10 000 square metres = 2·47105 acres.

TABLE I. Conversion factors – *cont.*

Volume

	m³	cm³	in³	ft³	gal
1 cubic metre	1	10⁶	$6 \cdot 10236 \times 10^4$	35·3146	219·969
1 cubic centimetre	10^{-6}	1	0·0610236	$3 \cdot 53146 \times 10^{-5}$	$2 \cdot 19969 \times 10^{-4}$
1 cubic inch	$1 \cdot 6387 \times 10^{-5}$	16·3871	1	$5 \cdot 78704 \times 10^{-4}$	$3 \cdot 60464 \times 10^{-3}$
1 cubic foot	0·0283168	28316·8	1728	1	6·22882
1 gallon (UK)	$4 \cdot 54609 \times 10^{-3}$	4546·09	277·42	0·160544	1

1 gallon (US) = 0·83268 gallon (UK).
1 cubic yard = 0·764555 cubic metre.
The *litre* is now recognized as a special name for a cubic decimetre, but is not used to express high precision measurements.

Velocity

	m/sec	km/hr	mi/hr	ft/sec
1 metre per second	1	3·6	2·23694	3·28084
1 kilometre per hour	0·277778	1	0·621371	0·911346
1 mile per hour	0·44704	1·609344	1	1·46667
1 foot per second	0·3048	1·09728	0·681817	1

1 knot = 1 nautical mile per hour = 0·514444 metre per second.

TABLE I – *cont.*

6-FIGURE CONVERSION FACTORS
SI, CGS AND FPS UNITS

Mass	kg	g	lb	long ton
1 kilogramme	1	1000	2·20462	$9·84207 \times 10^{-4}$
1 gram	10^{-3}	1	$2·20462 \times 10^{-3}$	$9·84207 \times 10^{-7}$
1 pound	0·453592	453·592	1	$4·46429 \times 10^{-4}$
1 long ton	1016·047	$1·016047 \times 10^{6}$	2240	1

1 slug = 14·5939 kg = 32·174 lbs.

Density	kg/m^3	g/cm^3	lb/ft^3	lb/in^3
1 kilogram per cubic metre	1	10^{-3}	0·062428	$3·61273 \times 10^{-5}$
1 gram per cubic centimetre	1000	1	62·428	$3·61273 \times 10^{-2}$
1 pound per cubic foot	16·0185	0·0160185	1	$5·78704 \times 10^{-4}$
1 pound per cubic inch	$2·76799 \times 10^{4}$	27·6799	1728	1

1 lb/gal (UK) = 0·0997763 kg/dm³.

Force	N	kg	dyne	poundal	lb
1 newton	1	0·101972	10^{5}	7·23300	0·224809
1 kilogramme force	9·80665	1	$9·80665 \times 10^{5}$	70·9316	2·20462
1 dyne	10^{-5}	$1·01972 \times 10^{-6}$	1	$7·23300 \times 10^{-5}$	$2·24809 \times 10^{-6}$
1 poundal	0·138255	$1·40981 \times 10^{-2}$	$1·38255 \times 10^{4}$	1	0·0310081
1 pound force	4·44822	0·453592	$4·44823 \times 10^{5}$	32·174	1

TABLE I. Conversion factors — *cont.*

Pressure

	N/m²	kg/cm²	lb/in²	atmos
1 newton per square metre	1	$1 \cdot 01972 \times 10^{-5}$	$1 \cdot 45038 \times 10^{-4}$	$9 \cdot 86923 \times 10^{-6}$
1 kilogramme per square centimetre	$980 \cdot 665 \times 10^{2}$	1	$14 \cdot 2234$	$0 \cdot 967841$
1 pound per square inch	$6 \cdot 89476 \times 10^{3}$	$0 \cdot 0703068$	1	$0 \cdot 068046$
1 atmosphere	$1 \cdot 01325 \times 10^{5}$	$1 \cdot 03323$	$14 \cdot 6959$	1

1 newton per square metre = 10 dynes per square centimetre.
1 bar = 10^{5} newtons per square metre = 0·986923 atmosphere.
1 torr = 133·322 newtons per square metre = 1/760 atmosphere.
1 atmosphere = 760 mmHg = 29·92 in Hg = 33·90 ft water (all at 0°C.).

Work and Energy

	J	cal$_{\mathrm{IT}}$	kWhr	btu$_{\mathrm{IT}}$
1 joule	1	$0 \cdot 238846$	$2 \cdot 77778 \times 10^{-7}$	$9 \cdot 47813 \times 10^{-4}$
1 calorie (IT)	$4 \cdot 1868$	1	$1 \cdot 16300 \times 10^{-6}$	$3 \cdot 96831 \times 10^{-3}$
1 kilowatt hour	$3 \cdot 6 \times 10^{6}$	$8 \cdot 59845 \times 10^{5}$	1	$3412 \cdot 14$
1 British Thermal Unit (IT)	$1055 \cdot 06$	$251 \cdot 997$	$2 \cdot 93071 \times 10^{-4}$	1

1 joule = 1 newton metre = 1 watt second = 10^{7} ergs = 0·73756 ft lb.
1 electron volt = $1 \cdot 60210 \times 10^{-19}$ joule.

TABLE 2. FUNDAMENTAL CONSTANTS

Constant	Symbol	Value	
		SI Units	Other Units
Electronic charge	e	$1\cdot60210 \times 10^{-19}$ coulomb	$4\cdot80298 \times 10^{-10}$ e.s.u.
Electronic rest mass	m_e	$9\cdot1091 \times 10^{-31}$ kilogram	$5\cdot48597 \times 10^{-4}$ a.m.u.
Electronic radius	r_e	$2\cdot81777 \times 10^{-15}$ metre	—
Proton rest mass	m_p	$1\cdot67252 \times 10^{-27}$ kilogram	$1\cdot00727663$ a.m.u.
Neutron rest mass	m_n	$1\cdot67482 \times 10^{-27}$ kilogram	$1\cdot0086654$ a.m.u.
Planck's constant	h	$6\cdot62559 \times 10^{-34}$ joule second	$6\cdot62559 \times 10^{-27}$ erg second
Velocity of light	c	$2\cdot997925 \times 10^{8}$ metres per second	$186\ 281$ miles per second
Avogadro's constant	L, N_A	$6\cdot02252 \times 10^{23}$ per mole	—

TABLE 2. Fundamental constants – *cont.*

Loschmidt's constant	N_L	$2 \cdot 68719 \times 10^{25}$ m^{-3}	$2 \cdot 68719 \times 10^{19}$ cm^{-3}
Gas constant	R	$8 \cdot 3143$ J K^{-1} mol^{-1}	$1 \cdot 9858$ calories °C.$^{-1}$mol^{-1}
Boltzmann's constant	$k = \dfrac{R}{N_A}$	$1 \cdot 38054 \times 10^{-23}$ J K^{-1}	$3 \cdot 29729 \times 10^{-24}$ calories °C.$^{-1}$
Faraday's constant	F	$9 \cdot 64870 \times 10^4$ C mol^{-1}	$2 \cdot 89261 \times 10^{14}$ e.s.u. mol^{-1}
Stefan-Boltzmann constant	σ	$5 \cdot 6697 \times 10^{-8}$ W m^{-2} K^4	$5 \cdot 6697 \times 10^{-5}$ erg cm^{-2} K^{-4}
Gravitational constant	G	$6 \cdot 670 \times 10^{-11}$ N m^2 kg^{-2}	$6 \cdot 670 \times 10^{-8}$ dyne cm^2 g^{-2}
Acceleration due to gravity	g	$9 \cdot 80665$ m s^{-2}	$32 \cdot 174$ ft sec^{-2}
Permeability of vacuum	μ_0	$4\pi \times 10^{-7}$ H m^{-1}	—
Permittivity of vacuum	ϵ_0	$8 \cdot 85418 \times 10^{-12}$ F m^{-1}	—

(International Atomic Weights, 1961, based on Carbon-12)

[*A.W. values in brackets denote mass number of the most stable known isotope*]

Element	*Symbol*	*At. No.*	*A.W.*
Actinium	Ac	89	[227]
Aluminium	Al	13	26·9815
Americium	Am	95	[243]
Antimony	Sb	51	121·75
Argon	Ar	18	39·948
Arsenic	As	33	74·9216
Astatine	At	85	[210]
Barium	Ba	56	137·34
Berkelium	Bk	97	[247]
Beryllium	Be	4	9·0122
Bismuth	Bi	83	208·98
Boron	B	5	10·81
Bromine	Br	35	79·904
Cadmium	Cd	48	112·40
Caesium	Cs	55	132·905
Calcium	Ca	20	40·08
Californium	Cf	98	[251]
Carbon	C	6	12·011
Cerium	Ce	58	140·12
Chlorine	Cl	17	35·453
Chromium	Cr	24	51·996
Cobalt	Co	27	58·9332
Copper	Cu	29	63·546
Curium	Cm	96	[247]
Dysprosium	Dy	66	162·50
Einsteinium	Es	99	[254]
Erbium	Er	68	167·26
Europium	Eu	63	151·96
Fermium	Fm	100	[257]
Fluorine	F	9	18·9984
Francium	Fr	87	[223]
Gadolinium	Gd	64	157·25
Gallium	Ga	31	69·72
Germanium	Ge	32	72·59
Gold	Au	79	196·967
Hafnium	Hf	72	178·49
Helium	He	2	4·0026
Holmium	Ho	67	164·930

TABLE 3. Table of elements, etc. – *cont.*

Element	Symbol	At. No.	A.W.
Hydrogen	H	1	1·00797
Indium	In	49	114·82
Iodine	I	53	126·9044
Iridium	Ir	77	192·2
Iron	Fe	26	55·847
Krypton	Kr	36	83·80
Lanthanum	La	57	138·91
Lawrencium	Lr	103	[257]
Lead	Pb	82	207·19
Lithium	Li	3	6·939
Lutetium	Lu	71	174·97
Magnesium	Mg	12	24·305
Manganese	Mn	25	54·938
Mendelevium	Md	101	[258]
Mercury	Hg	80	200·59
Molybdenum	Mo	42	95·94
Neodymium	Nd	60	144·24
Neon	Ne	10	20·179
Neptunium	Np	93	[237]
Nickel	Ni	28	58·71
Niobium	Nb	41	92·906
Nitrogen	N	7	14·0067
Nobelium	No	102	[255]
Osmium	Os	76	190·2
Oxygen	O	8	15·9994
Palladium	Pd	46	106·4
Phosphorus	P	15	30·9738
Platinum	Pt	78	195·09
Plutonium	Pu	94	[244]
Polonium	Po	84	[209]
Potassium	K	19	39·102
Praseodymium	Pr	59	140·907
Promethium	Pm	61	[145]
Protactinium	Pa	91	[231]
Radium	Ra	88	[226]
Radon	Rn	86	[222]
Rhenium	Re	75	186·20
Rhodium	Rh	45	102·905
Rubidium	Rb	37	85·47
Ruthenium	Ru	44	101·07
Samarium	Sm	62	150·35
Scandium	Sc	21	44·956
Selenium	Se	34	78·96
Silicon	Si	14	28·086

TABLE 3. Table of elements, etc. – *cont.*

Element	Symbol	At. No.	A.W.
Silver	Ag	47	107·868
Sodium	Na	11	22·9898
Strontium	Sr	38	87·62
Sulphur	S	16	32·064
Tantalum	Ta	73	180·948
Technetium	Tc	43	[97]
Tellurium	Te	52	127·60
Terbium	Tb	65	158·924
Thallium	Tl	81	204·37
Thorium	Th	90	232·038
Thulium	Tm	69	168·934
Tin	Sn	50	118·69
Titanium	Ti	22	47·90
Tungsten	W	74	183·85
Uranium	U	92	238·03
Vanadium	V	23	50·942
Wolfram (Tungsten)	W	74	183·85
Xenon	Xe	54	131·30
Ytterbium	Yb	70	173·04
Yttrium	Y	39	88·905
Zinc	Zn	30	65·37
Zirconium	Zr	40	91·22

TABLE 4. THE SOLAR SYSTEM

Planet	Equatorial Diameter (kilometres)	Mass (Earth masses)*	Mean Distance from Sun (millions of kilometres)	Sidereal period
Mercury	4840	0·054	57·91	87·969 days
Venus	12 300	0·8150	108·21	224·701 days
Earth	12 756	1·000	149·60	365·256 days
Mars	6790	0·107	227·94	686·980 days
Jupiter	142 800	317·89	778·34	11·86 years
Saturn	119 300	95·14	1427·01	29·46 years
Uranus	47 100	14·52	2869·6	84·0 years
Neptune	44 800	17·46	4496·7	164·8 years
Pluto	5900	0·1 (approx.)	5907	248·4 years
Sun	1 392 000	332 958	149·60†	—
Moon	3476	0·0123	0·3844†	27·32

* The Mass of the Earth is 5.976×10^{24} kilogrammes.
† Distance to Earth.

TABLE 5. TABLE OF AMINO ACIDS

Name	Formula	Molecular weight
Glycine	$CH_2(NH_2).COOH$	75·1
Alanine	$CH_3CH.(NH_2).COOH$	89·1
Phenylalanine	$C_6H_5CH_2CH.(NH_2).COOH$	165·2
Tyrosine	$C_6H_4OH.CH_2CH.(NH_2).COOH$	181·2
Valine	$(CH_3)_2CH.CH.(NH_2).COOH$	117·1
Leucine	$(CH_3)_2CH.CH_2CH.(NH_2).COOH$	131·2
Iso-leucine	$(CH_3).CH_2CH(CH_3)CH.(NH_2).COOH$	131·2
Serine	$CH_2OH.CH.(NH_2).COOH$	105·1
Threonine	$CH_3CHOH.CH.(NH_2).COOH$	119·1
Cysteine	$SH.CH_2CH.(NH_2).COOH$	121·1
Cystine	$[HOOC.CH(NH_2)CH_2S]_2$	240·3
Methionine	$CH_3.S.(CH_2)_2CH.(NH_2).COOH$	149·2
Asparagine	$NH_2CO.CH_2CH.(NH_2).COOH$	132·1
Glutamine	$NH_2CH.(CH_2)_2(CO.NH_2).COOH$	146·1
Lysine	$NH_2(CH_2)_4CH.(NH_2).COOH$	146·2
Arginine	$NH_2C(:NH).NH(CH_2)_3CH.(NH_2) COOH$	174·2
Aspartic	$COOH.CH_2CH.(NH_2).COOH$	133·1
Glutamic	$COOH.(CH_2)_2CH.(NH_2).COOH$	147·1
Histidine	$C_3H_3N_2.CH_2CH.(NH_2).COOH$	155·2
Tryptophan	$C_6H_4.NH.C_2H.CH_2CH.(NH_2).COOH$	204·2
Proline	$NH.(CH_2)_3CH.COOH$	115·1

TABLE 6. ELEMENTARY PARTICLES

Particle	Symbol	Charge	Spin	Mass (MeV)	Strange-ness	Lifetime (secs)	Decay Products
Proton	p	$+1$	$\frac{1}{2}$	938.26	0	Stable	—
Neutron	n	0	$\frac{1}{2}$	939.55	0	1010	$e^- + p + \bar{\nu}$
Xi-particles	Ξ°	0	$\frac{1}{2}$	1314.9	-2	2.9×10^{-10}	$\Lambda + \pi^\circ$
	Ξ^-	-1	$\frac{1}{2}$	1321.3	-2	1.7×10^{-10}	$\Lambda + \pi^-$
Sigma-particles	Σ^+	$+1$	$\frac{1}{2}$	1189.5	-1	8.1×10^{-11}	$p + \pi^\circ / n + \pi^+$
	Σ°	0	$\frac{1}{2}$	1192.5	-1	$\leqslant 10^{-14}$	$\Lambda + \gamma$
	Σ^-	-1	$\frac{1}{2}$	1197.4	-1	1.66×10^{-10}	$n + \pi^-$
Lambda-particle	Λ	0	$\frac{1}{2}$	1115.5	-1	2.5×10^{-10}	$p + \pi^- / n + \pi^\circ$
Omega-particle	Ω^-	-1	$\frac{3}{2}$	1672	-1	1.1×10^{-10}	$\Xi^\circ + \pi^- / \Xi^- + \pi^\circ / \Lambda + K^-$
Electron	e^-	-1	$\frac{1}{2}$	0.511	0	Stable	—
Neutrino	ν	0	$\frac{1}{2}$	0	0	Stable	—
Muon	μ^-	-1	$\frac{1}{2}$	105.66	0	2.2×10^{-6}	$e + \nu + \bar{\nu}^-$

NUCLEONS   HYPERONS

BARYONS   LEPTONS

FERMIONS

TABLE 6. Elementary particles – *cont.*

Particle	Symbol	Charge	Spin	Mass (MeV)	Strangeness	Lifetime (secs)	Decay Products
Eta-particle	η°	0	0	548·8	0	?	$2\nu/\pi^{\circ}+2\nu/3\pi^{\circ}$
Kaons	K_1°	0	0	497·8	-1	10^{-10}	$\pi^{+}+\pi^{-}/2\pi^{\circ}$
	K_2°	0	0	497·8	$+1$	$2\cdot8\times10^{-8}$	$\pi^{+}+\pi^{\circ}+\pi^{-}/3\pi^{\circ}/$etc
	K^{-}	-1	0	493·8	-1	$1\cdot2\times10^{-8}$	} various
	K^{+}	$+1$	0	493·8	$+1$	$1\cdot2\times10^{-8}$	
Pions	π^{+}	$+1$	0	139·6	0	$2\cdot6\times10^{-8}$	$\bar{\mu}^{+}+\nu$
	π°	0	0	135	0	1×10^{-16}	$2\gamma/\gamma+e^{+}+e^{-}$
	π^{-}	-1	0	139·6	0	$2\cdot6\times10^{-8}$	$\mu^{-}+\bar{\nu}$
Photon	γ	0	1	0	—	Stable	—

MESONS

BOSONS

437

TABLE 7. ELECTRON CONFIGURATIONS AND IONIZATION POTENTIALS OF THE COMMONER ELEMENTS

Element	Atomic Number	Electron Configuration Shell						Ionization Potentials (electron-volts)				
		1 K	2 L	3 M	4 N	5 O	6 P	I	II	III	IV	V
H	1	1						13·59				
He	2	2						24·48	54·40			
C	6	2	4					11·26	24·38	47·87	64·48	392·0
N	7	2	5					14·53	29·59	47·43	77·45	97·86
O	8	2	6					13·61	35·11	54·89	77·39	113·9
F	9	2	7					17·42	16·18	30·64	56·80	114·2
Ne	10	2	8					21·56	41·07	63·50	97·02	126·3
Na	11	2	8	1				5·14	47·29	71·71	98·88	138·4
Mg	12	2	8	2				7·64	15·03	80·14	109·29	141·2
Al	13	2	8	3				5·98	18·82	28·44	119·96	153·8
Si	14	2	8	4				8·15	16·34	33·49	45·13	166·7
P	15	2	8	5				10·48	19·72	30·16	51·35	65·0
S	16	2	8	6				10·36	23·40	35·0	47·29	72·5
Cl	17	2	8	7				13·01	23·80	39·9	53·50	67·8
Ar	18	2	8	8				15·75	27·62	40·9	59·8	75·0

TABLE 7. Electron configurations, etc. – *cont.*

Element	Atomic Number	Electron Configuration Shell						Ionization Potentials (electron-volts)				
		1 K	2 L	3 M	4 N	5 O	6 P	I	II	III	IV	V
K	19	2	8	8	1			4·34	31·81	46·0	60·9	82·6
Ca	20	2	8	8	2			6·11	11·87	51·2	67·0	84·4
Fe	26	2	8	14	2			7·87	16·18	30·6	56·8	—
Cu	29	2	8	18	1			7·72	20·30	36·8	—	—
Zn	30	2	8	18	2			9·39	17·96	39·7	—	—
Br	35	2	8	18	7			11·84	21·60	35·9	47·3	59·7
Kr	36	2	8	18	8			13·99	24·50	36·9	43·5	63·0
Ag	47	2	8	18	18	1		7·57	21·5	34·8	—	—
Sn	50	2	8	18	18	4		7·34	14·63	30·5	40·7	72·3
I	53	2	8	18	18	7		10·45	19·13	—	—	—
Xe	54	2	8	18	18	8		12·13	21·2	31·3	42·0	53·0
Cs	55	2	8	18	18	8	1	3·89	25·1	35·0	—	—
Ba	56	2	8	18	18	8	2	5·21	10·0	35·5	—	—
Hg	80	2	8	18	32	18	2	10·43	18·75	34·2	49·5	—

439

TABLE 8. PERIODIC TABLE OF THE ELEMENTS

IA	2A	3B	4B	5B	6B	7B	8			1B	2B	3A	4A	5A	6A	7A	0
1 H																	2 He
3 Li	4 Be											5 B	6 C	7 N	8 O	9 F	10 Ne
11 Na	12 Mg											13 Al	14 Si	15 P	16 S	17 Cl	18 Ar
19 K	20 Ca	21 Sc	22 Ti	23 V	24 Cr	25 Mn	26 Fe	27 Co	28 Ni	29 Cu	30 Zn	31 Ga	32 Ge	33 As	34 Se	35 Br	36 Kr
37 Rb	38 Sr	39 Y	40 Zr	41 Nb	42 Mo	43 Tc	44 Ru	45 Rh	46 Pd	47 Ag	48 Cd	49 In	50 Sn	51 Sb	52 Te	53 I	54 Xe
55 Cs	56 Ba	57* La	72 Hf	73 Ta	74 W	75 Re	76 Os	77 Ir	78 Pt	79 Au	80 Hg	81 Tl	82 Pb	83 Bi	84 Po	85 At	86 Rn
87 Fr	88 Ra	89† Ac															

←———— TRANSITION ELEMENTS ————→

*Lanthanides	57 La	58 Ce	59 Pr	60 Nd	61 Pm	62 Sm	63 Eu	64 Gd	65 Tb	66 Dy	67 Ho	68 Er	69 Tm	70 Yb	71 Lu
*Actinides	89 Ac	90 Th	91 Pa	92 U	93 Np	94 Pu	95 Am	96 Cm	97 Bk	98 Cf	99 Es	100 Fm	101 Md	102 No	103 Lr

TABLE 9. DIFFERENTIAL COEFFICIENTS AND INTEGRALS

y	$\dfrac{dy}{dx}$	$\displaystyle\int y.dx$
x^n	nx^{n-1}	$\dfrac{1}{n+1}.x^{n+1}$
$\dfrac{1}{x}$	$\dfrac{-1}{x^2}$	$\log_e x$
e^{ax}	ae^{ax}	$\dfrac{1}{a}.e^{ax}$
$\log_e x$	$\dfrac{1}{x}$	$x(\log_e x - 1)$
$\log_a x$	$\dfrac{1}{x}.\log_a e$	$x.\log_a\dfrac{x}{e}$
$\cos ax$	$-a.\sin ax$	$\dfrac{1}{a}.\sin ax$
$\sin ax$	$a.\cos ax$	$-\dfrac{1}{a}.\cos ax$
$\tan ax$	$a.\sec^2 ax$	$-\dfrac{1}{a}.\log_e \cos ax$
$\cot x$	$-\csc^2 x$	$\log_e \sin x$
$\sec x$	$\tan x.\sec x$	$\log_e(\sec x + \tan x)$
$\csc x$	$-\cot x.\csc x$	$\log_e(\csc x - \cot x)$
$\sin^{-1}\dfrac{x}{a}$	$\dfrac{1}{(a^2-x^2)^{\frac{1}{2}}}$	$x.\sin^{-1}\dfrac{x}{a} + (a^2-x^2)^{\frac{1}{2}}$
$\cos^{-1}\dfrac{x}{a}$	$\dfrac{-1}{(a^2-x^2)^{\frac{1}{2}}}$	$x.\cos^{-1}\dfrac{x}{a} - (a^2-x^2)^{\frac{1}{2}}$
$\tan^{-1}\dfrac{x}{a}$	$\dfrac{a}{a^2+x^2}$	$x.\tan^{-1}\dfrac{x}{a} - a\log_e(a^2+x^2)^{\frac{1}{2}}$

TABLE 10. SPECTRUM OF ELECTROMAGNETIC RADIATIONS

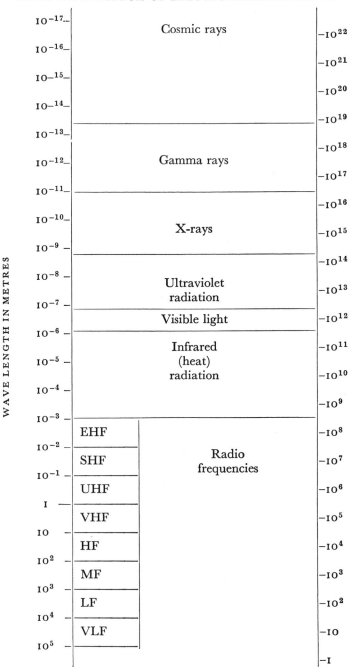

TABLE II. THE GREEK ALPHABET

Letters		Name
A	α	alpha
B	β	beta
Γ	γ	gamma
Δ	δ	delta
E	ϵ	epsilon
Z	ζ	zeta
H	η	eta
Θ	θ	theta
I	ι	iota
K	κ	kappa
Λ	λ	lambda
M	μ	mu
N	ν	nu
Ξ	ξ	xi
O	o	omikron
Π	π	pi
P	ρ	ro
Σ	σ	sigma
T	τ	tau
Υ	υ	upsilon
Φ	ϕ	phi
X	χ	khi
Ψ	ψ	psi
Ω	ω	omega